# Peak Lim

Alan James

## A guidebook to the sport and traditional climbing on Peak District Limestone

Text and topos by Chris Craggs and Alan James
Edited by Stephen Horne
All uncredited photography by Rockfax
Other photography as credited
Printed in Europe on behalf of Latitude Press Ltd.
Distributed by Cordee (www.cordee.co.uk)

All maps by ROCKFAX
Some maps based on original source data from openstreetmap.org

Published by ROCKFAX in May 2012
© ROCKFAX 2012, 2005, 2000, 1994

**www.rockfax.com**

**ISBN 978 1 873341 52 0**

Cover photo:
Julian Heath on *The Spider* (8a) - page 186
Plum Buttress, Cheedale. Photo: Christian Fox

This page:
Rich Mayfield on *Debauchery* (E1 5b) - page 352
High Tor, Matlock. Photo: Keith Sharples

Cheedale in the early season - don't forget the wellies. Photo: Chris Craggs

The Peak District National Park forms a much needed green lung for the many millions of city dwellers who live just over the horizon in almost every direction. The Park - the first in the UK (1951) lies within 50 miles of half the population of England. Despite its small size, it exhibits a rare variety of landscapes in such a small compass. From the desolate northern moors and their rugged gritstone edges, through the central farmland with its drystone walls, to the tranquil southern dales with their bubbling trout streams and white limestone towers; the area has a bit of almost everything and as such it attracts many visitors.

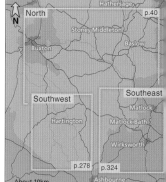

Of course climbers are just one such group and they are doubly blessed with two rock types to go at within the Peak Park, each with its own characteristics, unique settings and set of enthusiasts. *The Grit* remains the rock of choice for many, limestone being seen as the poor relative, and it appears likely that a superb set of grit area guidebooks over recent years is at least part of the reason for this. It is time to redress the balance a bit.

In this book we have the best of the limestone on offer in the Peak District. For trad climbing there are venues like the big three of High Tor, Beeston Tor and Chee Tor which rank with any limestone crag in the country for quality. Then there is the old forcing ground of Stoney - a place which can be warm and sunny when the near-by gritstone edges are cold and weather-beaten. Alternatively you could opt for some pleasant easier routes at Aldery Cliff, Wildcat, Ravensdale or Harborough - all great venues with a variety of climbing to suit most tastes, and this is not to mention a dozen other great crags.

Despite the pedigree of the limestone trad climbing, the most popular crags are the quarries that pockmark the Peak District landscape. These have been extensively explored and developed with most decent bits of rock now being bolted for sport climbing. They may not always be the most picturesque locations but crags like Horseshoe, Masson Lees and Harpur Hill have many quality routes towards the middle and lower end of the grade spectrum and are extremely popular and busy locations.

Those after harder sport routes on natural rock are spoilt for choice: the Mecca of Raven Tor, a couple of Cornices, loads of fine cliffs in Chee Dale, the fierce fingery walls of Water-cum-Jolly, plus a number of smaller crags dotted around to go at. This includes some world famous cutting edge routes offering great climbing from the mid grades right up to 9a.

Of the 2381 climbs described in this book, 1411 are sport routes (59%) and 970 are trad routes including classics of both genres. Sport climbing has become the norm on limestone for many nowadays, and at the same time trad limestone climbing has fallen out of fashion, though aficionados have continued to enjoy these fine climbs. New guidebooks always cause a spike in activity and we hope this one will provide a stimulus for anyone not familiar with climbing on Peak Limestone to get out there and give it a go, be it trad or sport.

*Alan James, Chris Craggs, March 2012*

John Crook on the wildly exposed
upper wall of *Armageddon* (E2
5c) - *page 62* - on Windy Buttress at
Stoney. Photo: Dan Lane
Dan's magnificent photo captures
Stoney very well - not the most perfect
of rock with some vegetation and flaky
holds, but bags of atmosphere!

Andy Hutchinson pulling hard on *Albatrossity* (8a+) - *page 248* - on the Water-cum-Jolly Cornice. Photo: Ryan Edwards

## The Book

This is the third ROCKFAX guidebook to Peak Limestone and it is 20 years since Alan James' first ever guidebook was produced back in 1992. Things have moved on considerably from the hand-drawn topos of this 1992 offering; nowadays lavish full-colour photo-topos have been used wherever possible and these are closely linked to detailed descriptions. Where the cliffs are heavily shrouded by trees we have used full-colour drawn topos. In a few cases we have actually used an amalgamation of both photo and topo (see Wild Cat - page 366). All crags are also feature a detailed approach maps with GPS parking locations.

## Coverage

We have given extensive coverage of all the major limestone crags in the Peak District, both sport and trad. In general, where a buttress or crag is included, we have included all the routes on that buttress although very minor eliminates may be excluded. This means that the book is a *selected crag guidebook* rather than a *selected route guidebook*. There are a number of large well-developed quarries - Intake, Halldale, Cawdor, Slayley Brook - that have been left out owing to legal restrictions placed on us by the land owners. Climbing is banned in these quarries anyway.

## History

The history of climbing on Peak Limestone stretches back over 100 years, every great climber of his generation has tested his mettle on these fingery classics. Most of the big lines were climbed, often with some aid, in the 1950 and 60s. As gear and fitness improved, many of these were free climbing and the intervening gaps were plugged by ever harder routes. Bolt protection arrived in the 1980s although initial acceptance was slow their use spread onto unclimbed sections of rock proved inexorable. Finally the development of sport climbing, introducing routes of the highest grade and allowed the development of many old quarries that had previously been dismissed as worthless. Beyond the first ascent details included with every route (where known), no other historical overviews are included here.

Laura Hudsen on making the rock-over move on *Body Machine* (7c+) -*page 216* - at Raven Tor. Photo: Adrian Berry. Up until 2008 the start of this route, *The Prow*, *Indecent Exposure* and many derivatives used an old tree to by-pass the dirty initial wall. This tree was cut down in July 2008 for no apparent reason and no-one has ever owned up to it. Since then the lower wall has been climbed by various alternative starts but the climbing is hard and the rock is filthy for much of the time - significantly longer than the rest of the crag. This senseless action has sadly tainted some of the best sport routes on Peak Limestone which, although still good, are not quite as good as they used to be.

## Key Previous Guides

The limestone areas in the Peak have been documented since 1913 when John Laycock included some climbs at Harborough and Brassington in his **Gritstone Climbs** book. Since then the documentation has shifted from area guidebooks with limestone and gritstone, to dedicated limestone guidebooks.
We are very grateful to all those who have worked on previous guidebooks. The key books are listed below.

**Northern Limestone** - Alan James, Mark Glaister and Chris Craggs *(ROCKFAX 2004)*

**From Horseshoe to Harpur Hill** - Gary Gibson *(BMC 2004)*

**Peak Limestone Wye Valley** - Geoff Milburn *(BMC 1999)*

**Peak Limestone** - Alan James *(ROCKFAX 1992)*

**Peak Limestone (3 Volumes)** - Geoff Milburn *(BMC 1987)*

**Northern Limestone** - Dave Gregory *(BMC 1980)*

**The Southern Limestone Area** - Paul Nunn *(BMC 1970)*

**The Northern Limestone Area** - Paul Nunn *(BMC 1969)*

**Rock Climbs on the Mountain Limestone of Derbyshire** - Graham West *(BMC 1962)*

2004

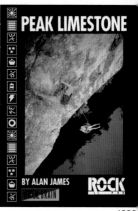

1992

## Web Site   www.rockfax.com

The Rockfax website is a mine of useful information about climbing all over Europe. It contains the Rockfax Route Database plus many PDF MiniGUIDES and updates both complementing the printed books produced by Rockfax and also covering new areas.

**Rockfax Route Database -** This database contains a listing of every route in the book (and most other Rockfax books as well). The Peak Limestone section has been available for over a decade and has logged a huge number of comments and votes on the routes. All this information has been vital in putting together this book, getting the grades and stars right and keeping a check on developments. Thanks to all those who have contributed.

The current version of the database has been updated to reflect the routes as described in this edition of the book so you can start using it again to keep everyone informed about any changes or your own opinions on grades, stars and the routes in general.

Don't forget that it is possible to use the database to construct a personal and printable tick-list of routes by using the advanced search function to select a location, grade band and star range of routes and return a list with tick boxes, and page references in this guide.

Rob Smith embroiled with *That was the River* (7b+) - *page 200* - in prime summer conditions on the Cornice in Chee Dale. Photo: Stu Littlefair When this crag finally dries out in early summer some courageous soul sets off up each route to begin the process of dusting it back down. It usually takes a few ascents before the routes clean up properly but they can stay that way until December if we are lucky.

Sabby Bacher crossing the powerful bulges of *Powerplant* (8a) -
*page 204* - on the Chee Dale Cornice. Photo: Mark Glaister

When we realised Northern Limestone was due to sell out (it actually sold better then we ever expected) and there was no queue to take on the rewrite, I thought I could squeeze in just one more project. Some guidebooks plead to be born and rush forth with barely a breaking of sweat from the grateful authors. Others have to be forced into existence by brute force and sheer bloody-mindness. The limestone guides always seem to slot into the latter category. The previous version; Northern Limestone, had the longest gestation of any Rockfax ever and although this volume has only taken a couple of years it has proved no exception to the rule. The reasons are various and obvious: new venues get developed, old ones become overgrown, holds break, bans are established and of course the trees get bigger year on year making the photography ever more challenging. Despite the tribulations we hope the final product does justice to these fine climbs.

Without the help of many climbers the book would never have happened. Jon Clark got in touch at an early stage and his encyclopedic knowledge of the Peak's hard sport routes has been invaluable, the Raven Tor section is a prime example of his great feedback. Graham Hoey has proof read the whole book and offered advice from his vast experience of hard trad routes throughout the Peak area, as has Gary Gibson - Mr Peak Lime himself! Others who have offered their advice/experience include Marc Bellingall, Bob Bennett, Dan Smith, Dave Johnson and Neil Foster. Apologies for anyone any I have missed. Kris Clemmow has provided excellent feedback as well as doing sterling work on access and rebolting. Jon Fullwood, Paul Bennett have read most of the text and offered plenty of feedback. Daimon Beail and Emma Harrington have been great proof readers.

As ever we have had the pleasure of browsing through and choosing from the galleries of many excellent photographers, their work adds immeasurable value to the book. Thanks to Adrian Berry, Ben Lea, Christian Fox, Craig Bailey, Dan Lane, David Bond, David Simmonite, Denise Hammer, Esther Bott, Jon Fullwood, Keith Sharples, Mark Glaister, Mike Hutton, Neil Foster, Nick Smith, Pete Clark, Ryan Edwards, Stu Littlefair; and also to those who offered photos; Mark Rankine, James Smith, James Reece, Thomas Bond, Tim Lounds and Tony Moody.

Graham and Dan Parkes were very helpful in getting many of the final (and more esoteric) action shots we needed (see pages 132 and 228). Stephen Horne has managed to make the complex production of these books a lot less complex and fraught. His support has been second to none - cheers for that.

As ever Sherri Davy has been standing right behind me, despite dragging her back from the sunny delights of winter in Kalymnos to tramp the muddy Derbyshire Dales - not once but twice! Alan James has been the guiding light behind this and every other Rockfax, accepting nothing less than perfection; with a mixture of cajoling and cudgelling I think we got there in the end.

*Chris Craggs, March 2012*

The bread and butter of this guidebook is the crags and the routes that it covers. Without the routes we have nothing to climb, and even with the routes we still need people to negotiate on our behalf to ensure continued access. We are very grateful to those who put in effort developing; people like Gary Gibson, Kris Clemmow, Jon Fullwood, Jon Clark, Graham Hoey and many more over the years. For access the whole Peak Area committee need a mention but especially Henry Folkard who deserves endless praise from every climber who ever touches rock in the Peak District.

It seems almost incredible that it was 20 years ago that I wrote my first acknowledgements in a Peak Limestone Rockfax. That particular effort - my first guidebook - was a life-changing event for me and took me in a direction I hadn't contemplated up to the point that Mick Ryan and Greg Rimmer gave me the opportunity. I am very grateful to both of them for having faith in me at that time.

Finally thanks to my family - 20 years ago there were just the two of us, now we have a house full and the place is so much more lively for it.

*Alan James, March 2012*

## Equipment Manufacturers

**Black Diamond -** *Outside back cover*
www.blackdiamondequipment.com

**Beta Climbing Designs** - *Page 17*
www.betaclimbingdesigns.com

**Mammut** - *Inside front cover*
www.mammut.ch

**Arc'teryx** - *Inside back cover*
www.arcteryx.com

**Entre-prise** - *Page 19*
www.entre-prises.com

**Rab** - *Opposite*
www.rab.uk.com

## Climbing Walls

**Awesome Walls** - *Page 2*
St. Alban's Church, Liverpool. Tel: 01512 982422
The Engine House, Stockport. Tel: 0161 494 9949
Sefton Road, Stoke-on-Trent. Tel: 01782 341919
www.awesomewalls.co.uk

**The Leeds Wall** - *Page 27*
Gelderd Road, Leeds. Tel: 0113 234 1554
www.theleedswall.co.uk

**Manchester Wall** - *Page 23*
St Benedict's Church, Manchester.
Tel: 0161 230 7006
www.manchesterclimbingcentre.com

## Shops

**Rock On** - *Page 21*
Mile End, London. Tel: 0208 981 5066
Craggy Island, Guildford. Tel: 01483 565635
Redpoint, Birmingham. Tel: 01213 598709
www.rockonclimbing.co.uk

**V12** - *Back cover flap*
The Old Baptist Chapel, Llanberis.
Tel: 01286 871534
www.v12outdoor.com

## Guiding

**James Thacker** - *Page 29*
Tel: 07887 992745
www.jamesthacker-mountaineering.co.uk

**Alternative Adventures** - *Page 29*
Tel: 028708 31258
www.adventurealternative.com

Rab®
At the heart of
Peak Climbing
since 1981
Rab® sponsored climber Tom Randall committed on an early ascent of The Great Tribulation, Hipley Hill. E6 6c. Photo: Mike Hutton.
www.rab.uk.com

# Peak Limestone Logistics

Mark Stevenson leading *Alcasan* (E2 5c) - *page 64* - at Stoney Middleton belayed by Rich Mayfield. Mark and Rich were on Day 16 of the Hard Rock Challenge where the two of them climbed all the routes in the book Hard Rock in a five week period. That's 6500m of climbing, 180 miles of walk ins, 4 ferry crossings, over 3,000 miles of driving and all at the mercy of the British weather which was pretty bad in July 2007. See page 1 for one of the 4 routes they did the previous day.
Photo: Dave Simmonite

> ## Mountain Rescue
> In the event of an accident requiring the assistance of Mountain Rescue:
> ## Dial 112 and ask for 'POLICE - MOUNTAIN RESCUE'
> All mountain rescue incidents in the Peak District area fall under the responsibility of Derbyshire Constabulary. If in any doubt request Derbyshire Police Operations Room.

## Mobile Phones

Many of the crags described in this section of the book have reasonable mobile phone coverage across the major networks. The exceptions are isolated and enclosed places like the depths of Chee Dale and Dovedale where coverage can be intermittent or not available at all. In an emergency, the only option is to climb to higher ground or find a phone box. It may be worth checking the situation before an emergency arises.

## Tourist Information Offices

If you are short of ideas of what to do on a wet day or need some accommodation, take a look at the Tourist Information Offices. They contain much more useful information than it is possible to include in these pages.

**Sheffield** - 14 Norfolk Row. Tel: 0114 221 1900
**Buxton** - The Crescent. Tel: 01298 25106
**Bakewell** - Old Market Hall, Bridge Street. Tel: 01629 816558
**Leek** - Market Place, Leek. Tel: 01538 483741
**Chesterfield** - Rykneld Square. Tel: 01246 345777/8
**Ashbourne** - 13 Market Place. Tel: 01335 343666
**Matlock** - Crown Square. Tel: 01629 583388
More information and other travel tips are at - **www.visitpeakdistrict.com**

## When to Go

Peak Limestone can offer something on most days of the year. There are several winter sun-traps like Beeston Tor and Horseshoe Quarry, which could well be pleasant and climbable in mid-winter. Conversely these same crags can be unbearably hot in the warmer months.
For harder routes many of the main crags of interest suffer from seepage and only come into condition from March and April onwards or later if we have a wet spring. If travelling from afar, take note of the crag seepage symbols to avoid disappointment. Once the summer arrives, the leafy dales offer plenty of shade and there is almost always something to go at even during a heat wave.

| Temperature °C | Jan | Feb | Mar | Apr | May | Jun | Jul | Aug | Sep | Oct | Nov | Dec |
|---|---|---|---|---|---|---|---|---|---|---|---|---|
| Average Max Temp (°C) | 6 | 6 | 9 | 10 | 14 | 17 | 20 | 19 | 15 | 12 | 8 | 5 |
| Average Min Temp (°C) | 1 | 1 | 3 | 3 | 6 | 9 | 11 | 11 | 8 | 6 | 3 | 1 |
| Average Rain Days/month | 9 | 10 | 8 | 6 | 6 | 5 | 6 | 6 | 7 | 7 | 8 | 6 |

## Getting Around

The easiest way to access most of the crags in this book is by car and the approach descriptions are written assuming you have access to one. Certain crags are accessible using public transport and train stations are marked on the maps. Bus coverage for the Peak District is reasonable. The best web site for finding train information is **www.thetrainline.com**. The best web site for finding bus information is **www.traveline.info**

# Beta Stick

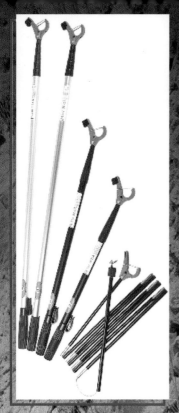

info@betaclimbingdesigns.com

**0114 2558882**
**www.betaclimbingdesigns.com**

## Accommodation

There are many campsites scattered throughout the area, from small and basic to plush. Over a hundred sites are listed (with map and phone numbers) at www.stilwell.co.uk

Other useful websites for all different types of accommodation are:
www.peakdistrictonline.co.uk
www.ukclimbing.com/listings
www.ukcampsite.co.uk/sites
www.thebmc.co.uk

**Youth Hostels -** There are numerous Youth Hostels in the Peak District, check out www.yha.org.uk

## Climbing Shops

More shops listed at -
www.ukclimbing.com/listings

**Crag X -** Unit 2  45 Mowbray Street, Sheffield. Tel: 0114 2769741
**Go Outdoors (Sheffield) -** Hill Street, Sheffield. Tel: 0114 2729733
**Go Outdoors (Hathersage) -** 6 Main Road, Hathersage. Tel: 01433 659 870
**Hitch 'n' Hike -** Mytham Bridge, nr Bamford, Hope Valley. Tel: 01433 651013
**Jo Royles -** 6 Market Place, Buxton. Tel: 01298 25824
**Nevisport -** The Square, Main Road, Hathersage. Tel: 01433 659666
**Outside -** Main Road, Hathersage. Tel: 01433 651936
**Outside -** Baslow Road, Calver. Tel: 01433 651936
**V12 -** Awesome walls, Stockport. Tel: 0161 4946008
**V12 -** Awesome walls, Stoke. Tel: 01782 333787

Duncan Bell on the ever-dry *Great Corner* (VS 4c) - *page 374* - at Willersley. Photo: Stu Littlefair

## Pubs

Pubs are an integral part of the climbing experience. The Peak District is blessed with many fine hostelries which make great locations for an après-climb pint where you can discuss the highs and lows of your day.

The list below are recommendations contributed by readers of the forums on UKClimbing.com. Most are marked on the relevant crag map near the crag they are closest to.

The view plaque at the Barrel Inn 'the highest pint in the Derbyshire'.

### Stoney and Horseshoe

**The Moon** (*page 42*), Stoney Middleton. An old favourite, with a sense of history.
**Miner's Arms** (*page 69*), Eyam. The staff seem really friendly and obliging.

### Chee Dale and Miller's Dale

**The Bull's Head,** Foolow. Good food and beer though quite small.
**The Barrel Inn,** Bretton. Good beer and magnificent views but gets busy.
**Three Stags Heads** (*page 211*), Wardlow Mires. Good atmosphere and beer but not to everyone's taste. Only open Friday, Saturday and Sunday. Doesn't serve lager, mobile phones must be off!
**The Red Lion** (*page 211*), Litton. A great pub in a tranquil location with fine beer and good meals.
**The Anglers Rest** (*page 214*), Miller's Dale. Passed on the way to Raven Tor.
**The Monsal Head** (*page 211*), near Water-cum-Jolly. Can be busy, but has good food and a fine selection of beers.
**The Packhorse,** Little Longstone. Great beer, but can get crowded because it is small.

### The Central Peak

**The Quiet Woman** (*page 267*), Earl Sterndale. Fine old country pub, lovely atmosphere, great beers, beautiful location. Handy for Aldery Cliff.

**The Queen's Arms** (*page 272*), Taddington. Small friendly country pub with small shop.

### Dovedale and Manifold

**The Bluebell Inn** (*page 280*), Tissington. Quite good for Dovedale and does reasonable meals.
**The Charles Cotton** (*page 282*), Hartington. Welcoming family pub and does good food.
**The Royal Oak Inn** (*page 284*), Wetton. Good food and beer, friendly staff, and £5 to camp behind the pub. Good for a weekend at Beeston Tor and Dovedale.

### Matlock Area

**The County & Station** (*page 343*), Matlock. Good food, real ales. A good pint of Pedigree
**The Princess Victoria** (*page 343*), Matlock. Good real ales and atmosphere, friendly staff and lots of nice bikes to look at on a weekend.
**The Boat Inn** (*page 372*), Cromford. Good for Willersley and near Scarthin Books.

### Wirksworth and Brassington

**The Barley Mow** (*page 385*), Bonsall. Great food and beer plus regular music nights and the annual international hen race!
**The Rising Sun** (*page 385*), Middleton. Friendly and local feel. Good food
**Ye Olde Gate Inn** (*page 394*), Brassington. Also handy for Harborough.
**The Miner's Arms** (*page 394*), Brassington. Also good for Harborough.

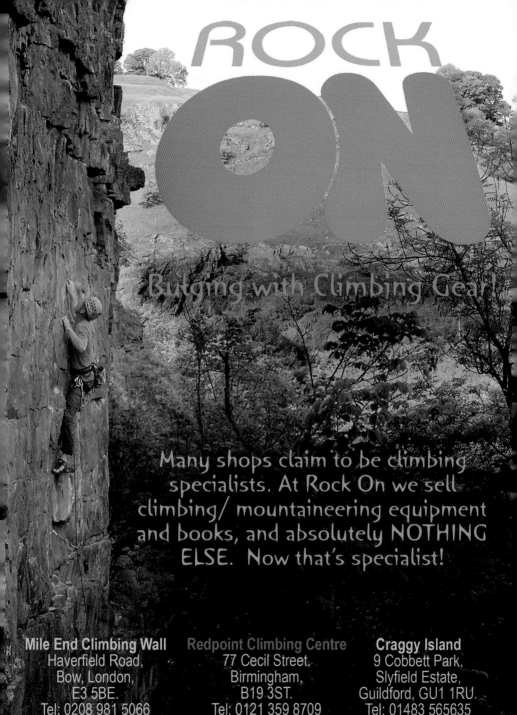

# ROCK ON

Bulging with Climbing Gear!

Many shops claim to be climbing specialists. At Rock On we sell climbing/ mountaineering equipment and books, and absolutely NOTHING ELSE. Now that's specialist!

**Mile End Climbing Wall**
Haverfield Road,
Bow, London,
E3 5BE.
Tel: 0208 981 5066

**Redpoint Climbing Centre**
77 Cecil Street,
Birmingham,
B19 3ST.
Tel: 0121 359 8709

**Craggy Island**
9 Cobbett Park,
Slyfield Estate,
Guildford, GU1 1RU.
Tel: 01483 565635

www.rockonclimbing.co.uk

Sam King on Windows 95, E6a+, Blackwell Halt                    Photo by Jess Garland

For those rare times of year when climbing on limestone isn't possible, the following climbing walls are well-worth considering. We haven't got enough room for approach directions so you will have to ring them up to find out how to get there. More information on the UKClimbing web site at **www.ukclimbing.com/walls/**

- Lead routes
- Bouldering
- Cafe
- Shop

**Awesome Walls** *Page 2*
The Engine House, Stockport.
Tel: 0161 494 9949
Large dedicated climbing centre.
**www.awesomewalls.co.uk**

**Awesome Walls** *Page 2*
Sefton Road, Stoke-on-Trent.
Tel: 01782 341919
Bouldering wall with some leading lines.
**www.awesomewalls.co.uk**

**The Climbing Works -**
Centenary Works, Little London Road, Sheffield.
Tel: 0114 250 9990
Opened in 2006, a dedicated Bouldering wall.
**www.climbingworks.com**

**The Edge, Sheffield**
John Street, Sheffield. Tel: 0114 275 8899
Dedicated climbing centre built in 1994 with new developments for each new season.
**www.sheffield-climbing.co.uk**

**The Foundry, Sheffield**
45 Mowbray Street, Sheffield. Tel: 0114 279 6331
Dedicated climbing centre built and added to by various people since 1991.
**www.foundryclimbing.com**

**Glossop Leisure Centre**
High Street East, Glossop. Tel: 01457 842272
Moulded concrete bouldering wall built by Bendcrete in 1990.

**The Leeds Wall** *Page 27*
Gelderd Road, Leeds.
Tel: 0113 234 1554
A dedicated climbing centre.
**www.theleedswall.co.uk**

**Manchester Wall -** *Opposite*
St Benedict's Church, Bennett Street,
Manchester, M12 5ND
Tel: 0161 230 7006
A dedicated climbing centre
**www.manchesterclimbingcentre.com**

**Nottingham Climbing Centre**
The Old Pool, 212 Noel St, Nottingham.
Tel: 0115 9988233
Dedicated climbing centre built in 2011.
**www.nottingham-climbing.co.uk**

**Rope Race**
Goyt Mill, Upper Hibbert Lane, Marple. Tel: 0161 426 0226
Dedicated climbing centre. Built and added to by various people since 1993.
**www.roperace.co.uk**

Time for the climbing wall maybe? Perhaps, but Horseshoe (aka Furness) was still busy with climbers when this shot was taken.

During the 1980s Peak Limestone was at the forefront of hard sport climbing and all the talk was of crags like Raven Tor and Chee Dale. The magazines and guidebooks of the time naturally focussed on these top routes and some of the older crags got forgotten and ignored. The general impression was that Peak limestone was only for those operating in the higher grades, however there always have been other places like Aldery Cliff, Harborough, Brassington, Ravensdale and Wildcat where there are plenty of excellent trad routes in the VS and below category. In this photo Ash Mellor, belayed by Dan Fawley, is on the classic *Clothesline* (S) - *page 271* - at Aldery Cliff. Photo: Dan Lane

# Peak Limestone Climbing

## Access

The limestone crags of the Peak District are managed by a variety of different land owners and conservation groups all of whom are keen to protect their own part of the natural landscape. This often brings them into conflict with climbers particularly over issues such as crag approach paths and nesting birds. The main issues in the Peak have been in Chee Dale and Water-cum-Jolly, and at some of the smaller crags like Ravensdale and Willersley. In most cases patient negotiating by members of the BMC Peak Area Committee have resulted in satisfactory solutions which enable climbing to continue, but sometimes with restrictions. All the specific details are given with the crag introductions. **Please familiarise yourself with this information before climbing.**

There are also some quarries described which have no formal access agreement. **Climbing has taken place in these quarries over the years, but it should be noted that their inclusion in this book doesn't imply that you have a right of access to climb on the crag.**

A crowded Ravensdale. Photo: Chris Craggs

## Good Practice Points for Crag Development and Maintenance

The following Good Practice Points for new routing, crag re-development, bolting and route cleaning have been suggested as a way of avoiding conflict. Please read them carefully especially if you are new routing or considering (re)placing any bolts.

**1)** Find out if the area intended for development or maintenance is protected for geological or biological reasons, or because of breeding birds.

**2)** Some cliffs may be in SSSIs (Sites of Special Scientific Interest). Drilling and vegetation-stripping on SSSIs will require consent from the land owner or the land manager. If you are unsure, make a note of as many of the details as possible - for example grid reference, nearest village. For all areas contact the local BMC Area Representatives (see below).

**3)** Adhere strictly to any bans or restrictions on drilling. If in any doubt seek advice from the BMC Access Officer or local Area Representative (see below).

**4)** If you encounter access problems when at a crag, DO NOT be confrontational, leave the crag politely and inform the local BMC Area Representatives (see below).

**5)** Ensure safe practice when cleaning or drilling particularly with respect to members of the public who may be below. Try to be discrete and don't drill at busy times and weekends.

**6)** Check on local ethical situation and consensus before bolting or replacing gear.

**7)** Avoid leaving krabs and threads on routes while working them.

## British Mountaineering Council

British Mountaineering Council, 177-179 Burton Road, Manchester, M20 2BB.
Tel: 0870 010 4878 Fax: 0161 445 4500. Web: **www.thebmc.co.uk** Email: **office@thebmc.co.uk**
The BMC is the official body representing climbers in Britain. If you have problems regarding access to any of the areas in this book, then get in touch with the BMC Access Officer at the address above.

## Gear

For the traditional routes on Peak Limestone a good sized rack with plenty of small and medium wires is required. A few cams should be carried but be wary of trusting them the same way you might trust a placement on gritstone since it is not unknown for them to strip out of smooth-sided limestone cracks when loaded. Around a dozen quick-draws will suffice for most routes and double 50m ropes (or 60m for High Tor) are essential. A selection of threads of various lengths and thicknesses will be found useful on many climbs for tying off old pegs, threading pockets and saplings, and extending runners.

For sport routes a single rope is the norm and, apart for a few exceptions, a 60m rope plus 12 quick-draws will be adequate. A rope sheet to keep the rope clean and a clip-stick to clip high 1st bolts may also be found useful.

## Bolting

The bolting history of the Peak area is the longest in Britain with many of the ethical debates being fought out here in the 70s and 80s. This has resulted in a variety of different bolts being littered across the crags varying in quality from solid to downright dangerous. Most of the quarries now have relatively good bolts and many of the old bolts on the harder crags have been replaced in recent years. Be wary of anything that looks like the photo to the right and support the local bolt funds each time you go climbing.

An old High Tor Bolt. Photo: Graham Hoey

### Bolt Funds in the Peak Area

The **Peak Bolt Fund** was set up in 2008 by local climbers who wanted to re-equip existing routes mainly on the old natural crags like Raven Tor and the Chee Dale Cornice. A lot of work has been done on these crags but there is still much to do.

The second bolt fund for the Peak limestone area is the **Gary Gibson Bolt Fund**. Gary has bolted thousands of routes across the country and is responsible for the majority of the bolting in the Peak quarries. Although Gary has established many new routes he also puts in a huge amount of effort in rebolting older climbs.

### How can I help?

The main way everyone can help is by making a donation. The simple gesture of a £10 online donation each time you go clipping bolts in the Peak can go a long way to providing the necessary funding. If you want to get more involved then there is always a need for volunteers to help with the hard work. Bolting is a difficult and time-consuming activity. If you are an experienced climber, or have a background in rope access, you could be a real asset to the Peak Bolt Fund.

If you wish to place some bolts yourself, please contact either the BMC or the Peak Bolt Fund first since they will be able to advise on bolting technique. It is important that all new bolts placed should be proper stainless steel bolts at least 10mm in diameter. For more information have a look at the BMC Better Bolts Campaign - www.thebmc.co.uk

To donate to the **Peak Bolt Fund** or the **Gary Gibson Bolt Fund** go to www.ukboltfund.org

The routes in this book are given one of two different grades depending on whether they are a trad route or a sport route. The table to the right gives a rough comparison of the sport and trad grade with other international grading systems.

On trad routes the majority of the gear is carried by the lead climber and is hand-placed.

A sport route is defined as one where all the major protection comes from gear fixed in the rock (bolts).

## British Trad Grade

**1) Adjectival grade (Diff, VDiff, Severe, Hard Severe (HS), Very Severe (VS), Hard Very Severe (HVS), E1, E2,.... to E10).**
An overall picture of the route including how well protected it is, how sustained and a general indication of the level of difficulty of the whole route.

**2) Technical grade (4a, 4b, 4c,..... to 7b).**
The difficulty of the hardest single move, or short section.

## Sport Grade

The sport grade is a measure of how hard it is going to be to get up a certain section of rock. It makes no attempt to tell you how hard the hardest move is, nor how scary a route is.

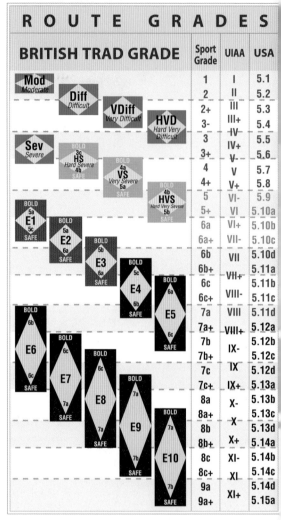

| ROUTE GRADES | | | |
|---|---|---|---|
| **BRITISH TRAD GRADE** | Sport Grade | UIAA | USA |
| Mod (Moderate) | 1 | I | 5.1 |
| Diff (Difficult) | 2 | II | 5.2 |
| VDiff (Very Difficult) | 2+ | III | 5.3 |
| HVD (Hard Very Difficult) | 3- | III+ | 5.4 |
| | 3 | IV / IV+ | 5.5 |
| Sev (Severe) 3c / HS (Hard Severe) 4b | 3+ | V- | 5.6 |
| VS (Very Severe) 4a 5a | 4 | V | 5.7 |
| HVS (Hard Very Severe) 4b 5a | 4+ | V+ | 5.8 |
| | 5 | VI- | 5.9 |
| E1 5a 5c | 5+ | VI | 5.10a |
| E2 5a 6a | 6a | VI+ | 5.10b |
| E3 5b 6a | 6a+ | VII- | 5.10c |
| E4 5c 6a | 6b | VII | 5.10d |
| E5 6b 6c | 6b+ | VII+ | 5.11a |
| | 6c | VIII- | 5.11b |
| | 6c+ | | 5.11c |
| E6 6b 6c | 7a | VIII | 5.11d |
| E7 6c 6c | 7a+ | VIII+ | 5.12a |
| E8 7a 7a | 7b | IX- | 5.12b |
| E9 7a 7a | 7b+ | IX | 5.12c |
| E10 7b 7b | 7c | IX | 5.12d |
| | 7c+ | IX+ | 5.13a |
| | 8a | X- | 5.13b |
| | 8a+ | X | 5.13c |
| | 8b | | 5.13d |
| | 8b+ | X+ | 5.14a |
| | 8c | XI- | 5.14b |
| | 8c+ | XI | 5.14c |
| | 9a | XI+ | 5.14d |
| | 9a+ | | 5.15a |

## Colour Coding

The routes are all given a colour-coded dot corresponding to a grade band. The colour represents a level that a climber should be happy at, hence sport routes tend to be technically harder than the equivalent coloured trad routes because the climber doesn't need to worry about the protection.

**❶ - Up to Severe / Up to 4+**
Mostly these should be good for beginners and those wanting and easy life.

**❷ - HS to HVS / 5 to 6a+**
General ticking routes for those with more experience.

**❸ - E1 to E3 / 6b to 7a**
Routes for the experienced and keen climber. A grade band which includes many of the Peak's great classics.

**❹ - E4 or 7a+ and above**
The really hard stuff including some of the top sport routes in the country.

Steve McClure climbing *The Bastard* (8c+) - *page 240* - at
Rubicon in Water-cum-Jolly. Photo Keith Sharples
The route follows the approximate line of an aid route by
Chris Craggs dubbed *Free That You Bastards*. This gauntlet
was picked up by the young Sheffield climbers of the
time who made several attempts to take up the challenge
resulting in initially *Zeke the Freak* to the left of the aid line
and finally *The Bastard* climbed by John Welford in 1995.

Since 2003 the routes on Peak Limestone have been open for voting on stars and grades on the ROCKFAX website and these graded lists have been based on the many votes we have received.

The list on this page covers the sport routes. Some additional routes have been added if the online database consensus wasn't sufficient. If you disagree with the list then please let us know by visiting the website and placing your votes - **www.rockfax.com**

Neil Foster pulling through the steep upper moves of *Circe* (E5 6b) - *page 60* - at Stoney Middleton. Photo: Keith Sharples

Rachael Crewe and Chris James on pitch 2 of *Froth* (VS 4c) -
*page 58* - at Stoney Middleton. Photo: Keith Sharples
Rachael won the 'Be In My Calendar' competition run by Keith
on UKClimbing.com. Each year he invites the lucky winner to
come on a photo-shoot and feature in the Calendar on a certain
month sponsored by UKClimbing.com

Dave Graham from the USA working
*Hubble* (8c+) - *page 218* - at Raven Tor.
Photo: Keith Sharples

## 7 c +

- ** Minos. . . . . . . . . . . . . . . . . 172
- ** High Torquing . . . . . . . . . . 345
- ** Michael Foot Jam . . . . . . . . 161
- ** Wil E. Coyote. . . . . . . . . . . 345
- ** Exit Wounds . . . . . . . . . . 363
- ** Let's Get Fossilised. . . . . . . 213
- ** Rooster Booster . . . . . . . . . 220
- ** The Vision . . . . . . . . . . . . 228
- ** The Weakling. . . . . . . . . . . 246
- ** Orange Sunshine . . . . . . . . 167
- ** Back to the Future. . . . . . . . 327
- ** Buried Alive . . . . . . . . . . . 285
- ** The Lockless Monster. . . . . . 161
- ** 666 . . . . . . . . . . . . . . . . 293
- *** Toys for the Boys. . . . . . . . 163
- ** A Vision of Loveliness. . . . . . 171
- ** The Tier Drop X-plodes. . . . . 171
- ** Communication Breakdown. . 171
- ** Boo . . . . . . . . . . . . . . . . 191
- ** Step on It. . . . . . . . . . . . . 327
- ** Pingham's Route. . . . . . . . . 139
- [50] Body Machine . . . . . . . . . . 216
- *** Proud Whore . . . . . . . . . . 218
- ** Pinging in the Rain . . . . . . . 139
- *** Spear of Odin . . . . . . . . . . 285
- *** Total Breakdown . . . . . . . . 171
- ** The Jug Jockey . . . . . . . . . . 199
- [50] Arch Enemies . . . . . . . . . . 312

## 7 c

- ** Knocked Out Loaded. . . . . . 228
- ** The Squealer. . . . . . . . . . . 341
- ** Hallowed be My Name . . . . . 381
- ** Fossil Wall . . . . . . . . . . . . 213
- ** Honoray Buoux . . . . . . . . . 294
- ** Obscene Toilet. . . . . . . . . . 222
- ** Wild in Me . . . . . . . . . . . . 225
- ** Jonah's Boner . . . . . . . . . . 312
- ** Stone the Loach . . . . . . . . . 154
- ** Sturgeon in the Cupboard. . . 155
- ** Fishing Without a Licence . . . 157
- ** Why Me?. . . . . . . . . . . . . 167
- ** À Bout de Souffle . . . . . . . . 177
- ** Taylor Made. . . . . . . . . . . . 198
- ** Another Toadside Attraction. . 222
- ** Esmerunga . . . . . . . . . . . . 163
- ** Let the Tripe Increase . . . . . 242
- ** Wright to Left . . . . . . . . . . 198
- ** Cordless Madness. . . . . . . . 206
- ** Laughing at the Rain. . . . . . . 139
- *** The Boltest . . . . . . . . . . . 362
- [50] Indecent Exposure . . . . . . . 216
- *** Cry of Despair. . . . . . . . . . 200
- ** Theology . . . . . . . . . . . . . 195
- ** Lightweight . . . . . . . . . . . 173
- ** Paulliac . . . . . . . . . . . . . . 251

## 7 b +

- ** A Bigger Tail . . . . . . . . . . . 239
- *** The Sea is a Brown Paper Bag. . . 171
- ** Moat People . . . . . . . . . . . 243
- ** Fire on Water. . . . . . . . . . . 252
- ** Pedal to the Metal . . . . . . . . 327
- ** Midgard Serpent . . . . . . . . 285
- [50] Sardine . . . . . . . . . . . . . . 222
- Bored of the Lies. . . . . . . . . 202
- ** Fenris . . . . . . . . . . . . . . . 285

- ** Barefoot in a Pool of Sharks . 157
- ** Stung. . . . . . . . . . . . . . . . 163
- ** Nervous Breakdown . . . . . . 171
- ** Meterol. . . . . . . . . . . . . . . 177
- ** The Naive and Sentimental Lover . 200
- ** Cathedral Taste . . . . . . . . . 177
- ** Dope . . . . . . . . . . . . . . . . 180
- ** Pump out the Squealies . . . . 349
- ** That was the River . . . . . . . 200
- ** Damson in Distress. . . . . . . 186
- ** Succubus. . . . . . . . . . . . . . 202
- ** The King of Ming. . . . . . . . . 67
- ** Soggy Biscuits. . . . . . . . . . . 99
- ** Power of Soul . . . . . . . . . . . 111
- ** Ratline . . . . . . . . . . . . . . . 126
- ** Cosmopolitan . . . . . . . . . . 206
- [50] Brachiation Dance . . . . . . . . 248
- [50] Moatorhead. . . . . . . . . . . . 243

## 7 b

- ** Deceptive . . . . . . . . . . . . . 341
- ** Tin Of. . . . . . . . . . . . . . . . 222
- ** Daylight Robbery. . . . . . . . . 168
- ** Good Time Emporium . . . . . 341
- ** Blockhead . . . . . . . . . . . . . 168
- ** Certificate X. . . . . . . . . . . . 273
- ** Secret Gudgeon Society. . . . 154
- ** XXXX. . . . . . . . . . . . . . . . 273
- ** Max Museum. . . . . . . . . . . 160
- ** Systems Malfunction . . . . . . 166
- ** Kiss My Arcy . . . . . . . . . . . 175
- ** Never to Look Back. . . . . . . . 179
- ** Witch in Stitch . . . . . . . . . . 181
- ** Snails of the Riverbank. . . . . . 201
- ** Big Zipper . . . . . . . . . . . . . 202
- ** The Third Order. . . . . . . . . . 206
- ** Virtual Insanity . . . . . . . . . . 99
- ** Old Man River . . . . . . . . . . 200
- ** Reward . . . . . . . . . . . . . . . 171

## 7 a +

- [50] Whose Line is it Anyway? . . . 202
- ** Countdown . . . . . . . . . . . . 167
- ** The Corniceman . . . . . . . . . 206
- ** The Main Motor Mile . . . . . . 139
- ** Tatanka Yotanka. . . . . . . . . 362
- ** Blessed are the Weak. . . . . . 381
- ** Incapacity Benefit . . . . . . . . 246
- ** Hungry Eyes . . . . . . . . . . . 154
- ** No Hiding Place . . . . . . . . . 155
- ** Max to the Wall . . . . . . . . . 159
- *** Kiss Me Hardy. . . . . . . . . . 175
- [50] Open Gate. . . . . . . . . . . . . 165
- ** Darl - Pitch 2 . . . . . . . . . . . 170
- ** Stealth. . . . . . . . . . . . . . . . 127
- ** Armistice Day . . . . . . . . . . 202
- ** Lost Contact . . . . . . . . . . . . 99

## 7 a

- [50] Rubicon. . . . . . . . . . . . . . 241
- ** Martial Music. . . . . . . . . . . 202
- [50] Cairn . . . . . . . . . . . . . . . . 127
- ** Fatal Attraction. . . . . . . . . . 176
- ** Much Monkey Magic . . . . . . 138
- ** Demolition Man . . . . . . . . . 83
- ** Can Boys . . . . . . . . . . . . . . 99
- *** Darl - Pitch 1 . . . . . . . . . . 167
- ** Case Adjourned. . . . . . . . . . 165

- [50] Clarion Call . . . . . . . . . . . . 202
- ** The Prophecy . . . . . . . . . . . 113
- ** Max Pax 'em In . . . . . . . . . . 159
- ** Supercrack . . . . . . . . . . . . 341
- *** White Gold. . . . . . . . . . . . 188
- ** Strait Jacket. . . . . . . . . . . . 365
- ** Quality Control. . . . . . . . . . 168
- ** High Society . . . . . . . . . . . 175
- ** Max Head Room . . . . . . . . . 159

## 6 c +

- ** Up the River Without a Paddle . . . 200
- ** The Max Works. . . . . . . . . . 159
- ** The Orcadian Donkey's Spotted Tail 362
- ** Run For Your Wife . . . . . . . . 82
- ** The Crystal Maze . . . . . . . . 100
- ** Four Telling Tales. . . . . . . . . 113
- ** Megalithic Man Direct . . . . . . 82

## 6 c

- ** An Ancient Rhythm . . . . . . . 83
- ** Legal Action. . . . . . . . . . . . 82
- ** Riding the Bullet . . . . . . . . . 100
- ** Say it With Flowers . . . . . . . 82
- ** Mouse Hunt. . . . . . . . . . . . 112
- ** Over the Hill . . . . . . . . . . . 113
- ** Max 'is Wall . . . . . . . . . . . . 159
- [50] Private Prosecution . . . . . . . 82
- ** Going Straight . . . . . . . . . . 101
- ** Rain Dance . . . . . . . . . . . . 80
- ** Litany Against Fear . . . . . . . 82

## 6 b +

- ** The Lime Arch. . . . . . . . . . . 312
- ** Megalithic Man . . . . . . . . . 82
- ** Shot Yer Bolt . . . . . . . . . . . 83
- ** Mr. Love Pants. . . . . . . . . . 100
- ** Recoil . . . . . . . . . . . . . . . . 365
- ** The Arapahoe Connection . . 150

## 6 b

- [50] Rocky Variations . . . . . . . . 110
- [50] Apollo Creed . . . . . . . . . . 110
- ** Shanacie . . . . . . . . . . . . . 100
- ** Calci-Mauve. . . . . . . . . . . . 113
- ** Rotund Rooley. . . . . . . . . . 81
- ** The Omen . . . . . . . . . . . . 113
- ** Outer Limits. . . . . . . . . . . . 126
- ** Windows 95. . . . . . . . . . . . 151

## 6 a +

- ** Open Season . . . . . . . . . . . 101
- ** School's Out . . . . . . . . . . . 81
- ** Bag of Bones. . . . . . . . . . . 112

## 6 a

- [50] Coral Seas. . . . . . . . . . . . . 110
- ** Supernatural . . . . . . . . . . . 113

## 5 +

- ** Senile Delinquents . . . . . . . 127

| Area | Crag | Routes | up to 4+ | 5 to 6a+ | 6b to 7a | 7a+ and up | Mod to S | HS to HVS | E1 to E3 | E4 and up |
|---|---|---|---|---|---|---|---|---|---|---|
| | | | SPORT ROUTES | | | | TRAD ROUTES | | | |
| Stoney Horseshoe | **Stoney** | 137 | - | - | - | 8 | 7 | 39 | 44 | 39 |
| | **Horseshoe** | 274 | 18 | 119 | 114 | 5 | - | 4 | 12 | 2 |
| Buxton Area | **Smalldale** | 51 | - | 9 | 33 | 8 | - | 1 | - | - |
| | **Harpur Hill** | 322 | 5 | 144 | 119 | 7 | - | 24 | 22 | 1 |
| | **Lovers' Leap** | 10 | - | 2 | 6 | 2 | - | - | - | - |
| | **Beerhouse Buttress** | 18 | - | 2 | 13 | 3 | - | - | - | - |
| | **Staden Quarry** | 59 | - | 2 | 11 | 14 | - | 7 | 19 | 6 |
| Chee Dale | **Chee Dale Upper** | 361 | - | 19 | 106 | 157 | 3 | 14 | 31 | 31 |
| | **Chee Dale Lower** | 162 | - | - | 23 | 76 | - | 7 | 27 | 29 |
| Miller's Dale | **Blackwell Dale** | 10 | - | - | - | 9 | - | - | 1 | - |
| | **Raven Tor** | 62 | - | - | 2 | 58 | - | - | - | 2 |
| | **Water-cum-Jolly** | 186 | - | - | 13 | 76 | - | 6 | 34 | 57 |
| | **Ravensdale** | 40 | - | - | - | - | 4 | 22 | 10 | 4 |
| Central Peak | **Aldery Cliff** | 26 | - | - | - | - | 2 | 20 | 4 | - |
| | **Taddington** | 22 | - | 3 | 11 | 8 | - | - | - | - |
| | **Rheinstor** | 13 | - | - | - | - | 1 | 7 | 4 | 1 |
| Dovedale Area | **Wolfscote Dale** | 15 | - | - | - | - | 1 | 5 | 6 | 3 |
| | **Manifold Valley** | 19 | - | - | - | 9 | 1 | 3 | 3 | 3 |
| | **Beeston Tor** | 37 | - | - | - | 5 | 1 | 13 | 12 | 6 |
| | **Dovedale** | 115 | - | - | 3 | 6 | 3 | 30 | 40 | 33 |
| | **Turkey Dip Rocks** | 11 | - | 1 | - | 10 | - | - | - | - |
| Matlock Area | **Masson Lees** | 75 | 6 | 13 | 40 | 16 | - | - | - | - |
| | **Pic Tor** | 13 | - | - | - | - | - | 3 | 8 | 2 |
| | **Lorry Park Quarry** | 20 | - | - | 4 | 13 | - | - | 2 | 1 |
| | **High Tor** | 83 | - | 2 | 10 | 8 | 1 | 7 | 21 | 34 |
| | **Long Tor Quarry** | 18 | - | - | 5 | 13 | - | - | - | - |
| | **Wildcat** | 38 | - | - | 3 | 4 | 1 | 24 | 3 | 3 |
| | **Willersley** | 53 | - | - | - | 2 | - | 24 | 16 | 11 |
| Wirksworth Area | **Colehill Quarry** | 33 | - | 17 | 14 | 1 | - | - | 1 | - |
| | **Harborough Rocks** | 50 | - | - | - | - | 34 | 15 | - | 1 |
| | **Brassington** | 29 | - | - | - | - | 18 | 11 | - | - |
| | **Hipley Hill** | 4 | - | - | - | - | - | 1 | 2 | 1 |

Region groupings (left margin): North, Southwest, Southeast.

More colour density means more routes and more quality.

| Approach | Sun | Sheltered | Dry in Rain | Multi-pitch | Restrictions | Summary | Page |
|---|---|---|---|---|---|---|---|
| 6 - 15 min | Sun and shade | | | | | Grand old venue with superb trad climbs in a busy setting. Lots of historical classics with some polish but a good year-round venue. | 42 |
| 5 - 8 min | Sun and shade | | | | | Probably the most popular crag in the book with loads of well-bolted sport routes in the mid-grades. A good sun-trap. | 68 |
| 5 min | Evening | | | | | North-facing walls with a good set of sport routes. A nice evening venue in summer. The best routes are in the 7a range. | 96 |
| 8 - 15 min | Sun and shade | | | | | The most extensive of the quarries with lots of sport routes on some good buttresses. Some poor sectors and it can be cold. | 102 |
| Roadside | Not much sun | Sheltered | | | | A very small ravine with a small set of routes. For the enthusiast who has climbed everywhere else, or a good place when very hot. | 132 |
| 5 min | Lots of sun | | | | | A small wall with some intense technical climbs. Access isn't easy but the crag faces south and is well bolted. | 134 |
| 1 - 6 min | Sun and shade | Sheltered | | | Restrictions | Two north-facing areas: a fine trad quarry and a steep natural sport buttress. Access problems in the quarry. A good venue for hot days. | 136 |
| 15 - 30 min | Sun and shade | Sheltered | Dry in the rain | Multi-pitch | | A very extensive area with sport and trad routes on natural buttresses. Sun and shade as required. Not much in the lower grades. | 146 |
| 18 - 20 min | Sun and shade | Sheltered | Dry in the rain | | | The continuation of the dale has two contrasting crags. Sunny and mid-grade trad, steep and shady hard sport. Both brilliant venues. | 188 |
| Roadside | Evening | Sheltered | Dry in the rain | | | A powerhouse crag with a set of short and hard sport routes. Easy access and dry in the rain but nothing easy. | 212 |
| Roadside | Lots of sun | Sheltered | Dry in the rain | | | One of the country's most important hard crags with world famous routes in the upper grades. A huge sun-trap but seepage a problem. | 214 |
| 5 - 25 min | Sun and shade | Sheltered | Dry in the rain | | | A mixture of mid-grade trad buttresses and hard sport crags on opposite banks of the river. Well sheltered with sun or shade. | 226 |
| 15 min | Sun and shade | | | Multi-pitch | | Mutli-pitch trad routes on a towering crag with some great routes. Few harder routes and some polish on the classics. | 254 |
| Roadside | Morning | | | | | An east-facing old quarry with a good set of slabby easier routes. Very quick access and a plesant secluded location. | 266 |
| 5 min | Not much sun | Sheltered | Dry in the rain | | | A small set of very technical sport routes in a shady setting above the A6. | 272 |
| 2 min | Afternoon | | | | | A small wall in an idyllic setting by a river. Short and bouldery routes on pockets. | 274 |
| 5 min | From mid morning | | | | | Nicely situated at the head of a picturesque dale. A small set of mid-to-hard trad routes. | 280 |
| 5 - 15 min | Sun and shade | Sheltered | Dry in the rain | | | A very popular (with walkers) cave with hard sport routes. Some seepage but cool when dry. Two smaller isolated crags as well. | 282 |
| 12 - 15 min | Lots of sun | | | Multi-pitch | | A beautiful sun-trap crag with fine routes in the mid-to-hard grades. Some great classics and multi-pitch routes. Year-round climbing. | 289 |
| 15 - 35 min | Sun and shade | Sheltered | | | | A set of pinnacles and buttresses with mostly trad routes in sunny and shady settings. Some great classics. | 298 |
| 10 min | Not much sun | Sheltered | Dry in the rain | | | Short, steep and hard. Sport routes in an incredibly secluded location. Some seepage but stays dry in the rain. | 326 |
| 10 min | Sun and shade | Sheltered | | | | A quarry with a decent set of sport routes in the mid-grades. Some friable rock. Sunny and shady walls. | 328 |
| 5 min | Not much sun | | | | | This small natural buttress of trad routes has some good climbing on pockets. Very shady and seldom busy. | 338 |
| 2 min | Late morning | | | | | Grotty quarry used for fly-tipping with a decent wall of mid-to-hard sport routes. Shady but not a nice location. | 340 |
| 10 - 15 min | Afternoon | | | Multi-pitch | | The best natural limestone crag in the Peak with stunning routes and rock. Superb lines and climbing, little seepage and plenty of sun. | 342 |
| 5 min | Morning | | | | | A secluded wall with hard sport routes in a very shady setting just seconds from the busy A6. | 360 |
| 15 min | Afternoon | Sheltered | | Multi-pitch | | A fine natural crag with multi-pitch trad routes in the lower-to-mid grades. West-facing with little seepage. | 364 |
| 5 min | Sun and shade | | | | Restrictions | North-facing and with access problems but good routes on some decent cracks, corners and walls. A good hot weather crag. | 372 |
| 2 min | Lots of sun | | | | Restrictions | A sunny quarry with technical sport routes. Access problems. | 386 |
| 10 min | From mid morning | | | | | Some delightful easy routes on a nice hillside. Only short but perfect rock quality and very sunny. | 390 |
| 10 min | Lots of sun | | | | | Short trad routes and bouldering on a picturesque hill. | 394 |
| 2 min | Sun and shade | | | | | Steep roadside crag with superb hard crack-line. North-facing. | 398 |

Faded symbol means that only some of the routes - are sheltered / are dry in the rain / are multi-pitch / are restricted

North | Southwest | Southeast | Stoney | Horseshoe | Smalldale | Harpur Hill | Lovers' Leap | Beerhouse | Craig-y-Biggs | Staden Q | Chee Dale U | Che Dale L | Blackwell D. | Raven Tor | Water-cum-Jolly | Ravensdale | Aldery Cliff | Taddington | Rheinstor

North | Southwest | Southeast | Stoney | Horseshoe | Smalldale | Harpur Hill | Lovers' Leap | Beerhouse | Cragg-Biceps | Staden Q | Chee Dale U. | Chee Dale L. | Blackwell D. | Raven Tor | Water-c-Jolly | Ravensdale | Aldery Cliff | Taddington | Rheinstor

# Stoney Area
## Stoney Middleton,
## Horseshoe Quarry

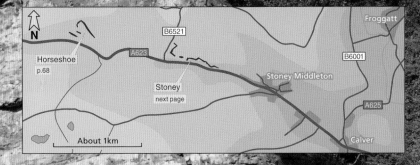

N

Horseshoe
p.68

B6521

A623

Stoney
next page

B6001

Froggatt

Stoney Middleton

A625

Calver

About 1km

Mark Rankin belaying and James Oswald
seconding on *Windhover* (E2 5c) - *page 62* - on
Windy Buttress at Stoney. Photo: Chris Craggs
The photograph was taken during the 2010
Stoney Climbers' Reunion when many old and
new faces turned up for a weekend of climbing,
reminiscing around a beer and barbeque. The
crag was busier than it had been for years and
many classic climbs were done.

| | No star | ☆ | ☆☆ | ☆☆☆ |
|---|---|---|---|---|
| Mod to S | 4 | 3 | - | - |
| HS to HVS | 10 | 19 | 9 | 1 |
| E1 to E3 | 12 | 18 | 8 | 6 |
| E4 / 7a+ and up | 9 | 21 | 11 | 6 |

Stoney is a crag which most climbers will encounter at some stage in their climbing career. This could be an early visit to tick the many mid-grade classic trad routes like *Padme*, *Pearly Gates*, *Froth* and *Sin*, or it could be at a later stage, as a seasoned campaigner coming to do battle with the essential yardstick routes like *Scoop Wall*, *Our Father*, *Bitterfingers*, *Wee Doris* and *Oliver*. Many folks' initial experiences at Stoney are off-putting - too much polish on the easy routes and too many hard moves on the hard routes. This is not always helped by the traffic noise though at least the quarrying has stopped. However, the one thing that all climbers who have experienced the fine climbing on the crag will agree on - the routes are certainly memorable. Nothing here drops into the done-once-quickly-forgotten category that might be levelled at routes in nearby Horseshoe. The best advice is to come here and try the routes for yourself with an open mind, but be prepared for the odd bit of loose rock, polished foothold, occasional awkward runner placements and some pretty solid grades. The crag has been an icon of Peak climbing for years - long may this continue.

## Approach    Also see map on page 41

The crag is perched above the A623, to the west of the village of Stoney Middleton. Park at a large lay-by on the left as you leave the village westwards, it can be very busy at weekends. From here it is a short walk up the road to Garage Buttress and the rest of the crag. Parking is no longer allowed on the sections of track underneath the buttresses. Do not park in front of the Electricity Sub-station by the Electric Quarry.

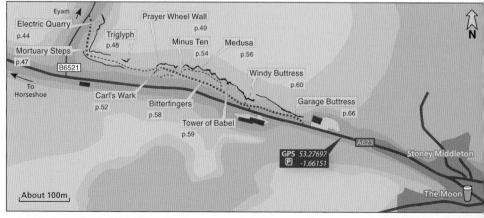

## Conditions

Stoney is fast-drying, sheltered and doesn't seep as much as many Peak limestone crags. Often when the nearby grit is being blasted by bitter winds, climbing can still be reasonably comfortable in the sheltered bays. The crag faces south and catches all the available sun, but can also be relatively cool in summer when the bays and trees give shade. The exception to these conditions is *Windhover* and its neighbours which are exposed to all the elements.

Luke Holmes stretched out on the crux of *Scoop Wall* (E2 5c) - *page 64* - on Windy Buttress at Stoney. Photo: Dan Lane Originally the route was a full blown aid climb but it didn't take long for the local dream team of Tom Proctor and Geoff Birtles to convert it into a classic free climb which is generally regarded as the best route at Stoney.

**❶ Helmut Schmitt . . .**   E6 6b

Often top-roped, but better as a testing lead if you are up to it. Climb a small groove in the arete, then move right along the break (direct is a fingery 6c). Up again to the first overlap, then pull over at a small groove. At the top overlap the hidden wire around to the left is worth seeking out. A final hard pull gains the upper wall.
*FA. Jerry Moffatt 1980*

**❷ Cabbage Crack . . . . . .**   E4 6a

The crack-line right of *Helmut* provides a fine workout. Steep and well-protected, the name is somewhat misleading as the crack is seldom used by those in the know!
*FFA. Tom Proctor, John Kirk 1979. Previously aided.*

**❸ Jasper . . . . . . . . . . .**   E3 6a

The easiest line on the wall, but still solid at the grade. Start as for *Cabbage*, or harder and more directly, up the wall to the right to gain the hanging groove. The last heave into the groove is hard, but once established you can bridge out for a breather. Finish straight up.
*FA. Jack Street, Geoff Birtles 1963*
*FFA. Tom Proctor 1975 then again in 1980 after losing a massive flake.*

**❹ Oliver . . . . . . . . . .**   E4 6a

One of the best routes at Stoney, with a great variety of bold and strenuous moves, and enough gear to make it safe - even if it doesn't feel like it. Save it for the lead instead of top-roping it. Follow the elegant groove to the roof, then move left and climb the tricky wall to a break (pumpy-to-place gear and scary position). Step right and stand in the break (baffling for some) then climb the still awkward upper wall. Wonderful.
*FA. Geoff Birtles 1979. Lost holds in the 1980s.*

**❺ Millionaire Touch . . .**   E4 6b

The first crack left of the corner gives a great pitch with a bit of a stopper move past a peg, the scene of much profanity, particularly for the short. After a good rest, the upper wall is less demanding, but demands respect. Thought by some to be the best route on the whole crag.
*FA. Geoff Birtles, Tom Proctor (1pt aid and a rest in the tree - long deceased) 1976 FFA. Nick Colton 1980.*

**❻ X Calibre . . . . . . . . .**   E6 6b

A poor eliminate. Start as for *Millionaire*, but move right below the roof. Climb direct (pegs) to the next break, where further hard moves gain easier ground and the cherty headwall.
*FA. Gary Gibson 2001*

**7 Brown Corner** .... 🌀👤🗲☐ HVS 5a

The huge corner at the back of the quarry is usually too grotty to be enjoyable. If loads of people have been up the thing and cleaned all the holds, then it may even be worth 3 stars.
*FA. Barry Webb, Charlie Curtis 1961. The route was very dirty and loose. There was also a massive tree in the corner which you could step into.*

*The wall to the right is* **One 'ard Move E6 6b** *(FA. Dougie Hall 1988)*

**8 Damocles** .......... 🌀🗲☐ E3 5b

Strenuous and sustained climbing up the long crack-line. Often loose and dirty, but good when clean. Needs traffic.
*FA. Ron Fawcett 1976*

**9 Golden Boy** ...... 🌀🖊🖊☐ E5 6b

The line to the left of *Emotional Rescue* following some faint crack-lines past 3 pegs. Dirty and rarely climbed.
*FA. Gary Gibson 1995*

**10 Emotional Rescue** . 🌀🖊▮☐ E5 6b

A big pitch which is seldom attempted. An inspection is probably advisable, since the gear is marginal, and the peg poor. Connect a series of cracks to an impasse at mid-height. Tricky moves lead past this, then up to the break. Follow easy corners to a ledge below a blank wall. Either power up this (direct rather than on the right) .... or cop-out and scuttle up the corner on the left.
*FA. Steve Bancroft, John Stevenson 1980*

**11 John Peel** .......... 🌀🖊☐ E2 5b

A reasonable old climb, but it is suffering from lack of traffic. Climb the long pumpy crack past a tricky bulge. Continue slightly left up the cleanest rock to the top.
*FA. Jack Street, John Ibbotson 1965. The second tried to lead the route first, but his attempts resulted in the route name.*

**12 Creeping Flesh** ...... 🗲🖊☐ E4 6a

The wall right of *John Peel* is loose and escapable.
*FA. Gary Gibson 2001*

## The Electric Quarry

This quarry contains arguably the finest wall at Stoney, but in its least-pleasant setting. There is something surreal about climbing while there is the gentle hum of the electricity substation coming from behind you, but the intricate technical moves usually provide enough of a distraction.

**Access** - Access here is a little touchy so keep well clear of any of the buildings (for your own safety if nothing else).

**Approach** - Although it is a little longer to walk, the best parking is the lay-by in the village. The crag-base path leads easily to the quarry (see map on page 41) or walk up the side of the main road. **Do not park in front of the substation.**

**Conditions** - This is another well-sheltered, often-dry sun-trap which is an excellent winter training ground, however it is desperate on hot afternoons in the warmer months.

North | Southwest | Southeast | Stoney | Horseshoe | Smalldale | Harpur Hill | Lovers' Leap | Beerhouse | Craig-y-Biceps | Staden Q | Blackwell D. | Che Dale L. | Chee Dale U. | Raven Tor | Water-c-Jolly | Ravensdale | Aldery Cliff | Taddington | Rheinstor

## The Slurper

Up the slope to the right of the quarry is a long wall running out to the jutting tower of *Mortuary Steps*. There are some decent routes here, though over the years they have become increasingly overgrown. Recent excavations have revealed some quality climbs, get them done whilst they are clean.

**Approach -** Although it is a little longer to walk the best parking is the lay-by in the village. The crag-base path leads easily towards the quarry (see map on page 41) the routes are just before the slope down to the quarry. **Do not park in front of the substation.**

**Conditions -** The wall gets the afternoon sun and generally the routes dry quite quickly though the surrounding trees make it sweaty and fly-infested in the summer.

**❶ Acrophobia . . . . . . . .** ☆ ⚏ ⬚ **HVS 5a**
The long corner gives a good pitch to possible tree belays on a good ledge. Move left and climb the clean groove to the summit meadows.
*FA. Jack Street and friends 1963*

**❷ J.Arthur . . . . . . . . . . . . .** ⚏ ⬚ **E1 5b**
Currently not as rank as the name suggests. Climb the crack right of the corner and its thinner continuation then trend out right to a stance on *The Slurper*. Finish as for this.
*FA. Jack Street and friends 1963*

**❸ Easy Action . . . . . . . .** ☆☆ ⚏ ⬚ **E1 5b**
The best route on this section. Climb the right-hand side of the wall into the left-hand of a pair of cracks. Up this with tricky moves left round the top bulge. Move right to join *The Slurper* at the ledges and finish as for this.
*FA. Dave Knighton, A.Bonnett 1976*

**❹ The Slurper . . . . . .** ☆ ⚏ ⚏ ⬚ **E1 5c**
The right-hand of two cracks can be dirty. It eases rapidly after a tough start and leads to a possible stance on grassy ledges. Continue up the crack on the left to the top. If you split the pitch with a belay on the ledge then the top section is worth 5b.
*FA. J.Street (2 pegs) 1965*

To the right the vegetation has smothered a small collection of routes that were of dubious worth when they were clean, best let them go. Beyond this, a long corner runs the full height of the crag.

**❺ Drainpipe Groove . . . . .** ⚏ ▨ ⬚ **VS 4c**
A good line though suffering from neglect, if clean and dry it would be just about worth a star. Climb the vegetated groove right then left to a ledge and possible stance (4b). A loose wall leads up to the base of a neat groove, finish up this.
*FA. Cioch Club members, about 1960*

Descent

25m

North | Southwest | Southeast | Stoney | Horseshoe | Smalldale | Harpur Hill | Lovers' Leap | Beehouse | Craig-y-Biceps | Staden Q | Chee Dale U | Chee Dale L | Blackwell D. | Raven Tor | Water-c-Jolly | Ravensdale | Aldery Cliff | Taddington | Rheinstor

## Mortuary Steps

The name is macabre, but the reality is less intimidating, especially the fine HVS up the centre of the buttress. The other routes are well-positioned, but see little traffic - so take care.

**Approach -** Follow the narrow level path north from under Prayer Wheel Wall, or walk up the track from the Electric Quarry.

*The next four routes all share an easy start up Mortuary Steps to the break. You can belay in this break to reduce rope drag.*

**6 Speed Kills** . . . . . . ⬚⬚⬚ **E4 6a**
A decent problem. From the break, pull over from the left into a scoop (peg with tat usually in place). Climb direct to the top.
*FFA. Tom Proctor 1979. FA. Bob Dearman 1977*

**7 The Morgue.** . . . . . . . . ⬚⬚ **E3 5c**
From the break pull over the bulge to gain a short crack. Climb this, then transfer left to another crack. Scary climbing, but good rock and moves.
*FFA. Tom Proctor 1979. FA. Bob Dearman, Al Evans 1977*

**8 Mortuary Steps** . . . ⬚⬚⬚ **HVS 5b**
The prominent groove gives a fine climb, though the approach has its fair share of dodgy rock. It may have a peg in it, but it doesn't need one. The main groove is pumpy fun.
*FA. Barry Webb, Charlie Curtis 1961*

**9 Cardiac Arrest** . . . . . . . ⬚⬚ **E4 6a**
From the break, move right and enter a short groove. Climb this, then exit rightwards with difficulty.
*FA. Tom Proctor, Ernie Marshall 1979*

**10 Beta Blocker** . . . . . . . . ⬚⬚ **E5 6b**
Start up *Little Capucin*, but climb the steep wall on the left to join *Cardiac Arete*. Very close to the next route in places.
*FA. Gary Gibson 2001*

**11 Little Capucin** . . . . . . . . . ⬚⬚ **HVS 5a**
The lower wall is solid up to a slightly loose middle section below the break, which needs a little care. Overall good climbing at the grade.
*FFA. Chris Jackson 1975. FA. Tony Howard, Pat Fearnehough 1961*

## The Triglyph

This isolated tower of rock has three classic old crack-climbs (mostly) with a classic old first ascensionist. Due to the removal of ivy, *Morning Crack* has been rediscovered. The routes here have been misdescribed in recent years, causing a few fluttery moments.

**Approach -** Follow the path to the right from *Mortuary Steps*, or left from below Prayer Wheel Wall.

**❶ How the Hell?** . . . . . . . VS 4c
The left-hand crack gives a good sustained pitch with a mixture of loose and polished holds. Finish either rightwards, leftwards or direct over the bulge.
*FA. Joe Brown 1950*

**❷ What the Hell?** . . . VS 4b
The central crack gives a fine little route, steep, sustained and often a bit of a struggle.
*FA. Jack Soper and members of SUMC 1957*

**❸ Hell Hath No Fury** . . . . . . E2 5b
The blunt arete between the two main cracks is bold.
*FA. Warren Trippett, David Law 1997*

**❹ Morning Crack** . . . . . . . . . S 4a
The right-hand crack has been unearthed from the ivy.
*FA. Joe Brown, Don Chapman 1950*

## Prayer Wheel Wall

The ever-popular and well-sheltered Prayer Wheel Wall is home to *Padme* and *Mani* which get plenty of ascents, but the slippery and tricky crack of *Om* is best left for the chanting.

**❺ Omlette** . . . . . . . . . . . . . E3 6a
A tiny route with a huge potential fall. It can be bouldered, but where are you going to put the mat?
*FA. Steve Bancroft 1976*

**❻ Om** . . . . . . . . . E1 5b
The battered crack above the right-hand edge of the cave entrance is harder than it looks, and slippery too.
*FA. J.Atkinson 1963. Previously aided.*

**❼ This Shit Wall** . . . . . . . . . . E2 5b
The un-noteworthy wall, starting 2m left of the scooped hole. The top section can be protected by a sneaky traverse into *Mani*.
*FA. John Reagan, Paul Mitchell 1979*

**8 Mani** . . . . . . . . . . . . **E1 5b**
Climb the wall just to the right of the scooped hole. Tricky moves at mid-height can be reachy. Above, it is just a matter of finding the right holds. Requires care to protect adequately.

**9 Padme** . . . . . . . . . . . . **HVS 5a**
The shallow groove gives a pleasant pitch with a tricky start and finish. Most people descend from the ledge, but there is a worthwhile upper pitch on the face above (4c) which can be done in one run-out with no change in grade. A little loose.
*FA. Barry Webb 1961*

**10 Asparagus** . . . . . . . . . . . . **VS 4b**
Follow the open corner, then trend right to ledges and a big tree with an in-situ belay.

**11 Robin** . . . . . . . . . . . . . . . **E2 5b**
An eliminate ,but with some decent moves. Climb the white wall and shallow groove then balance up the bold rib to easy ground.

**12 Cock-a-leekie Wall** . . . . **E2 5c**
A popular route at the grade requiring a tricky move to stand in the break and one sharp pull just above.

**13 Vinegar Fly** . . . . . . . . . . . **HVS 5a**
A balancy line up the short wall and blunt arete to the right of *Cock-a-Leekie Wall* passing a bush en route. The arete is loose, great care is needed.
*FA. Al Evans 1979*

**14 Minestrone** . . . . . . . . **HVS 4c**
Devious! The short angular groove leads to a roof - tricky gear and a loose flake. Pull left over this then trend left across the ledgy wall to reach the polished final section of *Asparagus*.
*FA. D.Johnson, T.Brooks, J.Wade, J.Childs 1957*

**15 Rosehip Wine** . . . . . . . . . **HS 4a**
The more pronounced groove to the right gives a nice pitch which has recently been re-excavated. Easy ground leads past a rose bush into the 1st groove, up this and its smaller continuation above to a belay in the trees. Abseil descent.
*FA. MGC members 1961*

To mid afternoon | 10 min | Sheltered

25m
12m
6m
18m

5 6 7 8 9 10 11 12 13 14 15

North
Southwest
Southeast
Stoney
Horseshoe
Smalldale
Harpur Hill
Lovers Leap
Beerhouse
Craig-y-Biceps
Staden Q
Chee Dale U.
Chee Dale L.
Blackwell D.
Raven Tor
Water-c-Jolly
Ravensdale
Aldery Cliff
Taddington
Rheinstor

**❶ Pollyanna** . . . . . . . **E1 5b**
The pushy crack in the sidewall leads to a cleaned leftward exit.
*FA. Geoff Birtles 1968*

**❷ Horizon.** . . . . . . . . . . . . . **S 4a**
Meander up the ledgy wall just right of the corner. The corner direct is quite a bit harder but artificial. Abseil from a fixed belay.
*FA. R.Salt, B.Salt 1957*

**❸ Juggernaut** . . . . . . . . . . . **VS 5a**
Climb easy rock into a shallow groove, up this and its left arete to reach a white band of rock. Move right to a groove to finish.
*FA. Brian Moore 1965*

**❹ Lost Horizon** . . . . . . . . . . . . . **S 4a**
Wander up ledges left of the arete of the cave then move left and mantle into the base of a groove. Up then left along ledges to join the easy upper section of *Horizon*. Abseil descent.
*FA. R.Salt, B.Salt 1957*

**❺ Aux Bicyclettes** . . . . . . . . . . . **VDiff**
The arete left of the cave leads to a ledge. Move left then back right to the continuation crack. Recleaned in early 2011.

*To the right is a deep rift with a couple of speleological trips. They are almost always dirty, slippery and potentially dangerous.*

**❻ Fingal's Flue** . . . . . . . . **HS 3c**
Start 12m back in the dark and climb up the back of the chimney into the roof of the cave to access the dim and distant skylight. Exit via this. The grade is nominal and a lamp will help a lot. Finish up a blocky gully. Madness.
*FA. JW.Puttrell, H.Bishop, D .Yeomans c1918. "VDiff with three matches".*

**❼ Fingal's Cave** . . . . . . . **HVS 5a**
Bridge up the inside of the cave (easier for the tall) to the roof then exit forward to daylight via the hole above the block that caps the cave. The gully above is a pleasant amble.
*FA. Eric Byne, Clifford Moyer, Frank Elliot 1933*

*A poor route, **The Groper, VS 4c**, follows the edge of the chimney.*

**❽ The White Knight** . . . . . . . . . . **VDiff**
An easy outing, once popular but now neglected and floral. Climb the face right of the cave rightwards to a ledge - possible stance. Continue up through a bulge to more ledges then move left to an easy finish up the gully between the towers.
*FA. Eric Byne, Clifford Moyer, Frank Elliot 1933*

**❾ Gabriel and the Pearly Gates** Top►50 **VS 4c**
A fine combination of two old routes gives a near-classic.
**1)** 4c, 18m. Climb the open-book corner to a ledge (peg). Awkward moves lead up and right around a bulge.
**2)** 4c, 15m. Traverse left to the arete, high or low, and follow the exposed groove above. Take care to avoid rope-drag.
*FA. (Gabriel) Jack Soper, Nev Crowther, Dave Johnson 1957*
*FA. (Pearly Gates) Dave Mellor, Dave Johnson 1959*

**10 Solitaire** . . . . . . . . 🏆1 🎯 📐 E1 5b
The right wall of the corner has some fluttery moments, with poor gear. High in the grade.
*FA. Jack Street (solo) 1966*

**11 St. Peter** . . . . . . . . . . 🏆1 🔧 E1 5c
The arete is usually approached from its right-hand side and is tricky at the roof. It can also be started from *Solitaire*.

**12 St. Paul** . . . . . . . . . . . . . 🎯 E3 5c
The bold wall just to the right is an eliminate.
*FA. Paul Cropper 1982*

**13 Parachute** . . . . . . . . . 🏆1 📐 VS 4b
Skate and slither up the corner to experience one of the most polished routes at Stoney.

**14 Roman Candle** . . . . . . . . . 🎯 VS 4c
The right side of the wall and left side of the upper arete.
*FA. MGC members 1961*

**15 Au Gratin** . . . . . . . . . 📐 🎯 HS 4a
The grooved right-hand arete has a tricky mantel early, another near the top and not much gear.

### Fingal's Cave and Pearly Gates
The scrappy looking area between *Padme* and *Gabriel and the Pearly Gates* is actually worth a second look. There are a few worthwhile easier routes on this section. The Pearly Gates Area itself has a couple of well-climbed routes and plenty of polished holds too.

North | Southwest | Southeast | Stoney | Horseshoe | Smalldale | Harpur Hill | Lovers' Leap | Beerhouse | Craigy-Bleps | Staden Q | Chee Dale U | Che Dale L | Blackwell D | Raven Tor | Water-cum-Jolly | Ravensdale | Aldery Cliff | Teddington | Rheinstor

**❶ Flake and Pillar** . . . . . . . . . . . . [ ] **E1 5b**
The name says it all. A hard start then easier going.
**Squeek, E5 6a** - The wall to the right of the upper section has been climbed. The crucial peg may be missing.
*FA. Unknown. FA. (Squeek) Nigel Slater 1991*

**❷ Bubbles Wall** . . . ☒☒ ☒ ☒ ☒ [ ] **E4 6b**
The polished line of tiny holds leading up right to the break is a desperate, fingery problem for most, and the pit makes it potentially nasty to fall from low down. Above, it relents and follows the enjoyable sustained bubbly wall left past a tricky thread.
**Bubbles Original, E3 5c** - Gain the upper section from *Flake and Pillar* for a less-scary experience.
*FA. Tom Proctor 1975. Originally Tom started from Flake and Pillar, but later he added the described direct start.*

**❸ Black Kabul** . . . . . . . . ☒ ☒ [ ] **E5 6b**
Originally this was a right-hand finish to *Bubbles Wall*, but many now start from *Carl's Wark Crack* since this is a pleasant **E5 6a** version without the ankle-snapping start of *Bubbles Wall*. A large cam is needed for the big pocket.
*FA. Jerry Moffat 1981*

**❹ Carl's Wark Crack** . . . . ☒ ☒ [ ] **E2 5c**
Start in the pit. After the slippery start, this gives great, sustained crack-climbing on knobbly jams. Not too polished, not too desperate and entertaining for spectators.
*Historical note: under the base of the crack is a cave that was once used to park carriages in. After a body was found there it became used as a rubbish dump. Eventually the ground reached its current level.*

**❺ Scarab** . . . . . . . ☒ ☒ ☒ ☒ [ ] **E6 6b**
A sustained wall-climb which is seldom led. Top-roping has made it desperate and not very much fun anymore.
*FA. Gabe Reagan (2pts) 1976. FFA. Tom Proctor (via a left variation) 1979.*

**❻ Green Crack** . . . . . . . . . . . ☒ [ ] **VS 4c**
The slippery open-book corner.
*FA. Stu Tyrrell, Brian Manton and others 1968*

**❼ Soapsuds** . . . . . . . . . . ☒ ☒ [ ] **E3 6a**
A technical little problem which is worth **E4 6b** if the direct line is followed. Can be dirty, especially at the top.
*FA. Al Evans and a cast of thousands 1979*

### Carl's Wark

Below Prayer Wheel Wall is a hidden bay with a steep back wall. The easy access to the top has made this a popular top-rope venue, consequently many of the routes are very polished. Don't be put off though, pack your rack and get involved with the cracks and you will have a good time. Just avoid the start of *Bubbles Wall* unless you are confident.
**Approach** - From above, find a path to the left of the wall (looking out). The wall can also be reached easily from below, via a short track off the main road.

Prayer Wheel Wall p.49

Stephen Horne taking on the mighty *Dead Banana Crack* (E1 5c) - *page 58* - at Stoney. Photo: Stephen Horne Collection Over the years these bays had become dank and dark due to the increasing tree cover. In 2009 there was a controlled felling on many of the trees which has opened up the rock faces once again.

North Southwest Southeast Stoney Horseshoe Smalldale Harpur Hill Lovers' Leap Beerhouse Craig-y-Biceps Staden Q Che Dale L. Chee Dale U. Blackwell D. Raven Tor Water-c-Jolly Ravendale Aldery Cliff Taddington Rheinstor

## Minus Ten Wall

The Minus Ten Area is another long-time training venue for the hard-core. However, these days most don't get much beyond s the first three metres of quality, polished bouldering. The eponymous route gives good jamming, and then there is *Traffic Jam* for those after hard and fingery face-climbing. The wall stays dry in the rain and doesn't seep.

**❶ Minus Wall . . . . . .** E1 5b
The thin crack and wall; neglected. The upper part is loose.
*FA. Dave Mellor, Dave Johnson 1959*

**❷ Minus Ten . . . . . . . . .** HVS 5a
Beef a way up the steep crack at the left end of the wall, it gives a smart bit of jamming which manages to be slippery and sharp at the same time. *Photo opposite*.
*FA. Dave Mellor, Dave Johnson 1959*

**❸ Great Escape . . . . . . . . . .** E1 5b
From the top of *Minus Ten* pump right along the dusty break (where are the footholds?) to finish up *Cointreau*. Pointless maybe, but aren't they all?
*FA. Geoff Birtles, Earnie Marshall, Al Evans 1976*

**❹ Jam Sandwich . . . . . .** E5 6b
The wall left of *Traffic Jam* has a thin crack, desperate climbing and two peg runners of dubious worth. Towards the top swing left to pockets.
*FA. Mark Pretty 1985*

North
Southwest
Southeast
Stoney
Horseshoe
Smalldale
Rubicon Hill
Lovers' Leap
Beanhouse
Craig-y-Biccos
Staden Q
Chee Dale U
Chee Dale L
Blackwell D
Raven Tor
Water-cum-Jolly
Ravensdale
Aldery Cliff
Taddington
Rheinstor

Graham Parkes pulling up the top section of *Minus Ten* (HVS 5a) - *opposite* - belayed by Steve Cunnington. Photo: Chris Craggs

**North** | **Southwest** | **Southeast** | **Stoney** | **Horseshoe** | **Smalldale** | **Harpur Hill** | **Lovers' Leap** | **Beehouse** | **Craig-y-Biceps** | **Stadem Q** | **Chee Dale L** | **Chee Dale U** | **Blackwell D** | **Raven Tor** | **Water-c-Jolly** | **Ravensdale** | **Aldery Cliff** | **Taddington** | **Rheinster**

**7** Cointreau . . . . . . . . .  **HVS 5a**
The jamming-crack on the right-hand side of the wall. Nearly always dry because of the angle and tree canopy.

*The dusty wall to the right has a solitary peg runner and is climbed by* **The Flashing Fisher, E3 5c.** *It is said to be a half-decent route though it sees few suitors.*

**5** Traffic Jam . . . . . . **E5 6b**
A popular training exercise. Straightforward climbing leads to half-height. Either traverse left (skinny fingers help) and climb the thin crack, or go straight up with stretchy moves past crozzles. The direct is harder but has fewer moves. Take care with the runner in the letter-box, it has been known to pull if not placed in the right spot.
*FA. Tom Proctor 1979*

**8** Thrutch . . . . . . . . . . . . . **HVS 5a**
The main angle of the bay is a worthwhile pitch and a good line with a taxing mantelshelf out right providing the crux. There are lots of rescue ledges along the way.
*FA. Don Whillans 1952*

**6** Double Scotch . . . . . . . **E2 5b**
The crack and big pockets on the right lead to an overlap (thread and weird rest) and a pumpy finale up the short wall. Escaping right is easier but is only for those lacking in scruples.
*FA. Martin Barnicott 1960s*

**9** Pygmies Walk Tall . . . . **E1 5b**
Climb *Thrutch* to the large ledge then step left and climb the wall to reach the roofs. Move up and right to the groove that splits the second overhang and finish steeply up this. Fine climbing that feels longer than it is.
*FA. Tom Proctor, Geoff Birtles 1967. The A Team resort to a peg for aid on what was then a HVS.*

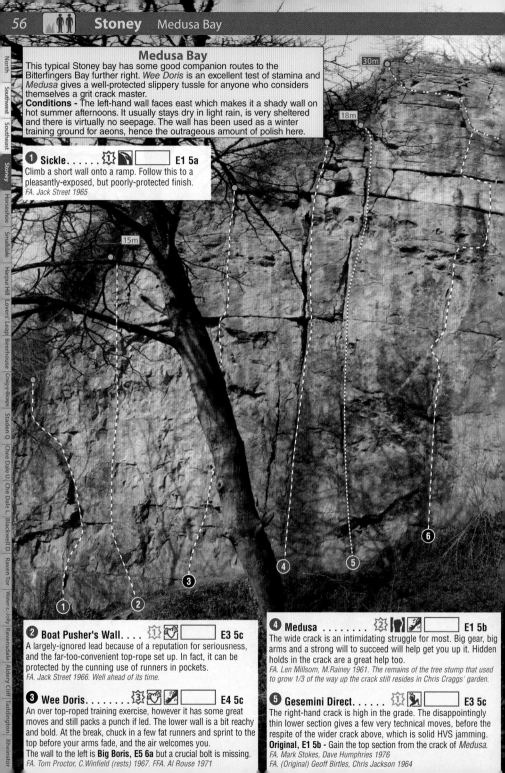

## Medusa Bay

This typical Stoney bay has some good companion routes to the Bitterfingers Bay further right. *Wee Doris* is an excellent test of stamina and *Medusa* gives a well-protected slippery tussle for anyone who considers themselves a grit crack master.

**Conditions -** The left-hand wall faces east which makes it a shady wall on hot summer afternoons. It usually stays dry in light rain, is very sheltered and there is virtually no seepage. The wall has been used as a winter training ground for aeons, hence the outrageous amount of polish here.

**1 Sickle......** E1 5a
Climb a short wall onto a ramp. Follow this to a pleasantly-exposed, but poorly-protected finish.
*FA. Jack Street 1965*

**2 Boat Pusher's Wall....** E3 5c
A largely-ignored lead because of a reputation for seriousness, and the far-too-convenient top-rope set up. In fact, it can be protected by the cunning use of runners in pockets.
*FA. Jack Street 1966. Well ahead of its time.*

**3 Wee Doris........** E4 5c
An over top-roped training exercise, however it has some great moves and still packs a punch if led. The lower wall is a bit reachy and bold. At the break, chuck in a few fat runners and sprint to the top before your arms fade, and the air welcomes you.
The wall to the left is **Big Boris, E5 6a** but a crucial bolt is missing.
*FA. Tom Proctor, C.Winfield (rests) 1967. FFA. Al Rouse 1971*

**4 Medusa ........** E1 5b
The wide crack is an intimidating struggle for most. Big gear, big arms and a strong will to succeed will help get you up it. Hidden holds in the crack are a great help too.
*FA. Len Millsom, M.Rainey 1961. The remains of the tree stump that used to grow 1/3 of the way up the crack still resides in Chris Craggs' garden.*

**5 Gesemini Direct......** E3 5c
The right-hand crack is high in the grade. The disappointingly thin lower section gives a few very technical moves, before the respite of the wider crack above, which is solid HVS jamming.
**Original, E1 5b -** Gain the top section from the crack of *Medusa*.
*FA. Mark Stokes, Dave Humphries 1976*
*FA. (Original) Geoff Birtles, Chris Jackson 1964*

North | Southwest | Southeast | Stoney | Horseshoe | Smalldale | Harpur Hill | Lover's Leap | Beehouse | Cragy-y-Bugbe | Staden Q | Chee Dale U | Che Dale L | Blackwell D | Raven Tor | Water-c-Jolly | Ravensdale | Aldery Cliff | Taddington | Rheinsto

**6 Pickpocket** .... E4 6a
A good start up the technical wall and ramp has some very hard moves. Above, the route loses its way amongst some big ledges and the final section is very escapable. Alternately, finish up *Golden Gate* or traverse right to the tree and abseil off.
*FA. Geoff Birtles, Tom Proctor (2pts) 1967. FFA. Ron Fawcett 1977*

**7 Frisco Bay.** VS 4c
The main corner is a good line, but is becoming very overgrown. The ivy needs trimming - again.
*FA. Don Whillans 1952. An atypical Whillans route.*

**8 Golden Gate** HVS 5a
Two contrasting pitches. Sadly the bottom pitch is very polished.
**1)** 5a, 20m. Climb the right-facing slippery cleft to the ledges.
**2)** 4c, 12m. Walk left into the corner then traverse out to the exposed arete and climb it to the top - the positions are superb.
*FA. Joe Brown, Slim Sorrell, Nat Allen, Frank Elliott 1950. Given HS for years.*

**9 Bingo Wall** E2 5b
The direct line through the eye is a fine route when clean and dry.
**1)** 5b, 18m. Passing the eye is tricky. Many abseil from the tree, but it is worth investigating further...
**2)** 4c, 10m. The cherty holds on the well-protected upper wall.
*FA. Jack Street 1966*

**10 Kelly's Eye** E4 6a
A good little micro-route which is losing its battle with the ivy. Climb the wall to the flake then swing left to make some hard moves up to the break (avoid the chipped hold). Save a bit for the thin crack above.
**Mind Blind, E6 6b -** The direct seam to the chipped hold is bold, but a side-runner (in *Kelly's Eye*) reduces the grade to only E5.
*FA. Tom Proctor, John Kirk 1979. FA. (MB) Paul Mitchell 1984*

**❶ Belinda . . . . . . . .** E4 6a
The crack and groove in the left wall of the main angle give a bold pitch. A side-runner makes the route a safer E3.

**❷ Froth . . . . . . . . . . . .** VS 4c
A polished old favourite with a first pitch which is like climbing a bar of soap. The second has some fine positions.
*Photo on page 35.*
**1)** 4b, 12m. Climb the corner to a ledge (optional belay).
**2)** 4c, 12m. Traverse right along the silica nodules. Either finish up the steep groove (more like HVS 5a in reality), or keep pumping along to the *Bitterfingers* tree.
*FA. Dave Mellor, Dave Johnson 1959*

**❸ Wallop . . . . . . . . . . . . . .** HS 4b
Escape out left from the belay on *Froth*.
*FA. Dave Mellor, Dave Johnson 1959*

**❹ Mottled Wall . . . . . . . .** E4 5c
18m. The wall just right has spaced gear and the odd rattly hold.
*FA. Gabe Reagan, Andy Barker 1976*

**❺ Dead Banana Crack . . .** E1 5c
A popular tick which has a reputation for sorting people out. The initial polished moves stop many attempts - succeed on these and you should be fine. Above, you can climb the crack or the flakes on the right to the break. Finish through the notch in the capping overhang for the full effect. *Photo on page 53.*
*FFA. Tom Proctor 1968. FA. Jack Street, Chris Jackson (1pt) 1965*

**❻ Bitterfingers . . . . . . . .** E4 6a
One of the classic test-pieces of the Peak which is a 'must do'. Polish is no excuse since it has been slippery for many years. Head diagonally right with testing moves to clip the old peg (beware of runners in the undercut; they may appear better than they are). Move up to the break, swing up and left and tackle the upper crack past an awkward-to-place runner.
**The Great Leveller, E6 6b** - Direct from the undercut flake on *Bitterfingers* via a painful mono move and long stretches. There is no gear once you leave the security of *Bitterfingers*.
*FA. Gabriel Reagan, Geoff Birtles 1976. FA. (GL) Paul Mitchell (solo) 1988*

**❼ Fe Fi Fo Fum . . . . .** HVS 5a
The very polished curving crack and arete.
*FA. Brian Moore, Geoff Birtles 1964*

**❽ Okra . . . . . . . . . . .** E4 6a
The substance of this route is the wall between *Bitterfingers* and *Fe Fi Fo Fum*, but is better as an alternative finish to *Bitterfingers*.
*FA. Al Rouse 1980s*

**❾ Beanstalk . . . . . . . . . . . . . .** E3 5c
The arete has good layaway moves and decent gear where it really matters.
*FA. Tom Proctor, Geoff Birtles 1971*

## Bitterfingers

At some stage every keen climber will find themselves below this wall contemplating an ascent of the notorious *Dead Banana Crack* or *Bitterfingers*; these routes should be on every serious climber's To Do List.
**Conditions -** The wall is well-sheltered in windy weather and can stay dry in the rain, but it is likely to be dank in the depths of winter even though there is no seepage. In the summer the trees used to give shade, though most have been felled now.

North
Southwest
Southeast
Stoney
Horseshoe
Smalldale
Harpur Hill
Lovers Leap
Beerhouse
Craig-y-Biorts
Staden Q
Chee Dale U
Che Dale L
Blackwell D
Raven Tor
Water-cum-Jolly
Ravensdale
Aldery Cliff
Taddington
Rheinstor

### ⑩ Augean . . . . . . . . 🔲🔲🔲 VS 4c
The crack right of the arete is quite steep and exhibits that Stoney oddity of being polished and loose at the same time. Finish round to the left as for *Fe Fi Fo Fum*.
*FA. Brian Moore, Geoff Birtles 1964*

### ⑪ Hercules . . . . . . . . . . . . . 🔲🔲 E4 5c
Start on the right and climb to a scary mantel onto a ledge; a runner in the corner and a second belayer out left are traditional. From the ledge, head up and left on mainly good holds to a crack and a tricky exit.
*FA. Tom Proctor, T.Rogers 1971*

### ⑫ Ivy Grotto Direct . . . . . . . . . . 🔲 HVS 5a
The long groove is a fine line with some interesting rock but the name is becoming more apt as the years roll by.

### ⑬ Mineshaft . . . . . . . . . 🔲🔲🔲 Mod
The deep rift over to the right is mostly used as a way down, though it gives an easy bit of chimneying.
*FA. Some miners.*

*To the right of Mineshaft (off the topo) is a rounded cave at 6m.*

### ⑭ Tantalus . . . . . . . . . . . . . 🔲🔲 HS 4b
Climb to the cave, traverse right for a couple of metres then up a groove to a ledge and tree belay. Traverse right again to a clean groove. Up this to finish via a short chimney.

## Tower of Babel
When viewed from Windy Ledge, this thin tower looks like it will fall down at any minute. However, it is standing the test of time and has three decent routes on it.
**Conditions -** It is more exposed than the bays further left and gets the sun in the summer.
**Descent -** Abseil off from fixed gear left (looking in) of the tower or thrash over leftwards and descend *Mineshaft*.

*The three routes described all start from a ledge and belay at the foot of the prominent twin grooves. This is gained up an easy but slippery chimney on the left.*

### ⑮ Glory Road . . . . . . . . 🔲🔲 VS 4b
A good, open route. Follow the left-hand groove.
*FA. Joe Brown, Ron Moseley 1951*

### ⑯ Sin . . . . . . . . . . . . . 🔲🔲 VS 4c
The right-hand groove gives steady, open climbing and bridging, on polished holds, with loads of gear. Amazingly, the route was originally graded Exceptionally Severe.
*FA. Ron Moseley 1952*

### ⑰ Lucy Simmons . . . . 🔲🔲🔲🔲 E2 5b
A lonely detour onto the front face of the tower gives a few good moves in a fine position. Try not to think about what is holding the tower up as you make a gripping series of lifting-a-fridge type of moves. A remarkably harrowing pitch for its relatively lowly grade.
*FA. Tom Proctor, Geoff Birtles 1967. Named after a girl in a calendar, or so they said.*

North | Southwest | Southeast | Stoney | Horseshoe | Smalldale | Harpur Hill | Lovers' Leap | Beehouse | Craig-Biceps | Staden Q | Chee Dale U. | Che Dale L. | Blackwell D. | Raven Tor | Water-c-Jolly | Ravensdale | Aldery Cliff | Taddington | Rheinstor

**North**

**Southwest**

**Southeast**

**Stoney**

**Horseshoe**

**Smalldale**

**Harpur Hill**

**Lovers' Leap**

**Beethouse**

**Craigy-Biceps**

**Staden Q.**

**Chee Dale U.**

**Chee Dale L.**

**Blackwell D.**

**Raven Tor**

**Water-cum-Jolly**

**Ravensdale**

**Aldery Cliff**

**Taddington**

**Rheinstor**

**❶ Inquisitor** . . . . . . . . 🔲 🔲 🔲 **E2 5c**
A popular route up the long flake on the left-hand side of the buttress. The lower wall is a bit thin, the bulge is a bit beefy and the upper groove is a bit wobbly.
FA. Geoff Birtles 1967 FFA. Ron Fawcett 1976.

**❷ Dies Irae.** . . . . . . . . . 🔲 🔲 **E2 5c**
Fine sustained face climbing through the bulges and thin crack above. Finish direct (maybe a bit loose, but much more satisfying) or traverse off left (along *Alcasan*). Top end of the grade.
*Photo opposite.*
FA. Tom Proctor, M.Peters 1967

*Some threads mark the start of* **Stuff the Turkey, E4 6b** *which follows a thin crack through the bulging wall.*

**❸ Circe** . . . . . . . . . 🔲 🔲 🔲 🔲 **E5 6b**
A good powerful line through the underlaps. An old bolt protects the crux, which is easier for the tall. After that it gets very pumpy, though on big holds. *Photo on page 33.*
FA. Tom Proctor, Steve Bancroft 1977

**❹ Gaspera** . . . . . . . . 🔲 🔲 🔲 **E5 6b**
Start up Kink and traverse left along a break. Pull through the bulge past a bolt and move up then left to finish as for *Circe*.
FA. Gary Gibson 1988

**❺ Kink** . . . . . . . . . . . . . 🔲 🔲 **E5 6b**
The prominent roof crack is sometimes wet. The hard climbing is reserved for the finishing moves over the bulge. Beware of protecting it with cams, they are inclined to pull out of the smooth-sided crack.
FA. Joe Brown, Ron Moseley 1951. FFA. John Kirk 1977

**❻ Kinky** . . . . . . . . . . . . 🔲 🔲 **7c**
The bulges to the right. There is no lower off, so either finish up the top crack of *Kink* or jump off onto the last bolt.
FA. Mark Pretty 2007

*The low opening is the Keyhole Cave, it gives an interesting speleological trip through to the other side of the buttress, especially without a torch. DO NOT use it as a toilet.*

🔆 Lots of sun  🧗 8 min

20m to ledge

(A)

18m to ledge

**④**

**⑥**

**⑤**

**②**

**③**

**①** . . . **Approach along Windy Ledge**

## Windy Buttress

The most impressive section of Stoney is the tall Windy Buttress which is home to many superb routes. The fact that they mostly start from the famous promenade of Windy Ledge gives instant exposure from the first move. **Conditions -** Although the name suggests otherwise, it can still give relatively sheltered climbing when grit crags are being battered by the wind. There is some seepage, but *Scoop Wall* is often dry.

**Descent -** The simplest descent is by abseil from the various trees marked on the topo. There is a fixed belay on the *Scoop Wall* tree and the one above *Inquisitor* is the sturdiest. For those who prefer to walk, head rightwards (looking in) and find a steep path which winds down the gully behind *Aurora*.

Chris Plant climbing *Dies Irae* (E2 5c) - *opposite* - above Windy Ledge. Photo: Chris Craggs
Another photograph take at the September 2010 Stoney Climbers' Reunion.

North · Southwest · Southeast · **Stoney** · Horseshoe · Smalldale · Harpur Hill · Lovers' Leap · Beerhouse · Craig-y-Biceps · Staden Q · Raven Tor · Che Dale U. · Che Dale L. · Blackwell D. · Ravensdale · Water-c-Jolly · Aldery Cliff · Taddington · Rheinstor

### 7 Kellogg......... E5 6b
A fine bouldery wall (remove heart flutter with a mat) leads to the break, then comes the hard bit. Entering and climbing the groove is desperate, but the route relents above.
*FA. Tom Proctor, Geoff Birtles 1969. FFA. Steve Haston 1976/7*

### 8 Nice in Nice..... E5 6b
The route has been rebolted above the break, but the lower-off mailons are on bolts about 3m apart (below the upper break). If you stick-clip the peg (used also by *Kellogg*) it is more like a 7b sport route. Boulder out the wall just right of *Kellogg* (mat) pass a peg to the break. Follow the line of gear up leftwards to below the break. Either lower off here or continue up and right into the final easy groove of *The Flakes*.
*FA. Gary Gibson 1987*

### 9 Kingdom Come. E5 6b
Originally given E4 6a, but lack of attention and subsequent loss of holds made a more serious proposition; now top end E5. Make very bold moves to pegs (stick-clip them or use a bouldering mat for E4). Move right to a groove and climb up to the break. Poor lower-off, better to finish up *The Flakes Direct*.
*FA. Dave Johnson, Dave Mellor 1959. FFA. John Kirk, Paul Mitchell 1978*

### 10 Special K.......... E4 6a
Another scary route suffering from a chronic lack of attention. The initial wall and bulge has poor gear. Above that it is around E2 5c. Cross *Armageddon* and climb direct until forced into *Windhover* by the ivy.
*FA. Tom Proctor, A.Dawson 1971. An impressive ascent for the time.*

### 11 The Flakes......... E2 5c
A good line following the obvious flaky feature.
**1)** 5c, 20m. Make a hard start up the *Windhover* arete (good wires) to a peg. Then trend leftwards under the roofs and finish with a tricky traverse to a neat hanging stance.
**2)** 4c, 10m. Step round left into the easy corner to finish.
*FA. Bob Dearman, M.Battersby 1964*

### 12 The Flakes Direct... E2 5c
Adds a good beefy finish to improve the original effort.
**1)** 5c, 20m. Follow *The Flakes* to a pleasant hanging stance.
**2)** 5c, 10m. Pull direct through the roofs then finish more easily.
*FA. Bob Dearman, M.Battersby 1964*

### 13 Armageddon....... E2 5c
Start up the *Windhover* arete to the base of the jamming crack then head diagonally across the excellent airy upper wall. The positions are almost unrivalled in the Peak. Once given an outrageous grade of VS and, although the start is now harder due to lost holds, the wild finish is the same as it ever was.
*Photo on page 5.*
*FA. Chris Jackson, B.Starkey 1964*

### 14 Windhover......... E2 5c
The arete is climbed on its left-hand side and is HVS after the start which can be baffling no matter how many times you have done it, but at least there are good wires. At the top, a crack gives limestone hand jams in a fine position. It originally finished round to the right of the arete up an easy but tottery groove.
*Photo on page 41.*
*FA. Dave Mellor, Dave Johnson 1960. FFA. Barry Webb 1960*

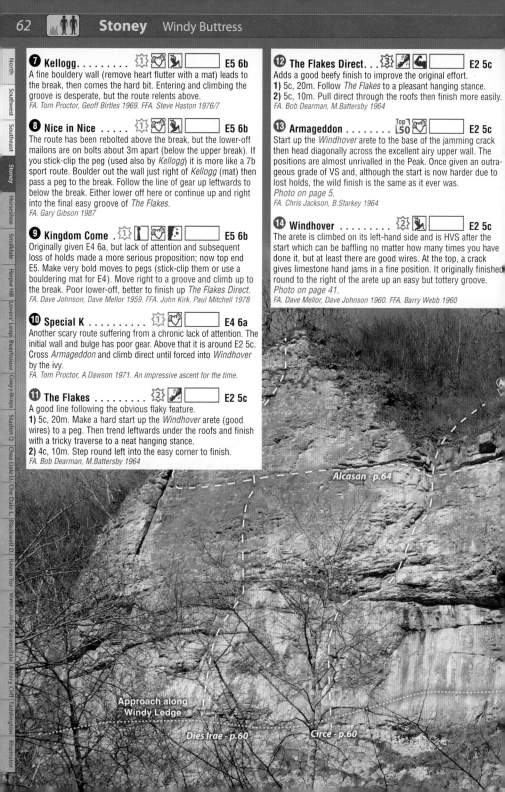

Alcasan - p.64

Approach along
Windy Ledge

Dies Irae - p.60

Circe - p.60

North
Southwest
Southeast
Stoney
Horseshoe
Smalldale
Harpur Hill
Lovers Leap
Beerhouse
Craigy-Bicaps
Staden Q
Chee Dale U.
Che Dale L.
Blackwell D.
Raven Tor
Water-c-Jolly
Ravenstide
Aldery Cliff
Taddington
Rheinstor

ots of sun 8 min

25m from ledge

n from ledge

Descent by
abseil or walk
down to the right

Alcasan - p.64

The steep, crumbly groove just round the arete is **Choss, E1 5b**.

**⑮ Scoop Wall** . . . . . . . . ⌈Top⌋ ⌈50⌋ □ **E2 5c**
The best route at Stoney. It follows the groove to a bulge, which
provides the first hard section, to a rest in a recess. Head up
the bulging crack above to an old peg, then make hard bridging
moves up and left to another crack. This last section is pumpier
on the legs than the arms, if you do it right.
*Photo on page 43.*
*FA. Rod Leeming 1965. FFA. Tom Proctor, Geoff Birtles 1967*

**⑯ Our Father** . . . . . . ⌈⅓⌋ □ **E4 6b**
A classic of the 60s, which was way ahead of its time.
**1)** 6b, 15m. A boulder-problem start leads to some fiddly flakes
and small wires - hard to place. Move up to a peg then step
right and make a long stretch for the undercut. Pull over and
climb more easily to a cave belay, Friend 3 useful. Abseil off
(indifferent belay) or safer and for the full tick ...
**2)** 5a, 10m. Step right to an easy, but well-positioned groove
and the summit meadows.
*FA. Tom Proctor, Geoff Birtles 1967. An awesomely impressive ascent for
the time and graded HVS. The roof is probably a V5 boulder problem that
Tom could do in his town shoes.*

**⑰ Menopause** . . . . ⌈⅓⌋ □ **E5 6b**
A neglected climb which was once a classic test-piece.
**1)** 6a, 15m. Make bold moves up the wall from the right-hand
end of the ledge. Often avoided by doing *Our Father*.
**2)** 6b, 10m. Desperate moves into the groove above the cave.
**Hysterectomy, E5 6c** - The groove to the right of pitch 2 is even
more technical.
*FFA. Chris Hamper (onsight) 1980. FA. Al Evans 1971*
*FA. (Hysterectomy) Jerry Moffatt 1981*

**⑱ Tiger Trot** . . . . . . . . . . ⌈⅓⌋ □ **VDiff**
A short exposed traverse where the ledge disappears. A good
combination is to connect it with the top section of *Aurora* to
give a great VS, or *Aurora Arete* for a HVS.

**⑲ Memnon** . . . . . . . . . ⌈⅓⌋ □ **E2 5c**
**1)** 5b, 25m. Worthwhile. Start below the buttress, on the track,
and climb the long open-book corner to the ledge.
**2)** 5c, 25m. Less worthwhile. Move right and climb a groove,
crumbling overhang and wall to the top.
*FA. Geoff Birtles, Chris Jackson (2pts) 1963*

**⑳ Aurora** . . . . . . . . . ⌈⅓⌋ □ **VS 4c**
An old favourite with good and varied climbing. The first pitch is
generally easy, but very bold. The upper corner is the opposite.
Start at the toe of the buttress.
**1)** 4c, 25m. Climb the bold wall out left then back right - care
needed on this pitch with loose rock and few runners.
**2)** 4c, 25m. Jam and bridge up the corner crack right of the
arete. At the top, move out left onto the arete for an astonish-
ingly exposed finish.
*FA. Frank Elliott 1933*

**㉑ Aurora Arete** . . . . . . . . ⌈⅓⌋ □ **HVS 5a**
Start from the stance of *Aurora* (or do *Tiger Trot*) climb the
exposed arete, starting up the groove and passing the bulge.
Some loose rock remains, but the positions are excellent.
*FA. Bob Dearman (2pts)1963*

**㉒ Alcasan** . . . . . . . . ⌈⅓⌋ □ **E2 5c**
The ubiquitous and excellent traverse (Hard Rock - say no more)
which crosses the buttress. Positions throughout are excellent,
and there is a lot of great climbing, but despite the passage of
many, there is still some suspect rock. *Photo on page 14.*
**1)** 5b, 40m. Climb *Aurora* (possible belay on the ledge) and
follow its second pitch before striking out left across the airy
wall to the *Our Father* cave stance. It is also possible to belay at
the start of the traverse, if moral support is needed.
**2)** 5a, 15m. Traverse left across the black wall (crumbly, but in
balance) to a small ledge on *Windhover*, just around the arete.
**3)** 5c, 15m. Traverse left again along the break, and then swing
under the roof to join *The Flakes* and follow it past the tricky
section to a hanging belay.
**4)** 5c, 35m. Traverse left to cross *Kellogg*, then left again across
the bay above *Kink*. Follow the break leftwards across the wall to
*Inquisitor*, then climb this to the top.
*FA. Chris Jackson, Jim Ballard, C.Moore (5pts) 1964*

*110m to the right of Windy Buttress is a white tower capped by
a substantial yew tree - see page 65. The hanging corner in the
right-hand side of this is:*

**㉓ Compositae Groove** . . . ⌈⅓⌋ □ **HVS 5a**
**1)** 4b, 28m. Graze up the grass bank to a bush belay.
**2)** 5a, 18m. Climb the groove past a couple of old pegs. At the
roof pull left and climb direct into the yew tree. Abseil descent.
*FA. Barry Web, Charlie Curtis 1961*

Steep descent down gully, or
abseil from above *Scoop Wall*

Lots of sun

8 min

25m from ledge

50m

22

22

Windhover - p.62

15

16

17

18

21

25m

19

20

23

North

Southwest

Southeast

Stoney

Horseshoe

Smalldale

Harpur Hill

Lovers' Leap

Beerhouse

Gadgy-Biceps

Staden Q

Chee Dale U.

Chee Dale L.

Blackwell D.

Raven Tor

Water-c-Jolly

Ravensdale

Aldery Cliff

Taddington

Rheinstor

**❶ Four Minute Tiler** . . 🎭 🖼 📓 ▭ E5 6b
A powerful direct route that sees few ascents. Climb to the break, then pull through the roof. Move up and right to some flakes. Continue up the tricky headwall past 2 old pegs.
*FA. Tom Proctor 1980. Tom's last new route at Stoney and also his hardest.*

**❷ La Belle et la Bete** . 🎭 🖼 🗡 ▭ E6 6b
Start as for *Colonel Bogey* to the 2 pegs, but head left to the break. Pull rightwards through the bulge (bolt) then make more hard moves into a groove (bolt) before swinging back to join and finish up *Four Minute Tiler*.
*FA. Mark Pretty 1986*

**❸ Colonel Bogey** . . . . 🎭 🖼 🖼 ▭ E4 6a
Another decent Stoney E4. A technical lower wall (a bit snappy) leads to hard moves past two pegs to gain the break. After a breather, tackle the bulge and groove above.
*FA. Tom Proctor 1979*

**❹ Helicon** . . . . . . . . 🎭 🗡 🥾 ▭ E3 5c
A good direct line. Start as for *Rippemoff* to the break, then continue direct in one long pitch. A bit loose but low in the grade.
*FFA. Jack Street, Paul Nunn 1970. Previously aided.*

## Garage Buttress
An impressive buttress with some big roofs in its upper section. The rock is a bit suspect in places and the lower wall is gaining vegetation too quickly.
**Conditions** - Relatively exposed, but it suffers little seepage and can be a sun-trap in winter.
**Descent** - Walk down the steep gully to the right (looking in).

🌞 Lots of sun  🚶 6 min

**❽ Ozone Bozo** . . . . . . 🎭 🖼 🖼 ▭ 7c
One of the earlier sport routes on this wall. It is now better to finish up the final groove of *Dig Deep for Victory*, avoiding the very dodgy looking large flake.
*FA. Paul Mitchell 1988*

**❾ The Big Apple** . . . . 🎭 🖼 🖼 ▭ 8a
Excellent and sustained climbing up the blank wall to an exciting finish. Low in the grade.
*FA. Kristian Clemmow 2007*

**❿ Little Plum** . . . . 🎭 🖼 🗡 🖼 ▭ 8a
A significant route from the early 80s. It is now climbed in one pitch as an easy 8a. A few wires are required for the easy middle section. The first pitch (a good 7c+ in its own right) is fingery and bouldery, and the upper section provides a nice contrast, being powerful and sustained in a great position.
*FA. Chris Jackson, Geoff Birtles 1963. The ascent took five days, they kept running out of pegs. A caving ladder was used to return to the high point.*
*FA. (P1) Geoff Birtles, John Kirk (some aid) 1979. FFA. Jerry Moffatt 1981.*
*FFA. (P2) Jerry Moffatt, Neil Molnar 1982*

**❺ Rippemoff** . . . . . . . . . 🎭 🖼 ▭ E1 5c
A popular route with a short and technical section on the first pitch.
**1)** 5c, 18m. Climb a groove, then make a hard, steep pull up left through a bulge. At the break, traverse right to a belay on the nose.
**2)** 5a, 12m. Pull onto the upper wall and finish straight up.
*FFA. Keith Myhill 1971. FA. (2pts) Chris Jackson, Geoff Birtles 1965*

**❻ Chewemoff** . . . . . . . . . 🎭 🖼 ▭ E4 6a
**1)** 5c, 18m. Pitch 1 of *Rippemoff*.
**2)** 6a, 15m. From the belay, move up and right through the roof via some complex moves (peg). Finish more easily above. Doesn't see much traffic.
*FFA. Tom Proctor 1979. FA. (1pt) Geoff Birtles, Tom Proctor 1968*

**❼ Dig Deep for Victory** . . . 🖼 🖼 ▭ 7c
The fingery wall just right of the ivy. Shared lower-off.
*FA. Kristian Clemmow 2006*

**⑪ Easy Skanking** . . . . . . E6 6b
A neglected trad route in two pitches 6b, 6a.
*FA. Andy Pollitt 1984*

**⑫ The Lovers' Leap** . . . . . 7b+
A short sport route through the roof to the left of the upper
section of *Little Plum*. It can be gained by the bottom pitch of
*Little Plum*, free or with aid.
*FA. Mark Pretty 2002*

**⑬ Ming the Merciless** 8a+
The wall just right of *Little Plum* is super crimpy and technical,
with some difficult clips.
*FA. Mark Pretty 2007. Done with a high pre-clipped bolt on Little Plum, due
to the hard clips. The route was done properly by Jon Clark in 2009.*

**⑭ The King of Ming** 7b+
One of the better sport routes on this buttress up the shallow
scoop with an exciting top section.
*FA. Mark Pretty 2007. Top section is on Big Nose (FA. Mark Pretty 1985).*

**⑮ Flycatcher** . . . . . . . . . . . E5 6a
A bold and seldom climbed route. A bolt on the left helps protect
it, but not very well.
*FA. Tom Proctor, Nick Stokes, Steve Bancroft 1978*

**⑯ Evasor** . . . . . . . . . . . . VS 4c
A fine top pitch which gives VS climbing in an amazing position.
**1)** 4b, 15m. An indifferent first pitch with spaced gear.
**2)** 4c, 20m. Trend up and left to the break. Follow this strenuously
leftwards to gain the hanging groove. Ascend this on superb holds
in an amazing position. The most exposed VS at Stoney.
*FA. Paul Nunn, Mike Richardson 1965*

**⑰ Aquiline** . . . . . . . . . . HVS 5b
**1)** 4b, 18m. Take the most stable line up the right-hand edge of
the buttress and belay on the break.
**2)** 5b, 15m. Climb the wall above leftwards past a peg then
move left into the finishing groove.
*FA. Bob Dearman, Richard Brown (1pt) 1965*

**⑱ Pendulum** . . . . . . . . . . HVS 5a
The well-named girdle can be started via *Aquiline* or better, from
the descent path. It features a lot of hunched up climbing and
sideways shuffling. Three pitches is normal, finish with a short
abseil from gear in the break.
*FA. Brian Moore, P.Fieldsend, much aid and many pendulums.*
*FFA. Jack Street, Chris Jackson 1960s*

| | No star | ⚀ | ⚁ | ⚂ |
|---|---|---|---|---|
| up to 4+ | 13 | 5 | - | - |
| 5+ to 6a+ | 87 | 34 | 2 | - |
| 6b to 7a | 76 | 38 | 11 | 1 |
| 7a+ and up | 3 | 4 | - | - |

North
Southwest
Southeast
Stoney
Horseshoe
Smalldale
Harpur Hill
Lovers' Leap
Beehouse
Craig-y-Biceps
Staden Q
Chee Dale U
Chee Dale L
Blackwell D.
Raven Tor
Water-c-Jolly
Ravensdale
Aldery Cliff
Taddington
Rheinstor

Chris Todd nearing the top of *Rotund Rooley*
(6b) - *page 81* - on the Main Wall at Horseshoe.
Photo: Ben Lea
It is interesting to think that the initial explora-
tions by climbers into this quarry concentrated
almost entirely on the Main Wall. It is after all
the best bit of rock here, however it was still
thought of as distinctly second fiddle to the real
routes back down the road at Stoney. Nowadays
these wall climbs have developed into fine routes
in their own right and almost certainly see many
more ascents than their Stoney counterparts.

Horseshoe Quarry was originally known as Furness Quarry; it was nicknamed Horseshoe-shaped Quarry by the first climbers to investigate the area. In early 1980s it was the Main Wall that first attracted climbers' attention. Chris Jackson and friends put up *Legal Action*, an E4 protected by some spaced pegs. Other climbers came to look, added routes and it became known as a good spot for sheltered winter sport. Gradually the routes spread out, often on rock of dubious quality, but providing low and mid-grade sport routes, for which the demand was huge.

It has become popular to denigrate the climbing at Horseshoe Quarry but it has given count-less climbers an introduction to outdoor sport. Most of the routes are worth doing and the best are very good indeed. Despite stabilisation work there is still plenty of loose rock to be found, wearing a helmet is advisable, particularly when belaying.

## Approach   Also see map on page 41

Horseshoe is situated 1km west up the A623 from Stoney, on the north side of the road. When driving from Stoney, look out for a track on the right-hand side where you can park. This is 0.8 mile from the Eyam junction. Don't block the turning circle. If this is full then continue a short distance further up the road to extra parking in lay-bys on either side. Be very aware of fast traffic on this road. Walk back to the track and follow it into the quarry. Leave no valuables in your car.

## Conditions

The main walls face southwest, and get plenty of sunshine. It is not as sheltered from the wind as you might expect, but it is still likely to be better than the grit, and there is little seepage so it is worth checking as a winter-sun venue. Some of the lesser walls face north and east, providing alternatives in hot weather.

## Access

Part of Horseshoe Quarry was acquired by the BMC in 2005. This includes the Main Wall rightwards as far as the Toilet Area. The other areas in the quarry remain in private ownership and, although there is no access agreement to any of these areas, in practice there should never be any problems climbing here. Horseshoe forms part of the Stoney Middleton Dale SSSI and the BMC land is dedicated for open access under CROW. The BMC wishes to acknowledge generous help from the Derbyshire Aggregates Levy Grant Scheme and the Peak District National Park's Vision for Wildlife Project along with their, and Derbyshire Wildlife Trust's ecologists, and the Ranger Service in developing and managing the site.

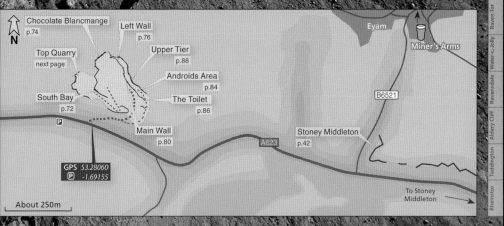

Chocolate Blancmange p.74 — Left Wall p.76 — Top Quarry next page — Upper Tier p.88 — Androids Area p.84 — South Bay p.72 — The Toilet p.86 — Main Wall p.80 — Eyam — Miner's Arms — B6521 — A623 — Stoney Middleton p.42 — To Stoney Middleton — GPS 53.28060 -1.69155 — About 250m

## Top Quarry

The first area described is in the top section of the quarry, home to a few minor routes. Many of these are polished, a reflection of their grade rather than their quality. There is some loose rock (and wobbly bolts!)

**Approach -** From the main quarry base, follow the ramp opposite the Main Wall up left and back right to reach the quarry.

Enterprise Wall

*On the way up to Top Quarry you pass a short wall above the track with two micro-routes on it.*

**❶ A Tracky Little Problem** . . . . . . ☐ 4
*FA. Mike Hunt, Jane Livingstone 2001*

**❷ A Tracky Little Bleeder** . . . . . . . ☐ 5
*FA. Mike Hunt, Jane Livingstone 2001*

*The next routes are on the short wall in the back-left corner of the bay on the Enterprise Wall.*

**❸ Gargle Blaster** . . . . . . . . . . . . ☐ 5+
Short and high in the grade. Using the crack on the right drops it to a steady 5.
*FA. Mike Hunt, Jane Livingstone 2001*

**❹ Uranus** . . . . . . . . . . . . . . . . . ☐ 3+
The crack-line on the left of the wall. A popular first lead.
*FA. Luke Hunt 1998*

**❺ Luke Skywalker** . . . . . . . . ☐ ☐ 4
The next crack has a tricky finish. Same bolts as *Uranus*.
*FA. Mike Hunt and others 1998*

**❻ Klingon** . . . . . . . . . . . . . . . . ☐ 4
An awkward move to gain a ledge and a steep finish.
*FA. Ross Pearson and others 1998*

**❼ Saturn's Rings** . . . . . . . . . . . . ☐ 4+
The right-trending crack to a steep finish.
*FA. John Pemblington and others 1998*

**❽ Vogon** . . . . . . . . . . . . . . . ☐☐ 6a
A tricky wall with a couple of long reaches.
*FA. Mike Hunt, Jane Livingstone 1999*

**❾ Dr. Who?** . . . . . . . . . . ☐ ☐ ☐ 6a
Climb the wall past a pale scar. Quite hard.
*FA. Gary Gibson 2001*

**Torchwood** . . . . . . . . . . 5+
The short line just right. Two bolts to a single-bolt lower-off.
*FA. Gary Gibson 2007*

**Beam me Across Scotty!** . . . . . . 5
This is a high-level girdle, but just climbing to the lower-off on
*Dr. Who?* is enough for most.
*FA. Bruce Goodwin, Tina Priestley 2001*

*Opposite the Enterprise Wall, above a scree slope, are some
slightly harder routes.*

**The Libertines** . . . . . . . . . . . . 6b
The short left-hand bolt-line.
*FA. Gary Gibson 2010*

**Taking Liberties** . . . . . . . . . . . 6c+
The right-hand bolt-line to a hard finishing move.
*FA. Gary Gibson 2001*

**Statuesque** . . . . . . . . . . . . . . 6a
The wall and crack.
*FA. Gary Gibson 2001. Takes the line of an old route Behold the Dustbuster.*

*Right of the scree slope is a prominent arete.*

**Mucker's Wall** . . . . . . . . . . . . 6a+
Climb the wall on the left-hand side of the arete, but without the
crack on the left. Using the crack is **A Fit of Peak, 6a**.
*FA. Gary Gibson 2001*

**Citzen's Arete** . . . . . . . . . 5
The uninspiring blocky arete.
*FA. Dave Williams, Geoff Middlehurst 2002*

**Freedonia** . . . . . . . . . . . . 6b
Head up the wall right of the arete. Care with the rock needed.
*FA. Gary Gibson 2010*

*There is another arete 10m to the right, two trad routes take the
left wall; **Drumming in a Lay-by, E1 5b** and **Greedor, E2 5b**.
Both are the work of Nick Taylor 1999.*

**The Whinger** . . . . . . . . . . . . . 6a+
This follows the arete with some decent moves.
*FA. Dave Williams, Geoff Middlehurst 2002*

**Off Limits** . . . . . . . . . . . . . . 6a+
The wall to the right of the arete. Follow the bolts.
*FA. Dave Williams, Geoff Middlehurst 2002*

Chocolate Blancmange

Heart to Heart

p.73

p.74

North
Southwest
Southeast
Stoney
Horseshoe
Smalldale
Harpur Hill
Lower's Leap
Beerhouse
Craig-y-Biceps
Staden Q
Chee Dale U.
Che Dale L.
Blackwell D.
Raven Tor
Water-c-Jolly
Ravensdale
Aldery Cliff
Taddington
Rheinstor

North
Southwest
Southeast
Stoney
Horseshoe
Smalldale
Harpur Hill
Lovers' Leap
Beerhouse
Craigy-Bleeps
Staden Q
Chee Dale U
Chee Dale L
Blackwell D
Raven Tor
Water-c-Jolly
Ravensdale
Aldery Cliff
Taddington
Rheinstor

## South Bay

This recessed bay is directly opposite the Main Wall. It offers cool climbing in hot weather.

**Approach** - The bay is opposite the Main Wall.
**Conditions** - This bay gives the best shady and cool climbing in the quarry, but it is slow to dry after rain.

**① NYD** . . . . . . . . . . . . . . . . . . `6a+`
Short wall behind a tree, 30m left of the bay.
*FA. Gary Gibson 2006*

**② Pig in a Poke** . . . . . . . . . . . . . `5`
Shallow groove on the left.
*FA. Gary Gibson 2010*

**③ Bad Boys Ink** . . . . . . . . . . . . . `6a`
A short rib with staples.
*FA. Gary Gibson 2001*

**④ Unruly Behaviour** . . . . . . . . . . `6a+`
The thin wall left of a crack.
*FA. Gary Gibson 2001*

**⑤ Treatment** . . . . . . . . . . . . . . . `6b`
The rib right of the dirty corner.
*FA. Gary Gibson 2001*

**⑥ Therapy** . . . . . . . . . . . . . . `6b+`
The blank wall has a very reachy crux.
*FA. Simon Cundy 1992*

Top Quarry

p.70

Five poor routes here

South Bay

← ① 30m

**7 Porgi Amor** . . . . . . . . . . . 🔲 **6a+**
The attractive central scoop is the best route on the wall and high in the grade. A difficult entry then some nice bridging moves above. Be aware of some loose rock near the top.
*FA. Nadim Siddiqui and others 1998*

**8 Foreign Tongues** . . . . . . . . . . . **6a**
Start up *Porgi Amor* then pull on the big jug to gain the right-hand groove. Avoid the block and finish up an arete.
*FA. Gary Gibson, Hazel Gibson 2001*

**9 Gouranga** . . . . . . . . . . 🔲 **6c**
A hard start (easier from the right) leads leftwards to the groove which has delicate balancy moves.
*FA. Nadim Siddiqui, Nick Colton 1998*

**10 You Crack Me Up** . . . . . . . . . . . **E1 5b**
The crack is a neglected trad route. Gear required.
*FA. Dave Simmonite, Gary Gibson 2007*

**11 MiniGrip** . . . . . . . . . . . . . . . . **7a+**
A fierce wall.
*FA. Gary Gibson 2006*

*The decaying wall at right-angles has a few more routes.*

**12 Unhung** . . . . . . . . . . . . . . . . . **6a+**
The rib right of the brambles.
*FA. Gary Gibson 2010*

**13 The Fire Hang** . . . . . . . . . . . . . **6b**
A narrow pillar right of a tree.
*FA. Gary Gibson 2010*

**14 Hang Fire** . . . . . . . . . . . . . . **6a**
The shattered rib above brambles.
*FA. Gary Gibson 2010*

**15 The Gobbler** . . . . . . . . . . . . . **5+**
Some disjointed cracks.
*FA. Gary Gibson 2010*

**16 Christmas Presence** . . . . . . . . . **6c+**
Up the arete by a large nose.
*FA. Gary Gibson 2010*

*There is a very short wall above a steep vegetated slope. This has five poor routes on it:* **Stepping on the Goose, 6c, Turkey Shoot, 6a+, Farmer's Seed, 6b, Chicken Feed, 6a** *and* **Top Gobbler, 5+**.

*Further right is the steep Heart to Heart Wall.*

**17 Nine Eleven** . . . . . . . . . . . 🔲 **6a**
A shallow groove leads steeply to a lower-off on the right
*FA. Gary Gibson 2010*

**18 Seven Eleven** . . . . . . . 🔲 **6b**
The left-hand side of the arete is decent enough.
*FA. Gary Gibson 2010*

**19 Tors Colon** . . . . . . . . . . . . . . **6c+**
The same arete is taken on its right-hand side.
*FA. Gary Gibson, Tim Parkinson 2001*

Not much sun | 8 min | Sheltered

16m to ground

12m

**Heart to Heart Wall**
The leaning wall on the far end of the quarry. The central crack was impressive enough to attract the attention of the early pioneers in the mid-80s. The routes are not popular and even the easy ones are hard!
**Approach -** The wall is to the left of the grassy slabs of the Chocolate Blancmange Area.
**Conditions -** It gets a small amount of sun in the morning only and can be cool in hot weather.

**20 Vent Your Spleen** . . 🔲 **7b**
Technical to start and pumpy to finish.
*FA. Gary Gibson 1998*

**21 Heart to Heart** . . . . . . . 🔲 **E4 6a**
The original route is the long crack-line. Requires trad gear.
*FA. Mark Pretty and others 1986*

**22 Sliver** . . . . . . . . . . . . 🔲 **6c+**
A bolted crack-line which is often damp if conditions aren't right.
*FA. Gary Gibson 1998*

**23 Stomach Pump** . . . . . . 🔲 **7a+**
Another thin crack-line is high in the grade.
*FA. Gary Gibson 1998*

**24 Skin Flint** . . . . . . . . . . . . . . . **6b+**
This one combines a hard start and an airy finish.
*FA. Gary Gibson 1998*

**25 The Blood Bank** . . . . . . . . . . . **6b**
The grey wall, starting from the top of the bank. A steep right-hand finish is better - **There Will be Blood, 6b**.
*FA. Gary Gibson, Hazel Gibson 2001. FA. (TWBB) Gary Gibson 2010*

North · Southwest · Southeast · Stoney · Horseshoe · Smalldale · Harpur Hill · Lovers' Leap · Beerhouse · Craig-y-Biceps · Staden Q · Chee Dale U. · Chee Dale L. · Blackwell D. · Raven Tor · Water-c-Jolly · Ravensdale · Aldery Cliff · Taddington · Rheinstor

## Chocolate Blancmange Wall

At the far end of the quarry is a large corner with a dirt slope beneath it - the line of *Chocolate Blancmange Gully*, a muddy scramble and the first route done here in 1982. The ascent required special ice climbing techniques and wellies. Left of the gully is a broken slab with several routes, some of which are two pitches. They are bolted, but there is some loose rock and reaching the base of the routes can be tricky. There are belay bolts in place. The routes are not of great quality, but they are easy and popular.
**Approach** - Walk to the far end of the quarry.
**Conditions** - Sunny and sheltered with little seepage.

**① Sharing Best Practice** . . . . . . . [    ] **6a+**
An arete in the back left-hand corner of the main quarry above a lot of rubble and grass.
FA. Gary Gibson 2001

**② Barney Rubble** . . . . . . . . . [ ] [    ] **5+**
The clean strip on the far left of the slab. Can be split at a belay giving two 5+ pitches.
FA. Michael Hunt, Jane Livingstone 2001

**③ Chauvi's Slab** . . . . . . . [ ] [ ] [    ] **5+**
The next line about 3m right of *Barney* is a bit better. Again it can be split, making it 5, 5+.
FA. Michael Hunt, Jane Livingstone 2000

**④ Still Nacht** . . . . . . . . . . . . [ ] [    ] **5+**
The centre of the face to the right is even looser than the other routes hereabouts.
FA. Gary Gibson 2007

The route *Trog* took the wall left of *Neanderthal* at 5+ but it has been debolted owing to rock instability.

**⑤ Neanderthal** . . . . . . . . . . [ ] [    ] **5**
Still a bit loose but better since rebolting and seeing a bit more traffic. If you split it the pitch grades are 4, 5.
FA. Michael Hunt, Jane Livingstone 2000

**⑥ Men at Work** . . . . . . . . . . [ ] [    ] **5**
The major groove on the left-hand side of the slab.
FA. Dave Williams and David Eaton 2010

**⑦ The Quarrymen** . . . . . . . . [ ] [    ] **6a**
The cleaned face left of *Excavator* improves with height.
FA. Dave Williams and David Eaton 2010

**⑧ Excavator** . . . . . . . . . [ ] [ ] [    ] **5+**
The line on the left-hand slab gives good climbing, hardest at the top. *Photo opposite.*
FA. Gary Gibson (solo) 1998. Bolted later by Michael Hunt.

**⑨ Slab Cake** . . . . . . . . . . . . . . [    ] **4+**
At the halfway break step left and follow the narrow slab.
FA. Michael Hunt, Jane Livingstone 1998

**⑩ Spare Rib** . . . . . . . . . . . . [ ] [    ] **5**
Follow *Slab Cake* to the break. Step right and climb the rib.
FA. Michael Hunt, Jane Livingstone 1998

**⑪ The Cake Walk** . . . . . . . . . [ ] [    ] **4**
The next cleaned slab.
FA. Gary Gibson 2001

**⑫ Christmas Pud** . . . . . . . . . . [ ] [    ] **4+**
Slightly cleaner than *Cake Walk*. *Photo opposite.*
FA. Luke Hunt, Michael Hunt Boxing Day 2001

**⑬ Sago Slab** . . . . . . . . . . . . [ ] [    ] **4**
The slab to the left of *Dream Topping*.
FA. Dave Glover 1998

**⑭ Dream Topping** . . . . . . . . [ ] [    ] **4+**
Harder than it looks. The slab on its right edge with care needed on the final moves.
FA. Michael Hunt, Jane Livingstone 1998

Chocolate
Blancmange
Gully - not
recommended

Morning  8 min  Sheltered

Rheinstor | Taddington | Aldery Cliff | Ravensdale | Water-c-Jolly | Raven Tor | Blackwell D. | Chee Dale L. | Chee Dale U. | Staden Q | Craig-y-Biceps | Beerhouse | Lovers' Leap | Harpur Hill | Smalldale | **Horseshoe** | Stoney | Southeast | Southwest | North

Climbers on *Excavator* (5+) and *Christmas Pud* (4+) - *opposite*. Belaying above the lower-off as illustrated, is not recommended. Photo: Chris Craggs

## Left Wall

The lower section of wall to the left of the Main Wall all the way to the large earth apron of Chocolate Blancmange Gully has been intensely developed with routes. Many of them have been excavated and consequently can be a bit dirty but they are cleaning up with traffic.

**Approach -** Walk past the Main Wall, the tallest section of rock on the right as you walk into the quarry - to a slightly lower face that is recessed back a bit.

**Conditions -** It gets the sun from mid-morning onwards, and can be unbearable in hot weather. In the winter months it makes a very pleasant sun-trap. It dries very quickly after rain.

**❶ Out of Africa** . . . . . . . . . . . . . 6b+
The wall left of the arete, avoiding the crack.
*FA. Dave Williams, Geoff Middlehurst 2002*

**❷ Madagascar** . . . . . . . . . . . 6b
Climb a short groove to tricky moves left to the arete. Nice rock.
*FA. Dave Williams, Geoff Middlehurst 2002*

**❸ Bird Island** . . . . . . . . . 6a
1) 6a, 16m. The left wall of the corner. Lower off or move right.
2) 6a, 15m. The exposed upper arete has some loose rock.
*FA. Dave Williams, Geoff Middlehurst 2002*

**❹ Seychelles** . . . . . . 6b
The steep wall and crack running to and through the roof.
*FA. Dave Williams, Geoff Middlehurst 2002*

**❺ Rainbow Warrior** . . 6c
Climb the slab leftwards to the overlap.
*FA. Bill Birch, Rick Gibbon 1998*

**❻ Weekend Warrior** . . . . . . . . 6b
Up the blunt arete.
*FA. Gary Gibson 2005*

**❼ Sam in Your Eye** . . . . . . . . 6a+
The yellow wall left of a crack.
*FA. Gary Gibson 2008*

**❽ During the War** . . . . . . 6a+
The wide awkward crack in the left-wall of the corner.
*FA. Dave Williams, Geoff Middlehurst 2009*

Upper Tier - Left

p.8

18m
18m
18m

**⑨ Before the War** . . . . . . . . . . . ☐ 5
The long and heavily-cleaned corner.
*FA. Dave Williams, Geoff Middlehurst 2009*

**⑩ Sahara** . . . . . . . . . . . . . . [🏃] ☐ 6c
This is the well-cleaned arete to the right of the corner.
*FA. Gary Gibson 2003*

**⑪ Union Jack** . . . . . . . . . . . [🏃] ☐ 5
This is the right-hand of the two massively-excavated corners.
There are a couple of stray bolts low down on this one.
*FA. Dave Williams, Geoff Middlehurst 2008*

**⑫ African't** . . . . . . . . . . . . . . . ☐ 6b+
The narrow wall to a high crux.
*FA. Gary Gibson 2005*

**⑬ Desperate Dan** . . . . . . . . . . . ☐ 6b
The long crack-line to the right - the first out of the corner.
*FA. Dave Williams, Geoff Middlehurst 2008*

**⑭ Fine and Dandy** . . . . . . . . [🏃] ☐ 6b
Weave up the wall, starting past a big white flake. Loose.
*FA. Dave Williams, Geoff Middlehurst 2008*

**⑮ African** . . . . . . . . . . . . . . . . ☐ 6a+
A better route up the thin cracks to a tricky upper bulge.

**⑯ Bloodguard** . . . . . . . . . . . [♡☐] ☐ 6c+
The left-hand side of the arete, starting from a mound. The third
clip is a touch scary.
*FA. Bill Birch, S.Coleman 1998*

**⑰ Grab Your Mandrakes** . . . . . . . ☐ 6b
From the ledge above the mound, climb the right-hand side of
the arete to the overhang and then the face above.
*FA. Gary Gibson 2002*

**⑱ Tirfin USA** . . . . . . . . . . . . . [🔒] ☐ 6a+
Up the groove to an awkward traverse right which reaches good
holds. Finish more easily. The link left is **Tirfin Mandrakes, 6a+.**
*FA. Dave Williams, Geoff Middlehurst 2002*

**⑲ Tirf's High** . . . . . . . . . . . . . . ☐ 6a+
A direct start to *Tirfin USA* up the wall on the right.
*FA. Dave Williams, Geoff Middlehurst 2002*

**⑳ Race of the Freuds** . . . . . . . . . ☐ 6b+
The thin crack through an overlap leads to an easier finish.
*FA. Nick Taylor, Sean McLaughlin 1999 (at E3 6a)*

**㉑ Peckling Fever** . . . . . . . . . [🖐] ☐ 5+
The short wall, crack and overlap lead to slabbier rock.
*FA. Nick Taylor 2000*

*The next three routes start from a pile of blocks.*

**㉒ Senter Home** . . . . . . . . . . . . ☐ 6a+
The rampline with a small overlap at half-height, and a choice
of finishes - although the central one is the best, with a delicate
move over the overlap.
**Left Spanner at Home, 6a+** - a left finish joins *Peckling Fever*.
**Write Back Home, 6a** - a right-hand finish.
*FA. Dave Williams, Geoff Middlehurst 2002. Including all the finishes.*

**㉓ Tirfer Off** . . . . . . . . . . . . . . . ☐ 6a+
Balance straight up a shallow groove to the right of a ramp.
*FA. Dave Williams, Geoff Middlehurst 2002*

**㉔ Maillon Sunday** . . . . . . . . . [🔒] ☐ 6b
From the top of the blocks, pleasant climbing leads up the wall.
Make a hard loop out right and back left onto easier ground.
*FA. Dave Williams, Geoff Middlehurst 2002*

**㉕ Bootiful Bernard Matthews** . [🔒] ☐ 6b
Climb the narrow face past the diagonal overlap to a crack.

**㉖ Foul's Bane** . . . . . . . . . . . [🔒] ☐ 6a
The narrow right-hand wall of the first shallow groove has some
nice moves. Climbing the corner direct (separate bolts) is **Nowt
Taken Out, 6a+.**
*FA. Bill Birch, Rick Gibbon 1998. FA (NTO) Gary Gibson 2011*

18m

North
Southwest
Southeast
Stoney
Horseshoe
Smalldale
Harpur Hill
Lover's Leap
Beerhouse
Craig-y-Biceps
Staden Q
Chee Dale L.
Che Dale U.
Blackwell D.
Raven Tor
Water-c-Jolly
Ravensdale
Aldery Cliff
Taddington
Rheinstor

**27 Drool Rock Worm** . . . . . . . . . . [ ] **6b**
Climb left of the borehole to a lower-off under the tree.
*FA. Bill Birch, Rick Gibbon 1998*

**28 Stone Throat** . . . . . . . . 🔟 [ ] **6b**
The route right of the borehole has a sloping start and a hard finish. Finishing just right (left hand in the borehole) is easier.
*FA. Bill Birch, Rick Gibbon 1998*

**29 Slay the Gray** . . . . . . . . . . . . [ ] **6b**
The next narrow pillar taken direct.
*FA. Gary Gibson 2006*

*The wall continues rightwards past a line of hangerless bolts, some tottering corners and dubious blocks. Just right of a prominent overhang at 6m there is a bolted arete.*

**30 Mr. Cellulite's Arete** . . . . . . [ ] [ ] **6a+**
The white and grey arete.
*FA. Gary Gibson 2001*

**31 Bandolier** . . . . . . . . . . . . [ ] **6a**
Up a long right-facing groove-line. Eases with height.
*FA. Gary Gibson 2001*

**32 Underslung** . . . . . . . . . . . . [ ] **6b+**
A tricky start leads to pumpier climbing above.
*FA. Gary Gibson 2008*

**33 The Little Thin Mexican across the Border**
. . . . . . . . . . . . . . . . . . . . 🔟 [ ] **6b**
The wall left of a short arete.
*FA. Dave Simmonite, Duncan Frisch 1994*

**34 Desperate Measures** . . . . . . . [ ] **6b+**
The wall and right-hand side of arete to the same finish.
*FA. Gary Gibson 2001*

**35 The Mexican takes Lexicon** . 🔟 [ ] **6a+**
The once-tottery wall has cleaned up and gives a nice pitch.
*FA. Gary Gibson 2003*

**36 Exceeding the Speed Limit** . . . . [ ] **6b**
Weave through the overhangs towards the top.
*FA. Jim Kelly, Bruno Marks 1993*

**37 Mind Your Head** . . . . . . . . . . . [ ] **6b+**
The fractured wall through an overlap. Exit left to *Exceeding...*
*FA. Gary Gibson 2003*

**38 Desperate Housewives** . . . . . . [ ] **6a**
Climb the narrow groove.
*FA. Gary Gibson, Hazel Gibson 2006*

**39 Collared** . . . . . . . . . . . . . 🔟 [ ] **6a**
Climb the flat face right of the left-facing groove.
*FA. Gary Gibson 2002*

**40 Spare Rib** . . . . . . . . . . . . . . [ ] **6b**
A route that skirts the left edge of the orange section.
*FA. Dave Williams 2000*

Lots of sun | 8 min | Sheltered

**41 Eddie McStiff.** . . . . . . . . . . . . [ ] **6a+**
A shallow groove-line that finishes up and left on easier ground.

**42 Pelvic Thrust** . . . . . . . . . . . . . [ ] **6b**
The right-hand side of the orange section up a groove.
*FA. Gary Gibson 2002*

**43 The Hippy, Hippy Shakes** . . [ ] [ ] **6a+**
Yet another long, shallow groove leads to a high belay. Care needed with the rock towards the top.
*FA. Gary Gibson 2008*

**44 Due Care and Attention.** . . . . . . [ ] **6a+**
Climb the groove to the top on spaced bolts. Polished.
*FA. Al Churcher 1987*

**45 Any Old Iron** . . . . . . . . . . . . . [ ] **6a**
Interesting moves and is (a bit) better than it looks. Taking the arete direct is around 6a+.
*FA. Gary Gibson 2001*

**46 Sunday Sport.** . . . . . . . . . [1] [ ] **6b**
Climb the well-bolted groove. Low in the grade.
*FA. Mark Pretty 1987. Extended with the harder finish in 2003.*

**47 Austin Powers** . . . . . . . . . [ ] [ ] **6b+**
The arete and shallow groove to its right. Sustained at the bottom and some poor rock higher up.
*FA. Gary Gibson 2001*

**48 The Big Fat Texan on the Corner**
. . . . . . . . . . . . . . . . . . . . . . [1] [ ] **6a**
The centre of the wall left of the big corner. Originally it was climbed direct, but now holds on the right are used. Climbed from *Austin Powers* gives a good 6b variation.
*FA. Dave Simmonite 1993*

**49 He Seems so Sumo** . . . . . . . . [ ] **6a**
The crack on the right starting from a block is sustained, though there is a good mid-height rest. Recently extended.
*FA. Gary Gibson 2004*

**50 Olive Oil** . . . . . . . . . . . . . . . [ ] **6a**
The juggy wall left of the big corner to an awkward exit.
*FA. Dave Williams, Geoff Middlehurst 2002*

**51 Removal Man** . . . . . . . . . . . . [ ] **4+**
The big corner has spaced bolts, some gear might help.
*FA. Dave Williams, Geoff Middlehurst 2002*

**52 Some Place.** . . . . . . . . . . . . . [ ] **6b**
A steep crack right of the corner to a neat finale above the roof.
*FA. Dave Williams, Geoff Middlehurst 2002*

**53 Sag Ponir** . . . . . . . . . . . . [1] [ ] **5+**
A short crack just left of the main arete - a one move wonder, mostly on good holds.
*FA. Gary Gibson 2002*

## Main Wall

The best routes at Horseshoe are on the Main Wall. This gives good clean climbing on stable rock with good bolts and lower-offs. Some of the routes are becoming polished.

**Approach -** The Main Wall is the tallest section of rock on the right as you walk into the quarry.

**Conditions -** It gets the sun from mid-morning onwards and can be unbearable in hot weather. In the winter months it makes a very pleasant sun-trap. It dries very quickly after rain.

Lots of sun | 6 min | Sheltered

**① Pale Rider** . . . . . . . . . . . ☆ ☐ **6a**
The main arete gives good, well-positioned climbing. Strictly speaking, the crack should be avoided, but this is a bit contrived.
*FA. Gary Gibson 2001*

**② Rain Dance** . . . . . . . . ☆ ☐ **6c**
The wall 3m right of the arete gives good climbing that eases with height. Exit over to the right. There are two poorer left-hand finishes: **The Colostomy Finish, 7a -** left towards the arete and over a small roof; and **Physical Fizz, 6c+** - continue slightly higher then move left below a bolt.
*FA. Ian French, Chris Wright 1985. FA. (PF) Mark Pretty 1986.*
*FA. (TCF) Lucian Cottle, Jim Kelly 1992*

20m

18m

*Sag Ponir
p.79*

① ② ③ ④ ⑤ ⑥ ⑦ ⑧

North | Southwest | Southeast | Stoney | Horseshoe | Smalldale | Harpur Hill | Lovers' Leap | Beethouse | Craig-Biceps | Staden Q | Chee Dale U | Che Dale L | Blackwell D | Raven Tor | Water-c-Jolly | Ravensdale | Aldery Cliff | Taddington | Rheinstor

Main Wall **Horseshoe** 81

North Southwest Southeast Stoney Horseshoe Smalldale Harpur Hill Lovers Leap Beerhouse Craig-y-Biceps Staden Q Raven Tor Blackwell D. Che Dale L Chee Dale U. Water-c-Jolly Ravensdale Aldery Cliff Taddington Sheinstor

**❸ School's Out** . . . . . . . ⟨2⟩ 🐾 ▭ **6a+**
A hard move on the lower arete leads to fine climbing up the higher groove. An excellent 6a combination is to start up *Rotund Rooley* and then move left.
*FA. Ian Riddington, Geoff Radcliffe 1985. FA. (New start) Gary Gibson 2003*

**❹ Rotund Rooley** . . . . ⟨2⟩ 🐾▯ ▭ **6b**
An easy start leads to a fine finish up the open scoop with a tiny hold on the crux pull. Polished and rather bold at the top.
*Photo on page 68.*
*FA. Mark Pretty, D.Whaley, Johnny Dawes 1986*

**❺ Waves of Mutilation** . . . ⟨1⟩ 🐾 ▭ **7a**
An eliminate with one tricky move. Low in the grade.
*FA. Simon Cundy 1992. FA. (New finish) Gary Gibson 2003*

**❻ First Days of Winter** . . . ⟨1⟩ 🐾 ▭ **HVS 5b**
Forgot your nuts? Pity - the disjointed groove/crack system is a decent pitch with a convenient lower-off.
*FA. Bill Gregory 1986*

**❼ Wall of Jericho** . . . . . . ⟨1⟩ 🐾 ▭ **6b**
This one has a couple of hard moves, one low down and again at half-height, A good pitch. *Photo this page.*
*FA. Steve France, Chris Wright, Ian French, Andy Goring 1986*

**❽ The Leading Line** . . . . . ⟨1⟩ ▯ ▭ **6b+**
The long lead vein has a stretch or two.
*FA. Gary Gibson 2001*

Mark Rankin on *Wall of Jericho* (6b) - *this page* - on the Main Wall at Horseshoe. Photo: Dan Lane

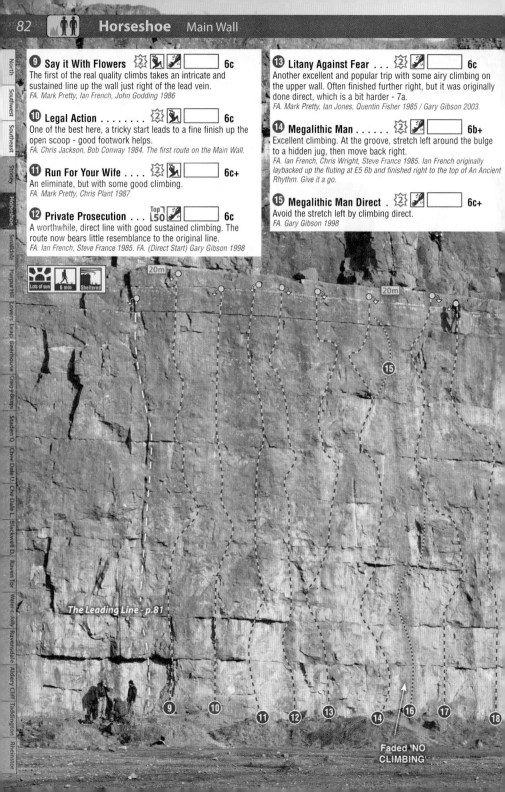

**9 Say it With Flowers**   6c
The first of the real quality climbs takes an intricate and sustained line up the wall just right of the lead vein.
FA. Mark Pretty, Ian French, John Godding 1986

**10 Legal Action . . . . . . . .**   6c
One of the best here, a tricky start leads to a fine finish up the open scoop - good footwork helps.
FA. Chris Jackson, Bob Conway 1984. The first route on the Main Wall.

**11 Run For Your Wife . . . .**   6c+
An eliminate, but with some good climbing.
FA. Mark Pretty, Chris Plant 1987

**12 Private Prosecution . . .**   6c
A worthwhile, direct line with good sustained climbing. The route now bears little resemblance to the original line.
FA. Ian French, Steve France 1985. FA. (Direct Start) Gary Gibson 1998

**13 Litany Against Fear . . .**   6c
Another excellent and popular trip with some airy climbing on the upper wall. Often finished further right, but it was originally done direct, which is a bit harder - 7a.
FA. Mark Pretty, Ian Jones, Quentin Fisher 1985 / Gary Gibson 2003.

**14 Megalithic Man . . . . . .**   6b+
Excellent climbing. At the groove, stretch left around the bulge to a hidden jug, then move back right.
FA. Ian French, Chris Wright, Steve France 1985. Ian French originally laybacked up the fluting at E5 6b and finished right to the top of An Ancient Rhythm. Give it a go.

**15 Megalithic Man Direct .**   6c+
Avoid the stretch left by climbing direct.
FA. Gary Gibson 1998

Lots of sun   6 min   Sheltered

20m

20m

(15)

The Leading Line - p.81

9   10   11   12   13   14   16   17   18

Faded 'NO CLIMBING'

North   Southwest   Southeast   Stoney   Horseshoe   Smalldale   Harpur Hill   Lovers Leap   Beehouse   Craig-y-Biceps   Staden Q   Chee Dale U.   Chee Dale L.   Blackwell D.   Raven Tor   Water-c-Jolly   Ravensdale   Aldery Cliff   Taddington   Rubicon

**16 Poisonality** . . . . . . . . 7a
A direct version of *Ancient Rhythm* with a tricky 2nd clip. The crux is a desperate trick move and is much easier when you know how.
*FA. Gary Gibson 1987*

**17 An Ancient Rhythm.** . . . 6c
A quality route with a hard, slippery and fingery pull past the second bolt, and fine crack-climbing higher up.
*FA. Mark Pretty, Chris Wright, Steve France 1986*

**18 Demolition Man.** . . 7a
A technical start and a finish that feels bolder than it is. There is also a finish to the right, which is harder, but less bold.
*FA. Ian French, Mark Pretty 1985.*

**19 Shot Yer Bolt.** . . . . . . . 6b+
Once the most popular route at Horseshoe, up the crack and groove. Showing its age a bit and high(ish) in the grade.
*FA. Ian French, Steve France, Mark Pretty, Chris Wright 1986*

**20 Southern Man** . . . . 7a+
Start direct (hard) or come in from the left. The finish is easier than it once was, but is still no pushover.
*FA. John Godding, Mark Pretty 1986*

**21 Nice Face, Shame about the Ledge**
. . . . . . . . . . . . . . . . . . . 6b+
The name sums it up, but the climbing is good.
*FA. Steve France, Ian French, Chris Wright 1985*

**22 Flat World.** . . . . . . . . 7a+
Technical climbing up the wall right of *Nice Face…* with a brutish finish. Powerful.
*FA. Gary Gibson 1998*

**23 Lost Monolith** . . . . . . 6b+
The easy ramp gives access to good climbing above.
*FA. Ian French, Steve France, Chris Wright, John Godding 1986*

**24 Screwy Driver** . . . . . . . . . . . . E1 5b
A hybrid route, which has been claimed several times. There are a couple of bolts, but it still requires some nuts.
*FA. Mark Pretty, Ian French 1986.*

*There is an eliminate up the narrow rib to the right -* **6c**.

**25 Spring Awakening** . . . . . . . . . HVS 5a
The long crack. Bits continue to drop off it, so care is needed.
*FA. S.Hennessy 1986*

20m

20m

24

19 20 21 22 23 25

Pink
'CLIMBING
PROHIBITED'

Prominent cracked arete

North | Southwest | Southeast | Stoney | Horseshoe | Smalldale | Harpur Hill | Lovers' Leap | Beerhouse | Craig-y-Biceps | Staden Q | Chee Dale U. | Chee Dale L. | Blackwell D. | Raven Tor | Ravensdale | Wavenscdle | Aldery Cliff | Taddington | Rheinstor

**1 Mutley stole my Route Man.** 6b
Covers the ground covered by an old route *Monkey Stole my Walkman* much of which was pulled down when stabilising the rock.
*FA. (MSMW) Nick Taylor 2000. Bolted in 2002 and again in 2009.*

**2 Winter Fingers.** 6b
Climb right of the gold bolts up the wall right of the pillar. .
*FA. Gary Gibson 2001*

**3 Broken to Bits** 6c+
*FA. Gary Gibson 2010*

**4 Down to the Last** 6b
A tricky start leads to a shallow groove system.
*FA. Gary Gibson 2007*

**5 Fragmented** 6c
Another shallow groove, a blunt rib and a technical finale.
*FA. Gary Gibson 2009*

**6 Mice Breaker.** 6b+
Gold bolts point the way up a friable wall.
*FA. Gary Gibson 2001*

**7 Finishing Off** 6b+
The left arete of the next groove - loose.
*FA. Gary Gibson 2009*

**8 Spectophotometry** E2 5c
The narrow groove leads to a high lower-off.
*FA. Sennen Hennassy, Ian French 1986*

**9 50 Bolts to the Gallon** 6a
The hanging arete is quite popular.
*FA. Nadim Siddiqui, Nick Colton 26.4.98*

**10 Like Ice, Like Fire** E1 5b
The wall just right of the arete with a borehole has 2 (staple) bolts, but needs gear too. Nice, but loose towards the top.
*FA. Chris Jackson, Bob Conway 1986*

**11 Galening Crack** HVS 5a
The long groove gives nice climbing - popular.
*FA. Bill Wintrip, Roy Small 1986*

**12 Compromise** E2 5b
Below the lower-off of *Galening Crack* is a brown groove. Start just to the right of this and climb left into it then up the groove (3 bolts) to an old peg. Finish up the groove on gear.
*FA. Bruce Goodwin, Dave Gregory, John Warburton 1997*

**13 Promises** 6a+
Climb the blunt arete, with a short awkward section. Soft (for the grade) and friable too.
*FA. Gary Gibson, Ian Milward, Nick Taylor 2007*

*Spring Awakening - p.83*

20m

**⑭ The Rottin' Word** . . . . . . . . . . ☐ **6c**
The wall has some tricky moves.
FA. Gary Gibson 1999

**⑮ Decaydence** . . . . . . . . . . . . . ☐ **6c**
Crusty climbing left of the pillar to a better finish.
FA. Gary Gibson 1999

**⑯ Order Number 59** . . . . . . . . 🔳 ☐ **E2 5c**
A trad route up the cracked wall just left of the orange scar.
FA. Chris Jackson, Al Churcher 1986

**⑰ A Right Earful** . . . . . . . 🔳🔳 ☐ **6a+**
The pillar on the left-hand side of the orange rock scar leads to a groove and a tough finale.
FA. Gary Gibson 2001

**⑱ Clean Your Mouth Out** . . 🔳🔳 ☐ **6c+**
The right side of the orange scar to a good finish. Hard.
FA. Gary Gibson 2001

**⑲ The Dust Bunnies** . . . . . 🔳🔳 ☐ **7a**
Steady climbing except for a stopper rockover near the top.
FA. Gary Gibson 1998

**⑳ Dalken Shield** . . . . 🔳🔳🔳 ☐ **6b**
The left-hand side of the arete left of the low cave has a tricky mid-height move.
FA. Bob Conway, Chris Jackson 1986. Now bolted on a different line.

**㉑ Hardcore! You Know the Score** 🔳 ☐ **6b**
The groove right of the low cave gives techinal climbing on small holds. It is becoming harder as it gets polished.
FA. John Cort, Jim Kelly 1992

**㉒ The Director's Cut** . 🔳🔳🔳 ☐ **6b**
The line of staples has a hard polished move at mid-height.
FA. Gary Gibson, Ian Milward, Nick Taylor 2003

**㉓ Blade Runner** . . . . . . . 🔳🔳 ☐ **6a+**
Head through the niche. It now has 3 bolts, but is still very run out for a sport route.
FA. Bill Gregory, Dave Gregory 1986

**㉔ Bruce's Bonus** . . . . . . . 🔳🔳 ☐ **6b**
The cleaned wall between the niche and the corner.
FA. Gary Gibson, Hazel Gibson 1998

**㉕ Do Androids Dream of Electric Sheep?**
. . . . . . . . . . . . . . . . . . . . . . 🔳 ☐ **E2 5c**
Follow the corner then traverse the wall rightwards (pegs/bolts) to a lower-off. The direct finish up the groove is easier (E1 5b), but less enjoyable. With a few wires it feels about 6a+.
FA. Mark Pretty, Ian Jones 1985

**㉖ Rage** . . . . . . . . . . . . 🔳🔳 ☐ **6b**
The good but devious wall eventually crossing *Androids*.
FA. Gary Gibson 2001

**㉗ The Running Man** . . 🔳🔳🔳 ☐ **6b**
Climb direct to *Androids* through some awkward roofs.
FA. Jim Kelly, Bruno Marks 1991

20m
18m
16m

Lots of sun | 5 min | Sheltered

⑮ ⑯ ⑰ ⑱ ⑲ ⑳ ㉑ ㉒ ㉓ ㉔㉕ ㉖ ㉗

Small cave

**Androids Area**
The main feature of this section is the open corner of *Do Androids Dream of Electric Sheep*. The walls either side of this corner are a bit unstable, and there have been rockfalls, although not all of these have been natural. The current crop of routes see plenty of traffic, and so any small loose stuff gets quickly cleaned off, but take care with the bigger blocks.
**Approach -** This wall is on the right as you walk into the quarry.
**Conditions -** It gets the sun from mid-morning onwards and can be unbearable in hot weather. In the winter months it makes a very pleasant sun-trap. It dries very quickly after rain.

North · Southwest · Southeast · Stoney · Horseshoe · Smalldale · Harpur Hill · Lovers' Leap · Beehouse · Craig-y-Biceps · Staden Q · Chee Dale U. · Chee Dale L. · Blackwell D. · Raven Tor · Water-cum-Jolly · Ravensdale · Aldery Cliff · Water-cum-Jolly · Teddington · Rheinstor

North
Southwest
Southeast
Stoney
Horseshoe
Smalldale
Harpur Hil
Lovers Leap
Beerhouse
Craig-y-Biceps
Staden Q
Chee Dale U
Che Dale L
Blackwell D
Raven Tor
Water-c-Jolly
Ravensdale
Aldery Cliff
Teddington
Rheinster

## The Toilet

The wall that greets you on arrival in the quarry proves that if you stick bolts in a bit of rock it will become popular, whatever its quality or the intrinsic value of the routes.

**Approach -** This is the first section which faces you as you enter the quarry.

**Conditions -** The sun hits here from about mid-morning onwards, making it too hot at times and a pleasant sun-trap at others. It dries quickly after rain.

**1 The Long Walk** ......... 🪨 [ ] 6c
An eliminate (gold bolts) up the left-hand side of the arete.
*FA. Gary Gibson 2010*

**2 The Dark Tower** ........... [ ] 6b+
Climb the pillar and pull through the overlap.
*FA. Gary Gibson 2006*

**3 The Drawing of the Three** ..... [ ] 6b+
Amble to the overlap and a wild finish.
*FA. Gary Gibson 2008*

**4 Willie the Kid** ......... 🔀 [ ] 6a+
Climb the angular, orange groove, exiting on the right.
*FA. Dave Williams, Geoff Middlehurst 2002*

**5 Calamity Jane** ............ [ ] 6b+
Start just right of *Willie..* and climb the steep right wall of the corner past loads of bolts.
*FA. Dave Williams, Geoff Middlehurst 2002*

**6 Jeff Garrett** ............ 🔀 [ ] 6a+
Climb the steep face, trending leftwards.
*FA. Dave Williams, Geoff Middlehurst 2002*

16m

Earth mound
below cave

**7 The Dogs** ............. 🪨 [ ] 6b
The well-bolted line left of a thin curving crack. Devious.
*FA. Dave Williams, Geoff Middlehurst 2002*

**8 Derailed** .......... 🔀🪨 [ ] 6a+
Climb left of the cave entrance to a steep final wall.
*FA. Gary Gibson, Nick Taylor 2002*

**9 Passage of Time** ..... 🔀🪨 [ ] 6b
The right arete of the cave to a surprisingly steep finale.
*FA. Jim Kelly, Bob Marks 1993*

**10 The Sewer** ............... [ ] 6a+
The easy rib leads to a steeper finish, trending rightwards.
*FA. Dave Williams, Geoff Middlehurst 2003*

**11 Latrine** ................. [ ] 5
The groove and wall.
*FA. Dave Williams, Geoff Middlehurst 2003*

*The next bunch of routes are getting polished and harder!*

**12 Armitage** ................ [ ] 6a
Behind the fallen blocks, the wall and left edge of an overlap.
*FA. Dave Williams, Geoff Middlehurst 2003*

**13 Shanks** ............... 🔀 [ ] 6a
The wall. This is the right-hand line behind the blocks.
*FA. Dave Williams, Geoff Middlehurst 2003*

**14 Potty** . . . . . . . . . . . . . . . . . [ ] **6a**
To the right of the blocks, pass the right-hand edge of the overlap.
*FA. Dave Williams, Geoff Middlehurst 2003*

**15 Psycho Ceramic** . . . . . . [ ] **6a+**
A steep start leads to the small, but tricky overhang.
*FA. Gary Gibson 2008*

**16 The Bog** . . . . . . . . . . . . . [ ] **6a**
From the lowest point of the wall, head around the right-hand edge of the roof. The start is tricky.
*FA. Dave Williams, Geoff Middlehurst 2003*

**17 Twyfords** . . . . . . . . . . . . . [ ] **6a**
Climb the shallow orange groove and crack.
*FA. Dave Williams, Geoff Middlehurst 2003*

**18 The Small Room** . . . . . . . . [ ] **6a+**
The next line right of the shallow, orange groove. Climb up to and over the roof.
*FA. Dave Williams, Geoff Middlehurst 2003*

**19 Thomas Crapper** . . . . . . . . [ ] **6a**
The white wall then jig right through the capping roof.
*FA. Dave Williams, Geoff Middlehurst 2003*

**20 Two Loos** . . . . . . . . . . . . . [ ] **4+**
Amble up the shallow groove.
*FA. Dave Williams, Geoff Middlehurst 2005*

**21 Montezuma's Revenge** . . . . . . . [ ] **6b**
Climb the right wall of the groove.
*FA. Dave Simmonite, Nadim Siddiqui 1998*

**22 Latrec** . . . . . . . . . . . . . . . [ ] **5**
Another shallow groove, trending leftwards to finish.
*FA. Dave Williams, Geoff Middlehurst 2005*

**23 Toilet Graffiti** . . . . . . . . . . . [ ] **5+**
Start up a short corner, leading to a steeper wall.
*FA. Dave Williams, Geoff Middlehurst 2005*

**24 Toilet Humour** . . . . . . . . . . . . [ ] **5**
A tricky start, but easier above. As dirty as you expected?
*FA. Gary Gibson 2007*

**25 De Throne** . . . . . . . . . . . . . [ ] **5**
Start up the shallow, orange groove.
*FA. Dave Williams 2005*

**26 On Uranus** . . . . . . . . . . . . [ ] **6a**
Pass left of the overhang into a shallow corner.
*FA. Dave Williams 2005*

**27 Eau de Toilette** . . . . . . . . . . . [ ] **6a**
Pull over the roof, then head up the pale rib.
*FA. Dave Williams 2005*

**28 Andrex** . . . . . . . . . . . . . . [ ] **6b**
Soft, strong and not very long.
*FA. Dave Williams, 2005*

**29 Easy Come, Easy Go** . . . . . . . . [ ] **3**
The right-hand arete of everything has an awkward start.
*FA. Gary Gibson 2006*

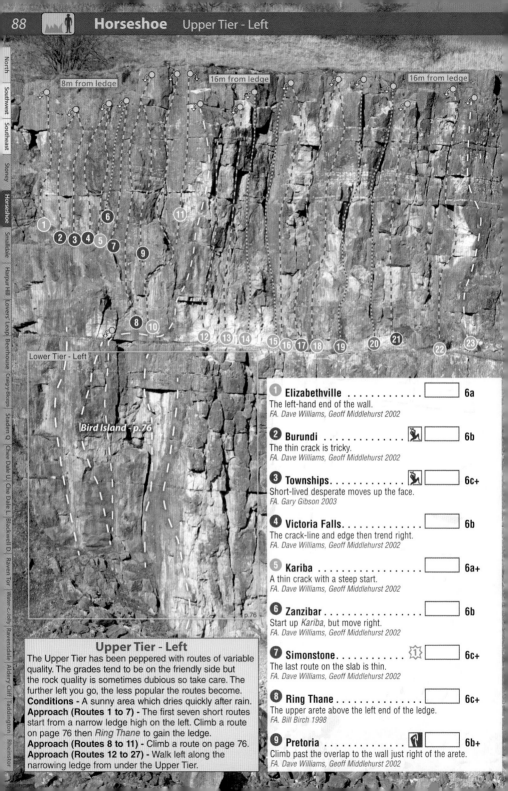

8m from ledge

16m from ledge

16m from ledge

Lower Tier - Left

Bird Island - p.76

p.76

## Upper Tier - Left

The Upper Tier has been peppered with routes of variable quality. The grades tend to be on the friendly side but the rock quality is sometimes dubious so take care. The further left you go, the less popular the routes become.

**Conditions -** A sunny area which dries quickly after rain.

**Approach (Routes 1 to 7) -** The first seven short routes start from a narrow ledge high on the left. Climb a route on page 76 then *Ring Thane* to gain the ledge.

**Approach (Routes 8 to 11) -** Climb a route on page 76.

**Approach (Routes 12 to 27) -** Walk left along the narrowing ledge from under the Upper Tier.

**1  Elizabethville** . . . . . . . . . . . . . ☐ 6a
The left-hand end of the wall.
*FA. Dave Williams, Geoff Middlehurst 2002*

**2  Burundi** . . . . . . . . . . . . . ☐ 6b
The thin crack is tricky.
*FA. Dave Williams, Geoff Middlehurst 2002*

**3  Townships** . . . . . . . . . . . . . ☐ 6c+
Short-lived desperate moves up the face.
*FA. Gary Gibson 2003*

**4  Victoria Falls** . . . . . . . . . . . . . ☐ 6b
The crack-line and edge then trend right.
*FA. Dave Williams, Geoff Middlehurst 2002*

**5  Kariba** . . . . . . . . . . . . . . . . ☐ 6a+
A thin crack with a steep start.
*FA. Dave Williams, Geoff Middlehurst 2002*

**6  Zanzibar** . . . . . . . . . . . . . . . ☐ 6b
Start up *Kariba*, but move right.
*FA. Dave Williams, Geoff Middlehurst 2002*

**7  Simonstone** . . . . . . . . . . . 11 ☐ 6c+
The last route on the slab is thin.
*FA. Dave Williams, Geoff Middlehurst 2002*

**8  Ring Thane** . . . . . . . . . . . . . ☐ 6c+
The upper arete above the left end of the ledge.
*FA. Bill Birch 1998*

**9  Pretoria** . . . . . . . . . . . . . ☐ 6b+
Climb past the overlap to the wall just right of the arete.
*FA. Dave Williams, Geoff Middlehurst 2002*

North | Southwest | Southeast | Stoney | Horseshoe | Smalldale | Harpur Hill | Lovers' Leap | Beerhouse | Craig-y-Biceps | Staden Q | Chee Dale U | Chee Dale L | Blackwell D | Raven Tor | Water-c-Jolly | Ravensdale | Aldery Cliff | Teddington | Rheinstor

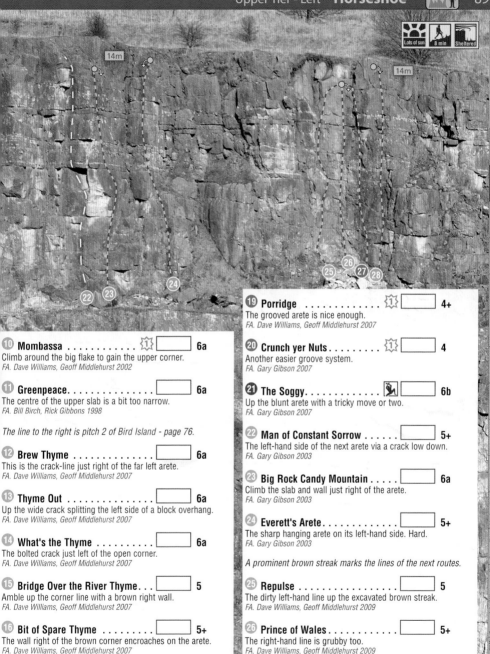

North
Southwest
Southeast
Stoney
Horseshoe
Smalldale
Harpur Hill
Lover's Leap
Beerhouse
Craig-y-Biceps
Staden Q
Chee Dale U.
Chee Dale L.
Blackwell D.
Raven Tor
Water-c-Jolly
Ravensdale
Aldery Cliff
Taddington
Rheinstor

**10 Mombassa** .......... 6a
Climb around the big flake to gain the upper corner.
FA. Dave Williams, Geoff Middlehurst 2002

**11 Greenpeace**. ............. 6a
The centre of the upper slab is a bit too narrow.
FA. Bill Birch, Rick Gibbons 1998

*The line to the right is pitch 2 of Bird Island - page 76.*

**12 Brew Thyme** ............. 6a
This is the crack-line just right of the far left arete.
FA. Dave Williams, Geoff Middlehurst 2007

**13 Thyme Out** ............. 6a
Up the wide crack splitting the left side of a block overhang.
FA. Dave Williams, Geoff Middlehurst 2007

**14 What's the Thyme** ......... 6a
The bolted crack just left of the open corner.
FA. Dave Williams, Geoff Middlehurst 2007

**15 Bridge Over the River Thyme**... 5
Amble up the corner line with a brown right wall.
FA. Dave Williams, Geoff Middlehurst 2007

**16 Bit of Spare Thyme** ........ 5+
The wall right of the brown corner encroaches on the arete.
FA. Dave Williams, Geoff Middlehurst 2007

**17 Fat Betty**. ................ 4+
The easy corner line has a white left wall.
FA. Dave Williams, Geoff Middlehurst 2007

**18 Take Your Thyme** .......... 5+
Meander up the right wall of the corner.
FA. Dave Williams, Geoff Middlehurst 2007

**19 Porridge** ............ 4+
The grooved arete is nice enough.
FA. Dave Williams, Geoff Middlehurst 2007

**20 Crunch yer Nuts**. ........ 4
Another easier groove system.
FA. Gary Gibson 2007

**21 The Soggy**. ............ 6b
Up the blunt arete with a tricky move or two.
FA. Gary Gibson 2007

**22 Man of Constant Sorrow** ...... 5+
The left-hand side of the next arete via a crack low down.
FA. Gary Gibson 2003

**23 Big Rock Candy Mountain** ..... 6a
Climb the slab and wall just right of the arete.
FA. Gary Gibson 2003

**24 Everett's Arete**. ........... 5+
The sharp hanging arete on its left-hand side. Hard.
FA. Gary Gibson 2003

*A prominent brown streak marks the lines of the next routes.*

**25 Repulse** ................ 5
The dirty left-hand line up the excavated brown streak.
FA. Dave Williams, Geoff Middlehurst 2009

**26 Prince of Wales**. .......... 5+
The right-hand line is grubby too.
FA. Dave Williams, Geoff Middlehurst 2009

**27 That Old DA Look**. ......... 4
A short wall leads to a groove with a tricky bulge.
FA. Gary Gibson 2011

**28 FOP** ................... 6a
The stapled pillar just to the right has some decent moves.
FA. Gary Gibson 2003

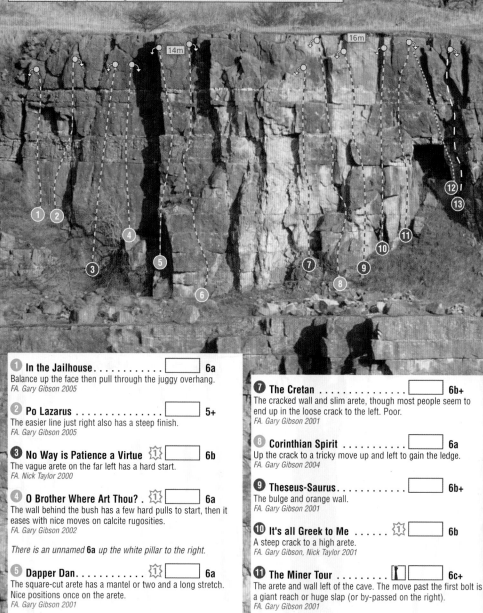

North
Southwest
Southeast
Stoney
Horseshoe
Smalldale
Harpur Hill
Lovers' Leap
Beehouse
Craig-y-Biam
Staden Q
Chee Dale U
Che Dale
Blackwell D.
Raven Tor
Water-cum-Jolly
Ravensdale
Aldery Cliff
Taddington
Rheinstor

## Upper Tier - Right

Shorter and less intimidating than the Main Wall, this section is great for catching the last rays of sun in the evening. Take great care not to knock stones off the ledge onto the climbers below. It is a wide ledge, but it has been known to happen.

**Approach -** From the right, via an easy-angled ramp as you enter the quarry, or a steeper (loose) gully to the right of Android Area.

**❶ In the Jailhouse** . . . . . . . . . . . 6a
Balance up the face then pull through the juggy overhang.
*FA. Gary Gibson 2005*

**❷ Po Lazarus** . . . . . . . . . . . . . . 5+
The easier line just right also has a steep finish.
*FA. Gary Gibson 2005*

**❸ No Way is Patience a Virtue** 🔄 6b
The vague arete on the far left has a hard start.
*FA. Nick Taylor 2000*

**❹ O Brother Where Art Thou?** . 🔄 6a
The wall behind the bush has a few hard pulls to start, then it eases with nice moves on calcite rugosities.
*FA. Gary Gibson 2002*

*There is an unnamed **6a** up the white pillar to the right.*

**❺ Dapper Dan** . . . . . . . . . . . 🔄 6a
The square-cut arete has a mantel or two and a long stretch. Nice positions once on the arete.
*FA. Gary Gibson 2001*

**❻ Babe the Blue Axe** . . . . . . . . . 5+
Awkward moves gain a ledge. Continue up the cleaned face.
*FA. Gary Gibson 2006*

**❼ The Cretan** . . . . . . . . . . . . . . 6b+
The cracked wall and slim arete, though most people seem to end up in the loose crack to the left. Poor.
*FA. Gary Gibson 2001*

**❽ Corinthian Spirit** . . . . . . . . . . 6a
Up the crack to a tricky move up and left to gain the ledge.
*FA. Gary Gibson 2004*

**❾ Theseus-Saurus** . . . . . . . . . . . 6b+
The bulge and orange wall.
*FA. Gary Gibson 2001*

**❿ It's all Greek to Me** . . . . . . 🔄 6b
A steep crack to a high arete.
*FA. Gary Gibson, Nick Taylor 2001*

**⓫ The Miner Tour** . . . . . . . . . 6c+
The arete and wall left of the cave. The move past the first bolt is a giant reach or huge slap (or by-passed on the right).
*FA. Gary Gibson 2001*

**⓬ Olympiakus** . . . . . . . . . . . 6c
Climb left to access the hanging groove left of *Her Aklion*.
*FA. Gary Gibson 2009*

14m

*P.M.'s Question Time - p.92*

*P.M.'s Question Time - p.92*

**⑬ Her Aklion.** . . . . . . . . . . . . . . . . . **6c**
Right of the cave, get into the right-hand hanging groove.
*FA. Gary Gibson 2001*

**⑭ Almost There** . . . . . . . . . . . . . **5**
The cracked arete of the cave system gives juggy fun.
*FA. Gary Gibson 2006*

**⑮ Into the Labyrinth.** . . . . . . . **6a**
The front face of the pillar has a tricky start. Nice.
*FA. Chris Wright, Mark Pretty, Andy Goring 1986 at E1 5b.*

**⑯ By Zeus** . . . . . . . . . . . **6a+**
The arete on the right of the pillar eases with height.
*FA. Gary Gibson 2001*

**⑰ Spiteful Rain.** . . . . . . . . . . . . . **5+**
Climb the groove and/or pillar to a ledge. The wall and overhang
lead to the top. The squeezed line just right is **Second Prize, 5**.
*FA. Nick Taylor 2001*

**⑱ Consolation.** . . . . . . . . . . . **5+**
Pull over the tricky overlap and plod up the face above.
*FA. Dave Williams, Geoff Middlehurst 2009*

**⑲ Tawny Owl Pie** . . . . . . . . **5**
An awkward right-facing groove to a leftwards exit.
*FA. Dave Williams, Gary Gibson 2006*

**⑳ The Owl** . . . . . . . . . . . . . **6c**
An eliminate to the right with a high crux.
*FA. Dave Williams 2006*

**㉑ White Dove** . . . . . . . . . . . **E1 5b**
The thin crack then swing right to the lower-off on *Nullo*.
*FA. Chris Wright, Ian French, John Godding, Ritchie Brooks 1986*

**㉒ Nullo in Mundo Pax Sincera** . . . **6c+**
Start at the blunt arete right of the white wall (at a bolt stud).
Up the white wall to the arete then as direct as possible without
using the crack on the left - if you can avoid it.
*FA. Nadim Siddiqui and others 1998*

**㉓ Supplementary Questions** . . **4+**
The shallow groove is followed throughout.
*FA. Chris Wright. Mark Pretty, Andy Goring 1986 at HVS 5a.*

**㉔ A Liberal Smear** . . . . . . . . . . **6c**
The wall leads to a hard finish. Close to the previous climb.
*FA. Gary Gibson 2001*

**㉕ Labour Relations** . . . . . . . . . . **6c+**
The thin slab and fine headwall above the overlap.
*FA. Gary Gibson 2001*

North Southwest Southeast Stoney Horseshoe Smalldale Harpur Hill Lovers' Leap Beerhouse Craig-y-Biceps Stadon Q Chee Dale U. Chee Dale L. Che Dale L. Blackwell D. Raven Tor Water-c-Jolly Ravensdale Aldery Cliff Taddington Rheinstor

North
Southwest
Southeast
Stoney
Horseshoe
Smalldale
Harpur Hill
Lovers' Leap
Beerhouse
Craig-y-Biop
Staden Q
Chee Dale U
Chee Dale L
Blackwell D
Raven Tor
Water-cum-Jolly
Ravensdale
Aldery Cliff
Teddington
Rheinstor

**26 P.M.'s Question Time** . . . . . . . ☐ E3 6a
Climb a crack to the left-hand end of the roof. Pull over, then move right and up the slab to finish.
**Avoiding the Issue, E4 6b -** climb direct past a solitary bolt.
*FA. Malcolm Taylor 1986. FA. (ATI) Gary Gibson 1999*

**27 Booker Prize** . . . . . . . . . . 🔟 ☐ 6a+
Up the front of the pillar to awkward moves onto the headwall. Clipping the lower-off is the crux.
*FA. Dave Williams, Geoff Middlehurst 2005*

**28 Sir Pryse** . . . . . . . . . 🔟 ◪ ☐ 6a+
The slab and narrow roof are worth seeking out.
*FA. Dave Williams 2001*

**29 Oy Missus** . . . . . . . . . . . . . . ☐ 6c+
The slabby face. Tricky to stay on the line.
*FA. Gary Gibson 2001*

**30 Mr. Blue Sky** . . . . . . . 🔟 ◪ ☐ 7a
A bit of a one-move-wonder on the tiny slab. Bold above.
*FA. Chris Wright, Steve France 1986*

**31 Esso Blue** . . . . . . . . . . . . . . ☐ HVS 5b
The short wide crack up the slab left of the arete.
*FA. Steve France, Ian French 1986. Probably climbed by Al Evans in the 1970s*

**32 Smoke Gets in Your Eyes** 🔟 ◪ ☐ 6c
A technical arete with hard moves past the 1st bolt. Old-skool bolting, so it's a bit bold too.
*FA. Steve France, Chris Wright 1986*

**33 Shell Super** . . . . . . . . . . . . . ☐ 6c
A tough micro-route on the sidewall (not visible on photo).
*FA. Gary Gibson, K.Bridgens 2008*

**34 Esso Extra** . . . . . . . . . . . . . . ☐ E1 5b
The groove to the right of the clean arete (not visible on photo). Step left at the roof to a crack. Lower-off on the left.
*FA. Steve France, I.Barton 1986*

**35 Mumble Jumble** . . . . . . 🔟 ◪ ☐ 7a
The wall and prominent overlap.
*FA. Gary Gibson 2001*

**36 Fargo** . . . . . . . . . . . . . . . . . . ☐ 6a+
The short straight crack is hardest at the top.
*FA. Gary Gibson 2001*

**37 Blue Sunday** . . . . . . . . . . 🔟 ☐ 6b
The short wall on reasonable rock.
*FA. Steve France, Ian French, Mark Pretty, Chris Wright 1986*

**38 Do It Yourself** . . . . . . . . . . . . ☐ 6b+
Climb direct above the small cave.
*FA. Gary Gibson 2001*

**39 New Bolts and Yankees** . . . . . . ☐ **6a**
A steep couple of pulls accesses the crack-line above.

**40 Kushti.** . . . . . . . . . . . . . . ☐ **6a+**
The steep crack immediately right of the shattered rock.
FA. Gary Gibson 2002

**41 Lovely Bubbly** . . . . . . . . . . . ☐ **6c+**
The wall left of the shattered, dirty groove has a hard crux.
FA. Gary Gibson 2002

**42 Slabby, but Nice** . . . . . . . ☐ **6a**
The right wall of the dirty groove has some nice climbing
towards the top. Spot the sneaky thread.

**43 Sam and Mary** . . . . . . . . . . . ☐ **5**
An initial crack leads to a steep finish.
FA. Dave Williams, Geoff Middlehurst 2009

**44 Ma Marmalade** . . . . . . . . ☐ **6a+**
A blunt, blocky arete leads to ledges and an awkward finish.
FA. Gary Gibson 2009

**45 Slam the Jam** . . . . . . . . . . ☐ **6a**
The groove and hand-crack splitting the white wall.
FA. Gary Gibson, Nick Taylor 2003

**46 Jam Slice** . . . . . . . . . . . . . . ☐ **6b**
Climb the wall and then the open groove above.
FA. Gary Gibson 2010

**47 Don't Try This at Home** . . . . ☐ **6c+**
The right-hand side of the face to a high crux.
FA. Gary Gibson 2009

**48 Red Rum** . . . . . . . . . . . . . . ☐ **5+**
Canter up the prominent corner system.
FA. Dave Williams 2010

**49 Nijinski.** . . . . . . . . . . . . . ☐ **E2 5b**
The centre of the recessed slab, small wires needed. The right-
hand side is **Seated Moon, E2 5b**
FA. Darren Hawkins, Malcolm Taylor 1986. FA (SM) Nick Taylor 2000

**50 The Party Animal** . . ☐ **6b+**
The blunt central arete has a technical middle section which can
be avoided round to the left at 5+. Check the lower-off and the
block it is attached to before using.
FA. Mark Pretty, Sean Coffey, John Godding 1986

**51 Café Bleu** . . . . . . . . . . . . . ☐ **E3 6a**
The right-hand side of the face on good rock.
FA. Malcolm Taylor, Darren Hawkins 1986

**52 Dinky Toy** . . . . . . . . . . . . . ☐ **E4 6b**
Climb the short grooves further right.
FA. Nigel Slater, Paul Grant 1986

**53 Corgi Registered** . . . . . . . . . . ☐ **6b**
A rounded arete complete with hidden holds gives the line.
FA. Gary Gibson, Mark Richardson 2006

**54 Hornby** . . . . . . . . . . . . . . . ☐ **6a+**
The final offering is this steep wall with a small overhang.
FA. Gary Gibson 2009

N

Smalldale
p.96

A6

Lovers' Leap
p.132

Beerhouse
p.134

Buxton

A53

A54

A515

Staden
p.136

Harpur Hill
p.102

A6

About 2km

# Buxton Area
## Smalldale, Harpur Hill
## Lovers' Leap
## Beerhouse Buttress
## Craig y Biceps
## Staden Quarry

Closing in on the lower-off on the line of *The Exclusion Zone* (6b+) - *page 112* - at the Prophecy Area at Harper Hill. The photograph shows Harpur Hill at its best, on a warm summer's evening. The first routes were put up here in the 1960s but they never proved popular. In 1994 Bill Birch and Nadim Siddiqui started to develop it as a sport climbing venue, though there was some initial opposition due to the bolting. Common-sense eventually prevailed and now it is one of the most popular venues in the Peak. Photo: Mark Glaister.

| | No star | ⊥1⊥ | ⊥2⊥ | ⊥3⊥ |
|---|---|---|---|---|
| **up to 4+** | - | - | - | - |
| **5+ to 6a+** | 5 | 4 | 1 | - |
| **6b to 7a** | 14 | 13 | 6 | - |
| **7a+ and up** | 1 | 4 | 3 | - |

Smalldale Quarry is a decent little venue with a couple of good walls developed for sport climbing - there is nothing of any significance here for the trad climber. The setting above a lorry park and brick factory isn't the best, but good climbing and occasional late afternoon sun can make it feel much more pleasant. The Main Wall has the best routes in the quarry with some excellent long pitches in the 6c to 7b range. The Crystal and Going Straight Walls offer routes at more friendly grades and are consequently quite popular.

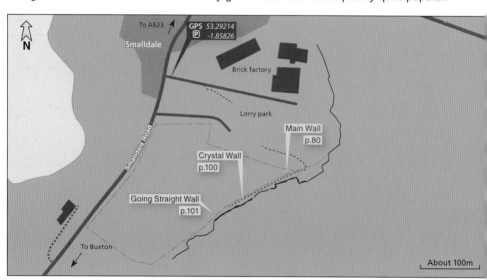

## Approach    Also see map on page 94

Smalldale village is situated near Peak Dale on a back road which cuts across from the A6 north of Buxton to Peak Forest on the A623. Just south of the village are two entrances to the quarry and a brick factory. Parking is possible by the side of the northern entrance to the brick factory on the surfaced road (bump your car up the kerb in case of big lorries). A small path to the right of the brick factory entrance leads to the lorry park area. Cross this and follow a path to the fence on the far side and the crag beyond. There is also a small amount of room to park at the southern entrance but tuck your car out of the way on the road side of the barrier in case it is locked.

## Conditions

The quarry faces north, but does get the late afternoon sun in summer. It is relatively sheltered and can give some entertainment in the rain although not for long as the water will start to run down the crag.

## Access

The crag is on private land but, as yet, there have not been any problems with access. It is important that cars are parked sensibly without blocking anything. The inclusion of the information in this book does not mean that you have a right of access to the crag.

North | Southwest | Southeast | Stoney | Horseshoe | Smalldale | Harpur Hill | Lovers' Leap | Beethouse | Craig-y-Bxepis | Staden Q | Chee Dale U. | Chee Dale L. | Blackwell D. | Raven Tor | Water-c-Jolly | Ravensdale | Aldery Cliff | Taddington | Rheinstor

Rachel Slater on *Upminster Kid* (6b) - *page 101* - on the
Going Straight Wall at Smalldale. Photo: Craig Bailey

The rest of the routes are on Main Wall, with the first few climbing various features on the north facing sidewall.

**8 Tawk the Squawk** ..... 7a
Balance and slap a way up the left-hand side of the arete.
*FA. Gary Gibson 2007*

**9 Squawkietawkie** ........ 7a
The right-hand side of the hanging arete, starting through the roof.
*FA. Gary Gibson 1995*

**10 Obelix** ............ 7a+
The middle of the sidewall tower, to a hard finish.
*FA. Gary Gibson 1995*

**11 Can'tgetmyfix** ....... 6c+
Start up *Obelix* and break right.
*FA. Gary Gibson 2007*

**12 Getafix** ......... 7a+
The right-hand arete of the tower. Another hard finish.
*FA. Gary Gibson 1995*

**13 Play it Again Sam** ....... HVS 5a
The angular groove - a good line, pity about the rock.

**14 Reservoir Frogs** ......... 6c
Good varied climbing right of the corner, starting up a crack.
*FA. Gary Gibson 1995*

Up and left of the Main Wall there is a bunch of short routes with very steep slopes below them.

**1 Beastiality** ............... 6a

**2 Killer Bee** ................. 6c

**3 Ladybird Killers** ........... 6c+

**4 Six Bee or Not Six Bee** ....... 6c+

**5 Bee Movie** ............... 6a+

**6 To Bee a Star** ............. 6a

**7 Terry and June** ............ 6c
*All above FA. Gary Gibson 1995*

### Main Wall

The impressive, tall face on the far left has a fine set of wall climbs, which are just a little too packed-in for their own good. In general though the routes are well bolted and offer some good, fierce face-climbing.
**Approach -** From the path by the fence, scramble up steep, blocky ground below the wall to a narrow ledge along its base. The routes on the sidewall and the short wall up and left are reached by a steep grassy scramble.

Not much sun / 5 min

**⑮ First Offence** . . . . . 🔆🎣📷⬜ **6c+**
Intricate and balancy climbing.
*FA. Bob Conway 1985*

**⑯ When Reason Sleeps** . 🔆🎣⬜ **7a+**
A very technical start leads to a bold-feeling upper wall.
*FA. Gary Gibson 1995*

**⑰ Stainsby Girls** . . . . . . 🔆🎣⬜ **7b**
Head straight up from the wide crack in the base of the wall,
then pull into the technical groove. Finish up this.
*FA. Chris Jackson 1985. FA. (Direct) Gary Gibson 1995*

**⑱ Virtual Insanity** . . . 🔆📿🎣⬜ **7b**
Popular and good. The fingery face leads straight up to a flake
and a thought-provoking finish. Lots of bolts and quite a few
tricky moves too. Stick to the line to claim the grade.
*FA. Nadim Siddiqui 1995*

**⑲ Soft Centre** . . . . . . . . 🔆📿⬜ **7a+**
A tiny groove and thin crack lead to the roof. Less good above, and
beware the loose block. Used to feel bold but it has been rebolted.
*FA. Jim Burton, Gary Gibson, Nadim Siddiqui 1995*

**⑳ Lies and Deception** . . . 🔆📷⬜ **7a**
A good lower wall and a hard move back right above the
(hollow?) roof to gain the final groove.
*FA. Gary Gibson 1995*

**㉑ Summat Outanowt** . . . . 🔆📷⬜ **7a**
The long slim groove leads to a tricky overlap and fine headwall.
*FA. Gary Gibson 2007*

**㉒ Lost Contact** . . . . . 🔆📷🎣⬜ **7a+**
The groove is easy, the crack and face above are sustained.
*FA. Bill Wintrip, Neil Foster 1985*

**㉓ Soggy Biscuits** . . . . 🔆📷📿⬜ **7b+**
A fingery climb with a hard finish.
*FA. Simon Lee 1995*

**㉔ Can Boys** . . . . . 🔆🐚📷📿⬜ **7a**
Some boys can. Superb climbing up the clean face.
*FA. Neil Foster 1985*

**㉕ Can Can Girls Can't** . . . . . . 🔆⬜ **6c**
The clean face just to the right.
*FA. Gary Gibson 2007*

*The thin crack and flake is **Little Lady, E3 5c**. It is rather scruffy
and unpopular.*

**㉖ Bedlam** . . . . . . . . . . . . . . 🐚⬜ **6c+**
The bolt-line on the far right.
*FA. Gary Gibson 1995*

**㉗ Noisy Neigbours** . . . . . . . . 📿⬜ **7a**
Start up *Beldam* and break right.
*FA. Gary Gibson 2007*

North · Southwest · Southeast · Stoney · Horseshoe · Smalldale · Harpur Hill · Lovers' Leap · Beehouse · Craig-y-Biceps · Staden Q · Blackwell D. · Chee Dale L. · Chee Dale U. · Raven Tor · Water-c-Jolly · Ravensdale · Aldery Cliff · Taddington · Rheinstor

*Between the two walls is a small isolated route on a short wall -* **Fringe Meeting, 6a**.

**1 Owd Biddy Flogger** . . . . . . 6a
The left arete has a loose start, but improves with height.
*FA. Gary Gibson, Nick Taylor, Andy Beaumont 2002*

**2 Floggin' a Dead Horse** . . . . 6b
The clean wall just to the right has neat moves.
*FA. Gary Gibson 2007*

**3 The Crystal Maze** . . 6c+
Head right then go direct; escalating difficulties.
*FA. Gary Gibson 1995*

**4 Hollow Inside** . . . . . . . 6b+
Climb the wall, keeping left of the pale rock via a useful flake, to hard moves for the break. Swing left to the lower-off.
*FA. Gary Gibson 1996*

**5 The Quartz Tricycle** . . . 6b+
A shallow groove leads past a bulge on the pleasant face above. Finish left then right up the crowning pillar.
*FA. Gary Gibson 1995*

**6 Friezian** . . . . . . . . . . 6b
The grey wall is technical early on, then easier above where it trends away to the right.
*FA. Gary Gibson, Nick Taylor 2002*

**7 Lady Luck** . . . . . . . . 6a+
A good climb left of the grotty central break. A hard start, with easier moves above.
*FA. Gary Gibson, Nick Taylor 2002*

**8 Just Passing Through** . . . . . . . 6b
The left-hand side of the pillar gives decent climbing to a final couple of difficult moves direct past the final bolt. You can slink left around this top bolt at 6a.
*FA. Gary Gibson, Nick Taylor 2002*

**9 Sock it to 'em** . . . . . . . 5+
A great pitch on weird rock up the right-hand side of the pillar. Steep and strenuous.
*FA. Gary Gibson, Nick Taylor 2002*

**10 Stone the Crows** . . . . . . . . . . 6b
Take the cracks, then pull out right onto the exposed tower.
*FA. Gary Gibson, Nick Taylor 2002*

**11 Learn the Lingo** . . . . . . 6c
Make good, sustained moves up the face. Pass some scars early on, then trend slightly left. Slightly suspect rock.
*FA. Gary Gibson 2002*

**12 Mr. Love Pants** . . . 6b+
Use the first clip of *Learn the Lingo*, but keep right and climb the rib passing the small overlap with sustained interest.
*FA. Gary Gibson 2002*

**13 Shanacie** . . . . . . . . . . 6b
Climb a tough wall to a small overlap, then move up to a roof and finish up a jamming-crack. The lower wall has a couple of hard moves on finger-locks. These are avoidable on the left at 6a.
*FA. Senan Hennessey, P.Faulkner 1985 (E2 5b). Bolted by Gary Gibson, 2002*

**14 Riding the Bullet** . . . . . 6c
Climb the centre of the technical face, trending slightly (but not too far) rightwards, then go direct to a good finish on the headwall.
*FA. Gary Gibson, Nick Taylor, Andy Beaumont 2002*

### Crystal Wall and Going Straight Wall
Two good faces on rock reminiscent of that at Staden, with some weird and wonderful formations on display. The right-hand wall is the most popular section of the quarry.
**Approach -** The walls are the right-most pieces of developed rock, which can be easily reached from the path below.

**15 Open Season** . . . . . . .  6a+

A steep start left of the adit entrance leads up the wall to a good finish up a crack.

*FA. Gary Gibson, Nick Taylor, Andy Beaumont 2002*

**16 More Chattery Teeth** . . . . . .  6b

Start just right of the adit entrance, and make tricky moves up to gain some cracks. Step left and finish more easily.

*FA. Gary Gibson, Jim Burton 2002*

**17 Upminster Kid** . . . . . . . . . .  6b

Climb the steep face through a patch of white rock, then step right for an exciting finale up the hanging tower.

*Photo on page 97.*

*FA. Gary Gibson, Nick Taylor 2002*

**18 Going Straight** . . . .  6c

Good climbing up the face to join and finish as for the previous climb. There are enough bolts, but only just.

*FA. Bob Conway 1985. Bolted in 2002.*

**19 Friend 15** . . . . . . . . . . . . .  6a+

Climb straight up the wall to the black stain and finish direct above it. You shouldn't need the eponymous piece of gear.

*FA. S.Hennessey (E2 5b) 1985. Bolted by Gary Gibson in 2002.*

**20 Shame on You** . . . . . . .  6a+

Balance up a short ramp then climb the wall by good moves.

*FA. Gary Gibson, Nick Taylor 2002*

**21 The Awesome Foursome** . . . . . .  6b+

A fierce little thing to the right.

**22 Single Decker** . . . . . . . . . .  6b+

A short route up white rock, several holds have gone west.

*FA. Gary Gibson, Jim Burton 2003*

**23 Triple Sec** . . . . . . . . . . . . .  6b

A wall leads to a ledge and loose cave. Climb the wall above.

*FA. Gary Gibson, Nick Taylor 2002*

**24 Double Wammy** . . . . . . . . . . .  6b+

The ledgy and technical wall split by a grass ledge.

*FA. Gary Gibson 2002*

| | No star | | | |
|---|---|---|---|---|
| **Mod to S / 4+** | 5 | - | - | - |
| **HS-HVS / 5-6a+** | 128 | 35 | 4 | 1 |
| **E1-E3 / 6b-7a** | 80 | 49 | 9 | 3 |
| **E4 / 7a+ and up** | 2 | 2 | 4 | - |

The quarried plateau of Harpur Hill is clearly visible on the hill overlooking Buxton. Its stark outline hides a large expanse of walls and quarries connected on different levels by tracks and paths. The setting can be delightful in places like The Playground and on much of the Upper Tier, but the Lower Tier with its rusty car wrecks and general grotty appearance makes it a less pleasant spot.

The development has been sporadic over the years. Initially there was a small collection of trad routes on Papacy Buttress then in the late 1990s the place saw a large number of sport routes added, again, mostly on the Upper Tier. It is a nice feature of the place that the original trad routes have retained their status in most cases and are still some of the better routes across the crag. *The Seven Deadly Sins*, *Seven Deadly Virtues* and *Nostalgia* are all great routes which it is worth packing your wires and cams for.

In more recent times all the walls have been dotted with sport routes of varying quality and some of the later additions on The Dark Side are pushing the bounds of what is worthwhile bolting.

**Safety note -** There is plenty of loose rock here and there have been accidents, a helmet is a good idea, as is belaying in a position that isn't directly below the leader.

## Approach　　Also see map on page 94

The quarry is situated to the southwest of the village of Harpur Hill which can be easily reached from the A53 Buxton-to-Leek road, or the A515 Buxton-to-Ashbourne road. Just to the west of the village, there is a steep well-signed side-road leading up left to an industrial estate. Follow this past a cafe as the road bends round to the right. Continue past the go-cart circuit and 150m up here is a lay-by on the left by a bus shelter. **Do not** park on any of the double-yellows closer to the crag, or obstruct access - you will get clamped and/or ticketed! Walk back to a gated track and follow a path through a field for 230m then bear right up the slope to enter the quarry directly in front of the Lower Tier. The easiest way to reach the Upper Tier is via a steep zigzag path that weaves up the slope just to the left of the Cairn Sector. The Dark Side and College are reached by following the main track.

There is also limited roadside parking on Grin Low Road close to the junction with Burlow Road. Walk up Fiddle Street to access the track leading to the quarry - see map opposite.

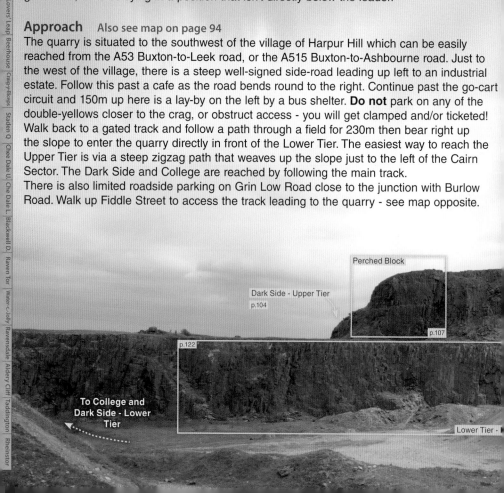

Perched Block

Dark Side - Upper Tier
p.104

p.107

p.122

To College and
Dark Side - Lower
Tier

Lower Tier -

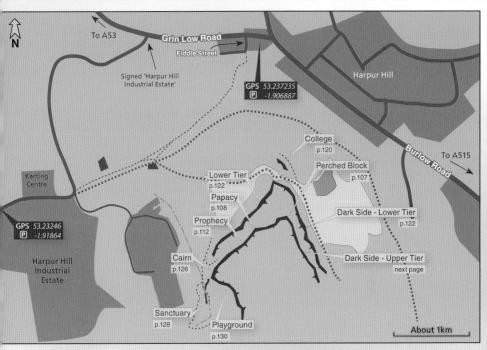

## Access

There is no formal access agreement to the quarry, and the inclusion of the information in this book does not mean that you have right of access to climb there. If asked to leave then please do so.

## Conditions

The main section of the cliff faces slightly west of due north, therefore it sees the sun from mid to late afternoon in the summer. The exceptions to this are The Dark Side, which gets the early morning sun only, and The Sanctuary and The Playground, which get sun from mid-morning onwards. The whole quarry takes little drainage, but it can be a cool and windy place and there is little shelter. It is an excellent retreat on hot summer days.

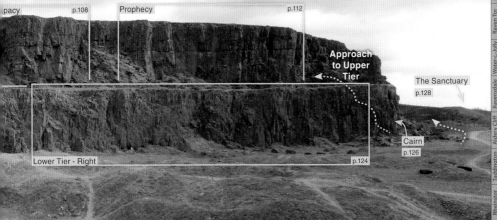

On the very far left-hand end are five short routes. From left to right these are: **This is the End, 5+**, **The End is Nigh, 5**, **Ending Now, 6a**, **Euroman Endeth, 4** and finally **Endeth, 5**. (All FA. Gary Gibson 2010)

**1 It has to End Somewhere** . . . . . ⬚ 6a
Climb the slab trending leftwards to a lower-off.
FA. Bill Birch, Peter Cowie 2006

**2 Will it Never End** . . . . . . . . . . ⬚ 4+
The left-hand pillar.
FA. Bill Birch, Peter Cowie 2006

**3 Is this the End?** . . . . . . . . . . . ⬚ 5
FA. Bill Birch, Peter Cowie 2006

**4 Coming to an End.** . . . . . . . . . ⬚ 6a+
The narrow pillar.
FA. Bill Birch, Peter Cowie 2006

**5 End Games** . . . . . . . . . . . . . . ⬚ HVS 5a
The cracks on the sidewall of the pillar to a lower-off.
FA. Bill Birch, Peter Cowie 2006

**6 In My Darkest Hour** . . . . . . . . ⬚ 5
The left-hand side of the slab.
FA. Gary Gibson 2010

**7 Endsville.** . . . . . . . . . . . . . 🦎⬚ 6a
The flat face on the far left has a tough finale.
FA. Gary Gibson, Nick Taylor 2002

**8 Centreville** . . . . . . . . . . . . . . ⬚ 6a
A crack to a flake.
FA. Bill Birch, Peter Cowie 2006

**9 Preston North End** . . . . . . . . . ⬚ 6c
The arete of the End Buttress.
FA. Bill Birch, Peter Cowie 2006

**10 Will They?** . . . . . . . . . . . . . . ⬚ 5
The short red wall.
FA. Gary Gibson 2010

**11 People Will Talk** . . . . . . . . . . ⬚ 5+
A slabby arete with a nice finish.
FA. Gary Gibson, Nick Taylor 2002

**12 The Parting of the Lips** . . . . 🧗⬚ 5
The narrow wall is gained by a scramble up and left.
FA. Gary Gibson 2002

**13 Ear to Ear** . . . . . . . . . . . . . . ⬚ 6a+
A thin face with a mid-height crux.
FA. Gary Gibson, Pete Clark 2002

**14 Uncreased** . . . . . . . . . . . . . . ⬚ VS 4c
The left-hand of a pair of cracks.
FA. Gary Gibson, Nick Taylor 2002

**15 Hairline** . . . . . . . . . . . . . . . . ⬚ VS 4c
The right-hand crack passing a good flake early on.
FA. Gary Gibson 2002

**16 The Mouth Waters** . . . . 🏅1 🧗⬚ 6b+
The narrowing black wall is one of the best hereabouts.
FA. Gary Gibson, Pete Clark 2002

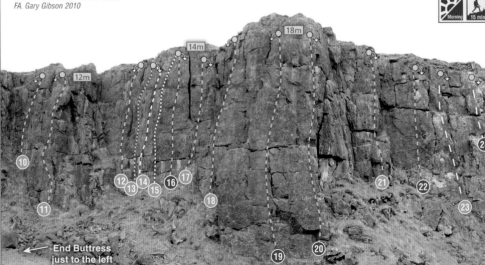

**17 I'm a Port Vale Dribbler** . . . . . . [ ] 6a
FA. Gary Gibson 2010

**18 George Stark Calling** . . [icons] [ ] 6a+
The fine arete of the buttress has some good moves.
FA. Gary Gibson, Pete Clark 2002

**19 Stark Disbelief.** . . . . . . . . [icon] [ ] 6c+
The centre of the face is unbalanced with a fierce crux section.
FA. Gary Gibson, Pete Clark 2002

**20 The Dark Half** . . . . . . [icons] [ ] 6b
A fine route with good moves on the upper arete.
FA. Gary Gibson 2002

**21 Graveyard Blues** . . . . . . . . . . [ ] 6a+
The arete in the recess around to the right.
FA. Gary Gibson 2002

**22 In Stark Contrast** . . . . . [icons] [ ] 6b+
After a hard start, climb past a pair of breaks to the lower-off.
FA. Gary Gibson, Hazel Gibson 2002

**23 Ghost Writer** . . . . . . . . . . . . . [ ] 5+
FA. Gary Gibson 2010

**24 Under the Lifeline** . . . . . . . . . . [ ] 6b
FA. Gary Gibson 2010

**25 Over the Deadline** . . . . . . . . . [ ] 6b
The left-hand line is the best on this short wall.
FA. Gary Gibson 2002

**26 Automatic Writing** . . . . . . . . . [ ] 6a
The middle line of bolts is tricky above mid-height.
FA. Gary Gibson 2002

**27 Fools Stuffing** . . . . . . . . . . . . [ ] 6a+
Awkward at mid-height. Try to avoid using the chimney.
FA. Gary Gibson 2002

## The Dark Side - Upper Tier

To the left of the main Papacy Buttress, the Upper Tier swings around to face east. This section features a collection of routes on blocky rock which can be dusty. There is also a small selection of indifferent trad routes amongst the sporty ones.

**Conditions -** The wall receives morning sun, but after that remains true to its name. It makes a welcome hot weather retreat, but when the cold wind blows, the place is pretty chilly.

**Approach -** From below Papacy Buttress, walk left around the corner for about 200m.

*To the right is a wall split into three buttresses in its upper section by a chequerboard of vertical and horizontal cracks.*

**28 Pillar of Wisdom** . . . . . . . . . . [ ] 6b
Scramble to the left-hand buttress and weave up it.
FA. Gary Gibson 2002

**29 The Invasion of the Creepazoid**
. . . . . . . . . . . . . . . . . . . . . [icon] [ ] 6c+
The central buttress improves after the start. Sustained.
FA. Gary Gibson 2002

**30 Later That Night.** . . . . . . . . . . . [ ] 6b
The right-hand buttress, finishing up a short crack.
FA. Gary Gibson 2002

**31 The Coming of the Sparrows** [icon] [ ] 5+
The thin slab leads to steeper moves up the cleaned rib.
FA. Gary Gibson, Hazel Gibson 2002

**32 Flight of the Finches.** . . . . . . . . [ ] 6c
The technical face and pillar above.
FA. Bill Birch, Peter Cowie 2006

The right-hand side of this area has a long groove left of a pillar. The steep black face to the left of this has three bolt-lines and one trad route.

**③③ Stop the Pigeon** . . . . . . . . [symbols] 6b+
Climb past a thin overlap and up a short rib.
FA. Gary Gibson, Nick Taylor 2002

**③④ Ken Dodd's Dad's Dog's Dead** . . [box] HVS 5b
The fingery crack to a lower-off on the right. A selection of gear is required.
FA. Gary Gibson, Nick Taylor, Alan Taylor 2002

**③⑤ Gathering Darkness** [symbols] 6c+
The short face is technical and sustained.
FA. Gary Gibson 2002

**③⑥ A Trip on the Dark Side** . [symbols] 6a+
A decent, but disjointed pitch. From the grotty groove head left up the fingery wall to ledges. Finish direct up the right-hand side of the arete above. The crack gives an easier finish.
FA. Gary Gibson, Hazel Gibson 2002

**③⑦ Feel My Presence** . . . . . . . . . [box] 6b+
Climb rightwards (higher is easier) out of the grotty groove to access the sharp arete which gives some technical laybacking.
FA. Gary Gibson, Jim Burton 2002

**③⑧ Tapenard** . . . . . . . . . . . . [symbol] 6b
Climb the pillar then work up leftwards.
FA. Gary Gibson, Nick Taylor 2001

**③⑨ Wild Olives** . . . . . . . . . . . [symbol] 6b
Climb through a cleaned area of rock then on via a couple of thin overlaps to a finish up the blocky rib. Better then it looks.
FA. Gary Gibson, Nick Taylor 2001

**④⓪ Gorignak** . . . . . . . . . . . . [symbol] 6b
Step left out of the groove and cross the overlap. Continue up the cracked wall above to an interesting finish.
FA. Gary Gibson, Nick Taylor 2002

**④① Galaxy Quest** . . . . . . . . . . [symbol] 5+
The crack-line.
FA. Gary Gibson 2011

**④② Omega 13** . . . . . . . . . [symbols] 6a+
Follow the thin crack to its end then continue up the face and blunt rib. A good last move if you stay direct.
FA. Gary Gibson, Hazel Gibson 2002

**④③ Dr Lazarus** . . . . . . . . . . . . . [box] 6a+
Pull through the overhang and follow cracks to a rightward exit. Short-lived sport with a high first bolt.
FA. Gary Gibson, Nick Taylor 2002

North | Southwest | Southeast | Stoney | Horseshoe | Smalldale | Harpur Hill | Lovers' Leap | Beerhouse | Craig-y-Biceps | Staden Q | Chee Dale U | Che Dale L | Blackwell D | Raven Tor | Water-c-Jolly | Ravensdale | Aldery Cliff | Taddington | Rheinstor

**Perched Block Buttress**

To the left of Papacy Buttress, the Upper Tier swings around to face east. At the junction of the faces is an impressive buttress with a set of sport routes on the left, and trad routes on the right. All of these are currently neglected.

**Conditions -** The right-hand side of the buttress receives evening sun in the summer. The left side gets virtually no sun at all. It is a useful hot weather retreat, but when the cold wind blows, the place is pretty chilly.

**Approach -** From below Papacy Buttress, walk left to the corner; about 100m.

① **What's the Paint?** . . . . . . . . . `5`
From the low point of the crag's grassy base a tricky start leads to easier ground.

② **Pity the Grafitti** . . . . . . . . . . . `5`
A similar line just to the right.

*The next three routes start from the grassy ridge on the right.*

③ **Set Fred Free** . . . . . . . . . . . . `6a`
The left-hand line has a steep finish.

④ **Wilky's Revenge** . . . . . . . . . . `5+`
The middle line off the ridge is nice enough.

⑤ **Making Plans for Nidge** . . . `6b`
Trend right into the cave then tackle the bulges that form its left-hand side.

⑥ **Helzapoppin'** . . . . . . . . `7a`
Good sustained climbing through the roof of the cave.

⑦ **Right Said Fred** . . . . . . . . `6b`
The right edge of the cave gives another beefy pitch.

⑧ **Coyote Club.** . . . . . . . . . . . . . `6a`
Head up the left edge of the lower wall. Single bolt lower-off.

*The tall face to the right has five decent-looking routes.*

⑨ **Wily E. Coyote.** . . . . . . . . . . . `E2 5b`
Start below and right of the poised block on a grassy ledge. Using a large pocket and sharing cam placements with *Road Runner* climb slightly left into a large scoop. Climb upwards and then trend slightly right after the poised block.
*FA. Jim Burton, A.Pedley 1998*

⑩ **Road Runner.** . . . . . . . . . . . . `E1 5b`
Start slightly right of *Wily E. Coyote*. Using the same large pocket climb straight up the face - cams after the first moves. Continue up and right to finish on vertical flutings.
*FA. A.Pedley, Jim Burton 1999*

⑪ **Zebedee** . . . . . . . . . . . . . . . `VS 4b`
Start on top of the grassy block and climb left to an overlap. Pass this on the right and move left into a shallow groove which leads to the mid-height ledge. Move right 3m and follow cracks then trend left to the top.

⑫ **Balance of Actions** . . . . . . . . . `HVS 5a`
Trend left towards a flake then climb direct up the face above.
*FA. Jim Burton, A.Pedley 1998*

⑬ **Greensleeves** . . . . . . . . . . . . `VS 4b`
Climb direct from the grassy block and traverse right to a crack which leads to an overhang. Move left to a thin crack and up this to the ledge. Finish up the wide crack above.

## Papacy Buttress

A fine buttress containing many of the best routes at Harpur Hill. It has some striking corners, and a big open groove separating the two walls. The quality sport routes are complemented well by a number of good trad lines, so bring your wires and cams.

**Approach -** From the Lower Tier, zigzag up the path left of Sector Cairn and head left to the buttress.

**Conditions -** The sun arrives in the mid-to-late afternoon. Before that it can be very cold if there is a wind blowing, but it is a good place on a hot summer day.

**1 Angleterre** . . . . . . . . . . . . . . . 5
The shallow groove on the left is normally a bit grubby.
FA. Gary Gibson 1998

**2 This England** . . . . . . . 7a+
A short, technical wall and blunt arete, starting up the slope.
FA. Gary Gibson 1998

**3 Pleasant Valley Sunday** . . . . . . E1 5b
The short, scooped crack is difficult to enter, then leads left to the lower-off on *This England*.
FA. Paul Harrison 1998

**4 Upthrutch** . . . . . . . . . . VS 4c
*The well-named water-worn groove leads to a steep exit.*
FA. Malcolm Baxter 1986

**5 Gritarete** . . . . . . . . 7a
A steep start leads to some unusual rounded holds above.
FA. Gary Gibson, Paul Harrison 1998

**6 Snake Eyes** . . . . . . . . . E3 5c
A fine, thin crack twists to the lower-off on *Gritarete*.
FA. Gary Gibson, Paul Harrison 1998

**7 Strangled at Birth** . . . . . 6b+
Start up the short arete and climb the thin wall above.
FA. Gary Gibson 1998

**8 Sincerely Yours** . . . . . . . . 6b
Nice climbing up the cracks and the harder wall above.
FA. Gary Gibson, Hazel Gibson 2007

**9 I'm in the Sin Bin** . . . . . 6a
More worthwhile climbing up the cracks that lead to a break.
FA. Gary Gibson, Hazel Gibson 2007

**10 Sin City** . . . . . . . . . E1 5b
Climb the groove then move right around a roof onto the ramp of *Seven Deadly Sins*. Move up left (loose block) then climb direct up the scoopy groove to a steep final crack.

**11 The Seven Deadly Sins** . . . . HVS 5a
A fine climb which follows an absorbing line up the buttress. Climb the short corner, then pull left onto a slab. Trend diagonally up left then direct to the main break. Move up a steep crack above to the next break then step back right before finishing up a well-positioned groove. Solitary stake belay a long way back.
FA. Bob Toogood, Bob Dearman 1966

North

Southwest

Southeast

Stoney

Horseshoe

Smalldale

Harpur Hill

Lovers' Leap

Beerhouse

Crag-y-Biceps

Staden Q

Chee Dale U.

Chee Dale L.

Blackwell D.

Raven tor

Water-c.-Jolly

Ravensdale

Aldery Cliff

Taddington

Rheinstor

North | Southwest | Southeast | Stoney | Horseshoe | Smalldale | Harpur Hill | Lovers' Leap | Beechouse | Craig-y-Biceps | Staden Q | Chee Dale U | Chee Dale L | Blackwell D | Raven Tor | Water-c-Jolly | Ravensdale | Aldery Cliff | Teddington | Rheinstor

**12 Coral Seas** . . . . . . . . `Top 50` ▢▯▢ **6a**
A superb route with a crux high on the wall. Easier than it appears. Climb the face right of the corner, then pull out onto the slab, and climb up to the break. Power through the bulge (the best hold has gone) then traverse up right to a lower-off.
*FA. Bill Birch, Nadim Siddiqui 1994*

**13 Avarice Allsorts** . . . . . . ▢▯▢ **6c+**
Start as for *Coral Seas*, but continue to the flat roof, then pull over on big positive holds to the next break. One more hard move gains easier ground, then the belay.
*FA. Gary Gibson, Dave Law 1998*

**14 Lust** . . . . . . . . . . . . . ▢▮▢ **VS 4c**
The central gully leads through a tricky overhang and into the open funnel above. A good line, but rarely climbed.
*FA. Bob Dearman 1966*

**15 Ask Mr. T. for Tea.** . . . . ▢▮▢ **6c+**
Climb just right of the big crack of *Lust* to a tricky move into *Rocky Variations*. Up left to cross the crack and finish up the sidewall on good rock.
*FA. Gary Gibson 2010*

**16 Rocky Variations** . . . . . `Top 50`▮▢ **6b**
A great climb with some testing moves through the hanging groove. From a block, step right onto the wall and climb to the groove. Pull out left and head up to a roof, step right to a groove then pull up and back left above the bulge (direct is 6b+ and on the left it is 6b). Finish up the easier grooved arete above.
*Photo on page 115.*
*FA. Bill Birch, Nadim Siddiqui 1994*

**17 Apollo Creed** . . . . . . . `Top 50`▯▢ **6b**
A fine and devious companion to *Rocky Variations* up the rock to its right. Start as for *Rocky Variations*, but trend rightwards up the slab. Make tough moves past the roof at its right-hand edge and continue to ledges. Pull up and right and finish up easier ground.
*FA. Bill Birch, Nadim Siddiqui 1994. May include the finishing section of One Deadly Variant (HVS 5b) the left-hand finish to Seven Deadly Virtues.*

**18 The Seven Deadly Virtues** . . ▢▢ **E1 5b**
A fine trad-route which follows the best line on the buttress. Start below the left-facing groove, and climb a crack up into it, then follow it to the roof. Traverse right past two bolt-lines to reach a loose groove on the right, which leads to the top. Alternatively, step left to a lower-off.
*FFA. T.Morris 1967. FA. Graham West, Barry Roberts (aid) 1960. The first route in the quarry, originally started up Lust, and traversed out right.*

**19 Luddite Thought Police** . . . . ▢▢ **E3 6a**
A direct finish to *Seven Deadly Virtues*, crossing the roof and powering up the steep crack above.
*FA. Gary Gibson 1998. Led on bolts in 1994 by Nadim Siddiqui.*

**20 Penal Servitude** . . . . . . . . ▢▢ **E2 5b**
Climb the crack on the right to reach the blunt arete forming the right-hand edge of the groove of *Seven Deadly Virtues*. Finish direct to a lower-off.
*FA. Nadim Siddiqui, Bill Birch 1994*

**21 Full Frontal** . . . . . . . . . ▢▮▢ **6c**
An eliminate up the front of the pillar is more independent than it looks. Make an awkward move in from the right (starting direct is an artificial 6c+). Another hard section leads up the pillar to the break. Finish up the easier wall above.
*FA. Bill Birch, S.Hunter, Nadim Siddiqui 1994*

**22 El Camino Real** . . . . . ▢▢ ▨▢ **E1 5b**
The compelling crack and groove to the right of the pillar give a fine sustained jamming pitch eventually joining and finishing up the groove of *Seven Deadly Virtues*.
*FA. Bill Birch (bolted) 1994. Led without bolts Gary Gibson 1998.*

**23 Power of Soul . . . .** 7b+
Climb the thin crack, which has an undercut start. Good climbing, but it is over all too quickly.
*FA. Nadim Siddiqui, Jim Burton 1994*

**24 Dementia Normale. . . . . . .** 6a
The cracks and groove lead to a lower-off.
*FA. Gary Gibson 1998*

**25 The Last Straw . . . . . . . . . . .** 6b
Start from blocks up right of the main wall. Climb past three close bolts, then easier moves lead up the edge above.
*FA. Gary Gibson 1998*

**26 Figure of Law . . . . . . .** 6c+
Up the slope to the right of the buttress. Climb the pillar past four bolts by some technical moves.
*FA. Gary Gibson, Dave Law 1998*

**27 I Am the Law. . . . . . . . . .** 6b+
The thin cracks soon ease, if you can do the start.
*FA. Gary Gibson 2006*

North | Southwest | Southeast | Stoney | Horseshoe | Smalldale | Harpur Hill | Lovers Leap | Beerhouse | Craig-y-Biceps | Staden Q | Cheer Dale U | Che Dale L | Blackwell D. | Raven Tor | Water-c-Jolly | Ravensdale | Aldery Cliff | Taddington | Rheinstor

## Prophecy Area

The most extensive section of the upper walls consists of a series of vertical faces, steep cracks and blocky buttresses. There are plenty of good lines here, and some patches of poor rock.

**Approach** - From the Lower Tier, zigzag up the path left of Sector Cairn, and follow the plateau to below the buttress.

**Conditions** - The sun arrives in the mid-to-late afternoon. Before that it can be very cold if there is a wind blowing, but it is a good place on hot days.

**1 Danny Cool** . . . . . . . . . . . . . . 5
The narrow rib has some decent moves.
FA. Gary Gibson 2007

**2 Cool Danny** . . . . . . . . . . . . . . 6b
Pleasant face climbing passing a thin roof early on.
FA. Gary Gibson 1998

**3 Screaming Wheels** . . . . . . . 6b
The attractive arete has a hard move at mid-height and a pumpy clip. Sadly it is easier to slink off to either side of the line.
FA. Gary Gibson 1998

**4 Swain's World** . . . . . . 6b
The right side of the long arete keeps on coming.
FA. Gary Gibson 2006

**5 No Man's Land** . . . . . . . . . . . 6b+
To the right of the arete, take the left-hand line of bolts.
FA. Gary Gibson 1998

**6 The Exclusion Zone** . . . . . . 6b+
As for No Man's Land, but follow the right-hand line.
Photo on page 94.
FA. Gary Gibson 1998

**7 The Iron Curtain** . . . . . . . . 6a+
The rib and shallow groove give a pleasant pitch.
FA. Gary Gibson, Hazel Gibson 1998

**8 Mouse Hunt** . . . . . . 6c
Start in a corner and climb the wall to a break right of a grassy ledge. The upper wall passing an overlap feels run-out.
FA. Gary Gibson 1998

**9 Slowly, Slowly Catch a Monkey**
. . . . . . . . . . . . . . . . . . . . . . 6a+
The crack and narrow pillar give a decent route.
FA. Gary Gibson, K.Bridgens, B.Bennt, Gordon Jenkin 2009

**10 Thing Thang** . . . . . . . . . . . 7a
The left-hand of two shorter routes up a scoop.
FA. Gary Gibson 1998

**11 Thang Thing** . . . . . . . . . . . 7a
The right-hand line, the crack on the right is taboo.
FA. Gary Gibson 1998

**12 Slab de Lune** . . . . . . . . . . . . . 6a
The rib on the recessed grassy slab.
FA. Gary Gibson 2001

**13 Master of a Lune** . . . . . 6b
A new route up the narrow face to the right.
FA. Gary Gibson 2010

**14 Stack of Stones** . . . . . . . . . 6a+
Start by using the flake on the left otherwise it is 6b. A new bolt has lowered the grip factor near the top.
FA. Gary Gibson, Hazel Gibson 1998

**15 Bag of Bones** . . . . . 6a+
A fine delicate rib left of the hammer-head block on excellent rock. The first bolt is tricky to reach if the grass is wet.
FA. Gary Gibson, Hazel Gibson 1998

**16 Plate of Scones** . . . . . . . . . . . 6b+
Scratch up the thin face just right of the hammer-head block and continue up a groove and crack.
FA. Gary Gibson 1998

**17 Sara Laughs** . . . . . . . . . . 6b+
The face above the blocks has a hard central section.
FA. Gary Gibson 1998

**18 Tenth Heaven** . . . . 6b
A tricky lower section leads to the easier crack.
FA. Gary Gibson, Nick Taylor 2008

**19 Calci-Mauve** . . . . . 6b
Start up the pillar to the break. The flowstone wall above has good moves. The right-hand finish is **Glas Double, 6c+**.
FA. Gary Gibson 1998

**20 Flaky Pastry** . . . . . . . . HVS 5a
An oddity, a decent mid-grade trad route up the big groove. There is a lower-off, thus removing the need to top-out.
FA. Gary Gibson 1998

**21 Over the Hill** . . . . . . . . 6c
An excellent sustained route up the cracks. Hard from the word go without ever being desperate and with a fine finish over the top roof - keep to the right for the better moves.
FA. Gary Gibson, Gordon Jenkin 2001

**22 Nostalgia** . . . . . . . . . . E4 6a
The long crack is a superb trad route with a new lower-off.
FA. Gary Gibson 1998

**23 The Omen** . . . . . . . . . 6b
Another of those long and worthwhile crack-systems.
FA. Gary Gibson, Tim Parkinson, Nick Taylor 2007

**24 Yogi Bare** . . . . . . . . . . 7a
A tricky wall climb. Finish left of the bolts. Can be dirty.
FA. Gary Gibson 1998

**25 Four Telling Tales** . . . . 6c+
The crack on the left-hand side of the arete is absorbing and technical with a tricky finish.
FA. Gary Gibson 1998

**26 The Talisman** . . . . . . . 6c+
The right-hand side of the arete is awkward and less satisfying than *Four Telling Tales*. Drilled pegs at the start.
FA. Gary Gibson 1998

**27 Bleingassen** . . . . . . . . . . 6c
The long open groove and blocky rib give a worthwhile pitch.
FA. Gary Gibson, Tim Parkinson, Nick Taylor 2007

**28 The Oracle** . . . . . . 7b
The fierce short wall to a roof is hard to onsight.
FA. Gary Gibson 1998

**29 The Prophecy** . . . . 7a
Worthwhile and popular though a bit of an eliminate. Climb to the roof and make long moves right past the bulge. The wall leads to the break and nice arete - avoid the crack on the right.
FA. Gary Gibson 1998

**30 Supernatural** . . . . . . . . . . 6a
Another long one and with plenty of good climbing too. Climb the long sustained crack to a high crux.
FA. Gary Gibson 2006

**31 The Indian Cottage** . . . . . . . . . 7a
Short and sharp climbing past the triangular roof.
FA. Gary Gibson 1998

**32 What a Load of Roti** . . . . . . 6a
Climb the crack to access the long soaring rib.
FA. Gary Gibson, Tim Parkinson, Nick Taylor 2007

**33 Aloo Gobi** . . . . . . . . . . 6c
A tough route up the technical wall above the roof.
FA. Gary Gibson 1999

**34 Z Victor 1** . . . . . . . . . . HVS 5a
Climb the groove to the cave, then the left wall. Exit to the right.

*Pappadum Groove - p.114*

North | Southwest | Southeast | Stoney | Horseshoe | Smalldale | Harpur Hill | Lovers' Leap | Beer House | Craig-y-Biceps | Staden Q | Chee Dale U | Chee Dale L | Blackwell D. | Raven Tor | Water-c-Jolly | Ravensdale | Aldery Cliff | Taddington | Rheinstor

**35 Pappadum Groove . . . . . . . . . ☐ 6a**
The groove to the ledge below the cave. Exit rightwards.
*FA. Gary Gibson 1998*

**36 Quartz Initial . . . . . . . . . . . . . ☐ 6b+**
The left-hand side of the short arete to the big ledge.
*FA. Gary Gibson 1998*

**37 Duma Key . . . . . . . ⛶🗝️🎒 ☐ 6a**
Climb the hand-crack in the corner above the huge block then follow the long finger-crack. Staple bolts.
*FA. Gary Gibson 2007*

**38 Viagra Falls . . . . . . . . ⛶🏊 ☐ 6c+**
The long technical wall leading to a hard roof. Avoiding the corner below the roof is tricky.
*FA. Gary Gibson 1998*

**39 Different Seasons . . . . . . . ⛶ ☐ 6a+**
The crack in the arete leads to a mid-height lower-off. If the first bolt is too high, start up the next route or use a wire.
*FA. Gary Gibson 1998*

**40 Apt Pupil . . . . . . . . . ⛶🗝️ ☐ 6c**
The steep wall right of the crack. The roof gives a hard finish.
*FA. Gary Gibson 1998*

**41 In the Gravy . . . . . . . . . . ⛶ ☐ 6a**
A poor start over blocks, and up a groove, leads to better climbing on the wall above the ledges.
*FA. Gary Gibson 1998*

**42 From Cradle to Grave. . ⛶🗝️ ☐ 6c**
The wall on the left-hand side of the gully. Start up the steep slope and avoid left-hand variants.
*FA. Gary Gibson 1998*

**43 Inception . . . . . . . . . . . . . . . ☐ HS 4b**
The prominent groove, a limestone *Green Gut* maybe?

**44 Calcite Claws . . . . . . . ⛶🏊 ☐ 6c**
The short, hanging arete has some tricky moves on interesting rock.
*FA. Gary Gibson 1998*

**45 So Veneer . . . . . . . . . . . 🏊 ☐ 6b**
Climb the wall just right of the arete.
*FA. Gary Gibson 1998*

**46 The End . . . . . . . . . . . . . . . . ☐ 6a**
Very poor, the short wall has a hard start leading past a break to a ledge and lower-off.
*FA. Gary Gibson, Gordon Jenkin 2001*

*Z Victor 1*
*p.113*

North
Southwest
Southeast
Stoney
Horseshoe
Smalldale
Harpur Hill
Lover's Leap
Beehouse
Craig-y-Biceps
Staden Q
Che Dale U.
Che Dale L.
Blackwell D.
Raven Tor
Water-c-Jolly
Ravensdale
Aldery Cliff
Taddington
Rheinstor

Meilee Rafe stretching for holds on *Rocky Variations* (6b) - *page 110* - on Papacy Buttress. Photo: Nick Smith

Papacy Buttress is a great example of trad and sport routes coexisting on the same bit of rock. Those that suggest that sport climbing will one day take over all Peak limestone crags should come and have a look here and see what can be done if you allow climbers to self-govern their bolting.

North · Southwest · Southeast · Stoney · Horseshoe · Smalldale · Harpur Hill · Lovers' Leap · Beehouse · Craig-Illops · Staden Q · Chee Dale U · Che Dale L · Blackwell D · Raven Tor · Water-cum-Jolly · Ravensdale · Aldery Cliff · Taddington · Rheinstor

## The Dark Side - The Racetrack Playa

The furthest section of the Lower Tier of the east-facing Darkside has been developed with a collection of mostly lower-grade routes. The area isn't especially popular and the rather gloomy and desolate setting doesn't really help.

**Approach (see map on page 103) -** The routes are most easily reached by walking left past the rest of the routes on the Lower Tier and through a quarried gap.

**Conditions -** Cool and shady for most of the day, only early-birds will climb in the sun here. Okay for hot summer days.

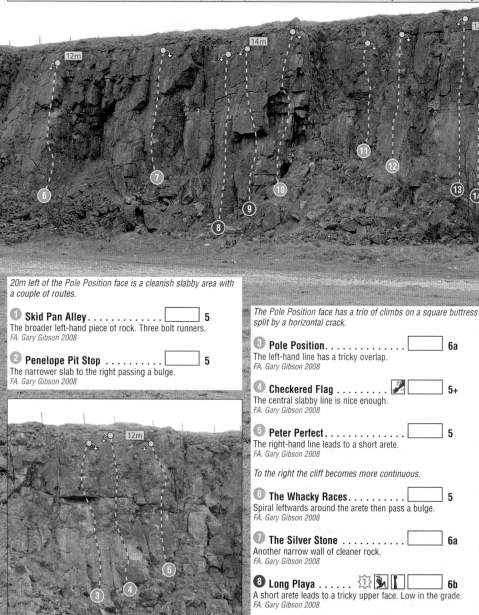

*20m left of the Pole Position face is a cleanish slabby area with a couple of routes.*

**❶ Skid Pan Alley** . . . . . . . . . . . . ☐ **5**
The broader left-hand piece of rock. Three bolt runners.
*FA. Gary Gibson 2008*

**❷ Penelope Pit Stop** . . . . . . . . . ☐ **5**
The narrower slab to the right passing a bulge.
*FA. Gary Gibson 2008*

*The Pole Position face has a trio of climbs on a square buttress split by a horizontal crack.*

**❸ Pole Position** . . . . . . . . . . . . . ☐ **6a**
The left-hand line has a tricky overlap.
*FA. Gary Gibson 2008*

**❹ Checkered Flag** . . . . . . . . ☐ **5+**
The central slabby line is nice enough.
*FA. Gary Gibson 2008*

**❺ Peter Perfect** . . . . . . . . . . . . . ☐ **5**
The right-hand line leads to a short arete.
*FA. Gary Gibson 2008*

*To the right the cliff becomes more continuous.*

**❻ The Whacky Races** . . . . . . . . . ☐ **5**
Spiral leftwards around the arete then pass a bulge.
*FA. Gary Gibson 2008*

**❼ The Silver Stone** . . . . . . . . . . ☐ **6a**
Another narrow wall of cleaner rock.
*FA. Gary Gibson 2008*

**❽ Long Playa** . . . . . . ☐ **6b**
A short arete leads to a tricky upper face. Low in the grade.
*FA. Gary Gibson 2008*

**❾ Dodgem Central** . . . . . . . . ☐ **6b**
Power through the middle of the detached (?) overhang.
*FA. Gary Gibson 2008*

North  Southwest  Southeast  Stoney  Horseshoe  Smalldale  Harpur Hill  Lovers' Leap  Beehouse  Craigy-Bicep1  Staden Q  Chee Dale U.  Blackwell D.  Che Dale L.  Raven Tor  Water-c.Jolly  Ravensdale  Aldery Cliff  Taddington  Rheinstor

To the right are five trad routes.

**16 Screaming Target.** . . . . . **E3 6a**
Fierce climbing up the blank face.
*FA. Nick Taylor 2003*

**17 Bone-man Connection** . . . . **E2 5c**
The thin crack and face above. Avoid the arete at the grade.
*FA. Nick Taylor 2003*

**10 Life's a Drag** . . . . . . . . . . . . . . **6a**
Meander up the right arete of the buttress and over the juggy overhangs.
*FA. Gary Gibson 2008*

**18 Fist to Fist is Done** . . . . . . . . . **VS 4c**
Wander up the right arete of the face, a small cam on the left helps protect the moves out onto the arete.
*FA. Nick Taylor 2003*

**11 TT Special** . . . . . . . . . . . . . . **5**
The short slab above the grass slope.
*FA. Gary Gibson 2008*

**19 Mikey Dread** . . . . . . . . **HVS 4c**
The crack and groove in the left wall of the corner.
*FA. Nick Taylor 2003*

**12 Brands Hatched** . . . . . . . . **6a**
The face eases after tricky initial moves.
*FA. Gary Gibson 2008*

**20 Scientist** . . . . . . . . . . **E1 5b**
The steep groove systems just right give a tussle.
*FA. Nick Taylor 2003*

**13 Trick Cyclist** . . . . . . . . . . **6b+**
The face and scoop right of the grim groove to a high crux.
*FA. Gary Gibson 2008*

**21 Speed Trials** . . . . . **7a**
Bolts again. The narrow face has a hard overlap.
*FA. Gary Gibson 2008*

**14 Speed Freak** . . . . . . . . . . . . . . **6b**
A similar line just right pulls through a small overhang.
*FA. Gary Gibson 2008*

**22 Quads.** . . . . . . . . . . . . . . . . . **5**
The short right arete of the face starts up the bank.
*FA. Gary Gibson 2008*

**15 Lap Times** . . . . . . . . . . . **5+**
The left arete of the next section features a beefy bulge.
*FA. Gary Gibson 2008*

**23 High Impact** . . . . . . . . . . **6a+**
The triangular face away to the right.
*FA. Gary Gibson 2008*

## The Dark Side - Long Wall

The right-hand side of the Lower Tier has some decent buttresses. Again the area isn't popular, mainly because it sees so little sun.
**Approach (see map on page 103) -** The routes are reached by walking left past the rest of the routes on the Lower Tier, then through a quarried gap. The Long Wall is on the right, just over the crest.
**Conditions -** Cool and shady for most of the day, making it pleasant on hot summer days.

*In the wilderness between the last sector and this are two sad routes: a wall with a circular orange scar is home to* **In Isolation** *(6a) and* **Strange Concept (4)** *up the left side of a grassy slab.*

**1** **Can't Pin it On Me** . . . . . . . . . . [____] 6a
Head up the arete of the block on the left.
*FA. Gary Gibson 2008*

**2** **Grow Fins** . . . . . . . . . . . . [icon][____] E2 5b
Balance up the bold left-hand arete of the main wall.
*FA. Nick Taylor 2003*

**3** **Cats 23** . . . . . . . . . . . . . . . [____] HVS 5a
Thuggier moves up the bubbly crack right of the arete.

**4** **Tricycle Man** . . . . . . . . . . . . [____] E2 5c
A thin crack leads to a hole at the break. Step right and finish up the thinner crack system above.

**5** **Get Peddling** . . . . . . . . . . [icon][____] 6c+
The bolted line up the rib and face just right is thin to start.
*FA. Gary Gibson 2008*

**6** **Face Value** . . . . . . . . . . . . [icon][____] E3 6a
Climb the niche then the face above trending right.

**7** **A Dip in Turquoise Nonsense** . . . [____] E3 6a
A more direct start up the face just right.
*FA. Gary Gibson, Paul Harrison 1997*

**8** **Faces in the Mirror** . . . . . . [icon][____] 6c
Thin moves up the face just left of the crack.
*FA. Gary Gibson 2008*

**9** **College Crack** . . . . . . . . . [icon][____] E1 5b
Plod up the straight crack, passing a ledge early on.

**10** **Permutation Wall** . . . . . [icon][icon][____] HVS 5b
The thin crack in the wall leads to an easier finish up a left-trending ramp and short crack.

**11** **Balance of Probabilities** . . . . . . [____] 6c
Balance up the arete to a ledge. Step right to finish.

**12** **Upthrutch** . . . . . . . . . . . . [icon][____] HVS 5b
An awkward groove leads to the base of the ramp. Climb up this.

**13** **Diamond Wall** . . . . . . . . . . . . [____] E1 5b
Climb the awkward, leaning groove and bulge to easy ground.

**14** **Pool Hand Fluke** . . . . . . . . . . [____] 6a+
The left-hand bolt-line on the final wall.
*FA. Gary Gibson 2008*

**15** **More Pool You** . . . . . . . . . . . . [____] 6a
… and the right-hand line.
*FA. Gary Gibson 2008*

*The square face on the left has a trio of routes:*

**16** **Sleeping Sickness** . . . . . . . . . [____] 6a
The short left-hand climb up the groove and face.

**17** **My Bed's Downstairs** . . . . . . . [____] 6a
A longer route up the steepening face has some nice moves.

**18** **Sleep On It** . . . . . . . . . . . . . [____] 6b
The tricky wall behind the tree. Keep right of the hanging groove.

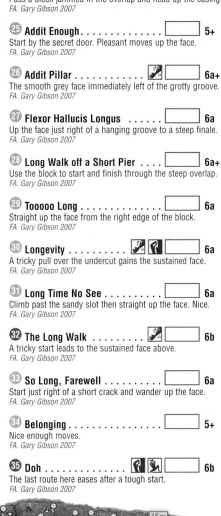

**24 You've Addit** . . . . . . . . . . . . . ☐ 6a
Pass a block jammed in the overlap and head up the easing face.
*FA. Gary Gibson 2007*

**25 Addit Enough** . . . . . . . . . . . . . ☐ 5+
Start by the secret door. Pleasant moves up the face.
*FA. Gary Gibson 2007*

**26 Addit Pillar** . . . . . . . . . . . ☐ 6a+
The smooth grey face immediately left of the grotty groove.
*FA. Gary Gibson 2007*

**27 Flexor Hallucis Longus** . . . . . . ☐ 6a
Up the face just right of a hanging groove to a steep finale.
*FA. Gary Gibson 2007*

**28 Long Walk off a Short Pier** . . . . ☐ 6a+
Use the block to start and finish through the steep overlap.
*FA. Gary Gibson 2007*

**29 Tooooo Long** . . . . . . . . . . . . . ☐ 6a
Straight up the face from the right edge of the block.
*FA. Gary Gibson 2007*

**30 Longevity** . . . . . . . . . ☐ 6a
A tricky pull over the undercut gains the sustained face.
*FA. Gary Gibson 2007*

**31 Long Time No See** . . . . . . . . . ☐ 6a
Climb past the sandy slot then straight up the face. Nice.
*FA. Gary Gibson 2007*

**32 The Long Walk** . . . . . . . . ☐ 6b
A tricky start leads to the sustained face above.
*FA. Gary Gibson 2007*

**33 So Long, Farewell** . . . . . . . . . ☐ 6a
Start just right of a short crack and wander up the face.
*FA. Gary Gibson 2007*

**34 Belonging** . . . . . . . . . . . . . . ☐ 5+
Nice enough moves.
*FA. Gary Gibson 2007*

**35 Doh** . . . . . . . . . . . . ☐ 6b
The last route here eases after a tough start.
*FA. Gary Gibson 2007*

**19 Regulo Mark 6** . . . . . . . . . . . ☐ 6b
The face and arete on the far left of the next long wall.
*FA. Gary Gibson 2007*

**20 Easy on the Gas** . . . . . . . . . . ☐ 5
The face to the right is tricky towards the top.
*FA. Gary Gibson 2007*

**21 The Pillar Talk** . . . . . . . . . ☐ 6a+
The next bolt-line to a high crux. A bit of an eliminate.
*FA. Gary Gibson 2007*

**22 The Pillar Walk** . . . . . . . . ☐ 5+
A shorter offering past scarred ledges.
*FA. Gary Gibson 2007*

**23 Addit and Scarper** . . . . . . . ☐ 6a+
Climb past two overlaps to a tricky finale.
*FA. Gary Gibson 2007*

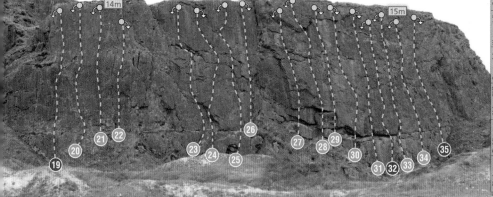

North  Southwest  Southeast  Stoney  Horseshoe  Smalldale  Harpur Hill  Lovers' Leap  Beerhouse  Craig-y-Biceps  Staden Q  Chee Dale U.  Che Dale L.  Blackwell D.  Raven Tor  Water-c-Jolly  Ravensdale  Aldery Cliff  Taddington  Rheinstor

Dark Side - Upper Tier

p.104

Dark Side - Long Wall

College Buttress

p.118

## College Buttress

The far right-hand end of the Dark Side has a decent chunky buttress with some reasonable routes.
**Approach (see map on page 103) -** The routes are reached by walking left past the rest of the routes on the Lower Tier and through a quarried gap. The cliffs are round to the left once through the gap.
**Conditions -** Cool and shady for most of the day, only early-birds will climb in the sun here. The area is fine for hot summer days though.

**❶ Old Fiends** . . . . . . . . 6c+
Climb through the centre of the butch overhang then the centre of the wall above.
FA. Gary Gibson, Gordon Jenkin, Mark Richardson, Rob Richmond 2006

**❷ Carvery** . . . . . . . . . . 6a+
The crunchy, crystalline crack leads to the contrasting delicate face above. Usually dirty.
FA. Gary Gibson, Gordon Jenkin, Mark Richardson, Rob Richmond 2006

**❸ The Wrong Unconquerable** . . . . 6b
The long crack on some odd rock leads to a layback flake finale. It is supposed to be a mirror image of *The Left Unconquerable*, on Stanage.
FA. Gary Gibson, Gordon Jenkin, Mark Richardson, Rob Richmond 2006

**❹ Fartless** . . . . . . . . . . 7a+
A tricky start leads to hard and fingery climbing above.
FA. Gary Gibson, Gordon Jenkin, Mark Richardson, Rob Richmond 2006

**❺ Strap a Doc to Me** . . . . . . . . . 6c
Decent climbing up nice scoopy rock, close to the right-hand edge of the face on the right.
FA. Gary Gibson, Gordon Jenkin, Mark Richardson, Rob Richmond 2006

Approach from quarried gap and Dark Side - Long Wall

*The rest of the routes are on the main chunky buttress.*

**6 The Gypsy Kings** . . . . . 6c

Balance up the arete to the left of the main buttress.
*FA. Gary Gibson, Gordon Jenkin, Mark Richardson, Rob Richmond 2006*

**7 Gooncrack.** . . . . . . 6b+

The crack in the sidewall of the buttress cleaves a high roof. Difficulties are short-lived, but quite intense.
*FA. Gary Gibson*

**8 Forfeit of Doom** . . . . . . . . 6b+

The left arete of the main buttress has some good moves.
*FA. Gary Gibson 2006*

**9 Meshrug a My Shoulders** . . 6b

Climb the face right of the arete, using the jammed block to pass the roof.
*FA. Gary Gibson 2006*

**10 Profitless** . . . . . . . . . 6b

Teeter up the face then climb the crack that splits the overlap strenuously. Varied.
*FA. Gary Gibson, Gordon Jenkin, Mark Richardson, Rob Richmond 2006*

**11 Merry Pheasant** . . . . . . . . . . . E1 5c

Trad climbing up the thin grassy cracks leads to bolder moves then another crack through the overhang.

**12 Moontalk** . . . . . . . . . 6b+

Nice face-climbing with a hard move in the middle and then again just below the top.
*FA. Gary Gibson, Gordon Jenkin, Mark Richardson, Rob Richmond 2006*

**13 Frantic Manoeuvres** . . . E2 5c

Balance up the ramp to reach the sanctuary of a ledge. Continue up the short crack (thread) to finish.

**14 Bonedigger** . . . . . . . . . . . . . . E1 5b

The thin crack splitting the slab would be a good little route if someone dug all the grass out.

**15 Prefect Day** . . . . . . . . 6b

Climb the pleasant face to harder moves through the overlap and up to the lower-off.
*FA. Gary Gibson, Gordon Jenkin, Mark Richardson, Rob Richmond 2006*

**16 Silent Sprung** . . . . . . . . . . . . 6b

*FA. Gary Gibson 2011*

**17 Thirty Nine and a Half Steps** . . . E1 5b

A neglected climb up vegetated steps to a better finish leftwards up the final slab.

**18 White Wind** . . . . . . . . . . . . . . 6a

The final line on the face is nothing special.
*FA. Gary Gibson, Gordon Jenkin, Mark Richardson, Rob Richmond 2006*

Morning    15 min

North | Southwest | Southeast | Stoney | Horseshoe | Smalldale | Harpur Hill | Lover's Leap | Beerhouse | Craig-y-Biceps | Staden Q | Chee Dale L | Che Dale U. | Blackwell D. | Raven Tor | Water-c-Jolly | Ravensdale | Aldery Cliff | Taddington | Rheinstor

## The Lower Tier

An extensive wall of rather scrappy rock. There are plenty of routes to go at here, and as long as you don't expect too much, you won't be badly disappointed.

**Approach** - This is the section of wall directly in front of you upon entering the quarry.

**Conditions** - The sun arrives about mid-afternoon. Before that it can be cold, though more sheltered than the Upper Tier.

**1 Thank-you Grooves** . . . . . . [  ] 5
The orange, scarred grooves right of the scree.
*FA. Gary Gibson 2010*

**2 Wallaclism** . . . . . . . . [  ] 6b
Trend left up the wall passing the crack/groove.
*FA. Gary Gibson 2010*

**3 Arteaclism** . . . . . . . . . . . [  ] 6a+
Teeter up the short, shattered arete.
*FA. Gary Gibson 2010*

**4 Overbored** . . . . . . . . . . . . [  ] 5
Climb the slabby rock right of a groove, leftwards.
*FA. Gary Gibson, Hazel Gibson, Nadim Siddiqui 2001*

**5 Gatting the Groove** . . . . . . . . . [  ] 5+
The groove with a steep start.
*FA. Gary Gibson, Hazel Gibson, Nadim Siddiqui 2001*

**6 Mine Anarchy** . . . . . . . . . . . . [  ] 5+
The left-hand line on the right-hand slab.
*FA. Gary Gibson, Hazel Gibson, Nadim Siddiqui 2001*

**7 Only Ken's Anarchy Will Do.** [  ] 6b
The second line on the slab. Tricky at the third bolt.
*FA. Gary Gibson, Hazel Gibson, Nadim Siddiqui 2001*

**8 Always Break the Rules** . . . [  ] 5+
Intricate moves right of a diagonal borehole.
*FA. Gary Gibson, Hazel Gibson, Nadim Siddiqui 2001*

**9 Snap Decision** . . . . . . . . . . . . [  ] 5+
The final line on the slab.
*FA. Gary Gibson, Hazel Gibson, Nadim Siddiqui 2001*

*30m to the right is the slabby Candy Store wall.*

**10 The Candyman** . . . . . . . [  ] 6a+
The left-hand line is quite sustained.
*FA. Gary Gibson, Hazel Gibson, Gordon Jenkin 2001*

**11 Flossy's Slab** . . . . . . . . . . . [  ] 6a+
A good little pitch.
*FA. Gary Gibson, Hazel Gibson, Gordon Jenkin 2001*

**12 Toy Story** . . . . . . . . . . . . . . [  ] 6a
Head past the edge of the flake and on to a rightward exit.
*FA. Gary Gibson 2001*

**13 Suck on This** . . . . . . . . . . [  ] 6a+
From the hanging flake, loop left then right up the wall.
*FA. Gary Gibson 2001*

Perched Block Buttress

p.107

10m

14m

12m

## 14 Jelly Beans ............ 6a+
*FA. Gary Gibson 2011*

## 15 Smartie People are Happy People
.................. 6a
The left-hand line on a grey slab. Avoid the route to the right.
*FA. Gordon Jenkin, Gary Gibson, Nadim Siddiqui 2001*

## 16 Candy Store ........ 6a
The right-hand arete of the slab.
*FA. Gordon Jenkin, Gary Gibson, Nadim Siddiqui, Hazel Gibson 2001*

## 17 Tempting Children ......... 6c+
Climb onto a pedestal right of the central crack, then power through two overlaps. Escape out right.
*FA. Gary Gibson, Gordon Jenkin 2001*

## 18 Would you like a Sweety?.. 6c
Good steep climbing through the double overlaps.
*FA. Gary Gibson, Gordon Jenkin, Nadim Siddiqui 2001*

## 19 Bolts 'R' Us......... 6b
A rib leads to an open, shallow groove, then a roof.
*FA. Gary Gibson, Gordon Jenkin, Nadim Siddiqui 2001*

## 20 Sing for Your Dinner...... 6b+
The right-hand line is steep and quite hard work.
*FA. Gary Gibson 2001*

## 21 Do Little ............... 6a
*FA. Gary Gibson 2010*

## 22 Playground Bully .......... 6b+
Muscle up the face right of the grotty red crack.
*FA. Gary Gibson 2010*

## 23 The Sweat Shop........... 6a
Up the narrow pillar.
*FA. Gary Gibson 2010*

## 24 Totti for England .......... 4
The solitary line on a slab.
*FA. Gary Gibson 2010*

Papacy Buttress

p.108

North · Southwest · Southeast · Stoney · Horseshoe · Smalldale · Harpur Hill · Lovers' Leap · Beerhouse · Craig-y-Biceps · Staden Q · Chee Dale L. · Che Dale L. · Blackwell D. · Raven Tor · Water-c-Jolly · Ravensdale · Aldery Cliff · Taddington · Rheinstor

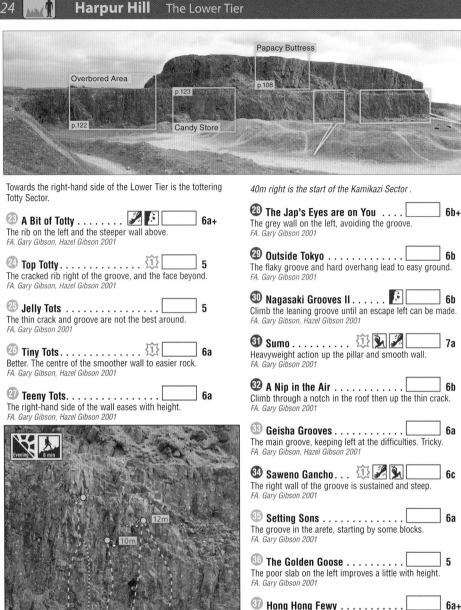

Papacy Buttress

Overbored Area

p.123

p.108

p.122

Candy Store

Towards the right-hand side of the Lower Tier is the tottering Totty Sector.

**㉓ A Bit of Totty** . . . . . . . 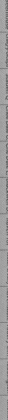 6a+
The rib on the left and the steeper wall above.
*FA. Gary Gibson, Hazel Gibson 2001*

**㉔ Top Totty** . . . . . . . . . . . . . 5
The cracked rib right of the groove, and the face beyond.
*FA. Gary Gibson, Hazel Gibson 2001*

**㉕ Jelly Tots** . . . . . . . . . . . . . . 5
The thin crack and groove are not the best around.
*FA. Gary Gibson 2001*

**㉖ Tiny Tots** . . . . . . . . . . . . . 6a
Better. The centre of the smoother wall to easier rock.
*FA. Gary Gibson, Hazel Gibson 2001*

**㉗ Teeny Tots** . . . . . . . . . . . . . 6a
The right-hand side of the wall eases with height.
*FA. Gary Gibson, Hazel Gibson 2001*

*40m right is the start of the Kamikazi Sector .*

**㉘ The Jap's Eyes are on You** . . . . 6b+
The grey wall on the left, avoiding the groove.
*FA. Gary Gibson 2001*

**㉙ Outside Tokyo** . . . . . . . . . . . . 6b
The flaky groove and hard overhang lead to easy ground.
*FA. Gary Gibson 2001*

**㉚ Nagasaki Grooves II** . . . . . . 6b
Climb the leaning groove until an escape left can be made.
*FA. Gary Gibson, Hazel Gibson 2001*

**㉛ Sumo** . . . . . . . . . 7a
Heavyweight action up the pillar and smooth wall.
*FA. Gary Gibson 2001*

**㉜ A Nip in the Air** . . . . . . . . . . . 6b
Climb through a notch in the roof then up the thin crack.
*FA. Gary Gibson 2001*

**㉝ Geisha Grooves** . . . . . . . . . . . 6a
The main groove, keeping left at the difficulties. Tricky.
*FA. Gary Gibson, Hazel Gibson 2001*

**㉞ Saweno Gancho** . . . 6c
The right wall of the groove is sustained and steep.
*FA. Gary Gibson 2001*

**㉟ Setting Sons** . . . . . . . . . . . . 6a
The groove in the arete, starting by some blocks.
*FA. Gary Gibson 2001*

**㊱ The Golden Goose** . . . . . . . . . 5
The poor slab on the left improves a little with height.
*FA. Gary Gibson 2001*

**㊲ Hong Hong Fewy** . . . . . . . . . . 6a+
The balancy left-hand edge of the buttress.
*FA. Gary Gibson 2001*

**㊳ The Rising Sun** . . . . . . . . . . . 5
The central line is high in the grade.
*FA. Gary Gibson, Hazel Gibson 2001*

**㊴ Kamikaze Clone** . . . . . . . . . . . 6a
The right-hand edge of the short, clean central buttress.
*FA. Gary Gibson 2001*

Evening  8 min

12m

10m

㉓ ㉔ ㉕ ㉖ ㉗

16m

14m

14m

28 29 30 31 32 33 34 35 36 37 38 39 40 41

**40m gap to next routes**

North | Southwest | Southeast | Stoney | Horseshoe | Smalldale | Harpur Hill | Lovers' Leap | Beehouse | Craigy-Biceps | Staden Q | Chee Dale L | Che Dale U. | Blackwell D. | Raven Tor | Water-c-Jolly | Ravensdale | Aldery Cliff | Taddington | Rheinstor

**40 Shang-Hai** . . . . . . . . . . . . . . . ☐ **6b**
Climb the slab and roofs directly above.
FA. Gary Gibson 2011

**41 Riding Shogun** . . . . ☐ **6a+**
Break right and weave through the bulges.
FA. Gary Gibson, Hazel Gibson 2001

30m to the right as the Tier fizzles out there is a final quartet of fairly unspectacular routes:

**42 Fuji Fantastic** . . . . . . . . . . . . . ☐ **6a**
The steep wall just right of a large, jutting flake.
FA. Gary Gibson 2007

**43 Picture This** . . . . . . . . . . . . . . ☐ **6a**
The upper part of the pillar is on better rock than the start.
FA. Gary Gibson 2007

**44 Jokoharma** . . . . . . . . . . . . . . . ☐ **VS 5a**
The deep groove is an oddity - a surviving trad route.
FA. Gary Gibson 2007

**45 The Bullet** . . . . . . . . . . ☐ **7a**
Tough climbing up the wall just right of the arete.
FA. Gary Gibson 2007

14m

42 43 44 45

The first routes are on the short wall above the path to the Upper Tier. Care is required here when it's wet.

**1 Inconsiderate Blinking** ...... ☐ 6a+
The thin crack on the left and the arete above.
FA. Gary Gibson, Nick Taylor 2002

**2 Unilateral Thinking** ...... 🔧 ☐ 6c
Climb the wall just to the right of a short arete low down on the upper section, trending right.
FA. Gary Gibson, Andy Grondowski 1999

**3 The Light** ......... 🎗 🪨 ☐ 7a
The wall further right has some good fingery climbing.
FA. Gary Gibson 1998

**4 Take Flight** ............. ☐ 6c+
The thin crack leads to a scoop and short arete.
FA. Gary Gibson, Nick Taylor 2002

The next three routes start from a bolt belay reached by scrambling out right across the grass slope - care required both with the access and if there are people climbing below.

**5 Buxton Goes French** ........ ☐ 6b+
Thin moves up the narrow slab. The right-hand arete is taboo if you really want the full tick.
FA. Bill Birch, Jonathan Bowden 1994

**6 Outer Limits** .......... 🎗 ☐ 6b
Climb the left-hand side of the striking sharp arete.
FA. Bill Birch, Nadim Siddiqui, Jonathan Bowden 1994

**7 Twilight Zone** ............ ☐ 6a+
The right-hand side of the arete to the same lower-off.
FA. Nadim Siddiqui, Bill Birch, Jonathan Bowden 1994

The rest of the climbs are on the more accessible lower walls.

**8 Argy Bargy** .............. ☐ 5
Tackle the steep sidewall of the buttress.

**9 The Misfits** ............ 🌂 ☐ 6a
The flake leads to a thin crack then a short-lived headwall.
FA. Gary Gibson, Jim Burton 2002

**10 Hissing Sid** ........ 🌂🔧 ☐ 6b
Climb to a small roof, pull over and balance up the wall.
FA. Bill Birch, Rick Hyde 1994

**11 Slippery Bill** .............. ☐ HVS 5a
Climb the orange crack and groove to the right.
FA. Rick Hyde, Bill Birch 1994

**12 Ratline** ........ 🎗🔧🖌 ☐ 7b+
The thin crack is harder than it looks and has great moves.
FA. Nadim Siddiqui, Bill Birch, Rick Hyde, Rehan Siddiqui 1994

### Cairn Area
The best of the harder routes at Harpur Hill is found on a fine wave formation on the lower walls; *Cairn* is well worth seeking out by all who are qualified. Most of the rest of the routes are rather better than their appearance may suggest.
**Approach -** This is usually the first section you arrive at on entering the quarry and heading slightly rightwards.
**Conditions -** The sun arrives in the mid-to-late afternoon. Before that it can be very cold, but it is a touch more sheltered than the Upper Tier.

Approach to Upper Tier

**13 Cairn** . . . . . . . . . 7a
The best route here but getting polished. Gain the wavey flake via a hard move, then climb this with powerful moves past the 3rd bolt to a jug. Swing left to better holds and up to the belay.
FA. Nadim Siddiqui, Bill Birch, Rick Gibbon 1994

**14 Stealth** . . . . . . . . . . . 7a+
A fine line spoilt by the horribly sharp finger-trashing pocket on the crux. Follow *Cairn* to the third bolt then stretch across to the pocket. Hang this then pull up to the lower-off.
FA. Nadim Siddiqui, Bill Birch 1994

**15 Great White** . . . . . . . . . . . . . 6a
Climb round the roof using the crack on the right. The direct version of the slab is **Orca, 6a+**.
FA. Bill Birch, Rick Gibbon 1994

**16 The Naked Spur** . . . . . . 5
The rather totty arete is the easiest hereabouts.
FA. Gary Gibson, Jim Burton 2002

**17 Assault and Battery** . . . . . . . . 6b+
The grotty wall in the alcove is marked by golden bolts.
FA. Gary Gibson, Jim Burton 2002

**18 Trial and Error** . . . . . . . . . . . . 7a
The angular, undercut arete gives some intense climbing, but the top arete is artificial. Rockfall may have affected the route.
FA. Nadim Siddiqui, Bill Birch 1999

**19 Senile Delinquents** . . . . . . 5+
The flake and wide crack to the roof then pull over this.
FA. Nadim Siddiqui, Bill Birch 1994

**20 Cabin Fever** . . . . . . . . . . . . 6b
The wall and overlap just right; a squeezed-in line.
FA. Keith Bridges 2003

The Playground p.130

**21 Fred Flintstone** . . . . . . . . . . . VS 4b
The brown wall is climbed past a worm feature. Belay on the ledge for this and the next two routes. The crack to the left is S 4a.
FA. Bill Birch, Rick Gibbon, Nadim Siddiqui 1994

**22 Barney Rubble** . . . . . . . . . . . VS 4c
Climb the crack just to the right to the same belay.
FA. Bill Birch, Rick Gibbon, Nadim Siddiqui 1994

**23 Yabba Dabba Doo!** . . . . . . . . . HS 4b
The short crack on the right-hand side of the wall.
FA. Bill Birch, Rick Gibbon, Nadim Siddiqui 1994

**24 Breakfast at Safeways** . . . 6b
The left-hand line on the clean final slab. Polished.
FA. Bill Birch, Nadim Siddiqui 1994

**25 Jam Butty Mines Crack** . . . . VS 4c
Balance up to the crack then follow it to the top.
FA. C.Trotter, P.Townroe 1966

**26 99p Special** . . . . . . . . . . 6b
From *JBMC*, climb the face just to the right. Avoid the arete.
FA. Bill Birch, Nadim Siddiqui 1994

**27 Food for Sport** . . . . . . . . . 6a
The arete has a problematic start.
FA. Bill Birch, Nadim Siddiqui 1994

**28 Over Easy** . . . . . . . . . . . 6a
The next little arete, on its right-hand side this time.
FA. Gary Gibson 2008

**29 Full Set** . . . . . . . . . . . 6a+
Technical face-climbing on the right-hand side of the wall.
FA. Gary Gibson 2008

**30 Short Sport** . . . . . . . . . . . . 6b
The small face. It can be climbed on the arete at an easier 6a.
FA. Dave Simmonite 2010

Path to The Playground along the fence

## The Sanctuary

The Sanctuary has a small collection of steep routes in an out-of-the-way setting. As with all quarried rock, care is required here; helmets are sensible, as is standing to the side of climbers in action.

**Approach (see map on page 103) -** The routes are most easily reached by descending the steep grass in front of the Cairn Area (poor path), then contouring round to the left (looking out).

**Conditions -** The sun arrives slightly earlier on this wall than the rest of the cliff, and it is a little more sheltered.

*The first routes are on the short wall on the far left.*

**1 By Caesarean** . . . . . . . . . . . . 5+
The left-hand line, left of the orange streak.
*FA. Gary Gibson 2002*

**2 New Arrivals** . . . . . . . . . . . . 6a+
Just to the right of the orange streak.
*FA. Gary Gibson 2002*

**3 Expecting** . . . . . . . . . . . . . . 5
The better rock on the right-hand side of the wall.
*FA. Gary Gibson 2002*

**4 Premature** . . . . . . . . . . . . 6a
Up the arete, left of a grotty groove that splits the face.

**5 Induction Program** . . . . . . 5
The narrower buttress to the right of a grotty groove.
*FA. Gary Gibson 2001*

**6 Safe Haven** . . . . . . . . . . . 5+
The first route on the main section of the face loops slightly left. Not the most solid pitch in the world.
*FA. Gary Gibson 2001*

**7 The Hollow Man** . . . . . . . . 5
Climb direct, treating the rock with care.
*FA. Gary Gibson 2001*

**8 Christian Salvage Man** . . . . 6a
A steep wall passing the overlap early on, with a sneaky finger-jug at mid-height. Good moves.
*FA. Gary Gibson, Hazel Gibson 2001*

To The Playground

**9 Which Depp-Artment** . . . . . . . [ ] 6a+
Pull through the overlap, then climb up and rightwards.
*FA. Gary Gibson, Hazel Gibson 2001*

**10 Ichabod** . . . . . . . . . . . . . . . . [ ] 5+
From the block, head straight up the wall, then left. Tricky.
*FA. Gary Gibson, Hazel Gibson 2001*

**11 Sleepy Hollow** . . . . . . [ ] 6a+
The blunt rib gives pleasant and tricky moves.
*FA. Gary Gibson, Hazel Gibson 2001*

**12 Bonny Helena** . . . . . . . . . . . . . [ ] 5
A squeezed-in line.
*FA. Gary Gibson 2011*

**13 Gone for a Tim Burton** . . . . [ ] 5
From broken flakes, climb left of the dirt streak.
*FA. Gary Gibson, Hazel Gibson 2001*

**14 The Height Below** . . . . . . . . . . [ ] 5
Take the brown streak almost into the groove, then trend left.
*FA. Gary Gibson 2001*

**15 The Sanctuarian** . . . . . . . [ ] 6c
The steep wall with a double overlap is tough.
*FA. Gary Gibson 2001*

**16 For Haven's Sake** . . . . . [ ] 6b
The right-hand side of the steep wall and overhang above.
*FA. Gary Gibson 2001*

**17 Downtown** . . . . . . . . . [ ] 6b
The shallow groove is nicely technical.
*FA. Gary Gibson 2001*

**18 What Lies Beneath** . . . . . . [ ] 6b
The next route has a tricky wall just below the lower-off.
*FA. Gary Gibson 2001*

**19 Haven or Hell** . . . . . . . . . . . . [ ] 6a
The final pillar gives a few steep moves.
*FA. Gary Gibson, Jim Burton 2002*

North | Southwest | Southeast | Stoney | Horseshoe | Smalldale | Harpur Hill | Lovers' Leap | Beehouse | Craig-y-Biorp | Staden Q | Chee Dale U | Che Dale L | Blackwell D | Raven Tor | Water-c-Jolly | Ravensdale | Aldery Cliff | Taddington | Rheinstor

## The Playground

Situated above the Cairn Area and the Sanctuary is a smaller quarry which is invisible from most of the rest of Harpur Hill. The location is more pleasant than much of the rest of the quarry and the aspect means it gets the sun much earlier in the day. The routes are on good quality rock, similar to the Papacy Buttress routes, but they are only short.

**Approach (see map on page 103) -** From beneath the Cairn Area, follow a small path on the left of the fence posts. This leads up to the next level where the walls can be seen on the far left. It can also be reached by way of a grassy ramp to the right of The Sanctuary.

**Conditions -** Sunny and more sheltered than the rest of Harpur Hill.

**1** Edge Play . . . . . . . . . . . . . . . . ☐ 5
The left-most line up a small corner.
*FA. Bill Birch, Peter Cowie 2007*

**2** Play Doh . . . . . . . . . . . . . . . ☐ 6a
The wall to the right of the corner.
*FA. Bill Birch, Peter Cowie 2007*

**3** Helter Skelterer . . . . . . . . . . . ☐ 6a+

**4** Groovy Player . . . . . . . . . . . . ☐ 6a+
*FA. Bill Birch, Peter Cowie 2007*

**5** Movie Player . . . . . . . . . . . . . ☐ 6a
*FA. Bill Birch, Peter Cowie 2007. Also claimed as Pachucho Cadaver by Nick Taylor in 2005.*

**6** Hard Player . . . . . . . . . . . . . . ☐ 6b+
*FA. Bill Birch, Peter Cowie 2007*

**7** I'm Not a Player . . . . . . . . . . . ☐ 4
The blocky groove and crack.
*FA. Bill Birch 2007*

**8** Playground Attraction . . . . . . . ☐ 7a+
The thin face above a block.
*FA. Gary Gibson 2008*

**9** The Hex . . . . . . . . . . . . . . . . ☐ 6c+
Short crack to a lower-off on the edge of the ramp.
*FA. Gary Gibson 2008*

**10** Ripsaw . . . . . . . . . . . . . . . . ☐ 6c+
Climb the blunt arete onto the ramp.
*FA. Gary Gibson 2008*

**11** Terror of the Towers . . . . . . . . ☐ 7a
Very thin wall to the ramp.
*FA. Gary Gibson 2008*

**12** Who is Casey? . . . . . . . . . . . . ☐ 6a
Wall past breaks.

**13** Leben Tod . . . . . . . . . . . . . . . ☐ 6a+
The rounded arete.

**14** Pinball Wizard . . . . . . . . . . . . ☐ 6b
A short wall with cracks.
*FA. Gary Gibson 2008*

**15** **Hamlet, Prince of Players** . . . . . [    ] 6a+
A wall with some nice cracks.
*FA. Bill Birch, Peter Cowie 2007*

**16** **William Plays Shakespeare.** . . . . [    ] 6a+
A thin face.
*FA. Bill Birch, Peter Cowie 2007*

**17** **Flog the Lune** . . . . . . . . . . . . [    ] 6a
The arete.
*FA. Gary Gibson 2008*

**18** **A Comedy of Played Errors** . . . . [    ] 6a+
The centre of the pillar.
*FA. Bill Birch, Peter Cowie 2007*

**19** **Did Romeo Play.** . . . . . . . . . . . [    ] 4
The wall and arete right of a crack.
*FA. Bill Birch, Peter Cowie 2007*

**20** **With Juliet** . . . . . . . . . . . . . . [    ] 6a+
Climb the right wall of a corner.
*FA. Bill Birch, Peter Cowie 2007*

**21** **A Merchant Played in Venice** . . . [    ] 4
The final arete.
*FA. Bill Birch 2007*

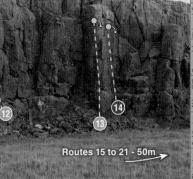

Routes 15 to 21 - 50m →

| | No star | ☆ | ☆☆ | ☆☆☆ |
|---|---|---|---|---|
| up to 4+ | - | - | - | - |
| 5+ to 6a+ | 1 | 1 | - | - |
| 6b to 7a | 6 | - | - | - |
| 7a+ and up | 1 | 1 | - | - |

Dan Parkes climbing *Down in the Sewer* (6a+) - *opposite.*

An esoteric crag with 10 sporty routes in a very secluded setting, have no doubt, you will have the place to yourself! Most of the routes were equipped and climbed by Gary Gibson in 2010 except for *Down in the Sewer* and *Z.C.T.* which he first climbed trad style in 1979!

## Approach    Also see map on page 94

The crag is hidden in the trees to the south of the A6, 0.4 of a mile to the east of the Morrisons' roundabout on the outskirts of Buxton. There is a small lay-by (two cars), just to the right of the entrance of the canyon (in front of a section of meshed-off crag) which is safest to access when west-bound. The first route is a minute away.

## Conditions

The canyon is recessed, tree-shaded, always cool and almost frequently humid and damp, especially underfoot. Pick the right conditions and a few hours fierce fingery red-spot sport is on offer here, in one of the Peak's more unusual venues.

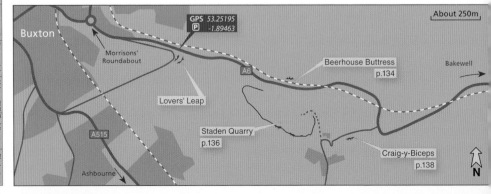

The first four routes are on the best bit of rock here, the tall flat wall rising above mulchy ledges on the far side of the gorge.

❶ **Rat's Rally** . . . . . . . . . . . . 🎫 ☐ **6c**
The hanging groove in the left arete.

❷ **The Falling** . . . . . . 🎫🎫🎫 ☐ **7a+**
Tackle the smooth left-hand side of the face - tough.

❸ **Down in the Sewer** . . . . 🎫 🎫 ☐ **6a+**
The pumpy flake-crack is the best route here. *Photo opposite.*

❹ **Z.C.T** . . . . . . . . . . . . . . . 🎫 ☐ **6b**
Balance up the right-hand side of the wall.

*The next two routes are further into the gloom on a short steep white wall.*

❺ **Unnamed** . . . . . . . . . . . . 🎫 ☐ **6c+**
A hard move gains the first decent holds - then go.

❻ **Unnamed** . . . . . . . . . . 🎫 🎫 ☐ **7b**
A hideous sequence reaches marginally easier ground.

*The final four routes are on the right-hand side (looking in) of the canyon. For consistency they are described left-to-right.*

❼ **Moss Marathon** . . . . . . . . 🎫 ☐ **6a**
The flat, mossy wall on the far left.

❽ **Mozzy Marathon** . . . . . . . 🎫 ☐ **6c+**
Climb the steep arete and crack above - if you can reach it.

❾ **My Life Led up to This** . . . . 🎫 ☐ **6c+**
Another short, steep and fingery pitch.
FA. Mark Pretty 2010

❿ **My Wife Led up to This** . . . . 🎫 ☐ **6b+**
The right arete.
FA. Paul Freeman 2010

| | No star | ☆ | ☆☆ | ☆☆☆ |
|---|---|---|---|---|
| **up to 4+** | - | - | - | - |
| **5+ to 6a+** | 1 | 1 | - | - |
| **6b to 7a** | 8 | 5 | - | - |
| **7a+ and up** | 1 | 2 | - | - |

This is another of those Peak venues which was ignored by earlier generations as being too small to bother with but, through the efforts of some dedicated new routers, it has been transformed into an attractive little crag in a pleasant location, though it has never proved popular. The climbing is quite deceptive since you expect short quick ticks but actually get some intense and technical problems. It is a natural buttress with compact rock giving routes of a fingery and sustained nature, with lots of small holds which are often hard to locate when unchalked. The pub after which it took its name has been closed down for years.

## Approach   Also see map on page 94

The crag is situated above the railway line that runs parallel to the A6 in Ashwood Dale, just to the east of Buxton. It is above the derelict pub, just west of the water treatment works. 100m west of the pub parking is a fenced concrete area with room for 3 or 4 cars - beware of fast traffic here. This is 1 mile from the Morrisons' roundabout. Pass round the left-hand side of the fencing then from the left-hand corner of the clearing, cross the fence and scramble up the steep loose bank until you pop out onto the railway line where the crag can be seen above you. A small path leads up rightwards to the crag.

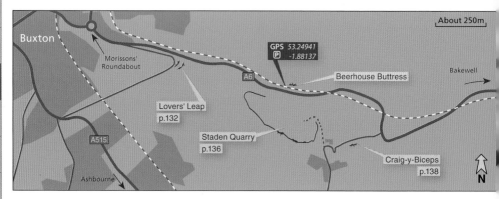

## Conditions
The wall faces south, suffers little from seepage, is well-sheltered and dries quickly after rain.

## Access
There is no formal access agreement to this crag and the inclusion of information here does not imply that you have right of access. It is illegal to cross a live railway line.

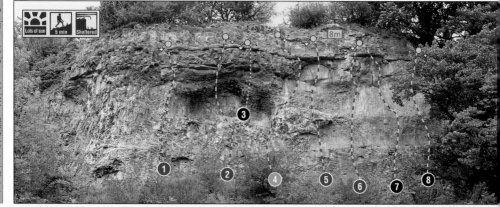

**❶ Nice Melons** . . . . . . . . . . 🔲 **6b**
Dreadful climbing up the rib left of the cave. Don't climb.
*FA. Gary Gibson 1997*

**❷ Gimme Shelter** . . . . . . . . 🔲 **7a**
A short technical problem over the bulge above the cave. Two moves of any significance but both hard ones.
*FA. Sid Siddiqui 1997*

**❸ And the Roof Fell In** . . . . . . 🔲 **7b**
Another very short but power-packed problem over the roof right of *Gimme Shelter*. Seldom climbed.
*FA. Gary Gibson 1997*

**❹ Intifada** . . . . . . . . . . . . . . . . 🔲 **6a+**
An easier route weaving through the caves and bulges.
*FA. Sid Siddiqui 1997*

**❺ Last Man First** . . . . . . . . . . 🔲 **7a**
A disjointed route with hard moves to a big ledge and the obligatory tricky finish over a roof.
*FA. Gary Gibson 1997*

**❻ Chain Reaction** . . . . . . 🔲 **7a**
The blunt rib leading to the left-hand side of the big scoop.
*FA. Sid Siddiqui 1997*

**❼ Jewfish** . . . . . . . . . 🔲 **7b**
Fierce technical climbing up the almost-blank wall marked by gold-coloured bolts. Finish by stepping left into *Chain Reaction*.
*FA. Gary Gibson 1997*

**❽ Jihad** . . . . . . . . . . 🔲 **7b**
Another fingery test-piece following a snaking line up the wall. More flashable than its neighbour but only just.
*FA. Sid Siddiqui 1997*

**❾ Here** . . . . . . . . . . 🔲 **7a**
The steep wall directly above the big tree has several tricky moves. Once again, it is difficult to onsight if unchalked.
*FA. Gary Gibson 1997*

**❿ We are not Alone** . . 🔲 **6b+**
The wall just left of a groove has two reachy moves.
*FA. Sid Siddiqui 1997*

**⓫ Little Brown Men** . . 🔲 **6c**
The vague corner has a technical crux.
*FA. Sid Siddiqui 1997. May have been soloed by Gary Gibson in 1979.*

**⓬ Clotted Cream** . . . . . . 🔲 **6a+**
The standard crag warm-up will give you a good impression of what to expect on the others. Move left at the low break although direct is also possible.
*FA. Gary Gibson 1997*

**⓭ The Age of Unreason** . . . . . 🔲 **6b**
The second most popular route on the crag is only a touch harder than *Clotted Cream*. It follows a slight groove to a steep finish.
*FA. Sid Siddiqui 1997*

**⓮ Savage Girth** . . . . . . . . . . 🔲 **6b+**
Start virtually as for *Age of Unreason* but pull right into a hanging corner.
*FA. Dave Simmonite, Sid Siddiqui 1997*

**⓯ Idiot Nation** . . . . . . . . . . . 🔲 **6c**
Steeper climbing with a serious 2nd clip. Aim for the big pinch above the second bolt. Finish out right onto a ledge.
*FA. Sid Siddiqui 1997*

**⓰ It's Uranus** . . . . . . . . . . . . . . 🔲 **6c+**
Steep and very thin climbing aiming for a left-facing groove. Gold-coloured bolts.
*FA. Gary Gibson 1997*

**⓱ Dripping Mercury** . . . . . . . 🔲 **6c+**
Another short and desperate little route.
*FA. Gary Gibson 1997*

**⓲ Men are from Mars, Women are from Venus**
. . . . . . . . . . . . . . . . . . . . . . . . . . 🔲 **6c**
A final diddy offering that packs a punch.
*FA. Sid Siddiqui 1997*

| | No star | ☆ | ☆☆ | ☆☆☆ |
|---|---|---|---|---|
| **Mod to S** | - | - | - | - |
| **HS-HVS** | 4 | 3 | 1 | 1 |
| **E1-E3 / 6b-7a** | 13 | 7 | 10 | - |
| **E4 / 7a+ and up** | 4 | 11 | 5 | - |

Staden Quarry is a bit of an anomaly, that rarest of beasts, a Peak limestone quarry with good rock and some great trad routes. Sadly the perfect tag is spoilt by the fact that the place faces north. There are three main chunks of rock of interest to climbers, with the Joint Effort Wall being the real showpiece of the crag. All the climbs listed here are worth doing, and there are some real classics amongst them.

Also covered here is the steep shady wall known as Craig-y-Biceps. This bulging face is unclimbable for much of the year because of seepage, but when dry, it gives some entertaining steep sport routes on decent rock. Recent developments have seen a re-equipping and the addition of several easier climbs on the wings.

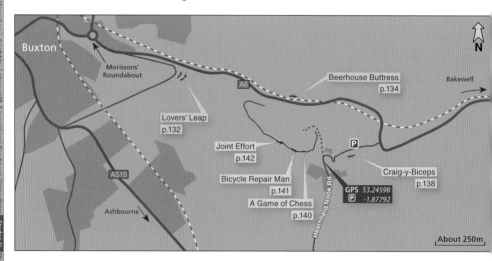

## Approach    Also see map on page 94

The quarry is situated just to the north of the tiny hamlet of Cowdale which can be reached via a minor road which branches northeast from the A515 Buxton to Ashbourne road, 2km southeast of Buxton. Cowdale can also be reached by turning south off the A6, 3km east of Buxton, on a minor road that runs steeply up past Craig-y-Biceps round a couple of acute (and slippery) bends. For both approaches, park on the verge on a bend in the village (see map). The quarry track starts here and loops round and down into the quarry. Watch out for protective cows when they have calves with them, they can be aggressive.

For Craig-y-Biceps there is room for one car (two at a squeeze) on the soft verge on the left side of the road opposite the crag. If this is full, park as for Staden and walk back down.

## Conditions

Both the quarry and the nearby Craig-y-Biceps face due north, so see little sunshine. The quarry makes a sunny venue on summer evenings but is most popular as a place to escape the summer heat, with plenty of shady rock available. At other times of the year it can be freezing cold, though at least it doesn't suffer from much in the way of drainage.

## Access

There are ongoing problems with access to Staden Quarry and at the time of writing (Feb 2012) access is not allowed. It is worth checking on the BMC RAD web site before planning a visit (**www.thebmc.co.uk**). If access is allowed again park sensibly and keep a low profile.

Dave Johnson grappling with the bulge on *Liquid Courage* (E1 5b)
- *page 143* - on the Joint Effort wall at Staden. Photo: Nick Smith

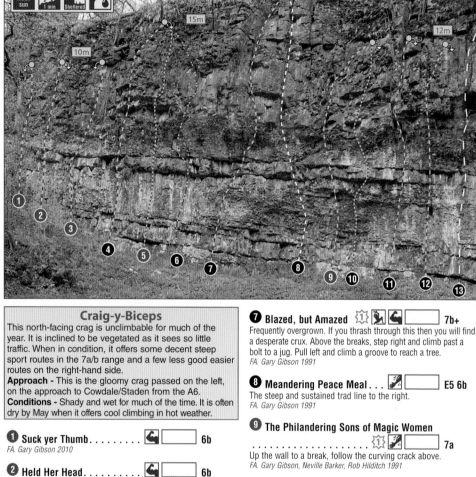

## Craig-y-Biceps

This north-facing crag is unclimbable for much of the year. It is inclined to be vegetated as it sees so little traffic. When in condition, it offers some decent steep sport routes in the 7a/b range and a few less good easier routes on the right-hand side.

**Approach** - This is the gloomy crag passed on the left, on the approach to Cowdale/Staden from the A6.

**Conditions** - Shady and wet for much of the time. It is often dry by May when it offers cool climbing in hot weather.

**❶ Suck yer Thumb** . . . . . . . . 6b
*FA. Gary Gibson 2010*

**❷ Held Her Head** . . . . . . . . . 6b
*FA. Gary Gibson 2010*

**❸ She didna Ken** . . . . . . . . . 6b+
*FA. Gary Gibson 2010*

**❹ J.L.N.O.E.** . . . . . . . . . 7b+
The left-hand side of the bulges requires a fair amount of power.
*FA. Gary Gibson 1991*

**❺ Much Monkey Magic** . . 7a
Excellent sustained climbing with some puzzling moves. Hard all the way including using the flat holds over the bulge.
*FA. Gary Gibson 1983*

**❻ Otto di Catania** . 7a+
A hard move over the mid-height bulge to gain a slot. Then move up to an edge by the bolt and make a hard stretch/jump for a good hold. Pull over the bulge and finish easily.
*FA. Gary Gibson 1991*

**❼ Blazed, but Amazed** 7b+
Frequently overgrown. If you thrash through this then you will find a desperate crux. Above the breaks, step right and climb past a bolt to a jug. Pull left and climb a groove to reach a tree.
*FA. Gary Gibson 1991*

**❽ Meandering Peace Meal** . . . E5 6b
The steep and sustained trad line to the right.
*FA. Gary Gibson 1991*

**❾ The Philandering Sons of Magic Women**
. . . . . . . . . . . . . . . . . . 7a
Up the wall to a break, follow the curving crack above.
*FA. Gary Gibson, Neville Barker, Rob Hilditch 1991*

**❿ A Wild Man from Way Back When**
. . . . . . . . . . . . . . . . . . 7a+
Start on the small ledge. Climb the wall past a prominent undercut block. There is a hidden bolt over the first bulge.
*FA. Gary Gibson 1991*

**⓫ Duelling Biceps** . . . . . . 7a+
Climb the steep wall to a roof, then gain a hanging groove above. Finish on the left.
*FA. Colin Binks, Chris Craggs, Graham Parkes 1989. Bolted later.*

**⓬ A Woman in Wellingtons** . . . 7b
*Hard, but easier in rock-shoes.*
*FA. Gary Gibson 2001*

**⓭ Wet yer Whistle** . . . 7b+
Climb to a break then tackle the bulges to a wide crack on the left. Haul over the roof and continue more easily up a groove.
*FA. Gary Gibson 1995*

**⑭ The Main Motor Mile** . . ⍟ 🔧 ☐ **7a+**
The best route on the crag. Climb up to the break, launch up the crack to the hole, move left (knee-bar?), then pull over and continue with gusto.
*FA. Gary Gibson 1983*

**⑮ Pingham's Route** ⍟ 🪨🧗🔧 ☐ **7c+**
The steepest route over the bulges at their widest point.
*FA. Paul Ingham 1995*

**⑯ Pinging in the Rain** ⍟ 🪨🧗 ☐ **7c+**
A good link between the routes on either side.
*FA. Mark Pretty 2011*

**⑰ Laughing at the Rain** ⍟ 🚪🔧 ☐ **7c**
The bulging right arete gives a modern classic. Climb a short wall and stretch past the lower bulge to reach jugs. Continue up the overhanging prow on great holds.
*FA. Gary Gibson 1995*

**⑱ Mesmerized** . . . . . . . . ⍟ 🔧 ☐ **7a+**
An indirect line, but in a fine position. Gain the hanging corner via hard moves in from the right. Climb the groove, then exit left under the roof to the lower-off of *Laughing*.
*FA. Gary Gibson 1987*

**⑲ You Know U.F.O.s** . . . . ⍟ 🔧 ☐ **7a+**
Start as for *Mesmerized*, but pull direct through the tiered-roof to a large flat hold on the lip. Make some fingery moves to a thin crack and a shallow groove which leads to a lower-off.
*FA. Gary Gibson 1991*

**⑳ E.T.** . . . . . . . . . . . . . . . ⍟ 🔧 ☐ **7b+**
The roof crack finish to *You Know U.F.O.s* is an epic struggle.
*FA. Mark Pretty 2011*

**㉑ Euphoric** . . . . . . . . . . 🔧🧗 ☐ **7a**
Climb through the bulging roofs on undercuts and breaks to gain a crack over the lip. Continue directly to join *U.F.O.s.*
*FA. Gary Gibson 1995*

**㉒ Pneumatic** . . . . . . . . . 🔧🚪 ☐ **6c+**
The powerful bulge followed by some stretches.
*FA. Gary Gibson 2010*

**㉓ Ecstatic** . . . . . . . . . . . . . 🔧 ☐ **6b**
Soon eases.
*FA. Gary Gibson 2010*

**㉔ Fantastic.** . . . . . . . . . . . . 🚪 ☐ **6b**
A juggy bulge and groove above.
*FA. Gary Gibson 2010*

**㉕ Traumatic** . . . . . . . . . . . . . . . ☐ **6b+**
Big holds and a bit of a heave.
*FA. Gary Gibson 2010*

**㉖ Check Out** . . . . . . . . . . . . ⍟ ☐ **6a**
The bulge leads to jugs. Up the crack and exit left.
*FA. Gary Gibson 2010*

**㉗ New Nomad** . . . . . . . . . . . . . . ☐ **6b+**
*FA. Gary Gibson 2010*

**㉘ Napped a Nod** . . . . . . . . . . . ☐ **6a+**
*FA. Gary Gibson 2010*

North
Southwest
Southeast
Stoney
Horseshoe
Smalldale
Harpur Hill
Lovers' Leap
Beerhouse
Craig-y-Biceps
Staden Q
Chee Dale U.
Che Dale L.
Blackwell D.
Raven Tor
Water-c.-Jolly
Ravensdale
Aldery Cliff
Taddington
Rheinstor

### ① Tout Comprendre . . . . . . . .    HVS 4c
The left-hand arete of the wall is rather light on gear. Start up the arete, or round to the left (easier, but less satisfying) to where it blanks out then keep to the right. Have you got that?

### ② A Game of Chess . .    E5 6b
A well-named slab route, which is desperate to figure out, and almost as hard to climb. Follow the hairline weakness in the left-hand side of the slab to the central bulge, and pass this phlegmatically. The grade is for side-runners, although it was originally climbed without and given E2! High in the grade.
*FA. Johnny Woodward, Andrew Woodward 1976*

### ③ Hammer into Anvil . . . .    E2 6a
From the centre of the slab, climb leftwards through the overhang to a niche, where things start to ease. A bit of a one-move-wonder.
*FA. Johnny Woodward, Andrew Woodward 1976*

### ④ Nice 'n' Sleazy. . . . . . . . .    E2 5b
Eazy does it up the right-hand side of the slab, trending left, to reach a flake where things ease. Side-runners in the previous route protect the lower section, otherwise it is nearer E4.
*FA. Gary Gibson 1979*

---

## A Game of Chess
The first section described in the main quarry is a short face on the left of the long back wall. This has some easy, and relatively popular, orange spot ticks, plus a couple of blank desperates including the fine route the wall is named after.

---

### ⑤ 96 Smears . . . . . . . .    E5 6c
Climb the steep, slabby wall to the right of *Nice 'n Sleazy* with desperation. Completely gearless, and almost holdless.
*FA. Gary Gibson 1991*

### ⑥ Rupert Bear Goes Hiking. . .    VS 4c
Hike up to the banana-shaped crack in the left side of the slab and follow it until it fizzles out. Finish direct awkwardly. Just about worth a star in the interests of spreading them around.
*FA. Johnny Woodward, Andrew Woodward 1976*

### ⑦ Bimbo the Exploding Lorry Driver's Gulch Eliminate
. . . . . . . . . . . . . . . . . . . . . .    HS 4b
The right-hand crack is straightforward and solid, apart from the exit. It gets a star for being the best HS in the quarry, either that or the route name - you choose.
*FA. Johnny Woodward, Andrew Woodward 1976*

### ⑧ Beau Jest . . . . . . . . . . . .    E1 5a
The right-hand arete of the short slab. The block round to the right that used to provide runners and holds has migrated south, though the scar remains
*FA. Al Evans 1976*

Not much sun | 6 min | Sheltered | Restrictions

Descent - - - -

12m

**9 Silent Manoeuvres....** E4 5c
The arete is tackled precariously on its right-hand side. Bold
laybacking, but sadly (or fortunately) escapable.
*FA. Gary Gibson, Derek Beetlestone 1980*

**10 Telescopic Demand** E3 6a
As reachy as the name suggests. Climb the sinuous crack in the
left-hand edge of the slab. A side-runner for the start is normal,
otherwise the route is E4. Continue up to and over the capping
overhang. Originally started up *Swan Song*.
*FA. Phil Wilson, Gary Gibson, Mark Walton 1979*
*FA. (Direct Start) Gary Gibson, Derek Beetlestone, S.Frazer 1981*

**11 Swan Song............** E1 5b
A bit of an eliminate high up. Climb right up the shallow ramp
until it is possible to reach a thin crack - small wires. Follow this
to easier ground and a finish over the overhang as for *Telescopic
Demand*.
*FA. Richard Davies, Simon Nadin 1983*

**12 Bicycle Repair Man** E1 5b
A classic. Crank up the thin crack (awkward to start) to a rest in
a tiny groove. Head left across the wall on surprising holds then
pull over the roof and pedal up a short, wide and deceptively
awkward crack. Becoming polished.
*FA. Mark Walton, Gary Gibson, Phil Wilson 1979*

**13 Charas........** E1 5b
Climb to the tree then tackle the thin finger-crack (poor
footholds and perfect runners) then the easier groove above.
*FA. Bob Dearman (4 points) 1969*
*FFA. Steve Worthington, Jim Worthington, Giles Barker 1977*

**14 Mosaic Piece..........** E4 5c
Step right out of *Charas* and leave the runners to balance up the
sketchy wall. A **Direct Start** is a bolder **E4 5c**.
*FA. Gary Gibson, Derek Beetlestone, S.Fraser (1 bolt runner) 1981*
*FA. (Direct Start) Bill Birch, Rick Gibbon 1990s*

**15 Wipe Out..........** E3 5b
Climb the thin crack to a ledge (tiny wires) then trend left up a
ramp before continuing directly to join the easy finishing crack.
This also has a bold **Direct Start, E4 5c.**
*FA. Gary Gibson, Mark Walton, Phil Wilson 1979*
*FA. (Direct Start) Bill Birch, Rick Gibbon 1990s*

**16 Paraplege..........** E3 5c
Start as for *Wipe Out*, but continue carefully in the same line up
the hairline crack to a creaky finish on the headwall.
*FA. Gary Gibson, Dave Williams 1979*

**17 Amatarasu............** VS 4c
The rather scruffy groove that bounds the wall on the right is
climbed passing a tricky overhang to enter the continuation.
*FA. K.Bridges (1pt) 1969*

## Bicycle Repair Man
A fine slab capped by a substantial tree, with another at
its base. It is split by two prominent cracks and is home
to a fine set of climbs, many of a 'fluttery' nature. It was
originally named after an old bike found underneath it
that needed some serious attention from the menders.

**Joint Effort Wall**
The showpiece of the quarry is this tall and rugged slab of dark rock. The right-hand side is steeper and forms a fine tufa-encrusted wall. Good technique and neat footwork pay dividends here.

Not much sun | 6 min | Sheltered | Restrictions

24m

28m

9

2

3

4

5

6

7

8

10

11

1

**❶ Suscipiat** ...... VS 4c
The left edge of the wall has a steep start up fluted rock then step left to the arete. Move back right (loose) and then follow the long crack on the right to a short grass bank.
*FA. Paul Nunn, W.Ward, John Smith (started round to the left) 1966*

**❷ Sunai** ............. E1 5b
Climb between *Suscipiat* and *The Nails* to a black wall. Go up the left-hand side of this then head right below a bulge to a niche. Leave this with difficulty for the grassy ledge above then continue up the short black slab trending right.
*FA. Bruce Goodwin, Alan Goodwin 1997*

North | Southwest | Southeast | Stoney | Horseshoe | Smalldale | Harpur Hill | Lovers' Leap | Beehouse | Craigy-Bicps | Staden Q | Chee Dale U | Che Dale L | Blackwell D | Raven Tor | Water-c-Joly | Ravensdale | Aldery Cliff | Taddington | Rheinstor

**Girdles -** At least four right-to-left rising diagonal girdles have been claimed on the wall. Although providing good moves, they have rather arbitrary lines and tend to interfere with the up and down climbs. The lines have been left for the inquisitive to rediscover, hopefully on quiet days.

**Descent**

24m

⑤ **Welcome to Hard Times**   **E3 5c**
Fine intricate face climbing. Climb deviously up the centre of the slab (small wires and threads) to the horizontal break. Take a deep breath and balance on up the slab, avoiding the option of a rightward escape into *Joint Effort*.
**Original Finish, E2 5c -** Step left to finish up *The Nails*.
FA. Andy Freeman, Pete Brayshaw, Giles Barker 1978
FA. (Direct) P.Stidever, R.Beadle 1983

⑥ **Joint Effort** . . . . . . . . Top⌐L50   **HVS 5a**
Excellent, the best of its grade here, following the sinuous crack-line that runs the full height of the face. A steep and technical start leads to easier sustained climbing (threads) and on up pleasantly sustained rock above.
FA. Bob Dearman (2 pts) 1969

⑦ **Badlands** . . . . . . . . . . . . . . **E3 6a**
Climb the slender pillar between *Captain Reliable* and *Joint Effort* leading to the start of *Private Gripped*. Finish up this (**E6**) or, more in keeping, move right to join *Captain Reliable*.
FA. Bill Birch, Rick Gibbon 1990s

⑧ **Captain Reliable** . . . . .   **E2 5c**
Climb the pleasant crack to the bulges and lace it with gear. Then pull up and right to find tricky-to-place runners and one more balancy move to reach easy ground.
FA. Phil Burke, Gary Cooper 1978

⑨ **Private Gripped** . . .   **E6 6b**
Follow *Captain Reliable* to the bulges. Step out left and tackle the desperately thin upper wall, with enough protection where needed. This is the original line although *Badlands* now makes a better start.
FA. Richard Davies 1986

⑩ **Extra Effort** . . . . . . . . . . .   **E2 5c**
An eliminate up the pillar between *Captain Reliable* and *Investal* is taken without recourse to either route for protection.
FA. Bill Birch, Rick Hyde 1990s

⑪ **Investal** . . . . . . . . . . . . . . . . .   **HVS 5a**
The rather scrappy looking crack and groove has some good moves on it. A pity about the vegetation.
FA. Jim Morgan 1969

⑫ **Clowning** . . . . . . . . .   **E2 5b**
The arete/wall right of *Investal*, and left of *Cathy's Clown*, is steep sustained and not too well protected.
FA. Bill Birch, Rick Gibbon 1990s

⑬ **Cathy's Clown** . . . . .   **E2 5c**
Fine sustained tufa climbing; technical and balancy despite its steepness. Climb the wall via a couple of bulges to an open groove and easier ground.
FA. Phil Burke, Gary Cooper 1981

⑭ **Liquid Courage** . . . . . .   **E1 5b**
The right-hand side of the wall is strenuous, sustained and high in the grade. Climb a scoop to the bulges and power diagonally right over these to a deep crack. More forceful climbing leads rapidly to easy ground. **Left-hand finish, E3 6a.**
*Photo on page 137.*
FA. Gary Gibson, Derek Beetlestone 1979

③ **The Nails** . . . . . . . . .   **E1 5b**
Not as hard as the name might suggest. Climb past the ancient ironwork and on up the pleasant crack to the base of a shallow groove. Balance up this using holds on the left arete and some neat footwork - poor gear. Nice.
FA. Paul Nunn, R.Olliphant (1pt) 1969

④ **Soft Times** . . . . . .   **E1 5c**
A pleasant eliminate weaving up the face between *Welcome* and *The Nails* to a finish up the black slab above and left of the final groove of *The Nails*. If you finish up *Welcome to Hard Times* the grade is worth **E3 5c.**
FA. Bill Birch, Rick Gibbon 1994.
FA. (finish as described) Bruce Goodwin, Gordon Mason 1995

North Southwest Southeast Stoney Horseshoe Smalldale Harpur Hill Lover's Leap Beerhouse Cadgy-Biceps Staden Q Chee Dale U Chee Dale L Blackwell D. Raven Tor Water-c-Jolly Ravensdale Aldery Cliff Taddington Rheinstor

North | Southwest | Southeast | Stoney | Horseshoe | Smalldale | Harpur Hill | Lovers' Leap | Beehouse | Craig-y-Biceps | Staden Q | Chee Dale U. Che Dale L. | Blackwell D. | Raven Tor | Water-c-Jolly | Ravensdale | Aldery Cliff | Taddington | Rheinstor

# Chee Dale

The leafy surroundings of Chee Dale provide a unique environment for climbers. Come here at the wrong time of year and you may well walk away disgusted at the thought of climbing anything, but visit on a warm summer or autumn day and the place will enchant you with is wonderful climbing and idyllic setting. No crag exhibits these extremes more than the Cornice. In the photo, Alan Royle tackles the sustained series of undercuts and sidepulls of the popular line *That was the River* (7b+) - *page 200*. Photo: Mark Glaister

North

Southwest

Southeast

Stoney

Horseshoe

Smalldale

Harpur Hill

Lovers' Leap

Beerhouse

Craig-y-Biceps

Staden Q

Chee Dale U.

Che Dale L.

Blackwell D.

Raven Tor

Water-c-Jolly

Ravensdale

Aldery Cliff

Taddington

Rheinstor

| | No star | ✪ | ✪✪ | ✪✪✪ |
|---|---|---|---|---|
| **Mod to S / 4+** | 2 | - | - | 1 |
| **HS-HVS / 5-6a+** | 22 | 15 | 2 | 1 |
| **E1-E3 / 6b-7a** | 74 | 80 | 25 | 7 |
| **E4 / 7a+ and up** | 69 | 106 | 84 | 35 |

Chee Dale has fallen in and out of fashion over the years as times and tastes have changed. There was a time in the late '80s and early '90s when it was the place to be and be seen, with new routes there for the taking, and climbers queuing up to make second ascents. Nowadays, many of the trad routes - especially the harder ones - have become neglected, and the lack of lower-grade sport routes means that many climbers are going elsewhere. In some ways, this situation sums up climbing in Chee Dale - the place is both intimidating and confusing to the uninitiated. However, a bit of exploration can turn to an obsession. It is doubtless the lack of easy to mid-grade sport routes which puts people off, although a tick-list of the classic trad routes should be enough to convince any sceptics of the quality of the climbing hereabouts. Chee Tor itself is a fine starting venue containing a set of routes that increases gradually in both difficulty and quality, culminating in superb routes like *Apocalypse*, *The Golden Mile*, *Ceramic Extension* and *Tequila Mockingbird*.

Fine though these trad routes are, the real wealth in Chee Dale climbing is its sport routes. Although there is little to get you going in the 6a/b grade range, above that, the climbing is as good as anywhere else in the Peak, with classics such as *Clarion Call*, *Countdown*, *The Sea is a Brown Paper Bag*, *Cry of Despair* and *Powerplant,* in the range 7a to 8a, to mention but a few.

Since the '60s, many of the big names of British climbing have made their mark here and mention should be made of all those who have contributed to the development of Chee Dale. In recent times that has involved tireless work in both bolting and access negotiation.

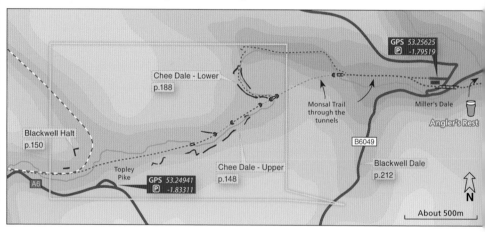

## Approaches

**Chee Dale Upper -** As the A6 from Bakewell to Buxton drops down the hill towards the River Wye, there is a large lay-by at Topley Pike overlooking the western end of Chee Dale. Locate a gate at the uphill end of the lay-by and skirt across the top of the steep slope to reach a path which cuts back left down Old Dale underneath the slope (**do not go directly up or down the steep slope**). At the bottom, turn right onto the old railway (or straight on for Blackwell Halt) and follow the track to the various buttresses.

**Chee Dale Lower -** From the tiny village of Miller's Dale on the B6049 below Tideswell, turn off uphill towards the old Miller's Dale Station and park here (pay). Walk (or cycle) along the track and through Chee Tor Tunnel to access the cliffs.

## Conditions

Much of Chee Dale takes a long time to dry out, and with the exception of the Embankment, the Sidings and Blackwell Halt - three possible winter-sun venues - a good spell of dry weather is required before the season can really begin. In autumn the walls can remain dry for several weeks after the weather has closed in. In the hotter months, shade can be found on most of the buttresses, with only Chee Tor, the Sidings and Blackwell Halt exposed to any afternoon sun. The high valley walls give good shelter from any wind.

Chee Dale stepping stones under the Cornice. Photo: Chris Craggs

## Access - IMPORTANT

Chee Dale is owned by the Derbyshire Wildlife Trust and is a site of international significance for flora and fauna. The DWT is prepared for climbing to continue to its current extent, but does not permit further development, this includes both trad and sport routes. The buttress approaches described in this book have been approved by the DWT, so please follow them closely. **Do not take a direct approach where no path exists**, the vegetation would make you regret such action anyway. There should be no new bolting, only replacement of old bolts and fixing of lower-offs to protect the crag-top vegetation. This should only be done after consultation with the BMC. With the exception of lower-offs, no extra gear should be left on the routes, this includes fixed slings and krabs. Crag gardening should be avoided.

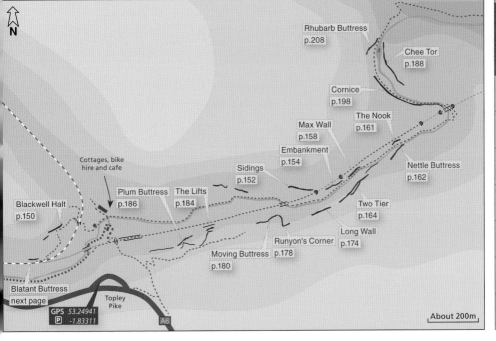

**1 Chug, Chug, Chug** ...... [ ] 6b
The short steep wall on the far left.
*FA. Gary Gibson 2006*

**2 For the Good of the Cause** .. [ ] 5
Start behind the tree and follow the broken groove above. The bolts are a bit spaced.
*FA. Brian Cropper, Nadim Siddiqui 1998*

**3 Close to the Edge** ..... [ ] 6a+
The short corner on the lower wall is awkward. Higher up, keep to the left of the arete.
*FA. Nadim Siddiqui, Brian Cropper 1998*

**4 Every Breath You Take** . [ ] 6b+
The longest section of good rock on the buttress but it is a wandering line. At the mid-height break you can climb direct up the wall then move left to the arete or climb the arete itself.
*FA. Nadim Siddiqui, Brian Cropper 1998. FA. (Start) Gary Gibson 2009*

**5 Eye Catching Cod Piece** [ ] 6b+
A direct line slightly spoilt by a ledge on the right higher up. Eschewing the ledge adds challenge and enjoyment.
*FA. Nadim Siddiqui, Brian Cropper 1998*

**6 Pipistrelle** ............ [ ] 6a
Share a start with the previous two routes then head right up the blunt arete and sadly, short wall.
*FA. Brian Cropper, Nadim Siddiqui 1998*

**7 Rave On** ................ [ ] 6a
Indifferent climbing not helped much by the dirty ledge at half-height.
*FA. Brian Cropper, Nadim Siddiqui 1998*

**8 Chill Out** .......... [ ] 6a+
The roof is easier than it looks (clip the bolt on *Feel the Beat* for added security). The final slab has one tricky move aided by a well-hidden side-pull. Shame about the ledge.
*FA. Nadim Siddiqui, Brian Cropper 1998*

## Blatant Buttress

This well-named little buttress is a bit too close to the active railway line for comfort, although the line is exclusively used by quarry traffic, so tends not to be used at weekends. Doing all the routes here in an evening is a good challenge - it has been done!

**Access -** Climbing here is not allowed and the descriptions are only included for completeness.

**Conditions -** The wall faces south and gets plenty of sun. It doesn't seep much and is quick-drying.

**Approach -** The best approach is from Blackwell Halt (next page) which avoids having to cross the railway line. Leave Blackwell Halt and find a small path which leads right (facing out) and down a steep drop to the side of the railway. Blatant Buttress is just along here.

North
Southwest
Southeast
Stoney
Horseshoe
Smalldale
Harpur Hill
Lovers' Leap
Beehouse
Craigy-Biceps
Staden Q
Chee Dale U.
Chee Dale L.
Blackwell D.
Raven Tor
Water-c-Jolly
Ravensdale
Aldery Cliff
Taddington
Rheinstor

**9 Feel the Beat** . . . . . . . . . . 🔲 6b
The best of the easier routes with hard moves to gain a rest above the break and a well-positioned final slab. There is a poorly placed lower-off which is invisible from below.
*FA. Nadim Siddiqui, Brian Cropper 1998*

**10 Emission Control** . . 🔲 7a+
After a taxing start the upper groove gives fine climbing on unhelpful lay-aways.
*FA. Nadim Siddiqui, Jim Burton 1998*

**11 Good Vibrations** . . . 🔲 7a+
Climb direct to reach a tricky groove. The best of the harder routes.
*FA. Nadim Siddiqui, Brian Cropper, Colin Struthers 1998*

**12 Wobbly Wheels** . . . 🔲 7b
Links the routes either side via some desperate moves.
*FA. Gary Gibson 2009*

**13 Loco-Motion** . . . . . . . 🔲 7a
The right-hand route can be started from the easy lower groove of *Love is a Swallow* or (harder) from *Good Vibrations*.
*FA. Nadim Siddiqui, Brian Cropper 1998*

**14 Love is a Swallow** . . . . . . . . . 🔲 6a+
The right-slanting groove on the right-hand end of the wall. Move back onto the wall near the top.
*FA. S.Barker, Nadim Siddiqui, Brian Cropper 1998*

**15 The Runaway Train** . . . . . . . . 🔲 6a+
A direct version of *Love is a Swallow*.
*FA. Gary Gibson 2006*

**16 Came down the Track** . . . . . . . 🔲 6b
A thin wall climb.
*FA. Gary Gibson 2006*

**17 One Track Offensive** . . . . . . . . 🔲 6a
Break right from *Came Down the Track* to a curving groove.
*FA. Gary Gibson 2009*

**18 Burning Rails** . . . . . . . . . . . . 🔲 5+
The final line, past a grassy ledge on the right.
*FA. Gary Gibson 2009*

Lots of sun | 15 min | Sheltered | Restrictions

18m

15m

**Approach from Blackwell Halt using a path further along the railway line**

North | Southwest | Southeast | Stoney | Horseshoe | Smalldale | Harpur Hill | Lovers' Leap | Beerhouse | Craig-y-Biceps | Staden Q | Blackwell D. | Che Dale L. | Chee Dale U. | Raven Tor | Blackwell D. | Ravensdale | Water-c-Jolly | Aldery Cliff | Taddington | Rheinstor

## Blackwell Halt

This compact wall has a good set of mid-grade routes. The setting is pleasant and there is plenty of picnic potential at the base.

**Conditions -** The wall faces south although the lower section is in the shade of the trees. There is little seepage and it is well-sheltered from the wind.

**Approach (also see page 146) -** From the Monsal Trail on the Chee Dale Upper Approach, head down towards the cafe/cycle hire. Cross the bridge and turn sharp left at the cottages and follow a small path along the edge of the river and past a pump house. This leads to a tunnel under the train tracks. On leaving the tunnel, cross the fence on the left and go up some hidden stone steps. From here a path leads up into the grassy field below the quarry.

*To the left of the main wall, and set in front of it, is a sidewall with a seven minor routes. These see little in the way of visitors.*

**1 Byte Size** . . . . . . . . . . . . . . . 6b
The left-hand line. An easy start to a tricky bulge.
*FA. Gary Gibson 2007*

**2 Ernie** . . . . . . . . . . . . . . . . 6c+
The second line, through the shattered roof - neglected.
*FA. A.Theaker, Sid Siddiqui, C.Struthers 1996*

**3 Defrag** . . . . . . . . . . . . . . . . . 6c
The next line - sad and lonely.
*FA. Sid Siddiqui, C.Struthers 1996*

**4 A Soldier's Diary** . . . . . . . . 6c
A tricky start leads to better things above.
*FA. Gary Gibson, Hazel Gibson 2007*

**5 Anoraks and Trainspotters** . . 6b
Start at a flake and head steeply up the wall. Dirty.
*FA. Sid Siddiqui, R.Siddiqui 1996*

**6 Micro-nerd** . . . . . . . . . . . 6b+
The penultimate route on this wall. Also dirty. The lower wall is the crux.
*FA. Sid Siddiqui, R.Siddiqui 1996*

**7 Nerd the Absurd** . . . . . . . . 6b
The last offering here is teeny tiny.
*FA. Gary Gibson, Hazel Gibson 2007*

*The rest of the routes are on the taller, cleaner face over to the right. The first climbs start from a high ledge reached by an easy scramble.*

**8 Micro-chip** . . . . . . . . . . . 6c+
Fingery moves past the first two bolts then it's all over.
*FA. Bill Birch, Rick Gibbon 1995*

**9 Modem** . . . . . . . . . . . 6a
Deceptively pumpy for such a short route, high in the grade but still the most popular warm-up here.
*FA. Bill Birch, Rick Gibbon 1995*

**10 C.D. Romp** . . . . . . . . . . . E2 5c
A trad route up the crack is high in the grade. Tree belay.
*FA. Rick Gibbon, Bill Birch 1995*

**11 The Arapahoe Connection** 6b+
A good route with mostly positive holds which somehow feels steeper than the other routes on this wall.
*FA. Bill Birch, Rick Gibbon 1995*

**12 Hard Drive** . . . . . . 6b+
A hard start leads to good holds and a tricky clip above. High in the grade and pumpy too.
*FA. Bill Birch, Rick Gibbon 1995*

**13 Megabyte** . . . . . . . . . . . 6b
Steady climbing to tricky moves on the upper wall.
*FA. Bill Birch, Rick Gibbon 1995*

To mid afternoon | 15 min | Sheltered

8m

5m

① ② ③ ④ ⑤ ⑥ ⑦

A path here leads across to
**Blatant Buttress**

North | Southwest | Southeast | Stoney | Horseshoe | Smalldale | Harpur Hill | Lovers' Leap | Beerhouse | Crag-y-Brysg: | Staden Q | Chee Dale U | Che Dale L | Blackwell D | Raven Tor | Water-c-Jolly | Ravensdale | Aldery Cliff | Taddington | Rheinstor

**14** Gopherspace . . . . . 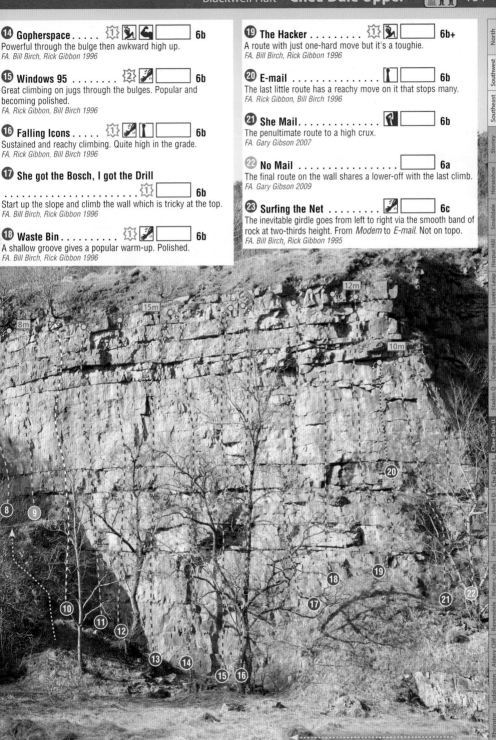 **6b**
Powerful through the bulge then awkward high up.
*FA. Bill Birch, Rick Gibbon 1996*

**15** Windows 95 . . . . . . . . **6b**
Great climbing on jugs through the bulges. Popular and becoming polished.
*FA. Rick Gibbon, Bill Birch 1996*

**16** Falling Icons . . . . . **6b**
Sustained and reachy climbing. Quite high in the grade.
*FA. Rick Gibbon, Bill Birch 1996*

**17** She got the Bosch, I got the Drill
. . . . . . . . . . . . . . . . . . . . **6b**
Start up the slope and climb the wall which is tricky at the top.
*FA. Bill Birch, Rick Gibbon 1996*

**18** Waste Bin . . . . . . . . . **6b**
A shallow groove gives a popular warm-up. Polished.
*FA. Bill Birch, Rick Gibbon 1996*

**19** The Hacker . . . . . . . . . **6b+**
A route with just one-hard move but it's a toughie.
*FA. Bill Birch, Rick Gibbon 1996*

**20** E-mail . . . . . . . . . . . . . . **6b**
The last little route has a reachy move on it that stops many.
*FA. Rick Gibbon, Bill Birch 1996*

**21** She Mail . . . . . . . . . . . . . **6b**
The penultimate route to a high crux.
*FA. Gary Gibson 2007*

**22** No Mail . . . . . . . . . . . . . . . . **6a**
The final route on the wall shares a lower-off with the last climb.
*FA. Gary Gibson 2009*

**23** Surfing the Net . . . . . . . . **6c**
The inevitable girdle goes from left to right via the smooth band of rock at two-thirds height. From *Modem* to *E-mail*. Not on topo.
*FA. Bill Birch, Rick Gibbon 1995*

# The Sidings

Although not one of Cheedale's premier venues, this is a compact buttress with short and technical routes on good rock. It gets plenty of sun, a consideration in the winter. The mid-grade routes are worth seeking out since there aren't many on the pages which are coming up. The harder routes are typical vertical limestone horrors which you either love or avoid like the plague.

**Approach (also see page 146)** - From the Monsal Trail on the Chee Dale Upper Approach, cross the fence **carefully** and find a small path up left, just before the first tunnel, that runs under the buttresses.

**Conditions** - It dries quickly, doesn't suffer from seepage and is a good winter sun-trap (when little else in Chee Dale is climbable).

*There are two isolated routes about 200m left of Fizzy Buttress on a small overhanging wall above a lower section of crag.*

**❶ Galswegian Kiss** . . . . . 7c+
The left-hand line.
*FA. Mark Pretty 2011*

**❷ Strawberry Kiss** . . . . . . 7b
The right-hand line.
*FA. Alisdair Hannah, Ian Dunn 1996*

*The first routes are on a lone barrel-shaped buttress about 50m left of where you arrive at the crag.*

**❸ Up the Creek** . . . . . . . . E5 6a
The loose wall has little to recommend it.
*FA. Neil Foster, Al Rouse, Richard Hazsko 1984*

**❹ Hupsters** . . . . . . . . . . 7a+
The left-hand line of 2 bolts has some hard moves. Holds going AWOL hasn't helped. Finish at the lower-off on the right.
*FA. Tony Coutts, Ed Morgan 1994*

**❺ Fizzy** . . . . . . . . . . . . . 6c+
The right-hand two bolts to the same lower-off. Surprisingly sustained for such a short route.
*FA. Tony Coutts 1991*

*The next routes are situated on the clean buttress about 10m left of the main area.*

**❻ Sleepers** . . . . . . . . . . . . . . . . HVS 5a
The left-hand side of the pillar. The curving flake on the left gives an alternative start.
*FA. Brian Cropper 1977*

**❼ Lust in the Dust** . . . . . . . . E1 5b
The short thin crack on the left-hand side of the pillar. A long reach is required to leave the crack.
*FA. Jim Rubery, Dave Gregory 1985*

**❽ Platonic Desire** . . . . . . E1 5c
The centre of the pillar past a faded thread. At the top break, head left to the tree.
*FA. Bill Birch, Rick Gibbon, J.Woodhead 1987*

**❾ Spring is Here** . . . . . . . . . . . . HVS 5a
The groove on the right-hand side of the buttress leads to a small overlap. Finish up the crack and overlaps above, heading left to the belay. Quite high in the grade.
*FA. Loz Francombe, Brian Cropper 1977*

*The best climbing is on the main right-hand section.*

**❿ I Drink Therefore I Am** . E4 6b
A micro-classic with some fierce fingery moves. Climb up to clip an inverted peg on the right. Climb back to the ground. Now start again slightly left to gain another peg and a diagonal crack. Keep going to the tree.
*FA. Nadim Siddiqui, Paul Cropper 1982*

**⓫ The Dukes of Hazard** E5 6c
Fine precarious climbing up the central groove-line with a desperate last move. Slinking off right before the crux is **E4 6b**.
*FA. Paul Cropper and others 1982*

**⓬ County Time** . . . . . . . . E3 5c
A precarious wall climb with some good moves. Hidden small wires protect.
*FA. Gary Gibson, Hazel Gibson 1999*

North | Southwest | Southeast | Stoney | Horseshoe | Smalldale | Harpur Hill | Lovers' Leap | Beerhouse | Craig-y-Biceps | Staden Q | Chee Dale U. | Chee Dale L. | Blackwell D. | Raven Tor | Water-c-Jolly | Ravensdale | Aldery Cliff | Teddington | Rheinstor

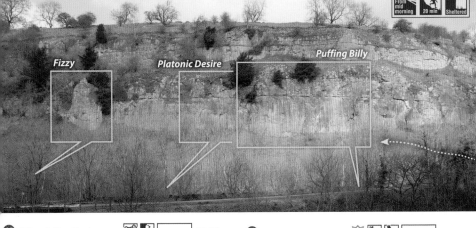

**13** **A Touch Too Much** . . . . **E1 5b**
A poor non-line up the arete. It is easier if you use holds on *Puffing Billy*.
FA. Paul Cropper, Nadim Siddiqui, D.Campbell 1982

**14** **Puffing Billy** . . . . . . . . . . . **VS 4b**
The corner crack direct to the yew tree - pleasant.
FA. Tony Howard, John Amatt 1960s

**15** **A Sign of the Times** . . . . . . . . **VS 4c**
Start up *Sprint Start* but climb the grassy wall to the left.
FA. Gary Gibson 1979

**16** **Sprint Start** . . . . . . . . . . . **E1 5a**
The thin rightwards-leaning flake is hard to get gear behind. Above this, climb the wall on hidden holds.
FA. Jon Walker, Gary Gibson 1979

**17** **Lethal Dose** . . . . . . **E3 6b**
The thin cracks (small wires) lead to a reachy crux move. A notorious stopper route.
FA. Loz Francomb, M.Harrison, Paul Cropper 1977

**18** **Fame But No Fortune** . . . . . . . . **E2 5c**
Use the dominating tree and the thread for protection. To avoid the painful experience of hitting the tree, don't fall off.
FA. Simon Nadin 1982

**19** **Fireman's Frolic** . . . . . . . . . . . **Diff**
The tree-choked crack - it is climbing but not as we know it. Escape off right with care.

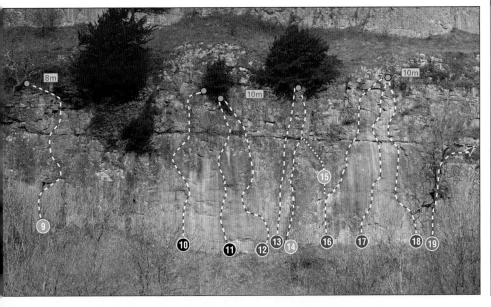

## The Embankment

The Embankment was transformed during the late '80s into the first of the true sport crags in the Peak. Over the years the original gear has been replaced and reaching the first bolt is no longer such an ordeal. The drawback is that some of the routes are now very polished and most of the original holds have gone!

**Approach (also see page 146) -** From the Monsal Trail on the Chee Dale Upper Approach, walk around to the right of the first tunnel. Pass some ramparts to get to the buttress just beyond.

**Conditions -** It suffers less from seepage than other steep Chee Dale crags except when it has been very wet. It can also get sunshine in the winter and is sheltered from any wind.

*The arete of the tunnel passed on the approach gives Chee Dale's easiest sport route -* **Unzipping the Wild Physique, 4+.**

**❶ The World According to Tommy Trout**

. . . . . . . . . . . . . . . . . . . . . .   6c+

Loose and seldom climbed. From the first rest on *Hungry Eyes*, swing left under a bolt. Make a hard move up into a groove then pull out right onto the headwall. Climb up to a tree and then traverse right to the lower-off on *Hungry Eyes*.
*FA. Mark Liptrot, John Welford 1988*

**❷ Hungry Eyes . . . . .**   7a+

Climb the fingery wall to a rest in the recess; then tackle the flake and layaways to a jug at the top. Move left and pull up the headwall. There is a poor left-hand start through the bulges.
*FA. Dave Lee, Adam Haynes (as an E6 6b) 1982. It was bolted in the mid-90s. The flake-line was formerly an aid route.*

**❸ Beef It . . . . . . . .**   7b

From the niche of *Hungry Eyes*, reach up and start an excellent sequence of cross-throughs until the lower-off is reached well to the right.
*FA. Mark Pretty 1987*

**❹ Secret Gudgeon Society**   7b

The line trends right in its upper section along a vague overlap. Finish straight up to the lower-off. Polished.
*FA. Gary Gibson, Mark Elwell 1987*

**❺ Stone the Loach. . . . . .**   7c

The hardest of the set has a very taxing middle section using crimps and side pulls.
*FA. Gary Gibson 1988*

**❻ Mind of a Turbot . . . . .**   7b

A typical Embankment route; a fiddly lower wall then a rest at the break followed by a bit of a pull onto the headwall.
*FA. Gary Gibson 1987*

**❼ The Man Who Fell to Earth**   6c+

Just left of the central groove. Getting to the overlap at the break is okay then a reachy pull provides the main difficulties. Finding the correct hold is usually the crux.
*FA. Keith Sharples, Nigel Slater 1989*

### 8 Arachonothera Direct .. 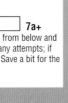 6b+

The easiest route up the buttress. Climb the wall to enter the groove which is more awkward than it looks. Finish with a difficult move above the overlap.
*FA. Jim Campbell, Chris Addy, Mick Horlov (left-hand finish at E3) 1976. Bolted in 1996 with the finish. FA. Tony Howard, R.Holt (aid) 1960s.*

### 9 Prawnography .... 6c

A squeezed-in line just right of the groove gives surprisingly independent climbing even though you use holds on the adjacent routes. The section above the break requires some determined pulling on sloping layaways.
*FA. Ian Dunn, Alisdair Hannah 1996*

### 10 Bream in Black ...... 7a+

The old warm-up route has shed some holds and become harder and more sustained and so less popular.
*FA. Pete Oxley, Gary Gibson 1987*

### 11 Breamtime .... 7a+

The central line of the wall gains the arch-overlap from below and left. The move past the bolt at the break stops many attempts; if you are struggling, try a dyno - it is a good hold. Save a bit for the finishing move left from the arch using a mono.
*FA. Gary Gibson, John Codling 1987*

### 12 The Barracuda Bass Sound . 7a+

Climb direct to the break and pull over to a junction with *Breamtime*. Finish over the arch. Pumpy and high in the grade.
*FA. Gary Gibson 1987*

### 13 Pump up The Bass .......... 7a+

A variation finish over the right side of the roof.

### 14 No Hiding Plaice ..... 7a+

A quality sport route. Climb to the break then pull right into a crack which leads to the right-hand end of the overlap. Finish up and left to the lower-off.
*FA. Chris Wright (as an E5 6b) 1987*

### 15 Sturgeon in the Cupboard 7c

A good hard route. It follows a big 'S' shape up the wall around the small bulge requiring some big pulls on small sharp holds. It eases with height but not by much.
*FA. Gary Gibson 1987*

### 16 Whiting on the Wall 7c

A direct version of *Sturgeon* is high in the grade. Not a great route as it uses the polished footholds on *Sturgeon* as handholds.
*FA. Darren Hawkins 1995*

### 17 The Black Widow..... E1 5b

The big beefy corner that bounds the wall never gets done.
*FA. Tony Howard (aid) mid-1960s. FFA. Jim Campbell, Con Carey, Chris Addey 1976*

**18 Silence of the Clams** .. 7a
Up to and over the small fish-tail roof right of the corner. The final moves provide the main difficulties.
**Future Paradox, E3 6a** - take the right-hand side of the fish-tail to the same lower-off as *Clams*. Rarely done.
*FA. Gary Gibson, Doug Kerr 1991 FA. (FP) Richard Davies 1984*

**19 Over the Rainbow Trout** 6c+
A crooked line but with some good moves.
*FA. Gary Gibson 1987*

**20 Night of the Guppy** . 7b
The sustained bulges just left of the big hanging corner give a short, but power-packed, pitch. It has shed some holds and is now high in the grade.
*FA. Gary Gibson 1988*

**21 The Red Spider** . . . . . . . . E3 5c
The steep and neglected hanging groove to a grotty exit.
*FA. Tony Howard (aid) mid-1960s. FFA. Gabe Regan, Jim Moran, John Regan 1976*

**22 Lamprey on Ice** . . . . . . . . 7a+
A poor eliminate squeezed up the rib right of *Guppy*. Undercut right across the initial roof to a rest, then pull back left and continue steeply.
*FA. Gary Gibson 1999*

**23 The Zander Welfare Club** 7b
A steep line up the wall right of the groove. Climb through the bulge to better holds then move up right to a jug. Stand on this then continue to the roof and pull over to the lower-off. The rock near the bottom is slightly dodgy.
*FA. Gary Gibson 1987*

**24 Red Snapper Meets the Dog Fish**
. . . . . . . . . . . . . . . . . . . 7a+
A unlikely-looking climb up the left-hand side of the steep bulging recess. In the end there is only the one hard pull but the rest is still uphill.
*FA. Gary Gibson 1999. The lower bulge was the aid route The Web.*

**25 Name That Tuna** . . 7b+
The enticing groove above the right-hand side of the recess is very hard to reach. Once there, the bolts leads up the left sidewall more easily to the lower-off. The old finish was the groove.
*Formerly an aid route.1960s. FFA. Chris Hamper 1988.*
*FA. (New finish) Gary Gibson 1999*

Sturgeon in the Cupboard - p.155

North — Southwest — Southeast — Stoney — Horseshoe — Smalldale — Harpur Hill — Lovers' Leap — Beerhouse — Craig-y-Biceps — Staden Q — Chee Dale U. — Che Dale L. — Blackwell D. — Raven Tor — Water-c-Jolly — Ravensdale — Aldery Cliff — Taddington — Rheinstor

**㉖ Garfish Serenade** . . . . . 🔒 📷 ☐ **7a+**
An eliminate up the rib right of *Name That Tuna*. The initial wall is hard and often dynamic. Higher up it needs a fingery pull.
*FA. Gary Gibson 1999*

**㉗ The Open Secret** . . 🔆 📷 ☐ **E5 6b**
The impressive hanging groove is desperate to enter past a bolt runner. It is likely that the rock needs care since it sees few ascents these days.
*FA. Dave Lee, Mike Raine 1983. Previously aided.*

**㉘ Fragile Earth** . . . . . . . 📷 🔒 ☐ **E5 6b**
An unlikely looking and rarely repeated line following some thin flakes to the right of the groove of *Open Secret*.
*FA. Dave Lee, Mark Pretty 1983*

**㉙ Something Fishy** . . . . . 📷 🔒 ☐ **7c**
The desperate fingery wall just left of the ivy shroud.
*FA. Danny Brooks 1992*

*The right-hand section of the buttress is almost always gloomy and shaded by trees hence it is slow to dry. However it can be cool in hot weather. The ivy is starting to take over.*

**㉚ Fishing Without a Licence**
. . . . . . . . . . . . . 🔆 📷 🔒 ☐ **7c**
Good technical climbing up through the short hanging scoop which is hard for most of its length. The route needs traffic to keep the ivy at bay.
*FA. Alan Doig, Mike Radcliffe 1989*

**㉛ Barefoot in a Pool of Sharks**
. . . . . . . . . . . . . 🔆 📷 🔒 ☐ **7b+**
An excellent route which deserves more traffic. The bulge is hard but above that a reachy move and a hard rock-over provide the major difficulties.
*FA. Gary Gibson 1987*

**㉜ Kiss the Mackerel** . 🔆 🔒 ☐ **7c**
A short and desperate route. The initial bulge is awkward and above that comes a reach that stops many.
*FA. Gary Gibson 1999*

**㉝ The Life of a Stickleback** 📷 🔒 ☐ **7b+**
Another short, desperate route starting up the slope. Use a jug to start a horrendous sequence up the technical wall.
*FA. Gary Gibson 1987*

**㉞ Minnows as a Substitute for White Bait**
. . . . . . . . . . . . . . . . . 🔆 ✂ ☐ **6c**
A curious traverse along the top break which gives an entertaining pitch (and useful for sneaking a quick look at the harder routes). There are two bolts then clip the lower-offs on the other routes. Finish at the lower-off of *Fishing*....
*FA. Gary Gibson 1999*

## Max Wall

This popular buttress has experienced several waves of activity over the years to leave a good wall of solid rock with some decent routes. On the left-hand side, *Max Headroom* and *The Max Works* are two of the more popular sport routes in Chee Dale. The right-hand side turns a bit nasty with steep and powerful starts over the bulges.

**Approach (also see page 146) -** From the Monsal Trail on the Chee Dale Upper Approach, drop down before the first tunnel). Walk under the Embankment and drop down to the river and continue for 100m.

**Conditions -** It suffers from seepage but when dry will give sheltered and mostly shady (tree-covered) climbing in light rain. It can be okay in dry winter spells.

*Up the bank on the left are a couple of short and pretty poor sport routes. The sloping take-off doesn't help.*

**① Mix and Match.** . . . . . . . . . . . . ☐ 6a
The left-hand line part-way up the bank.
*FA. Gary Gibson 2003*

**② Maximum Potential** . . . . . . . . ☐ 6a
The right-hand line.
*FA. Gary Gibson 2003*

*The dirty corner is* **Maxi, HVS 5a.**

**③ Pepsi Max.** . . . . . . . . . . . 🔖 ☐ 6c+
The bolts just right of the corner. The roof is awkward to cross and has some very worrying large blocks in it. Avoid.
*FA. Gary Gibson, Simon Rice 1999*

**④ Max Factor** . . . . . . . . . . . . ⚝ ☐ E2 5b
A good little trad route up the wall between the two bolt-lines. The crux is probably placing the second wire. At the roof step right and continue up to the tree.
*FA. Gary Gibson, Phil Gibson, Hazel Carnes 1982*

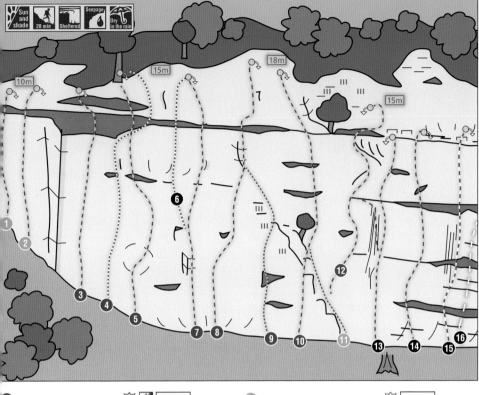

**5** **Max Head Room** . . . . . 🔄 ✏️ [ ] **7a**
A popular route with some hard moves in the middle section.
The bolts are in a straight line but the moves snake around a bit.
FA. Gary Gibson 1986

**6** **Max Wall** . . . . . . . . . 🔄 🐦 [ ] **E5 6a**
A bold wall climb which sees few ascents. Start just right of the
cable and climb into a hanging corner. Tackle the thin wall above
whilst ignoring the bolts to the right.
FFA. Gary Gibson 1979. FA. Gabriel Reagan (1 rest - on what?) 1976.

**7** **Max Pax 'em In** . . . . . . 🔄 🐦 [ ] **7a**
The direct version of Max Wall with bolts.
FA. Gary Gibson 2003

**8** **Max 'is Wall** . . . . . . . . 🔄 🐦 [ ] **6c**
A popular route with one hard move past the second bolt. At the
top, move right to a fine finish on the upper wall.
FA. Keith Sharples, Graham Hoey 1985. FA. (Finish) Gary Gibson 1999

**9** **Lunatic Fringe** . . . . . . . 🔄 🐦 [ ] **6c+**
Gain the diagonal vegetated ramp via a boulder problem start.
Follow it for a move or two then finish up Max 'is Wall.
**Black Max - E1 5b.** The ramp all the way, never gets done.
FA. Richard Davies (solo) 1985. FA. (BM) Jim Moran, L.Holmes 1977

**10** **Max Pact** . . . . . . . . . . 🔄 🐦 [ ] **6b**
Start by pulling through a small bulge to gain the ramp. Wander
up onto cleaner rock above to finish in a small groove.
FA. Gary Gibson 1985

**11** **Max Pact Indirect** . . . . . . . 🔄 [ ] **6a+**
Starting up the ramp gives a popular easier route.
FA. Gary Gibson 1985

**12** **The Max Works** . . . . . . 🔄 ✏️ [ ] **6c+**
A fine route which is high in the grade and popular too. Start
from the ramp, then move right and up to the bulge. Move past
this then stretch right to an overlap. Finish straight up.
FA. Gary Gibson 1983

**13** **Max to the Wall** . . . 🔄 ✏️ 🐦 [ ] **7a+**
A direct line up the green streak and then right over the bulge to
a lower-off. Good climbing.
**Incandescent Courage, E6 6a -** The original route here was a
direct start to The Max Works taking a line left of Max to the Wall.
FA. Gary Gibson 1985 using bolts on the right. New bolts shortly after.
FA. (IC) Richard Davies (solo after practice) 1986

**14** **Max-a-Million** . . . . . . . 🔄 ⫿ [ ] **7b**
Hard to grade; the crux reach is straightforward for the very tall
(7a or less) but for average people it is a desperate dyno. There
is a short person's method as well which is also 7b using some
miserable little holds.
FA. Gary Gibson 1985

**15** **Afterlife** . . . . . . . . . . 🔄 🐦 [ ] **E6 6b**
No gear and plenty of hard moves to the break, then a couple of
threads before a hard finish. Often top-roped, seldom led.
FA. Richard Davies (solo after practice) 1983

North | Southwest | Southeast | Stoney | Horseshoe | Smalldale | Harpur Hill | Lovers Leap | Beerhouse | Craig-y-Biceps | Staden Q | Chee Dale U. | Che Dale L. | Blackwell D. | Raven Tor | Water-c-Jolly | Ravensdale | Aldery Cliff | Taddington | Rheinstor

**16 Maxonomy** ...... 🎲 🔋 🏃 ☐ 7a+
A barely independent route which uses holds on both adjacent lines. At the break pull straight over and finish with a hard move to reach the belay.
*FA. Gary Gibson 1991*

**17 Max Museum** .... 🎲 🔋 🔫 ☐ 7b
The unlikely-looking bulges require a determined sequence of pulls on some unhelpful, but just sufficient, holds and pockets.
*FA. Gary Gibson, Richard Davies 1985*

**18 Maxwell House** ... 🎲 🔋 🏃 ☐ 7b+
Steep and powerful moves are required to make your way past the bulges and two bolts. At the break move right around the top bulge. A hard second clip.
*FA. Chris Wright 1991*

**19 Rough Justice** .. 🎲 🔋 🏃 🔫 ☐ 7c
The direct to the finish of *Maxwell House*. Complex moves.
*FA. Keith Sharples 1991*

**20 A Bigger Max** .. 🎲 🔋 🏃 🔫 ☐ 7b+
A desperate fingery series of moves. Both bulges are hard and, if you miss the second clip, you may end up in the drink.
*FA. Gary Gibson 1985*

**21 The Max They Love To Hate** 🔫 ☐ 7b
A fingery and technical set of bulges.
*FA. Gary Gibson 1991*

**22 Dream Thief** ....... 🔫 🏃 ☐ 7a+
A boulder problem start over the first bulge leads to another bulge and another hard move. Above this, move left to find the lower-off on *The Max They Love To Hate*.
*FA. Richard Davies (solo after practice) 1986*

⊝ **Access (all routes to the right of** *Dream Thief***)** - *Avoid these routes when the stepping stones are required by walkers.*

*The vegetated scoop is the start of* **Orgasimus Maximus, HVS 5a.**

**23 Tyrannosaurus Max** ...... 🎲 ☐ E3 5c
An entertaining route around the left-hand side of the big roof starting from the 12th stepping stone.
*FA. Gary Gibson 1985*

**24 Let the Max Increase** .. 👟 🔋 ☐ 7b
The centre of the roof moving left past 4 bolts to a tree. The direct finish is **Krankius Maximus, 7b+**, no lower-off.
*FA. Gary Gibson 1991. FA. (KM) Mark Pretty 2011*

**25 Maxing Around** ...... 👟 🔋 ☐ 7a+
The next line of bolts over the wide roof.
*FA. Gary Gibson 1991*

**26 Maximuscle** ...... 🎲 👟 🔋 ☐ 7b+
The final line. You need to reverse aid it to get the gear.
*FA. Mark Pretty 2011*

## The Nook

A small buttress with some steep and hard neglected sport routes that are not often in condition.

**Approach (also see page 146) -** From the Monsal Trail on the Chee Dale Upper Approach, drop down before the first tunnel, walk past the Embankment and Max Buttress and along the stepping stones. Once back on land, walk on for another 200m (Nettle Buttress to your right, across the river) to the crag on the left.

**Conditions -** It suffers from bad seepage but when dry gives sheltered shady (tree-covered) climbing even in light rain.

*To the left of the cave is a scrappy wall with three poor trad routes; all about E2 and with dodgy names.*

**❶ The Dukes of Earl (Grey)** 🦺❘ ⬜ **7c**
The bolt-line starting at the foot of the slope. The bulge requires a long reach and some good foot work.
*FA. Keith Sharples 1994*

**❷ Michael Foot Jam** . ⛺🦺🆒 ⬜ **7c+**
The left-hand side of the main roofs. A powerful climb where the obvious clue is in the route name and the crux move involves using a sloper.
*FA. Chris Plant 1989*

**❸ A Cure for Arapiles.** . . . . . . . . ⬜ **(7b)**
The central line was originally climbed using a big block which has since fallen off. It awaits a reascent.
*FA. Gary Gibson, Adam Hudson 1985*

**❹ Santiano.** . . . . . . . . . . 🆒🆒 ⬜ **E5 6a**
Totally neglected these days but a fine effort in its day. The line goes over the widest section of the roof via a niche. The gear is mostly the old pegs placed over 3 decades ago.
*FA. Tom Proctor, Chris Gore 1979. Previously aided.*

**❺ Rock Umbrella.** . . . . ⛺🆒🦺 ⬜ **7b**
A savage roof test-piece with old gear. Climb up to a thin crack in the roof and finish standing at the lip. Connecting these two positions is somewhat tricky.
*FA. Daniel Lee 1982. A free version of the aid route 'The Storm'.*

**❻ The Storm.** . . . . . . ⛺🆒🦺 ⬜ **7b+**
Yet more steep roof work just right of *Rock Umbrella*. The trick here is connecting the 2 jugs, one halfway across the roof and one at the lip.
*FA. Jerry Moffatt 1982. Climbed before the previous route was freed so for a time there were 2 'Storms' albeit for a few days only.*

**❼ A Bit of Nooky** . . . . ⛺🦺🆒 ⬜ **8a+**
Now things start getting really tricky. Super-steep moves lead up to a hard move past a bolt. Slap out right to a jug then climb straight up by yet more hard moves to the lower-off.
*FA. Mark Pretty 1989*

**❽ The Lockless Monster** ⛺❘ 🆒 ⬜ **7c+**
The best of the hard routes. Climb a steep wall to the roof and cross this on good holds to a stopper move. Success here accesses a small niche, pull out left to finish. Used to be the most flashed 8a in the Peak.
*FA. John Hart 1989*

**❾ Theoria.** . . . . . . . . ⛺🦺🆒 ⬜ **8a+**
An excellent route with moves suited to those who have been campusing. The desperate start is often by-passed by using the tree. Above this, gaining a good hold in the niche on *Lockless* is hard. Finishing out left has also been known to spit people off.
*FA. John Hart 1989. FA. (Start) Ben Moon 1989.*

**❿ There's Life in the Old Log Yet**
. . . . . . . . . . . . . . . ⛺🦺🆒 ⬜ **7c**
The short but hideously steep wall right of the tree. No rests in the tree are allowed and it may be harder than 7c.
*FA. Mark Pretty 1993*

*Further right are a few more bouldery trad routes before the wall deteriorates to nothing.*

North
Southwest
Southeast
Stoney
Horseshoe
Smalldale
Harpur Hill
Lovers' Leap
Beehouse
Craig-y-Biceps
Staden Q
Chee Dale U.
Che Dale L.
Blackwell D.
Raven Tor
Water-c-Jolly
Ravensdale
Aldery Cliff
Taddington
Rheinstor

## Nettle Buttress

The name doesn't inspire, but the buttress is worth a visit in hot weather. *Summer Wine* is the classic route but the powerful *Stung* receives more attention.

**Conditions -** The crag dries slowly but is sheltered and cool in hot weather. The base gets thick with vegetation.

**Approach (also see page 146) -** From the Monsal Trail on the Chee Dale Upper Approach, drop down under the Embankment before the first tunnel. Continue over the stepping stones until the crag appears on the right on the other side of the river. Wade across to it. The same point can also be reached from the Chee Dale Lower approach. Do not form a path up the opposite bank of the river which would disturb the vegetation.

**Access -** This buttress is in the wildlife reserve managed by Derbyshire Wildlife Trust. Only use the described approach and do not walk along the crag base further than the described routes.

*There are some old routes to the left of here but these have been debolted and should now be avoided.*

**❶ Snail Mail.** . . . . . . . . . . . . . . . 6b
A disjointed route up the sidewall with a steep little start.
FA. Gary Gibson 1998

**❷ Harmonious Harmonica** . . . . . . 6c
A very poor climb up the arete.
FA. Gary Gibson 1998

**❸ Symmetrical Systems** . . . . . . . 6b
The left-hand side of the scoop is steeper than it looks.
FA. Hazel Gibson, Gary Gibson 1998

**❹ Balanced Ballistics** . . . . . . 6b
The right-hand side of the scoop to a blind finish.
FA. Gary Gibson 1983. Bolted in 1998

**❺ Suryanamasker** . . . . . . . . . . . E5 6b
The hanging groove has yet to be tidied up.
FA. Keith Sharples 1984

**❻ Long Dead Train** . . 7b
The rounded arete gives a good fingery route starting from *Suryanamasker*. The direct start is a hard problem making the route a bold-feeling 7b+.
FA. Gary Gibson 1998

**❼ Stuffed Badger.** . . . . E5 6b
A *technical* pitch up the blank wall, past a bolt, to the big groove which has adequate protection. Start from *Suryanamasker* for the original route but the bouldery direct is more famous and better.
**Brock the Start, V8** (and **E6 6c**) - a mini-classic of the '80s.
FA. Jerry Moffatt 1982

**❽ Summer Wine** . . . . . E5 6a
A recently cleaned classic. The upper wall is usually reached from the block on the right (although there is a desperate direct at 6b). Above that it gives pumpy, scary climbing - old skool E4. There is a right-hand finish past a bolt which is **The Eve Syndrome, E5 6c**.
FA. Dave Lee, Neil Foster, Tim Freeman 1983. FA. (ES) Malc Taylor 1989

**❾ First Light** . . . . . . . . . E2 5b
Good balancy climbing up the vague ramp-line starting from the top of the block. Unaffected by more recent additions.
FA. Gabriel Reagan 1976

**❿ Epidavros** . . . . . . . . . . . . 6b+
A good counter diagonal to *First Light* with two tricky sections split by a good rest. The nervous might want a wire for the section shared with *First Light*.
FA. Gary Gibson 1982. Bolted in 1998

**⓫ Light Ideas** . . . . . . . . . 6c
The line of glue-ins before the corner is much steeper than it looks and is really fiddly near the top with few positive holds.
FA. Gary Gibson 1998

**⓬ Stravandrabellagola** 7b
The left-hand side of the roof. One powerful snatch on the lip for the tall, the rest move left and heel-hook the lip at 7b+.
FA. Gary Gibson 1998

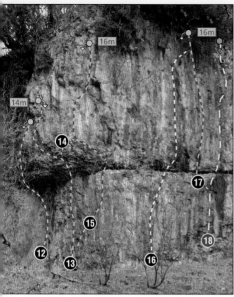

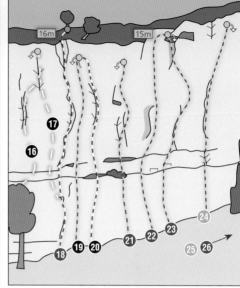

### ⑬ Esmerelda .... ⬛🔲🔲🔲🔲 7b+
Start under the widest part of the roof and follow the pillar to the break. Make a series of large spans (or powerful moves) between decent holds to a jug on the lip. Span left and climb the hanging groove (still very uphill) to the lower-off.
*FA. Mike Lea 1998. Originally Quasimodo, A3.*

### ⑭ Esmerunga ...... 🔲🔲🔲🔲 7c
Up *Esmerelda* to the good jug on the lip. Move up and right as for *Stung*. The hardest (and best?) way up the buttress.
*FA. Ed Brown 2008*

### ⑮ Stung ............ 🔲🔲🔲 7b+
Start as for *Esmerelda*, but trend right to the break and a rest on the right. Traverse strenuously back left along the lip then up to gain a stuck-on hold in a faint groove. Fight back right from this (moving low is a cop-out!) to follow the large flake to the belay. Phew! Some of it was climbed before by **Major Incontinence** which passes the lone bolt on the right at **E5 6c**.
*FA. Gary Gibson 1998. FA. (MI) Dave Pegg 1988*

*The final, and easiest line up the buttress is **Ouch, 7b+**. Start as for Stung and follow this route leftwards to finish up Esmerelda.*

### ⑯ General Incompetance . 🔲🔲🔲 E7 6b
The slim groove on the right-hand side of the wall gives this route which was well ahead of its time in 1984. There is some fixed gear but it must be of dubious worth now. Lower-off *Toys*...
*FA. Dougie Hall 1984. Retrobolted briefly but the bolts were removed immediately to preserve one of the few E7s on limestone.*

### ⑰ Toys for the Boys ... 🔲🔲🔲🔲 7c+
A fine route that now sees plenty of traffic. Climb the wall left of the corner of *No Light*.
*FA. Chris Gore 1994*

### ⑱ No Light ........... 🔲🔲🔲 E3 5c
An excellent trad route up the corner. Much pumpier than it looks with the crux at the top. Becoming vegetated.
*FA. Gabriel Reagan 1976*

### ⑲ Subterra ........... 🔲🔲🔲 7b
Climb the fingery pillar to a technical finish.
*FA. Gary Gibson 2002*

### ⑳ Terra Incognita ...... 🔲🔲🔲 E5 6b
A steep and attractive line up the scoops in the wall. Destined to become a neglected relic but as good as the others here.
*FA. Dave Lee 1983*

### ㉑ Gobblin' Women ........ 🔲🔲 6b+
The steep wall and groove above a hard start.
*FA. Gary Gibson 1999*

### ㉒ Little Girl Eater/Fish-u-Like.... 🔲 6b
Climb past the flying fin and up a short, slabby wall.
*FA. Dave Knighton 1976. FA. (Direct start and bolts) Gary Gibson 1999*

### ㉓ Fishlock ........... 🔲🔲 6b+
The middle scoop-line. Dirty at the bottom and precarious in the middle but with a nice move or two.
*FA. Gary Gibson 1998*

### ㉔ Kakaho ................. 🔲 6a+
The slightly larger groove-line is an easier proposition with just one tricky move near the top.
*FA. Gary Gibson 1998*

### ㉕ Cock-a-hoop ............. 🔲 6a
Up a short groove to a headwall.
*FA. Gary Gibson, Jim Burton 2002*

### ㉖ Bursting Out ........ 🔲🔲 6c
A fingery, white scoop, finishing leftwards.
*FA. Gary Gibson 2002*

Up the slope is another buttress with four routes on it;
**Magician's Enemy, 6b - Birthday Boy, 7b+ - Pulsar, 7a - War Locks, 6c+**. *It can also be reached from the left side of Two Tier Buttress.*

North | Southwest | Stoney | Horseshoe | Smalldale | Harpur Hill | Lovers' Leap | Beerhouse | Craig-y-Biceps | Staden Q | Chee Dale U. | Che Dale L. | Blackwell D. | Raven Tor | Water-c-Jolly | Ravensdale | Aldery Cliff | Taddington | Rheinstor

## Two Tier - Left

The tall left-hand side of Two Tier Buttress contains some great long sport routes. The far left-hand side is becoming somewhat overgrown but the main Open Gate Wall has some fine rock above the break. Several eliminates and filler-in routes have been added around the long corner of *Thoth*.

**Approach (also see page 146) -** From the Monsal Trail on the Chee Dale Upper Approach, drop down under the Embankment to the river. A short distance down-stream is a crossing point. It has stepping stones when the river is low, but often needs wading.

**Conditions -** This side of Two Tier dries quite quickly but it can still have crucial damp patches into the summer. It receives the evening sun, is well-sheltered and cool in hot weather.

*The first routes are on the barrel-shaped wall up and left of the main section. It is reached by a tricky scramble up leftwards. The first route on this wall is - Home from Home, E5 6b.*

**❶ Another Brick in the Wall** . . . 7b+
The left-hand bolt line. The second bolt is twinned.
*FA. Keith Sharples 1990*

**❷ Osher, Osher, Osher** . . . . . . 7a+
Tackle the lower bulge from the right. Finish at a tree. There is a project to the right.
*FA. Gary Gibson 1985*

**❸ The Bride and the Groom** . . 6c+
After the bulging start, things get easier above.
*FA. Chris Wright 1990*

**❹ The Burqa King** . . . . . . . . 7b
Another steep start then the undulating wall above.
*FA. Gary Gibson 2000s*

**❺ The Incredible Pierre** . . 7a+
From the right-hand end of the ledge, move up and make hard moves to gain a tricky slab finish.
*FA. Gary Gibson 1985*

**❻ Short Sharp Shock** . 7c
Desperate technical climbing which keeps shedding holds. The current best line is to move right after the 3rd bolt on the headwall, into *Poor Dill*. You could move back left above this at hard 7c, or try and climb direct at an artificial 7c+.
*FA. Dave Pegg 1987*

**❼ Poor Dill** . . . 7c
Good climbing past a glued-on hold. A long left arm helps and it is easier for the tall.
*FA. Gary Gibson 1999. Named in memory of Gary's dog.*

**❽ Open Gate** . . . . . Top50 7a+
A superb route which, despite being rebolted, is still a scary proposition. The lower crack is straightforward but the upper wall proves taxing for its whole length with a particularly testing fingery rock-over. Many will find the final run-out worthy of E5 (it used to be a bit longer, and above a hand-placed bolt).
*FA. Gary Gibson 1985*

**❾ Case Adjourned** . . . 7a
A great climb, again with a final scary run-out which may make it feel like an E5. After a fingery start, continue more easily to the break. Crank upwards to the final bolt, chalk your hands up and go - right has more holds but straight up has a good flake.
*FA. Gary Gibson 1985. Gary also added the direct start in 1999.*

**❿ Smelting Point** . . . . . . . . . 6c
A poor route when compared to its neighbours. Climb straight up the left-hand side of the open groove of *Thoth*, then span out left. Continue artificially up the left-hand arete to the break. The upper wall requires a hard fingery left-hand pull. Move up to the belay without touching the crack on the right.
*FA. Gary Gibson, Phil Gibson 1982 as Melting Point. Direct start and finish added in 1999 and the whole route renamed.*

**⓫ Thoth** . . . . . . . . . . . . . . . . . . E1 5b
Two pitches up the lower corner and upper flake.
**1)** 5b, 15m. The corner to the break. Move right to belay.
**2)** 5a, 15m. Follow the big flake to the lower-off on *Melting Pot*.
*FFA. Paul Nunn, Mike Richardson 1965*
*FA. Paul Nunn, Oliver Woolcock (aid) 1964*

**⓬ Cockerel Cry** . . . . . . . . 6c+
Climb directly up the line right of the corner, over two bulging sections, finishing high on the buttress.
*FA. Gary Gibson 2001*

**⓭ Jackson's Browned Off** . . . . 6c
A short route up the wall above the raised ledge. Clip the first bolt (tricky) then swing out right and up before stepping back left to an undercut flake. Direct to this point is an artificial 6c+. Move past the flake and continue to a thread lower-off.
**Running on Empty, E5 6a** - A bold solo up the wall right of *Jackson's*, to the small grass ledge above and right.
*FA. Gary Gibson 1999. FA. (RoE) Ron Fawcett 1981*

*The next three routes start from a belay on a small grass ledge which is best reached by Jackson's Browned Off. The rock on this wall is a little crusty and these routes have regularly lost holds.*

**⓮ Just Pullet** . . . . . . . . . 7a+
The upper wall above *Systems Malfunction* has a barn-door crux move to a huge hold. (Hint: this route was constructed by a tall person).
*FA. Gary Gibson 1999*

**⓯ Evidently Chickentown** . 7c
The desperate wall and thin crack. Climb left of the bolts above the break, then move right. The star is for the position, not the quality of the climbing.
*FA. Gary Gibson 1999*

**⓰ Poultry in Motion** . . . . . . . . 7b+
Move right from the belay and attack the bulge.
*FA. Gary Gibson 2001*

From wading point on the river

North | Southwest | Southeast | Stoney | Horseshoe | Smalldale | Harpur Hill | Lovers' Leap | Beerhouse | Craig-y-Biceps | Staden Q | Chee Dale L. | Chee Dale U. | Blackwell D. | Water-c-Jolly | Ravensdale | Aldery Cliff | Taddington | theImstor | Raven Tor

North
Southwest
Southeast
Stoney
Horseshoe
Smalldale
Harpur Hill
Lovers' Leap
Beeehouse
Craig-y-Biceps
Staden Q.
Chee Dale U.
Chee Dale L.
Blackwell D.
Raven Tor
Water-cum-Jolly
Ravensdale
Aldery Cliff
Teddington
Rheinstor

**❶ Mega-Bites** . . . . . . . . 🗲 ▢ **7b**
The powerful roof left of *Systems Malfunction*.
FA. Gary Gibson 2001

**❷ Systems Malfunction** . . 🗲 ▢ **7b**
The roof on the left side of the wall is a hard problem. It is easy to reach but turning the lip proves to be extremely taxing and the short will have the last laugh.
FA. Gary Gibson 1985

**❸ Titter ye Not** . . . . . 🗲 ▢ **8a**
A desperate roof problem which is slow to dry. Climb the open scoop (of *Offal*) and turn the lip by a variety of poor holds, slaps and knee-bars. Proceed to the lower-off.
**Offal, E3 6a -** The original wandering line through the roofs.
FA. Lucien Cottle 1990. FA. (Offal) Phil Gibson, Gary Gibson 1982

**❹ Waffle** . . . . . . . . . . . ▢ **7b+**
A desperate direct line through *Offal*. The crux roof (above a hands-off rest) requires some nasty moves.
FA. Gary Gibson 1999

**❺ Malnutrition** . . . . . ▢ **E4 6a**
A good trad route with two contrasting sections. Start up the left-hand of two red grooves (the right-hand one is a 6b direct start) then move right. Climb the wall, then make a bold pull over the roof. Move up and left to a tree belay.
**Ghee Force, E4 6b -** Direct above the starting groove, past a bolt.
FA. Gabe Reagan, Jim Reading 1976. FA. (GF) Simon Lee 1991

**❻ Split Infinitive** . . . . ▢ **E5 6c**
The best line of the various grooves and corners on this bit of wall is spoilt by having some hideously difficult climbing and it is seldom attempted. Climb the groove all the way to the roof, pull right past a thread and up into the trees.
**Isolate, E4 6b -** The left-hand start to *Split Infinitive* was the first route on this section.
**Nerefaun, E5 6c -** *The first attempt to climb the corner ended in an escape rightwards up the rounded arete.*
FA. Richard Davies 1985. FA. (Isolate) Gabe Reagan, Al Evans 1976
FA. (Nerefaun) Richard Davies 1984

## Two Tier - Centre
This wall probably contains the best quality rock in the Dale; clean and compact with only a few loose patches. It has sport routes from 6c to 8b and a few excellent trad challenges, less seepage than other buttresses and is shady until late afternoon in summer.
**Approach (also see page 146) -** From the Monsal Trail on the Chee Dale Upper Approach, drop down under the Embankment to the river. A short distance down-stream is a crossing point. It has stepping stones when the river is low, but often needs wading.
**Conditions -** The compact rock on this area dries out more quickly than the walls to the left. It is the first section to catch the evening sun and is well-sheltered and cool.

**7 Stogumber Club...** 🔲🔲🔲 **7c**
Fingery and technical. Once at the break, traverse right to *Entrée* and continue up this to the lower-off.
*FA. Richie Patterson 1996*

**8 Entrée** ...... 🔲🔲🔲🔲 **8a**
A superb little boulder problem with some very fingery moves. Passing the first two bolts provides the meat of the route. Lower off at the very top or jump off after the hard bit.
*FA. Chris Gore 1990*

**9 Kali Yuga** ..... 🔲🔲🔲🔲 **8b**
An immaculate hard route on perfect rock. It is now finished direct with the addition of a new belay.
*FA. Rupert Davies 2003*

**10 Countdown** ...... 🔲🔲🔲 **7a+**
A great climb on perfect rock which is one of the best sport routes in the Dale. The move off a pocket, above the bulge, proves to be a stopper for some, especially those who are a little on the short side. A wire or two might help on the final section.
*FA. Ron Fawcett 1981. Bolted by Gary Gibson in 2002, at the same time as Darl, with respect to the positions of the original gear.*

**11 Darl - Pitch 1** ...... 🔲🔲🔲 **7a**
A classic route from the '70s which gives a great companion to *Countdown*. The bouldery wall leads to a hanging groove where a poor rest is possible. Move back left and up to the lower-off. A wire might help. Pitch 2 is described with the Upper Tier.
*FA. Gabriel Reagan, Al Evans 1976. Both pitches were climbed but a point of aid was used on P2. P1 was harder than most things around at the time.*

**12 Why Me?** ....... 🔲🔲🔲 **7c**
Extremely powerful climbing up the wall right of *Darl* with a thuggish crux. The initial wall is hard enough but at the bulge it really starts to pack a punch.
*FA. Gary Gibson (1 point of aid) 1986*

**13 Orange Sunshine** .. 🔲🔲🔲 **7c+**
A milestone which is an 'old style' sport route with regard to the bolting. The tricky lower wall leads to a poor undercut above the second bolt. Make a couple of desperate moves upwards to a good slot. Finish left into *Why Me?* To the right is an old project with pegs in it.
*FA. Bob Dearman, G.Riley (aid) 1970. FFA. (P1) Jerry Moffatt 1984. P2 awaits a free ascent. Bob Dearman promised free beer for life to the first person to do this. Take a look before you decide to accept the challenge.*

**14 Boring** .............. 🔲🔲 **7c**
A poor route which avoids the main difficulties by slinking into the base of *Ninth Life*.
*FA. Seb Grieve 1990*

20m

16m

7   8   9   10   11   12   13   14

**From wading point over the river**

**Access -** This buttress is in the wildlife reserve managed by Derbyshire Wildlife Trust. Only use the described approach and do not walk along the crag base further than the described routes.

North | Southwest | Southeast | Stoney | Horseshoe | Smalldale | Harpur Hill | Lovers Leap | Beerhouse | Craig-y-Biceps | Staden Q | Chee Dale L | Chee Dale U. | Blackwell D. | Raven Tor | Water-c-Jolly | Ravensdale | Aldery Cliff | Taddington | Rheinstor

North
Southwest
Southeast
Stoney
Horseshoe
Smalldale
Harpur Hill
Lovers' Leap
Beerhouse
Craig-y-Biggs
Staden Q
Chee Dale U.
Che Dale L.
Blackwell D.
Raven Tor
Water-c-Jolly
Ravensdale
Aldery Cliff
Taddington
Rheinstor

### ⑮ Ninth Life . . . . . . . ☒ 🪝 ▦ [ ] E7 6c

The slanting groove is one of the few really hard trad routes on Peak Limestone. Rarely climbed, it remains an important tick for the aspiring. The hard lower wall (the 6c bit) is protected by wires in the break and the bolt on *Boring*. Above this, only tenacity and a will to survive will get you to the top. There is a wire to aim for, and a good skyhook, but there is a ground-fall to worry about before you reach it.

*FA. Jonny Woodward 1982. Named for Jerry Moffatt who used one of his lives when not quite making the first ascent by falling from the last moves.*

### ⑯ Daylight Robbery . . ☒ 🪝 ▯ [ ] 7b

It looks unlikely at the grade but once you get on it the climbing is good and the moves are surprisingly independent. Start by heading towards the groove of *Ra*, then hang-a-left onto the steeper section above, where it is easy to get lost and take a whipper. A long move enables the upper wall to be reached, teeter up this to the lower-off.

*FA. Chris Hardy 1989. The name refers to what happened to a sack of gear which was left at the bottom of the route.*

### ⑳ Rising Sap . . . . . . . . . . . 🪝 [ ] 6b+

A slightly artificial line to the left of the flake of *Osiris*. Either start direct (a hard but artificial **6c**) or more logically from *Osiris*. Climb the wall above trying to keep out of the corner but most put their right foot in it at least once.

**Osiris, E1 5a** - The flake/corner into the trees.
*FA. Gary Gibson 1999. FA. (Osiris) John Loy, Ernie Marshall 1971.*

*The next two routes are popular so expect a bit of polish. Originally they crossed each other and had better, more natural lines. You could swap the starts and finishes to recreate this.*

### ㉑ Subterfuge . . . . . . . . ☒ 🪝 [ ] 6b+

Start up the steep wall past a good hold. Continue with more hard moves and unhelpful holds up the upper rib; avoid the leftward temptations.
*FA. Gary Gibson 1998*

Evening | 20 min | Sheltered | Seepage | Dry in the rain

### ⑰ Ra . . . . . . . . . . . . . . . . . . [🪝] [ ] E4 6a

Less good than the line would suggest. Gain the hanging groove and layback up it to easy ground and the trees above.
*FFA. Jim Reading 1976. FA. G.Armstrong 1971*

### ⑱ The Cruise Brothers . . . ☒ [🪝] [ ] 7a+

A strenuous, sustained sequence of laybacks with some very demanding clips.
*FA. M.Farrar, Steve Brown 1987*

### ⑲ Some Coincidence . . . . 🪝 🪝 [ ] 7a+

The left-hand side of the compact wall. The middle section proves to be awkward to onsight with some insecure pulls on rounded holds. A bit too close to the loose arete near the top.
*FA. Gary Gibson 1986*

### ㉒ Quality Control . . . . . ☒ [🪝] [ ] 7a

Now climbed direct with two good sections. Start up a steep and technical wall and head for the groove, following this to the lower-off.
*FA. Gary Gibson 1985*

### ㉓ Nogads . . . . . . . ☒ 🪝 🪝 [🪝] [ ] 7b+

After a powerful start it relents to just technical and fingery climbing until the last move above an undercut shake. Finish direct using a sloper and gain the lower-off. Trending left into *Quality Control* before the last move is a good **7b**.
*FA. Martin Crocker 1988*

### ㉔ Blockhead . . . . . . . ☒ 🪝 🪝 [ ] 7b

The wall left of the scoop is one of the more popular routes here. Start from the right then climb direct up the rib.
*FA. Chris Wright 2002*

### 25 Reasons to be Cheerful 7b+
The open groove gives a difficult route. The bolts are to the right of the groove, as are most of the holds. It is unbalanced with one short hard section after an easy start.
*FA. Gary Gibson 1985*

### 26 The Inbetweenies..... 7a+
A steep but relatively straightforward start leads to an impasse at the bulge. Quick thinking is required here. Short but sweet.
*FA. Gary Gibson 1999*

*The next couple of routes are grassing over.*

### 27 Wot a Waste.......... 6c+
A short wall past a chunky ledge, with a frustrating crux.
*FA. Chris Gore 1982*

### 28 Tippers........... 6c+
A short and intense wall climb.
*FA. Gary Gibson 1999*

James Garden climbing *Aberration* (8a) - *page 172* - on Secteur Nadin. Photo: Christian Fox

North · Southwest · Southeast · Stoney · Horseshoe · Smalldale · Harpur Hill · Lovers' Leap · Beerhouse · Craig-y-Biceps · Staden Q · Chee Dale U. · Che Dale L. · Blackwell D. · Raven Tor · Water-c-Jolly · Ravensdale · Aldery Cliff · Taddington · Rheinstor

## Two Tier - Upper

This hanging garden of exposure is one of only two buttresses in the Peak which require an abseil approach to get to them. The setting is unique with a good set of hard routes in a spectacular position.

**Approach -** From the Two Tier Centre (page 166), follow the path under Secteur Nadin, around to the right, up and over the buttress to a small cave with abseil station.

**Descent -** Abseil from the new ab station but take great care since there may be people below. Derbyshire Wildlife Trust have requested that climbers don't abseil down the gully below *Sibser*.

**Access -** This buttress is in the wildlife reserve managed by Derbyshire Wildlife Trust. Only use the described approach and do not walk along the crag base further than the described routes.

12m

*Darl (pitch 1) p.167*

**❶ Laurels for Hardy . .　　7b+**
Way off to the left is a lone route. Start off the left end of the ledge (bolt belay). Climb over a tree to a break. Follow a scoop and the wall above rightwards to a lower off.
*FA. Chris Hardy 1992. Reclimbed by Alisdair Hannah in 1998 and named 'Far From the Madding Crowd' after a lot of holds had fallen off.*

**❷ In Tiers. . . . . . . . . . . . . .　　8b+**
A short desperate outing left of the groove of *Darl*.
*FA. Steve McClure 2009*

**❸ Darl - Pitch 2 . . . . .　　7a+**
A historic pitch which is more popular than it used to be due to extra bolts. Start up the crack then make hard moves past a blank section to the break. Finish up a groove.
*FFA. Kim Carrigan, Jerry Moffatt (with pre-clipped runners) 1981. In its present state Ian Dunn 1997. FA. Paul Nunn, Oliver Woolcock 1965*

*Breaking left out of Darl is an open project.*

**❹ Hardcore Junkie . .　　8b**
A desperate start leads to a jug and a rest. Make a hard fingery sequence up and left to the break. The final bulge is a little easier. It is also possible to do a right-hand start via the adjacent route at 8a+.
*FA. Alisdair Hannah 2002*

**❺ Welcome to my World .　　8a**
Excellent climbing. A reachy start gains the jug on *Hardcorejunkie*, then make a series of fingery moves up and right to gain the break. Finish up a short groove to the belay.
*FA. Mark Pretty 2009*

**From path right of Secteur Nadin**

After another desperate project are more routes on a wall below a large roof.

**6 The Curse of the Mummy**  8a
Formerly an E6 that lost holds including a big ledge. It has been rebolted and reclimbed. Finish up *A Vision of Loveliness*.
FA. Simon Nadin 1986

**7 A Vision of Loveliness** .  7c+
A good route but slightly spoilt by the amount of glue. A hard initial wall leads to a good rest. From here make a beautiful dynamic move and a frustrating crimpy move to finish.
FA. Ian Dunn 1999

**8 A Picture of Perfection** .  8a
The wall and bulge with a sneaky rest on the next route.
FA. Mark Pretty 2009

**9 The Sea is a Brown Paper Bag**
. . . . . . . . . . . . . . . . . .  7b+
A great route which is a top-end 7b+ and shorties may find it 7c. The initial wall is technical and the break gives only a poor rest. Steeper ground above leads to a final thin wall. A hard left-hand finish is **Recycled, 7c**.
FA. Simon Nadin 1986. FA. (Recycled) Mark Pretty 2009

**10 The Tier Drop X-plodes.**  7c+
Sustained and technical climbing with a great finish around the top roof. The lower wall has one hideous move on it using a nasty shallow mono.
FA. Simon Nadin 1986

**11 Reward** . . . . . . . . . . . .  7b
Excellent climbing. Climb the initial wall by a subtle sequence to gain the break and a semi-rest. The roof above proves awkward, but delights await for the tenacious - or lucky.
FA. Simon Cundy 1991

**12 Monster Mouse Resurgent** .  6c+
Start below the right-hand end of the roof. A low rock-over and a stretch at the top provide the difficulties. A pumpy warm up for the harder challenges to the left.
FA. Richard Davies 1986. Originally E5 but it was bolted in 1991.

**13 Aggrieved** . . . . . . . . . . . .  6c+
Start up *Monster Mouse..* and clip the first bolt, then move up right past 2 more bolts to the lower-off. An unbalanced route with a very hard crux sequence.
FA. Claudie Dunn 2000

**14 Sibser** . . . . . . . . . . . . . .  7b+
A short and technical wall .
**Disjointed Might, E5 6a** - A bold route to the left past a flake.
FA. Unknown. The name stands for 'Slmon's Bolts Someone Else's Route'.

**15 Communication Breakdown** .  7c+
Start up *Darl - Pitch 2* and traverse right, frantically at first till things ease before reaching a lower-off on *the Mummy*.
FA. Alisdair Hannah, Ian Dunn 1997

**16 Nervous Breakdown** . . .  7b+
Start up *Reward* then traverse left to the *Mummy*.
FA. Ian Dunn, Alaisdair Hannah 1996

**17 Total Breakdown** . . .  7c+
Mega; the biggest sport pitch in the Peak with 27 bolts and lots of pump. Follow *Communication Breakdown* then reverse *Nervous Breakdown* and finish up *Monster Mouse*.
FA. Gareth Parry 1999

North | Southwest | Southeast | Stoney | Horseshoe | Smalldale | Harpur Hill | Lovers' Leap | Beerhouse | Craig-y-Biceps | Staden Q | Chee Dale U | Che Dale L | Blackwell D. | Raven Tor | Water-c-ho;y | Ravensdale | Aldery Cliff | Taddington | Rheinstor

## Two Tier - Secteur Nadin

A tall buttress right of the bulk of Two Tier which takes its name from its main developer in the early 1980s when the routes here were amongst the hardest in the Dale. More routes have been added and many of the older lines have been tidied up.

**Approach** - See page 166.

**Conditions** - There can be seepage here but it is seldom a problem. It gets the evening sun and is sheltered.

**1 The Chicken Run** . . . . . . . 🗓️ [ ] **HVS 5a**
One of the better easy routes in the Dale with an nice finale.
**1)** 5a, 18m. Follow the corner and belay on a ledge on the left.
**2)** 5a, 15m. Originally it finished direct but the huge flake has fallen down. Instead, traverse right along the break in a good position and pull up into the trees. Abseil off.
FA. Tony Howard, Tony Nicholls, John Amatt 1964

**2 A Rooster in the Hen House** 🗓️ [ ] **6b+**
A long, wandering pitch which has a few worthwhile moments. Start just right of *Chicken Run* and make difficult moves up the initial wall to a short pillar. Easier climbing follows then move right and make long moves up a clean wall to the lower-off.
FA. Jim Burton 2002

**3 Goldfinger** . . . . . . . . . 🗓️ 🖐️ [ ] **E2 6a**
Unbalanced with a hard start. Make a hard pull past bolts and head up a big flake. Step left to another flake and climb to the break. Move right past the bulge to the lower-off of *Rooster*.
FFA. Jim Campbell 1976. FA. Jeff Morgan, Bob Toogood (2pts) 1970

**4 The Flight of Icarus** . . . 🗓️ 🖐️ [ ] **E6 6b**
An excellent but imposing route which sees few ascents. Start up *Goldfinger*. Above the second bolt move slightly right and up a short groove to a good hold and runners. Traverse right to a small roof, a rest and good gear. Pass this via a flake on its left and climb up to the bulges (good cam). Cross these with difficulty to a lower-off.
FA. Simon Nadin, Richard Davies 1984

🚫 **Access** - This buttress is in the wildlife reserve managed by Derbyshire Wildlife Trust. Only use the described approach and do not walk along the crag base further than the described routes.

**5 Aberration** . . . . . . 🗓️ 🖐️ 🐦 [ ] **8a**
A long diagonal pitch (30m) with some good climbing. Low in the grade. Start up *Goldfinger* to the second bolt. Traverse right into the semi-rest of *Minos*. Continue right via a very hard move almost to the belay of *Gonads*. Climb straight up to the top.
*Photo on page 169*.
FA. Simon Nadin, Richard Davies 1984

**6 Minos** . . . . . . . . 🗓️ 🖐️ 🖐️ 🖐️ [ ] **7c+**
A great direct line. Make powerful starting moves then move up and span left into a scoop on *Aberration*. Climb up to the roof and a rest. Cross this, then balance back right and climb the rib to the break. Finish leftwards over the bulges to a lower-off.
**Celebration, 7c** - Start up *Aberration* and continue up *Minos*.
FA. Chris Wright 1996

**7 Buster** . . . . . . . . . 🗓️ 🖐️ 🖐️ [ ] **8a+**
A desperate start to *Gonads* heading for the base of its final groove.
FA. Steve McClure 1997

**8 Gonads** . . . . . . 🗓️ 🖐️ 🖐️ 🖐️ [ ] **8a+**
One of the more significant sport routes of its day. Start steeply then make a demanding traverse left via a mono to the bottom of a groove and a slight rest. Climb the still-tricky groove.
FA. Simon Nadin 1987. Remained unrepeated for several years.

Evening | 20 min | Sheltered | Seepage | Dry in the rain

25m
22m
15m
4
5
6
7
9
1
2
3

**⑨ Ultralight** . . . . . . . 🗒🧗✏️☐ **8a+**
Direct from the start of *Gonads*. Missing holds have
compounded the difficulties.
*FA. Chris Cubbitt 2000s*

**⑩ Seven Pounds Overweight. .** ✏️☐ **8a**
A scary sport route which has been largly usurped by its
neighbours. Follow *Gonads* to the first bolt. Traverse up right to the
groove on *Spizz Energy*. Climb this then launch leftwards along the
curving undercut and flake (wire useful) to gain a belay above.
Swinging in from *Lightweight* drops the grade to 7c+.
*FA. Simon Nadin 1986*

**⑪ Lightweight** . . . . . . 🗒🧗🪨☐ **7c**
The direct start to *Seven Pounds* is now more popular than the
original. Climb direct to the groove on *Spizz Energy* then finish up
*Seven Pounds*. A wire is useful on the top traverse. Alternatively
you can finish up *Spizz Energy*.
*FA. Chris Wright 1995*

**⑫ Spizz Energy** . . . . . [50] 🧗🐚☐ **E5 6b**
One of the great routes of Chee Dale which has absorbing
climbing and gear when you need it. Climb up past a bolt and peg
to a good flake. Make a tenuous traverse down and left into the
groove (bolt and a rest). Climb this to a bolt up right. Pass the
peg above and somehow end up standing on the jug. Squirm up
the awkward finishing groove.
*FA. Ron Fawcett 1980*

**⑬ A Touch of Class** . . . . . . . . 🗒☐ **E4 6a**
A fine hybrid with two good independent sections. Follow *Spizz
Energy* to the flake then climb up right to join *Mad Dogs*. Pull
over as for this then climb the steep groove above.
*FA. Chris Hardy, Chris Addy 1989*

**⑭ Spazz Energy** . . . . . . . 🗒🧗☐ **7a+**
An inferior companion to big brother *Spizz*. Reasonable climbing
low down but not of the same class overall.
*FA. Gary Gibson, Gordon Jenkin 2000*

**⑮ Mad Dogs and Englishmen .** [50]☐ **E3 5c**
A fine and devious route which is one of the best of its grade in
the Peak. Very sustained, though with a harder move to reach
the roof. Climb a flake to a peg. Step across left to another flake
then pull up with difficulty (peg above) to below the roof. Pull
over to gain a bucket then tiptoe right across the slab. Climb
direct to the top and a dirty exit.
*FFA. Gabriel Reagan, Al Evans 1976. FA. Brian Moore, Jim Ballard 1969.
A 7c sport route was added close to Mad Dogs changing the character of
this route so much that the bolts were removed.*

**⑯ Machineries of Joy** . . . . . . 🗒☐ **E1 5b**
**1)** 5b, 32m. Climb the flake of *Mad Dogs* to the roof. Undercut
right along this into the grass and nettles and descent path.
**Ape Index, E5 6c** - A long reach through the bulge above the
traverse on pitch 1 of *Machineries of Joy*.
**2)** 5b, 10m. Climb a groove above a large projecting block.
*FA. Al Evans, Dave Knighton 1976. FA. (Ape Index) Chris Gore 1982*

**⑰ Within Reach** . . . . . . . . . 🗒☐ **6c**
A worthwhile route filling the gap to the right. Trend rightwards
and climb the technical slab to the roof which provides an
interesting contrast to the fingery moves below.
*FA. Mike Przygrodzki, Clive Edmunds 2003*

⊘ *The short wall up and right - Vista Wall - has been mostly
deboltted. Please don't re-develop this wall.*

**Vista Wall**

**To Upper Tier**

## Long Wall

Long Wall provides four distinct sections. On the left is an area which takes a lot of seepage which can make the routes dirty long into the summer. Once cleaned up they provide some good sport with *High Society* and *Kiss Me Hardy* being two of the classic ticks of the Dale. The central section bulges impressively above an easier vertical wall. The routes tend to be short and powerful. Further right is the cut-away which is often dirty but does have a few items of interest. Right again the wall rears up in a continuous section of steep rock which gives fine technical and sustained routes and even that rare thing - hard limestone slab climbing.

**Approach (also see page 146) -** From the Monsal Trail on the Chee Dale Upper Approach, drop down under the Embankment to the river. A short distance down-stream is a crossing point. It has stepping stones when the river is low, but often needs wading (as for Two Tier). Follow the path right under Two Tier and keep going through the vegetation to reach Long Wall. Derbyshire Wildlife Trust have requested that climbers don't approach Long Wall from below or from Runyon's Corner.

**Conditions -** The wall gets little sun, is very slow to dry and can be dirty. All sections are well-sheltered from the elements and cool on hot days.

*The first route described is on a barrel-shaped buttress 50m left of Long Wall.*

**❶ Super Orchic** . . . . . . . 🔲🔲⬜ **7b**
Short and technical moves past three bolts. 5m long.
*FA. Tony Coutts, Ed Morgan 1994*

*The first route on Long Wall proper is just left of the cut-away, starting behind a big tree.*

**❷ Columnus** . . . . . . . . . . . . 🔲⬜ **7b+**
A powerful route through bulges on the left of the cut-away. The start is a bit obscured by a large tree.
*FA. Gary Gibson 1996*

**❸ The Orange Order** . . . . . . 🔲⬜ **6c**
Right of the corner with a finish over the roof.
**Banana Republic, E2 5c -** The left-hand corner of the recess.
*FA. Gary Gibson 2000s. FA. (BR) Chris Jackson 1983*

**❹ Orange Free State** . . . . . . 🔲⬜ **6b+**
Steep jug pulling through the centre of the cut-away. The final move proves to be a bit of a stopper. Often dirty.
*FA. Gary Gibson 1996*

**5** **Berried** . . . . . . . . . . . **6c**
A hard start and a blind finish over the widest part of the roof which requires a bit of a reach. Often dirty. Pass a small sapling at half height.
*FA. Gary Gibson, Hazel Gibson 1996*

**6** **Black Rights** . . . . . . . . **7b**
A technical wall leading to a rest at the break. The bulge above is awkward. The cleanest of the bunch.
*FA. Gary Gibson 1996*

**7** **High Society** . . . . . **7a**
The first and still one of the best additions to Long Wall. Easier than it looks, but no pushover, with a final teasing move. Climb the bulge and steep wall above the bush to a break and semi-rest. Take the wall above past a sloper to finish at a tree.
*FA. Keith Sharples, Graham Hoey 1984. Bolted in 1999*

**8** **Kiss Me Hardy** . . . . . **7a+**
An excellent route, the best of its grade on the wall. Climb the bulge right of *High Society*, either from the left or direct (both ways are hard since the loss of holds). Continue more easily to the break, above which a final test of your fitness awaits.
*FA. Chris Hardy 1989*

**Access -** This buttress is in the wildlife reserve managed by Derbyshire Wildlife Trust. Only use the described approach and do not walk along the crag base further than the described routes.

**9** **Kiss My Arcy** . . . . . **7b**
A good companion to *Kiss Me Hardy* with similar climbing - a hard bulge then sustained moves above.
*FA. Gary Gibson 1999*

**10** **Mystical Attainment** **7b+**
A straightened out old trad route with a new direct finish. The bulge has a very reachy crux.
*FA. Richard Davies (at E6 6b) 1986. Bolted later and renamed 'Demystified' with a new direct finish.*

**11** **Mouldwarp Wall** . . **7c**
Direct through the steepest section of bulges on very thin holds requiring two long reaches (or a desperate alternative sequence) to gain a good hold. The first bolt may be missing.
*FA. Andy Popp 1993*

**⑫ Brothers in Arms** . . 7b+
The lower part is beefy climbing on undercuts but getting into the top groove is the crux.
*FA. Keith Sharples, Chris Hardy 1989*

**⑬ Rouge Total**. . . . . . . . 7b
Hard moves through the bulge eject you onto the steep upper wall. The easiest line through these bulges. There is an old project to the left which makes finding the line a bit tricky.
*FA. Gary Gibson, John Codling 1991*

**⑭ Total Rock**. . . . . . . . . 7c
The next line through the right side of the bulges.
*FA. Clive Edmunds 2004*

**⑮ Jungle Rock** . . . . . . . 7b+
A veritable banquet for the biceps, this fine route demands a powerful approach. A spike hold marks the way. It lost some crucial holds and is now much harder.
*FA. Keith Sharples 1989*

**⑯ Some Things Change** . . 7b+
A powerful bulge low down with undercuts and side-pulls, and a few tricky moves above. One final hard pull. Tricky second clip.
*FA. Gary Gibson 1996*

**⑰ Fatal Attraction** . . . . . . 7a
The easiest line hereabouts kicks off straight away with strenuous moves to gain the flake-line. Sporty moves up this lead to the roof and a possible knee-bar rest before the fun really begins. Not the best warm-up for the Wall, but it's all there is.
*FA. Keith Sharples, Phil Burke, Rory Gregory 1989. An old route Chain of Command, E4 6b (FA. Gary Gibson 1982 ) wandered over this area.*

**⑱ Lucky Finger** . . . . . 7b
The bulging arete is sustained, technical and seldom climbed. Tricky to onsight and it can be dusty.
*FA. Gary Gibson 1996*

*The big corner is the forgettable* **Monopedagogue, E2 5b**.

**⑲ The Balancing Act** . . . . 7a+
A hard route with contrasting technical sections. Finish over the top roof to a lower-off.
**Rolling Stone, E4 6b** - The wall just to the right has seen little attention and may be the same routes as *Balancing Act*.
*FA. Gary Gibson 1999. FA. (RS) Keith Sharples 1990*

**⑳ Trick Show** . . . . . . . . 7b+
The centre of the recess. The start gives some very hard moves but there is a good breather before the final roof.
*FA. Gary Gibson (1pt) 1982. The aid was removed (Matt Boyer) in 1994 but he didn't finish the pitch. First ascent is unknown, it was bolted in 1999.*

**㉑ Casamance** . . . . . . . . . . . 7a+
Steep moves through bulges lead to the reachy finishing roof. This is easier if you don't use the obvious holds.
*FA. Gary Gibson 1991*

**㉒ Macumba** . . . . . . . . . . . . 7a+
An inferior and easier right-hand start to *Casamance*.
*FA. Gary Gibson 1991*

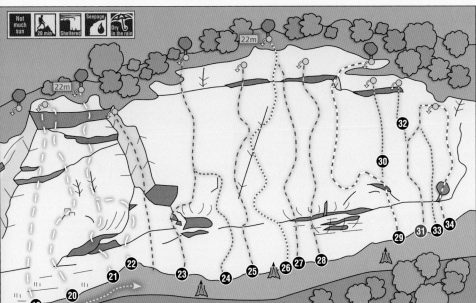

The big corner is the line of **Freeway, HVS 5a**. A defunct route - **Big News Manmouth**, *traversed right out of this onto the arete but the huge block you traversed on has gone. The line up the sidewall is a project; a grade of 7b+ has been mooted.*

**㉓ Atlantic Realm. . . .** 7b+
Start below the big square roof. Good hard climbing and more sustained than it used to be when there was a huge hanging block under the roof. Low in the grade.
FA. Chris Wright 1990

**㉔ Gob on the Mountain** 7c
A short, sharp route right of the big roof, unfortunately it is rather unbalanced. Reach the first break then make a desperate move on tiny holds and no footholds to gain a big flake above. Above this join *Atlantic Realm* for a fine finish.
FA. Martin Crocker 1988

**㉕ Meterol . . . . .** 7b+
Quality climbing up the wall just to the right. Climb the wall to the break and stand in it. Step right then make hard pulls to a good hold. Climb to a down-pointing spike then move left to another good hold. Move back up right to the belay at the break.
FA. Chris Wright 1996

**㉖ Breathless . . . .** E6 6c
A wandering line with some fine climbing. Sadly the difficulty of the second pitch makes it a serious undertaking and its bolted neighbours means it is now largely ignored. Climb the wall to the right of the slim groove and make a crucifix span left to reach the down-pointing spike of *Meterol*. **7c+** with the second clip sorted.
FA. Dave Pegg 1987

**㉗ Cathedral Taste . . .** 7b+
Excellent, at last something for the aficionados of balance (well after the start). Crimp through the bulge to gain the (steep) slab above. Climb this thoughtfully.
FA. Gary Gibson, Rehan Siddiqui 1996

**㉘ À Bout de Souffle. .** 7c
Another very technical and fine wall climb. Climb up to a stump, move up to undercuts - hard for the short - then make a desperate move onto the slab above. Trace a line delicately up the slab to the easier final bulge.
FA. Ian Dunn, Alisdair Hannah, John Hartley 1996

**㉙ Multiplex . . . . . . . . . .** E4 6b
A neglected route with good climbing. Move up to the overlap then stretch left to a jug (bolt). Make a wild drop down to the ledge and finish more easily up the excellent wall above. **Smutt, E5 6c -** The direct start past an old peg.
FA. Gary Gibson, Phil Wilson 1982. FA. (Smutt) Allen Williams 1987

**㉚ Child Lock. . . . . . . . .** 7a+
A reachy direct finish to *Multiplex* with a hard clip.
FA. Chris Wright 1990

**㉛ Hot Panties . . . . . . . . .** 7a
Technical moves which keep on coming to a tricky finish.
FA. Mike Annesley 1987

**㉜ Steaming Strides . . . . .** 7a+
Desperate moves up left from the 2nd bolt on *Hot Panties*.
FA. Gary Gibson, Nadim Siddiqui 1996

**㉝ Nookie Bear . . . . . . . .** 7a+
Direct to the lower-off on *Hot Panties* via three hard moves.
FA. Gary Gibson 1996

**㉞ Child's Play. . . . . . . . . . .** E4 6a
The last climb on the wall requires a runner or two, and a peg to protect it. Finish at the lower off of *Hot Panties*.
FA. Chris Wright 1990

*20m further right is a poor route **Skid Marks, 6b+**. 2 bolts, 2 pegs and a lower-off in the break.*

**❶ Watch This Space** . . . . . . . 🧗 [____] **6c**
The left-most bolt-line has some tricky moves.
*FA. Jim Burton, Gary Gibson, Nadim Siddiqui 1995*

**❷ Robert's Roberts** . . . . . . . . 🧗 [____] **7a+**
Hard undercut moves lead through the bulge up a short wall.
*FA. Gary Gibson 2010*

**❸ Kill the Bill** . . . . . . . . 🧗 ✊ [____] **7b+**
The blank wall right of two cracks. The mid-height reach above
the second bolt is a bit of a stopper.
*FA. Chris Wright 1990*

**❹ Overslapped** . . . . . . . 🏔1 🧗 [____] **7a**
Probably the best route on this bit of wall; connecting a series of
small jugs before trending left to a lower-off.
*FA. Gary Gibson, Jim Burton, Nadim Siddiqui 1995*

**❺ Slappy, Happy Chappy** . . . . ✊ [____] **7a**
Beefy moves are needed to pass the small overhang.
*FA. Gary Gibson 2010*

**❻ Thunderstrapped** . . . . . . . . ✊ [____] **7a**
The left-hand side of the overlap. Lower off the tree.
*FA. Gary Gibson 1995*

**❼ Overclapped** . . . . . . . . ✊🪜 [____] **7a**
The centre of the overlapping roof to hard moves above.
*FA. Gary Gibson 1995*

**❽ Megaflapped** . . . . . . . . . . 🧗 [____] **6c**
Climb up to a short corner in the roof. Pull over and continue up
right to the belay. Often damp.
*FA. Gary Gibson, Hazel Gibson 1996*

**❾ Runyonectomy** . . . . . . . . . . . . [____] **6b**
The line left of the huge grass-filled angle of the bay is often
damp and greasy.
*FA. Gary Gibson 1996*

**❿ The Jury's Out** . . . . . . . . . . . . [____] **6b+**
Just left of a corner up a vague rounded pillar.
*FA. Gary Gibson, Jim Burton, Nadim Siddiqui 1995*

**⓫ Community Service** . . . 🏔1 🪜 [____] **6c+**
The best in Runyon's Corner. Start below a left-facing flake.
Climb up to this then pull over onto the wall above. The holds
lead up and left before a move back right gains the belay.
*FA. Gary Gibson 1995*

## Runyon's Corner

This is not the best sector in Chee Dale but it does have a few
pleasant little routes and is in a delightful and secluded setting. Over
the years the routes have become rather neglected.

**Access -** This area is very sensitive. Please only use the small path
below the crag and don't stray into the vegetation. Also, don't use
this as an approach to Long Wall.

**Approach (also see page 146) -** From the Monsal Trail on the Chee
Dale Upper Approach, scramble up to Moving Buttress (page next
page) and turn the corner on the left.

**Conditions -** Sheltered and shady in windy or hot weather but it
stays damp for long periods after rain.

**Access -** This buttress is in the wildlife reserve managed by
Derbyshire Wildlife Trust. Only use the described approach and
do not walk along the crag base further than the described routes.

**12 Open Verdict** . . . . . . . . 7a+
A hard start and difficult moves above before finishing back left past a crack.
*FA. Gary Gibson, Nadim Siddiqui 1995*

**13 In the Defence** . . . . . . . . . 6c
The wall left of a thin crack is awkward. There is a peg in the first break. The final moves to the belay are tricky.
*FA. Gary Gibson, Hazel Gibson 1996*

**14 The Fifth Amendment** . . 6c
*The front of the pillar has a tricky start and some decent moves.*

*The next two routes are on the short left-facing sidewall.*

**15 For the Prosecution** . . . . . 6c
The very short line on the left-hand edge of the sidewall.
*FA. Gary Gibson 1996*

12m

10m

**16 Witness This** . . . . . . . . . . 6c+
The right hand edge of the sidewall appears too short to be worthwhile. Don't be fooled, there are plenty of moves.
*FA. Gary Gibson, Howard Lancashire 1996*

**17 The Plea** . . . . . . . . . . . . . 6a+
A decent recent addition up the pillar to the right.
*FA. Gary Gibson 2010*

**18 Guilty** . . . . . . . . . . . . . . . 6c
Awkward moves gain a ledge and easier climbing above.
*FA. Gary Gibson 2010*

**19 No Intent** . . . . . . . . . . . . 6b+
Climb up to a short flake and make hard moves above to the upper break. Finish up right. At the top, most people slink leftwards almost onto the arete before coming back right.
*FA. Gary Gibson, Jim Burton, Nadim Siddiqui 1995*

**20 As Loose As This?** . . . . 6c+
Times and tastes change - as long as there are some solid bolts. Good moves, fingery pulls at mid-height provide the interest.
*FA. Gary Gibson 1987*

**21 In the Stox** . . . . . . . . . 7a
A short and technical wall climb.
*FA. Gary Gibson 1990s*

**22 Stax a Time** . . . . . . . . 7b
The line of bolts 2m left of the arete gives a desperate pitch with an unusual crux move.
*FA. Gary Gibson 1996*

**23 Never to Look Back** . . . 7b
A well-positioned climb up the left-hand side of the arete.
*FA. Gary Gibson 1991*

Early morning | 20 min | Sheltered | Seepage

North | Southwest | Southeast | Stoney | Horseshoe | Smalldale | Harpur Hill | Lovers' Leap | Beehouse | Craig-y-Biceps | Staden Q | Chee Dale L. | Chee Dale U. | Blackwell D. | Raven Tor | Water-c-Jolly | Ravensdale | Aldery Cliff | Taddington | Rheinstor

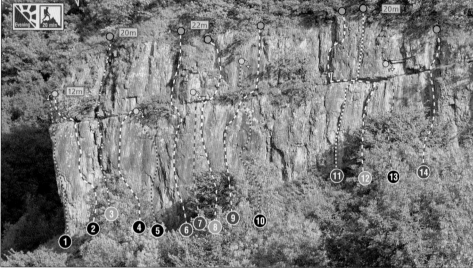

## Moving Buttress

This fine wall stands proudly above the railway and was one of the first walls in the Dale to be developed mainly because it has a number of good groove and crack-lines. **Approach (also see page 146)** - From the Monsal Trail on the Chee Dale Upper Approach, just before crossing a bridge, turn right and climb over a stile and head steeply up to the wall.

**Conditions** - This wall gets little sun, except on summer evenings. It dries quickly and doesn't seep much but gives no shelter in the rain. The nettles and undergrowth can make the crag base difficult to navigate in the summer.

❶ **I Had a Black Shirt .**  **7a+**
The right-hand side of the arete. Tricky to flash.
*FA. Gary Gibson 1996*

❷ **Protest and Survive . . .**  **E4 6a**
A good wall climb with reasonable gear on the crux but an extremely unhelpful flake above can give a few worrying moments. Lower-off to the left.
*FA. Nadim Siddiqui 1992*

❸ **Whistling Crack . . . . . .**  **VS 4b**
The wide crack is thoroughly traditional.
*FA. John Arrundale, Graham West 1960*

❹ **Gander Meat . . .** 🔲🔲🔲🔲 **E6 6c**
A tendon-tearing exercise up the clean, white wall. Gear consists of a peg and some hard-to-place wires. Finishing leftwards at mid-height is a bit of a cop-out - **E5 6b**.
*FA. Chris Gore 1984*

❺ **Dope . . . . . . . .** 🔲🔲🔲🔲 **7b+**
Thin climbing with a desperate move above the third bolt.
*FA. Tony Coutts 1995. Also claimed as 'Foie Gras' and 'Meat and Two Veg'.*

❻ **Autonomon . . . . . . . . . . .** 🔲 **E1 5b**
Climb easy rock leftwards to a ledge. Finish up the vegetated groove above. Abseil off.
**Spirit of the Age, E5 6a** - the bold wall to the left.
*FA. Paul Nunn 1966. FA. (SotA) Mark Liptrot 1985*

❼ **Automoton . . . . . . . . . . .** 🔲 **7a**
Thin fingery climbing leads to a lower-off.
*FA. Gary Gibson 2002*

❽ **Monoton . . . . . . . . . . . . . . .** 🔲 **VS 4b**
Climb the groove to gain the break. Finish up the corner above and abseil off. Originally it finished up the groove of *Autonomon*.
*FA. Paul Nunn, J.Smith 1966*

Access - This buttress is in the wildlife reserve managed by Derbyshire Wildlife Trust. Only use the described approach and do not walk along the crag base further than the described routes.

20m

8m

10m

**20** **21** **22** Big Boned... p.182

**17** **18** **19**

**15** **16**

---

**❾ Vibrator** . . . . . . . . . . . **E2 5c**
The thin crack and steep slab lead to a grassy ledge. Step right and tackle the final awkward crack. Abseil from a tree.
*FA. Brian Griffiths, Rod Brown 1976*

**❿ Witch in Stitch** . . . . **7b**
Progress above the second bolt is made by a desperate static move or an ungradeable jump.
*FA. Gary Gibson 1986*

*The next section of wall has four trad routes on loose rock. Further right is a better wall with a prominent roof.*

**⓫ Thin Lizzy** . . . . . . . . . . . . . **E1 5b**
A tricky lower crack leads to the break (threads). Then make a hard move to get established over the roof. There may be a bolt at the top of the route, if not, do battle with the horrid exit then abseil off.
*FA. Bob Conway, Chris Jackson, Giles Barker 1979*

**⓬ Swinging Wall** . . . . . . . . . . . . **VS 4c**
A counter-diagonal to *Thin Lizzy* but not quite as good. Climb the crack to a thread in the break then traverse left to an easier corner.
*FFA. Bill Tweedale 1970. FA. B.Whittaker, N.Smith 1969*

**⓭ A Man Called Horse** . . . **7b+**
Extremely technical moves up the wall.
*FA. Seb Grieve 1990*

**⓮ Dynamic** . . . . . . . . . . **E1 5c**
The shallow groove to the right of the smooth wall is balancy and not well protected. Finish up a flake and on into the trees.
*FA. Brian Griffiths, Rod Brown 1976*

**⓯ Orchrist** . . . . . . . . . . . . . . . **VS 4c**
The groove just left of the larger groove of *Osculation*.
*FA. D.Irons (aid) 1970*

**⓰ Osculation** . . . . . . . . **HVS 5a**
The large open groove gives a fine pitch. Take care with a dangerous loose block which may still lurk halfway up the route.
*FA. Brian Griffiths, Rod Brown 1976*

**⓱ Wise Up! Sucker** . . . . . . . . . **6c+**
A short sport route with a good rock-over move.
*FA. Simon Cundy 1989*

**⓲ Your Rotten Thoughts** . . . . . **7a+**
Two hard moves on the black wall.
*FA. Gary Gibson 2002*

**⓳ Priming the Pump** . . . . . . . **E4 6a**
The thin curving crack is sustained and seldom climbed.
*FFA. Chris Plant, Dave Lee 1982. Formerly aided.*

**⓴ Oh No! It's the Wall to Wall Birthday Party**
. . . . . . . . . . . . . . . **7a+**
The thin crack and bulge has some loose holds.
*FA. Chris Wright 1990*

**㉑ Fresh Jive** . . . . . . . . . . **7c**
Short and hard. No lower-off.
*FA. Tony Coutts 1996*

**㉒ Shaking Crack** . . . . . . . **E2 5b**
The diagonal crack gives the best route on this section of wall. A struggle from the very first move but well protected.
*FA. Jerry Frost, Ernie Marshall 1976. Formerly aided.*

North | Southwest | Southeast | Stoney | Horseshoe | Smalldale | Harpur Hill | Lover's Leap | Berthouse | Cornbe Bisset | Station Q | Chee Dale U. | the Dale | Blatwell D. | Brown Tor | Water-c-Jolly | Ravensdale | Plum Buttress | Aldery Cliff | Tiddington | Blackrocks

North

Southwest

Southeast

Stoney

Horseshoe

Smalldale

Harpur Hill

Lovers Leap

Beehouse

Craig-y-Bic

Staden

G----hill

Che Dale

Rivelwell

Raven Tor

Water-- J-lly

Ravensdale

Aldery Cliff

T-dd-----n

Rhentir

**23 Big Boned Backside Melon .** ▨ ☐ **7b+**
Short-lived technical interest. Lower off the last bolt.
*FA. Tony Coutts 1996*

*The next two routes start above the big block.*

**24 Dangleberry** . . . . . . . . . . ⛰1 ☐ **VS 4c**
An old-style piece of route finding which skirts around the main
roofs. Climb a thin groove to a niche below the roof. At the
break, traverse left for 4m then climb a groove to the top.
*FA. Graham West, Brian Bamford pre-1961*

**25 Thor's Hammer** . . . ⛰2 🔨📷 ☐ **E1 5b**
A big struggle through the roofs and onto the hanging flake
above. Start up *Dangleberry*. Can also be started direct.
*FA. Bill Tweedale, J.Greenwood 1970. Previously aided.*

**26 Socialism** . . . . . . . . . . ⛰ 📷 ☐ **E3 5c**
An eliminate, cutting through the two main roof challenges. Start
from the embedded block and climb the blank slab to the break.
Pull through the roofs onto a thin flake above.
*FA. Ian Jones, Neil McAdie 1982*

*Shaking
Crack p.181*

**27 Colon** . . . . . . . . . . . . . E1 5b
Start up *Thin Thin Groove* to the break then traverse left until below a fine groove. Follow this to the top.
FA. Ken Jones, E.Finney, Brian Moore (aid) 1962

**28 Thin Thin Groove** . . . . . . . . VS 4c
The right-hand side of the roofs has a thin thin hanging groove. Gain this and follow it to the top.
FA. Barry Roberts, Graham West pre-1961

**29 Quake.** . . . . . . . . . . . . . . E1 5b
A delightful set of short grooves. Awkward in the middle.
FFA. Jim Moran 1976. Previously aided.

**30 The Price of Fame** . . . . . . . E4 6b
Climb flakes then cross *Vibration* to a lower-off up right.
FA. Mark Liptrot 1985

**31 Vibration.** . . . . . . . . . . . E1 5b
Follow the scoops up left past a thread and some better gear to finish up *Quake*. The scene of a few big falls.
FA. Jim Moran, Geoff Milburn 1976

**32 Family Fortunes.** . . . . . . . . 7a+
A direct above the thread on *Vibration*. Leaving the ramp is the crux; above that it relents, but not by too much.
FA. Gary Gibson 1997

**33 Pushed to the Hilti** . . . . . . . 6c
Start up *Vibration* but climb direct past 2 old bolts. Wires will be needed to get to the first bolt.
FA. Simon Cundy 1989

**34 Shock the Monkey** . . . . . . . E4 6a
The rising diagonal cracks to the top of *Pushed to the Hilti*.
FFA. Chris Plant, Dave Lee 1982. FA. T.Rogers, B.Samuels

**35 Gibbon Take** . . . . . . . . . . . . 6c
A short filler-in squeezed into the right-hand end of the buttress. 3 bolts to a lower-off
FA. Gary Gibson 1997

North | Southwest | Southeast | Stoney | Horseshoe | Smalldale | Harpur Hill | Lovers Leap | Beerhouse | Craig-y-Biceps | Staden Q | Blackwell D. | Chee Dale L. | Chee Dale U. | Raven Tor | Water-c-Jolly | Ravensdale | Aldery Cliff | Taddington | Rheinstor

## The Lifts

The Lifts have become less fashionable of late and parts are slowly retreating behind the ivy. Although none of the routes are outstanding, many are worthwhile and are in a fantastic position; the closest we have to the Cheddar experience in the Peak.

**Conditions -** The crag gets evening sun making it a good evening venue. It suffers no seepage but is exposed.

**Approach (also see page 146) -** From the car park at Topley Pike on the A6, follow the signed path leading away to the right to reach the shallow valley. Go down this, until a footpath leads off to the right and zigzags up the hill eventually joining the main Blackwell path. Continue on this for about 200m. Careful navigation is required to locate the gully to the right (looking out) of the Lifts. This leads down steeply to the crag base. The tree above *Ragged Arete* is a good marker since this is about 50m left (looking out) of the main Third Lift buttress.

**Access -** This buttress is in the wildlife reserve managed by Derbyshire Wildlife Trust. Only use the described approach and do not walk along the crag base further than the described routes.

Ragged Arete tree

**❶ Fingerpops** . . . . . . . . 🔲 **7b+**
A short and horribly technical climb using nasty pockets.
*FA. Gary Gibson 1997*

**❷ Crank it Up** . . . . . . . . . . . . 🔲 **6c+**
The centre of the wall. Better than its neighbours.
*FA. Gary Gibson 1987*

**❸ An Uplifting Experience** . . . . . . 🔲 **6b+**
Climb the wall using the crack. 7a if you avoid the crack.
*FA. Gary Gibson 1997*

*There is a gap of chossy rock with some poor trad routes.*

**❹ Access all Areas** . . 🔲 **7a+**
The wall right of the crack is a bit artificial but has some good moves. No touching the crack at this grade.
*FA. Gary Gibson 1997*

**❺ Elephant Talk** . . . . 🔲 **7a+**
Hard climbing leads to a friable flake. Pass this and continue on some still-loose rock to the lower-off.
*FA. Dave Pegg 1987. FA. (Direct) Gary Gibson 1997*

**❻ Hamish** . . . . . . . . . . . 🔲 **7a**
A direct line past the right-hand side of the flake.
*FA. Tony Coutts 1995*

**❼ Five Miles High** . . . . . . 🔲 **6c+**
A reasonable route passing the short groove.
*FA. Gary Gibson 1997*

**❽ All Fall Down** . . . . 🔲 **7a+**
A wandering line with sustained moves. The 2nd clip is a gripper.
*FA. Gary Gibson 1995*

**❾ High Scream Sunday** . . . . . 🔲 **6c**
A well-positioned route up the arete. Slightly escapable at the bottom (6b+ if you go too far right) but good higher up.
*FA. Gary Gibson 1997*

**❿ Succulent Corner** . . . . . 🔲 **S 4a**
The wide thrutchy crack in the back of the corner is reached up the grassy wall - juicy.

**⓫ The Sting** . . . . . . . . . . . . 🔲 **HVS 5b**
Gain the tricky hanging groove from the left or direct.
*FA. P Bagnell, D Gibbinson (2 pts aid) 1965*

**⓬ The Siberian Hamster** . . . . . 🔲 **7a**
A hard start past an old bolt (slink left if you don't trust it) leads to a break. Pull over the roof and up the arete to finish.
*FA. Gary Gibson, Nadim Siddiqui 1997*

*Routes on the walls to the right rise above a narrow path. They never get done and are overgrown so are not described here. The final route is an old easy classic. The best access is to abseil from the tree mentioned in the approach.*

**⓭ Ragged Arete** . . . . . . . . . 🔲 **S 4a**
A great little route. Start on the right of the arete and climb a flake on the left moving back right towards the top - jugtastic.
*FA. John Arrundale, John Lancashire pre-1961*

*The rest of the routes are on the Second Lift - reached by continuing down the approach gully.*

**⓮ Mississippi Burning** . . . . . . 🔲 **7a**
A technical wall leading to a small roof and crack.
*FA. Gary Gibson 1997*

**⓯ Tricky Dicky** . . . . . . . . . . . 🔲 **6c+**
A poor route with a glued jug and an artificial start. The crack to the left is **Black Momma, VS**.
*FA. Gary Gibson 1997*

**⓰ The Black and White Minstrel Show**
. . . . . . . . . . . . . . . . . . . 🔲 **7b**
A narrow gap with some hard technical climbing.
*FA. Gary Gibson 1991*

**⓱ Rusty Lee** . . . . . . . 🔲 **7a**
The best route on the crag following the attractive little grooves. Three hard moves, three long reaches.
*FA. Gary Gibson 1991*

**⓲ Daddy's Riding the Range** . . 🔲 **7a+**
Hard moves up the unprotected and loose wall lead to a friable undercut and a long move to a chipped hold. Poor.
*FA. Gary Gibson 1997*

**⓳ Close Control** . . . . . . . . . 🔲 **6b**
A pleasant little route through the steep groove just left of the arete. The groove is less helpful than it looks and the third bolt difficult to clip. One of the originals - check out the bashee.
*FA. Gary Gibson 1983*

**⓴ White Riot** . . . . . . . . . . . 🔲 **6a**
Good climbing up the right-hand side of the arete with some large holds.
*FA. Gary Gibson, Hazel Gibson 1997*

*The line just right, following the flakes, is **Phase Contrast, E1 5b**. To the right are two cracks (both HVS) and a long, low roof.*

**㉑ Iron Filings** . . . . . . . . . . . 🔲 **6c**
The left-hand route of three taking the easiest line over the first roof via a big flake. The crack on the left is out-of-bounds.
*FA. Gary Gibson, Hazel Gibson 1997*

**㉒ Steel on Steel** . . . . . . . 🔲 **7a**
Passing a bolt in the roof requires a huge reach. Climbing up left then traversing back right avoids this.
*FA. Gary Gibson 1982/1997 - The original route started on the right.*

**㉓ Mettle Fatigue** . . . . . . . . . . 🔲 **6c**
The roof is easy, the upper wall requires more tenacity.
*FA. Gary Gibson, Hazel Gibson 1997*

**㉔ Pop the Rivet** . . . . . . . . . 🔲 **6a**
An awkward move past the first bolt. Can feel harder if you don't find the right holds. Not a good warm-up.
*FA. Gary Gibson, Hazel Gibson 1997*

## Plum Buttress

A magnificent buttress which dominates the western end of the Dale and has a small set of top-notch routes, both trad and sport. Only three of the routes are within the ticking reach of most climbers but these are all of the highest quality, and include *Sirplum*, one of the finest E1s in the country.

**Approach (also see page 146)** - From the Monsal Trail on the Chee Dale Upper Approach, Plum Buttress is the first major buttress you encounter when walking down the Dale. Cross a stile directly below the crag and drop down steeply then up to the buttress. Do not cross this fence earlier (where there is also a stile) and keep away from the scree slope.

**❶ Wilderness Years** .... 🎣 ⅋ ☐ **7b+**
The once-disputed line left of the arete was bolted to give a tricky sport route with a desperate crux and some loose rock.

**❷ The Stalk** ............ ⅋ ☐ **VS 4c**
The open-corner on the left of the buttress gives a great outing on good holds with plenty of solid runners after a vegetated start. At the top break, move out left to escape. There may be an abseil station in place, if not, walk round. If you thought it a push-over, consider the next route as a suitable extension.
*FA. Harold Drasdo, G.Mansell 1955*

**❸ Aplomb**. . . . . . . . . . ⅋ ☐ **E1 5a**
A superbly exposed trip through unbelievable territory at the grade. The grade reflects the overall sustained nature of the route rather than the protection, which is more than adequate. There are a number of variations, including an extended start from over on the left and an independent finish, but none as good as this particular combination.
1) 4c, 25m. Climb all of *The Stalk* to its belay.
2) 4c, 15m. Move up and right across a grassy and slightly loose wall to belay above the roof of *The Big Plumb*.
3) 5a, 25m. A mega-pitch which requires a confident second. Drop down and make a wild hand traverse of the break to a spike on *Sirplum*, and a hanging belay. Plenty of fixed gear to clip.
4) 5a, 20m. Finish up *Sirplum*. Originally it finished up the shallow groove further to the right - this is grassy nowadays.
*FA. Jeff Morgan, Bob Toogood 1968*
*FA. (Sarin) Paul Nunn, Trevor Briggs 1966*

**❹ Victoria** . . . . . . . . . . . . . ⅋ ☐ **E3 5c**
A neglected trad route which is seldom climbed.
1) 5a, 25m. Climb leftwards across the wall then up to the break.
2) 5c, 10m. Pull over the roof (pegs) then left and back right to gain the upper groove. Bolt belay, abseil off.
*FA. Keith Myhill 1971*

**❺ Mrs Brown** . . . . . . 🎣 ☐ **7c**
Climb the wall left of the Big Plum groove to the break. Move left and pull over as for *Victoria*, then move back right and up to reach the upper groove of *Victoria*. Bolt belay, abseil off.
*FA. Mark Pretty 2011*

**❻ Raisin Roof**. . . . . . . . 🎣 ☐ **E5 6b**
The first route over the big roof to be freed. From the first stance on *The Big Plum*, move up left and pull through the roof with difficulty. Move back right to join *The Big Plum*.
*FA. Dominic and Daniel Lee 1992*

**❼ The Big Plum** . . 🎣 ☐ **E6 6c**
Once this was the big challenge of Chee Dale but the resulting free version is not quite the mega-route that was hoped for. Apart from the section crossing the roof, it is all straightforward. It is around 7b+ as a sport route. The use of aid on the roof section offers the potential of an exciting trip up one of the Peak's finest features at an amenable grade (VS and A1).
1) 4b, 20m. Climb the pod-shaped groove to a ledge.
2) 6c, 10m. Climb up to the roof and cross this past a desperate move (long reach) at the lip to an exposed stance just above.
3) 4c, 10/20m. Plod up the groove above to the grass terrace. A finish can be made up the groove in the final tower if required.
*FFA. Neil Foster 1987. FA. Graham West, Barry Roberts 1960*

**❽ Damson in Distress** 🎣 ☐ **7b+**
The sport version of the *Big Plum* is bolted from the roof upwards, finishing rightwards up the final section of *The Spider*. To make it a full sport route use the bolted start of *The Spider* (long draws). Take care on the upper section - some loose rock here.
*FA. Mark Pretty 2011*

**❾ The Spider** . . . . . . . 🎣 ☐ **8a**
A major route tackling the roof at its widest point which gives good moves separated by decent rests and the odd bit of dodgy rock. The best positioned sport route in the Peak! It is usually done in one huge (40m) pitch but then lowered-off in stages.
*Photo on cover.*
*FA. Kristian Clemmow 2004. Almost freed in 1987 by Andy Pollitt (1pt) although the new version takes a different line through the main roof.*

**❿ Sloe Gin** . . . . . 🎣 ☐ **E6 6b**
A superb hard route which is well protected by pegs and bolts.
1) -, 10m. Climb *Sirplum* to a hanging belay in a scoop.
2) 6b, 15m. Climb up to the break (not as easy as it looks). Then reach out to holds on the lip, whilst trying to keep your feet on the rock. Swing around onto the face above and pull up flakes to reach the break. Traverse left to a big thread belay.
3) 6a, 18m. Pull out right and then climb direct to reach the final groove on *Sirplum*. Finish up this.
*FA. Neil Foster, Rory Gregory 1987. Described by Neil as "Mountaineering in complete safety".*

**⓫ Sirplum** . . . . . . . 🎣 ☐ **E1 5b**
One of the great ticks in the Peak which reaches positions that other E1s don't - an amazing outing. Apart from one technical move at the start of pitch 2, it is never desperate, but it is pumpy and committing. Retreat from the nose is problematical so take your Prusiks if you are nervous. For this reason it makes it a poor route for an inexperienced second.
1) 4c, 25m. Climb up and right across the buttress to a comfortable ledge on the right of the main roofs.
2) 5b, 25m. Move left and make a powerful couple of pulls over the roof. Climb up left to a breather on a pedestal then surge up and left again on big holds, with increasingly brain-jellying exposure, to reach the very edge of the world. A hard pull gains a bridged rest (at last) in the final groove then amble up this with a grin as wide as the valley. Good gear mostly, although the effort of fixing the monster thread under the roof is probably not worth expending unless you are REALLY scared.
**The Plumb-line Finish, E1 5b** - From the big thread, pull through the small roof above and finish direct into the jungle. A good alternative.
**The Defector, E2 5c** - Another worthwhile variation up the crack and over the roof above the pedestal - beware of loose rock.
*FA. Bob Dearman (aid) 1964. FFA. Unknown*
*FA. (Plumbline Finish) Al Evans, Geoff Birtles 1976*
*FA. (The Defector) M Warwick, D Beaver 1979*

**Conditions -** The crag gets shade for most of the day but it can get good late-afternoon sun. It doesn't seep very much and dries quickly. The nettles at the base, and on the descent, can be a problem so wear your long pants.

**Access -** This buttress is in the wildlife reserve managed by Derbyshire Wildlife Trust. Only use the described approach and do not walk along the crag base further than the described routes.

Descent

50m

40m

25m

25m

North
Southwest
Southeast
Stoney
Horseshoe
Smalldale
Harpur Hill
Lovers' Leap
Beerhouse
Crag-y-Biceps
Staden Q
Chee Dale U.
Che Dale L.
Blackwell D.
Raven Tor
Water-c-Jolly
Ravensdale
Aldery Cliff
Taddington
Rheinstor

**1 White Gold** . . . . . . . . 7a

Excellent climbing on good rock; a quality route. Climb the groove via long pulls to the small roof. Move up left and traverse left to enter a scoop a little nervously. From the break, swing right and up with difficulty to gain the finishing scoop and lower-off. A direct link between the two roofs is hard 7b and reachy.
FA. Chris Gore, Dominic Lee 1982

**2 Nobody's Hero** . . . . E5 6b

Sadly neglected, when clean this provides good climbing. Start up *White Gold* but traverse diagonally right until a long and scary move up gains a good hold and protection. Continue direct with interest.
FA. Gary Gibson 1984

**3 The Myrmidon** . . . . E5 6b

Another fine route suffering from a lack of attention. Climb the lower wall to a drilled peg and make a huge move or leap to gain holds way above. A semi-rest can be taken at the break before tackling the only slightly easier section above. Seldom flashed.
FA. Keith Sharples 1984

**4 The Ogre** . . . . . . 8a

The left-hand line on the red wall is desperate for shorties. There is a left-hand variation too.
FA. Chris Gore 1986

**5 Igor** . . . . . . . . . . 7c

The right-hand line on the wall gives a pushy pitch.

**6 Two Sunspots** . . . . . . . E2 5c

Deservedly popular; a fine route linking the weaknesses in the steep wall to the right. Climb the flake-line to the break, then try and find the easiest traverse line into the crack on the left. Follow the scoop above to tree belays.
FA. Gary Gibson, Barry Holmes, Tony Bailey 1980

**7 Midnight Summer Dream** E5 6a

A good first limestone E5. Although the crux section may induce some butterflies, the fall is both safe enough and long enough to encourage success. Climb to the leftward-leaning crack and on to the bolt. Continue above this until it is possible to escape leftwards into *Two Sunspots*.
FA. Gary Gibson, Adam Hudson 1983

**8 Midnight at the Oasis** . . E6 6b

From the bolt on *Midnight Summer Dream* teeter up rightwards to an oasis. Continue direct past a peg to finish.
FA. Alan James 1992

**9 Sergeyenna** . . . . . . . . . . . E1 5b

Good climbing up the steep wall, although a little wandering is required for the grade. From the thin crack, head for the roofs. Traverse under these (think about rope-drag!) until a groove allows access to the trees.
FFA. Jerry Peel and team 1976. FA. Bob Dearman, Dave Gill 1966

**10 Heart of Darkness** . . . . E3 5c

A very good mirror image of *Sergeyenna* with some surprising holds and protection. From atop the pinnacle, step left and climb the fine wall to the roofs. Old school thuggery is needed to cross these. Finish at a tree.
FA. John Fleming and team 1980

**11 Hergiani** . . . . . . . . . . . . . E2 5b

Climb to the top of the pedestal from its right-hand side. Step right and continue up the tricky crack then step right and head up some grooves. Abseil off, or do the top pitch which tackles the wall above via two grooves, at 4c.
FA. Paul Nunn, Oliver Woolcock (aid) 1965

**12 Absent Friends** . . . . . . E3 5c

Better protected and not as hard as it looks, this is a fantastic route tracing a line up the steep wall to the right. Above the mid-height crux, continue past a rest ledge to finish up a short groove to a tree. Abseil descent, do not lower around the tree.
FA. Mark Stokes, Mike Browell 1979

**13 Nostradamus** . . . . . . . . . . E1 5b

A sustained pitch with lots of quality moves and rests up the groove-line to the right.. The crux is low-down and nowhere are the difficulties excessive. Start right of *Absent Friends* and climb to a thin break. An awkward move leads to another one to gain the groove which is followed to a lower-off on the right.
FA. Jeff Morgan, Dave Lester (aid) 1970

## Chee Tor - Left

The open left end of this excellent crag has a fine wall with a good set of routes which are as popular as any of the trad routes in the Dale.

**Conditions -** The extreme left-hand end can appear a little dank but the Sergeyenna Wall is the first section of the crag to dry and cleans up pretty quickly in early summer. The crag is very sheltered but it will get wet in any rain.

**Approach (also see page 146) -** Use the Chee Dale Lower Approach. Drop down from the Monsal Trail and double back under the bridge heading downstream. Chee Tor is the first big crag on the right-hand side. It can be reached via the island in the river at the far end. Negotiate this by careful use of the stepping stones, or wading if the water is high.

25m

8  6  7  9  10  11  12  13

**Access -** This buttress is in the wildlife reserve managed by Derbyshire Wildlife Trust. Only use the described approach and do not walk along the crag base further than the described routes.

**⓮ Rave On** . . . . . . . . ⚿ 🧗 🪝 ☐ **E3 5c**

Excellent beefy climbing up the prominent right-facing flake, with good but hard-won gear. Start below and left of the flake (there's a bold direct version at E4 5c). Move right and fight upwards. At the top step left to the lower-off on *Nostradamus*.
*FA. Geoff Birtles, Ernie Marshall, Al Evans 1976*

**⓯ Boobs** . . . . . . . . ⚿ 🪝 🔒 🪝 ☐ **8a**

The line of bolts right of *Rave On* gives a technical pitch which is low in the grade. After the 3rd bolt, trend right into *Boo* and finish up this.
*FA. Andy Popp 1996. Superseded 'No Bolts We're British' (FA. Mark Pretty 1988) which used a similar start but went left into Rave On.*

**⓰ Boo** . . . . . . . . . . ⚿ 🪝 🪝 ☐ **7c+**

A fine, technical and safe companion route to *Tequila* which proves relatively amenable until the sharp and fingery finish. Reaching the first pair of bolts is easy, but then things steadily become more demanding as moves left lead to the crux finale.
*FA. Ben Masterson 1985*

**⓱ Tequila Mockingbird** ⌐Top⌐50 🪝 🪝 ☐ **E6 6b**

An outstanding route marking a step forward in trad limestone climbing. A serious start and long moves between distant gear put this at the upper limit of the grade. Start below the rather high first bolt. Good luck. The route had a controversial history but hopefully now it will remain in its 2 pegs, 2 bolts state. To do a 7c sport route, pre-clip the first bolt above the initial run-out then those climbers who want to attempt a classic E6 still can. The start is harder than it used to be because holds have gone.
*FA. Ron Fawcett 1982. Originally climbed with yo-yo techniques. Visiting Frenchman Jean-Pierre Bouvier red-pointed the route and renamed it 'Gandalf Le Magicien' claiming he had made the first real ascent. Since then the route has twice gained bolts on its initial wall against the wishes of the 1st ascensionist, and then had them removed.*

**⓲ Basic Channel** . . . . ⚿ ①  🪝 🪝 ☐ **8a**

A bolted start to *Eyes of Fire*, some gear is needed for the shared section of the route. Follow the line of bolts (some twinned) to a junction with *Eyes of Fire*. For those who want an 8a sport route lower off at the final pair of bolts.
*FA. Craig Smith 1998*

**⓳ Eyes of Fire** . . . . . . ⚿ 🪝 🗺 ☐ **E6 6c**

A traditional solution to the gap right of *Tequila* which has seen only a handful of ascents. A demanding route which is very difficult to onsight. Start below the large flake on *Mortlock's* and climb to this. Make a desperate traverse left to clip a bolt then continue directly up with no respite to gain a shallow groove and crucial small nut protection (difficult to place). Finish direct to the belay of *Mortlock's*.
*FA. Simon Nadin, Richard Davies 1984. It was bolted in 1988 and received many ascents at 7b+. The bolts were removed later.*

**⓴ Mortlock's Arete** . . ⌐Top⌐50 🧗 🪝 ☐ **E4 6a**

Quite simply, done in its entirety, this is one of the best E4s on limestone in the country.
**1) 6a, 25m.** Climb up a scoop to a bulge (normally with some rotten stuck wires). Pull past these (old peg) and gain the beckoning flake. Thug your way up this to final taxing moves (the scene of many failures) leading to a belay on a small ledge.
**2) 6a, 15m.** The steep, and well-protected groove (an old peg and good wires) above is a contrast to the pitch below requiring subtlety rather than brute strength.
*FFA. Tom Proctor, Geoff Birtles 1976 after a race against Fawcett and Livesey. FA. Colin Mortlock, Lynne Noble, P.Hutchinson 1962. The line they took incorporates Apocalypse P2.*

*The wall up and left of the top pitch of Mortlock's Arete has four pitches. You have to do Mortlock's pitch 1 to get to them.*

**㉑ The Freeman Trap** . . . . . . . . . ☐ **6c+**

Climb slightly leftwards before moving back right at the top.

**㉒ Mantrap** . . . . . . . . . . . . . . . . . ☐ **7b+**

Start with a bulge.

**㉓ The Poverty Trap** . . . . . . . . . . . ☐ **7b**

The tricky bulge and wall.

**㉔ The Freedom Trap** . . . . . . . . . ☐ **E5 6b**

The wall just left of *Mortlock's* top groove. Climb up a rising diagonal and follow this to the break. Belay at the top.
*FA. Simon Nadin 1984*

**㉕ The Golden Mile** . . ⌐Top⌐50 🗺 🪝 ☐ **E5 6b**

Vying with *Supersonic* on High Tor as the best E5 on Peak limestone; but this one is almost a full grade harder. E3 5c climbing leads up the groove with good holds and adequate protection to a rest ledge on the right (bomber crucial nuts). Now climb deviously and determinedly up and left to pockets (in-situ thread) below the sloping ledge. Getting established on this is difficult and leads to a semi-rest, but beware, the upper wall climbed from left to right has taken many scalps. Traverse left to the *Mortlock's* belay or continue up *Apocalypse*.
*FA. Pete Livesey, Alec Livesey 1980. Livesey's last great route in the Peak which was named because Livesey had told Ron Fawcett that he was going to Blackpool for the day, but instead he sneaked here to pick this plum.*

**㉖ The Dream Mile** . . . ⚿ 🗺 🪝 ☐ **E5 6b**

A tight line fitted in right of *The Golden Mile*. Start up *Apocalypse* then break right after 5m and climb the wall direct to the top pitch of *Apocalypse*. Finish up this. A long pitch.
*FA. Mark Pretty 2010*

**㉗ Apocalypse** . . . . . . . ⚿③ 🪝 🗺 ☐ **E4 6a**

Yet another superb Peak E4. Pitch 1 has the technical well-protected crux, but pitch two provides the real challenge.
**1) 6a, 22m.** Easy climbing leads into the corner which is followed with increasing difficulty. Returning from a slight detour onto the left wall provides the crux shortly before the break is reached. Lash yourself in.
**2) 5c, 18m.** Pull over the roof to gain the flake and follow it strenuously on good holds, pausing on occasion to frantically stuff in gear. Save some courage for the final moves off the flake. Move left to follow *Mortlock's* to finish.
*FA. Steve Bancroft, John Allen - the only E6 in Bancroft's 1977 Recent Developments guide. As this was full of notorious sand-bags he must have had a torrid time on this route.*

## Chee Tor - Centre

The central section of Chee Tor has some great long pitches from HVS to E5. Many of the routes are classics but probably *Meditation* and *Ceramic* are the pick of the bunch. Some of the routes look a bit grassy but, once you get on them, their true quality soon shows through.

**Conditions -** Because of the trees the central wall is inclined to hold humidity and is slower to dry but also stays cool in hot weather (until you pop your head above the trees on the crux). The wall is very sheltered.

**Approach -** See page 189.

**Access -** This buttress is in the wildlife reserve managed by Derbyshire Wildlife Trust. Only use the described approach and do not walk along the crag base further than the described routes.

**❸ Meditation** . . . . . . . . . [Top⎺ 50] ▧ [____] **E1 5b**

Although a little polished, this Chee Tor classic offers great climbing at the grade with two distinct and contrasting crux sections. Climb the groove to a rest and thread. Delicate moves right allow access to the upper groove which is left with a hard pull past good gear to excellent finishing holds.
*FA. Jim Moran, George Traish 1977*

**❹ Less Than Zero** . . . . . . ▨[▯][____] **E3 5c**

Worth attempting as an introduction to the grade since there is only one relatively short and well-protected hard bit. From the top of the first groove of *Meditation* continue up and left via a long move to easier climbing.
*FA. Jim Moran, Geoff Milburn, Simon Horrox 1978*

**❶ Alfresco** . . . . . . . . . . . . . . . [____] **HVS 5b**

Sadly a bit of a drainage line otherwise it would see more action.
**1) 5b, 25m.** Start as for *Apocalypse* but traverse right out of the corner when it gets tricky. Climb the flake to a belay at the break.
**2) 5b, 16m.** Move left and pull over into a grotty groove.
**Suddenly, E5 6b -** The wall right of the starting groove of *Alfresco* to reach and cross that route.
*FA. J.Taylor, Graham West (aid) 1960s. FA. (Suddenly) Gary Gibson 1983*

**❷ One Night** . . . . . . . . . . . . ▨[____] **E1 5b**

Pull direct over the bulge above the belay of *Alfresco* into a finely-positioned groove.
*FA. Keith Sharples, Ian Riddington 1983*

**❺ Valentine (pitch 1)** . . . . . . . ▨[____] **E1 5b**

The first pitch gives an excellent counter-diagonal to *Meditation*. Climb the wall left of *Ceramic* past two small trees. Cross over the scoop and holes on *Meditation* and continue up leftwards to the break. There is a second pitch, up the steep groove above, past some old rotten bolts at solid E5.
*FFA. (P2) Jerry Moffatt 1981 with pre-clipped gear.*
*FA. Jeff Morgan, H.Mares (aid on P2) 1970.*

**❻ Approaching** . . . . . . . . ▨[▯][____] **E3 5c**

Another fine climb at the bottom end of the grade, tracing a devious line on good rock with adequate rests. Protection is good, but spaced at times. Start 2m left of *Ceramic* and climb the wall, trending left into a shallow scoop (avoid a rightward line near *Ceramic*; this is E4). Continue up and left to finish up *Meditation*.
*FA. Gary Gibson, Adam Hudson 1983*

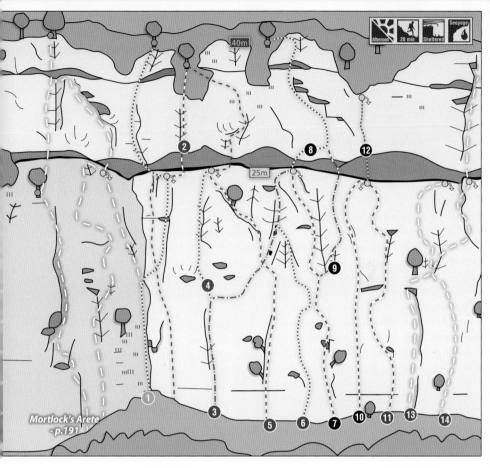

**❼ Ceramic** . . . . . . . . . . 🔲📖☐ **E4 5c**
A Chee Tor rite of passage with a massive reputation for its fall from the crux (which is actually a safe if daunting prospect). Start under the hanging groove and climb up to arrange bomber gear. Run it out up this then escape left at its top to safety; that is unless you are thinking of carrying on up:
*FA. Gabriel Reagan, Mark Stokes 1976*

**❽ Ceramic Extension** . . 🔲📖☐ **E5 6a**
A great old-school E5; sloping holds, bags of exposure, a long run out, awkward-to-clip old gear, but ultimately safe (just tell anyone below to look out.) From the top of *Ceramic*, pull over the bulge and traverse right with difficulty past a peg until, at last, decent holds and easier climbing arrive. Absolutely superb.
*FA. Johnny Woodward, Dave Lee 1982*

**❾ Terrorcotta** . . . . . . 🔲📖☐ **E6 6c**
A bold eliminate. From the base of the *Ceramic* groove step right, place some micro-wires then balance up the wall, with a move right past a tiny tree, to the break. Dump your gear in the break, apart from 1 quickdraw, pull over the bulge on tiny slopers and side-pulls. Run it out up to the peg on *Ceramic Extension* and finish up this.
*FA. Seb Grieve, Jez Portman 1998*

**❿ Laughing** . . . . . . . . . 🔲📖☐ **E6 6b**
Good climbing with an exciting finish. It is possible to inspect it from *Splintered Perspex* but this isn't very encouraging. Climb the wall left of *Splintered Perspex* to a scoop. Pull over the bulge at a streak then move up to a hole. Swing left to a bolt and climb boldly to the break.
*FA. Gary Gibson 1985*

**⓫ Splintered Perspex** . . . . 🔲📖☐ **E3 6a**
A lesser-known Chee Tor gem which gives fine sustained moves and a well-protected crux. Climb the wall to a rest on the left. Make hard moves up and right, past a wafer-thin flake, into a groove. Climb this then keep going up left until one final hard pull gains the break.
*FA. John Fleming (1 pt) 1981. FFA. Ducan Critchley 1981*

**⓬ A Nasty Farming Accident** 🔲📖☐ **7b**
An extension to *Splintered Perspex* past 3 bolts to a lower-off.
*FA. Andy Popp 1996*

Mortlock's Arete - p.191

North | Southwest | Southeast | Stoney | Horseshoe | Smalldale | Harpur Hill | Lovers' Leap | Beerhouse | Craig-y-Biceps | Staden Q | Chee Dale U. | Chee Dale L. | Blackwell D. | Raven Tor | Water-c.-Jolly | Ravensdale | Aldery Cliff | Taddington | Rheinstor

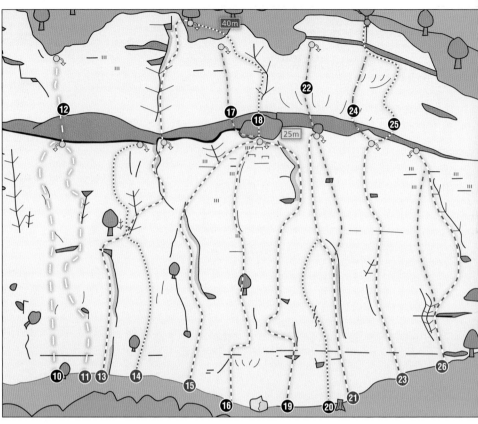

**13 Great Central Route . . .** 〔23〕🏃 ▢ **E2 5c**
A popular climb with two worthwhile and contrasting pitches.
**1) HVS 5a, 25m.** Follow a flake/groove then move right past a
tree to gain a bigger flake/corner. Climb this to the break. Often
done in its own right and pleasant enough.
**2) 5c, 15m.** Struggle desperately past a peg on the bulge and
thrash up the groove above and on into the trees.
*FA. Rod Brown, Alan Wright (aid) 1963*

**14 Of Youth . . . . . . . . . . .** 〔1〕🐾 ▢ **E3 5c**
A counter line to *Great Central* giving good open climbing. Low
in the grade as there is only one short hard section adequately
protected by small wires. Climb the wall past a small tree then
move up and left to the traverse (and tree) of *Great Central*. The
wall above provides a testing finale.
*FA. John Fleming 1981*

**15 Shake. . . . . . . . . . . . . .** 〔1〕 ▢ **E1 5b**
Climb up to reach the large left-facing flake and follow this to
easier ground and the break. Traverse rightwards across the wall
to a yew tree belay.
*FA. Chris Jackson, Tom Proctor 1971*

**16 Two Generations . . . . .** 🏃🕊 ▢ **E6 6b**
A neglected route with a short hard section past a thread on its
lower section. Above, it wanders more easily up the wall.
*FA. Gary Gibson 1985*

**17 Captain Ahab. . . . . . . .** 🏃🦀 ▢ **7b+**
The bulge and wall.
*FA. Mark Pretty 2011*

**18 The Body Line . . . . . . .** 〔1〕🏃 ▢ **E4 6a**
The groove above the yew tree belay for *Shake*. Entry requires
liberal use of the tree which can be a scratchy experience.
The groove itself is very technical although not particularly
sustained. Finish out left to a tree.
*FA. Jim Moran, Geoff Milburn 1983*

**19 Autobahn . . . . . . . . . .** 〔23〕🏃 ▢ **E5 6b**
Another route known for its safe, but juicy fall. Climb the wall to
the flake and good protection. From here, traverse leftwards and
up with difficulty to a small undercut (crucial small wires). Make
one last hard move past this to easier ground.
*FA. Ron Fawcett 1981*

**20 Lily Street. . . . . . . . . .** 🗝🚪 ▢ **E5 6b**
An eliminate left of *Queer Street*. Climb to a thread, move up left
to a bulge (thread) and make a long move over to gain the step
left on *Queer Street*. Check the threads before climbing.
*FA. Gary Gibson 1986*

North | Southwest | Southeast | Stoney | Horseshoe | Smalldale | Harpur Hill | Lovers' Leap | Beerhouse | Craigy-Biceps | Staden | Chee Dale L | Chee Dale U | Blackwell D | Raven Tor | Water-c-Jolly | Ravensdale | Aldery Cliff | Taddington | Rheinstor

**㉑ Queer Street** . . . . . . . 🏷🪧⬜ **E3 6a**
A fantastic, but often frustrating and energy sapping route which is getting rather polished. Very safe, but strenuous to make it so. Climb to the groove and bridge up this until a layback sequence is demanded. If successful, move left to easier climbing leading to the break. **Direct finish** - straight up from the top of the groove.
*FA. Tom Proctor, Chris Jackson 1971*
*FA. (Direct Finish) Gary Gibson, Ian Riddington 1984*

**㉒ Moby Dick** . . . . . . . 🏷🪧🔵⬜ **7c**
The steep bulging wall above the belay of *Queer Street*.

**㉓ 42nd Street** . . . . . . . . 🏷🔵⬜ **E3 5c**
A fine and popular pitch to push your E-grade on. It has a few bold sections but overall it is low in the grade and adequately protected if you stay cool. Start 3m left of the groove of *Sunny Goodge Street*. Climb diagonally leftwards past a hard bit to a rest. Move up then right onto some smooth holds and a decent runner or two. Continue slightly leftwards with difficulty then up onto easier ground and a belay in the break.
*FA. Tom Proctor, Chris Jackson 1971*

**㉔ Theology** . . . . . . . 🏷🪧🔵⬜ **7c**
A good route on the upper wall. From the belay of *42nd Street* climb the steep line left of *Duel in the Sun* past 4 bolts and a peg. Finish up the thin crack of *Duel in the Sun* and abseil off a tree.
*FA. Andy Popp 1996*

**㉕ Duel in the Sun** . . . 🏷🔵🔵⬜ **E5 6b**
A fine though seldomed climbed pitch on the upper wall. From the belay on *42nd Street*, pull over the bulge and clip a peg on the right. Move back left (wire) then pull up and right over the bulge using a hidden hold. One final desperate move gains a break. Move left and finish up the thin crack on the left.
*FA. Dave Lee 1983*

**㉖ Sunny Goodge Street** . . 🏷🔵⬜ **E2 5b**
Features some good moves near the bottom but above the hard section the route rather fizzles out. Follow a short groove then make hard moves across right to an undercut flake. Pull over this and climb the groove above.
**Hatred, E4 5c** - A bold direct version.
*FA. Al Evans, Jim Moran 1977 FA. (Hatred) Gary Gibson 1982*

North | Southwest | Southeast | Stoney | Horseshoe | Smalldale | Harpur Hill | Lovers' Leap | Beerhouse | Craig-y-Biceps | Stadem Q | Chee Dale U. | Chee Dale L. | Blackwell D. | Raven Tor | Water-c-Jolly | Ravensdale | Aldery Cliff | Taddington | Rheinstor

## Chee Tor - Right

On the right-hand end of the crag the rock and route quality drop a notch but there are still a few things worthy of attention. The most important route here is the start of the famous Girdle.

**Approach and Conditions - See page 189.**

**Access - This buttress is in the wildlife reserve managed by Derbyshire Wildlife Trust. Only use the described approach and do not walk along the crag base further than the described routes.**

*The dirty bay to the right of Sunny Goodge Street has four poor neglected routes -* **The Last Laugh, HVS 5a - Pink Panther, E5 6a - Grinning Chimney, HVS 5b - Hooligans, E3 5c.**

**❶ Match of the Day** . . . . . . . 🔏 [    ] **E2 5c**
A good little route which packs a lot into its height. Climb the sustained lower wall to a flake. Follow this with difficulty to easier ground.
*FA. Jim Moran, Al Evans 1976*

**❷ Goal of the Month** . . . . . . . 🔏 [    ] **E3 5c**
Speedy climbing if you do it right. Climb the wall two metres left of the thin crack of *The Chopper* past 2 threads.
*FA. Gary Gibson 1984*

**❸ The Chopper** . . . . . . . . . . 🔏 [    ] **VS 5a**
The thin crack left of the big flake gives a pleasant and testing pitch for the grade. Where the crack runs out, step left into another flake and continue to the belay on the left. Commonly used to start the shorter version of the girdle.
*FA. John Amatt and others 1964*

*There are two poor routes up the front of the big hanging flake,* **Sleepwalkers, HVS 5b** *and* **Pleasant Dreams, HVS 5c.**

**❹ Rape** . . . . . . . . . . . . . 🔏 [    ] **E2 5b**
The right-hand side of the hanging flake gives a worthwhile pitch. Gain it from below and right. There is a second pitch which pulls directly into the vegetable garden above.
*FA. Tom Proctor, Ernie Marshall 1976*

*The bold wall and shallow groove from 5m up the next route is* **Grapple and Grope, E5 6a** *(FA. Gary Gibson 2010)*

**❺ Gulle Gulle Groove** . . . . . . . 🔏 [    ] **VS 4c**
Enjoyable climbing up the open groove left of a big tree.
*FA. Tony Howard and others (aid) 1965*

**❻ Flycatcher** . . . . . . . . . . . 🔏 [    ] **E1 5b**
A poor man's *Snap Dragon* but with good climbing. Climb the wall behind the tree to a flake then move up and left to the edge of the wall. Climb up to join, and finish up, *Gulle Gulle Groove* to the break.
*FA. Jim Moran, G.Traish 1977*

**❼ Snap Dragon** . . . . . 🔏 💬 🔨 [    ] **E5 6b**
An unsung gem. From behind the big tree, climb up to a flake. Move up right to a second flake and then back left to a thread. Launch up the wall above and don't expect any more gear since your right hand will occupy the only decent slot.
*FA Gary Gibson 1984*

**❽ Leering Wall** . . . . . . . . . . 🔏 [    ] **HVS 5b**
An unlikely looking line at the grade. Start up a left-leaning flake. Choose your level and step out right onto the wall, lower is easier, then stand up on some good holds and continue to a tree.
*FA. Tony Howard and others (aid) 1965. FFA. Unknown*

**❾ Dagenham Dave** . . . . . . . . . . [    ] **E1 5b**
Climb the wall to a bulge then make hard moves to gain a groove. Finish at the break.
*FA. Gary Gibson, Phil Wilson 1979*

**❿ Clive's Route** . . . . . . . . . . . . [    ] **VS 4c**
Some thin cracks lead up the wall to a scoop on the right. Finish at a tree.
*FA. Clive Rowland 1965*

*The narrow wall just right is* **Switch, E2 6a** *(FA. Gary Gibson 2010)*

**⓫ Changeling** . . . . . . . . 🔏 🔨 [    ] **E4 6a**
A desperate technical problem which sees few ascents.
*FA. Richard Davies 1984*

**⓬ Doggone Groove** . . . . . . . . . . [    ] **VS 4b**
The groove on the far right of the crag and is usually used as a start to the *Girdle*. There is also a second pitch which follows two grooves to the right (**VS 4b**).
*FA. Malc Baxter, Jim Heys 1961*

**What Aches?, E3 5c** *is the vague rib to the right;* **Otaix, E1 5b** *is 5m right of Doggone Groove and* **Negative Earth, E1 5b** *is 10m right of Doggone Groove.*

Chee Tor - Centre

Chee Tor - Left

p.188

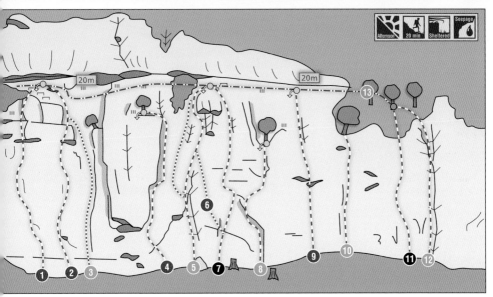

**⑬ Chee Tor Girdle** . . . . . . . . . [Top 50] [ ] **VS 5a**

**172m.** One of the classic VS routes of the Peak which provides a great outing with amazing situations for the grade. Not a good route for a busy weekend but fun and fairly dry (certainly the hardest bits) in light rain. The long version starts up *Doggone Groove* but you can miss the first traverse pitch by starting up *The Chopper*.

**1) 4b, 30m.** Climb *Doggone Groove* to a belay on the left.

**2) 4b, 42m.** Traverse the break to a tricky descent to easy ground. Belay above *Match of the Day*.

**3) 4a, 35m.** Traverse into the gully then out to reach a yew tree above *Queer Street*. The scenery is starting to get better.

**4) 5a, 30m.** Follow the break past many belays and threads, with a hard move above *Ceramic*, to a great hanging stance.

**5) 4c, 35m.** Keep going across the groove of *Alfresco*, tricky crossing the left wall, until you reach the tree/lower-off of *Mortlock's Arete*. Abseil off - 20m to the ground.

*FA. Chris Jackson, J.Atkinson, B.Starkey 1964*

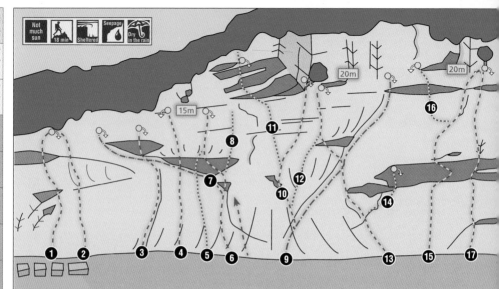

## Cornice - Left

The left-hand side of the Cornice is one of the most impressive bits of rock in the Peak, although in winter, it is difficult to see that it will ever give any dry climbing. When dry, the routes here give some great challenges. **Conditions -** This section is so slow to dry, some years, it doesn't. Even when it is dry it takes a long time for the routes to clean up and requires someone to do the dirty work. Once dry and clean it will remain so for many months and there have even been ascents of *Monumental* in December. It is extremely sheltered from wind and any rainfall no matter how heavy. It is also very cool and shady. In summer the whole of the left and centre part of the crag can be prone to condensation early in the morning and be damp on a dry day. **Approach (also see page 146) -** Use the Chee Dale Lower Approach. Drop down from the Monsal Trail and double back under the bridge heading downstream and cross a wooden bridge to reach stepping stones which lead to the crag.

**❶ Forehead Trombone . . .** 7b+
Start from the second stepping stone and follow a flake to a roof. Pulling over this gives the hard crux. Lower-off on the right. Usually dirty.
*FA. Malcom Taylor, Matt Szabo 1989*

**❷ Sharp Practice. . . .** 8a+
Start from the 1st stepping stone and climb to good holds by the 1st bolt. Make a desperate slopy pull and then attempt to gain holds on the lip. Dyno for a pinch, then move up to the lower-off. Usually dirty.
*FA. Keith Sharples 1995*

**❸ Masculine Power Trip** 8a+
A power problem up the steep seam in the lower wall leaves you below the bulges. Crank this for the full tick. Usually dirty.
*FA. Ben Moon 1989. Extended by Keith Sharples 1994. Formerly aided as 'The Crack'.*

**❹ Mescaline Power Trip. .** 8a
Another desperate start, or use stones and/or the first bolt to gain a finger edge, then start climbing. The rock-over onto the slab is tricky, the roof above, less so; however there is still one obstacle before the lower-off. Usually dirty. Old bolts.
*FA. Mark Pretty 1989*

**❺ Wright-On . . . . . . .** 7c+
Another route which was started by sitting on the first bolt although this one has been bouldered out upping the grade to 8a. The first bolt may be missing anyway. If it is re-bolted then the tricky bit above the start proves to be the intricate footwork needed to cross the roof. Finish at the lower-off on *Taylor Made*.
*FA. Chris Wright 1994*

**❻ Taylor Made . . . . .** 7c
Start up the groove to a rest below the roof (high first bolt). Push on over the roof before making a tricky traverse left. A hard pull upwards remains. A very good route when clean. There is a hard old project to the right which finishes up *Taylor Made*.
*FA. Malcom Taylor 1989*

**❼ Wright to Left . . . .** 7c
A rising traverse that follows the overhanging groove-line crossing the previous three routes to the lower-off on *Sharp Practice*. Usually dirty and the bolts may be rusty.
*FA. Chris Wright 1995*

**❽ Feminine Ego Trip . . . .** 8a
Start as for *Taylor Made* to the rest in the groove. Hard moves on undercuts are needed to gain the hollow flake. There is no lower-off so you have to drop back onto the top bolt to escape. Not very popular and usually dirty.
*FA. Malcom Taylor 1989. Formerly the aid route 'The Groove'.*

**9 Monumental Armblaster** 8a+

One of the best lines in the Peak up the monumental diagonal groove. The climbing is hard and sustained with plenty of knee work and egyptians necessary (knee-pads). There is a bit of a shake at half-height and the finish requires a long reach. It often spits off attempts from high up which can be frustrating. Loss of footholds has made it a bit harder.
*FA. Sean Myles 1989. Formerly the aid route 'Monumental Alabaster'.*

**10 Nemesis** 8a+

From kneebars on *Monumental*, move left to a sika'd crimp, then make powerful moves up and then left to gain a sika'd boss. Move back right to finish with relative ease.
*FA. Keith Sharples 1994. Formerly the aid route with the somewhat comical name of 'The Slab'.*

**11 Clematis** 8b

A left-hand finish to *Nemesis*. Jugs on top of the crag must be held before reaching down to a lower-off bolt.
*FA. Kris Clemmow 2011*

**12 Bricktop** 8b

A fine direct finish to *Nemesis*. Climb direct up the steep wall after the hard start, finishing up the final part of *Malcolm X*. Photo on page 207.
*FA. Kris Clemmow 2010*

**13 Malcolm X** 8b+

A counter diagonal line to *Monumental* with fewer knee bars and significantly harder moves. Start up *Last Eggs* then break left into the rest on *Monumental*. Leave this and head for the lower-off. **Malcolm Armblaster, 8b**, Connects the start of *Malcolm X* to the finish of *Armblaster*.
*FA. Steve McClure 1999. FA. (MA) Dan Varian 2010*

**14 Last Eggs Before the M1** 7c+

Half a route which still awaits an extension. It includes the start of *Malcolm X*.
*FA. John Hart 1991*

**15 Gran Techo** 8b

Climb the wall left of *Jug Jockey* via dynamic moves to the roof. An improbable sequence and seemingly impossible reaches lead to the lip. A final stiff move deposits you onto the slab. A few delicate shuffles along the ramp lead to a rest point before the final pull to the ledge.
*FA. Kris Clemmow 2011*

**16 Techno Prisoners** 8b+

A super reachy finish up the wall above the roof of *Gran Techo*.
*FA. Bob Hickish 2011*

**17 The Jug Jockey** 7c+

A roof climb tackling the obvious weakness in the centre of the long roof. Climb the lower wall through a right curving overlap to a rest below the roof. Swing out along the flake across the roof and make a hard pull onto the upper wall.
*FA. Keith Sharples 1990*

**18 Easy Rider** 7c+

From the roof of *Jug Jockey*, follow the hollow break rightwards until large undercuts and other holds deposit you on the headwall and easier climbing.
*FA. Mark Pretty 2010*

**19 Dreadnaught** 8c

The hardest roof climb in the Peak, tackling the roof at an unobvious weakness. A big ring bolt in the roof marks the line. An old project breaks out right on the upper wall.
*FA. Steve McClure 1999*

**20 The Roof Warrior** 8a

A superb route with three hard sections. The tricky lower wall leads to a shake-out at the roof. Gaining a good hold in the roof is difficult, then easier moves lead to the lip. One more tricky section pulling leftwards around the roof leads to the lower-off.
*FA. Keith Sharples 1991*

**㉑ Cry of Despair . . . . .** 7c
Follow the steep wall to the weakness through the right end of the large roof. The crux is on the bottom wall but many fall off from high up (hence the name) so remember to milk the mid-height rest.
*FA. Chris Hardy 1990*

**㉒ That was the River .** 7b+
An energy-sapping pitch featuring a very tough move to get established on the line of undercuts. From a good jug halfway, easier climbing leads to a wild last couple of moves.
*Photo on pages 9 and 144.*
*FA. Chris Hamper 1988*

**㉓ Rapid City . . . . . . .** 8a
A fine climb which would only be 7c if you didn't have to do the powerful start of *That was the River*. After the start follow the flakes above until a desperate sloper move gains the roof. Many stop here now due to loose holds above on the roof.
*FA. Dougie Hall 1990*

**㉔ Streamline . . . . . . . . .** 7c+
A poor route crossing *That was the River*, sadly it keeps losing holds. The hard moves may be unclimbable now.
*FA. Mike Lea 1994*

**㉕ This is the Sea . . .** 7c+
The direct start to *That was the River* is a contrast. One hard move proves to be the only barrier to success; it is very technical and fingery. One of the first hard routes to dry out.
*FA. Mark Pretty 1988*

**㉖ Old Man River . . . . . . .** 7b
The 1st of the routes up the River via a prominent blunt flake. Crossing the first bulge is tricky. The flake gives a shake-out and the moves above are unobvious but okay when wired.
**Zippy's Direct Finish, 7b+ -** head straight up to the belay on *The Naive and Sentimental Lover.*
**Dirty Old Man, 7c+ -** link this route with *Naive and....*
*FA. Gary Gibson, Matt Ward 1986. FA. (Zippy's Direct) Mark Pretty 1995 FA. (Dirty Old Man) Mark Pretty 2010*

**㉗ Up the River Without a Paddle**
**. . . . . . . . . . . . . . . . .** 6c+
An unlikely climb which is seldom dry but proves popular when in condition. Pull over the first overhang to a shake, then tackle the second overhang and move up and right to gain and follow a strenuous flake-line leading right to the lower-off.
*FA. Gary Gibson 1984*

**㉘ The Naive and Sentimental Lover**
**. . . . . . . . . . . . . . . .** 7b+
Start up *the River Without a Paddle* but break left from the niche above the roof to a flake-line; difficult. A higher method is possible for the short. Climb the wall above on small holds.
*FA. Mark Pretty 1986*

### 29 Snails of the Riverbank 〰️⟦⟧ 7b
The direct that has two hard roofs. The first requires a fingery pull and the second seems very unlikely until you go for it.
*FA. Gary Gibson 1986. FA. (Direct start) Ian Dunn 1997*

### 30 The Spiders from Mars . . . . ⟦⟧ 6b
A poor route with some loose rock. Cross the roofs at a step in the overhangs and plough on up to the lower-off.
*FFA. Neil Molnar, J.Taylor 1983. FA. Chris Jackson, Rod Haslam 1976*

### 31 The Monday Club . . . . . . . . ⟦⟧ 7a+
A dirty start leads to the better top wall. Both overlaps prove tricky to cross.
*FA. Chris Hardy 1989*

### 32 Trampled Underfoot . . . 〰️ ⟦⟧ 7a
A devious route which winds through the roofs to an excellent finish. From *Monday Club* move out right under the roof and make a hard pull into the groove. Avoid the roof by stepping right and left then tackle the upper wall via thin moves.
*FA. Chris Hardy, G.Gilmore 1989*

### 33 Gardener's Question Time. . . 〰️⟦⟧ 7a
Start left of a leaning block and climb the wall past two hard sections to the roof. Heave over this and finish up the wall above. The original line - **Rue Morgue, E4 6a** - gained the same finish by the wall above the block (now *The Goldfish*).
*FA. Seb Grieve 1994. FA. (Rue Morgue) Chris Jackson 1979*

### 34 The Goldfish . . . . . . . . 〰️⟦⟧ 7a+
Climb the wall then move up right to a notch in the main roof. Pull up and around the roof and finish up the rounded slab.
*FA. Gary Gibson, Mark Pretty 1986*

### 35 Crowd Control . . . . 〰️⟦⟧⟦⟧ 7c
A stopper move at the roof and a superb rounded finish. If you can't hack the roof crux, then tag the upper wall onto *Une Crime Passionel* for an easier version - 7a+.
*FA. Keith Sharples 1989*

**❶ Une Crime Passionel** . . . . . 🔁 [____] **E4 6a**
One of the few trad routes on the Cornice that gets ascents.
Start up an open groove to a bolt. Climb past this to a bulge
then move left (bolt) and up to the final crack. Feels about 6c+
with a few wires required.
*FA. Gary Gibson 1982*

**❷ Fey** . . . . . . . . . . 🔁 🖋️ 🐾 [____] **E4 5c**
A good line but usually dirty from neglect. The upper section
gets done as part of *War Memorial*.
**A Basic Power Problem, E6 6b -** A forgotten line to the left
direct through the bulges.
*FFA. Jerry Frost 1980. FA. Bob Conway, Chris Jackson (1pt) 1979.*
*FA. (ABPP) Richard Davies 1989*

**❸ War Memorial** . . . . . . . 🔁 [____] **6c**
A route with some good face climbing. A large cam or wire
might be needed for the top but the climbing is easy.
*FA. Gary Gibson 1983*

**❹ Succubus** . . . . . . . 🔁 🖋️ 🐾 [____] **7b+**
A filler-in but with some good climbing. Hard to grade as the
crux section is reachy, powerful and desperate, but it is quite
short and is much more amenable to redpoint.
*FA. Seb Grieve 1994*

**❺ Shazam** . . . . . . . . . . . 🔁 🐾 [____] **E4 6a**
A thin crack-line leads to a superb move into the top groove.
Lower off from *Martial Music*. Seldom climbed.
*FFA. Jerry Moffatt 1982. FA. Gabriel Reagan, M.Dewsbury (1pt) 1976*

**❻ Martial Music** . . . . . . . 🔁 🐾 [____] **7a**
Neat climbing just right of the crack. Save something for the
move across the top bulge, a common take-off point.
*FA. Gary Gibson 1983*

**❼ Clarion Call** . . . . . . . . . [Top 50] 🐾 [____] **7a**
The first of a great trio, although the lower wall is beginning
to suffer from polish. Probably the most popular climb on the
Cornice. Although the first wall has the hardest move, the top
will sort out those lacking fitness.
*FA. Gary Gibson 1983. Led without bolts by Nick Dixon 1984. Bolts gradu-
ally replaced over the years.*

**❽ Poppy Fields** . . . . . 🔁 🐾 🖋️ [____] **7b+**
Start up *Armistice Day* but pull over the bulge to its left. Up the
technical wall on small edges, pull over the next bulge and make
sustained moves just right of *Clarion Call* to its belay.
*FA. Simon Lee 2004*

**❾ Armistice Day** . . . . . . . 🔁 🖋️ [____] **7a+**
The central line has great climbing interspersed with good rests
including a hands-off knee-bar before the final tricky wall.
*FA. Gary Gibson 1984*

**❿ Whose Line is it Anyway?** [Top 50] 🖋️ [____] **7a+**
The hardest of the trio. Start by going left via an undercut
pocket, then traverse right before breaking back out left to a
boulder problem to gain the niche. Then climb the wall before
heading out left to finish on the scarily-thin jug.
*FA. Jon deMontjoye, Neil Foster 1989*

**⓫ Big Store** . . . . . . . . . . 🔁 🐾 [____] **E5 6b**
Seldom climbed these days but a worthy route with a decent
line. Climb the groove to the bulge then pull left to finish up
*Whose Line*. Two wires should cover it. Will need a clean.
**The Egyptian Bizarre, E5 6b (7a) -** The direct finish past two
bolts. To turn it into a 7a put a long sling on the lower bolt.
*FA. Gary Gibson 1984. FA. (Egyptian Bizarre) Jon deMontjoye 1989*

**⓬ Big Zipper** . . . . . . 🔁 🐾 ▯ [____] **7b**
Gives good independent climbing. Snake around the first bolts
before heading straight to the right edge of the roof. Move up to
the handrail and make a long move up right to a finishing jug; a
popular place to fall from.
*FA. Gary Gibson 1986*

**⓭ Beelzebub** . . . . . . . 🔁 🐾 🖋️ [____] **7b+**
Move left over the bulge from the rest on *Big Zipper*.
*FA. Seb Grieve 1996*

**⓮ Bored of the Lies** . . . . . 🔁 🖋️ [____] **7b+**
This product of an earlier age now appears to have an odd
line, though there is a logic to it; worth doing. The lower wall
is sustained to a semi-rest at a junction with *Big Zipper*, finish
up this. The original finish traversed right and dropped down to
what is now *Ouijaboard*.
*FA. Mark Pretty 1986*

**⓯ Ouijaboard** . . . . 🔁 🐾 🐾 🖋️ [____] **8a**
An excellent route, more independent than it looks. Climb the
wall 2m right of *Bored* on tiny holds, pockets and undercuts to
join and finish for the original *Bored*. Choosing which move is
the crux proves difficult as they're all desperate. Very sequency
and reachy in places but well worth the effort.
*FA. Dave Cross, Carl Dawson 1997*

## Cornice - Centre

The central section of the Cornice is by far the most popular bit with plenty of great routes in the 7a to 7b category. Most are now well bolted with good lower-offs.

**Conditions** - The central section dries more quickly than the steeper walls. It is well sheltered and gives dry climbing in heavy rain.

**Approach** - Page 198.

Not much sun | 18 min | Sheltered | Seepage | Dry in the rain

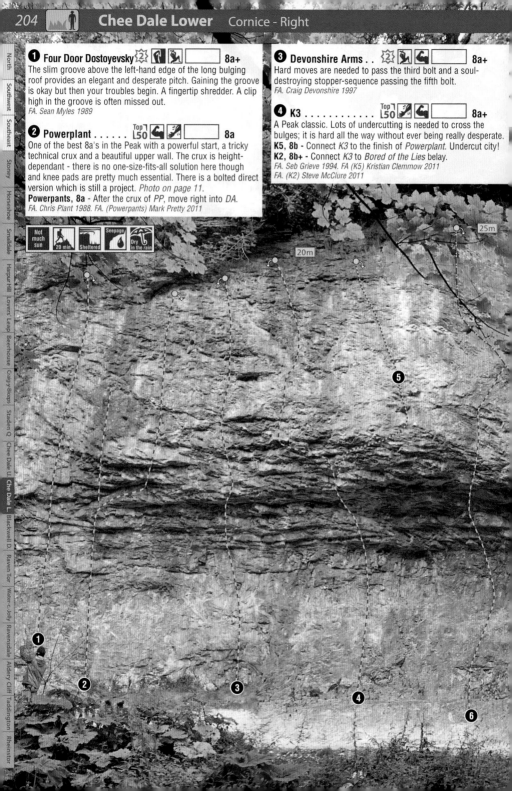

**❶ Four Door Dostoyevsky** 8a+
The slim groove above the left-hand edge of the long bulging roof provides an elegant and desperate pitch. Gaining the groove is okay but then your troubles begin. A fingertip shredder. A clip high in the groove is often missed out.
*FA. Sean Myles 1989*

**❷ Powerplant** [Top 50] 8a
One of the best 8a's in the Peak with a powerful start, a tricky technical crux and a beautiful upper wall. The crux is height-dependant - there is no one-size-fits-all solution here though and knee pads are pretty much essential. There is a bolted direct version which is still a project. *Photo on page 11*.
**Powerpants, 8a** - After the crux of *PP*, move right into *DA*.
*FA. Chris Plant 1988. FA. (Powerpants) Mark Pretty 2011*

**❸ Devonshire Arms** 8a+
Hard moves are needed to pass the third bolt and a soul-destroying stopper-sequence passing the fifth bolt.
*FA. Craig Devonshire 1997*

**❹ K3** [Top 50] 8a+
A Peak classic. Lots of undercutting is needed to cross the bulges; it is hard all the way without ever being really desperate.
**K5, 8b** - Connect *K3* to the finish of *Powerplant*. Undercut city!
**K2, 8b+** - Connect *K3* to *Bored of the Lies* belay.
*FA. Seb Grieve 1994. FA. (K5) Kristian Clemmow 2011*
*FA. (K2) Steve McClure 2011*

Not much sun | 20 min | Sheltered | Seepage | Dry in the rain

North · Southwest · Southeast · Stoney · Horseshoe · Smalldale · Harpur Hill · Lovers Leap · Beehouse · Craig-y-Biceps · Staden Q · Chee Dale U · Chee Dale L · Blackwell D. · Raven Tor · Water-c-Jolly · Ravensdale · Aldery Cliff · Taddington · Rheinstor

**5** 42 . . . . . . . . .  8b
A powerful route breaking right out of *K3* using a combination of undercuts and wild slaps. Neglected in recent years.
*FA. John Hart 1995. His age at the time.*

**6** 32 . . . . . . . . . . . .  8b+
Desperate moves through the bulges to join *R'n'P*.
*FA. Kristian Clemmow 2007. His age at the time.*

**7** R'n'P . . . . . . . . .  Top 50  8a+
The best line here following the right-to-left diagonal through the bulges. The climbing is powerful through these then the upper wall proves less-steep, but still pumpy.
*FA. John Hart 1990*

**8** Snatch . . . . . . .  8b
Desperately thin climbing direct up the smooth wall after the starting bulges of *R'n'P*.
*FA. Kristian Clemmow 2003*

**9** Barney Ragin' . .  8b+
A super-sustained pitch that links *R'n'P* with *Love Amongst the Butterflies* tackling the bulges via a good slot.
*FA. James McHaffie 2010*

**10** Love Amongst the Butterflies
. . . . . . . . . . . . . .  8b
A technical nightmare. Start by pulling over onto the slab and a virtual hands-off rest. Crimp up the blankness above to an undercut then make a final desperate move to gain the belay.
*FA. Seb Grieve 1996*

**11** Asia Shadow Player  8b
A right-hand finish to *Butterflies* starting from its rest is more crimpy and technical than its parent, if that's possible.
*FA. Steve McClure 1997*

**12** Somehow Super . .  8c
Start up *Love Amongst..* and climb direct up the desperate wall.
*FA. Steve McClure 2008*

20m

*Cosmopolitan - p.206*

**Cornice - Right**
The best routes on the cornice are on the elegant central wave of rock which hangs over the path. The multi-layer bulges and steep walls provide some complex challenges, all in the higher grades. Further right is a lesser wall which still has plenty to offer and at slightly lower grades.
**Conditions -** The main bulges are slow to dry but give very sheltered climbing once they get there. The right-hand side dries more quickly.
**Approach -** Page 198.

North  Southwest  Southeast  Stoney  Horseshoe  Smalldale  Harpur Hill  Lovers' Leap  Beerhouse  Craig-y-Biceps  Staden Q  Chee Dale U.  Chee Dale L.  Blackwell D.  Raven Tor  Water-c-Jolly  Ravensdale  Aldery Cliff  Taddington  Rheinstor

North
Southwest
Southeast
Stoney
Horseshoe
Smalldale
Harpur Hill
Lovers' Leap
Beerhouse
Craig-y-Biceps
Staden Q
Chee Dale U
Che Dale L
Blackwell D
Raven Tor
Water-c-Jolly
Ravensdale
Aldery Cliff
Taddington
Rheinstor

| Not much sun | 20 min | Sheltered | Seepage | Dry in the rain |

Somehow Super - p.205

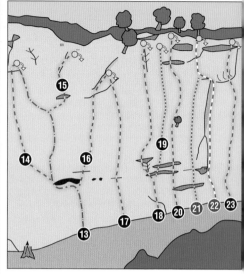

**⑬ Cosmopolitan** . . . . 🔲🔲🔲 **7b+**
A fine climb. Climb up to a wide slot. Swing left then climb direct and slightly left to a stopping point. Step left and make thin moves up and left via a small groove to the lower-off.
FA. Gary Gibson 1985

**⑭ Unleashing the Wild Physique**
. . . . . . . . . . . . . . 🔲🔲🔲🔲 **8a**
One of the original routes here but now much harder due to loss of holds. Climb to the slot on *Cosmopolitan* then traverse left onto the blank wall. Hard technical moves up here gain the belay.
FA. Mark Pretty 1986

**⑮ Cordless Madness** . . . . 🔲🔲🔲 **7c**
A direct finish to *Cosmopolitan* with some fine climbing. Where *Cosmo* goes left mooch right on an undercut - poor footholds - then climb direct.
FA. Nigel Slater, Rosie Brown, Alan Doig 1989

**⑯ Mandy** . . . . . . . . . . . 🔲🔲 **7b+**
From the right-hand end of the slot make a hard fingery pull up to a jug. Finish more easily up the wall and flake above.
FA. Mark Pretty 1986

**⑰ Flowers in the Dirt** . 🔲🔲🔲 **7b**
A disproportionately hard crux provides the main difficulties although the gap between bolts 3 and 4 may be worrying for some. Take a small wire if you are unsure.
FA. Keith Sharples 1989

**⑱ The Third Order** . . . . . . 🔲🔲🔲 **7b**
A short-lived hard section to pass the niche followed by delicate climbing above. This section is particularly difficult when dirty.
FA. Gary Gibson 1985

**⑲ Loco** . . . . . . . . . . 🔲🔲🔲🔲 **7b+**
Hard over the lower bulge, easier above.
FA. Gary Gibson 2002

**⑳ Too Pumpy for Grumpy** . 🔲🔲🔲 **7b+**
Direct over the bulges then up the wall past a small tree.
FA. Nigel Slater 1989

**㉑ Further Adventures in Greendale**
. . . . . . . . . . . . . . . . . . . . . 🔲🔲 **6c**
The red wall left of a flake has a tricky clip or two. The easiest and most logical line heads straight for the lower-off. Passing the lonely bolt out on the right is either a long reach or simply desperate.
FA. Keith Sharples 1989

**㉒ Old Man's Gambit** . . . . . . . 🔲🔲 **E2 5c**
Gain the hanging corner from below. Climb it and escape left at the top into the trees.
FA. Chris Jackson, D.Sant, Rod Haslam 1976

**㉓ The Corniceman** . . 🔲🔲🔲🔲 **7a+**
The wall right of the flake, moving left over the bulge.
FA. Gary Gibson 1986. New finish added when it was rebolted.

 *No climbing to the right of here.*

North
Southwest
Southeast
Stoney
Horseshoe
Smalldale
Harpur Hill
Lovers' Leap
Beehouse
Cadgy-Bicaps
Staden Q
Chee Dale U.
Chee Dale L.
Blackwell D.
Raven Tor
Water-c-Jolly
Aldery Cliff
Ravensdale
Taddington
Rheinstor

Jordan Buys on *Bricktop* (8b) - *page 199* -
on the Cornice. Photo: Mike Hutton

North
Southwest
Southeast
Stoney
Horseshoe
Smalldale
Harpur Hill
Lovers' Leap
Beerhouse
Craig-y-Biceps
Staden Q
Chee Dale U
Chee Dale L
Blackwell D
Raven Tor
Water-c-Jolly
Ravensdale
Aldery Cliff
Taddington
Rheinstor

From mid morning | 20 min | Sheltered | Seepage / Dry in the rain

10m    14m

① The Way of the Gone Wives. . . . ☐ 6b+
Behind a tree at the left-hand end of the wall. An easy lower wall and thin flake higher up. Gold bolts.
FA. Gary Gibson, Simon Rice, Tim Gallagher 1998

② Custard Pie in yer Eye . . . . ☐ 6c
A shallow groove and a bulge. Belay on the tree above.
FA. Gary Gibson, Simon Rice 1998

③ Cry Havoc. . . . . . . . . . . . . . . ☐ 6c
A short wall and groove.
FA. Gary Gibson, Simon Rice, Tim Gallagher 1998

④ Fallout Zone . . . . . . . . . . ☐ 6c
The wall with a bulge just to the right of Cry Havoc.
FA. Gary Gibson, Dave Law 1998

⑤ Gaseous Exchange . . . . ☐ 6c+
Climb the wall to a bulge. Pull around this (hard clip) and finish up the technical wall above.
FA. Gary Gibson, Dave Law 1998

⑥ Chemical Weapons ☐ 7a
An easy wall leads to a difficult bulge. There is more hard climbing on the wall above.
FA. Gary Gibson 1988

⑦ Rhubarb, Rhubarb, Rhubarb ☐ 6b+
Climb easily to reach a technical rib, above and right of the roof. Cross this to the lower-off.
FA. Gary Gibson, Dave Law 1998

⑧ Semolina Sunday. . . . . . . . . . ☐ 6c+
The easy wall leads to a ledge and the break. Above this a few sharp pulls are needed to gain the belay. Can be slimy as it follows a drainage streak.
FA. Gary Gibson 1998

⑨ The Bee's Knees . . . . . . . . ☐ E1 5a
Seldom climbed and probably filthy. The groove right of Semolina to the break. Move up and right to gain a groove leading to a roof. Pull over to the lower-off on Semolina Sunday.
FA. Chris Jackson, Bob Conway 1979

⑩ The Garlic Twist. . . . . . . . . ☐ 6b+
Start right of the groove of The Bee's Knees. It has a hard start and a tricky move on side-pulls above the bulge.
FA. Gary Gibson, Dave Law 1998

⑪ Brief Camouflage . . . . . ☐ 6c
A good route up the clean wall with some technical moves above the break on layaways.
FA. Gary Gibson 1982. Bolted in 1998.

⑫ The Day of the Long Knives . ☐ E6 6b
Given 7b+ by some but it isn't really a sport route in its current condition. After the start, head right to the break. Make some desperate thin moves up the wall above.
FA. Keith Sharples 1989

⑬ Feline Fine . . . . . . . . . . . . ☐ 6c
Good climbing on the lower wall but above the break the main difficulty is keeping out of the groove.
FA. Gary Gibson, Dave Law 1998

⑭ Fat Ginger Cat . . . . . . ☐ 7a+
Start just right of the short crack of Feline Fine. Climb the hard wall to the break then continue with more difficulty to a lower-off on the right.
FA. Malcom Taylor, Jon deMontjoye 1989

## Rhubarb Buttress

The name gives you the right impression - a buttress that is more about vegetation than rock. However, after some hard work by Gary Gibson in the late 1990s, the wall contains a selection of well-bolted sport routes. Of the trad routes, *Blood Lust* is worth a look.

**Approach (also see page 146) -** Use the Chee Dale Lower Approach. Drop down from the Monsal Trail and double back under the bridge heading downstream. Continue under the Cornice and along the boardwalk until the crag appears on the left.

**Conditions -** Although it does receive some sunshine, the wall is shaded by the trees and as such can be a bit damp and green. It is well-sheltered but it gets dirty during the winter and needs to be cleaned up before most of the routes can be climbed - bring a brush when you climb here.

### ⑮ Turbo-charged Monster Mouse

......................... **7a**

The centre of the tallest section of the wall has some excellent technical moves.
*FA. Richard Davies 1986. Bolted in 1998.*

### ⑯ Thrash Your Woodie **7b**

Climb the right-hand side of the wall to a high arching overlap. Finish by heading left.
*FA. Simon Lee 1989*

### ⑰ Me Tarzan......... **7b+**

Tackle the left-hand edge of the long bulging roof.
*FA. Allen Williams 1989*

### ⑱ De Vine....... **8a**

Just to the left of the hanging ivy. A desperate short bulge is ideally suited to those with strong tiny fingers.
*FA. Ruth Jenkins 1994*

*The big cave with a big bulging roof had three routes crossing it. The gear is very old on these now and the cave contains some rare ferns. Please don't climb these routes.*

### ⑲ Blood Lust......... **E2 5c**

A worthwhile trad route. Climb a line of scoops and undercuts to the groove. Finish up the fine flake on the right to a tree. It can be climbed direct on the lower wall at E3 6a.
**Bloodworm, E3 6a -** The dirty wall left of *Blood Lust*.
*FA. Unknown. FA. (Bloodworm) Gary Gibson 1982*

### ⑳ Bad Blood............ **E5 6a**

An old-style trad route with little protection on the lower wall. At the break, avoid the roof by a crafty traverse before moving back left above. The direct line has been climbed with side-runners at E5 6c.
*FA. Gary Gibson 1982*

### ㉑ Blood Transfusion....... **E5 6b**

The right-hand edge of the wall. The start to the bolt needs bouldering out and then comes the crux. At the break, pull over as for *Bad Blood* but continue direct to the trees.
*FA. Chris Hardy 1989*

*The last two routes are on a small white buttress directly above the path, opposite Chee Tor.*

### ㉒ Lady's Finger....... **7a+**

Climb the left-hand line of bolts. Much easier when chalked.
*FA. Gary Gibson 1998*

### ㉓ The European Female.. **7a**

A good route worth cleaning. Although short, it is no pushover; from the first move to the last it hardly lets up.
*FA. Gary Gibson 1983. Bolted 1998.*

North | Southwest | Southeast | Stoney | Horseshoe | Smalldale | Harpur Hill | Lovers' Leap | Beerhouse | Craigy-Biceps | Staden Q | Chee Dale U | Che Dale L | Blackwell D. | Raven Tor | Water-c-Jolly | Ravensdale | Aldery Cliff | Taddington | Rheinstor

One unfortunate feature of hard limestone routes on crags like Raven Tor is their tendency to shed holds and change grade over the years. Usually they become harder as holds break off and the grades creep up which has happened on many routes at Raven Tor. In this photo Toby Dunn is on the latest version of *The Toilet* (8a now but 7c+ in 1988) - *page 222*. Photo: Stu Littlefair

# Miller's Dale
## Blackwell Dale, Raven Tor
## Water-cum-Jolly
## Ravensdale

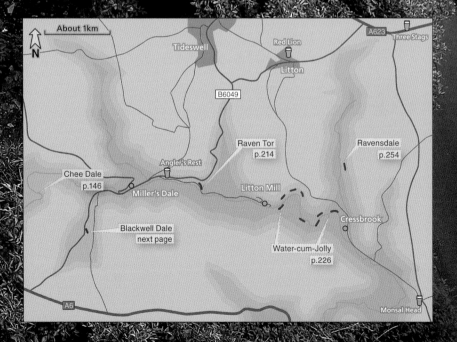

About 1km

N

Tideswell
Red Lion
A623
Three Stags
Litton
B6049

Raven Tor
p.214

Ravensdale
p.254

Chee Dale
p.146

Angler's Rest
Miller's Dale

Litton Mill

Blackwell Dale
next page

Cressbrook

Water-cum-Jolly
p.226

A6

Monsal Head

| | No star | 🌣 | 🌣🌣 | 🌣🌣🌣 |
|---|---|---|---|---|
| **up to 4+** | - | - | - | - |
| **5+ to 6a+** | - | - | - | - |
| **6b to 7a** | 1 | - | - | - |
| **7a+ and up** | 4 | 1 | 4 | - |

Blackwell Dale is the small unspectacular dale leading up from Miller's Dale towards the A6. Beginners' Wall itself is hidden in the trees above the road and, if you drive too quickly, you will miss it. Further up the road is a cave known by its most famous route/problem - *Sean's Roof*. Beginners' Wall itself must be one of the most inappropriately-named crags in the Peak. There is very little for the beginner here although it was originally given the name because it was a good place to learn aid climbing. These days it is most popular as a bouldering venue although the sport routes do get occasional ascents. The main attraction is the route from which the crag takes its name. Most of the other quality routes are really just derivatives of this. There are a few exceptionally bouldery routes on the left-hand side of the crag for those who found the main routes a bit straightforward.

## Conditions
The crag catches little sun, except occasionally in the evening, however even then it is usually filtered through the trees. It is very sheltered from the wind and will give dry climbing in the rain providing it isn't already seeping.

## Approach    Also see map on page 211
Blackwell Dale is situated on the B6094 between Miller's Dale and the A6.
**From Miller's Dale,** head up the hill and after a bend or two there is a small lay-by on the left. The crag is above this.
**From the A6,** drop down the hill. As the dale narrows there is a huge cave on the right (*Sean's Roof*). The lay-by for Beginners' Wall is 200m after this cave.

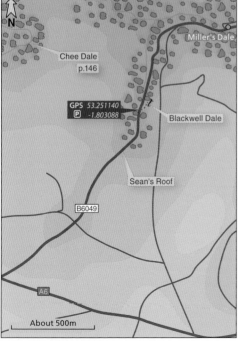

The first route is in the road-side cave, about 100m further up the road from the small lay-by for Beginners' Wall.

**❶ Sean's Roof** . . . . . 🌣 🗡️🔩 [    ] 8b+
Originally climbed as a sport route but it is now more usually bouldered above mats at Font 8a+/V11. Follow the bolts on the left-hand side of the cave to finish on the hold by the last bolt.
*FA. Jerry Moffatt 1995*

There is more bouldering in this cave plus several problems on a wall on the other side of the road.

**❷ The Midges Bite Back** . . . . . 🔩 [    ] 7a+
An occasionally well-named route, two metres left of *Citadel*. Cross the two roofs with small rests in between.
*FA. Paul Reeve 1989*

**❸ Citadel** . . . . . . . . . . . 🗡️🎖️ [    ] E1 5b
The big leering groove. Go on, you know you want to.
*FA. Geoff Birtles, Ron Fawcett (1pt) 1972. FFA Ron Fawcett 1970s*

**❹ O'Leanna the Butler Dunn It!** . . . [    ] 7c+
A short and desperate boulder problem two metres right of *Citadel* to an easier finish up the steep flake-line.
*FA. Richard Patterson 1995*

**❺ The Love of Money is the Root of All Evil**
. . . . . . . . . . . . . . . . . . . . . . 🔩 [    ] 8a+
Desperate crimpy climbing with a dynamic move to gain an often-wet pocket. Continue up the flake-line of the previous route to finish.
*FA. Richard Patterson 1998*

**6 Fossil Wall** . . . . 🏃📖📙🔧⬜ **7c**
A powerful route following the line of substantial glue-in bolts.
Start on the left-hand side of the juggy ledge then undercut left
to gain a crack. Follow this up and then make a hard stretch
rightwards to gain another crack. Finish more easily.
*FA. Ron Fawcett 1986*

**7 Let's Get Physical** . 🏃📖📙⬜ **8a+**
Great moves straight up the steepest section of the buttress.
Single bolt lower-off.
*FA. Mark Pretty 1988*

**8 Let's Get Fossilised** . . . 🏃🔧⬜ **7c+**
Links the start of *Let's Get Physical* with the upper section of
*Fossil Wall*. Climb *LGP* to near the 3rd bolt, then span left with
difficulty to gain the upper flake on *Fossil Wall*. Finish up this.
*FA. Jon Clark 2009*

**9 Beginners' Wall** . . . . . . 🏃📖⬜ **7b+**
The most popular route here is used as a power training
exercise. Jump to start then heave up the pockets above.
*FA. Paul Mitchell 1984*

*The lower section has been developed with a number of boulder
problems around the start of Beginners' Wall.*

**10 Middle Age Spread** . . . . . . 📙⬜ **7b+**
The wall 4m right of *Beginners' Wall*. A minor variation is **A
Bigger Slap** which goes direct to the lower-off by a harder move
but the same overall grade.
*FA. Mark Pretty 1988*

| | No star | ⚝ | ⚝⚝ | ⚝⚝⚝ |
|---|---|---|---|---|
| up to 4+ | - | - | - | - |
| 5+ to 6a+ | - | - | - | - |
| 6b to 7a | 1 | 1 | - | - |
| 7a+ and up | 4 | 23 | 18 | 15 |

Raven Tor is the most famous Tor in the Peak, even the French have heard of this one! The main reason for its fame is the sheer number of dramatic hard routes it has produced over the years. Almost every recent wave of development in climbing standards in Britain has produced a route at this crag - *The Prow*, once proclaimed as the hardest route in the World; *Revelations*, one of the first 8a+'s in the World; *Hubble*, the World's first 8c+ (or even 9a?); and now *Mutation*, one of only a hundred or so 9a routes in the World. The crag still has more to offer and the bulging roof right of *Hubble* is set one day to push the notch higher again.

Unlike many steep limestone crags in Yorkshire, and abroad in France and Spain, the very hard routes at Raven Tor tend to be more bouldery and powerful, with short but intensely difficult sequences rather than sustained stamina plods. This makes repeats of the top routes even harder to come by since you can't just get fitter, you need to get stronger as well. The routes a grade or two below the top routes are now mainly used as training pieces by local climbers. *Sardine* and its many variations have become somewhat polished over the years but they should still be regarded as excellent worthwhile challenges by any aspiring sport climber. *Indecent Exposure* and *Body Machine* are both fine, sustained lines and *The Prow* itself is probably the best of the lot, offering a great free route with a devious line up the centre of the crag. For the less experienced climber, Raven Tor has little to offer except big grades to oggle at. Boulderers will find plenty to keep themselves busy, especially on the right-hand side of the crag.

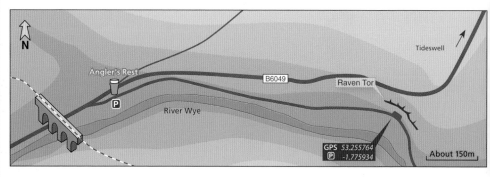

## Approach    Also see map on page 211

Raven Tor is the perfect crag for the roadside generation. It should be approached from the B6049 at Miller's Dale, just south of Tideswell. A sharp turn off this road (signed to Litton Mill) leads past the Angler's Rest and on for about 1km to the crag, which is un-missable above the road on a bend (although it was famously missed once by an underwhelmed visiting American rock star). Parking is limited, if it is full DO NOT block the road as this has caused problems in the past. Alternative parking is available a 5 min walk further on at the bottom of Tideswell Dale.

## Conditions

A majestic sun-trap and early starts are needed in summer to beat the sunshine onto your chosen redpoint route. A moment too late and the place becomes an unappealing sweat bowl where holding onto even the biggest of jugs becomes impossible. In wetter and colder weather the crag can be a great place to head for. The capping roof gives shelter from the heaviest of rain.

## Access

Raven Tor is on land owned by the National Trust who are willing to allow access to the crag. Make sure that you park carefully and don't block the road - alternative parking is available 5 minutes walk away at the base of Tideswell Dale. Also, please avoid unnecessary disturbance of the vegetation and bird life, particularly at nesting time.

Simon Wren on *Obscene Gesture* (7c) - *page 222*. Photo: David Bond

1982 was a big year for Raven Tor with free ascents of many old aid routes. One odditiy from this period was Dominic Lee's ascent of *Obscene Gesture* which he graded E6 6b and named after its mono move. It remained one of the few hard trad routes here until it was finally retro-bolted in 2009 on a slightly different line. Not surprisingly, it has become very popular since then.

North | Southwest | Southeast | Stoney | Horseshoe | Smalldale | Harpur Hill | Lovers' Leap | Beerhouse | Craig-y-Biceps | Staden Q | Chee Dale U. | Chee Dale L. | Blackwell D. | Raven Tor | Water-c-Jolly | Ravensdale | Aldery Cliff | Taddington | Rheinstor

North | Southwest | Southeast | Stoney | Horseshoe | Smalldale | Harpur Hill | Lovers' Leap | Beerhouse | Craig-y-Biceps | Staden Q | Chee Dale U | Chee Dale L | Blackwell D | **Raven Tor** | Water-c-Jolly | Ravensdale | Aldery Cliff | Taddington | Rheinstor

*The first couple of routes hardly ever dry out now due to changes to the drainage in the fields above the crag.*

**❶ Koran Direct** . . . . . . . . . . 🖾 [    ] **7a+**
A fully bolted route that is hardly ever climbed these days due to the fact it takes a long time to dry out and clean up.
*FA. Nigel Slater 1985. FA. (Koran) Tom Proctor, D.Baker 1966.*
*FFA. (Koran) Pete O'Donovan, Chris Craggs 1982*

**❷ Ayatollah** . . . . . . . . . . . . 🖾 [    ] **6c+**
Once a popular warm-up route, but now it is usually wet and dirty and sees little attention.
*FA. Pete Oxley, Brian Tilley 1988.*

**❸ Barely Decent** . . . . 🖾 🔦 🎿 [    ] **7a+**
Originally this started at 7b+ just to the left of the direct start to *Indecent Exposure*, to join it briefly at the break. A new left-hand start has now been bolted (the start of the old route *Hubris*) which makes a more logical combination with the rest of the route but is much slower to dry. The line leads up and leftwards through the flakes to finish up the final section of *Ayatollah*.
*FA. Mark Pretty 2008*

*The left-hand bolted start of Barely Decent, and the loose rock above it, is the line of* **Hubris** *- initially an epic aid route and then a seriously loose E5 free climb.*

*The sad loss of the tree traditionally used to start Indecent, Body Machine and The Prow has slightly spoilt some of the routes here especially when the lower wall is slimy and wet, as it usually is, since then a stick clip is required to start them.*

*The old tree. Dave Turnbull belaying. Photo: Neil Foster*

**❹ Indecent Exposure** . [50] 🔦 🎿 [    ] **7c**
Climb up the awkward bottom wall to the break, then pull over a bulge and continue up a large chalked-up flake. (Stick clip the second staple for the 7b+ tick if the bottom is wet). Move up to undercuts and rightwards to climb a short fingery section. Then head back left and up to the break. Continue up the pumpy groove above to a high lower-off (28m). When very dry you can do the start to *Barely Decent* and move right at 7b+ for the full route from the ground. If you climb to the top of the crag from here then you've done **The Full Monty, 7c+**. Originally the route used the stance on *The Prow* and then swung round the hanging arete to the right (E5 6a) to access the top of the crag - this was the pitch that gave the route its name.
*FFA. Ron Fawcett 1982. FA. (The Full Monty) Mark Pretty 2005*
*FA. Jeff Morgan, H.Mares (as the Prowler) 1970*

**❺ Body Machine** . . . . [50] 🔦 🎿 [    ] **7c+**
A classic route with great moves throughout its full length, and includes a finish which can spit you off. Climb up the technical and fingery bottom wall, just to the right of the *Indecent Exposure* start, to the break and a rest at a flake. (Stick clip the second or third bolt when the bottom wall is wet - 7c for the full route from here). Move up and rightwards and make a hard rock-over to a good hold. More good moves lead to the next break and bit of a rest. Pull over and sort out which holds to use to shimmy rightwards before a final big heave over the top bulge.
*Photo on page 7.*
**Half Decent, 7c** - Climb *Body Machine* to the first break, then make tricky moves up and slightly left to join *Indecent Exposure* at its crux. Continue up that route to finish.
*FA. Ron Fawcett 1984. FA. (Half Decent) Mark Pretty 2008*

**❻ An In and Out of Body Experience**
. . . . . . . . . . . . . . . . . 🔯 🤚 🎿 [    ] **8a**
An fine extension to *Body Machine* climbing the wall up and left of the belay to powerful moves around the top roof.
*FA. Mark Pretty 2007*

**❼ Body Builder** . . . . . 🔯 🤚 🎿 [    ] **8a+**
Climb *Body Machine* to the big hole in the upper break, then pull up and rightwards and attack the powerful bulge, rejoining *Body Machine* at the end.
*FA. Mark Pretty 2007*

## Raven Tor - Left

The tallest section of the crag is on the left-hand side beneath the prominent prow. The trio of *Indecent*, *Body Machine* and *The Prow* are the big routes here with each being a superb and a historically significant route. Further left on the scrappy left-hand side, the routes are not in the same class.

**Conditions -** A sheltered sun-trap. It seeps in the wetter months and only gives limited cover in the rain although the big three routes should stay dry.

*The Prow - p.218*

North
Southwest
Southeast
Stoney
Horseshoe
Smalldale
Harpur Hill
Lovers' Leap
BeeHouse
Craigy-Biceps
Staden Q
Chee Dale U
Che Dale L
Blackwell D
Raven Tor
Water-c-Jolly
Ravensdale
Aldery Cliff
Taddington
Rheinstor

**❶ The Prow** . . . . . . . ⬜[50] 🔲🔲🔲 **8a**

One of the historic landmark routes of the Peak. The way to climb it these days is in one giant pitch from the ground for an amazing 8a tick, although it is still a good 7c+ tick done in one pitch to the belay of *Body Machine*. Climb up the *Body Machine* start then traverse rightwards past a belay and up the technical wall to a big hole in the break. Move slightly right again and then straight up the tufa line via superb moves. Enter the massive groove line above and get a sneaky rest at the *Body Machine* belay. Finally climb up to the giant roof and exit via very powerful moves to a belay up and right.
FA. Ron Fawcett, Gill Fawcett 1982 (over 3 days). Followed the line of some of the aid route 'The Prow Route' (Bob Dearman, J.Gerrard 1963) although not the start or middle section. Repeated in a single day by Jerry Moffatt. Claimed as the 'hardest route in the world' in High magazine.

**❷ Jehovah Kill** . . . . . 🔲🔲🔲🔲 **8b+**

A desperate technical exercise up the wall to the right of The *Body Machine* start. Lower-off at the first break.
FA. Jon Welford 1993

**❸ The Crucifixion** . . . . 🔲🔲🔲🔲 **8a**

Climb *The Prow* to the base of the final groove, then pull directly over the small roof above and a brief rest then make a big span left (hence the route name). Continue up the headwall up and left to another hard move and a shared belay with *The Prow*. Very pumpy.
FA. Neil Foster 2006

**❹ Proud Whore** . . . . . . 🔲🔲🔲 **7c+**

Climb *The Prow* to the top of the tufa line and then continue straight up past a tricky move to enter the steep groove line above. Continue up this on better holds to a lower-off. Excellent.
FA. Mark Pretty 2003 The top section was the line originally taken by Andy Pollit's 1987 route Whore of Babylon.

**❺ Brazen Strumpet** 🔲🔲🔲🔲 **8a**

A complicated and very long (40m) pitch requiring some careful rope work. Start up *The Prow* to the belay on *Revelations* then climb the wall diagonally up and rightwards past some undercut flakes to the high break. From here move right along the ledge and climb up the crux headwall via some desperate bouldery moves. A brief diversion into *Proud Whore* and back right will deposit you underneath a small roof. Pull around this to gain the belay. Best done on a quiet day.
FA. Mark Pretty 2006

**❻ Revelations** . . . . . ⬜[50]🔲🔲 **8b**

A great historic route that still regularly repels attempts. A desperate start (which has got harder over the years) using a poor pocket gains the groove and a knee-bar rest. Swing out right, then pull up and onto the technical slab to the lower-off.
FFA. Jerry Moffatt 1984 A free version of The Prow Direct start. Soloed by visiting Frenchman Anthoine le Menestral in 1985!
FA. Bob Dearman, M.White 1965

**❼ Rage** . . . . . . . . 🔲🔲🔲🔲 **8b**

The significant continuation of *Revelations* is the true line of the old aid route *The Prow*. Follow *Revelations* to the belay then continue up the first part of *The Prow* to the hole in the break. Climb directly up a thin flake to a hard move to the break. Then move up and left via tricky moves to the belay of *Body Machine*.
FFA. Malcolm Taylor 1992. FA. (The Prow) Bob Dearman, J.Gerrard 1963.

**❽ Hubble** . . . . . . . . . 🔲🔲🔲 **8c+**

Climb directly over the bulges below and right of *Revelations*, moving slightly left above. Another historical landmark, being the world's first 8c+, and one which is still very rarely repeated. Rumoured to be hard for the grade! *Photo on page 36*.
FA. Ben Moon 1990. A replica of the route was even built in a Sheffield cellar. Repeated only twice over the next 10 years.

To the right of *Hubble* is an infamous project, *Brandenburg Gate*, rumoured to be in the 9b range.

**❾ Make It Funky** . . . . 🔲🔲🔲 **8c**

A breach of the lower bulges that packs in a lot of hard climbing. Follow the bulges leftwards to a blank section and the infamous mono move - an old bolt hole. Move right to the flake and lower-off of *Mecca*. A drier direct start has also been added at the same grade.
FA. Mark Pretty 1993. Originally known as Mega.

**❿ Mega Whore** 🔲🔲🔲🔲🔲 **8c**

An extension to *Make It Funky* is a good, but slightly unbalanced, pitch which has never become popular. Climb the original route past the mono move, then continue straight up the wall to join *Brazen Strumpet*. Finish at the *Mecca* lower-off.
FA. Steve McClure 1998. The route Whore of Babylon (FA. Andy Pollitt 1987) had 3 points of aid to by-pass what is now Hubble and reach the upper wall. FA. (as Brandenburg Gate) Brian Moore, Jim Ballard 1966.

**⓫ Mecca - The Mid-life Crisis**
. . . . . . . . . . . ⬜[50]🔲🔲🔲🔲 **8b+**

A fine, historic route from the 80s, which has some stopper moves and regularly repels redpoint attempts. Start in the cave and swing out to gain the wall. Reaching the hanging groove up and left is taxing, climbing it is only marginally easier. Finish by stretching left to the big flake and lower-off, or try the next route.
FA. Martin Atkinson 1988. The hardest route in the country at the time and completed the day before Martin moved to Switzerland.

**⓬ Mecca Extension** 🔲🔲🔲🔲 **8c**

The full version is an incredible stamina test which packs an 8a+ on top of the already desperate 8b+. There is a rest at the *Mecca* flake and a breather higher up before the upper crux.
FFA. Steve McClure 1998. It had been a long-standing project of Mark Leach's but, after working the top section, he was unable to repeat Mecca in order to attempt the link. FA. Graham West, Barry Roberts 1960. The original aided line is well to the left of the free line of Mecca although several lines were taken on the early aid attempts.

**⓭ Hajj** . . . . . . . . . 🔲🔲🔲🔲 **8c**

Another extension to *Mecca*, which is slightly harder and more bouldery than the original. Follow *Mecca Extension* to the good hold just before the top crux, then climb the black wall up and leftwards via desperate moves to the top ledge and a traverse right to the original belay.
FA. Steve McClure 2004

**⓮ Kaabah** . . . . 🔲🔲🔲🔲🔲 **8c+**

A stunning direct extension to *Mecca* which avoids the big flake at the belay. At the top of *Mecca's* groove continue direct up the thin flake-line to a brief rest in a small recess. Continue direct up the desperate wall above to join *Mecca Extension* near the top.
FA. Steve McClure 2004

### Raven Tor - Centre

The centre of the cliff is savagely undercut, a barrier which put off all attempts at free climbing until Moffatt breached it in 1984 with *Revelations*. Developments since then have almost all been with ground-breaking ascents of major projects, often at a new grade level. Many of the routes are content simply to cross the lower roofs (at an average grade of around 8b), but more recently some have been extended upwards. The end result is the most concentrated collection of hard routes in the country.

**Conditions -** A well-sheltered sun-trap, giving dry climbing in the heaviest of rain, but it suffers from seepage, and is slow to dry in the spring.

Lots of sun | Roadside | Sheltered | Seepage | Dry in the rain

40m

28m

20m

*Body Machine - p.216*

10m

*Evolution - p.220*

North · Southwest · Southeast · Stoney · Horseshoe · Smalldale · Harpur Hill · Lovers' Leap · Beehouse · Crag-y-Bicsps · Staden Q · Chee Dale U. · Chee Dale L. · Blackwell D. · Raven Tor · Water-c-Jolly · Ravensdale · Aldery Cliff · Taddington · Rheinstor

**⑮ Evolution** ........ 8c+

Moffatt's last significant route at the Tor was a major achievement in every respect, although it has now been over-shadowed by *Mutation*. Lower-off above the small flake which is reached after a crucial span left.
*FA. Jerry Moffatt 1995*

**⑯ Mutation** ...... Top 150 9a

The most impressive of McClure's awesome additions to the crag and the current hardest in the Peak. Before the hard span near the top of *Evolution* gain a pinch after a hideous cross-over move. Continue up the wall above to the lower-off on *Chimes*.
*FA. Steve McClure 1998*

*A couple of high level link-ups have been completed.*
**Stevolution, 9a** – *Climb Evolution to the belay and continue into Kaabah.*
*(FA. Steve McClure 2009)*
**Devolution, 8b+** – *Climb Evolution to past the roof then pull out right to finish up Chimes of Freedom. (FA. Rupert Davies 2005)*

*The next section of rock has a number of very complicated lines and link-ups.*

**⑰ Chimes of Freedom** . 8a+

One of the more popular hard routes at the Tor. There are several methods to pull around the bottom roof, all are hard and powerful. Some lower-off at the first break above the roof for an 8a tick, but the wall above is superb and considerably easier (7c), to finish at a lower-off in a scoop.
*FA. Andy Pollitt 1986. The initial roof had a huge block on it which made the route much easier. It was reclimbed by Ben Moon in 1990 after this had fallen off. FA. (Free and Easy) Chris Craggs, Colin Binks, Martin Veale 1982*

*In addition to the plentiful bouldering available in the cave, there is also a fun traverse:*
**Mecca Traverse, 8a+** - *A right to left of the entire cave. Start as for Weedkiller, cross Chimes and Evolution at a high level under the lip, then swing across jugs and down-climb the start of Mecca. (FA. Kristian Clemmow 2004)*

**⑱ Major Waddage** .... 8b

A superb long extension to *Chimes of Freedom*. The route misses out the *Chimes* belay and continues straight up the technical wall with a hard move to gain the big break. After a good rest here move up and left and make a desperate reach (or dyno) to a good hold, then back right via tricky moves to below the small roof at the top. Pull over this to the belay.
*FA. Steve McClure 2003*

**⑲ The Green Alternative** 7c+

The short roof to the right of *Chimes* shares the same start then pulls up right and through the roof via campus style moves to a belay. It can also be linked into the upper wall of *Chimes of Freedom* to give **Chimes Alternative, 8a**.
*FA. Mark Pretty 2007. FA. (Chimes Alternative) Jon Clark 2009*

**⑳ Weedkiller** ...... 7c+

A typical Raven Tor boulder problem route. Reaching the roof is tricky but crossing it is another ball game altogether.
*FA. Tim Freeman 1984. Reclimbed by Steve Lewis in 1990 after he himself had spectacularly pulled a small but crucial block off it.*

**㉑ Rooster Booster (P2)** 7c

A seldom-climbed pitch which is a little loose in places, however, the position and moves are good. It can be gained by aiding up to the start belay or, better still, start up *The Green Alternative* and link into it - **The Green Rooster, 8a**.
*FA. Jerry Moffatt 1982.*
*FA. (The Green Rooster) Ted Kingsnorth 2009*

**㉒ Fowl Play** ....... 8a

Start up *Weedkiller* to the belay then climb *Rooster Booster* (pitch 2) to the high break. Pull over the bulge up and leftwards to a junction with *Waddage* just below the top.
*FA. Mark Pretty 2004*

**㉓ Jive Turkey** ...... 7b+

A worthwhile pitch with good moves. From the *Weedkiller* belay, head up and right via a thin flake-line to the break and a rest. Then head up and rightwards via fingery moves to the belay. Starting up the *Green Alternative* gives **Let's Get Green, 7c+**.
*FA. Mark Pretty 1987.*
*FA. (Let's Get Green) Ted Kingsnorth 2009*

**㉔ The Missing Link** ..... 8a

Start up *Weedkiller* then follow *Jive Turkey* to the thin break-line. From here climb direct up the snappy black wall above and then a traverse left into *Rooster Booster* (P2) to finish. Can also be started via *The Green Alternative* at the same grade.
*FA. Mark Pretty 2007*

**㉕ The Exterminator** .. 8a+

Climb *Weedkiller* to the belay, then make a short traverse rightwards for about 2m to gain the thin wall and then continue straight up to a junction with *Jive Turkey* at the break. Finish up that route to the belay. Can also be started via *The Green Alternative* at the same grade.
*FA. Mark Pretty 2007*

**㉖ Rooster Crossing** .. 8c

A desperate direct start to *The Exterminator*. Climb through the roof to the right of *Weedkiller* via grim moves to the thin break, then slightly left to join *The Exterminator* at its crux. Continue up this to finish.
*FA. Steve McClure 2007*

**㉗ Rooster Booster**... 7c+

The distinct traverse line left from the start of *Sardine* gives a powerful and strength-sapping pitch which suits those with small fingers. The original second pitch is now usually climbed as a route on its own reached from a different start.
*FA. Jerry Moffatt 1982. FA. (as The Cambridge Bolt Route) Rod Brown, Michael White 1964. Ello Ethique is a weird combination climbed by Jean Baptiste Tribout in 1985. It combined Weedkiller with a reverse of Rooster Booster and then most of Sardine - bizarre but impressive.*

North
Southwest
Southeast
Stoney
Horseshoe
Smalldale
Harpur Hill
Lovers' Leap
Beerhouse
Craig-y-Biceps
Staden Q.
Chee Dale L.
Chee Dale U.
Blackwell D.
Raven Tor
Water-c.-Jolly
Ravensdale
Aldery Cliff
Taddington
Rheinstor

Lots of sun | Roadside | Sheltered | Seepage | Dry in the rain

Sardine - p.222

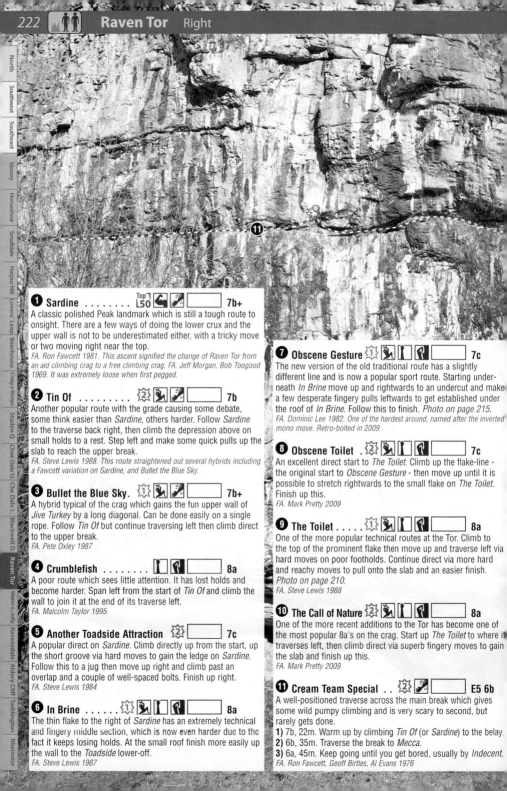

**① Sardine** . . . . . . . . `Top 50` 7b+

A classic polished Peak landmark which is still a tough route to onsight. There are a few ways of doing the lower crux and the upper wall is not to be underestimated either, with a tricky move or two moving right near the top.

FA. Ron Fawcett 1981. This ascent signified the change of Raven Tor from an aid climbing crag to a free climbing crag. FA. Jeff Morgan, Bob Toogood 1969. It was extremely loose when first pegged.

**② Tin Of** . . . . . . . . 7b

Another popular route with the grade causing some debate, some think easier than *Sardine*, others harder. Follow *Sardine* to the traverse back right, then climb the depression above on small holds to a rest. Step left and make some quick pulls up the slab to reach the upper break.

FA. Steve Lewis 1988. This route straightened out several hybrids including a Fawcett variation on Sardine, and Bullet the Blue Sky.

**③ Bullet the Blue Sky.** 7b+

A hybrid typical of the crag which gains the fun upper wall of *Jive Turkey* by a long diagonal. Can be done easily on a single rope. Follow *Tin Of* but continue traversing left then climb direct to the upper break.

FA. Pete Oxley 1987

**④ Crumblefish** . . . . . . . . 8a

A poor route which sees little attention. It has lost holds and become harder. Span left from the start of *Tin Of* and climb the wall to join it at the end of its traverse left.

FA. Malcolm Taylor 1995

**⑤ Another Toadside Attraction** 7c

A popular direct on *Sardine*. Climb directly up from the start, up the short groove via hard moves to gain the ledge on *Sardine*. Follow this to a jug then move up right and climb past an overlap and a couple of well-spaced bolts. Finish up right.

FA. Steve Lewis 1984

**⑥ In Brine** . . . . . . 8a

The thin flake to the right of *Sardine* has an extremely technical and fingery middle section, which is now even harder due to the fact it keeps losing holds. At the small roof finish more easily up the wall to the *Toadside* lower-off.

FA. Steve Lewis 1987

**⑦ Obscene Gesture** 7c

The new version of the old traditional route has a slightly different line and is now a popular sport route. Starting underneath *In Brine* move up and rightwards to an undercut and make a few desperate fingery pulls leftwards to get established under the roof of *In Brine*. Follow this to finish. *Photo on page 215.*

FA. Dominic Lee 1982. One of the hardest around, named after the inverted mono move. Retro-bolted in 2009

**⑧ Obscene Toilet** . 7c

An excellent direct start to *The Toilet*. Climb up the flake-line - the original start to *Obscene Gesture* - then move up until it is possible to stretch rightwards to the small flake on *The Toilet*. Finish up this.

FA. Mark Pretty 2009

**⑨ The Toilet** . . . . . 8a

One of the more popular technical routes at the Tor. Climb to the top of the prominent flake then move up and traverse left via hard moves on poor footholds. Continue direct via more hard and reachy moves to pull onto the slab and an easier finish. *Photo on page 210.*

FA. Steve Lewis 1988

**⑩ The Call of Nature** 8a

One of the more recent additions to the Tor has become one of the most popular 8a's on the crag. Start up *The Toilet* to where it traverses left, then climb direct via superb fingery moves to gain the slab and finish up this.

FA. Mark Pretty 2009

**⑪ Cream Team Special** . . E5 6b

A well-positioned traverse across the main break which gives some wild pumpy climbing and is very scary to second, but rarely gets done.
1) 7b, 22m. Warm up by climbing *Tin Of* (or *Sardine*) to the belay.
2) 6b, 35m. Traverse the break to *Mecca*.
3) 6a, 45m. Keep going until you get bored, usually by *Indecent*.

FA. Ron Fawcett, Geoff Birtles, Al Evans 1976

## Raven Tor - Right

This section is the training wall. The prolific number of eliminates and combination pitches is a result of endless hours spent by the top climbers working out (often so that they can walk 30m to the left and try a route there). As the wall tails off to the right the routes become much more intense power problems compared to the stamina-fests around *Sardine*. This is also a popular section for bouldering.

**Conditions -** As sheltered and hot as the rest of the crag. It stays dry in most rain and dries out more quickly than the other sections. In dry winter months it can make an excellent venue.

22m

20m

Rooster Booster - p.220

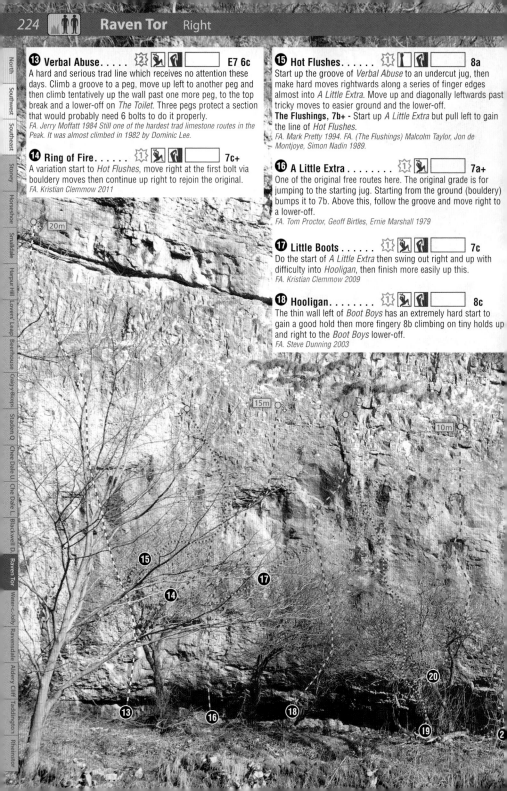

**13 Verbal Abuse.....** E7 6c
A hard and serious trad line which receives no attention these days. Climb a groove to a peg, move up left to another peg and then climb tentatively up the wall past one more peg, to the top break and a lower-off on *The Toilet*. Three pegs protect a section that would probably need 6 bolts to do it properly.
*FA. Jerry Moffatt 1984 Still one of the hardest trad limestone routes in the Peak. It was almost climbed in 1982 by Dominic Lee.*

**14 Ring of Fire......** 7c+
A variation start to *Hot Flushes*, move right at the first bolt via bouldery moves then continue up right to rejoin the original.
*FA. Kristian Clemmow 2011*

**15 Hot Flushes......** 8a
Start up the groove of *Verbal Abuse* to an undercut jug, then make hard moves rightwards along a series of finger edges almost into *A Little Extra*. Move up and diagonally leftwards past tricky moves to easier ground and the lower-off.
**The Flushings, 7b+ -** Start up *A Little Extra* but pull left to gain the line of *Hot Flushes*.
*FA. Mark Pretty 1994. FA. (The Flushings) Malcolm Taylor, Jon de Montjoye, Simon Nadin 1989.*

**16 A Little Extra........** 7a+
One of the original free routes here. The original grade is for jumping to the starting jug. Starting from the ground (bouldery) bumps it to 7b. Above this, follow the groove and move right to a lower-off.
*FA. Tom Proctor, Geoff Birtles, Ernie Marshall 1979*

**17 Little Boots......** 7c
Do the start of *A Little Extra* then swing out right and up with difficulty into *Hooligan*, then finish more easily up this.
*FA. Kristian Clemmow 2009*

**18 Hooligan........** 8c
The thin wall left of *Boot Boys* has an extremely hard start to gain a good hold then more fingery 8b climbing on tiny holds up and right to the *Boot Boys* lower-off.
*FA. Steve Dunning 2003*

20m

15m

10m

15

14

17

13

16

18

20

19

**⑲ Boot Boys** ...... 8a+
A desperate technical wall climb which is best suited to those with small fingers and high pain tolerance. Boulder up to a jug in the break. Make an extremely hard pull on a tiny mono pocket to gain another pocket above. More thin pocket pulling leads to the second bolt. Another hard sequence leads to a scary clip. Finish above up the relatively easy slab.
*FA. Andy Pollitt 1987. Freed only 2 days after a sky-hook aided ascent had been made. Some of the holds were 'comfort-ised'.*

**⑳ Out of My Boots** ...... 7c
Start as for *Boot Boys* to the jug and then pull out right to finish up *Out of My Tree*.
*FA. Steve McClure 1998*

**㉑ Out of My Tree** .... 8a
Another painful boulder problem start leads to the break and a jug, then make one more hard pull leftwards to gain the flake-line. The upper wall is comparatively easy. Missing the start by balancing up the old tree was **Perfidious Primate, E4 6b**.
*FA. Andy Pollitt 1987. FA. (PP) Ron Fawcett, Geoff Birtles 1976*

**㉒ Dialectics** ....... 8a+
From the jug on *Out of My Tree*, move up right and then make a few tough moves on sloping holds to gain a lower-off.
*FA. Mark Pretty 1993*

**㉓ Pump up the Power** ... 8a+
Only short but it packs it in. Pull past a pocket to a short groove then make a desperate exit from this to a lower-off.
*FA. Ben Moon 1987*

**㉔ Rattle and Hump** .. 8a
Short and sharp. Boulder up to the jug then make a desperate move left. Finish more easily up and right to the ledge.
*FA. Malcolm Taylor 1989*

**㉕ Seraphim** ....... 8b+
The wall to the right of *Rattle and Hump* has a desperate start on tiny holds and then a marginally easier upper wall.
*FA. Rupert Davies 2007*

**㉖ Wild in Me** ...... 7c
A reachy and bouldery start past two flakes leads to a finger rail and then a few tricky pulls on the upper wall to a belay.
*FA. Richard Davies 1986. Climbed as a bold E6 6c but it relied on chipped holds. Reclimbed by Mark Pretty in 1993 after these had been filled in.*

**㉗ Super High Intensity Body Building**
............ 7a
A well-named end to the activities here. Boulder up a flake to a good hold then move right and up the wall to the belay above the grass.
*FA. Steve Lewis, John MacKenzie 1986*

*At the far right-hand end of the crag is a short wall above a slab with three routes. Left is* Mortal Combat, 7b+ *right is* Gran Turismo, 7b *but the best of the trio is:*

**㉘ Tomb Raider** ..... 8a
The central line past 4 bolts. A tricky slab at the bottom leads to powerful moves through the bulge. Easier for the tall.
*FA. Tony Coutts 1998*

*Further down the road, at the entrance to Tideswell Dale, is a small overhanging crag hiding in the trees.*

**㉙ Culloden** ........ 8a+
This has been re-bolted and is a worthwhile route if you enjoy the short bouldery offerings at Raven Tor.
*FA. Ben Moon 1990*

Lots of sun | Roadside | Sheltered | Dry in the rain

| | No star | | | |
|---|---|---|---|---|
| Mod to S / 4+ | - | - | - | - |
| HS-HVS / 5-6a+ | 9 | 2 | 1 | 1 |
| E1-E3 / 6b-7a | 23 | 28 | 5 | 2 |
| E4 / 7a+ and up | 45 | 59 | 35 | 12 |

The River Wye continues south and west from Chee Dale, past Miller's Dale, into Water-cum-Jolly. In many ways this is Chee Dale's neglected little sister, the routes and buttresses are shorter and often the rock is of a lesser quality. On the plus side, a good track runs through the valley, it has a pleasant open aspect and quite a number of the cliffs catch the sun, with another set offering shady retreat in hot weather. Many of the routes in Water-cum-Jolly have been neglected in recent years. Those which rely on fixed gear are slowly being rebolted but others should be regarded now as unclimbable. This is especially true on Lammergeyer Buttress, and some of Moat and Central Buttresses - these routes have been included in this book since they may be rebolted in the future. Apart from the ever-popular Rubicon Wall, and the Cornice when it is in condition, you are very likely to have most of the routes here to yourself.

## Approach   Also see map on page 211

**Litton Mill Approach -** From the B6049 Tideswell to Miller's Dale road, take the sharp turn towards Litton Mill and past the Angler's Rest pub. Park at the small parking spot about 200m past Raven Tor and just before the signs dissuading you from continuing to the village. Follow the road on foot and continue past the old mill (now apartments) onto the valley bottom path.

**Cressbrook Approach -** Descend into Monsal Dale and follow the valley bottom road all the way to Cressbrook. Park here on the roadside opposite the new flats development in the old mill. A well-marked path leads up into the dale proper. As Rubicon Wall comes into view there is a bridge on the left which leads to the south bank and the Cornice.

## Access

**Access in WCJ is very sensitive so please follow the described approaches and notes included with each buttress introduction very carefully.** The rights to the north riverbank in WCJ is owned by an angling club. They are willing to allow climbers and walkers access to the dale but please do nothing to disturb their fishing activities. The section including Jackdaw Point, Upper Circle and Ping Pong Area is a wildlife reserve owned and managed by Derbyshire Wildlife Trust. They are willing to allow climbing on these three buttresses but only within strict limits and providing climbers use the described approaches only. There should be no new routes and no gardening of any kind on these buttresses. The other sections, including the south bank, are owned by various land owners. Access to these buttresses isn't a problem but climbers should make as little disturbance as possible since the whole dale is important for wildlife of all kinds. Apart from lower-offs, no extra gear should be left on the routes, this includes fixed slings and krabs.

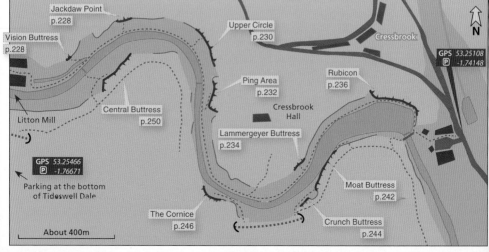

## Conditions

WCJ is well sheltered from the wind and offers both winter sun venues (Upper Circle) and summer heat (the Cornice, Central and Moat). There is some seepage on the north-facing crags and Rubicon Wall. The bottom end of the Dale (Rubicon) often floods in wet weather, making it impassable without wellingtons.

Adrian Berry half way across *Rubicon* (7a) - *page 241* - on Rubicon Wall. Photo: Nick Smith This impressive roof was first climbed on aid in 1960 by Jim Curtis. Geoff Birtles nearly freed it in 1976 before Tom Proctor managed a completely free ascent in 1979 after what was described at the time as 'selective cleaning'. Since then it has been properly bolted, shed holds and settled down as a 7a sport route.

North · Southwest · Southeast · Stoney · Horseshoe · Smalldale · Harpur Hill · Lovers' Leap · Beehouse

Craig-y-Biceps · Staden Q · Chee Dale U · Che Dale L · Blackwell D. · Raven Tor · Water-c-Jolly · Ravensdale · Aldery Cliff · Taddington · Rheinstor

Left margin (vertical): North | Southwest | Southeast | Stoney | Horseshoe | Smalldale | Harpur Hill | Lovers' Leap | Beerhouse | Craig-y-Biccas | Staden Q | Chee Dale U | Chee Dale L | Blackwell D | Raven Tor | Water-c-Jolly | Ravensdale | Aldery Cliff | Taddington | Rheinstor

## Vision Buttress

Vision Buttress is the first crag encountered on the Litton Mill approach and offers two hard routes which have both been re-bolted. These routes are not on a topo.

**Conditions -** The wall is well-sheltered and receives whatever sun manages to filter through the tree canopy. It is steep and seeps badly after wet spells but will give dry climbing in light rain.

**Approach (also see page 226) -** From the Litton Mill end, walk down the path until just past the small weir near Central Buttress. Tip-toe across ditch on the left using a large tree and make your way through the vegetation up to the crag which may well be hidden (in summer) above and to the left.

**❶ The Vision** . . . . 🔲 🔲 🔲 🔲 🔲 **7c+**
One of the original Peak test-pieces from the 1980s with a desperate crux move/leap.
FA. Ron Fawcett 1982

**❷ Knocked Out Loaded** 🔲 🔲 🔲 🔲 **7c**
A right-hand version of *The Vision* which shares the same start. At the break scuttle right then pull up to the lower-off.
FA. Andy Pollitt 1987

## Jackdaw Point

A neglected buttress with a neat little set of mid-grade routes. Most of the gear is good, but watch out for the odd loose hold, especially on the finishes.

**Conditions -** A well-sheltered sun-trap. It is great on warm days in the spring and winter, and suffers little from seepage. In summer, the trees give some shade, but it can still be very hot.

**Approach (also see page 226) -** From the Litton Mill end, walk down the path until level with the right-hand end of Central Buttress on the opposite bank, by a block on the path. Take a small path here direct to the buttress.

**Access -** This buttress is in the wildlife reserve managed by Derbyshire Wildlife Trust. Only use the described approach and do not walk along the crag base further than the described routes.

Dan Parkes stretching on *Erithacus* (E2 5b) - *opposite* - on Jackdaw Point proving that even on cold grey winter days Peak Limestone offers some action.

Only approach on this path and do not walk beyond the routes on this topo

No climbing further left

No climbing further right

**③ Ground Control** . . . . . . . . . . .  E1 5b
The hanging corner to the left of the buttress.
**Skyline Pigeon - E5 6b** exits right from the groove, past a peg.
*FA. Bill Wintrip, Chris Jackson 1985*

**④ Armed With an Empty Gun** .  E4 6a
A thin eliminate but with some good moves. Start up *Erithacus* or (better) up *Ground Control*. Climb over the bulge via some thin cracks.
*FA. Chris Jackson, Bill Wintrip, Roy Small 1985*

**⑤ Erithacus** . . . . . . .  E2 5b
Climb a series of flakes - sustained and tricky to protect the start. These lead to a ledge with threads over to the right. Abseil from here. *Photo opposite.*
*FFA. John Hesketh, Dave Tait 1977. FA. (1pt) Alan Sanderson, Mick Walsh 1977*

**⑥ Army Dreamers** . . .  E2 5c
A good little route with a hard crux - high in the grade. Climb the wall to a slight bulge (old peg). Pull over this to the ledge.
*FA. Ron Fawcett, Gill Fawcett 1981*

**⑦ Fledgling Flakes** . . . . .  HVS 5b
Climb the wall to some flakes. Pull up these to the ledge. Abseil from threads.
*FFA. Tom Proctor 1976. Previously aided.*

**⑧ Burning Up Time** . . . . .  E3 6a
Climb the thin wall to the overlap. Pull right to reach a single bolt lower-off, or finish at the ledge above.
*FA. Gary Gibson 1979*

**⑨ Nervous and Shaky** . . . . . . . .  E4 6a
A well-named filler-in up the wall right of *Burning Up Time*.
Finish at a single bolt lower-off, or at the ledge above.
*FA. Simon Cundy 1990*

**⑩ Fledgling** . . . . . . . . . . . . . .  VS 4c
The groove in the right-hand side of the wall past a tree. Finish on the ledge and abseil off.

*The next routes all finish at trees. Abseil from these and avoid disturbing the cliff-top vegetation.*

**⑪ First Flight** . . . . . . . . . . . . . .  HVS 5a
The slim hanging groove is awkward to reach.
*FA. Mick Walsh, Alan Sanderson 1976*

**⑫ Palmolive** . . . . . . . . .  E1 5c
Short and sweet past a peg. Top end and harder than it looks.
*FA. Chris Hardy 1983*

**⑬ Endless Flight** . . . . . .  E2 5c
This steep crack packs a lot in and was a real sandbag at E1.
*FA. Alan Sanderson, Mick Walsh 1978*

**⑭ Fear of Flying** . . . . . . . . . .  E2 5b
A short and technical wall climb. A flake and a peg mark the line which rises diagonally across the wall.
*FA. Paul Cropper, Bill Brook 1978*

**⑮ Flight Path** . . . . . . . . . . . .  VS 4b
The corner to the right.
*FA. Alan Sanderson, Mick Walsh 1978*

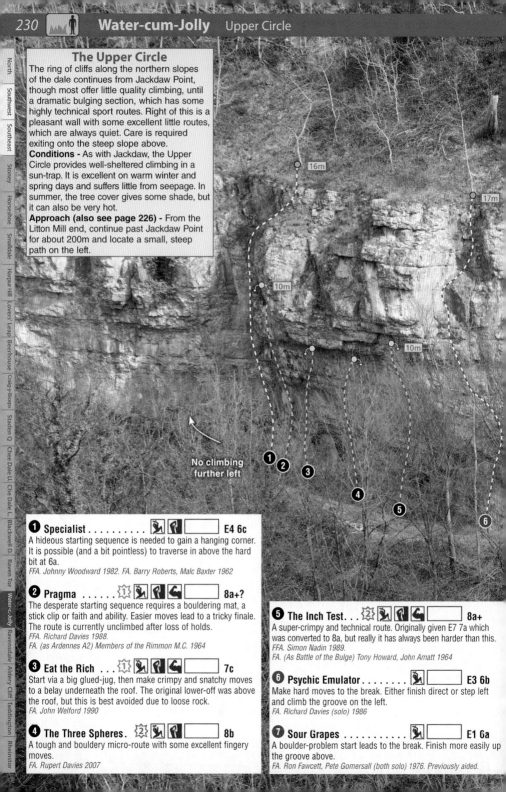

## The Upper Circle

The ring of cliffs along the northern slopes of the dale continues from Jackdaw Point, though most offer little quality climbing, until a dramatic bulging section, which has some highly technical sport routes. Right of this is a pleasant wall with some excellent little routes, which are always quiet. Care is required exiting onto the steep slope above.

**Conditions -** As with Jackdaw, the Upper Circle provides well-sheltered climbing in a sun-trap. It is excellent on warm winter and spring days and suffers little from seepage. In summer, the tree cover gives some shade, but it can also be very hot.

**Approach (also see page 226) -** From the Litton Mill end, continue past Jackdaw Point for about 200m and locate a small, steep path on the left.

No climbing further left

**❶ Specialist . . . . . . . . . .** ▣ E4 6c
A hideous starting sequence is needed to gain a hanging corner. It is possible (and a bit pointless) to traverse in above the hard bit at 6a.
*FFA. Johnny Woodward 1982. FA. Barry Roberts, Malc Baxter 1962*

**❷ Pragma . . . . . .** ▣ 8a+?
The desperate starting sequence requires a bouldering mat, a stick clip or faith and ability. Easier moves lead to a tricky finale. The route is currently unclimbed after loss of holds.
*FFA. Richard Davies 1988.*
*FA. (as Ardennes A2) Members of the Rimmon M.C. 1964*

**❸ Eat the Rich . . .** ▣ 7c
Start via a big glued-jug, then make crimpy and snatchy moves to a belay underneath the roof. The original lower-off was above the roof, but this is best avoided due to loose rock.
*FA. John Welford 1990*

**❹ The Three Spheres.** ▣ 8b
A tough and bouldery micro-route with some excellent fingery moves.
*FA. Rupert Davies 2007*

**❺ The Inch Test. . .** ▣ 8a+
A super-crimpy and technical route. Originally given E7 7a which was converted to 8a, but really it has always been harder than this.
*FFA. Simon Nadin 1989.*
*FA. (As Battle of the Bulge) Tony Howard, John Amatt 1964*

**❻ Psychic Emulator . . . . . . . .** ▣ E3 6b
Make hard moves to the break. Either finish direct or step left and climb the groove on the left.
*FA. Richard Davies (solo) 1986*

**❼ Sour Grapes . . . . . . . . . . .** ▣ E1 6a
A boulder-problem start leads to the break. Finish more easily up the groove above.
*FA. Ron Fawcett, Pete Gomersall (both solo) 1976. Previously aided.*

**Access -** This buttress is in the wildlife reserve managed by Derbyshire Wildlife Trust. Only use the described approach and do not walk along the crag base further than the described routes.

North
Southwest
Southeast
Stoney
Horseshoe
Smalldale
Harpur Hill
Lovers' Leap
Beerhouse
Craig-Biceps
Staden Q
Blackwell D.
Che Dale L.
Chee Dale U.
Raven Tor
Water-c-Jolly
Ravensdale
Aldery Cliff
Taddington
Rheinstor

No climbing further right

---

**⑧ Splinter in the Mind's Eye . .** [icon] E2 6b
A boulder problem which becomes a route higher up.
*FA. Richard Davies (solo) 1986*

**⑨ Sweet William. . . . . . . . .** [icon] E2 5c
A good little route. Climb a thin crack to a roof. Pull over with difficulty and climb to ledges above.
*FFA. Tom Proctor 1976. Previoulsy aided.*

**⑩ Western Samoa . . . . . . . .** [icon] E4 6b
The roof right of *Sweet William* has a hard move at the lip.
*FA. Alan James 1991*

**⑪ Dead Tree Groove . . . . . . .** [icon] E2 5c
A pleasant groove, typical of the routes on the Upper Circle. Follow the slab rightwards, then finish up the groove above, care needed with the exit.
*FA. Jim Curtis, Pete Hanson (aid) 1960*

**⑫ Palace of Tyranny . . . . . .** [icon] E1 5b
A hugely over-dramatic name. Poor climbing up the left-hand side of the blank, bulging wall right of *Dead Tree Groove*.
*FA. Gary Gibson 1979*

**⑬ Trench Warfare . . . . . . . .** [icon] E2 5b
The right-hand companion to *Palace of Tyranny*.
*FA. Richard Davies (solo) 1988*

**⑭ Sweet FA . . . . . . . . . . . . . .** E1 5b
Left of the groove of *Dead Tree Crack* is another smaller groove above a bulge. Reach this from below and right. High in the grade - both of them.
*FA. Jim Moran, Con Carey 1976*

**⑮ Dead Tree Crack . . . . . . . .** [icon] E1 5b
One of the more popular routes here. It tackles the prominent corner and feels about twice as long as it looks. The prickly finish is ugly.
*FA. Jim Curtis, Pete Hanson (aid) 1960*

No climbing
further left

**❶ Deception . . . . . . .** E4 6a
A fine route with unlikely-looking climbing for the grade. Climb
the steep wall to the break, pull up right into a thin crack then
make a delicate move back left, past a similar crack, to an easier
finish. The old peg has now gone but the route is still E4.
*FFA. Ron Fawcett 1981. FA. Mick Walsh, Alan Sanderson 1977*

**❷ Confidence Trick . . . . . . . . . .** 7b+
Climb a tiny groove in the arete then trend left up the wall
passing spaced bolts (small wires needed) at the start. Finish at
a lower-off as for *Rio Verde*.
*FA. Mark Pretty 2006*

**❸ Rio Verde . . . . . . . . .** E4 6b
Hard climbing up the capped groove right of *Deception*. Pull
left from the top of the groove and climb the tricky upper arete.
Check whether the crucial peg is in place or not.
*FA. Al Rouse, Andy Bailey 1984*

**❹ Mandrake . . . . . . .** E5 6a
An excellent headwall is the main attraction on this reclusive
test-piece. Climb the loose wall to a ledge, the thin crack above
is technical and it isn't all over when you get the hidden jug.
Check whether the crucial solitary peg is in place or not, before
you get to the jug preferably.
*FFA. Ron Fawcett 1981. FA. Mick Walsh, Alan Sanderson 1977*

**❺ The Ponger . . . . . . . . . . . . . .** VS 4b
Start up *Ping*, or further up left, and climb the left edge of the
buttress, finishing up a left-facing corner. Poor.
*FA. Mick Walsh, Alan Sanderson 1976*

**❻ Ping . . . . . . . . . . . . .** HVS 5b
A fine crack climb which provides one of the (few) real gems of
the Upper Circle, pumpy and quite awkward to protect. It starts
on the lower left toe of the buttress and follows the prominent
crack on the right to a lower-off. Good value.
*FFA. Keith Myhill 1970. Together with Ping Pong, this ascent marked the
change from aid climbing to free climbing in the 1970s.
FA. Graham West, Barry Roberts 1959*

**❼ Ping Pong . . . . . . . . .** E1 5b
The superb flake is a great companion to its left-hand sister
offering another pumpy number. Start on the centre of the
buttress and follow a couple of loose-ish grooves to reach the
flake. Steam up this then, at its top, move left to the lower-off.
*FFA. Keith Myhill 1970. Previously aided.*

## Ping Pong Area

This area has two isolated buttresses with a few quality routes between them. Mandrake Buttress is worth a visit if you are looking for some stern trad routes. Ping Buttress has two great mid-grade routes which will not disappoint.

**Conditions -** Both walls are well-sheltered from the wind and suffer little from seepage. They face due west and get the afternoon sun.

**Approach (also see page 226) -** From the Litton end. Continue past the upper Upper Circle until a steep gully leads up and back left towards Ping Buttress. Mandrake Buttress is reached a little further along.

**Access -** This buttress is in the wildlife reserve managed by Derbyshire Wildlife Trust. Only use the described approach and do not walk along the crag base further than the described routes.

18m

15m

No climbing further right

---

**8 Desmond Douglas** .... ✰ **E2 5c**
The combi-route had to be climbed but, unlike in most cases, this one has a worthwhile (and reachy) move, past a thread. High in the grade.
*FA. Gary Gibson 1988*

**9 Pong** ............... **E1 5b**
The other table-tennis route avoids the decent rock on the buttress. This one starts up *PP* but then makes the mistake of heading up the 'orrid groove. A bit of a stinker and best avoided.
*FA. Graham West, Barry Roberts (aid) 1959*

*Round to the right was **Virgin's Crack**, VS 4b. This has been lost behind the ivy, please leave it that way.*

North
Southwest
Southeast
Stoney
Horseshoe
Smalldale
Harpur Hill
Lover's Leap
Beehouse
Craig-y-Biceps
Staden Q
Chee Dale U
Chee Dale L
Blackwell D
Che Dale L
Raven Tor
Water-c-Jolly
Ravensdale
Aldery Cliff
Taddington
Rheinstor

North | Southwest | Southeast | Stoney | Horseshoe | Smalldale | Harpur Hill | Lovers' Leap | Beerhouse | Craig-y-Biceps | Staden Q | Chee Dale U | Chee Dale L | Blackwell D | Raven Tor | Water-cum-Jolly | Ravensdale | Aldery Cliff | Taddington | Rheinstor

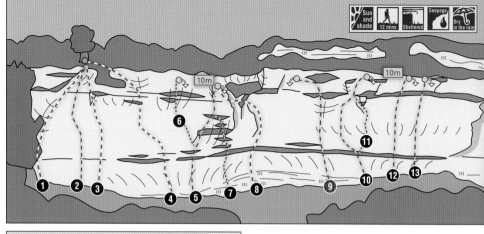

## Lammergeyer Buttress

This buttress has been almost entirely ignored for many years and all the routes should be considered as unclimbable in their present state. The fixed gear which is crucial for most routes, is in a terrible state and much of the rock is terminally loose. If re-bolted the buttress will give a series of intense and powerful sport routes. The descriptions are included to show the lines.

**Approach (also see page 226)** - From the Cressbrook end, pass Rubicon Wall and continue for about 400m until a small steep wall can be seen above you to the right, opposite Moat Buttress.

**Conditions** - Well-sheltered and receives whatever sun manages to filter through the tree canopy. The walls are steep and seep badly after wet spells but will give dry climbing in light rain.

**❶ The Lammergeyer Twins** ⬚⬚ **E5 6b**
A once-good route up the scoop is now mostly behind ivy.
*FA. Paul Mitchell 1983*

**❷ As Summers Die** ..... ⬚⬚ **7a+**
A desperate technical problem on which success depended on how flexible you were. Two bolts and a peg show the line.
*FA. Mike Lea 1989*

**❸ One Way Reflection** ⬚⬚⬚ **E5 6b**
The routes started over a bulge to a small hole, then up the wall (bolt) and back right to a break where there was once a lower-off.
*FA. Richard Davies, A. Stewart, Mark Delafield 1986*

**❹ Final Apocalypse** .......... **E5 6b**
A technical diagonal line started over a steep lower bulge then it went left across a smoother wall and up to the break. The original route finished in the trees.
*FA. Richard Davies 1987*

**❺ The Myth of Masculinity** ⬚⬚ **7a+**
Extremely steep and sustained. The line is indicated by a couple of old pegs.
*FA. Paul Mitchell, Andy Barker, Mark Pretty 1985*

**❻ Mr. Puniverse** ....... ⬚⬚ **7a+**
This route shared its start with *Myth* to its second peg then it broke out left up the wall and over the steep bulges.
*FA. Chris Wright 1989*

**❼ The Ego has Landed** ⬚⬚⬚ **7b+**
A direct start to *Myth* over heaps of bulges. Two bolts and a peg are in place before the final peg on *Myth*.
*FA. Mike Lea 1989*

**❽ The Amnicolist Spies on the Black Submarine**
................... ⬚ **E5 6b**
The flakes in the centre of the buttress provided a thoroughly desperate struggle. The original finish headed left to the *Myth* lower-off. A harder right-hand finish exists - *Periscope Voyeur*, still **E5 6b** for the whole route.
*FA. Paul Mitchell, John Kirk 1985. FA. (PV) Andy Barker, Ben Moon 1985*

**❾ Living with a Porcupine** ... ⬚ **7a**
A slightly more friendly route but still the same dubious rock and insubstantial fixed gear. The line is marked in a scoop by a thread and 2 pegs to a lower-off out left.
*FA. Gary Gibson 1988*

**❿ Once upon a Time** .... ⬚⬚ **7a+**
Again the line is indicated by two bolts and a peg at the break.
*FA. Richard Davies 1986*

**⓫ Tree Surgeon.** ........ ⬚⬚ **7b**
A left-hand version of *Once Upon a Time* past a bolt.
*FA. Richard Davies 1987*

**⓬ The Fall** ........ ⬚⬚⬚ **7c+**
This one gave extremely technical climbing. Two pegs and a bolt.
*FA. Chris Wright 1989*

**⓭ Vindicator.** ....... ⬚⬚⬚ **7c**
The final line on the wall, below a prominent undercut.
*FA. Richard Davies 1987*

In the winter of 2011/12 some routes were added to the left-hand end of Rubcion Wall proving that there are still new lines to be found on old well-developed crags. Although it may not be a classic, *Welsh Rarebit* (6b+) - *next page* - is a worthy addition, as Graham Parkes finds out. Photo: Chris Craggs

Rheinstor | Taddington | Aldery Cliff | Ravensdale | Water-cum-Jolly | Raven Tor | Blackwell D. | Che Dale L. | Chee Dale U. | Staden Q. | Cragg-Brepo | Beerhouse | Lovers' Leap | Harpur Hill | Smalldale | Horseshoe | Stoney | Southeast | Southwest | North

Lots of sun | 5 mins | Sheltered

10m

8m

## Rubicon Left

The most celebrated buttress in Water-cum-Jolly is the splendid sweep of rock known as Rubicon Wall. The left-hand side of this crag has a mix of sport routes and trad routes. Although none are as popular these days as they used to be, *Honeymoon Blues*, *Dragonflight* and the hard sport found around *Caviar* remain top quality challenges. There are also some technical routes in the central section which are usually done above bouldering mats.
**Conditions -** The wall is a well-sheltered sun-trap which can make it too hot at times. Some of the crag seeps badly, although the section around *Dragonflight* less so.
**Approach (also see page 226) -** From the Cressbrook end. Rubicon Wall is the first crag you encounter on the right when following the riverside path.

**❶ Alimoany** . . . . . . . . . . . . 7b+
The steep crack leads to a big ledge. Follow the bolts above, with some difficulty, to the lower-off.
*FA. Malcolm Taylor 1994*

**❷ Honeymoon Blues** . . . . E5 6b
A route of two halves, both with great climbing. Weave around on the lower wall below some threads in the bulge, then reach up to these, and make a hard move up onto the half-time ledge. Step left, then make a hard move past a large block. Pull right and climb a groove to the tree. Abseil off.
*FA. Ron Fawcett 1981*

**❸ Salar** . . . . . . . 8a
The groove bulge and wall give a very technical route. The first ascensionist managed somehow to move direct past the final bolt (at least 8a+) but most now go left. Supersedes *Dapper Slapper,* which used the same start, but then traversed off rightwards to *Lapin*. A good first 8a for boulderers, the tall and those who can jump.
*FA. (Direct ) Malcom Taylor 1992. FA. (DS) Paul Mitchell 1984*

**❹ Slapin** . . . . . . . . . . . 7c
Start up *Salar* but break right up the bulging wall.
*FA. Mark Pretty 2012*

**❺ Slapdasher** . . . . . . 7a
Thin climbing up the white wall.
*FA. Paul Freeman 2011. Climbed on Christmas Eve.*

**❻ Lapin** . . . . . . . . . . . . . . E3 5c
The flake-line looks more attractive now that you can use the lower-off on *Welsh Rarebit*. May still be a bit loose.

**❼ Welsh Rarebit** . . . . . . . . . 6b+
Right of the flakes of *Lapin*. Photo on previous page.
*FA. Paul Freeman 2012*

The next routes start right off the riverside path. Please be aware of other users by keeping the noise down and not blocking the path.

**❽ Changing Fortunes. . . .** 　　　　　 **E4 6b**
A one-move-wonder. Crossing the bulge past the peg is the hard bit. After that, finish rightwards up *Dragonflight*.
*FA. Keith Sharples, Chris Hardy 1988*

**❾ Chair's Missing . . .** 　　　　　 **E4 6b**
A reachy move past a bulge provides the difficulties. Similar to its left-hand neighbour, but a bit easier.
*FA. Ron Fawcett 1981. Named after Ron's squatted landing position on a previous attempt at the route.*

**❿ A Tall Story . . . . . .** 　　　　　 **E5 6c**
The third of the trio of reachy problems requires the longest arms.
*FA. Quentin Fisher 1983*

**⓫ Dragonflight . . . . . . . .** 　　　　　 **E3 5c**
A super little route which is quite tricky for the short. The climbing is delicate and exposed but never quite as serious as it feels. Climb to the flake and lace it, and the break, with wires. Make a tricky step up to stand on the holds on the flake, commit to some slopers and reach the upper groove. Finish more easily to a single-bolt lower-off.
*FA. Chris Jackson, Dave Sant, Rod Haslam 1976. Given HVS originally because Chris didn't think he was good enough to lead extreme. The grade stuck for 13 years.*

**⓬ The Dragonflight Traverse** 　　　 **V3**
The name says it all. Do it in either/both directions. Polished.

**⓭ Jezebel. . . . . . . .** 　　　　　 **E5 6a**
A harder version of *Dragonflight*. Boulder up to a break right of *Dragonflight* then clip the bolt above. Make hard moves past this to another break (cam). Traverse right and climb a slim groove and bulges to the lower-off.
*FA. Daniel Lee, Dominic Lee 1981. Previously aided, hence the bolt. The minor direct start (as described) was added by Andy Barker.*

**⓮ Kingfisher. . . . . . .** 　　　　　 **E5 6c**
A direct line with one hideously technical move and requiring a baby-bouncer approach to protect. Clip the bolt on *Jezebel* and reverse to the ground. Starting to the right, climb direct past 2 pegs to the finish of *Jezebel*.
*FA. Quentin Fisher 1985*

**⓯ Jaws . . . . . . . . . .** 　　　　　 **E5 6b**
This early Fawcett offering has some superb climbing. Climb up to a good hold by a peg. Stand up above the peg and continue up the wall to the ledge. Cross the final bulges to the left of the obvious line. Tree belay.
*FA. Ron Fawcett 1981*

**⓰ Plectrum Maxilla Direct . . .** 　　 **E7 6c**
Serious and bouldery moves are required to reach a protruding peg on the bulging wall. Continue direct to the top break then step left into *Jaws*. Originally it traversed into the peg from *Jaws*.
*FA. Malcom Taylor 1992. FA. (original) Paul Mitchell 1986*

North
Southwest
Southeast
Stoney
Horseshoe
Smalldale
Harpur Hill
Lover's Leap
Beehouse
Craig-y-Biceps
Staden Q
Chee Dale U
Chee Dale L
Blackwell D.
Raven Tor
Water-cum-Jolly
Ravensdale
Aldery Cliff
Teddington
Rheinstor

**⑰ Barracuda** ...... 8b
The desperate left-hand start to *Caviar*. Only a short crux section at the bottom, but very hard and fingery. The route has become slightly easier than when first done due to hold crumblage.
*FA. Andy Harris 2008*

**⑱ Caviar** ....... 8a+
A sport route for boulderers, which has become a popular first 8a+, although it isn't an easy one. Aim for the good hold, then manoeuvre back up and left, by whatever means you can manage, to gain the top break. Above is still uphill.
*FA. Tony Ryan 1986. The second 8a+ in the Peak.*

**⑲ Beluga** ........... 8a+
A right hand/direct version of *Caviar* is slightly harder than the original. Break right after the first bolt, then climb direct to rejoin *Caviar* at the break.
*FA. Jon Fullwood 2008*

**⑳ Eugenics** .......... 8b+?
Intensely fingery and technical climbing. Still unrepeated since the loss of a crucial hold, and reported to be rather unpleasant.
*FA. Mark Pretty 1993*

**㉑ Let the Tribe Increase** .. 8a
Very technical and sequency climbing up an old bolt-ladder. Loss of a crucial hold has upped the grade.
*FA. Quentin Fisher 1986. Previously aided.*

**㉒ Dangerous Tribes** ..... 8a
A link up of *Dangerous Brothers* and *Tribes*. Climb *Dangerous Brothers* to the second bolt, then make fingery crux moves up and left to the glued hold on *Tribes,* and finish up that.
*FA. Jon Clark 2010*

**㉓ The Dangerous Brothers** 8a
Three bolts and a bolt at the break show the way. There are two methods of doing the crux, one for crimpers and one for those keen on rockovers. Most people finish at the break, although the FA did complete the bulge at no change in grade.
*FA. Martin Atkinson 1987*

**㉔ Too Old to be Bold** . 7c
Once derided as too short and too polished - now that short is a virtue, and everything else is just as polished it doesn't seem so bad. Hard and slippery all the way.
*FA. Mark Pretty 1987. Named when the trad/bolt argument was at its peak.*

**㉕ Coot** ............. E4 6a
The first of the routes on the central section is poor. The grade may be gentler than the routes to either side, but the hollow flakes and brambles above spoil things. From the top break, step right to finish up the upper wall - harder than it looks.
*FA. Unknown and nobody has come forward to claim it.*

**㉖ Piranha** ...... E6 6b
A fine, bold climb which still sees few ascents although it makes a good highball above a couple of mats. Use the drilled monos, then tiny crimps and layaways with a tear-jerking move required to reach the break. Above, move right and up to the next break.
*FA. Ron Fawcett 1981*

18m

12m

m

㉖ ㉗ ㉘ ㉙ ㉚ ㉛ ㉜ ㉝ ㉞

North
Southwest
Southeast
Stoney
Horseshoe
Smalldale
Harpur Hill
Lovers' Leap
Beehouse
Craig-y-Biceps
Staden Q
Chee Dale U.
Blackwell D.
Che Dale L.
Raven Tor
Water-c-Jolly
Ravensdale
Aldery Cliff
Taddington
Rheinstor

㉗ **Cora** . . . . . . . . **E6 6c**
A harder version of *Piranha* sees even fewer ascents. The hard section is below the first break, so sliding right from here gains the hole of *Miller's Tale* and an easy descent. This is a better option than tackling the top section.
*FA. Andy Pollitt 1986 starting on the left. Ben Moon added the direct.*

㉘ **White Bait** . . . . . . **E5 6c**
Similar to its left-hand neighbours, but with the crux situated conveniently low on the wall. Climb on pockets to a peg at the break. A scuttle rightwards is advised, or continue up over the bulges (various decaying pegs) to an ugly finish.
*FA. Daniel Lee 1981*

㉙ **Flake Out Shake Out** . . . **E4 6c**
A short bouldery route up the wall between *White Bait* and *Miller's Tale* via a flake. At the break, finish which ever way you want, but right and down is easiest.
*FA. Steve Earnshaw, Jon Cort 1987*

㉚ **A Miller's Tale** . . . . **E5 6b**
Another old test-piece showing its age. The lower section with the good climbing is still in good nick. Boulder out to the big hole (V4 - harder than it looks). Sort out gear in the break (peg) and stretch or jump to good holds above. The rest is easy, though dirty and the pegs are old. There is a new lower-off.
*FFA. Andy Barker, Paul Mitchell, Steve Wright 1981*
*FA. (as Souwester) Chris Craggs, Colin Binks 1981*

㉛ **Hot Fun Closing** . **8a**
A boulder problem start (**Kudos, V7** easy way using layaways on right, **V9** hard way going direct) leads to a shattered flake. Continue to gain the break and then up the wall above.
*FA. Ben Moon 1986. FA. (Kudos) Chris Gore 1986*

㉜ **A Bigger Tail** . . . . . **7b+**
Jump to gain small edges which lead up and right, via a pocket, to the break (a V7 problem to here). Continue direct.
*FA. Tim Freeman 1985. The finish was bolted in 2010.*

㉝ **The Press** . . . . . . . . . . **V9**
A desperate problem. Gain the jug on *A Bigger Splash* by using tiny, opposing layaways. The sit down start is **V11**.

㉞ **A Bigger Splash** . . . **V7**
From low jugs on the right gain a good jug via some leftward-leaning flakes. Some of the footholds double as mirrors.
*FA. Dominic Lee 1981*

Lots of sun | 5 min | Sheltered | Seepage | Dry in the rain

14m

① ② ④ ⑤ ⑥ ⑦ ⑨ ⑪ ③

**① Last But Not Least .** ⬚🧗🪢⬚ **7a**
The wall just right of the first big tree. A short, reachy bulge at the top provides the main difficulties.
*FA. Paul Freeman 2010*

*Two old trad routes tackle the wall above and right of the ivy patch -* **Sperm Worm, E5 6a** *on the left and* **Dumb Animal, E5 6a** *on the right.*

**② The Pinch Test. . . .** ⬚🧗🪢⬚ **7c+**
The upper wall to the left of *The Angler.* A desperate and frustrating boulder problem on poor pinches provides the difficulties.
*FA. Mark Pretty 2009*

**③ The Angler . . . .** ⬚🧗🪢🪢⬚ **E6 6c**
A desperate one-move problem. Climb direct to a ledge just right of the ivy. Somehow use tiny holds to gain a flake above (peg and thread).
*FFA. Dominic Lee 1981. FA. Chris Craggs, Colin Binks 1981*

**④ The Wimp. . . . . . . . .** ⬚🧗⬚ **7c**
Take *The Sissy* to the fourth bolt, then move over left and up into *The Angler* to finish. Some gear is needed for the top.
*FA. Mark Pretty 2010*

**⑤ The Sissy . . . . . . .** ⬚🧗🪢⬚ **8a**
Typical of Rubicon; short, hard and becoming harder as bits drop off. The difficulties are confined to the steep middle section where a powerful rock-over is required. There is a lower-off just below the final bulge.
*FA. Chris Plant 1989. Named after Ben Moon's comment on routes which require footwork.*

**⑥ Zeke the Freak. .** Top 50 🧗🪢🪢⬚ **8b**
A classic product of the 1980s which has held its grade in spite/because of various snapping holds. The middle section around the slight hanging groove can be climbed direct using an undercut to leave the scoop, or via a right-hand detour using pockets. Finish up the flake.
*FA. Ben Moon 1987*

**⑦ The Bastard. . . .** ⬚🧗🪢🪢⬚ **8c+**
The tiniest of fingery holds and a hard section packed into a few intense metres gives the ultimate Rubicon route (only two repeats in 15+ years), which may only be surpassed if the wall right of *Caviar* is ever climbed. Easy 8c+ - what an oxymoron! *Photo on page 31.*
*FFA. John Welford 1995. FA. (Aided as Free That You Bastards) Chris Craggs, Graham Parkes 1986*

## Rubicon Right

The right-hand side of Rubicon Wall is probably more popular these days with boulderers particularly on the fine technical climbing around *The Press*. The routes on this section tend to be extended boulder problems anyway with most of the hard climbing low down, before the first break. Around the big *Rubicon* roof, the bouldering remains on the lower band, whilst the routes launch themselves up and outwards into some very steep territory.
**Conditions (also see page 226) -** The wall is a well-sheltered sun-trap which can make it too hot at times. There is a lot of seepage and the path floods in winter.
**Approach -** From the Cressbrook end. Rubicon Wall is the first crag you encounter on the right when following the riverside path.

12m

**8 Truly Awesome** ...... 🗓 🧗 [ ] **7a+**
A little brother to the main route to the right. Despite the name, it's not as good, but still worthwhile. The route has also been known as *Totally Awesome*.
*FA. Ian Dunn 1991*

**9 Rubicon** .......... Top⌐50 🧗 [ ] **7a**
Excellent roof climbing up the main line of the roof, which is more of a sprint than a marathon. Scramble up to the ledge then reach out and clip a bolt or two. Take a deep breath and move into upside-down mode. The first and last pulls are the hardest. Said to be low in the grade by muscle-bound gorillas.
*Photo on page 227.*
*FFA. Tom Proctor, Geoff Birtles 1979. They used a completely different set of holds at about E3. The old pegs were replaced with bolts in 1991.*
*FA. Jim Curtis, Ian Bretherick 1960*

**10 Zeitgeist** ........ 🗓 ❗ 🧗 [ ] **7b**
A harder version of *Rubicon*, with more bolts than you can usually clip. More independent than it looks, but still a bit of sideline attraction when compared to the main event just to the left.
*FA. Ian Dunn, Claudie Dunn, Neil Critchlow 1991*

**11 No Jug, No Thug** .. 🗓 🧗 🪛 [ ] **E5 6b**
A wild traverse above the hard routes on mostly fixed gear (**7b**-ish). Climb *Rubicon* (belay) then traverse the break left to the flake at the end. Cams useful for the last moves. A continuation **Cruising the Seven Seas, E6 6b,** keeps going at break level, crossing *The Angler* and finishing at *Last but not Least*.
*FA. Andy Barker 1983. FA. (Cruising...) Chris Plant 1989*

**12 The Bomb is Coming** 🗓 🧗 🪛 [ ] **7a**
More fun roof climbing. Run up the lower wall to the break then blast across it with a testing snatchy move at the end.
*FA. Paul Mitchell 1983*

**13 Toenail Pie** ........... 🧗 [ ] **E2 5b**
Start up *The Bomb* but break right and follow the easiest line through the roof to the right (1 peg). Finish in the trees.
*FA. Tom Proctor, Geoff Birtles, Ernie Marshall 1975*

**14 Small but Perfectly Formed** .... [ ] **7a+**
The small overhanging prow with two bolts. Jump off onto the second bolt after gaining the jug above it.
*FA. Mark Pretty 2010*

*The right-hand side of the bay is a super-popular bouldering area, and it is often dry. There are four popular and polished traverses here. **High, V1 Middle, V3** and **Low, V4** as well as **Warm Up, V1** where everything goes.*

North | Southwest | Southeast | Stoney | Horseshoe | Smalldale | Harpur Hill | Lovers' Leap | Beerhouse | Craig-y-Biceps | Staden Q | Chee Dale U | Chee Dale L | Blackwell D | Raven Tor | Water-cum-Jolly | Ravensdale | Aldery Cliff | Teddington | Rheinstor

## Moat Buttress

Moat Buttress's Gold Rush year was way back in 1988; the Rubicon dam burst, and climbers flocked to the newly-accessible crag; in no time it was covered with routes. Before and since then, it has been avoided by most climbers, despite the restored water level only denying access to four routes. It isn't the most solid of crags, and much of the fixed gear is now old although this is now being replaced.

**Conditions -** It faces northwest and gets late afternoon sunshine. There is some winter seepage.

**Approach (also see page 226) -** Approach from Cressbrook. Cross the bridge below the dam and turn right onto the path that leads up onto the hillside above the dale. Follow this path for about 500m, until you are above Moat Buttress. For routes 1 to 4, drop down carefully and walk along the water's edge. For the rest of the routes, continue along the cliff-top path to a fence above a gully. Drop down the gully and turn right under Crunch Buttress, then go onwards to the main Moat Buttress.

**① Sheerwater** . . . . . . . . . ☷ ▮▮   **E1 5b**
A traverse with good positions though it is seldom climbed.
**1)** 4c, 20m. Starting up the bank on the left of the crag, move up rightwards to gain the break. Follow this to a ledge and belay - old pegs may be in place.
**2)** 5b, 10m. Climb up and over the bulge and finish with a stiff pull into a groove over the small roof. Belay on the tree.
**2a) Sheer Indulgence**, E2 5b, 10m. Climb a line 2m right of pitch 2 of *Sheerwater*.
*FA. Geoff Birtles, Al Evans 1976. FA. (SI) Paul Dearden 1988*

**② Nude Moatorcycle Girl** . ▮▮ ▮▮   **7a**
The first bolt-line starts from the small beach.
*FA. Simon Cundy, R.Harrison 1991*

*The next two routes can be done from hanging belays above the water (use the first bolt of Nude MG to guide your ropes away from the water) or access the upper sections from the lower wall of Nude MG.*

**③ Out of the Shadows** ☷ ◣ ▮▮   **7b**
The upper bulge requires a determined approach and leads to an entertaining tree lower-off.
*FA. Keith Sharples, Graham Hoey 1988*

**④ Another Moatside Attraction**
. . . . . . . . . . . . . . . . . ☷ ▮ ▮▮   **7a+**
A bouldery start is awkward. Above this are some hard bulges split by a hands-off rest on a ledge.
*FA. Gary Gibson 1988*

*Four routes start from the water (they were climbed in 1988). From left to right they are* **Moat Madness E5 6b, Shear Power E5 6b, The Lady of the Lake E5 6b, D.T.'s Route E5 6b.** *The gear on these routes is mostly fixed and over 20 years old and they are best left until the crag finally fills in along its base and they get rebolted.*

*The next routes can sometimes be reached from the right. If the path below Rubicon is flooded then you can only get as far as Moatorhead. When the Rubicon path is dry you can reach Excalibur, and Drawbridge... with good wellies.*

**⑤ Drawbridge Down When the Levee Breaks**
. . . . . . . . . . . . . . . . . ▮▮ ▮▮   **E6 6c**
Old bolts up a very neglected line up the grooves left of the steeper central section. It was once thought to be 7c.
*FA. Malcolm Taylor 1988*

**⑥ Excalibur** . . . . . . ☷ ◣ ▮▮   **E6 6b**
A fine line and a fine pitch, which is worth the effort of the approach. The gear is mainly in place (7b+?), although best bring a small rack. Three hard sections give the difficulties.
*FFA. Andy Pollitt 1986. FA. Brian Moore, Jim Ballard 1967*

**⑦ No Mud, No Thud** . . . . . . . . . .   **E6 6b**
Start up a small groove to arrive at the rising traverse of *Excalibur* from directly below. Bits of old gear and wires.
*FA. Chris Plant 1988*

**⑧ Let the Tripe Increase** ☷ ◣ ▮   **7c**
Start up a flake then tackle the bulge by an intense bouldery sequence. Continue more steadily up the wall above.
**A Bigger Splat, 7a -** A half route that reaches the ledge on the right.
*FA. Chris Plant 1988. FA. (ABS) Malcolm Taylor 1988*

**⑨ All Hands to the Pump** . ▮▮ ▮   **7c+**
Solo onto the ledge via the easy crack on the right. Powerful climbing leads to a slight rest below the bulge. Full on moves lead to a jug and belay.
*FA. Mark Pretty 2012*

15m       22m

①   ② ③ ④   ⑥   ⑩   ⑭   ㉒

**Flooded section**

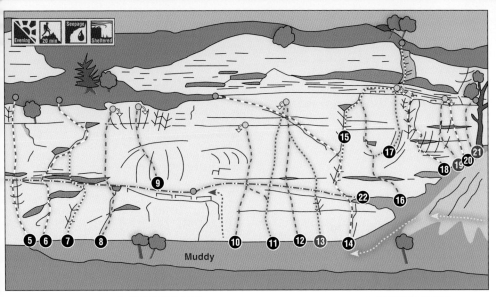

Muddy

**⑩ Moatorhead.** . . . . . 🎒🏊🥾[    ] **7b+**
A good climb which has been re-bolted with a direct start. The
original start is up *Coming Up for Air* at no change in grade. It
would be 7c if it wasn't for the no-hands rest.
*FA. Gary Gibson 1988. FA. (Direct) Kris Clemmow 2012*

**⑪ Coming Up for Air** . 🎒🏊🎒[    ] **7c**
Climb direct up to the break, pass left of the small roof, then
go right at the top of the slab to the base of a large crack/flake.
Follow this (run-out) to a lower-off just below a ledge.
*FA. Kevin Woodhead 1999*

**⑫ Moat People** . . . . . . . 🎒🏊[    ] **7b+**
Re-bolted and better for it.
*FA. Gary Gibson 1988*

**⑬ Afloat in the Moat** . . . . 🎒⬛[    ] **6c+**
Start up a small groove. Re-bolted.
*FA. Gary Gibson 1988*

**⑭ Piranha Wall** . . . . . . . . . . 🎒[    ] **E?**
An old trad route that hasn't been climbed for years. It starts
below the high corner then takes a diagonal line leftwards. Once
given E3 5c although it is probably much more serious than that.
*FA. Chris Jackson 1976*

**⑮ Triton** . . . . . . . . . . . . . 🐚🎒[    ] **E4 5c**
A series of corners lead to the main break. Move right to tackle
the clean upper groove to the trees. Not climbed for many years
with old pegs and much loose rock.
**Jaws II, E4 6b -** The direct finish over the roof above the lower
corners.
*FA. Chris Jackson, Bob Conway 1976. FA. (Jaws II) Chris Plant 1984*

**⑯ Two Sheep to Leicester.** 🎒🎒[    ] **7a+**
Pull over the loose bulge, then climb the technical wall above.
*FA. Paul Dearden, Alan James 1991*

**⑰ Searching for the Yeti** 🎒🏊🎒[    ] **7b**
Start as for *Two Sheep*... but break out right up the steep arete.
May well be harder due to the loss of holds.
*FA. Alan James 1991*

*The routes to the right are all old and suffering from neglect.
They are currently unclimbable but may well be rebolted in the
future hence we have included the descriptions.*

**⑱ Moat Wall** . . . . . . . . . . . . 🎒[    ] **E?**
Gain the hanging groove somehow. Not reclimbed since losing
crucial holds. It was given a grade of 7c originally.
*FA. Chris Wright 1989*

**⑲ Moat Race** . . . . . . . . . . . . 🎒[    ] **6c+**
An old peg and a bolt mark the line.
*FA. Gary Gibson 1988*

**⑳ Moat Puddings** . . . . . . . . . 🎒[    ] **E?**
The bolt has fallen out of this one. It was originally E4 6a.
*FA. Gary Gibson 1988*

**㉑ Castle Puddings.** . . . . . . . . 🎒[    ] **6b+**
The wall has three old pegs and leads to a tree belay.
*FA. Nigel Slater 1985*

*Finally for those after an almost sea-cliff-like adventure, there is
a major girdle along the break.*

**㉒ The Flying Dutchman** . . 🎒🎒[    ] **E6 6c**
A free ascent of the old aided girdle-traverse of the buttress.
Start on the terrace below and right of the *Triton* groove.
**1)** E4 6a, 10m. Traverse the break to the big scoop ledge.
**2)** E6 6c, 15m. Continue along the break to a hanging belay in
the middle of the wall. Mostly fixed gear - about 7c+.
**3)** E5 6a, 10m. Continue to the *Sheerwater* belay. About 7a+.
**4)** VS 4c, 15m. Reverse *Sheerwater* to finish back on the
ground.
*FFA. Andy Cave, Andy Perkins, Tony Parkes 1999*
*FA. J Ballard, B.Moore (A3) 1966*

*Over to the left of the Majorca Alternative are five more routes which rely mostly on fixed gear. Much of this gear is old and none of the routes have good lower-offs. They may be re-bolted sometime in the future.*
*From left to right they are:* **Rhyme Cryme E4 6b, Rhyme and Reason E3 6a, Happy Days E4 6a, Oh Dear! E4 6a.**

**❶ The Majorca Alternative . . .** 〔1〕☐ **7a+**
This one has been rebolted. It starts about 5m left of the big tree. Head up the steep wall past some overlaps.
*FA. Bill Gregory, Keith Sharples 1988*

**❷ Costa del Jolly . . . . . . .** 〔1〕◧☐ **7a**
Fingery climbing up the smart wall.
*FA. David Simmonite 2011*

**❸ Wish you Were Here . . . . . . . .** ☐ **6b**
Start to the right and climb up behind the tree.
*FA. David Simmonite 2011*

**❹ Mission Impossible** 〔1〕◧◧☐ **8a+**
The left-hand line has a desperate bouldery middle section requiring a horrendous lock-off to a small side-pull.
*FA. Tony Coutts 1998*

**❺ Karma Killer . . .** 〔2〕◧◧◧◧☐ **8b**
Superb technical climbing up the steep wall involving a desperate mono-move and then a sustained finish.
*FA. Tony Coutts 1999*

**❻ Agent Provocateur .** 〔2〕◧◧☐ **8a+**
Excellent climbing up the bulging rib. A powerful start via small undercuts leads to the break and a rest, then a very exciting finishing bulge. *Photo opposite.*
*FA. Tony Coutts 1998*

**❼ Perfecto . . . . . . . . . .** ◧◧☐ **7c+**
A very reachy start leads to a short and fierce wall and then up the wall left of a groove to the lower-off of *Trainer Tamer.*
*FA. Tony Coutts 1997*

**❽ Trainer Tamer . . . . . .** ◧◧☐ **7b+**
A tricky wall leads to an easier scoop and a lower-off on the ledge above.
*FA. Tony Coutts 1997*

**❾ Breakbeat . . . . . . . . . .** 〔1〕◧◧☐ **8a**
A pumpy right-to-left traverse of the upper break line. Follow *Trainer Tamer* to the break then traverse this leftwards to finish up the final section of *Mission Impossible.*
*FA. Tony Coutts 1998*

**❿ One to One . . . . . . . .** ◧◧☐ **7a+**
Climb the wall to the left of the big flake of *Under Western Eyes.* There is currently no lower-off for the route and the upper wall is a tad loose. The short bottom wall is probably more useful as a boulder problem warm-up if you are attempting harder things to the left.
*FA. Mike Lea, Chris Wright 1990*

**⓫ Under Western Eyes . . .** ◧◧☐ **E5 6b**
Climb the leaning flake to a roof (peg). Pull over to gain a big ledge. Either walk off rightwards, or tackle the groove above for the summit experience (5c), but be warned; it is loose and hard.
*FFA. Andy Barker 1981. FA. Graham West 1962*

**Crunch Buttress**
The steep wall, passed on the way to Moat Buttress, has been developed with some intense and hard sport routes.
**Conditions -** Well-shaded and dry in the rain, but it suffers from seepage in winter and is slow to dry.

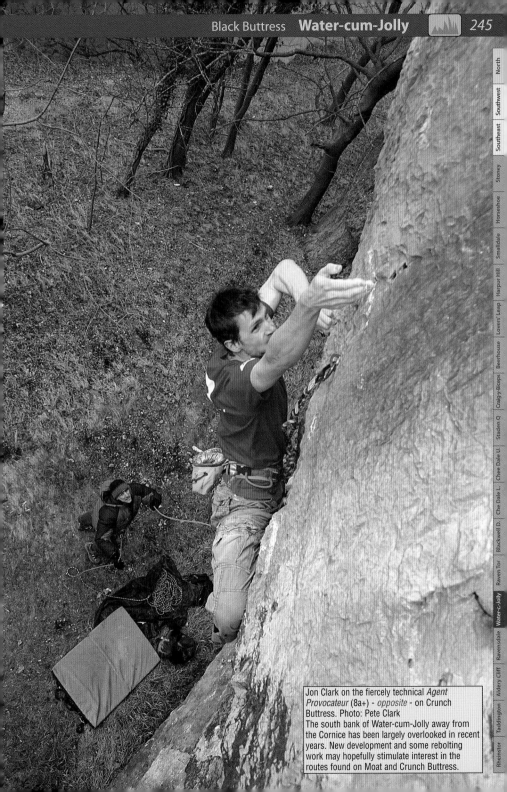

North
Southwest
Southeast
Stoney
Horseshoe
Smalldale
Harpur Hill
Lovers' Leap
Beerhouse
Craigy-Bleeps
Staden Q
Chee Dale U.
Che Dale L.
Blackwell D.
Raven Tor
Water-c-Jolly
Ravensdale
Aldery Cliff
Taddington
Litheinstow

Jon Clark on the fiercely technical *Agent Provocateur* (8a+) - *opposite* - on Crunch Buttress. Photo: Pete Clark
The south bank of Water-cum-Jolly away from the Cornice has been largely overlooked in recent years. New development and some rebolting work may hopefully stimulate interest in the routes found on Moat and Crunch Buttress.

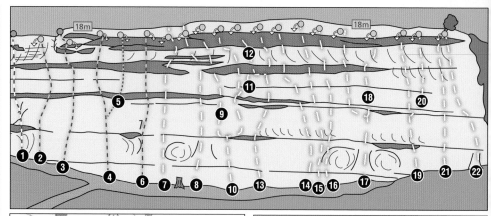

Brachiation Dance - p.248

## The Cornice

The second of the Peak's Cornices is in the form of a single crashing wave of rock which befits its name better than its Chee Dale counterpart. Most of the routes build slowly up the lower wall to hard and strenuous moves around the bulges, often with desperate reaches or powerful pulls to reach the crest.

**Conditions -** This Cornice is very slow to dry, some years it never fully dries out. Once dry, it remains climbable for weeks after the weather has turned. It is very sheltered from the wind and rain, and never gets sun; a fine retreat in hot weather.

**Approach (also see page 226) -** From Cressbrook, cross the bridge below the dam, then pick up a low sheep-track that skirts the edge opposite Rubicon. Follow this to a fence (Moat Buttress below), cross over and drop down to the Monsal Trail. Walk along this to a path on the right of the cutting, before the next tunnel - where the fencing ends. Follow this for about 50m, until you can drop down under a buttress through the trees. When at river level, follow the path past a couple of steps to the Cornice.

### ❸ The Dole 1989 . . . .  7c
Start direct (**The Restart**) to the first bulge. After that it is standard stuff to the first lower-off; only one hard move but it is a toughie. Adding an extra move or two above the lower-off was formerly **The Enterprise Allowance Finish**, 7c+, although few do this anymore.
*FA. Malc Taylor, John Hart 1989. FA. (The Enterprise Allowance Finish) Mark Pretty 1989. FA. (The Restart) Steve Earnshaw.*

### ❹ Yorkshire 8b . . .  8a
The first of the hard routes. It is now finished left at the top (easy 8a) instead of the original right-hand finish, which has lost crucial holds and is now worth 8a+.
*FA. Ben Masterson 1989. The name was a dig at the Yorkshire scene on the late 1980s where there seemed to be a few too many 8b routes appearing.*

### ❺ Ape Index . . . . . . .  8b+
Follow *Yorkshire 8b* to the roof. Step right and make desperate fingery moves upwards to a slightly easier finish. *Photo opposite.*
*FA. Steve McClure 2001*

### ❻ The Weakling . .  7c+
One of the few routes which is significantly harder for the tall, the difficulties start at the first main roof.
*FA. Ben Masterson 1988*

### ❶ The Bulge 1984 . . . . . . . .  E5 6b
On the far left-hand end of the crag, climb out of a scoop to the break - old thread. Move up left and pull through the final roof via a notch. Belay above.
*FA. Andy Mitchell 1984*

### ❷ Incapacity Benefit . . . .  7a+
A popular warm-up with a long history. Start 6m left of where the path arrives. It starts in roughly the same position as an old route - *The Thatcher Years* - but uses a completely new set of holds, and has a different line.
*FA. Kristian Clemmow in 2006*
*FA. (Thatcher Years) Bill Gregory, Keith Sharples (as an E5 6b) 1988.*
*FA. (Nothing to Help the Poor) Paul Mitchell 1984. Started on the left.*

North | Southwest | Southeast | Stoney | Horseshoe | Smalldale | Harpur Hill | Lovers' Leap | Beehouse | Craig-y-Biceps | Staden Q | Chee Dale U | Che Dale L | Blackwell D | Raven Tor | Water-c-Jolly | Ravensdale | Aldery Cliff | Taddington | Rhenstor

Steve McClure pulling hard through the bulges on *Ape Index* (8b+) - *opposite* - on the WCJ Cornice. Photo: Keith Sharples

North Southeast Stoney Horseshoe Smalldale Harpur Hill Lovers' Leap Beehouse Craig-y-Biceps Staden Q Chee Dale U. Che Dale L. Blackwell D. Raven Tor Water-c-Jolly Ravensdale Aldery Cliff Taddington Rheinstor

**7 Brachiation Dance** . . . . 🔝50 7b+
A classic, up an awesome line on decent holds for the most part. Low-(ish) in the grade. Start direct (**Dance Direction**) to the break, the original came from the left. Pull away to a poor rest below the final roof then crank this to the top. Either reverse and lower off from the last bolt or scratch up the slope to a tree.
*FFA. Tim Freeman 1984. Led with one rest by Dominic Lee in 1980*
*FA. (as Nemesis) Graham West, Barry Roberts 1959*
*FA. (Dance Direction) Steve Earnshaw, Mark Shearer 1990*

**8 The Free Monster**. . . 8a
A fine climb with a chequered history. Start by the stump and climb up the easy stuff until things blank out, once the sight of a bolted on flake-hold. Crank past this and keep going through the final roof to reach the top. Drop back down and lower off the last bolt.
*FA. John Welford 1991. Nigel Slater climbed the route as The Tea Monster in 1990. His dubious bolted-on flake had a short life.*

**9 The Auctioneer** . 8a+
An excellent route. Start up *Rumble* but climb slightly left on pockets and an undercut to a crimpy finish. The full tick requires pulling past the belay to jugs just above it.
*FA. Keith Sharples 2001*

**10 Rumble in the Jungle** 8a+
Head up the wall then traverse right along the break until below the big flake. Climb up to this then use a prominent sloper to gain the upper break. Traverse this left until sloping holds allow a dyno to a sharp jug. Continue to the lower-off.
*FA. Andy Pollitt 1989. Jean Baptist-Tribout had almost completed the route but sportingly grabbed a quickdraw near the top to invalidate the ascent.*

**11 Monsterosity** . . . . . . 8b
A superb pitch. Start up *Rumble* to its big flake, then climb up right by powerful undercutting. Cross the final roof to join *Albatrossity*.
*FA. Simon Reed 2001*

**12 Barbarosity** . . . . 8a+
The direct finish to *Monsterosity*.
*FA. Ben Heason 2010*

**13 Albatrossity**. . . . 🔝50 8a+
Strenuous and excellent. Climb the thin initial wall and over the first of the bulges. The middle bulge requires a wing-span to match the route name. Originally it traversed right but the direct is better and more logical involving hard pulls on slopers to the top break. *Photo on page 6.*
*FA. Robin Barker 1992. FA. (Direct version) Simon Reed 1994*

**14 Superfly** . . . . . . 8a+
More hard roofs requiring big spans and powerful moves. The middle roof is what gives the route its name. Above that it is still tricky all the way to the last move.
*FA. Neil Bentley 1995*

**15 Superocity** . . . . . . . . . 8a+
Start as for *Superfly* (the original method) or more direct.
*FA. Simon Reed 2007*

**16 Eclipsed** . . . . . . 8a+
A hard start leads to an even harder finish requiring a desperate pull on a two finger pocket, a harder replica of the *Glue Machine*.
*FA. Steve Fearn 1999*

### ⑰ The Disillusioned Glue Machine
..................  **8a**
Well named. Climb to the break then move left to the roof, which
is crossed using the V-pockets and a heel-hook. It is easier to
miss out the final bolt giving an exciting fall potential. At the top,
pull past the lower-off, before slumping back for the full tick.
*FA. Mark Pretty 1989*

### ⑱ Empire Burlesque ....  **7c+**
The first of the easier routes at this end of the crag. Climb direct
from where *Glue Machine* heads left using power and finger
strength. Leaving the hole on the final roof is tasty.
*FA. Andy Pollitt 1986*

### ⑲ The Nasty Man ... **7c**
Make snappy, crimpy moves to the break. Step left then head up
the wall past the big undercut to a hard move on tiny crimps.
Pull through the roof to finish. Originally started up *Empire
Burlesque*.
*FA. Jon Barton, Robin Barker 1998*

### ⑳ Goldcrest ..... **8a**
Follow *The Nasty Man* to the break. Then move up to a crimp
and make a hard move right. Another hard move gains the break
under the top roof and a kneebar helps solve the powerful finish.
*FA. Jon Barton 1999*

### ㉑ Sirius.......... **7c+**
Steep climbing leads to a final hard pull over the top roof which
you can either do, or you can't and most can't. Tree belay.
*FA. Chris Wright 1989*

### ㉒ Atilla the Hun .......... **7a+**
Like most routes on the edges of hard crags, this one is easier
and not quite as good as its neighbours. A steep start and roof
finish provide the difficulties.
*FA. Keith Sharples 1989*

### ㉓ Catch the Rainbow.......... **6c**
The final shorter line.
*FA. Dave Simmonite 2010*

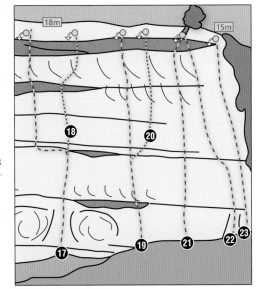

## Central Buttress

The biggest crag in the dale was once popular, and routes like *Behemoth* and *La Chute* were amongst the top routes of their day. The place now sees few visitors and the grass has taken over on many of the routes. Recently, a number of the old rotten pegs have been replaced with bolts, maybe the crag will see a much deserved renaissance.

**Approach (also see page 226) -** The easiest approach is to wade the weir from the main path, just before the crag appears on the right. The water is very shallow, except in flood. Alternatively, cross a bridge in the village, and follow a path up to the railway. Turn left on here and skirt around the tunnel entrance onto the hillside. After a short distance, drop down a steep gully (the second one) and contour around to the crag.

**Conditions -** The crag is well sheltered, and can be very pleasant on summer evenings when it gets the sun. There isn't much seepage for such a big crag.

**❶ Hammy Hamster's Last Rites** [ ] **E3 5c**
A poor loose route on the left.
*FA. Richard Davies 1986*

**❷ Chiming Crack . . . . . . .** [ ] **E4 6a**
The line follows a series of ringing flakes left of the cutaway of *Hemmingway's Horror*. Climb up to the bulge and pull into the crack then heave up it to the top.
*FFA. Tom Proctor, Jim Reading, Ernie Marshall 1976*
*FA. Eric Fairhurst, Sonny Lee 1950s*

**❸ Dangerous Liaisons . . .** [ ] **E5 6b**
A gap-filler with some good powerful climbing. Nearly a sport route at **7b**. Climb the wall to a peg. Two bolts on the wall above are both difficult to clip. Snake around them to gain a thin crack above.
*FA. Keith Sharples, Chris Wright 1990*

**❹ Hemmingway's Horror . . . .** [ ] **E2 5c**
The original line up this section wanders a bit but has some good moves. Gain the cutaway then climb the right-hand side to the bulge and pull up right into a groove. Make a tricky move up to a flake which leads more easily to the top.
*FFA. Tom Proctor 1975. FA. Graham West, Barry Roberts 1950s*

**❺ Carillon Crack . . . . . . .** [ ] **E3 5c**
The steeply undercut crack is savage. Gain the cutaway on its left side. Pull up into the left-hand crack and climb it.
*FFA. Ron Fawcett and others 1976. FA. Graham West, Barry Roberts 1950s*

**❻ Silent Storm . . . . .** [ ] **E5 6a**
A filler-in that gives better climbing than its neighbours. From the centre of the cutaway, pull over the bulge (runner in *Carol's Crack*) to gain a thin crack above. Climb this to the top.
*FA. Richard Davies, Simon Nadin 1987*

**❼ Carol's Crack. . . . . . . .** [ ] **E3 5c**
More beefy climbing up the crack which leaves the right-hand side of the cutaway. Approach direct then thug away.
*FA. Ron Fawcett 1976*

**❽ The Importance of Being Ernest .** [ ] **E4 6a**
A thin crack at the start leads to the wall right of *Hemmingway*.
*FA. Keith Sharples 1985*

**❾ The Bellringer . . . . . . . . . .** [ ] **E2 5c**
The broken flakes and cracks.
*FA. Tom Proctor 1975*

**❿ Vapour Stream . . . . . . . . . . . .** [ ] **E4 6a**
Direct over the double overlap. It originally had a single peg.
*FA. Richard Davies 1986*

**⓫ La Belle Age . . . . . . . . . . . . .** [ ] **E5 6b**
The crucial pegs have been replaced by bolts.
*FA. Richard Davies 1986*

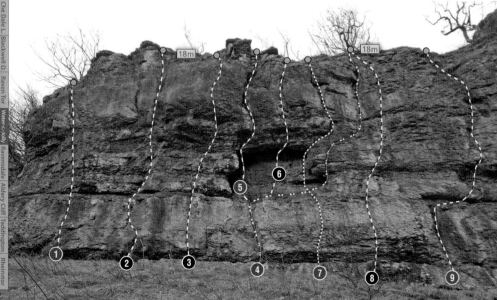

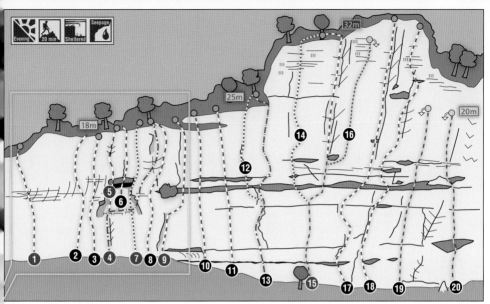

**⑫ En Masse Descendre** . . 🔆🏕️ ☐ **E6 6b**
Move left over the bulge from *In Bulk* and climb the desperate
wall. The crucial pegs have been replaced with bolts.
*FA. Richard Davies 1986*

**⑬ In Bulk** . . . . . . . 🔆 🧗🏕️ ☐ **E6 6b**
Climb the big flake of the original start to *St. Paul* then move up
to a slim groove (bolt). Pull up and right to gain a short corner.
Make some hard and fingery moves up the blank section above
to easier ground.
*FA. Jerry Moffatt 1982*

**⑭ Leviathan** . . . . . . . 🔆🏕️🧗 ☐ **E5 6b**
A serious undertaking. Start up *St. Paul Direct* to the ledge.
Climb through the bulge above to gain a short crack. Move right
then climb to easier ground above.
*FFA. Dominic Lee, Daniel Lee 1981*
*FA. (as Damascus Road, a hard A2) Brian Moore, Jim Ballard 1966*

**⑮ St. Paul Direct** . . . . . . 🔆🎿 ☐ **E3 6a**
One of the few easier routes on the buttress but still quite an
undertaking. It originally started on the left (*In Bulk*) and used
the ledge to gain the upper groove. This option can still be
climbed at E3 5c but the direct version is better. From the ledge
head right up the steep wall (bolt) to gain the grassy cracks
which lead to the top.
*FFA. Andy Parkin, Pete O'Donovan 1976. FA. Dave Peck, Paul Nunn 1960.*
*FA. (Direct Start) Richard Davies (solo) 1987*

**⑯ Paulliac** . . . . . . 🔆🧗🧗🎿 ☐ **7c**
The slim pillar between the two main crack-systems via a
tenuous line of tiny grooves and overlaps. Start up *St. Paul
Direct* to the first bolt in the upper groove. Step right below a
small bulge to climb the thin seam, which is sustained, fingery
and technical.
*FA. Seb Grieve 2009*

**⑰ Behemoth** . . . . . . . . . . ⌈Top⌉🎿 ☐ **E5 6b**
                                ⌊50⌋
The finest route in WCJ has a hard start. Once past this, the
route follows a superb, sustained finger and hand crack. Climb
left of a lower crack to a bulge (peg). Pull through with difficulty
to the ledge above then head up the wall to gain the crack.
Thrash up this (off-fingers and small cams), the hanging corner
is your target; make it that far and you're home.
*FFA. Ron Fawcett, Pete Livesey 1976. FA. Paul Nunn, Brian Barlow, Barry
Ingle 1960. FA. (Direct Start) Jim Moran, Geoff Milburn 1980*

**⑱ That'll Do Nicely** . . 🗯️🎿🦶 ☐ **E5 6b ?**
The pegs have gone making this *much* more serious than it
used to be - it has not been re-led. Climb the lower wall past the
bulge to a ledge. Move right then climb up into a crack to reach
a short groove. Climb this and the right-facing corner above to
a loose finish.
*FFA. Ian Parsons, Howard Lancashire 1989. The upper section was climbed
as Yankee Dollar by Jim Moran in 1980. FA. Bruce Andrews, Brian Moore
1970. This followed the original aided line of Behemoth to start.*

**⑲ The Treadmill** . . . . 🔆🦶🧗 ☐ **7b**
Tackle the steep right-hand side of the buttress starting at a
small hole in the loose wall. Climb up left into a left-facing
groove then step right to a ledge. Climb the wall then a right-
facing flake to a lower-off. Originally loose it is supposed to be
cleaning up and might settle at 7a+. Pumpy, rattly fun either way.
*FA. Seb Grieve 2009*

**⑳ Fort Knox Direct** . . . . 🔆🦶🧗 ☐ **7b ?**
Climb to the roof and move right before powering through it.
Climb the wall, bulge and loose flake-crack to a lower-off. It
has lost a crucial hold above the roof since the first ascent. It is
possible to by-pass the roof on either side at a lesser E5-ish.
*FA. Seb Grieve 2009. FA. (Fort Knox) Jim Moran, Geoff Milburn. This
avoided the hard roof by a loose loop out left and back right.*

**The Troll, E2 5c, 5a,** *tackles the broken cracks and grooves to
the right in two pitches.*

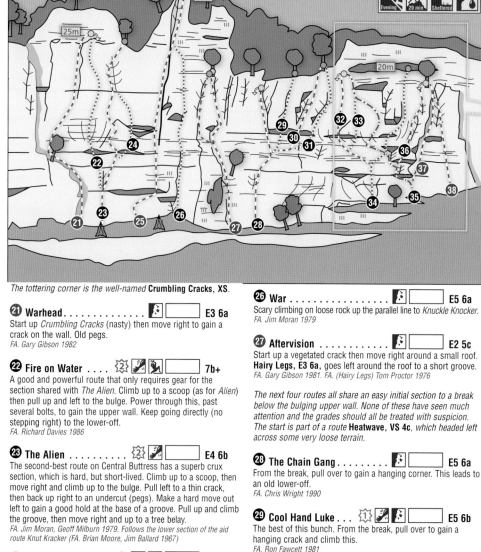

*The tottering corner is the well-named* **Crumbling Cracks**, *XS*.

**㉑ Warhead** . . . . . . . . . . . . **E3 6a**
Start up *Crumbling Cracks* (nasty) then move right to gain a
crack on the wall. Old pegs.
*FA. Gary Gibson 1982*

**㉒ Fire on Water** . . . . **7b+**
A good and powerful route that only requires gear for the
section shared with *The Alien*. Climb up to a scoop (as for *Alien*)
then pull up and left to the bulge. Power through this, past
several bolts, to gain the upper wall. Keep going directly (no
stepping right) to the lower-off.
*FA. Richard Davies 1986*

**㉓ The Alien** . . . . . . . . . . **E4 6b**
The second-best route on Central Buttress has a superb crux
section, which is hard, but short-lived. Climb up to a scoop, then
move right and climb up to the bulge. Pull left to a thin crack,
then back up right to an undercut (pegs). Make a hard move out
left to gain a good hold at the base of a groove. Pull up and climb
the groove, then move right and up to a tree belay.
*FA. Jim Moran, Geoff Milburn 1979. Follows the lower section of the aid
route Knut Kracker (FA. Brian Moore, Jim Ballard 1967)*

**㉔ Aliens** . . . . . . . . . **E6 6c**
Start up *Alien*, but break right onto the wall. The middle section
shares some ground with a route called **White Fright, E6** which
tackled the loose rock between *Alien* and *Knuckle Knocker*.
*FA. (Aliens) Mike Lea 2000. FA. (White Fright) Ron Fawcett 1981*

**㉕ Knuckle Knocker** . . . . . **E3 5c**
A fine crack-climb, spoilt by its start. The loss of a crucial block
has made it hard. Start below a long, thin roof. Climb up to a
peg, then traverse right (peg), and pull up to gain a ledge at the
base of the crack. Follow the crack to a tree belay at the top.
*FA. Keith Myhill 1970*

**㉖ War** . . . . . . . . . . . . . . . . . **E5 6a**
Scary climbing on loose rock up the parallel line to *Knuckle Knocker*.
*FA. Jim Moran 1979*

**㉗ Aftervision** . . . . . . . . . . . **E2 5c**
Start up a vegetated crack then move right around a small roof.
**Hairy Legs, E3 6a**, goes left around the roof to a short groove.
*FA. Gary Gibson 1981. FA. (Hairy Legs) Tom Proctor 1976*

*The next four routes all share an easy initial section to a break
below the bulging upper wall. None of these have seen much
attention and the grades should all be treated with suspicion.
The start is part of a route* **Heatwave, VS 4c**, *which headed left
across some very loose terrain.*

**㉘ The Chain Gang** . . . . . . . . **E5 6a**
From the break, pull over to gain a hanging corner. This leads to
an old lower-off.
*FA. Chris Wright 1990*

**㉙ Cool Hand Luke** . . . **E5 6b**
The best of this bunch. From the break, pull over to gain a
hanging crack and climb this.
*FA. Ron Fawcett 1981*

**㉚ Disparagement** . . . . . . **E5 6a**
From the break, gain the hanging groove and climb it.
*FA. Jim Reading 1976*

**㉛ Time Warp** . . . . . . . . . . . . **E4 6b**
Traverse right along the break and pull over into the right-most
hanging groove.
*FA. Jim Moran 1980*

**㉜ Fatal Attraction** . . . . . . . . **E5 6a**
Start up *Sox* but break left up the wall.
*FA. Chris Wright 1990*

**33 Fatal Hesitation . . .** 🪝🐾 ▐ ⬜ **E6 6c**
Direct from *Fatal Attraction* to the lower-off on *La Chute*.
*FA. Richard Davies 1986*

**34 Sox . . . . . . . . . . . .** ⚙️🪧 ⬜ **E5 6a**
A counter-diagonal to *La Chute*, leading to a fine finish. Start left of a tree, and climb past a bolt to the break. Traverse right into a groove, then climb up and leftwards through the bulges (bolts). Move back right to gain a hanging flake and layback up this to easier ground and the top.
*FA. Jim Moran, Geoff Milburn 1982*

**35 La Chute . . . . . . . . . .** ⚙️🪧 ⬜ **E5 6b**
The original line on this section has some good climbing, the old gear has been replaced by bolts. Start below *Coldity Groove*, but move left (bolt) and follow a groove (bolt) to a break. Traverse left (*Sox* in reverse), then move up to a bolt in the bulge. A hard series of pulls gains the wall above. Cross this diagonally to the lower-off.
*FA. Ron Fawcett 1981*

**36 La Route . . . . . . . . . .** ⚙️🪝 ⬜ **E4 6a**
A fine climb with a crucial hidden hold on the crux. Climb *La Chute* to the break and continue direct above up a flake-crack. Move right into a groove and climb direct to a lower-off.
*FA. Keith Sharples, Mike Browell 1985*

**37 Coldity Groove . . . . . . . . .** 🪧 ⬜ **E3 5c**
The long groove-line is reached by a hard pull from below. Use the lower-off on *La Route*.
*FFA. Jim Campbell, Con Carey 1976. FA. Pete Bagnell, Dan Murphy 1964*

**38 Coldity Crack . . . . . . . . . . . . .** ⬜ **E1 5b**
The crack and groove on the right, to a leftward exit.
*FFA. Pete O'Donovan, Mark Stokes 1976. FA. Pete Bagnell, Dan Murphy 1964 starting up the current line of Coldity Groove.*

North | Southwest | Southeast | Stoney | Horseshoe | Smalldale | Harpur Hill | Lovers' Leap | Beerhouse | Craig-y-Biceps | Staden Q | Chee Dale U. | Che Dale L. | Blackwell D. | Raven Tor | Water-c-Jolly | Ravensdale | Aldery Cliff | Taddington | Rheinstor

| | No star | | | |
|---|---|---|---|---|
| **Mod to S** | 5 | - | - | - |
| **HS to HVS** | 9 | 16 | 8 | 2 |
| **E1 to E3** | 3 | 16 | 7 | 1 |
| **E4 and up** | 2 | 17 | 19 | 11 |

A fine tall west-facing buttress that rises above the attractive wooded valley of Cressbrook Dale and has a good set of middle-grade climbs. The main face is Raven's Buttress, rising directly above the cottages, this has several fine climbs and a fair smattering of loose rock and ivy. For something less intimidating there is a good cluster of shorter climbs surrounding the impressive natural arch of the Flying Buttress Area over to the left. Currently most of the worthwhile routes are reasonably clean and solid, although there may still be some loose rock, and some of the holds are very polished. Encroaching vegetation is an ever-present problem.

## Approach    Also see map on page 211

The cliff is located in Cressbrook Dale. From the B6465 Ashford in the Water to Wardlow road, take either of two lanes down into Monsal Dale, one of which starts by the Monsal Head pub - a recommendable spot. Once in the dale, pass the entrance to Water-cum-Jolly, and keep right up the hill. After about 500m, a minor road on the right leads down to cottages below the crag, with parking space for about eight cars. If the parking is full, leave your car back down at the mill. From the right-hand side of the parking, a track leads down to the river (often dry) and up the steep wooded bank to the base of the cliff.

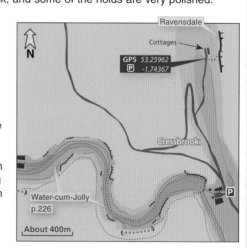

## Conditions

The crag faces west, and catches the afternoon sun. It does not suffer much from seepage, but the larger Raven's Buttress gets any wind going.

## Access

The crag is managed by English Nature as part of a National Nature Reserve. They ask that climbers approach the crag on the marked concessionary path from the parking by the cottages, and only climb on the crags covered in this guide. Additionally, English Nature may impose restrictions to safeguard nesting birds. These are indicated by signs on the approach path and on the BMC website. Please do not ignore these.

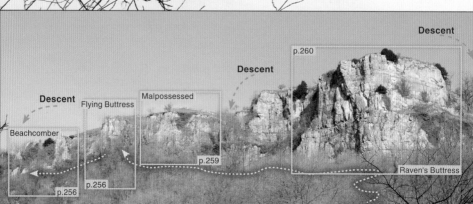

North

Southwest

Southeast

Stoney

Horseshoe

Smalldale

Harpur Hill

Lovers Leap

Beerhouse

Craig-y-Biceps

Staden Q

Chee Dale U.

Chee Dale L.

Raven Tor

Blackwell D.

Water-c-Jolly

Ravensdale

Aldery Cliff

Taddington

Rheinstor

Tony Payne on the polished crack of *The Gymnic* (HVS 5a) - *next page* - on Flying Buttress at Ravensdale. Whilst some of the more popular routes at Ravensdale are a bit polished, they are probably no more polished than they were when the authors first climbed them over 30 years ago!

*50m left of the Flying Buttress is a slim tower of rock, with ivy on its left side, and one worthwhile climb. Beyond this are a couple more interesting offerings, then a descent gully.*

**❶ Pedestal Branch** . . . . . . . [icons] **VDiff**
Start up the chimney but branch left behind the ivy to locate the Pedestal. Finish up the crack above this.
*FA. John Loy 1960*

**❷ Bifurous Chimney.** . . . . . . . [icons] **VDiff**
The deep and wide rift on the left is interesting.
*FA. Don Morrison 1961*

**❸ The Bigot Direct.** . . . [icons] **E3 6a**
The steep thin cracks just left of the arete are fierce, but soon ease. Originally the route came in from the left at HVS 5b.
*FA. (Direct) Gary Gibson 1979. FA. (Original) John Fleming 1976*

**❹ Beachcomber** . . . . . . . . . [icons] **HVS 5a**
Climb the face of the tower, and the short crack to the overhang. Step left to pass this, then move back right to finish up the well-positioned face above. Do it before the ivy wins.
*FA. Chris Jackson, Rod Haslam 1978*

*Of most interest at this end of the crag is the Flying Buttress and its surrounding walls.*

**❺ Gruesome Groove** . . . . . . . . . [icon] **VS 4c**
The not-too-gruesome groove to a choice of exits.
*FA. John Loy, G Armstrong 1965*

**❻ Scorpion.** . . . . . . . . . . [icons] **E2 5c**
Climb to a niche, then pull right (hard) to the hanging flake. Go up this with difficulty, to reach the easier, but looser final arete.
*FA. M.Quinn, J.Dutton, B.Samuals (2 pegs) 1966*

**❼ The Gymnic.** . . . . . . . . . . . [icons] **HVS 5a**
Left of the through-cave, tackle the twin cracks and the bulge to access the interesting groove above. Although highly polished, it remains popular. Exit either side of the final roof.
*Photo on previous page.*
*FA. John Loy, Harry Gillott, Brian Stokes, Ted Howard 1960*

**❽ Freedom Slaves.** . . . . . [icons] **E4 6c**
Climb the groove right of *The Gymnic* to the overhang then go straight through the roof (rumoured to be more solid than it looks) and finish up the arete above.
*FA. Paul Fearn 1994*

**❾ Cold Shoulder** . . . . . . . . . [icons] **E1 5b**
Start up *Amain*, then make an exposed traverse left above the main overhang to finish up the left arete above *The Gymnic*.
*FA. Mark Kemball, Bill McKee 1981*

**❿ Amain** . . . . . . . . . . . [icons] **HVS 5a**
The hanging crack right of the cave opening is entered by a tough struggle. Follow the easier corner crack above. Exit left or right with no change in grade.
*FA. John Loy, Dave Johnson, Dave Mellor 1960*

**⓫ Russian Roulette** . . . . . . . . . . [icons] **HVS 5b**
An eliminate following the crack squeezed between *Amain* and the arete to the right. Finish out on the arete itself.
*FA. Mick Horlov, Bob Dearman 1978*

**⓬ Looking at Blue** . . . . . . . . . [icons] **HVS 5b**
Another contrived line starting up the thin crack left of *Impendant* and finishing out on the arete of *Russian Roulette*.
*FA. Gary Gibson 1979*

**⓭ Impendant** . . . . . . . . . [icons] **VS 4c**
A bit of an oddity, a limestone jamming crack that proves to be worthwhile, popular and sustained at the grade.
*FA. John Loy, Dave Mellor 1960*

**⓮ Shattered Crack.** . . . . . . . . . . . [icon] **VDiff**
From the foot of *Impendant*, step right over the void and move up onto a suspect block. The crack above is less shattered than the name suggest. Finish with care up steep grass.
*FA. John Loy, R.Precious 1959*

Descent

20m

20m

20m

16m

Abseil descent

⑨

⑦ ⑧ ⑩ ⑪ ⑫ ⑬ ⑭

⑥ ⑤

North
Southwest
Southeast
Stoney
Horseshoe
Smalldale
Harpur Hill
Lower's Leap
Beerhouse
Craig-y-Biceps
Staden Q
Chee Dale U.
Chee Dale L.
Blackwell D.
Raven Tor
Water-c-Jolly
Ravensdale
Aldery Cliff
Taddington
Rheinstor

## Flying Buttress
To the left of the big face of Raven's Buttress is a hidden natural archway with an angular bay to its right. There is a good collection of climbs here, though the best of these are now very polished. Care is required with many of the exits, which are grassy and/or loose.
**Approach -** Walk left from under the Main Buttress and cross a fence. Then continue on the path up towards the *Wilt* wall and the natural arch.
**Belays -** Belays at the top are difficult to find.
**Descent -** Walk left along the cliff-top and drop down a steep gully 50m left of *Beachcomber*. Abseiling from the tree above *Tria* is an alternative.

Afternoon
15 min
18m
Shattered Crack - p.256
To The Gymnic
15
16
17
18
19

A
18m
18m
20m
19
20
21
22
23
24

**15 Amnesiacs** . . . . . . . . . . . . . . . . **E1 5b**
Climb the awkward cracks and groove in the south-facing wall to a convenient tree.
*FA. Graham Parkes, Dave Vincent, Chris Craggs 2005. So called because, when it came to write it up, we couldn't remember anything about it.*

**16 Cave Corner** . . . . . . . . . . . **S 4a**
The left corner of the square alcove is approached up the juggy wall. Care is needed with blocky rock and grass at the top.
*FA. John Loy 1959*

**17 Ash Crack** . . . . . . . . . . 2 **VS 4c**
Climb the sustained central crack in the back wall of the alcove. Well glossed and well protected - it eases with height.

**18 Hydrolysis**. . . . . . . . . . 1 **E1 5b**
A bit of an eliminate line, though moves are neat. Up the thin cracks and the narrow wall between *Ash Crack* and *Tria*.
*FA. Gary Gibson, J.Norris 1979*

**19 Tria** . . . . . . . . . . . . . . . . . 2 **HS 4b**
The right-hand corner of the alcove is worthwhile, giving enjoyable bridging, marred only by the polished holds. Exit left.
*FA. Dave Johnson, Dave Mellor 1960*

**20 Cut Loose or Fly** . . . . . 🎚️ 🔳 ⬜ **E3 5c**
Climb the crack and wall on the right, avoiding the urge to bridge into the groove on the left.
FA. Phil Burke, Keith Myhill 1978

**21 Wilt** . . . . . . . . . . . 🎚️ 🔳 🔳 ⬜ **E5 6b**
Start up the crack of Cut Loose or Fly, then, from good holds, traverse right and climb the desperately faint crack.
FA. Ron Fawcett 1982

**22 Pagan Man** . . . . . . . . 🎚️ 🔳 ⬜ **E5 6b**
Follow the technical scoop above the Wilt traverse, then the bulge above to easy ground.
FA. Johnny Dawes, Tony Kartawick 1984

**23 The Wilt Alternative** 🎚️ 🔳 🔳 ⬜ **E5 6c**
A fierce direct start to the faint crack; a peg and a thread protect the hardest moves.
FA. Quentin Fisher 1985

The wide wall to the right is rather loose and vegetated, though there is a trio of grooves and a neat finger crack worth seeking out, if you have done everything else. There are other routes on the wall, but they never get done.

**24 Malpossessed** . . . . . . . 🎚️ 🔳 ⬜ **HVS 5b**
The groove right of the arete is approached by trending right-wards on the lower wall to the bulges. Pull up into the groove on the right-hand side of the block overhang then move left into its continuation and finish up this.
FA. Ernie Marshall, John Loy (2 pegs) 1968
FFA. Ken Myhill, Terry King 1970

## Malpossessed
Between the delights of the Flying Buttress Area and the main Raven's Buttress, is a wide wall with over 20 recorded routes. Sadly, the amount of loose rock and vegetation here means that most of them never get done. The best four lines are described in the hope that a bit of traffic will help clean them up.
**Approach (also see page 254)** - Walk left from under the Main Buttress and cross a fence. The routes are just beyond a steep descent gully.
**Belays** - Belays at the top are difficult to find, many climbers simply get well back and dig their heels in.
**Descent** - The gully to the right gives a scrambly descent. It is steep, care needed, especially if it is at all damp. You can also abseil or use the walking descents at either end of the crag.

**25 Sneck** . . . . . . . . . . . . . . . 🔳 ⬜ **HVS 5b**
Climb the wall or the flake to the left (harder) to the bulges. Move left and pull through into the base of the angular groove. Up this and the floral wall above to finish right of the overhang.

**26 The Wick** . . . . . . . . . . . . 🔳 ⬜ **VS 4b**
The long, angular groove on the right passes a substantial tree at 10m. Exit rightwards up near vertical meadows. A bit (or maybe a lot) of traffic might clean up the grass and enable the reinstatement of the route's lost star.
FA. John Loy, M.Walsh, G.Armstrong 1969

20m to the right is a prominent, thin crack that is also worth seeking out.

**27 Rock Biter** . . . . . . . . . 🎚️ 🔳 ⬜ **HVS 5a**
Nice, well-protected climbing up the thin cracks 10m left of the next descent gully starting from a grassy ledge.
FA. Chris Jackson, D.Sant 1978

Descent

North
Southwest
Southeast
Stoney
Horseshoe
Smalldale
Harpur Hill
Lovers' Leap
Beerhouse
Craigy-Biceps
Staden Q
Chee Dale U.
Chee Dale L.
Blackwell D.
Raven Tor
Water-c-Jolly
Ravensdale
Aldery Cliff
Taddington
Rheinstor

## Raven's Buttress

The main event at Ravensdale is the superb barrel-shaped buttress that juts out towards the cottages and parking place far below. The situations on the cliff are as impressive as might be expected, with superb views out to the west and the cliff catching the evening sun full on. The downside is the fact that some of the best routes have become very polished over the years and care with the rock is required over much of the cliff. Some of the less edifying experiences here are returning to well-deserved obscurity.

**Belays -** Belays at the top are difficult to find. There are a couple of stakes, well-buried in the grassy cliff top, but on many of the routes you will need to use your ingenuity.
**Descent -** Walk right (looking in) to reach the descent gully.

❶ **Solitaire** . . . . . . . . . . . . . . . . HS 4b
The short crack in the face to the left of *Conclusor*. Tree belay, scramble off left. Unremarkable and also unpolished.
*FA. John Loy (solo - who would have guessed?) 1960*

❷ **Conclusor** . . . . . . . . . . Top 50 HVS 5a
A fine route with good climbing and a reachy couple of moves just before easy ground is gained. The best route on the crag - possibly. Make sure to take a decent sized rack especially if you intend to do it as a single pitch. Start under the soaring groove.
**1)** 4c 12m. Follow the small groove to a stance on the ledge.
**2)** 5a, 30m. Climb the well-defined groove-line running up the left side of the main face.
*FA. Clive Rowland, Paul Nunn 1964*

*The rock to the right was once climbed by the hellish Hades, though it has largely disappeared under vegetation.*

❸ **Delusor** . . . . . . . . . . . . . . . HVS 5a
**1)** 5a, 12m. Make a hard (5b?) first move to gain a left-slanting crack/ramp-line then continue to a grassy landing onto a stance under a bulge.
**Original Start, VS 4c -** Start up *Conclusor* then traverse diagonally right to the stance. Very scruffy now, but it avoids that first move.
**2)** 4c, 30m. Climb the groove above to a bulge. Pass this and climb the continuation groove, making good use of its right wall, to join and finish up the final section of *Medusa*.
*FA. Dave Johnson, Dave Mellor 1960*

❹ **Medusa** . . . . . . . . . . VS 4b
The original classic has become polished over the years. It is still worth doing but be prepared for a slippery time. Start from a narrow grassy ledge above and left of the large tree growing left of the toe of the buttress.
**1)** 4b, 18m. Climb the glossy flake-crack then step right onto a short, steep, shattered wall above (some suspect holds). Step out right and belay left of a large pinnacle.
**2)** 4b, 26m. Climb to the top of the pinnacle, then slide up the shiny crack to a possible stance. Climb the pleasant ramp, in a superb situation, to finish up the grassy groove. Belay on the ledge on the right or find a well-hidden iron spike in the grass.
*FA. Dave Johnson, Dave Mellor 1960*

❺ **Via Vita** . . . . . . . . . . E1 5c
A fine finish via the hanging prow out in space is the highlight. Short-lived but thrilling and very exposed. *Photo on page 263.*
**1)** 4b, 26m. Follow the slippery flake of *Medusa* to the shattered wall, then continue up the steep groove to reach a cramped stance on the slabby gangway. The way on is where you don't want it to be; out into space.
**2)** 5c, 22m. Climb up the ramp a little way then swing right and up to a tiny ledge. Gain the undercut crack on the right with difficulty and follow it to the top. Well protected but wild.
**The Sinister Finish, E1 5b -** From the small ledge it is also possible to head left to a crack. Even more exposed.
*FA. John Loy, Dave Mellor (1pt) 1960*

❻ **Via Vita Direct** . . . . E2 6a
The striking overhanging groove high on the crag leads from the stance on *Medusa* straight up to the crux of the normal route, via some fierce finger-jamming. Short and sharp though fortunately very well protected.
*FA. Chris Jackson 1976*

*The next climbs all share a belay on the terrace at half-height, below the prominent upper scoop. They all have some loose rock; helmets and a little care are sensible precautions.*

❼ **Mealy Bugs** . . . . . . . . . VS 4c
**1)** 4c, 20m. Climb the shallow groove with a wide crack just right of the tree at the foot of the face - steeper than it looks - then as it fades trend right to a belay and good stance on the terrace. *Photo on page 263.*
**2)** 4c, 25m. Follow the slabby left wall of the open groove then trend up left again up the loose and grassy scoop above. Finish up the fine but short-lived jamming crack high on the left.
*FA. Dave Johnson, Dave Mellor 1960*

❽ **Mealystopheles** . . . . . . VS 5a
**1)** 5a, 22m. Start at a shallow groove to the left of the toe of the buttress and climb this and enter the awkward left-facing groove above. Follow the continuation groove to the terrace and a belay.
**2)** 4c, 24m. Follow *Mealy Bugs*, but once in the scoop, traverse round the arete and finish up the wide crack that lurks there. This is awkward to start but soon eases.
*FA. Bob Dearman, Rod Brown 1965*

❾ **Bullets** . . . . . . . . . . . . HVS 5b
Forges a very direct line up the face, offering some good climbing and a fine finish. Start at the toe of the buttress.
**1)** 5a, 22m. From the lowest point of the buttress, climb into and up a shallow groove that leads to the break. Move left via a thin flake, then climb the rounded arete to a stance on the terrace.
**2)** 5b, 22m. Climb the arete to a bulge, and pull over this to reach a wide crack and a well-positioned finish.
*FA. Gary Gibson 1980*

❿ **Mephistopheles** . . . E1 5b
A good climb that starts just left of the toe of the buttress, below an evil-looking hanging flake.
**1)** 5a, 22m. Climb a groove, then move right past the wedged flake with care. Continue awkwardly up the thin crack until tricky moves right gain the belay.
**2)** 5b, 24m. Climb the crack above the stance to steeper rock, then pull through the bulges to join the wide crack that forms the final section of the upper pitch of *Mealystopheles*. Steep.
*FA. Paul Nunn, Oliver Woolcock (1pt) 1964*

North
Southwest
Southeast
Stoney
Horseshoe
Smalldale
Harpur Hill
Lovers' Leap
Beerhouse
Cragg-Biceps
Staden Q
Chee Dale U.
Chee Dale L.
Blackwell D.
Raven Tor
Water-c-Jolly
Ravensdale
Aldery Cliff
Taddington
Rheinstor

North
Southwest
Southeast
Stoney
Horseshoe
Smalldale
Harpur Hill
Lovers' Leap
Beehouse
Craig-y-Biceps
Staden Q
Chee Dale U
Che Dale L
Blackwell D
Raven Tor
Water-cum-Jolly
Ravensdale
Aldery Cliff
Taddington
Rheinstor

45m

45m

Descent

45m

22m

22m

### ⓫ Purple Haze ..... 🏕🔧🔨 ☐ E1 5b
A fine climb with a good open finish, high on the wall. Start by the thorn tree under a left-facing flake, leading to an overhang.
**1)** 5b, 22m. A thin flake, overhang and groove above lead awkwardly to easier grooves and the terrace.
**2)** 5a, 24m. Follow the wide flake-crack from the terrace, then the fine steep wall and corner to finish.
*FA. Bob Dearman, D.Riley (2pts) 1970*

### ⓬ Ploy.............. 🏕🔨 ☐ VS 4c
The crack and long twisting groove right of the thorn tree.
**1)** 4c, 22m. Climb the groove, then move right and up into a niche. Climb up and slightly left to a grassy ledge.
**2)** 4c, 26m. Follow the wide flake-crack to its top, then traverse right easily, passing a yew tree. Climb the groove, pulling out left on to the wall (peg) in a good position. Finish direct.
*FA. Oliver Woolcock, Rod Brown 1964*

### ⓭ Frore ............. 🏕🔨 ☐ VS 5a
**1)** 5a, 20m. Start 2m right of *Ploy*, and climb up to a blank open groove. Follow this delicately, then continue diagonally up rightwards over some vegetated rock. Belay on the terrace.
**2)** 4c, 23m. Follow easy rock right of a crack to a ledge (and junction with *Ploy*). Continue up the groove of *Ploy* for 3m, then make a rising traverse right to the top.
*FA. John Loy, W.Woodward 1958*

North

Southwest

Southeast

Stoney

Horseshoe

Smalldale

Harpur Hill

Lover's Leap

Beehouse

Craigy-Biceps

Staden Q

Chee Dale U.

Che Dale L.

Blackwell D.

Raven Tor

Water-c-Jolly

**Ravensdale**

Aldery Cliff

Taddington

Rheinstor

Climbers on the finishing groove of *Via Vita* (E1 5c) and *Mealy Bugs* (VS 4c) - *page 261*. On the latter the leader appears to have made some efforts to avoid the jamming crack which is the highlight of the pitch!

North
Southwest
Southeast
Stoney
Horseshoe
Smalldale
Harpur Hill
Lover's Leap
Beerhouse
Craig-y-Biceps
Staden Q
Chee Dale U
Chee Dale L
Blackwell D
Raven Tor
Water-c-Jolly
Ravensdale
Aldery Cliff
Taddington
Rheinstor

# The Central Peak
## Aldery Cliff, Taddington Rheinstor

Caroline Taylor on *eXit Stage Left* (6a) - *page 273* - at Taddington. Photo: Craig Bailey

This secluded little crag has a set of short but fairly intense routes which require both technique and tenacity. There aren't many 'thank god' jugs on this crag and usually the main difficulty is finding the best of a multitude of poor holds to use.

North | Southwest | Southeast | Stoney | Horseshoe | Smalldale | Harpur Hill | Lovers' Leap | Beehouse | Craig-y-Biceps | Staden Q | Chee Dale U. | Che Dale L. | Blackwell D. | Raven Tor | Water-c-Jolly | Ravensdale | Aldery Cliff | Taddington | Rheinstor

| | No star | 😊1 | 😊2 | 😊3 |
|---|---|---|---|---|
| **Mod to S** | 1 | 1 | - | - |
| **HS to HVS** | 10 | 8 | 2 | - |
| **E1 to E3** | 1 | 2 | 1 | - |
| **E4 and up** | - | - | - | - |

Aldery Cliff is a secluded and slabby crag that offers a decent set of clean trad routes on fairly solid rock and some reasonable grades. Its popularity means that many of the routes are polished. It is an ancient quarry, but it has been abandoned so long that if feels more like a natural edge. This, coupled with a pleasant and sheltered setting (morning sunshine), makes it a delightful place to climb. Another advantage is that you can park right under the crag.

The routes are mostly on steep slabs, seamed with cracks that generally provide good protection, often from small wires. Belays at the top can sometimes be a problem, using the nearest tree is usually the best idea though be aware that these may be off to one side. Many of the trees have substantial cables/fixed karabiners on them to facilitate abseil descents, please respect these. There have been occasional rockfalls here, and a section of the cliff on the far right is currently deemed unsafe. As with all quarried limestone a little care and common sense is needed.

The crag is owned and managed by the BMC, so access should never be a problem. In 2010, the gate was locked on occasions to discourage local youths from using the quarry base as a party venue - there is limited roadside parking when this happens - ensure not to block the road, it is narrow and used by BIG farm traffic. From time to time, the vegetation gets a little out of hand. If this is the case, then let the BMC know and a cleaning/pruning session will be organised.

Walk descent

## Approach   Also see map on page 264

Aldery Cliff is situated just to the southwest of the tiny village of Earl Sterndale, indeed the crag is sometimes referred to as Earl Sterndale. From the A515 south of Buxton, follow signs for Longnor. Earl Sterndale is signed off these roads. The crag is about 500m south of the village, right next to the road, and you can park in the area in front of the crag. Please make sure you close the gate at all times.

## Conditions

The crag faces east, and gets the morning sun. It is very well-sheltered from westerly winds. In hot weather it is a good late afternoon venue. Generally the quarry is quick drying and doesn't suffer from seepage.

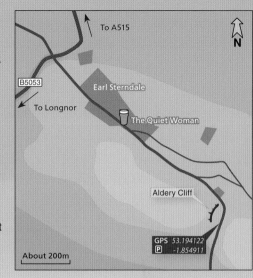

To A515

B5053

To Longnor

Earl Sterndale

The Quiet Woman

Aldery Cliff

GPS 53.194122
-1.854911

About 200m

Abseil descent

17

23

## Aldery Cliff

An ancient quarry that offers an unusual array of lower grade slabby limestone routes. The crag is popular and the routes are polished. It gets morning sun.
**Descent -** The easiest descent is to abseil from one of the crag-top trees - **be aware of climbers below**.
**Approach -** Cars can be parked in the base of the quarry, please keep the gate closed.

*The first routes are over on the far left on the last (first?) decent piece of rock; a relatively clean buttress with a conspicuous thin crack splitting its front face - Cooper's Peg Route. Left of this is a corner - Jackorner - and the crack left of the corner is* Therianthropic, HVS 5a *which is overgrown in its upper parts. Other routes have been recorded even further left but they are pretty poor and never get climbed nowadays.*

**1 Jackorner** . . . . . . . . . . . . . . . ☐ **VS 4c**
Climb the corner to a rightwards exit onto vegetated ground.
*FA. John Woodhouse, Andrew Sansom, Graham Hoey 1974*

**2 Cooper's Peg Route** . . . 🔁 🔩 ☐ **E2 6a**
A good little exercise for the connoisseur. Climb up the ramp and arrange some gear. Move back left and make a hard pull up the crack above to easier ground and a tree. Abseil off.
*FFA. Al Evans 1977. Formerly aided.*

**3 November Wall** . . . . . . 🔁 🔩 ☐ **E2 5b**
Start at a flake, or start as for *Cooper's Peg Route* and move right. Climb the boldish wall (wires behind some dubious flakes) to the trees. Abseil off.
*FA. J.Holt, I.Barber, K.Yates 1977*

*Next is an attractive slab and a neat left arete.*

**4 The Arete** . . . . . . . . . . 🔁 🖼 ☐ **E1 5a**
The best route in the quarry, following the fine arete. Make tricky starting moves past some unconvincing wires/micro-cams to gain the break. Finish more easily up the arete and belay on a tree. Harder for the short.
*FA. G.R.Fiddles, A.T.Braddock 1959*

**5 Mitre Crack** . . . . . . . . . . . 🔁 ☐ **VS 4c**
The zigzag cracks give a good little route. Sometimes has bats.
*FA. G.R.Fiddles, A.T.Braddock 1959*

**6 Chance in a Marillion** . . . . . 🖼 ☐ **E3 6a**
A bold and technical eliminate up the slab between the cracks. Hard moves near the top and less escapable than it looks from below.
*FA. Duncan Lee, Gary Thornhill 1986*

**7 The Cardinal** . . . . . . . . . . 🔁 ☐ **VS 4c**
The rightward-slanting crack into the corner. The corner itself provides a trickier-than-expected finish.
*FA. G.R.Fiddles, A.T.Braddock 1959*

**8 The Actress/The Bishop** 🔁 🖼 ☐ **HVS 5b**
A combination of two old routes which used the huge block (which now lies under the wall). This new line follows the corner all the way to the top, fingery and slippery crux at the start and joining *The Cardinal* to finish. *Photo opposite.*
*FA. (Actress) Richard Davies 1985. The Bishop used the block to gain the right-hand arete which it followed to the top. The Actress was a direct start to The Cardinal which tackled the block as well.*

**9 Sycamore Crack** . . . . . . . . . . . ☐ **HS 4b**
The tree-choked fissure up the slab to the right has been spruced up recently. An ascent requires as much tree climbing ability as rock climbing skills. Reaching the first tree is the crux.

**10 Carmen Jones** . . . . . . . . . **VS 4c**
The left arete of the narrow slab up and right has been given a wash and brush-up. Worth doing.
*FA. G.R.Fiddles, A.T.Braddock 1959*

**11 Carmen** . . . . . . . . . . . . . **VS 4c**
A nice pitch up the clean slab. Follow the left-hand crack to reach another crack trending right (polished) which leads to a tree. Continue easily to the top, or abseil off.
*FA. G.R.Fiddles, A.T.Braddock 1959*

*More ex-routes exist to the right but beyond this, and opposite the entrance gate, things improve dramatically.*

Graham and Dan Parkes enjoying the fine upper section of *The Actress/The Bishop* (HVS 5b) - *opposite* - at Aldery Cliff, having tackled the slippery crux start.
Photo: Chris Craggs

The mossy left-hand edge of the slab and the grassy groove round to the left are the substance of **Ash Tree Arete, HVD.**

**⓬ Anti-Digestant** . . . . . . . . . . . . ☐ **HVS 5a**
Climb the slab, just left of a short left-facing corner, passing a tricky section. Follow a crack to a ledge and continue to a tree belay. Abseil off.
FA. Gary Gibson, Derek Beetlestone 1979

**⓭ Ash Tree Slab** . . . . . . . . . ☼ ☐ **HS 4a**
Climb the left-facing corner to a ledge on the right, it can also be started direct, **The Nonsense Man Start, 5a** . Follow the cracks above to another ledge and then climb a steep corner to the top.
FA. G.R.Fiddles, A.T.Braddock 1959

**⓮ Nettlerash** . . . . . . . . . . . . . ☼ ☐ **HS 4a**
The central crack of the slab gives an interesting pitch, with plenty of protection, and polish. At the tree stump, finish left into the corner and up to a solid tree. A popular alternative finish can be made up the left-hand side of the detached flake, joining Broken Toe or finish direct at 4b.
FA. G.R.Fiddles, A.T.Braddock 1959

**⓯ Broken Toe** . . . . . . . . ☼ ☐ **HVS 4c**
The blank line on the right-hand side of the slab. Climb past thin cracks (which don't take wires) and make a series of mantel-type moves to the first runner at about 10m. The rest is steady, but take care on the big detached flake. Belay on the big tree. A side-runner in Nettlerash is possible, dropping the grade to VS.

**⓰ Central Arete** . . . . . . . . . . . . . ☐ **HVD**
The blocky arete leads to a ledge. Step left and use the trees to reach a belay ledge, or go direct at 4b. A top section can be done up the pillar and flake-crack right of a tree at scruffy 4b.
FA. G.R.Fiddles, A.T.Braddock 1959

**⓱ Janbaloo** . . . . . . . . . . ☼ ☐ **HVS 5b**
Straightforward slab-climbing, but light on gear. Start on the left-hand side of the slab, and climb to a break. Step up, then place a runner in Surface Plate (or ignore this at E1) and make thin moves up to a good slanting crack. Step left to climb the slab and arete to a good ledge. Belay on the tree, then either finish up the arete on the right, or abseil off. The obvious direct finish is a bold-feeling E1 5b.
FA. P.Barber, R.Shaw 1978

### ⑱ Surface Plate .......... 🔆 ☐ HVS 5a
One of the more popular routes in the quarry, giving some testing slab moves. Overall however, it is low in the grade. Climb the thin crack direct to the wider crack on *Janabaloo*. Climb this crack to a ledge and tree. Finish as for *Janabaloo* or abseil off.
*FA. G.R.Fiddles, A.T.Braddock (aid) 1959*

### ⑲ Clothesline ........ 🔆 ☐☐ S 4a
Climb the diagonal crack into the corner. Follow another crack here to the ledge. Awkward belays on wires behind, or drop down to the tree. Finish up the flake-crack in the right wall above. *Photo on page 24.*

### ⑳ The Fly ................ ☐ HVS 5a
Start up *Clothesline,* but move right onto the wall. Climb this into a corner and find a tree to belay on. Abseil off.
*FA. J.Holt, I.Barber, K.Yates 1977*

### ㉑ The Spider ........... 🗺 ☐ VS 4c
Climb the groove to the right of the main slab towards a tree. Step left before you reach it, onto an arete, and climb this to the tree to belay - quite bold. Abseil off.

### ㉒ Burst ............... 🗺 ☐ HVS 4c
Scramble up to a ledge below a groove. Climb this, and the crack above to the tree on *The Spider.* Abseil off.
*FA. Gary Gibson 1979*

### ㉓ The Bender ........... 🔆 ☐ HVS 5a
Climb the scoop to the left of the arete to the big ledge - optional belay on the left here. Climb the slab above to a crack and left-facing corner. At its top, move back right round the arete to a crack which leads into the trees. Abseil off.

### ㉔ Terrace Wall ....... 🏔 🗺 ☐ VS 4b
Climb the arete which is awkward at the top. Possible belay on the ledge. Move up into a groove and step right into a slabby corner. Follow this to the top. There is a slightly harder direct variation which tackles the left edge of the overhang.

### ㉕ A Question of Palance ....... ☐ VS 4b
The shallow groove just to the right of the lower arete and a continuation between the two finishes of the previous climb.
*FA. Gary Gibson 1979*

### ㉖ Right Arete ........... 🏔 ☐ VS 4b
Amble up the blunt right-hand arete to the terrace, then more of the same and an awkward mantle to reach the groove above and a tree belay.

*There are a few more routes to the right, these are not described here and this section of rock is unstable.*

| | No star | ⟨1⟩ | ⟨2⟩ | ⟨3⟩ |
|---|---|---|---|---|
| up to 4+ | - | - | - | - |
| 5+ to 6a+ | 3 | - | - | - |
| 6b to 7a | 7 | 4 | - | - |
| 7a+ and up | 4 | 2 | 2 | - |

Taddington, or Crag 'X' as it is often known, is a compact crag situated above the A6. There is nothing of any great quality here, but the routes are well-bolted and there are a few interesting lines, especially for those leading in the 7a/b range. Most of the routes follow a similar pattern - relatively easy starts, sometimes on slightly loose rock, leading to a rest, then an intense hard section follows, on small crimpy holds, where the crux is often locating the best ones to use. Higher up, some of the routes ease off and others keep going all the way to the belays.

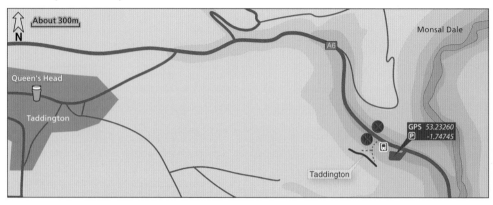

## Approach   Also see map on page 264

Taddington crag is situated just off the A6, between Buxton and Bakewell. The best approach is from Deep Dale car park, which is just off the A6 opposite the base of Monsal Dale. From the car park, head up the road, past a bus stop, to a point where there are two clearway signs on opposite sides of the road. From these signs, a path leads steeply up through the trees to the crag.

## Conditions

In winter the crag is visible from the main road, but it seeps badly, and is rarely in condition. When the place dries out in the summer, the dense tree-cover hides the crag, although it is still within earshot of the busy road. It gets virtually no sun, making it a good hot-weather retreat. It is also very sheltered, and some of the routes will stay dry in quite heavy rain.

Rachel Slater on *Red X* (6c) - *opposite* - at Taddington. Photo: Craig Bailey

The first routes start from a raised platform on the left-hand side of the crag, by a vast cave.

**❶ Bag of X** . . . . . . . . . . . . . 🏃 [ ] **6c+**
An odd line traversing above the cave. The crux is the first bulge.
*FA. Gary Gibson 1995*

**❷ Xactly** . . . . . . . . . . . . . . 💪 [ ] **6b**
Up the wall then trend left up steeper rock.
*FA. Gary Gibson 2010*

**❸ X Box** . . . . . . . . . . . . . 💪 🎖 [ ] **6b**
Step out right from the last route then head up the wall.
*FA. Gary Gibson 2010*

**❹ X Marks the Spot** . . . . . . . . . . [ ] **6a+**
The easiest route on the crag has been extended downwards!
*FA. Nadim Siddiqui 1994*

**❺ Ham and X** . . . . . . . . . . . . 💪 [ ] **6b**
*FA. Gary Gibson 2010*

**❻ Xtermination** . . . . . . . . . . 🏃 [ ] **6a+**
*FA. Gary Gibson 2010*

**❼ Xageration** . . . . . . . . . . . 🏃 [ ] **6b**
*FA. Gary Gibson 2010*

**❽ In the X Team** . . . . . . . . . 🏃 [ ] **6b**
*FA. Gary Gibson 2010*

**❾ eXit Stage Left.** . . . . . . . . . . . . [ ] **6a**
Start up a short groove, then climb the wall above.
*Photo on page 264.*
*FA. Nadim Siddiqui 1994*

**❿ The X Files** . . . . . . . . 💡 🏃 [ ] **6b**
Make a hard start left past the first bolt.
*FA. Nadim Siddiqui 1994*

**⓫ Xtra Time** . . . . . . . . . . . . . 🖐 [ ] **6b+**
Just independent of *Red X* but shares the last move or two.
*FA. Nadim Siddiqui 1994*

**⓬ Red X.** . . . . . . . . . . . . . . . 💡 [ ] **6c**
Start from the right end of the platform and climb the slight rib.
*Photo opposite.*
*FA. Nadim Siddiqui 1994*

The rest of the routes start from just above the approach path.

**⓭ Great eXpectations.** . . . . . . 💡 [ ] **6c**
A broken start, but good rock above. Hard moves past the first bulge and a hard finish from the scoop.
*FA. Nadim Siddiqui, Jim Burton 1994*

**⓮ Certificate X** . . . . . . . . 💡 🎖 [ ] **7b**
An excellent route past the large mid-height hole on the crag. The finish is harder now some holds have gone AWOL.
*FA. Nadim Siddiqui, Jim Burton 1994*

**⓯ Malcolm X** . . . . . . . . . 💡 🎖 [ ] **7a+**
An entertaining right-hand finish to *Certificate X*.
*FA. Nadim Siddiqui 1994*

**⓰ Top MarX** . . . . . . . . . . 💡 🕯 [ ] **7a**
A direct line, which is easier than it looks. A long reach helps.
*FA. Gary Gibson 1995*

**⓱ XXXX** . . . . . . . . . . 💡 🏃 🎖 [ ] **7b**
A quality climb with intricate moves through the bulge, and sustained climbing above. Difficult to flash.
*FA. Nadim Siddiqui 1994*

**⓲ Little Blue Lies** . 💡 🕯 🎖 🏃 [ ] **7b+**
A fingery wall-climb which is harder for shorties.
*FA. Gary Gibson 1995*

**⓳ Y Should I?** . . . . . . . . . . . 💪 [ ] **7b+**
Powerful and blind moves through the roof lead to a tricky finish.
*FA. Gary Gibson 1995*

**⓴ Xcursion** . . . . . . . . 💪 🏃 🎖 [ ] **7c+**
The hardest on the crag with fierce moves through the bulges.
*FA. Gary Gibson 1995*

**㉑ XTC** . . . . . . . . . . . . . 🏃 💪 [ ] **7a+**
A short hard section through the roof.
*FA. Gary Gibson 1995*

**㉒ X Partridge** . . . . . . . . . . . 💪 [ ] **7a+**
..and the final line over the small roof.
*FA. Gary Gibson 1995*

Not much sun | 5 min | Dry in the rain | Seepage | Sheltered

| | No star | 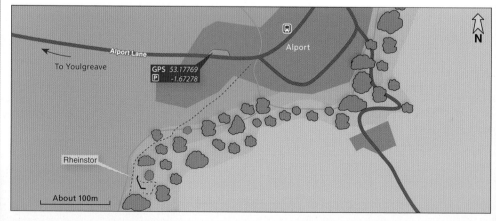 1 star | 2 star | 3 star |
|---|---|---|---|---|
| **Mod to S** | 1 | - | - | - |
| **HS to HVS** | 2 | 4 | 1 | - |
| **E1 to E3** | - | 6 | - | - |
| **E4 and up** | - | 1 | - | - |

A lovely little cliff in a sylvan and sunny setting by the River Bradford, just south of Alport. The crag gets plenty of sun, and is only a couple of minutes from the car, making it a great spot for a quick evening session. The climbing offers a contrast to the welcoming and friendly setting, being quite fierce and technical on sharp pockets, although the routes which follow cracks tend to be more amenable. There is also plenty here to interest boulderers especially on the compact lower wall. A few problems have been marked but the potential is vast with many eliminates and variations possible.

The polish on the lower holds is testament to its popularity many years ago although of late it has seen little traffic. If you do pop by then bring a rope and gear and tick *Le Crepsule* for starters and you won't be disappointed.

## Approach   Also see map on page 264

Rheinstor is situated to the south of Bakewell and Haddon Hall off the B5056 which in turn is off the A6. Head towards Youlgreave and Alport on a minor road. There is parking available on either side of the road, just to the west of Alport where it starts to rise up towards Youlgreave. On the south side of the road, a good track leads down towards the river through a couple of gates, and on to the crag, which is located just around the bend - an easy five minutes from the car.

## Conditions

Rheinstor faces southwest, gets the afternoon and evening sun, dries quickly after rain, and is generally sheltered from the wind.

## Access

There used to be a plaque bolted to the rock which stated that climbers operated here at their own risk. The plaque has gone, though it's doubtless this still applies. The very public nature of the place means that it is a bit of a showcase for climbers, so please keep the noise level down and refrain from any other anti-social behaviour that might offend reserved ramblers. Please don't lower-off or abseil from the trees that grow on the cliff top, use the walking descent down to the right (looking in) of the crag.

Dan Parkes with his sights firmly set on
the first bit of gear on *Mjolinir* (E1 5c)
- *next page*. The shot shows the decent
pocketed rock here. Photo: Chris Craggs

## Rheinstor

A small selection of routes on a lovely little buttress of excellent, pocketed rock in a sunny riverside setting.
**Descent -** Scramble to the top of the buttress, then descent steeply to the right (looking in) through the trees to a stile in the fence. **Please do not abseil from the crag-top trees.**

**1 Wotan** . . . . . . . . . . . . . . **VDiff**
Climb the chimney and the continuation groove.
FA. Trevor Morris, Anne Morris 1964

**2 Fenris.** . . . . . . . . . . . . . . **VS 4b**
From the chimney, trend rightwards up the wall via ledges to enter and climb a short groove. Dirty (and a bit loose) at the moment. A direct start up the flaky wall below the ledge might have a move of 5a.
FA. Trevor Morris, Dave Thorpe 1965

**3 Le Crepuscule** . . . . **VS 5b**
The shallow groove has a fierce polished start, though protection is perfect. The rest of the route is pleasant ambling, though there is a bit of loose rock towards the top.
FA. Trevor Morris, Dave Thorpe late 1960s

**4 Wizard of Aus** . . . . **E4 6a**
Climb the wall just right of where the sign used to be, with a stretch for the break. Continue to cross Le Crepuscule to a finish up the rib on the left.
FA. Gary Gibson 1979

**5 Meridian.** . . . . . . . . **E3 6b**
Climb up the blunt rib to a crux stretch of the break then step right and continue via the upper rib and groove.
FA. Gary Gibson 1979

**6 Ron's Route** . . . . . **E3 6a**
The face and shallow groove just to the right, again the lower wall is the crux.
FA. Ron Fawcett 1981

The next routes are all steep and worthwhile. The finishes are rather interchangeable though the crack on the right is best.

**7 Mjolinir** . . . . . . . . **E1 5c**
From right of the ground-level pocket, climb up then trend slightly right via a bee-hive niche to the break. Climb the rib to an easy prickly groove or better, move right up the steep groove/crack joining and finishing as for Valhalla.
Photo on previous page.
FA. Andy Parkin, Mike Browell 1976

**8 Valhalla** . . . . . . . . . . **HVS 5b**
Head up the wall to the right to enter a groove-system then follow the upper cracks to a steep finish and tricky exit.
*FA. Trevor Jones, A.Dunlop, C.Astill, Steve Read 1974*

**9 Asgard** . . . . . . . . . . . **HVS 5b**
Two metres left of the fence, climb the wall then move right to a ramp. Up this to the big hole and finish up *Valhalla*.
*FA. Trevor Morris, Dave Thorpe late 1960s*

*The last two routes are by the bounding fence. On both of these the ivy is starting to invade.*

**10 Loki** . . . . . . . . . . **HVS 5a**
The cracks above the fence leads steeply (keep right on the rib) to a good ledge. The finish is steep and has a big wobbly flake.
*FA. Trevor Morris, Dave Thorpe late 1960s*

**11 Baldur** . . . . . . . . **HVS 5a**
Beyond the fence lurks this jamming crack, which is steep and butch towards the top. The ivy is currently in charge here.
*FA. Trevor Morris, Dave Thorpe late 1960s*

*There are several girdles on offer here that may be worth a look if you have done all the proper routes, and are still infatuated with the place, or if you just want a good workout.*

**12 Traverse of the Gods** . . . . . . . **HVS 5a**
The high girdle starts up *Fenris*. Climb past the perched flake (possible stance) on *Meridian* to reach the hole on *Asgard*. Continue right and up then move right to the top of *Baldur*.
*FA. T.Morris, D.Thorpe 1960s*

**13 Spirit Chaser** . . . . . . . **E2 5c**
The lower break from right to left, a good pumpy solo for the confident at about V2. Start from *Baldur* and finish when it fizzles out around *Crepuscule*.
*FA. John Codling 1979*

**14 Upper Boulder Traverse** **V5**

**15 Lower Boulder Traverse** **V6**

Afternoon | 2 min | Sheltered

# Dovedale Area
## Wolfscote Dale, Manifold Valley
## Beeston Tor, Dovedale

North
Southwest
Southeast
Wolfscote Dale
Manifold Valley
Beeston Tor
Dovedale

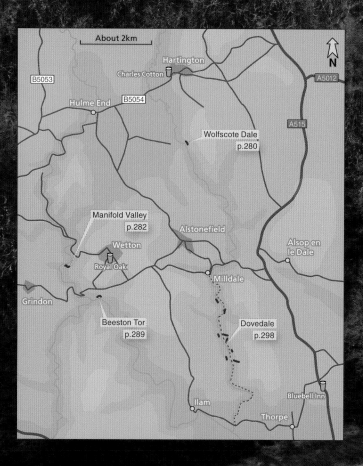

About 2km

N

Hartington

Charles Cotton

B5053

A5012

Hulme End

B5054

A515

Wolfscote Dale
p.280

Manifold Valley
p.282

Alstonefield

Wetton

Alsop en
le Dale

Royal Oak

Milldale

Grindon

Beeston Tor
p.289

Dovedale
p.298

Ilam

Bluebell Inn

Thorpe

Charles Capel follow the long traverse on the
Dovedale classic of *John Peel* (HVS 5a) - *page 316* -
on Tissington Spires. Photo: David Bond
The fine rock architecture of Dovedale was acknowl-
edged by the National Park when they felled many of
the trees in the dale to expose the pinnacles and faces
for all to see. As is the way with trees, they have
started to grow back but most of the crags still have
excellent views down to the valley below.

North

Southwest

Southeast

Wolfscote Dale

Manifold Valley

Beeston Tor

Dovedale

| | No star | ☼ | ☼☼ | ☼☼☼ |
|---|---|---|---|---|
| Mod to S | 1 | - | - | - |
| HS to HVS | 3 | 2 | - | - |
| E1 to E3 | 3 | 2 | 1 | - |
| E4 and up | - | 3 | - | - |

Tucked away in an idyllic setting in Wolfscote Dale in the southern Peak are a couple of rocky towers. The Right Celestial Twin is a scruffy overgrown mess, but the Left Celestial Twin is well worth a visit if you want somewhere out of the ordinary - chances are you will have the place to yourself, apart from the occasional walker taking a look at the cave at the crag base. The routes don't see much traffic, but the rock is quite solid.

Wolfscote Dale is owned by the National Trust, who are willing to allow access to the crag. Please avoid disturbance of the vegetation and bird life, particularly at nesting time.

## Approach   Also see map on page 278

There is parking for about a dozen cars at the lower end of the minor road (signed Beresford Dale) that runs south from Mill Lane - the road between Hartington and Warslow. This is 2km west of Hartington. Keep left at both junctions and stop before the ford. Cross the footbridge and follow the path across the meadow to the cliff.

## Conditions

The main cliff is sheltered, low lying and southwest facing. It catches the afternoon sun and is often in condition. However, it sees little traffic and some of the routes have become a bit overgrown over the years.

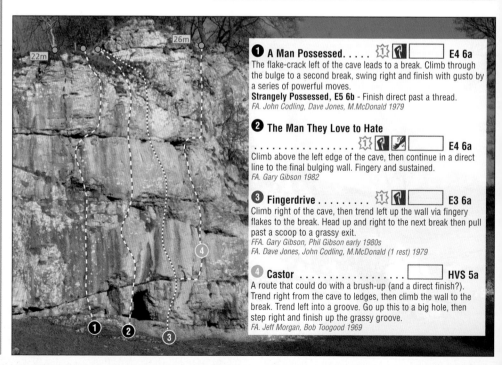

**❶ A Man Possessed.** . . . . ☼ 🔒 ☐ **E4 6a**
The flake-crack left of the cave leads to a break. Climb through the bulge to a second break, swing right and finish with gusto by a series of powerful moves.
**Strangely Possessed, E5 6b** - Finish direct past a thread.
*FA. John Codling, Dave Jones, M.McDonald 1979*

**❷ The Man They Love to Hate**
. . . . . . . . . . . . . . . ☼ 🔒 ✍ ☐ **E4 6a**
Climb above the left edge of the cave, then continue in a direct line to the final bulging wall. Fingery and sustained.
*FA. Gary Gibson 1982*

**❸ Fingerdrive** . . . . . . . . ☼ 🔒 ☐ **E3 6a**
Climb right of the cave, then trend left up the wall via fingery flakes to the break. Head up and right to the next break then pull past a scoop to a grassy exit.
*FFA. Gary Gibson, Phil Gibson early 1980s*
*FA. Dave Jones, John Codling, M.McDonald (1 rest) 1979*

**❹ Castor** . . . . . . . . . . . . . . . . . ☐ **HVS 5a**
A route that could do with a brush-up (and a direct finish?). Trend right from the cave to ledges, then climb the wall to the break. Trend left into a groove. Go up this to a big hole, then step right and finish up the grassy groove.
*FA. Jeff Morgan, Bob Toogood 1969*

The remainder of the routes are located up and right, above a grassy terrace that rises from right to left. This is reached by a short scramble.

**5 Arrundale's Crack** . . . . . . . . . □ **S 4a**
The right-hand groove near the end of the terrace. The groove further left is **Definitely Devilish, VS 4c.**
FA. J.Arrundale 1961

**6 Raquel Welch** . . . . . . . . . [icon] □ **HVS 4c**
The wall and bulges just right of the corner.

**7 Applause** . . . . . . . . . . . . [icon] □ **HVS 5a**
Trend rightwards up the wall to enter the flaky groove. Up this to the top with the expected grassy exit.
FA. Graham West 1961

**8 Bright Eyes** . . . . . . . . . . . . . . □ **E2 5c**
Swing left out of the leaning groove, then climb the wall.
FA. John Codling, R.Cope 1979

**9 Fever Dream** . . . . . . . [icons] □ **E3 5c**
Climb the leaning groove (often wet) out to the arete, swap sides, then balance up it in a dramatic position.
FA. John Codling, Jerry Codling 1979

**10 Roberts Roberts** . . . . . . . . . . □ **HS 4a**
The right-angled groove throughout.
FA. B.Roberts, M.Roberts 1961

**11 Thread, Butter and Wheeze** . [icon] □ **E2 5c**
The centre of the wall, right of the groove, on (mostly) good holds. A couple of old threads may be in place.
FA. Alan Williams, Gary Gibson 1983

**12 Strawberry Window** . . . . . . [icon] □ **E2 5b**
The left edge of the cave, then the shallow groove above.
FA. John Codling 1979

**13 Going Tornado** . . . . [icons] □ **E5 6b**
The right wall of the cave is climbed leftwards - tough.
FA. Ron Fawcett 1981

**14 Paraffle** . . . . . . . . . . . . . . . . □ **HVS 5b**
The tricky, curving groove to a hard and scruffy exit.
FA. Bob Dearman, Mick Horlov 1978

**15 Plink, Plink Fizz** . . . . . . . . [icon] □ **E1 5c**
The short white wall on the far right.
FA. Clive Allen, Rob Wright 1986

Routes 1 to 4

| | No star | ☆ | ☆☆ | ☆☆☆ |
|---|---|---|---|---|
| **Mod to S** | - | - | - | - |
| **HS to HVS** | - | 1 | - | 1 |
| **E1 to E3** | - | 2 | - | 2 |
| **E4 / 7a+ and up** | - | 3 | 4 | 4 |

The imposing orifice of Thor's Cave overlooks the upper Manifold Valley and is a very popular stop-off for walkers making it a crag which almost always feels busy although you will rarely find too many climbers there. Until recently the cave was mostly the domain of aid climbers with the odd free route plus a fine west-facing wall overlooking a steep gully that drops down to the valley bottom - *Tower Direct* and *West Window Groove* are the two main ticks here, but the other routes are worth looking at if you have the time. In the last few years the insides of the cave have been developed with a series of routes that can be best described as a climber's playground and a guidebook-topo-maker's nightmare. The complex internal architecture and upside down route lines makes for a confusing picture, however the climbing is of a spectacular nature for all those up to the grades.

Also covered in this chapter are the outlying crags of Ossam's Crag, with its mid-grade route, and The Chimney, with its pair of contrasting offerings.

## Approach    Also see map on page 278

Thor's Cave is situated in the Manifold Valley, to the north of Beeston Tor. It can be approached either from Wetton Village, or from the valley below, starting from the parking used for Beeston Tor. From the parking in Wetton village, follow the road west until you have just left the village. Take the track on the left, Thor's Cave can now be seen ahead of you. From the end of the track, follow the path across the fields to the crag.

For the lower approach, take the road leading towards Grindon down into the valley. Park on the right, just over the bridge, and walk up the valley until you are below the cave. A well-marked path leads steeply up from here.

The other two small buttresses are best approached from limited parking at the north end of the valley by the junction of the cycle track and a minor road.

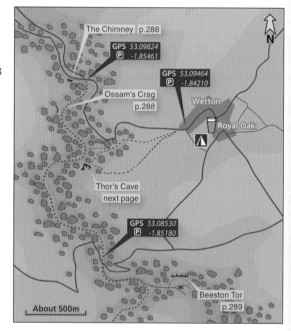

The Chimney p.288
GPS 53.09824 P -1.85461
GPS 53.09464 P -1.84210
Ossam's Crag p.288
Wetton
Royal Oak
Thor's Cave next page
GPS 53.08530 P -1.85180
Beeston Tor p.289
About 500m
N

## Conditions

The main cave faces north, and gets little sun, although the West Window is well-placed for the late afternoon sun. The cave seeps badly during the winter, and is slow to dry. Once dry, the internal cave routes can be climbed in virtually any weather and the place makes a good retreat when it gets hot.

## Access

The Manifold Valley is owned by the Chatsworth Estate who are willing to allow access to the crag. Please avoid unnecessary disturbance of the vegetation and please remember that you are on public display most of the time here so be on your best behaviour.

North · Southwest · Southeast · Wolfscote Dale · Manifold Valley · Beeston Tor · Dovedale

Ed Hammer aiming for the lip of the cave on *Thormen's Moth* (8a) - *next page* - in Thor's Cave. Photo: Denise Hammer
Although usually wet the routes on this most-public of caves are quite popular when they do dry out. Amazingly though you can also climb in almost perfect isolation just metres away if you venture through the cave to the West Window area, even on a Bank Holiday weekend.

North

Southwest

Southeast

Wolfscote Dale

Manifold Valley

Beeston Tor

Dovedale

North
Southwest
Southeast
Wolfscote Dale
Manifold Valley
Beeston Tor
Dovedale

## Thor's Cave - Inside

The main cave has a set of harder routes. There are a couple of trad routes on the left-entrance wall, but of most interest are the sport routes inside the depths of the cave. These follow complex lines and end in the middle of nowhere but offer great climbing. There are also a number of other aid routes (not described) which confuse the lines in the cave.

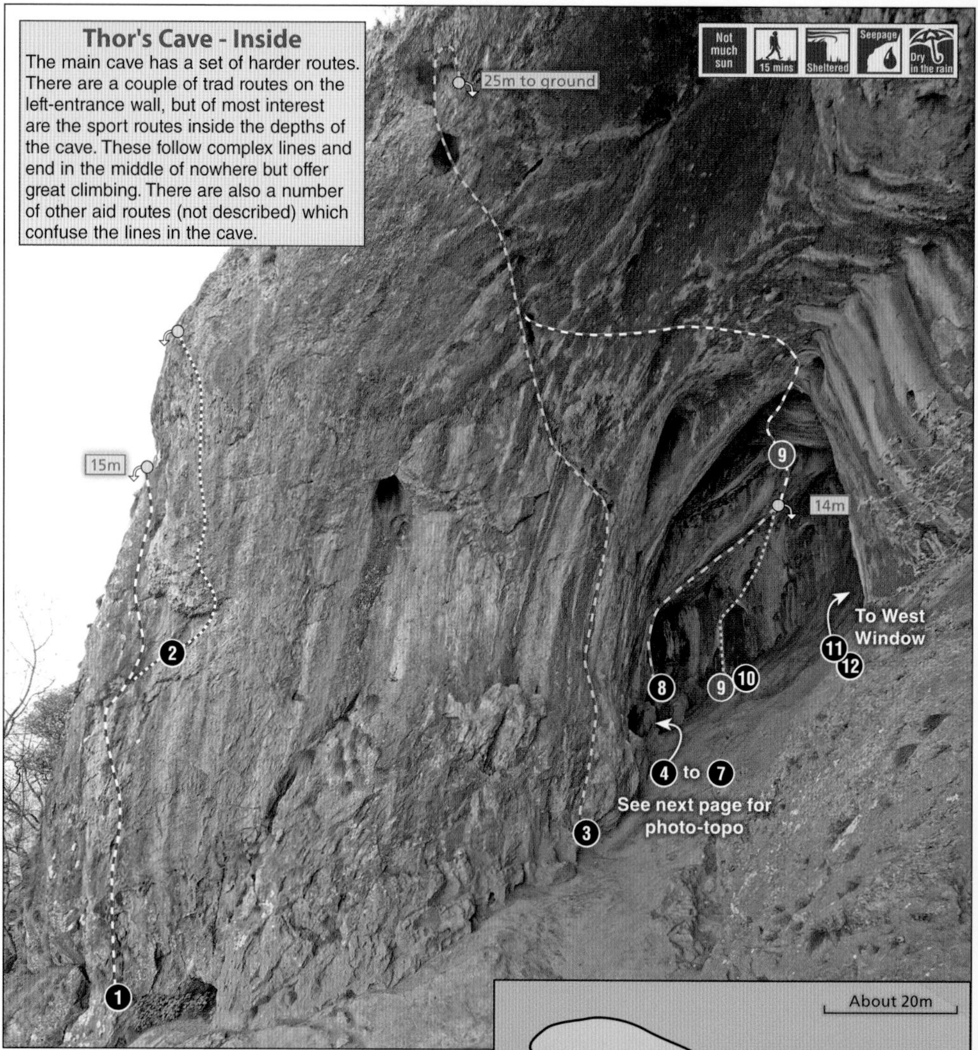

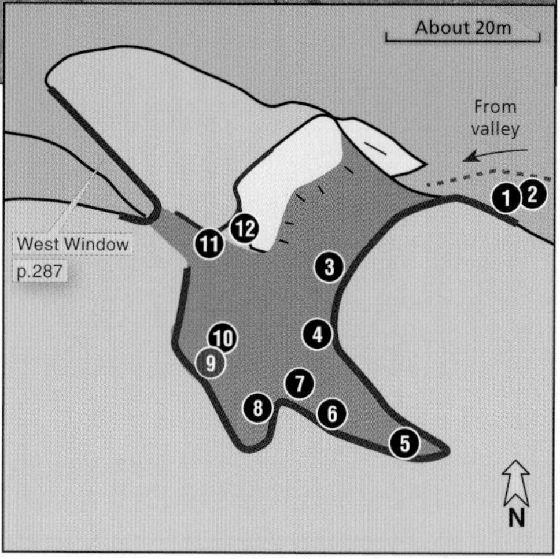

Not much sun | 15 mins | Sheltered | Seepage | Dry in the rain

25m to ground

15m

14m

**To West Window**

② ⑨ ⑩ ⑧ ⑪ ⑫

④ to ⑦

**See next page for photo-topo**

③

**① Doctor Blake** . . . . . . . . 🎖 💔 ☐ **E5 6a**
From the left edge of the cave, climb the bold wall into a groove to a tree and an escape. Rarely repeated.
*FA. Dominic Lee, Daniel Lee 1982*

**② Blake's 7** . . . . . . . . . 🎖 💔 ☐ **E6 6b**
Break right out of *Doctor Blake* and attack the bulges (old peg) to a lower-off. Another route that hardly ever gets done.
*FA. Andy Taylor 1992*

*The next climb is on the inner left-hand sidewall of the cave.*

**③ Thormen's Moth** ᵀᵒᵖ 50 🪝🧗‍♂️🪝 ☐ **8a**
A free ascent of the aid route *Thor*, gives a low 8a, sadly it is almost always wet. Climb the sidewall then link the pockets across the roof to reach the jug just *above* the big fat chain.
*Photo on previous page.*
*FFA. Andy Pollitt 1988. FA. Bob Dearman, A Cornish, Jeff Morgan 1969*

About 20m

From valley

West Window
p.287

⑪ ⑫ ① ②
③
⑩ ④
⑨ ⑦
⑧ ⑥
⑤

N

*The rest of the routes are even further back in the gloom. Three of the climbs use very different approaches to reach a lower-off hidden high in the roof in a recess know as The Belfry.*

**4 Spear of Odin** . . . . ⛰️🥾🪜⬜ 7c+
Technical climbing up a string of odd features. Climb the striped wall opposite the pillar 7m right of *Thormen's Moth*, trending right to the apex of the arch then continuing up into The Belfry to locate the well-hidden lower-off.
*FA. Jon Fullwood 2006*

**5 Buried Alive** . . . 🧗🪜🪜⬜ 7c+
1) 6b+, 2) 6c+, 3) 7c+, 4) 7b+, 5) 6a, 6) HVS 5a, 80m.
An astounding expedition through the dark lands, linking the deepest recess of the cave with the West Window. Start at the back of the west passage and forge a way to daylight at the West Window. Head torch essential. Stick-clip the 1st bolt - or climb to it at E3 - then get exploring.
*FA. Jon Fullwood 2006/7*

**6 Escape to Valhalla** . . . . 🧗🪜⬜ 8a
More amazing climbing. The long side of the grey pillar opposite *Spear of Odin* leads to the same lower-off. Step in from the right and follow pockets (hidden 1st bolt - the easy runout can be protected with a large cam). Trend right at the 2nd bolt by wild moves into and out of a hueco. From an awkward rest blast straight up and out to a hands-off rest in The Belfry.
*Photo on next page.*
*FA. Jon Fullwood 2006*

**7 Ragnarok** . . . . . . . 🧗🪜🪜⬜ 8a
Start up *Escape to Valhalla* but head right and follow the lower of the two fault lines in the roof to its termination above the West Window. Wild and unusual, not to mention thrutchy.
*FA. Jon Fullwood 2006*

**8 Midgard Serpent** . . 🧗🪜🪜⬜ 7b+
In the middle of the chamber is a broad grey pillar. Follow the old aid bolts up the right side of this then break out up the 60 degree leaning trench. Finish at the chain - easy 7b+. Originally it finished by climbing to holds above the chain - at hard 7b+.
*FA. Jon Fullwood 2006*

**9 Kyrie Eleison** . . . . . . . . . . 🧗⬜ A1
60m. The longest roof climb in the Peak and a fun introduction to aid climbing as it is fully bolted. From the back right corner of the cave, climb into a niche then follow the fixed gear across the undulating roof, even downhill in places until *Thormen's* is joined. Lower off at the lip. Great wet weather sport. Be aware that if you let your belay ropes dangle to the floor of the cave, people will walk all over them.
*FA. Bob Dearman, K.Bridges, Bob Toogood 1972. The first ascent was spread over three days, though with all the gear in place the route can be done in a couple of hours. FFA. Dream on!*

To Belfry lower-off
West Window
Approach to West Window
West Window p.287
Thor's Cave
From Wetton
From valley

**10 Fenris** . . . . . . . . . 🧗🪜🪜⬜ 7b+
The line of pods and huecos on the back wall of the cave (as for *Kyrie Eleison*) right of the grey pillar. Steady climbing up the pods to a tough crux, finish at the belay of *Midgard Serpent*.
*FA. Jon Fullwood 2006*

**11 Loki the Trickster** . . . . . 🧗🪜⬜ 7c
The arete and wall right of the West Window, as seen looking out towards the West Window. Pockets and a hanging flake lead to a hard move left into the groove/flake. Finish at the break by the roof.
*FA. Jon Fullwood 2006*

**12 Móoguo** . . . . . . . . 🧗🪜🪜⬜ 8b
Starting right of *Loki the Trickster*. Climb an easy wall to a pod below a prominent line of weakness leading back towards the apex of the cave. A hard boulder problem gains the weakness which is followed to a good knee-bar rest before the final bouldery crux to gain The Belfry belay.
*FA. Dan Varian 2009*

North
Southwest
Southeast
Wolfscote Dale
Manifold Valley
Beeston Tor
Dovedale

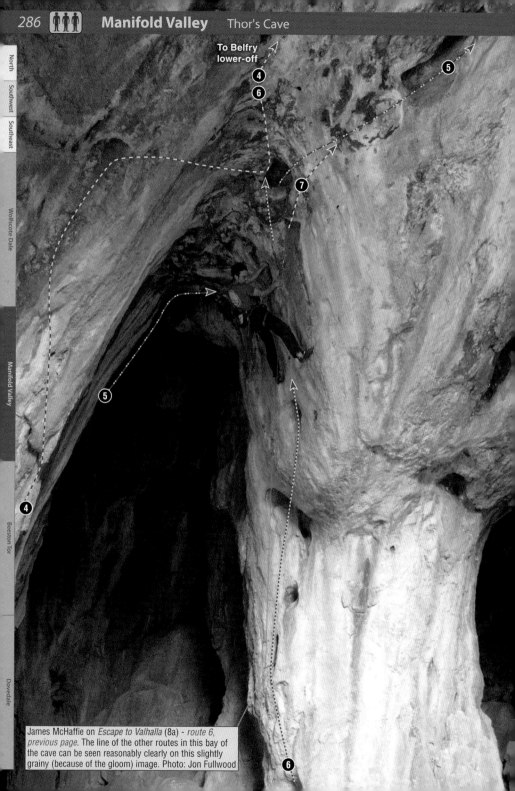

North

Southwest

Southeast

Wolfscote Dale

Manifold Valley

Beeston Tor

Dovedale

To Belfry
lower-off

④

⑥

⑤

⑦

⑤

④

⑤

⑥

James McHaffie on *Escape to Valhalla* (8a) - *route 6, previous page*. The line of the other routes in this bay of the cave can be seen reasonably clearly on this slightly grainy (because of the gloom) image. Photo: Jon Fullwood

North

Southwest

Southeast

Wolfscote Dale

Manifold Valley

Beeston Tor

Dovedale

**13 Slanting Crack. . . . . VS 4c**
Scramble out to a stance at the foot of the chimney in the left-hand side of the face. Follow this (wide and awkward) until it develops into a long crack. Continue up this steeply to a grassy bay (possible stance) and a final short groove. It can also be started from further down the gully with a grassy first pitch, though this sees even less action than the normal approach.
*FA. Roy Leeming (VS and A2) 1950s*

**14 Deep Freeze . . . . . . . . . . E2 5c**
From the stance on *Slanting Crack*, move back right then climb the fingery rib (threads) to enter a shallow groove. Up this to rejoin *Slanting Crack* on easy ground.
*FA. Gary Gibson, Mark Elwell, Phil Gibson 1983*

**15 Tower Direct . . . . . . . . E3 5c**
A great route up the centre of the white wall. From a stance in the base of the window, climb leftwards into a thin crack. Up this until it fizzles out then step left into a second crack. This gradually eases to ledges and an exit corner.
*FFA. Tom Proctor, Chris Jackson 1971. FA. Roy Leeming early 1950s*

**16 Twilight of the Tired Gods . . E3 5c**
The hanging flake to the left of the window gives a butch pitch.
**1) 5c, 16m.** Traverse out as for *Tower Direct* but follow the undercut flake to a small stance on *West Window Groove*.
**2) 5b, 20m.** Step back left to the flake and follow it to its end. Move left over grass and exit via an easy groove.
*FA. Roy Leeming 1950s. FA. Jerry Frost, John Codling, Mike Browell 1979*

**17 West Window Groove . . HVS 5a**
The other great classic of the cliff is easier for the supple and/ or long legged.
**1) 5a, 16m.** Climb cracks that split the left-hand face (looking out) and move right to a small stance.
**2) 5a, 20m.** Climb up until it is possible to straddle the groove (exposed) then continue to a niche on the left - possible stance. Finish up the chimney and right-trending grassy ramp above.
*FA. Joe Brown, Ron Moseley early 1950s*

### West Window
The rest of the climbs are located around the impressive vertical gash of the West Window which is the tall slit that lets light into the back of the main cave.
**Approach -** The only easy way to reach this wall is by scrambling through the cave and out of the Window.
**Descent -** Abseil from trees at the crag top or walk off the top and round and down via the top approach path.

North
Southwest
Southeast
Wolfscote Dale
Manifold Valley
Beeston Tor
Dovedale

## Ossam's Crag

A great grassy lump of a crag that was once the home to nine climbs of dubious merit. In these ecologically aware times these have been allowed to return to nature. The line of the crag however remains well worth calling in for.

**Descent** - Steep open slopes to the right of the crag lead back to the base.

**Approach (also see page 278)** - The crag is a short walk from the limited parking at the north end of the valley.

**1 Cummerbund** ....... 🎗️ 🧗 ▭ **VS 4b**

A fine climb up a strong line that sees few ascents nowadays. The 1st pitch is thoroughly unpleasant and there is some loose rock on the rest of the climb, but despite this it is well-worth seeking out. Be aware of any bird/access restrictions.

**1)** 4a, 24m. From the fence climb grassy rock into a shallow groove and over a bulge to a stance just below the break.

🌄 Morning | 🚶 10 mins

**2)** 4b, 22m. Traverse round the arete and follow the break as it rises across the face with the occasional moves on the slab below to avoid the steep bits. There is a stance just short of some flakes.

**3)** 4b, 20m. Traverse right below the flakes to a niche then climb up and right to regain the break. Continue to a stance and thread and/or tree belays in an open niche.

**4)** 10m. Easy grassy scrambling leads to the ridge.
*FA. D.Burgess, J.Allen 1965*

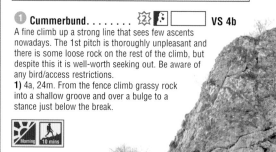

**2 The Chimney** ......... 🎗️ ▭ **Mod**

The tube through the cliff gives a fun outing to the skylight window. Onward progress is possible but pointless so return the same way. A bum-slide is possible but not recommended.

**3 Rain Games** ..... 🎗️ 🧗 🧗 ▭ **E5 6b**

The right edge of the cave and the hanging seam above give a great challenge. Needs cleaning and re-equipping.
*FA. Ian Dunn, Paul Ingham 1984. Originally aided as Chimney Direct.*

## The Chimney

Another forgotten cliff, that was once home to seven routes of dubious worth. The eponymous Chimney is worth calling in for as a Peak curio and the two hard routes listed here would benefit from a bit of a spring clean.

**Approach (also see page 278)** - The crag is a short walk from the limited parking at the north end of the valley. Walk along the cycleway until just before a hump-backed bridge, then cross the dry river bed and scramble up the steep bank to the cliff. The area of interest is away to the right hidden behind the bushes.

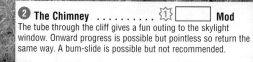

🌄 Morning | 🚶 5 mins | Sheltered | 💧 Seepage

| | No star | ⟨1⟩ | ⟨2⟩ | ⟨3⟩ |
|---|---|---|---|---|
| **Mod to S** | - | 1 | - | - |
| **HS to HVS** | 3 | 6 | 2 | 2 |
| **E1 to E3** | 2 | 3 | 5 | 2 |
| **E4 / 7a+ and up** | 1 | 5 | 5 | - |

Beeston Tor is fine high dome of pocketed white limestone tucked away in one the Peak's most secluded settings. There is a great range of high quality trad climbs here often on rock that is superb and as an extra positive the location is both sheltered and sunny. As for the downside (there always is one) large sections of the lower slabby walls are very vegetated, which makes access to many of the climbs a bit of a pain in the dry and downright dangerous when wet. There are some well-used tracks and bits of fixed rope where care is needed. Once on the smooth walls above the vegetation the positions are unbeatable.

## Approach   Also see map on page 278

The Tor is hidden away in the Southern Peak, and is best approached from the villages of Wetton or Grindon. From both villages, the road drops down steeply into the valley, by the Manifold Way which is popular with cyclists - free parking here. Take the left-hand of two tracks on the other side of the road which lead after 0.4 of a mile to parking in the field just short of where the track crosses a bridge and bends left towards the farm - a small fee (50p) is usually charged. A gate on the left leads to some stepping stones over the often-dry river, and on up to the base of the crag arriving at the ever-dry recess where *The Thorn* starts. The approaches to the various sections of the crag are complex and can be dangerous in damp conditions - great care is needed, see the route pages for details.

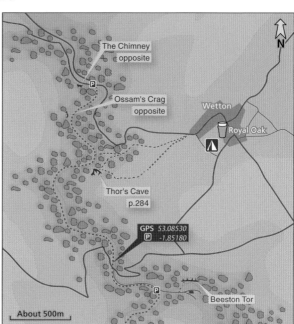

The Chimney opposite

Ossam's Crag opposite

Wetton

Royal Oak

Thor's Cave p.284

GPS 53.08530 -1.85180

Beeston Tor

About 500m

## Conditions

The cliff is the best sun-trap in the Peak, and clear winter days here can be excellent, since there is little seepage. However, this information is well known and the crag can become crowded when conditions are right, with congestion likely on the routes around the Ivy Gash. After rain, the steep access-tracks to the various parts of the cliff become slippery and dangerous - great care is needed in slick-soled climbing boots. The same applies to the descent gully if there is any dampness. In the warmer months Beeston Tor can be unbearably hot.

## Access

Beeston Tor is owned by the National Trust, who are willing to allow access to the crag. Please avoid unnecessary disturbance of the vegetation and bird life, particularly at nesting time.

North
Southwest
Southeast
Wolfscote Dale
Manifold Valley
Beeston Tor
Dovedale

## The West Wall

The left-hand side of the main section of the cliff is a little disappointing at first acquaintance - the lower two-thirds look more like steep pastureland than good climbing terrain. Higher up there is a fine wall of excellent, pocketed rock which give most of the routes their quality climbing.

**① West Wall Climb . . . . . . .** 🔲 **VS 4c**

A wandering outing up the left flank of the cliff with a bit of a bushwhack early on, although it manages to raise its head with some nice climbing in the upper reaches. Done in dry conditions, it provides a surprisingly worthwhile trip - despite appearances to the contrary. Start by a tree on the approach path.
**1)** 4a, 22m. Follow the cleaned line between the vegetation to the second tree on the wall.
**2)** 4b, 15m. Trend right across the wall to a niche. Step right out of this, then climb the wall past a bulge to a good, sheltered stance at the break.
**3)** 4c, 15m. Step left and climb the awkward crack, then slabby rock leftwards to easy ground.
*FA. D.Burgess 1966*

**② Enough Time . . . . . . . . . .** 🔲 **HVS 5b**

A right-hand finish to *West Wall Climb* following the line that *Beeston Eliminate* should have taken.
**1)** 4b, 25m. Pitch 1 of *West Wall Climb* but belay further right.
**2)** 5a, 12m. Climb the wall above to the cave stance.
**3)** 5b, 25m. Follow the break rightwards strenuously to join the top of *The Thorn*.
*FA. Gary Gibson, Derek Beetlestone 1978. Graham Hoey had previously climbed the last pitch in mistake for Beeston Eliminate. The pitch was first described in the 1970 Southern Limestone guide as an aided direct version of the Eliminate (2 pegs and many threads).*

*The next routes start in the central section of the crag at the ever-dry gearing up spot under the big diagonal slab that is the first pitch of The Thorn.*

**③ Patience . . . . . . . . . . . . .** 🔲 **HVS 5b**

A reasonable start and finish are linked by some rock and a lot of vegetation in the upper half of the first pitch.
**1)** 5b, 28m. Climb the crack in the left wall of the slabby groove to bulges, then traverse left to easier rock. Graze up the rib and grotty terrain to a belay below cleaner rock. A tough pitch. The wall to the left gives a harder variant - **The Direct Start, E2 5c**.
**2)** 5a, 14m. Trend left up the wall to a niche, then climb up and slightly leftwards to belay in the cave.
**3)** 4c, 15m. Finish leftwards, as for *West Wall Climb*.
*FA. Des Hadlum, G.Smith (3pts) 1968*

**④ The Beest . . . . . . .** 🔲 **E3 6a**

A cracking eliminate with a lot of fine fingery climbing and just a little unsavoury grass to remind you where you are.
**1)** 6a, 28m. Follow *Patience* to the bulge, then make fingery moves through this. Keep slightly right to avoid the vegetation until a horizontal traverse leads to a stance below cleaner rock.
**2)** 5c, 20m. Climb steeply rightwards to a rest in a shallow groove. Climb the groove, then trend slightly left to the bulges. Step right then pull leftwards onto the headwall and climb this, passing a man-sized hole, to easy ground and the holly.
**The Beesty Boys, E3 6a** - This follows the fixed gear up the wall, and through the bulge left of the *The Beest* pitch 2.
*FA. Jeff Morgan, Zep Dyszlewicz (8pts) 1970. FA. (TBB) Nigel Slater 1987*

**⑤ Principle of Moments . .** 🔲 **E3 5c**

The wall to the right of the upper pitch of *The Beest*. A worthwhile pitch, although it sees little attention. Step right from the stance on *The Beest* and climb the wall direct, except for a short jig left along thc juggy holds of *The Beeston Eliminate* (page 297). Tackle the bulges right to left then finish straight up.
*FA. John Fleming, Jim Shackleton 1983*

Descent

The West Wall

Ivy Gash

Central Wall

Bertram's Chimney

p.292

p.294

p.294

*The Thorn - p.293*

*Lots of sun* | *12 min* | *Sheltered* | *Multi-pitch*

North
Southwest
Southeast
Wolfscote Dale
Manifold Valley
Beeston Tor
Dovedale

45m

2

*Beeston Eliminate - p.297*

35m

4

5

A 28m

2

25m

22m

4

*The Thorn - p.293*

1

3

1 3

Descent

48m

30m to ledge

35m

Beeston Eliminate - p.297

18m to ledge

The Beest - p.290

28m

Central Wall - p.294

Approach from the right is possible - p.297

## Ivy Gash

This section is the showpiece of the crag with a set of fine intricate climbs which take complex lines to reach some magnificent positions high on the wall. On its left-hand side is *The Thorn* - one of the Peak's finest limestone climbs. In the middle of the crag is a fine shield of perfect pocketed rock. This exceptional wall has several good routes although the black streak taken by *Black Grub* is head and shoulders above the rest.

**Descents -** For routes which finish in the Ivy Gash, abseil from the substantial belay on *The Thorn* stance. Take care if there are people below you. If it is very busy, then why not consider finishing up the route *Ivy Gash*? For the routes which top out, walk leftwards (looking in) to a slippery gully.

**6 The Thorn** . . . . . . . . . Top⌐ 50⌐ 🦶 ☐ **HVS 5a**
One of the Peak's best limestone climbs and the classic of the crag. A superb central line, with a well-positioned crux. A pull on the peg of the crucial bulge lowers the grade to a solid VS.
**1)** 4b, 28m. From the ever-dry cave, climb the slabby right wall, right then left into the main groove, before easier climbing leads to threads (chains) under the huge overhangs.
**2)** 5a, 20m. Move out left and climb the short juggy rib to the bulges (several old pegs). Pull rapidly over to easier-angled ground in the groove above, continue to a belay in the big holly.
*FA. Joe Brown, Ron Mosley (some aid) 1954*

**7 Flying Doctor.** . . ⟨↥⟩ 🔩 🔲 🎨 ☐ **E5 6b**
Devious but exciting, especially in its upper reaches.
**1)** 5c, 38m. Climb *The Thorn* for 12m then move left and up into a shallow hanging groove. At its top, follow the rib and then do the crux of *The Thorn*. Move out right to a small stance in a groove.
**2)** 6b, 22m. Traverse right on the lip of the roof and enter a shallow scoop with difficulty. Climb up the scoop to a roof then through this via a useful flake to a grubby exit.
*FA. Phil Burke, Pete (the eponymous flying doctor) Thexton 1980*

**8 Double Top** . . . . . . ⟨↥⟩ 🔩 🦶 ☐ **E4 6a**
Another devious routes that seeks out difficulties and exposure and finds plenty of both.
**1)** 4b, 28m. Pitch one of *The Thorn* gives a pleasant prelude.
**2)** 6a, 12m. The pocketed crack-line gives a hard way through the roof. Continue to a restricted stance a short distance above.
**3)** 6a, 18m. Step out right and climb past a ledge and then a peg to a narrow hanging slab and follow this out right to the expected grubby exit.
*FFA. Phil Burke, Rab Carrington 1980. FA. Bob Dearman (aid) 1966*

**9 Ivy Gash** . . . . . . . . . . ⟨↥⟩ 🔲 ☐ **HVS 5b**
Short-lived and unbalanced but it follows a strong natural line.
**1)** 5a, 28m. Take pitch 1 of *The Thorn* to the chains.
**2)** 5b, 28m. Scramble along the cave (stance) then make tricky moves along the break, to a big hole (on *Black Grub*). Enter a steep groove which soon eases to floral scrambling.
*FA. John Sumner late 1950s*

*The hanging wall below the right-hand side of the Ivy Gash has some fine fingery climbing. The lack of a good line on some of the routes is made up for by the quality of the moves.*

**10 Stagnation** . . . . . . . . . . ⟨↥⟩ ☐ **VS 4c**
From the point where *The Thorn* heads back left into the gully, climb straight up the pocketed wall to reach a short diagonal crack that leads into the Ivy Gash.
*FA. Gary Gibson R.Hewitt 1978*

**11 Nocturne.** . . . . . . . . . . . . . ⟨↥⟩ ☐ **VS 4c**
Follow *The Thorn* until a traverse leads out right to a ledge (possible stance to the right if required) then climb the face via a short crack and the wall above up a shallow groove running up towards the ivy. Cut left under this to reach the Ivy Gash.
*FA. Nat Allen D.Burgess 1970*

*The next four routes all start at a ledge under the white wall below the Ivy Gash. This is best reached using the first section of Nocturne.*

**12 Pocket Symphony.** . . . . . ⟨↥⟩ 🔩 ☐ **E1 5b**
From the ledge, head left to a diagonal break/crack then climb direct up the excellent pocketed wall (threadable surprises aplenty) to pass right of the ivy and escape into the Ivy Gash.
*FA. Dave Jones R.Cope 1978*

**13 Deaf Dove.** . . . . . . . . . ⟨↥⟩ 🔩 ☐ **E2 5c**
More pocket-pulling though fiercer than most hereabouts. Despite that, the route is quite low in the grade. Don't forget the threads. Climb the steep wall to the left of the shallow scoop, and directly above the stance, crossing a small bulge to join the last couple of moves of *Central Wall*.
*FA. John Codling 1979*

**14 Evensong** . . . . . . . ⟨↥⟩ 🔩 🔲 ☐ **E1 5a**
The right-hand side of the face gives a fine pitch. Climb the shallow scoop/groove directly above the stance then continue up the pleasantly sustained wall and bulge above to cross *Central Wall* into the Ivy Gash.
*FA. Dave Jones, R.Cope 1978*

**15 Midnight Mass.** . . . . . . . 🔩 🎨 ☐ **E3 5c**
A boldish rarely climbed pitch up the right side of the face. Some threads might need to be (re)placed. Climb the right-hand side of the face, avoiding the vegetation until the ramp of *Central Wall* is reached. Climb straight up the wall until an escape into the Ivy Gash is possible.
*FA. Gary Gibson 1983*

*Linking Double Top with The Beesting is an open project that should be about 8b. The removal of the ivy curtains from the roof of the Ivy Gash has allowed the development of a series of short hard sport routes in a wild setting. The 1st pitch of The Thorn is the quickest approach.*

**16 The Beesting** . . . . . . . ⟨↥⟩ ▯ ☐ **8a**
A huge leap gains a hole and exciting sideways climbing.
*FA. Kristian Clemmow 2006*

**17 The Beeston Bomber** ⟨↥⟩ 🦶 ▯ ☐ **8a+**
Very reachy climbing through the roof right of centre.
*FA. Kristian Clemmow 2007*

**18 666** . . . . . . . . . . . . . . ⟨↥⟩ 🔩 ☐ **7c+**
The original line here with fierce pocket climbing.
*FA. Simon Nadin 1989*

**19 Beast It!** . . . . . . . . . . . 🔩 🦶 ☐ **7b**
A short line up the bulge on the right.
*FA. Mark Pretty 2006*

**20 Pat-trick** . . . . . . . . ⟨↥⟩ 🔩 🎨 ☐ **E4 6b**
Reachy moves in and out of the hanging niche.
*FA. Mark Elwell, Andy Grondowski 1982*

North · Southwest · Southeast · Wolfscote Dale · Manifold Valley · Beeston Tor · Dovedale

**㉑ Central Wall** . . . . . . . . . . 🔲 VS 4b
An amenable classic taking a good line up the smooth-looking wall on the right-hand side of the cliff. Scramble up grubby ledges to a fat peg belay below the wall. Follow the diagonal break that runs leftwards across the wall, passing between some much blanker terrain. Low in the grade.
*FA. D.Burgess 1966*

**㉒ Catharsis** . . . . . . . . . 🔲 E3 5c
An eliminate that ultimately proves a worthwhile experience. From *Central Wall*, climb rightwards via a bulge to a rest in a scoop close to *Black Grub*. Step back left and climb the pocketed wall until an escape left into *Ivy Gash* is possible or, better, follow it to the top.
*FA. Dave Jones 1979*

**㉓ Black Grub** . . . . . . . . 🔲 E3 5c
The black streak running down the right-hand side of *Central Wall* is a fingery classic. Follow *Central Wall* then move right to the base of the streak. Climb straight up this which is sustained and fingery all the way to its top (a rest is possible on the left, in the scoop of *Catharsis*, for the harassed). At the top of the streak, pull up and finish up the *Ivy Gash*.
*FA. John Yates 1974*

**㉔ Cleo's Mood** . . . . . . . 🔲 E5 6a
Makes the most of the rock to the right of *Black Grub*, though it is eventually forced left in search of easier ground to join *Black Grub* at the big hole.
*FA. Gary Gibson 1983*

**㉕ The Fly** . . . . . . . . 🔲 E3 6a
From the start of *Central Wall*, climb rightwards to enter the shallow left-trending groove and follow it to where it fizzles out. Make difficult moves leftwards across the wall to reach easier ground, and a finish up the grass.
*FA. G.Smith, Nat Allen, B.Metcalfe (5pts) 1968*

**㉖ The Web** . . . . . . . . . . . . . . . . 🔲 HVS 5a
The climbing on offer is rather overshadowed by the jungle crossed. Follow *The Fly* to where it steepens, then swing out right and follow a ramp to a crack and the matto grosso. An abseil from the first solid tree is probably the best idea.
*FA. D.Burgess, Nat Allen (1pt) 1966*

**㉗ The Spider** . . . . . . . . . . . 🔲 HVS 5a
Devious, but interesting and worthwhile; good rope-work is a must. Follow *The Fly* until it is possible to traverse the wall to the right descending slightly to reach the lip of the diagonal overhangs. Climb the ramp/groove rightwards, then the wall slightly left to tree belays and an escape.
*FA. G.Smith, Nat Allen (3pts) 1968*

**㉘ Solution Pollution** . . . . . . . 🔲 E1 5b
Short, but not without interest. Start left of the ivy and climb the steep pocketed wall until forced right into *The Spider*. Finish up this, or bale from one of the lower-offs.
*FA. Gary Gibson 1983*

**㉙ Majolica** . . . . . . . . . . 🔲 E3 5c
Good fun and almost a sport route at about 6b if you clip gear on the previous route. Climb the groove past some threadable pockets and the remains of the old pint-pot handle hold, to blanker rock. Press on up this to join *The Spider*. Finish up this or lower off.
*FA. Gary Gibson 1983*

**㉚ Faience** . . . . . . . . 🔲 E4 6a
More Black Country butchness. Climb the arete of the cave to steeper terrain. Stretch up this to reach a groove, pull over the bulge that caps it and gain *The Spider*. Lower off or finish up *The Spider*. Check the state of the old threads.
*FA. Gary Gibson 1983*

**㉛ Budgie** . . . . . . . . . 🔲 E4 6a
Steep and powerful climbing up the edge of the cave of *Bertram's Chimney*. Start inside the cleft and climb for 10m, then swing out left to gain the front face. Power up this (old pegs) until it is possible to swing left and gain some respite on *The Spider*. Finish up this.
*FA. John Codling, T.Bristling 1979*

**㉜ Honoray Buoux** . . . 🔲 7c
Continues where *Budgie* escapes left. From halfway along its traverse, blast up the leaning prow on two-finger pockets until a high break allows an escape left. A direct finish awaits. An old abandoned project with tatty bolts.
*FA. Mark Pretty 2005*

**㉝ Bertram's Chimney.** . . . . . . 🔲 VDiff
A smelly experience, but taking in some impressive rock. The big diagonal rift on the right-hand side of the cliff is climbed via its slabby right-hand wall until it is possible to escape away to the right and reach vegetated scrambling. At certain times of the year, breathing in the depths of the chimney is difficult. In the summer the top undergrowth can be difficult to get around.
*FA. Nat Allen, D.Burgess 1963*

**㉞ Gary Gobstopper** . . . . . . . 🔲 HVS 5a
Makes the most of the right-hand wall of the chimney. Climb via a couple of disjointed and slightly totty grooves. Above the second one, head left (old peg) to join *Bertram's Chimney*. Finish up or down this.
*FA. Dave Jones, R.Cope 1978*

*There are more lost routes in the rocky jungle to the right and they are best left that way.*

*The Thorn - p.293*

Lots of sun | 15 min | Sheltered

**Descent**

30m to ledge

## Central Wall and Bertram's Chimney

The right-hand side of the cliff has some worthwhile climbs, though the best of these are quite hard. The clean wall of *Black Grub* is an immaculate classic with some hard companions on either side. The wall immediately left of *Bertram's Chimney* is steeper with some good routes but sadly only short-lived. This area of the cliff is normally quieter than the rest of the place.

**Approach (also see page 278) -** From below *The Thorn*, follow the precarious path with fixed ropes along the bottom of the crag. Once below *Bertram's Chimney*, scramble up the fixed ropes to the crag. **Take great care, especially if it is wet** - one slip and you're gone.

**Descent -** For routes which top out, walk leftwards and scramble down a gully. For the routes around *Bertram's Chimney*, either use one of the lower-offs, or find a tree to abseil, or scramble up and walk off leftwards.

22m to ledge

20m to ledge

26

22

33

23

27

20m

24

32

*dnight Mass - p.293*

31

21 25

28

**Approach from**
***Nocturne* - p.292**

29  30  33  34

**Fixed rope approach - also see p.297**

Lots of sun | 15 min | Sheltered

North
Southwest
Southeast
Wolfscote Dale
Manifold Valley
Beeston Tor
Dovedale

30m to le

① 

35m

② 

West Wall

③ 

Ivy Gash

Ⓐ

28m

Central Wall

① 

The Thorn - p.293

22m to ledge

Bertram's Chimney

**The fixed rope
approach to
*Bertram's Chimney***

All three girdles start up *West Wall Climb* - see page 290.

## The Girdles

There are three very good girdles of Beeston Tor on offer that make the most of the exposure. *Beeston Eliminate* is the best and won't interfere with other climbers very much. The other two cross some excellent rock but you will get in everyone's way if the crag is busy.
All three girdles start up *West Wall Climb* - see page 290.
**Descent -** From the cliff's crest, cross the crest to locate the easy gully on the other side which leads round the left edge of the cliff.

### ❶ Beeston Eliminate . . 🧗🗺️🔦 ⬜ HVS 5a

The long rising-diagonal, and highest of the three girdles, is one of the major lines on the cliff and offers a superb outing with some astounding positions at the grade. Harder for the tall and potentially a bit of a gripper to second.
**1)** 4b, 28m. Start by the tree on the path, 10m right of a small cave and follow the cleaned path of *West Wall Climb* (see p.290) for two pitches to the sheltered stance at the start of the break.
**2)** 5a, 22m. Traverse down and right across the wall following the line of good holds (don't forget the second man) to reach the groove of *The Thorn* then climb this to the holly tree belay.
**3)** 5a, 26m. Climb back down rightwards again and get past the horrible spiky bush then cross the fingery wall to regain the break. Follow this (threads) in a wild position, to a grassy rake (thread belays up and left) and an easy escape to the ridge.
*FA. G.Smith, T.Burnell 1966*

### ❷ Lord of the Dance . 🧗🔦🪝 ⬜ E3 6a

The middle girdle offers a lot of fine fingery climbing with a sting-in-the-tail crux. Start as for *Beeston Eliminate*.
**1)** 4a, 15m. Climb the cleaned stripe to a big tree.
**2)** 5b, 30m. Follow *Beeston Eliminate* to below the overlap just short of the stance. Traverse right descending slightly all the way to below the crux bulge of *The Thorn*. Climb down into the cave to belay.
**3)** 5b, 16m. Descend the diagonal crack/ramp then pull right over the bulge and follow a gently rising line to a small stance on the polished ramp of *Central Wall*.
**4)** 6a, 34m. Traverse right to gain the left-slanting groove of *The Fly*. Up this to hard moves left (old pegs) then easier grassy climbing to the top.
*FA. John Codling, Dave Jones 1979*

### ❸ Perforation . . . . . . . . 🧗🪝 ⬜ HVS 5a

The lowest girdle is a long trip with a fair bit of vegetated rambling early on but it improves as the miles roll by. Start as for *Beeston Eliminate*. Some pitches can be combined.
**1)** 4a, 15m. Climb the cleaned stripe to a big tree.
**2)** 4c, 30m. Follow the base of the steep wall rightwards (vegetated) until it is possible to climb down the upper part of P1 of *The Thorn* and belay where a ramp runs out right.
**3)** 5a, 16m. Follow the ramp rightward to a small stance on the polished ramp of *Central Wall*.
**4)** 5a, 14m. Continue in the same line to a small stance in the groove of *The Fly*.
**5)** 5a, 18m. Swing right to access a ramp then continue up and right across a mixture of rock and grass to the top.
*FA. Paul Nunn, T.Briggs 1969. Recorded at the time as Armadillium.*

North · Southwest · Southeast · Wolfscote Dale · Manifold Valley · Beeston Tor · Dovedale

| | No star | ☆ | ☆☆ | ☆☆☆ |
|---|---|---|---|---|
| **Mod to S** | 1 | 2 | - | - |
| **HS to HVS** | 14 | 8 | 5 | 3 |
| **E1-E3 / 6b-7a** | 10 | 21 | 11 | 5 |
| **E4 / 7a+ and up** | 11 | 15 | 5 | 8 |

The north-south gash of Dovedale has a fine set of climbs on the various bits of rock scattered along its length, and has long been a firm favourite with limestone climbers. Many of the climbs finish on proper summits which is an added attraction. The Dale is the most popular tourist destination in this guidebook; in summer hoards travel up and down the valley gazing in awe at the spires, fins and arches that make up the superb rock architecture scattered along the Dale. Ascents of the free-standing tower of Ilam Rock, and the climbs around the Doveholes in particular will always draw a crowd of onlookers and the Pickering Pinnacle and Tissington Spires are also quite public, though fortunately there are plenty of more discreet bits of rock for those who don't perform well in front of a crowd. Whatever your chosen destination, many pieces of rock described here are only home to a small set of quality routes, to get the most out of a good day's climbing out of a visit you will need to go to more than one buttress.

## Approach    Also see map on page 278

Dovedale is the valley between Thorpe Village at its southern end and Milldale at its northern end. It runs parallel to the main A515 Buxton to Ashbourne road which is the best road to gain access to the villages at either end. There is a large free car park in Milldale, and a large expensive car park just past the Izaak Walton Hotel at the Thorpe end. A substantial path follows the east bank of the river for the entire length of the dale and this gives access to Bailey Buttress, Dove Holes, Pickering Tor and Tissington Spires. The one bridge gives access to Ilam Rock but Dovedale Church and Ravens Tor usually require a spot of wading. More detailed approaches are given with each buttress.

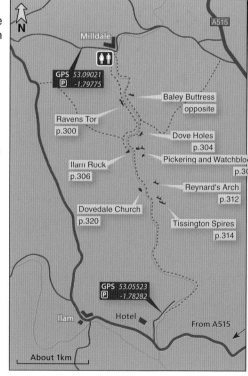

## Conditions

The wide variety of rock formations present different faces hence climbing is possible in sun or shade as desired often even on the same buttress. The high sides of the valley, and the heavy tree cover, shelter all crags from the wind. There is little seepage but the shady crags of Dove Holes and Ravens Tor are slow to dry.

## Access

Dovedale is owned by the National Trust who are willing to allow access to the various crags. Please only use the described approaches and avoid unnecessary disturbance of vegetation and bird life, particularly at nesting time.

**① Ribit . . . . . . . . . . . . .**  🔲 🔲 🔲 **E4 6b**
Start 2m left of the groove of *Claw Left-hand* and climb a
left-slanting weakness (hard) and a short rib to a ledge. Use
undercuts to gain the smooth wall above, then climb this direct
(peg) on pockets and flakes - gradually easing - passing a thread
runner just below the top.
*FA. Bill McKee 1999*

**② Claw Left-hand . . . . . .** 🔲 🔲 🔲 **HVS 5b**
Battle up the slippery and strenuous groove to where the angle
eases, then move up right to the hanging chimney of *The Claw*.
Climb up this awkwardly to a ledge on the left - possible stance
and escape route to the left, or take the rather scruffy ramp
rightwards to easy ground (4c).
*FA. Jack Street, Al Evans 1966*

**③ The Claw . . . . . . . . . . . .** 🔲 🔲 **HVS 5a**
Climb the tricky, thin crack to a recess (and a cop-out lower-off).
Battle up the awkward, leaning chimney to a ledge and possible
stance on the left. Finish as for *Claw Left-hand* along the ramp
or by escaping leftwards.
*FFA. Jack Street, Al Evans 1967. FA. A Critchlow, R Hassell (1pt) 1965*

## Baley Buttress
The first piece of decent rock on the east bank of the
river is a sheltered, south-facing tower of rock with a
couple of good lines on it.
**Approach -** From the riverside path, scramble up the
steep bank to the prominent buttress, which is virtually
opposite Ravens Tor.
**Conditions -** This is a south-facing sun-trap which is well
sheltered and dries quickly.

**④ Swallow Tails . . . . . . .** 🔲 🔲 **E3 6a**
Climb the thin and fierce crack, then continue through the right-
hand side of the black bulges above. Follow the groove to reach
the diagonal break of *The Claw* and finish direct. Variation starts
are available to the left (5c) and right (5b).
*FA. Dave Jones, R Cope 1979*

**⑤ Bill Baley . . . . . . . . . .** 🔲 🔲 🔲 **VS 4b**
Start on the right below parallel cracks. Climb the right-hand
crack for 8m, then climb the groove and loose wall on the left to
a niche. Climb the crack above to join the diagonal break on the
upper section of *The Claw*. Finish as for this.
*FA. R Hassall, A Critchlow (3pts) 1965*

## Ravens Tor

A fine steep cliff, northeast-facing and seamed by a selection of cracks and grooves, giving some of the best climbing in the dale. As with some other crags, the ivy is encroaching.

**Approach (also see page 298) -** The easiest approach is by wading the river below the cliff, using one of the weirs. For those who wish to avoid getting wet feet, the path on the west bank starts behind the public toilets in Milldale and is a pleasant walk. The path continues down the west bank all the way to Ilam Rock.

**Conditions -** The cliff is perhaps best used as a shady retreat on hot summer days, though it is well sheltered from the prevailing winds at all times. There is little seepage, although it is slow to dry after rain.

Descent

15m to ledge

32m

30m

20m

15m

20m

Morning · 20 min · Sheltered

North · Southwest · Southeast · Wolfscote Dale · Manifold Valley · Beeston Tor · Dovedale

**1 Tennessee Waltz . . . . .** HVS 5b
**1)** 5a, 18m. The thin crack leads to a dubious flake that is climbed to a small stance, where the angle falls back.
**2)** 5b, 18m. Head left up the steep wall and pull into a shallow groove which leads to a classic Dovedale grassy exit.
*FA. A Hill, G.Dunn 1972*

**2 Southern Rib . . . . . . . . . .** E1 5b
Popular and excellent, though inevitably a little polished.
**1)** 5b, 18m. Bold moves reach the crack, then power up it until it fizzles out then take the flake to its end and swing left to the stance on *Tennessee Waltz*.
**2)** 5a, 30m. Climb the narrowing slab to a small overhang, pass the left-hand end of this then move right then back left to a groove which leads to a worry exit onto the meadows above.
*FFA. Rod Leeming 1965. FA. Joe Brown (2pts) 1950s*

**3 The Temptress . . . . . . .** E5 6a
The bold, bulging rib between the crack systems is a stern test. The grade assumes that several pegs are in place. Climb the scoop and face, trending left to the overhang. Pull right over this to reach a crack, and follow this steeply to a stance in the bay above. Finish as for *Southern Rib*.
*FA. John Codling, Dave Jones 1980. Originally done in two pitches.*

**4 Left-hand Route . . . . . .** E1 5b
The steep and pumpy groove gives a fine sustained pitch. Climb the groove until it is possible to pull over to less awkward ground. Continue to a good stance. Abseil off or continue up *Brown's Blunder*.
*FFA. Jack Street, Geoff Birtles 1967. FA. John Sumner, Brian Knox 1950*

**5 Deltoid Shuffle . . .** E4 5c
A taxing wall with some absorbing climbing which is not as bold as grit routes of the same grade.
*FA. John Codling, Dave Jones 1979*

**6 Raven . . . . . . . . . . . . . . .** E2 5c
Two worthwhile pitches split by a ramble up *Brown's Blunder*.
**1)** 5c, 24m. Climb the right-hand crack in the lower wall to its end then gain the ramp with difficulty. Move left and then back right to a stance in the base of a groove (thread belays).
**2)** 5b, 18m. Climb the steep groove then at its top swing boldly up and right to gain a standing position with difficulty. Finish up and right again, more easily.
*FA. Keith Myhill, Bill Hayley (almost free - 1 nut aid) 1971*

**7 Brown's Blunder . . . . . . . .** VS 4c
The easiest route up the cliff, which follows a good line although it is a touch vegetated and there is some loose rock.
**1)** 4c, 20m. Follow the diagonal break (threads) until awkward moves past a bulge gain a good stance.
**2)** 4b, 12m. Climb the steep groove on the left (where the great man made his blunder) then move left again to easy ground and graze-a-way to the top.
*FFA. Pete WIlliams, John Amies 1963. FA. Joe Brown (aid on P2) 1950s*

**8 Aquarius . . . . . . . .** E2 5c
A steep start leads to some fine crack climbing. Climb the ramp of *Brown's Blunder* for 8m (thread - possible stance) then pull rightwards though the bulges to gain the crack splitting the wall above. Follow this with interest, passing a small resting ledge at half-height to a steep grass exit.
*FA. Jack Street, Tom Proctor 1968*

**9 Central Wall . . . . . . .** E3 5c
Fine climbing up thin cracks splitting the central white wall.
**1)** 5c, 20m. Climb to the thin crack and follow it with difficulty until it is possible to move right to a small ledge and belay.
**2)** 5b, 14m. Climb up then left into the hanging groove and bridge up this to easy ground.
*FFA. Tom Proctor, Keith Myhill (1pt) 1969.*
*FA. Rod Leeming (aid) 1950s.*

**10 Central Wall Direct . . .** E4 6b
The thin right-trending crack directly above the stance.
*FA. Chris Hamper 1978*

*There are two short and fierce pitches up the wall to the right of the direct finish to Central Wall.*

**11 Judas . . . . . . . . . . . .** E5 6b
Follow *Central Wall* to the stance, but tackle the fierce crack in the headwall to the right of the *Direct Finish*.
*FA. Jim Moran, Geoff Milburn 1982*

**12 The Doldrums . . . . . . . . . .** E3 5c
The right-hand crack in the headwall is rarely visited.
*FA. Jim Moran, Geoff Milburn 1982*

*Venery - p.302*

North / Southwest / Southeast / Wolfscote Dale / Manifold Valley / Beeston Tor / Dovedale

### ⑫ Venery . . . . . . . . . . . ⚝📷☐ HVS 4c

The left-hand parallel crack in the right side of the face is a popular outing and follows a strong natural line. The 1st pitch is disappearing under the ivy.
**1)** 4b, 15m. Climb a bulge into the groove that falls from the crack-line and follow it to a stance on the right.
**2)** 4c, 15m. Step back left and follow the sustained crack, passing a small bulge a short way below the top.
*FFA. H.Smith 1963. FA. Joe Brown 1950s*

### ⑬ Parrot Face . . . . . . . . ⚝📷☐ HVS 5a

**1)** 4b, 15m. Take the first pitch of *Venery* to the stance.
**2)** 5a, 15m. The right-hand crack is also sustained and has a couple of tricky overhangs to maintain the interest. Pumpy.
*FA. Jack Street 1966*

### ⑭ Skewball. . . . . . . . . . . . . . . . ☐ VS 4c

Climb a crack then step right into its continuation. Head up the grassy ramp right again to finish.

### ⑮ Jugbit. . . . . . . . . . . . . . . . . . ☐ E2 5c

Climb the smooth wall to the roof then move left to enter the groove of *Skewball*. Up this and the grassy ramp above.
*FA. Nick Dixon 1985*

### ⑯ Tendonitis Sucks . . . . . . . . . . ☐ E5 6b

From the first peg on *Jugbit*, step right onto the wall and climb it with difficulty.
*FA. Nick Dixon 1985*

Andy Turner on *Easter Island* (E1 5b) - *page 307* - on the dramatic pinnacle of Ilam Rock in Dovedale. Photo: David Simmonite

Easter Island was perhaps the most curious choice for inclusion in the book Extreme Rock since it isn't really in the same class as the other routes featured. The line and position are amazing, but the climbing less good and too much time is spent on the grotty north (right in this photo) face. It is still a good route though and well worth doing if only for that summit feeling you get on the top where you can usually wave to the appreciative spectators.

North
Southwest
Southeast
Wolfscote Dale
Manifold Valley
Beeston Tor
Dovedale

## Dove Holes

The twinned sockets provide one of the Peak's more unusual climbing venues - a pair of water-worn caves where the dark art of aid climbing can still be practised. For those after the free routes, *Police and Thieves* and *The Umpire* are well worth seeking out.

On busy weekends you will be the centre of attention. Although there isn't much loose rock to dislodge, take care, especially with ropes and gear, since people will wander about beneath you.

**Approach (also see page 298) -** walk down the main path from Milldale and you can't really miss the huge double cave directly above the path.

**Conditions -** This is a cool summer haven, and it gets little sun. There is a lot of seepage, and the crag is slow to dry. For those into aid climbing, there is plenty to do here in the heaviest of rain.

**❶ The Archers. . . . . . . . . . . .** 🖾 ☐ **E5 6b**
The pillar to the left of the smaller cave leads to an overhang. Move right under this and sprint for the trees.
*FA. Mark Pretty 1988*

**❷ The Ball . . . . . . . . . .** 🖾🖾 ☐ **A2**
An interesting aid route exiting the smaller left-hand cave, including a bit of downhill climbing to pass the lip. The gear is mostly in place. Abseil off.

**❸ Pumping Iron . . . .** 🖾🖾🖾 ☐ **E5 6b**
The right-slanting overlap between the caves is as strenuous as the name suggests. From the ledge, undercut and layaway along the overlap until it is possible to pull over the square roof to reach a lower-off tree.
*FFA. Craig Smith Johnny Dawes 1984*
*FA. John Codling, Steve Allen, J.Lockett (1 rest) 1983*

**❹ Restricted Practices . . . . . .** 🖾 ☐ **E5 6b**
The right-hand side of the wall between the caves is technical to start. Trend left through the overhangs, and pull through to reach the trees. Abseil off.
*FFA. Keith Sharples 1990. FA. Zep Dyszwicz, P.Pearson 1969*

*There have been a number of new aid-routes added to these caves by Dave Williams, Geoff Middlehurst, Mike Whittaker and others. These new lines have confused the existing lines.*

**❺ The Wicked . . . . . . . . . . .** 🖾 ☐ **A2**
Start inside the left-hand edge of the arch, and climb the pillar and thin crack in the roof out to join *The Bat*.
*FA. Chris Craggs, Colin Binks 1982. Rapidly neutered by the addition of many extra bolts.*

**6 The Bat. . . . . . . . . . .** ⬜⬜⬜ **A2**
A classic aid route which is pretty straightforward with solid bolts. Climb the central pillar, then cross the roof bat-style, past a reachy section in the middle, to a lower-off on the lip.
*FA. Al Evans 1969*

**7 Middle Stump . . . . .** ⬜⬜⬜ **A2**
Back breaking work up the right-hand leaning wall, following a vague line of weakness and joining *The Bat* just short of the lip. Spaced bolts in places.
*FA. Colin Binks, Chris Craggs 1980s*

**8 Follow the Bear . . . . . . . .** ⬜⬜ **E5 6b**
From the base of the pillar on the right, trend left, hugging the lip of the cave following the line of fixed gear. Don't fall.
*FA. Malc Taylor 1988*

**9 Police and Thieves.** ⬜⬜⬜ **E4 6a**
A fine, devious pitch, with plenty of good climbing. Climb the awkward wall for 5m, then head left past a crumbly flake. Climb direct to a hidden peg, then tackle the pushy bulge to better holds on the headwall. Climb this direct, until a traverse right leads to a good tree belay/lower-off.
*FA. Jim Moran, Nick Plishko, Steve Webster, Chris Addy 1982*

**10 The Umpire . . . . . . . .** ⬜⬜ **E3 5c**
Start as for *Police and Thieves,* but continue up an awkward little groove until a ledge on the right can be gained. Climb the wall leftwards to undercuts, then sprint up the final wall to reach a good tree. Lower off.
*FA. John Codling, Dave Wiggin 1978*

North
Southwest
Southeast

Wolfscote Dale

Manifold Valley

Beeston Tor

Dovedale

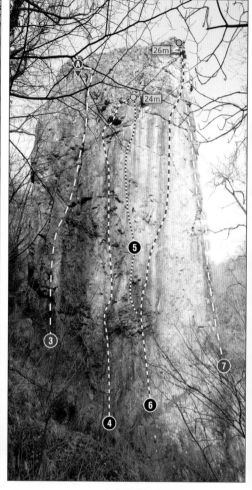

## 1 Original Route . . . . . . . HS 4a

Poor, but the easiest way up the tower, and one of the earliest limestone routes in the Peak. From the col at the back of the tower, traverse left and climb the loose grassy wall.
*FFA. Seigfreid Herford 1914. FA. Samuel Turner 1903, on a top-rope. He completed his ascent with an impressive headstand on the top.*

## 2 The Wong Edge . . . E3 6a

The once-pegged cracks in the uphill face of the tower give a strenuous tussle. From the resting ledge on the right, step back left, and finish up the still-tricky upper wall.
*FFA. Ron Fawcett, Chris Gibb 1976. FA. Joe Brown, Don Whillans 1950s.*

## 3 The Groove . . . . . . . . E2 5c

Bridge and battle into, then up, the leaning corner to reach relief on a shelf. Finish up the more amenable groove behind.
*FFA. Jack Street, Alan McHardy 1969. FA. Slim Sorrel, Nat Alan 1950s.*

## 4 The Gladiator . . E4 6a

An unequal battle for many. Climb the rib, then the sustained pocketed crack with difficulty (old peg) to an eventual breather on a ledge on the left. Pull up and right, through the bulge, then swing rightwards to the lower-off.
*FFA. Ron Fawcett, Chris Gibb 1976. FA. Rock and Ice members early 1950s*

## 5 Steve's Route . . . . . . . E6 6c

Start up *Eye of the Tiger* but break left and climb the wall via some desperate fingery climbing to the lower-off.
*FA. Steve McClure 2007*

## 6 Eye of the Tiger . E7 6c

Cue the Rocky music. A big bruising pitch up the finest bit of rock in the valley. Mega-classic and about sport 7c. From the ever-dry ledge under the face, climb into a niche, then follow the searing crack into ever more desperate terrain. At the horizontal crack, swing right for respite in the final section of *Easter Island*. A direct finish would be nice. With several pieces of fixed and old jammed gear it is nearer E6. *Photo on page 323.*
*FFA. Ron Fawcett 1982. FA. Pete Williams, John Amies 1963*

28m

**❼ The White Edge** . . . . . . E3 6a

Once a spectacular aid route and now a worthwhile free outing. Climb the crack just left of the arete, with a breather around rightwards on *Easter Island*. Get back left and continue in the same vein, until the final groove can be entered, not before time.
*FFA. Ron Fawcett 1978. FA. Joe Brown, Ron Mosley early 1950s*

**❽ Easter Island** . . . . . . . . . . E1 5b

Almost a great classic, though the grassy grot just to the right of the lower section is a bit of a spoiler - you will either love it or hate it. Care with the ropework is required. From the gearing-up ledge above the river, pull onto the front face, and climb the arete and wall (or grubby easy ground further right) to a big thread. Swing up and left to enter the hanging groove, and finish spectacularly over the left-hand side of the capping overhang. *Photo on page 303.*
*FA. Ed Ward-Drummond, Hamish Green-Armytage 1972*

## Ilam Rock

The finest pinnacle in the valley is in a dramatic setting, leaning out over the river and the ogling walkers. The routes are perhaps not as good as you might expect, and *Easter Island* itself has been over-sold in the past, however, there are still some great ticks, all of which finish with that rare summit feeling.

**Approach (also see page 298)** - Walk down the main valley path, and the pinnacle is obvious by the first bridge. In summer it can be reached direct from Ravens Tor, via a narrow and muddy path.

**Conditions** - The leaning wall faces south, and gets plenty of sun. It is well sheltered, and *Gladiator* and *Eye of the Tiger* will stay dry in the rain for the most part.

**Descent** - Abseil from the substantial chains at the summit.

⑦
⑧
⑥

From the bridge

North | Southwest | Southeast | Wolfscote Dale | Manifold Valley | Beeston Tor | Dovedale

30m

10

Thunderball
p.310

20m

## Pickering Pinnacle

Pickering Pinnacle is the slender, grassy tower opposite Ilam Rock. It offers some good climbing on the retiring south-facing white wall hidden high above the crowds gawping at Ilam. None of the routes described here are popular and many rely on old fixed gear which should be treated with suspicion.

**Approach (also see page 298)** - The first three routes are easily reached above the main valley path. The other routes can be reached by a steep path around the back of the pinnacle which leads to a col level with the starts. Alternatively you can approach from *Adjudicator Wall*.

**Conditions -** Most of the routes get plenty of sun and dry quickly. It is well sheltered and there is little seepage.

**Descent -** Abseil from old pegs (long overdue for replacement) directly above the pinnacle's shortest side.

1

2

3

4

Ilam Rock
p.306

Pickering Pinnacle

Thunderball
p.310

Watchblock
p.311

North
Southwest
Southeast
Wolfscote Dale
Manifold Valley
Beeston Tor
Dovedale

A 18m to ledge

**① Pickering Ridge** . . . . . . . . VS 4b
The long riverside arete is a good climb, at least in retrospect.
Gain the arete from the bank on the left, then follow it
throughout, and plant your flag on the summit.
*FA. Joe Brown early 1950*

**② What Crisis?** . . . . . . . . . . . . . HVS 5a
The left-hand arete of the cave leads to a block, move right
above the lip to the steep grass above the cave. Climb direct
up a corner to a tree, then escape rightwards or finish as for
*Pickering Ridge*.
*FA. John Flemming, Tom Carruthers 1978*

**③ Crisis** . . . . . . . . . . . . . E5 6c
Short and fierce. Climb the overhang above the right-hand rib of
the cave past several old peg-runners. Continue up the groove
above and belay. Escape rightwards.
*FFA. Johnny Woodward 1982. FA. Chris Calow, Richard Haszko (3 pegs)
1978*

**④ Daylight Robbery** . . . . . . . . . . . E1 5b
Start up *Crisis*, but move right along a break to a ledge. Pull
round a bulge to a crack and climb this to a belay. Escape right.
*FA. Clive Allen, Rob Wright 1992*

*The next routes are reached from the narrow grassy col behind
the pinnacle. Escape from the summit is via an abseil back down
the short side. The bits of fixed gear are relics.*

**⑤ Monsieur Mange Tout** . . . . . . E5 6b
Climb the fine white wall directly, past 2 pegs and a thread to a
lower-off. Good positions, but the gear is old.
*FA. Mark Pretty 1987. Originally climbed as Point Blank, E5 6b but this
stepped left to avoid the last move. FA. Andy Grondowski 1983*

**⑥ The River** . . . . . . . . . . . . E4 6a
An eliminate up the rounded arete left of *Pickering's Overhang*.
Keep going until you can no longer avoid rejoining the parent
route near the top.
*FA. Mark Elwell, Andy Grondowski 1983*

**⑦ Pickering's Overhang** . . . . . E1 5b
The flaky groove requires some hard work to pass the bulge.
The wall above (old pegs) is also tricky.
*FA. Joe Brown 1950s*

**⑧ The Flake** . . . . . . . . . E1 5c
A compelling line. Short-lived, but hard work.
*FA. S.Read (aid) 1969. FFA. Unknown*

**⑨ Chunky Punky** . . . . . . . . . . . . . HVS 5a
The short side of the tower soon eases.
*FA. John Codling, D.Wiggin 1978*

**⑩ Original Route** . . . . . . . . . . . . S 3c
Traverse the grassy north wall (tree runners) out to the even
grassier ridge (possible stance) then gibber up the crest.
*FA. Frank Elliott 1932*

Lots of sun  25 min  Sheltered

North
Southwest
Southeast
Wolfscote Dale
Manifold Valley
Beeston Tor
Dovedale

The col by Pickering Pinnacle

## Thunderball

A sunny wall in a very secluded setting. Apart from *Thunderball,* the routes see zero traffic - expect grass and loose rock.

**Approach (also see page 298) -** The usual approach is from the main valley path, up a steep, vegetated gully just south of Lion Rock (a small buttress over the path) passing under the Watchblock Buttress. The area can also be reached from the col of Pickering Pinnacle.

**Conditions -** The face gets plenty of sun and is well sheltered. There is little seepage.

**❶ Final Witness** . . . . . . . 🎒 E2 5b
1) 5b, 14m. Climb straight up the wall, initially via a groove, then by steeper pocket climbing to reach a ledge on the left.
2) 4a, 12m. The easy chimney offers an escape.
*FA. John Codling, P.Douglas, Dave Jones, Chris Calow, Mike Browell 1978*

**❷ Thunderball.** . . . . . . . . 🧗 E1 5b
Worth the bushwack, offering interesting and devious climbing.
1) 5b, 16m. Climb straight up the wall, then trend out right and climb the steepening wall above to a small stance on the left below the capping bulges.
2) 4c, 12m. Climb awkwardly up the groove to reach the roof, then scuttle left around this to easier rock. A rightward exit is harder (5a), and perhaps more in keeping with the lower pitch.
*FFA. Bob Dearman 1976. FA. Roy Leeming (4pts) 1965*

**❸ Red Eye** . . . . . . . . . . . . . . . HVS 5b
1) 5b, 14m. Climb onto the lower end of the diagonal ramp (crux), then follow it to a ledge and belay. The tree here has gone.
2) 4c, 14m. Climb up grassy rock behind the stance to the overlap that caps the wall, then follow this rightwards (thread). It is possible to escape out right onto the slab via the dry stone wall. Climb up and right (grass) to finish.
*FA. Chris Calow, Mike Browell,, Dave Jones, John Codling 1978*

**❹ Suspended Sentence** . . 🎒 🧗 E5 6b
Short, but action packed. Climb straight up the bulging, pocketed wall to a diagonal flake that leads leftwards to join *Red Eye.* Bailing out from the stance is the best idea.
*FA. John Codling (solo) 1978*

**❺ Harold Wilson** . . . . . . . . . . . E2 5b
Odd. Gain a ramp, then a black pocket to reach a flake. Up this to the grassy ledges and a possible stance. Climb up to the overlap and follow it left to join *Red Eye* at the thread. Finish as for this.
*FA. Jack Street, Alan McHardy 1970*

**❻ Palsy Wall** . . . . . . . . . . . 🧗 HVS 5a
Follow the major flake system across the face, right to left, to exit as for *Red Eye.*

## The Watchblock

One of the best walls in Dovedale is the superb Watchblock Buttress, home to the classic *Adjudicator Wall*. It is much more secluded than some of the other crags in the Dale, although it is high on the ticklist of other climbers all after the same route. If it is busy, try some of the other delights while you are waiting.

**Approach -** The most usual direct approach is from the main valley path up a steep vegetated gully just south of Lion Rock (a small buttress over the path).

**Conditions -** Most of the routes get afternoon sun and are well-sheltered. There is little seepage.

**❼ Wall of Straws.....** 🔲🔲🔲🔲 **E5 6b**

A fine pitch - devious, technical, sustained and superb. Climb the rib at the left-hand edge of the face then hand-traverse out right to gain a hanging ramp. Climb up and right via a shallow groove to eventually gain *Adjudicator Wall*. Climb the groove to its end then pull onto the wall above before swinging right to gain easy ground and some respite.
*FA. Ed Cleasby, Rob Matheson, B.McKinley 1981*

**❽ Three Piece Combo .....** 🔲🔲 **E4 6a**

A reasonable line but over-shadowed by its neighbours. Follow *Wall of Straws* to the base of its crucial groove, then swing left onto the face, climb past a creaky jug and then onwards up a line of flakes to join the final section of *Adjudicator Wall*.
*FA. Chris Plant, Mike Hammill 1984*

The line of bolts up the back of the scoop to the right are an open project - it is about 8a.

**❾ Adjudicator Wall ..** 🔲🔲🔲🔲 **E3 5c**

Judge, jury and harsh taskmaster. A magnificent climb; the best in the valley. From the toe of the buttress, trend up and left following good finger holds and a line of threads. Swing down and left to access a steep groove and sprint up this to an old peg at its top. Swing left and, before gravity takes over, layback up into the welcome shade of the capping yew tree.
*Photo on page 319.*
*FA. Jack Street, Geoff Birtles (one rest) 1969*

**❿ Nancy Whisky .........** 🔲🔲 **E1 5b**

A worthwhile climb amd a good warm-up for *Adjudicator*. From the start of the traverse of *Adjudicator Wall*, climb the shallow groove directly above to reach a possible stance out right. Traverse back left past trees to the final juggy wall.
*FFA. B.Whittaker, K.Mercer, Brian Cropper 1973. FA. Nat Allen 1960s*

**⓫ Watchblock Direct .........** 🔲 **HVS 5b**

From the base of the buttress, climb to, and through, the bulge, then trend rightwards up the crusty wall. Continue up the slabs to finish right by the Watchblock. Tree belay to the left.
*FFA. B.Whittaker 1973. FA. Nat Allen, D.Carnell (1pt) 1965*

The Watchblock

## Reynard's Arch

A popular attraction, at least since all the trees that used to hide it were cut down. There is a small selection of spectacular sport routes here in a bizarre setting.

**Approach (also see page 298)** - The Arch is clearly visible midway between The Watchblock and Tissington Spires. It is reached by a steep scramble.

**Conditions** - The face is mostly shaded from sun due to its angle. It is well sheltered. There is a lot of seepage for much of the year, though once dry it will remain so for quite a while, including in light rain.

**❶ The Lime Arch . . . . . . 🎯🔗 ⬜ 6b+**
The steep red wall forming the left wall of the arch is much easier than it looks. After a straightforward start, head up and right to a good flake then either go left to the first hole, or straight up on good crimps to a big finish.
*FA. Gary Gibson 1982. Bolted in 2010*

**❷ Jonah's Boner . . . . 🎯🔗⬜ 7c**
The right-hand side of the cave 50m further up from *Arch Enemies* is home to this retiring toughie. Knee-bars and other chicanery might help.
*FA. Simon Lee 1995*

**❸ Arch Rival . . . . . . . . . 🎯🔗⬜ 7a**
Start at the top of the slope on the right. An easier lower wall leads to a good jug at half-height. Make hard moves through the bulge using pockets and layaways, finishing with a long move to gain the jug on *Arch Enemies*.
*FA. Jon Clark 2010*

**❹ Arch Enemies . . . . ⬜50🔗⬜ 7c+**
Follow the central line of bolts under the arch and out to a belay around the back. Sustained and powerful. A stunning and unusual route for the Peak - not to be missed. *Photo opposite.*
*FA. Andy Pollitt 1987*

**❺ Sworn Enemy . . . . . . . 🎯🔗⬜ 8a**
Excellent steep climbing with a hard sequency crux. Starting on the right, climb up the vertical wall to a good hold under the roof. Move left along a series of good pockets to an impasse, then using small pockets and poor edges power up desperately to the good hold on *Arch Enemies*. Suitably rested, crank through the crux of *Arch Enemies* to the finishing jug.
*FA. Jon Clark 2010*

**❻ Things Ain't Like They Used to Be**
**. . . . . . . . . . . . . . . . . 🎯🔗⬜ 7a+**
Climb the thin pocketed flake-line, past several hard moves to a brief rest then make a big move to the break and a lower-off.
*FA. Gary Gibson 1984. Bolted in 2010*

North
Southwest
Southeast
Wolfscote Dale
Manifold Valley
Beeston Tor
Dovedale

The most obvious omission from the 2004 Northern Limestone Rockfax was Reynard's Cave with its classic *Arch Enemies* (7c+) - *opposite* - here being climbed by Dave Bond. We have corrected that in this edition and the good news is that another trio of routes have been added in the mean time improving the place's appeal.
Photo: Dave Bond Collection

## Tissington Spires

The finest collection of towers and spires in the Dale forms a complex set of walls and gullies that require careful navigation to properly locate yourself. They form a series of fins of rock which are generally accessed by the steep gullies between the fins.

**Approach (also see page 298) -** The Spires can be approached from either end easily using the main valley path. Each of the buttresses then has its own approach requirements described with the routes.

**Conditions -** Most of the walls described face southwest and get the afternoon sun. They are well sheltered from the wind and dry quickly. There is little seepage.

## Campanile Pinnacle

The tower has a grassy front face of little interest, its right side has better rock. The most obvious feature is a right-curving overlap taken by *Whacko*.

**Approach (also see page 298) -** Direct from the main path.

**Descent -** Abseil from the crest.

**❶ Campanile** . . . . . . . . **S 4a**

From the base of a groove, move left and climb a flake, then the groove above. Move up to a ledge and possible stance. Climb a groove on the right, then follow a ramp to the arete, cross this rightwards and finish over a small overhang.

*FA. Steve Read, Ron Leeming, D.Carnell, P.Brown, Steve Hunt 1956*

**❷ Whacko** . . . . . . . . **E3 5c**

Climb to a flake and follow it strenuously (good gear, pumpy to place) to its end. A short leap or long stretch gains a jug, then sprint to join *Campanile* and follow it to the top.

*FFA. Malc Taylor 1976. FA. R.Leeming S.Read late 1950,*

**❸ The Man with X-Ray Eyes** **E2 5b**

Start 3m right of *Whacko*, and climb to the slanting roof which is followed rightwards to its end. Head back left briefly, then rightwards up the juggy arete, until it is possible to ease leftwards and to *Whacko* above its crux. Finish easily.

*FA. Gary Gibson, Phil Gibson 1983*

Campanile Pinnacle — this page
Silicon Wall — opposite
Ten Craters — opposite
John Peel — p.316
South Gully Buttress — p.318

## Silicon Wall Area

In the middle of the pinnacles are two small walls with a set of good pitches on clean rock.

**Approach (also see page 298)** - Hike up from the path. For *Ten Craters*, pick out a path that leads up either side of a lesser pinnacle/fin below the main Silicon Wall. This should leave you at a col behind the fin.

**4 A Secret State** . . . . . . . **E3 5c**
Start below the left-hand of two crack-systems and climb the wall leftwards (old threads) to a groove, which leads to the break. Press on up the final wall then exit rightwards.
*FA. Gary Gibson, Hazel Carnes 1983*

**5 Under Pressure** . . . . . . . . . . . **HVS 5b**
Climb up and left into a shallow cave, and pull round its left edge steeply to enter the easier (and floral) upper groove.
*FA. Bill Wintrip, Chris Jackson 1984*

**6 Silicon** . . . . . . . . . . . . . . **HS 4b**
Worth seeking out. Climb up and right to enter the right-hand of the parallel cracks. Finish up this by sustained climbing.
*FA. Steve Read, Ron Leeming, D.Carnell, P.Brown, S.Hunt 1956*

**7 Manna Machine** . . . . . . . . . **VS 4c**
Climb the lower wall rightwards to the arete, then step back to the left and take the thin crack to the crest.
*FA. Gary Gibson 1981*

*Up the gully right of Silicon is a hidden wall with a set of juggy routes. Descend to the right or by abseil. The first four routes share a common lower pitch.*

**8 Rose Bowl** . . . . . . . . . . . **HVS 5b**
The face on the left of the cleanest section of rock.
**1) 4b, 10m.** Climb the short wall to a good ledge - tree belay.
**2) 5b, 20m.** From the left-hand end of the ledge, climb the gradually-easing wall on spaced jugs.
*FA. John Codling, Chris Calow 1979*

**9 Don van Vliet** . . . . . . . . . **E1 5c**
An eliminate between *Rose Bowl* and *Ten Craters*, offering nice, but escapable climbing. Start at a thread just left of the start of *Ten Craters*. Follow the technical wall on small pockets.
*FA. Nick Taylor 1995*

**10 Ten Craters of Wisdom** . . . . **VS 5a**
**1) 4b, 10m.** As for *Rose Bowl*.
**2) 5a, 20m.** Step left and pull through a notch in the overhang to the left of a large hanging flake, onto the slab above. Continue up the face on good holds, trending slightly leftwards. A fine pitch with many (even 10 perhaps) surprising holds.
*FA. Chris Calow 1978*

**11 Simeon** . . . . . . . . . . . . . **VS 4c**
Devious, but worthwhile. Some good moves.
**1) 4b, 10m.** As for *Rose Bowl*.
**2) 4c, 22m.** Climb through the bulge directly above, then trend right and back left, following the line of large and well-travelled holds, until it is possible to join *Simeon Direct* above its crux.
*FA. Nat Allen, D.Carnell (1pt) 1965*

**12 Simeon Direct** . . . . . . . . . **HVS 5a**
Only a small independent section but worth a separate entry.
**1) 4b, 10m.** As for *Rose Bowl*.
**2) 5a, 20m.** Climb through the bulge directly above, then continue up the slab and easier, steeper rock to reach the left-hand end of a ledge. Exit to the right.

**13 Archibald the Grim** . . . . **E2 5c**
Makes the most of the rock on the right. Climb a cleaned strip to a notch in the bulge. Pull up and left onto the wall with difficulty, then continue more easily to the right-hand end of the final ledge on *Simeon*. Finish easily.
*FA. Chris Jackson, Bill Wintrip 1983*

North | Southwest | Southeast | Wolfscote Dale | Manifold Valley | Beeston Tor | Dovedale

Afternoon | 30 min | Sheltered

## The John Peel Wall

The tallest and best rock at Tissington Spires is the John Peel Wall. Most of the routes start in the awkward, narrow gully below the face, but soon reach majestic positions on the face above. *George* itself is a classic by anyone's reckoning, but the others are also worth a look while you are there.

**Approach (also see page 298)** - Follow the well-marked path under South Gully Buttress up to the face.

**Descent** - Most of the popular routes have fixed anchors. Either abseil from these, or continue to the tree at the top and abseil. Alternatively follow the ridge to the right then scramble and slither back down the gully.

**① Mandarin** . . . . . . . . . . . . . . . . HVS 4c
On the left-hand side of the face is a right-trending overlap. Climb this to its end then pull up to reach a narrow ledge. Climb the wall to a large orifice then trend right to reach the crest of the wall. Finish up the grotty ridge on the right for the full tick, or (more sensibly) escape by abseiling from the tree.
*FA. Paul Nunn, Ken Jones 1970*

**② Brutus** . . . . . . . . . . . . E1 5b
The thin crack that runs up to the grassy col gives a pleasant pitch. Climb the crack to its end at a small overlap then step out right and head for the ridge and the abseil tree.
*FA. Pete O'Donovan, Mark Stokes 1976*

**③ There Will Be Blood** 8a
Start up *Caesar* (wires) then move out onto the smooth wall and climb this with great difficulty on a series of razor edges.
*FA. Mark Pretty 2010*

**④ Caesar** . . . . . . . . E4 6a
The thin seam running up to the right-hand edge of the col gives a fierce pitch, with a short blank section passed by determined finger jamming. An upper pitch up the groove right of the arete doesn't add a lot to the experience; send up your hapless second-man, abseil off or use the lower-off to the left.
*FA. John Codling, Chris Calow 1978*

**⑤ George** . . . . . . . . . . . Top 50 E1 5b
One of the best routes in the Dale - a big pitch, steep sustained and in a superb situation. Several old pegs remain though plenty of more modern alternatives are available. Climb straight up the tricky fingery wall under the base of the slanting fault of *John Peel*. Follow this until it starts to lean to the right when awkward, exposed moves can be made out onto the face on the left. Climb steeply into the long crack and then follow it all the way to the cliff top. Superb.
*FA. Steve Read, Rod Leeming, D.Carnell, P.Brown, S.Hunt mid 1950s*
*FFA. (well almost - 2pts) Paul Nunn, Jeff Morgan 1969*

**⑥ Destot's Gap** . . . . . . . . E5 6c
Bold, devious, desperate and seeing little attention. A direct version would be even harder - but at least it would be logical. Gain the bulging wall by a hard descending traverse from *George* then climb the flake to its end. Swing up left onto the wall then trend back right to rejoin *George*. What a palaver.
*FA. Jim Moran, Geoff Milburn 1983*

**⑦ Bye, George** . . . . . . . . E3 5c
Follow *George* to the base of the long crack then move out left to access a shallow groove. Climb this and grassy rock above to the summit meadows.
*FA. Mark Pretty, Jon Haswell 2003*

**⑧ John Peel** . . . . . . . . HVS 5a
Another classic, taking a long diagonal line and giving strenuous but well-protected climbing with good rests. *Photo on page 278.*
1) 5a, 25m. From a large tree in the gully, trend left to reach the base of the crack (junction with *George*) then climb it as it leans over. Traverse right and climb up to a tiny stance.
2) 5a, 25m. Continue in the same line to where the mighty yew used to be, and finish leftwards to the ridge or abseil from the fixed gear attached to the tree's remains.
*FA. Pete (Trog) Williams, John (who peeled) Amies 1964*

**⑨ Black Flip** . . . . . . . . . . . . E4 6a
A hard route although the 1st pitch is good at HVS 5a.
1) 5a, 22m. Start as for *John Peel* but follow the lower break out right then climb up to the stance under the overlap.
2) 6a, 20m. Pull into the steep groove above and climb it (ancient ironmongery) until it is possible to get out left onto the wall. Continue up this steeply until it eases and finish via grass and some poor rock.
*FFA. John Codling, Steve Allen 1983*
*FA. Paul Nunn, Jeff Morgan (5pts) 1969*

**⑩ Wild Bill** . . . . . . . . . . . . . E2 5c
Climb *John Peel* for 4m then head up the wall to a break and traverse right to the solid tree runner. Step back left and climb straight up to the stance on *John Peel*. Abseil off.
*FA. John Codling, D.Wiggan 1978*

**⑪ Crazy Horse** . . . . . . . . E3 5c
An eliminate, but a good direct line with some fine climbing. Start just left of *Yew Tree Wall* and climb to where *Wild Bill* comes in from the left. Cross this and continue (hard) until it can be rejoined on the right. Follow it for a couple of moves then trend right to join and finish up *Yew Tree Wall*.
*FA. Mark Pretty, Paul Freeman 2007*

**⑫ Yew Tree Wall** . . . . . . . E1 5c
Tricky moves straight up the wall to a solid (non-yew) tree then continue in the same line to a fingery flake. Step right and press on to the remains of the big yew. Escape right along the break, or abseil from the fixed gear. Almost a sport route now with all the threads.
*FA. Paul Nunn, Jeff Morgan (1 sling) 1969*

**⑬ Geronimo** . . . . . . . . . . . . E3 6a
Up *Yew Tree Wall* to the tree then climb the wall to the right until forced back left to rejoin *Y.T.W.*
*FA. Paul Nunn, Jeff Morgan (1 sling) 1969*

**⑭ Orange Peel** . . . . . E3 6a
Long, arduous and rarely done. Not marked on the topo. Start left of *Brutus*, join and follow it to the ridge. Descend 5m then cross the steep wall to reach the base of *George's* crack. Continue down right then across to the stance on *John Peel*. Climb up and right via a shallow groove, traverse right to the end of all things.
*FA. John Codling, Chris Calow, Pete Douglas 1978*

## South Gully Buttress

The last of the Tissington Spires is known as South Gully Buttress. The routes described here vary from the classically mild to the modern desperate but none of them are outstanding.

**Approach (also see page 314) -** Direct from the main path.
**Descent -** From the top of the pinnacle, a short downclimb gains the gully below John Peel Wall. It is also possible to abseil.

**❶ Zulu Dawn** . . . . . . . .  **E5 6b**
Hard work, though it has a load of fixed gear. The rounded arete of the buttress is climbed initially on the right to bulges. Swing left, then power up the steep wall by sustained climbing on spaced holds.
*FA. Gary Gibson 1985*

**❷ And the Weather** . . . . . . . **E1 5b**
The bulging wall left of the main groove is climbed via the wide crack to reach the bulges. Cross these on the right via a short and strenuous crack, then step left and climb the wall to a right-trending crack. Finish up this.
*FA. Gary Gibson 1982*

**❸ Dr Livingstone** . . . . . . . . **VS 4b**
The deep groove is less of a darkest Africa experience than you might expect. Climb steeply into the groove, then bridge up to the roof (loose blocks) which is passed on the right to a stance. Step left and finish up the easier groove. Abseil or scramble down the short back wall.
*FA. Tony Howard, Tony Nicholls, Bill Tweedale 1963*

**❹ Stanley Wall** . . . . . . . . . . . . **VS 4c**
Follow the wide crack right of the arete, then move right to another crack in the wall to the right until the stance on *Dr Livingstone* is reached. Finish up this. Grassy. Descend as for *Dr Livingstone*.
*FA. Tony Howard, Tony Nicholls, Bill Tweedale 1963*

**❺ The Mystery Tour** . . . . . . . . . **HS 4b**
A natural extension to the previous routes for those who crave more of a wilderness experience. From the belay on the col, climb down 5m, then traverse the wall to the left before climbing up to a small overhang. Continue left to reach the far arete. Scramble up this to the top.

North
Southwest
Southeast
Wolfscote Dale
Manifold Valley
Beeston Tor
Dovedale

The Watchblock Buttress is typical of the climbing in Dovedale - an isolated wall with excellent rock and a handful of great routes. The best of these is *Adjudicator Wall* (E3 5c) - *page 311* - a classic rising diagonal line with absorbing climbing. Here Rik Battye sets out across the first tricky section. Photo: Mike Hutton

## Dovedale Church

Dovedale Church East Face has a great selection of routes ranging from the amiable VS 4c of *Snakes Alive*, through to the fierce E6 6b of *Amazona* and with a fair bit in between. Once you start exploring the labyrinthine delights of the inner sections, there are plenty more routes to be found although none are of the quality of the routes on the main face. In recent years the place has seen little traffic and some of the routes have become overgrown.

**Approach (also see page 298)** - For this one you have to get your feet wet. The Church is located slightly upstream from Tissington Spires on the opposite bank of the river to the main path. Wade the river at a diagonal weir, slightly upstream from the crag, and fight your way through the undergrowth to its base.

**Conditions** - The main face catches the morning sun only and is well sheltered from wind. There is some seepage and the place makes a good summer retreat in hot weather.

Wade the river at the diagonal weir

N

Map not to scale

*The first routes listed are the ones tucked around the back of the pinnacles. They are all around 10m to 14m long and marked on the plan map starting with the two on the downstream face.*

**1 Bob Can't Cope** . . . . . . . . . . . E3 5b
The centre of the face on the left and the grotty arete left are not especially edifying.
*FA. Nick Dixon 1983*

**2 Bob Hope** . . . . . . . . . . . . . . . E2 5b
Climb the wall trending right to the arete then step back left and finish direct.
*FA. Gary Gibson, Derek Beetlestone, Phil Gibson 1980*

*The route* **Meeting Across the River, E4 6a**, *used to take a line up the sidewall of the back pinnacle but it is now overgrown.*

**3 Crypt Route** . . . . . . . . . . . S 4a
Creep up the rib left of the arch until it is possible to step into the chimney. Bridge up this and through the eye-hole to emerge on the other side of the cliff. Top out to a sling belay.

**4 No Turning Back** . . E5 6b
The crack in the wall right of the arch of *Crypt Route* is gained by a steep bulging wall (three bolts). Climb the crack on wires to finish over the roof (and up the grass). Harder for the short. It is possible to obtain a rest by using *Crypt Route* behind you.
*FA. Andy Taylor, Alison Taylor, Malc Taylor 1992*

**5 Sold Down the River** . . . . . . E5 6b
Connect two flakes in the rear pillar of the back pinnacle, to the left of the arch. An ancient thread marks the line and this is usually pre-clipped from the left.
*FA. Gary Gibson 1984*

**6 Unknown** . . . . . . . . . . . . . . . ?
*A bolted line for which no further details are known.*

**7 French Technique** . . . . . 7a
A very short route up the red wall opposite the window in the back pinnacle. Two bolts lead to an old lower-off.
*FA. Malcolm Taylor 1988*

**8 American Style** . . . E4 6b
The once-pegged crack is short but action packed. It gives well-protected but arduous finger-jamming and laybacking and is about as American as Bakewell Tart.
*FFA. Keith Sharples 1982. Previously aided.*

**9 Bolt it and Believe it** . . . 7c
Short and sharp climbing up the wall left of *Tales of the Riverbank*. Two bolts and a peg to a lower-off.
*FA. Mark Pretty 1988*

**10 Tales of the Riverbank** . E5 6a
A superb sustained pitch, on which the gear is perfect, but hard work to place. A loose wall (old peg and good small wires) leads to the bulge that guards the crack, pull over this then press on rapidly up the soaring line. A couple of bridged rests are available for the long legged but the ability to press on will be found of more use.
*FFA. (nearly) John Fleming, Chris Calow (1pt) 1978. FFA. Ron Fawcett 1978*
*FA. Steve Read, Roy Leeming, Derek Carnell, Phil Brown, Steve Hunt 1950s*

**11 Pogles' Wood** . . . . . . . . . . E4 6a
Climb direct up some flakes from *Tales* to join *The Rattler*.
*FA. Neil Foster 1988*

**12 The Rattler** . . . . . . HVS 5b
Start up *Anaconda* but move out left to a good crack and follow this to the ledges above.
*FA. Bill Wintrip 1988. Much of this was the original line for Anaconda.*

**13 Anaconda** . . . . . . . . . . E1 5b
A good climbs that snakes about less than you might be expecting. Bridge and jam the long groove up to the overhang then pass this with difficulty to gain the continuation corner. Continue up the crack, eventually stepping right to finish on the grassy crest. There are abseil anchors up there, honest.
*FA. Roy Leeming (1pt aid) 1965. The original finish moved left above the roof to join what is now The Rattler.*

**14 Phil's Route** . . . . . . . . E2 5c
A magnificent line, great for aficionados of slippery limestone fist-jamming. Follow the crack-line throughout. The main difficulties are concentrated in passing the lip of the biggest roof. Marks will be deducted for shoddy style, use of knees and any squealing.
*FA. Steve Read, Roy Leeming, Derek Carnell, Phil Brown, Steve Hunt (aid) 1956. Phil Brown returned 25 years later to attempt the route free. Unfortunately he fell off*

**Descent -** The grassy island in the sky of the main summit is best quitted by abseil. There is a fixed belay on the back (west) side of the pinnacle and a tree above *Snakes Alive* and *Amazonia*.

Morning | 35 min | Sheltered | Seepage

30m

30m

*Jungle Land - p.322*

North
Southwest
Southeast
Wolfscote Dale
Manifold Valley
Beeston Tor
Dovedale

**15 Jungle Land** . . .  **E5 6b**
A big butch pitch through the right-hand side of the roof and with plenty of relics from the iron age. Climb the wall to the roof then power through this and the smaller overhang above until it is possible to move right to finish up cracks in the airy arete, first on the right then the left. Move right to the tree and abseil.
*FFA. Dominic Lee 1982. FA. Steve Read and others 1950s*

**16 Amazona.** . . . . . **E6 6c**
Start up *Snakes Alive* then make a desperate traverse left into a thin crack. Climb the crack and continue up the smooth wall above, using a line of barely adequate pockets, that lead up and right to a belay on a small tree.
**Wild Country, E5 6c -** Join the start of *Amazona* with the finish of *Jungle Land*. It has been superseded by the former.
*FA. Dominic Lee, Daniel Lee 1982. FA. (Wild Country) John Codling, R.Cope (tension) 1979. FFA. Dominic Lee, Daniel Lee 1982*

**17 Snakes Alive** . . . . . . . . . . **VS 4c**
The soaring groove is the main feature of this side of The Church. Bridge up it, passing the bulge on the left, to reach ledges complete with belay/abseil pegs.
*FA. Pete Williams, John Amies 1963*

**18 Judge Jeffries** . . . . . . **HVS 5c**
Links the groove of *Snakes Alive* with the right-hand arete by an interesting traverse. From 3m up the groove, head right until the final section of *Quiet Life* can be used to reach the tree.
*FA. John Codling, Dave Jones 1979*

**19 Quiet Life** . . . . . . . . . **E3 6a**
The elegant scoops in the right-hand side of the wall succumb to technical bridging. Descent is awkward - best continue upwards to find a substantial tree to abseil from.
*FA. Chris Calow, N.Channon 1977*

**20 Blue Sister** . . . . . . . . . **E4 6a**
An eliminate though with some good climbing. Start up *Quiet Life* but gain the face on the left at the earliest opportunity. Move left then climb the face centrally before trending back right to the top of *Quiet Life*.
*FA. Gary Gibson 1983*

Sun and shade | 35 mins | Sheltered

*Phil's Route - p.320*

North

Southwest

Southeast

Wolfscote Dale

Manifold Valley

Beeston Tor

Dovedale

Gus Hudgins on *Eye of the Tiger* (E7 6c) - *page 306* - on Ilam Rock in Dovedale. Photo: David Simmonite

North
Southwest
Southeast
Turkey Dip
Masson Lees
?ic Tor
Lorry Park Q.
High Tor
Long Tor Q.
Wildcat
Willersley
Colehill Q.
Harborough
Brassington
Ripley Hill

The climbing at Wildcat usually involves slightly indifferent starts, which are often dank due to the tree cover, but build to excellent upper sections with fine moves in dramatic situations. Here Dom Sellars moves into the sun on *Sphynx* (VS 5a) - *page 371* - High Crag at Wildcat. Photo: Dan Lane

# Matlock Area
## Turkey Dip, Masson Lees
## Pic Tor, Lorry Park Quarry
## High Tor, Long Tor Quarry
## Wildcat, Willersley

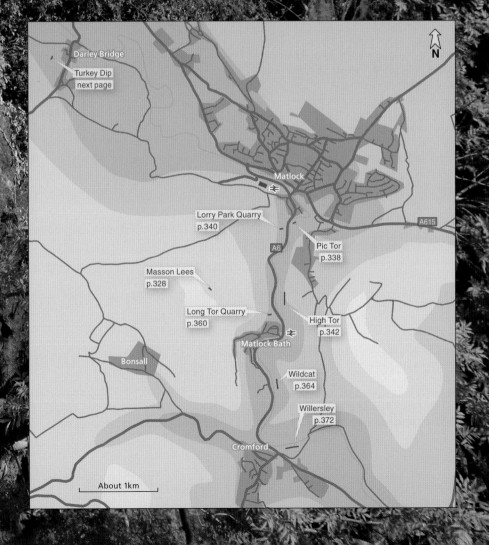

Darley Bridge

Turkey Dip
next page

N

Matlock

Lorry Park Quarry
p.340

Pic Tor
p.338

A6

A615

Masson Lees
p.328

Long Tor Quarry
p.360

High Tor
p.342

Matlock Bath

Bonsall

Wildcat
p.364

Willersley
p.372

Cromford

About 1km

North | Southwest | Southeast | Turkey Dip | Masson Lees | Pic Tor | Lorry Park Q. | High Tor | Long Tor Q. | Wildcat | Willersley | Coldhill Q. | Harborough | Brassington | Hipley Hill

| | No star | ✪ | ✪✪ | ✪✪✪ |
|---|---|---|---|---|
| **up to 4+** | - | - | - | - |
| **5+ to 6a+** | 1 | - | - | - |
| **6b to 7a** | - | - | - | - |
| **7a+ and up** | - | 7 | 3 | - |

A hidden and secluded crag, with a small selection of hard and harder routes. The crag has been climbed on for well over 20 years. It is likely that the first free routes here were predated by aid ascents of the most obvious crack-lines - these were then freed in 1987. More recently, the place has been given a complete overhaul and it is now well worth a visit by anyone looking for steep routes in the high 7s and above.

## Approach   Also see map on page 325

The GPS indicated is roadside parking for a couple of cars. From here walk back towards the village to locate a gate on the right (Private Property sign). If there isn't space here then there is limited parking in Darley Bridge - **please park considerately** - and walk along Oldfield Lane for 180m from the village square to the third gate on the left. This gives access to a good gravel track running into the woods. Follow the track into the woods for around 240m, until it splits just before a footbridge. As the path runs round the side of the pond, take the left-hand fork, then scramble up the bank on the right to locate the cliff - well-hidden.

Simon Wren cruising up *Pedal to the Metal* (7b+) - *opposite*. Photo: David Bond

## Conditions

The crag is exceptionally sheltered by the surrounding trees and its overhanging nature. It gets little sun, and will stay dry in the rain. By the same logic, it will be slow to dry once it gets properly wet-through.

## Access

The crag is an amazingly secluded setting, overlooking a pond deep in a wood. The wood is actually a plantation owned by H.J. Enthoven & Sons, who have a large industrial setup on the opposite side of the main road. Signs by the gate and again at the cliff suggest that climbing isn't tolerated here. The crag is listed here for completeness.

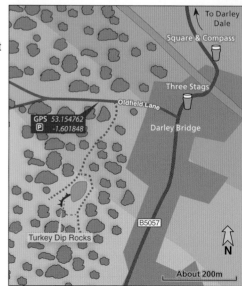

North
Southwest
Southeast
Turkey Dip
Masson Lees
Pic Tor
Lorry Park Q.
High Tor
Long Tor Q.
Wildcat
Willersley
Colehill Q.
Harborough
Brassington
Hipley Hill

**14m**

**14m**

**14m**

Not much sun | 10 min | Sheltered | Seepage | Dry in the rain

**❶ Land of the Lost** .. 🔲 8a+
Short and very bouldery. Start on the left slab briefly, before moving right along the break and then climb desperately up the white wall above using small crimps and poor slopers.
*FA. Jon Clark 2008*

**❷ Back to the Future** . 🔲 7c+
A good pitch, crossing the two cracks. From the left slab, move right along the break, then make bouldery moves to join *Step On It* at the halfway jug. Move right again (crux) using a small crimp, to finish up *The Land That Time Forgot*.
*FA. Jon Clark 2008*

**❸ Step on It** ..... 🔲 7c+
A fine, sustained classic up the searing crack-line. Fiercely technical, pumpy and fingery too.
*FA. Malcolm Taylor 1987*

**❹ The Land that Time Forgot** 🔲 7c
The crack to the right may be marginally easier.
*FA. Darren Hawkins 1987*

**❺ Animal Antics** .......... 🔲 7b+
The steeply-leaning groove is often wet. Move out right from the previous route, then climb the groove and the hanging block.
*FA. Chris Plant 1987*

**❻ Pedal to the Metal** ....... 🔲 7b+
A right-hand finish gives a better (and harder) climb. From the jug in the groove, swing right to access the front of the leaning prow. Only the crux remains, pinch your way to glory.
*Photo opposite.*
*FA. Jon Clark 2007*

**❼ Onslaught** ....... 🔲 8a
Start up *Animal Antics* to the jugs in the groove, then make bold and desperate moves right around the bulging arete. Ape rapidly along the lip of the roof to finish at *Unleashed*'s lower-off.
*FA. Jon Clark 2007*

**❽ Unleashed** ......... 🔲 7c
Start up the big black groove on the right, and cross the roof with difficulty to jugs, then take the easier groove above.
*FA. Jon Clark 2007*

**❾ Overkill** ........ 🔲 8a
Up *Unleashed* to the jugs, reverse *Onslaught* and finish up *Pedal To The Metal* for a full body workout.
*FA. Jon Clark 2008*

**❿ Annihilator** ......... 🔲 7c+
Taxing climbing up the right-hand wall of the big groove, accessing the hanging niche provides the main difficulties.
*FA. Jon Clark 2007*

**⓫ Beat It** ................. 🔲 6a+
The warm-up for the crag is nothing special.
*FA. Jon Clark 2007*

North
Southwest
Southeast
Turkey Dip
Masson Lees
Pic Tor
Lorry Park Q.
High Tor
Long Tor Q.
Wildcat
Willersley
Colehill Q.
Harborough
Brassington
Hipley Hill

Alison Martindale on *Pocket Rocket* (6c) - *page 332* - at Masson Lees. Photo: Mark Glaister
As with many of the limestone quarries, the rock quality is not always the best, but the presence of bolts means the routes see plenty of traffic which keeps them relatively clean. Care is needed though, especially here at Masson Lees due to the friable nature of the rock.

| | No star | | | |
|---|---|---|---|---|
| **up to 4+** | 4 | 2 | - | - |
| **5+ to 6a+** | 9 | 4 | - | - |
| **6b to 7a** | 20 | 19 | - | - |
| **7a+ and up** | 2 | 15 | - | - |

The Peak District is riddled with old quarries, many provide climbers with sport but a lot of these are not the nicest places to spend time. Masson Lees is a bit of an exception and is far and away the most pleasant of all the recent discoveries. It was first developed by Gary Gibson in 2004 and he pretty much added all the routes himself with his climbing companions. There are over 70 sport routes here now with good bolts and lower-offs and the quarry has no known access problems at the moment. Wall climbing and strenuous pocket pulling are the main things on the menu.

## Approach    Also see map on page 325

Masson Lees is situated only half a mile from the middle of Matlock, though once in the quarry, you could be a 1000 miles away from the place. From the traffic lights near Sainsbury's in Matlock, follow the new road up the hill for 0.3 miles and turn left on to Snitteton Road. 0.4 miles down here is a sharp right turn onto Salter Lane. Drive up this for almost exactly a mile to a wide opening on the left, the track leading to Low Farm. Park here without restricting access and walk up the track (DO NOT DRIVE UP THE TRACK) and where it bends right continue across the fields, keeping left at a vague fork. The quarry soon appears on the right, walk past the first section and descend into the second one.

## Conditions

The steeper north-facing walls take a lot of drainage, are slow to dry, and only really come into condition from about May onwards. The easier routes on the south-facing walls are almost always in good condition.

## Safety Warning

The rock in the quarry is friable (rather than actually loose) and holds can break without warning. There have been several accidents, seconds need to be extra vigilant when belaying here.

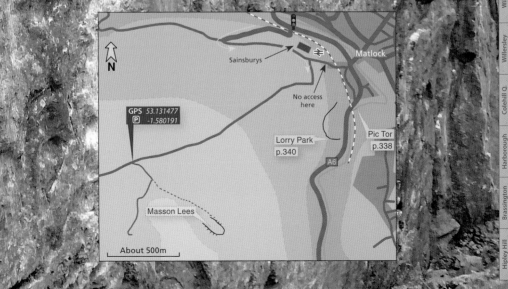

Lorry Park p.340    Pic Tor p.338

North
Southwest
Southeast
Turkey Dip
Masson Lees
Pic Tor
Lorry Park Q.
High Tor
Long Tor Q.
Wildcat
Willersley
Colehill Q.
Harborough
Brassington
Hipley Hill

## Red Wall

On the left-hand side of the quarry at the foot of the descent is a sunny crusty wall with a popular set of easier routes. Some of the rock is loose, care needed **Conditions** - Sunny, sheltered and quick to dry.

**1 Wake Up Call** .... 6b
A hard lower wall and beefy roof make this worth seeking out.
*FA. Gary Gibson, Pete Clark 2004*

**2 Crack o' Dawn** . . . . . . . . . . . . 5
Aim for the groove. Things soon ease.
*FA. Gary Gibson, Pete Clark 2004*

*The next four routes are below some unstable rock which has collapsed on the right-hand side (taking one lower-off with it).*

**3 Mourning has Broken** . . . . . 6a+
*FA. Gary Gibson, Pete Clark 2004*

**4 Slumberland** . . . . . . . . . . . 5
*FA. Gary Gibson, Pete Clark 2004*

**5 Dawn's Chorus** . . . . . . . . . 4+
*FA. Gary Gibson, Pete Clark 2004*

**6 Wake Me Up Before You Go Go**
. . . . . . . . . . . . . . . . . . . . . 4
Finish at the lower-off on *Dawn's Chorus*.
*FA. Gary Gibson, Pete Clark 2004*

**7 Oh to Lie In** . . . . . . . . . . . . 5
*FA. Gary Gibson, Pete Clark 2004*

**8 Sludge Money** . . . . . . . . . . . . 4
*FA. Gary Gibson, Pete Clark 2004*

**9 Five Years and Waiting** . . . . . . 4
*FA. Gary Gibson, Mark Richardson 2009*

*To the right is a better collection of climbs. The first couple pull out of a low cave to start.*

**10 Auto Pilot** . . . . . . . . . . . . 6c
The start is tough, it is easier and looser above.
*FA. Gary Gibson, Ian Milward 2004*

**11 Moov Over** . . . . . . . . 6b
Power out of the cave via a pig (or cow) of a move then weave through the overlaps above. Direct is (a bit) harder.
*FA. Gary Gibson, Ian Milward 2004*

**12 Have a Cow** . . . . . 6a+
Just right of the cave via a faint rib to a big last mooove.
*FA. Gary Gibson, Ian Milward 2004*

**13 Udderley** . . . . . . . . . . . . . 5+
Head up the groove then move left into *Have a Cow*.
*FA. Gary Gibson 2010*

Lots of sun | 10 min | Sheltered

14m

12m

**14 Featherlite Arete** . . . . . . . 6a
The arete of the wall taken on its right-hand side - poor.
*FA. Gary Gibson 2010*

**15 Red and Ribbed for Your Pleasure**
. . . . . . . . . . . . . . 6c
The technical pale wall and groove on the left-hand side of the face has sustained layaway moves and some crusty rock.
*FA. Gary Gibson, Pete Clark 2004*

*The routes to the right are the best and most popular here, though they will always be a bit dusty and crusty.*

**16 Who Sat on my Satsuma?** 6a
Up the left-hand side of the red wall with the odd tricky move linking the mostly good holds.
*FA. Gary Gibson, Pete Clark 2004*

**17 A Life of Grime** . . . . . . 6a
The centre of the wall is nice and sustained and has a long reach or two. Pumpy.
*FA. Pete Clark, Gary Gibson 2004*

**18 Fun in the Sun** . . . . . . . . . 6a+
Possibly the best here. Climb the right-hand arete of the wall to a tricky finale.
*FA. Pete Clark , Gary Gibson 2004*

**19 End o' Taffs Corner** . . . . . . 4
The angular corner right of *Fun in the Sun*. Often dusty.
*FA. Gary Gibson, Ian Milward 2004*

**20 The Chemistry Mates** . . . . . 3
Scramble up the ledgy wall right of the corner.
*FA. Gary Gibson 2010*

**21 Physics Too** . . . . . . . . . . 6b+
This is the longer line up the face slightly up and to the right. Easy and loose ground leads to crux near the top - poor.
*FA. Gary Gibson 2010*

North
Southwest
Southeast
Turkey Dip
Masson Lees
Pic Tor
Larry Park Q.
High Tor
Long Tor Q.
Wildcat
Willersley
Colehill Q.
Harborough
Brassington
Hipley Hill

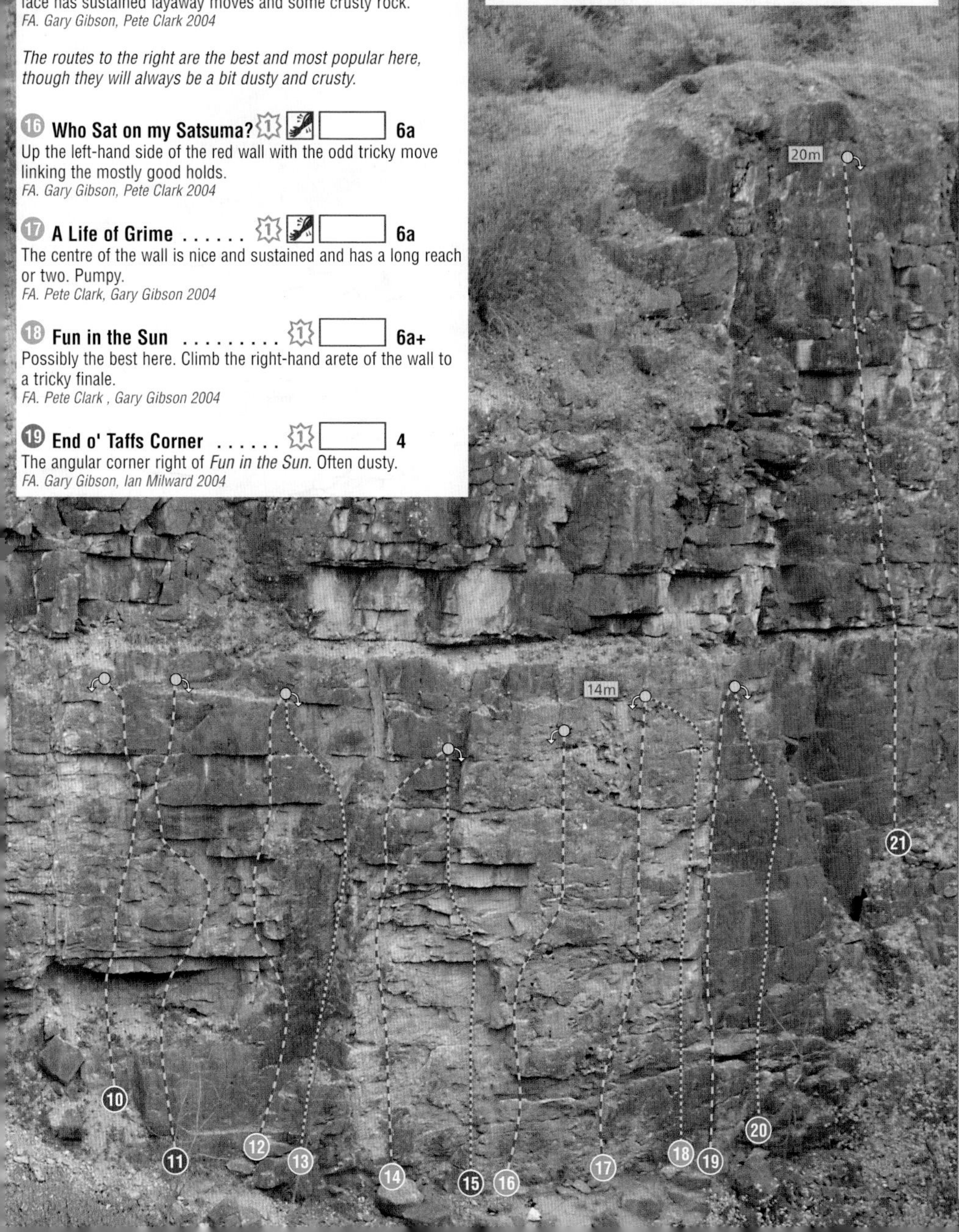

## Overhanging Wall

On the left-hand side of the shady wall is a popular venue with a good set of steep and mostly hard routes. The rock is a bit dusty and soft despite the traffic.

**Conditions -** The crag faces northeast and effectively receives no sun. It also suffers severely from seepage after heavy rain, though once dry (May usually) it can be in condition through to October.

**❶ Reactn** . . . . . . . . . . . . . . . . . . ⬜ 6b+
The hidden groove and wall left of the main arete.
*FA. Gary Gibson, Pete Clark, Roy Thomas, Ian Milward 2004*

**❷ Java Script** . . . . . . 🔆⬜ ⬜ 7a+
The soaring arete has a hard move getting back round right.
*FA. Gary Gibson 2004*

**❸ In the Pocket** . . . . . 🔆⬜⬜ 6c+
A series of good pockets leads to a reachy (especially desperate for the short) finish. Crusty.
*FA. Gary Gibson 2004*

**❹ Pocket Rocket** . . . . 🔆⬜⬜ 6c
Fine steep pocket-pulling via a left-facing flake system.
*Photo on 328.*
*FA. Pete Clark, Gary Gibson 2004*

**❺ Eye, Eye** . . . . . . . 🔆⬜⬜ 6b+
A superb eye-catching pitch via a series of crusty pockets that runs up the leaning wall. Eases with height. *Photo on page 12.*
*FA. Gary Gibson 2004*

**❻ Exorcised** . . . . . 🔆⬜⬜⬜ 7b
Excellent sustained and fingery climbing up the ochre wall. The rock turns a bit dodgy towards the top.
*FA. Gary Gibson, Pete Clark, Nick Taylor 2006*

**❼ Exo6** . . . . . . . . . . 🔆⬜⬜ 7a
More sustained and fingery climbing with some neat manoeuvres up the pale streak. Holds have come and gone.
*FA. Gary Gibson 2004*

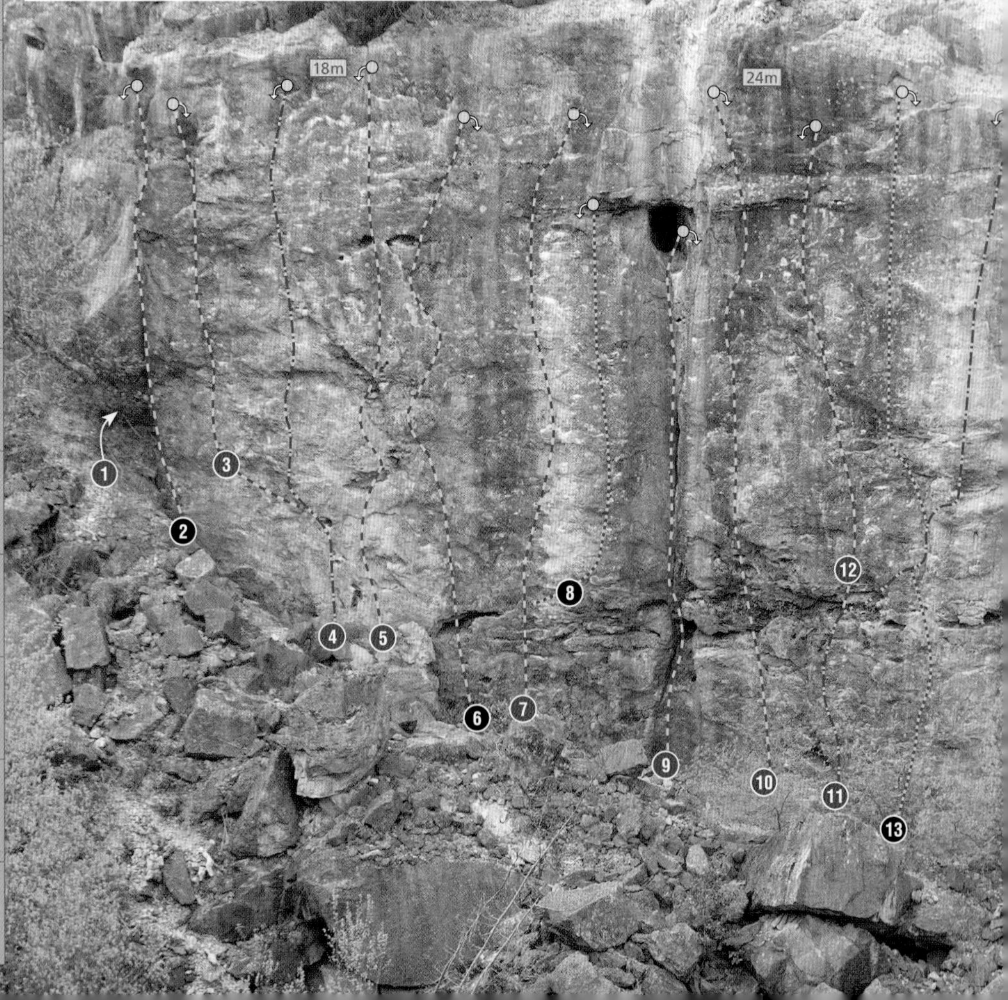

18m

24m

**⑧ Bison Fute** . . . . 7b
Start up the previous route then swing right to tackle the blunt rib left of the long crack-line. Reachy and fingery, though most of the holds are good.
*FA. Gary Gibson 2004*

**⑨ Pierluigi Galena** . . . . . 7a
The long (galena) speckled crack-line gives a couple of big pulls. Can be muddy early in the season.
*FA. Gary Gibson 2004*

**⑩ Second Class Citizen** . . 6c+
More sustained, fingery (and dirty) climbing up the orange face right of the crack. The finish is tricky and often damp too.
*FA. Gary Gibson, Ian Milward, Mark Richardson, M.Elwell, Gordon Jenkin 2006*

Not much sun | 10 min | Seepage | Sheltered

**⑪ Handy Borehole** . . . . . . 6c+
Climb to the break then move out right and head up the fine wall above the prominent borehole. Sustained and good.
*FA. Gary Gibson, Ian Milward 2004*

**⑫ Quatrieme Quartier** 7a
One of the best routes of the grade here with sustained, pumpy climbing on good holds. From the break of *Handy*, move up (crux, reachy) to good holds and continue first leftward then back right to gain the lower-off.
*FA. Gary Gibson 2004*

**⑬ The Premier Club** . . . . . 7a+
Climb the tricky wall rightwards to reach *Handy*'s traverse, do the borehole move, then continue direct via long spans up the steep wall.
*FA. Gary Gibson 2006*

**⑭ The Pete Clark Diaries** . 7a
A difficult lower wall leads leftwards to the break. Climb the wall above to a jug then move right and up on good holds to an easing. Follow the rib/groove to the lower-off.
*FA. Gary Gibson 2004*

**⑮ The Masson Chronicles** 7b
Start as for *The Pete Clark Diaries*, but at the break move right and up the excellent grey rock(!) via some sharp pulls to reach good holds. Finish up *Pete's Diary*.
*FA. Gary Gibson 2008*

**⑯ Nice One Masson** . . . . . 7a+
Climb past the huge orange scar and on up the sustained wall. Care is needed with the rock near the top.
*FA. Gary Gibson 2004*

**⑰ Woof Justice** . . . . . . . . 7a+
Move left out of the groove at a flake and climb the tricky wall to reach a resting ledge. The face above is easier.
**Direct start** - 7a+ for tall people, harder for shorties.
*FA. Pete Clark, Gary Gibson 2004*

**⑱ Grand Theft Auto** . . 7a
The long groove line finishing via the easier wall above. This is a sport route that manages to feel like a trad route.
*FA. Pete Clark, Gary Gibson 2004*

24m

*The Cows, The Cows - p.334*

North | Southwest | Southeast | Turkey Dip | Masson Lees | Pic Tor | Lorry Park Q. | High Tor | Long Tor Q. | Wildcat | Willersley | Colehill Q. | Harborough | Brassington | Hipley Hill

## Black Wall

On the central section of the long shady wall is another set of steep and mostly hard routes. The rock is a bit dusty and soft despite the traffic.

**Conditions -** The crag gets faces northeast and effectively receives no sun. It also suffers severely from seepage after heavy rain, though once dry (May usually) it can be in condition through to October.

**❶ The Cows, The Cows** . . 7a+
Good climbing starting up the right arete of the prominent groove. A technical start leads to easier ground above.
*FA. Pete Clark, Gary Gibson 2004*

**❷ Masson Accomplished** . 7a+
Another good route tackling the full height of the wall. The start is hard, the middle is reachy and the finish is pumpy.
*FA. Nick Taylor, Gary Gibson, Ian Milward, Mark Richardson 2006*

**❸ Unveiled** . . . . . . . . . . 7a
A fingery, reachy start leads to a reachy and sandy finale.
*FA. Gary Gibson 2010*

North
Southwest
Southeast
Turkey Dip
Masson Lees
Pic Tor
Lorry Park Q.
High Tor
Long Tor Q.
Wildcat
Willersley
Colehill Q.
Harborough
Brassington
Hipley Hill

### 4 Seventh Time Lucky . . . 7b
A hard start reaches easier climbing which leads to a long reach to complete the initial difficulties. The extension is **Plucked, 7b+**.
*FA. Gary Gibson 2004. FA. (Plucked) Gary Gibson 2010*

### 5 Never to Rise . . . . . . . 7a+
A difficult start via a faint rib leads to fine technical face climbing and a tough finish; hard for the short. The excellent extension is a good bit harder **Resurrection, 7b+**.
*FA. Gary Gibson 2004. FA. (Resurrection) Jon Clark 2007*

### 6 Long Black Veil . . . 7a+
Start up a left-facing flake then continue up the centre of the fine face above via sustained and very fingery climbing. Another great route, if it is dry - get on it.
*FA. Gary Gibson 2004*

### 7 Fuck Your Gods . . . . . . 7a
The climbing is better than the name, featuring some sustained and fingery moves.
*FA. Nick Taylor, Gary Gibson 2004*

### 8 Cattle Mutilation Expedition 6c+
Good wall climbing with an awkward start and high crux. Sustained but pretty low in the grade.
*FA. Nick Taylor, Gary Gibson, Pete Clark 2004*

### 9 Masson Impossible . . . . . . 6c
The black face has the crux at half-height. Eliminate-ish.
*FA. Nick Taylor, Gary Gibson 2004*

### 10 The Numbers Game . . . . . . 6b
Balance up the shallow groove - a half-height crux again.
*FA. Gary Gibson, Pete Clark 2004*

### 11 Lifelong Learning. . . . . . . . . . . 5+
Another shallow groove with just a couple of tricky moves.
*FA. Gary Gibson, Pete Clark 2004*

### 12 Closing Chapter. . . . . . . . . 6b+
Awkward climbing with one hard move for good measure.
*FA. Gary Gibson, Pete Clark 2004*

### 13 Opening Salvo. . . . . . . . . . 6b+
Trend right up the face to a steeper finale.
*FA. Gary Gibson, Pete Clark 2004*

### 14 Last Offence . . . . . . . . . . . 6b+
Start under the block that overhangs the top of the crag and climb the wall via some reachy moves.
*FA. Gary Gibson 2010*

### 15 Better Luck Next Time Steve 6b+
The short and technical wall on the far right. The start is tricky and the finish is steep.
*FA. Gary Gibson, Pete Clark 2004*

## White Wall

The pale right-hand side of the long shady wall has a selection of routes, several of which follow steep cracks and grooves. The rock is a bit dusty and soft and watch out for the odd loose block.

**Conditions -** The crag faces northeast and effectively receives no sun. It also suffers severely from seepage after heavy rain, though once dry (May usually) it can be in condition through to October.

*On the far left (and just right of the White Wall) is a prominent square arete with two routes.*

**① Maitre d'Hotel** . . . . . . . . . . . . ☐ **6a**
The arete on its left-hand side throughout.
*FA. Gary Gibson, Pete Clark, Nick Taylor 2004*

**② Major Dormo** . . . . . . . . . . . . . ☐ **5**
The scruffy right-hand side of the arete has tricky initial moves.
*FA. Gary Gibson, Pete Clark, Nick Taylor 2004*

**③ Four by Four** . . . . . . . . . . . ☐ **6c+**
The steep wall above the ledge has a tough crux.
*FA. Gary Gibson, Nick Taylor 2008*

**④ Leap of Fete** . . . . . . . . . . ☐ **7a**
A dyno to start and some neo-gritstone weirdness to finish.
*FA. Gary Gibson 2008*

**⑤ Tapering Out** . . . . . . . ☐ **7a**
Gain the narrowing groove with difficulty. Finish up the wall and crack above by some worrying moves.
*FA. Gary Gibson 2004*

**⑥ Last Orders** . . . . . . ☐ **6c**
A hard start from a rocky ledge gains easier ground.
*FA. Gary Gibson, Mark Richardson 2004*

**⑦ Smear for yer Beer** . . . . . . ☐ **7b**
The lower wall leads to a ledge and a desperate finale.
*FA. Gary Gibson 2004*

**⑧ Calling Time** . . . . . . . . ☐ **7a+**
Steady wall climbing leads to another tough finish.
*FA. Gary Gibson 2004*

**⑨ Lager than Life** . . . . . . . . . ☐ **7b**
A hard start leads to more of the same.
*FA. Gary Gibson 2009*

**⑩ Leffe and Out** . . . . . . . . . . . ☐ **6b+**
Tackle the front face of the big flake via the odd nice move.
*FA. Gary Gibson 2010*

**⑪ From Beer to Eternity** . . . . . . . . ☐ **7a**
Stagger up the left-slanting flake to hard moves above.
*FA. Gary Gibson 2009*

14m

North
Southwest
Southeast
Turkey Dip
Masson Lees
Pic Tor
Lorry Park Q.
High Tor
Long Tor Q.
Wildcat
Willersley
Colehill Q.
Harborough
Brassington
Hipley Hill

**⑫ The Crash Test Dummies** 7a
The first of three longer wall climbs. A long stretch is required to pass the bulge at the top. A bit snappy.
*FA. Gary Gibson 2004*

**⑬ Bish, Bash, Bosch .** 6c
The long thin crack in the wall gives a worthwhile pitch.
*FA. Gary Gibson 2010*

**⑭ Twist of Feet . . . . .** 7a+
The wall between the two crack-lines has hard moves, especially towards the top. The big loose block is tricky to avoid.
*FA. Gary Gibson 2004*

**⑮ Elbowed Out . . . . .** 6b+
Tackle the imposing flaky crack-system, it gives a worthwhile pitch that is intimidating but low in the grade.
*FA. Gary Gibson 2010*

**⑯ Hilti Sound System** 7a
The wide, pale wall gives fine sustained climbing despite the Sika. It is quite fingery but not too hard for the grade.
*FA. Gary Gibson 2004*

**⑰ Forefinger Exercise . . .** 7a
Head up the thin right-slanting crack, with crux moves where it thins using a sharp-edged hold to bridge the gap.
*FA. Gary Gibson, Nick Taylor 2004*

**⑱ Piano Fingers . . . . . . . . . .** 7a
The shallow leaning groove in the arete gives a tricky pitch that is nearly always dirty.
*FA. Gary Gibson 2004*

*Over the slope to the right is a short wall (7m) with three teeny offerings - not marked on the topo.*

**⑲ The Doldrums . . . . . . . . . . . . .** 6b
The left arete via a yellow scoop.
*FA. Gary Gibson 2009*

**⑳ Hole in the Wall . . . . . . . . . .** 6c+
The central bulges and rib.
*FA. Gary Gibson 2009*

**㉑ Snapping Turtle . . . . . . . .** 7a
A bouldery problem on the right.
*FA. Gary Gibson 2009*

Not much sun | 10 min | Seepage | Sheltered

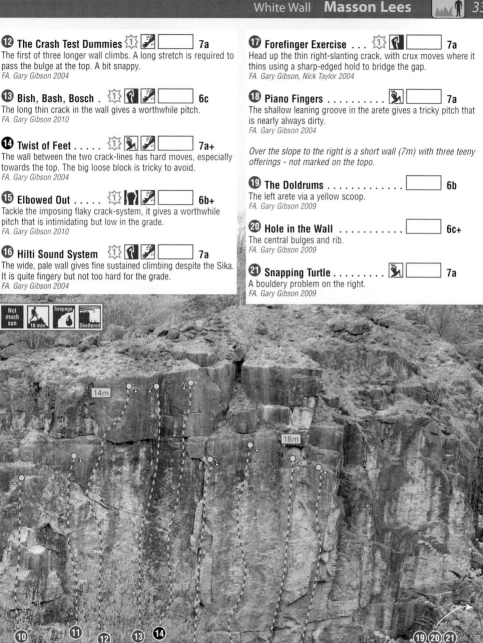

14m · 18m

| | No star | ⚜ | ⚜ | ⚜ |
|---|---|---|---|---|
| **Mod to S** | - | - | - | - |
| **HS to HVS** | - | 3 | - | - |
| **E1 to E3** | 1 | 4 | 3 | - |
| **E4 and up** | 1 | 1 | - | - |

Pic Tor is a small buttress of good quality rock hidden in Matlock, just a short distance from the River Derwent and the A6. The rock is pocketed and the climbing tends to be fingery and sustained. Protection is usually good - bring plenty of small wires. The crag is a level five minute walk from an extensive car park and is a good spot to grab a few routes when passing.

The routes have been popular for years and many of them are rather polished, though this doesn't distract too much from the quality of the climbing.

**Bend Tor -** This small natural crag can be seen from the parking for Pic Tor. It has a handful of routes, including two decent-but-ageing 7a's on the tall white wall on its left-hand side.

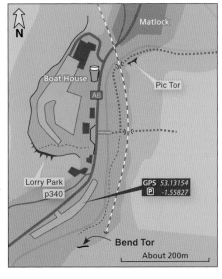

## Approach    Also see map on page 325

From the large public parking (pay) just south of Matlock on the A6, walk back towards Matlock, and cross a large green bridge over the river. On the far side, turn left along the riverside path and continue for 150m. The crag is on the right just after the railway arch.

## Conditions

The crag faces north, and sees little sun, making it a great place for hot summer days. It is very sheltered and slow to dry, although there isn't much seepage.

Graham Parkes climbing *Cistron* (E1 5b) - *opposite* - at Pic Tor. Photo: Chris Craggs

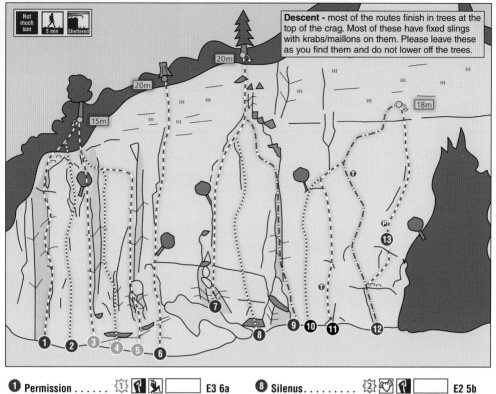

**Descent** - most of the routes finish in trees at the top of the crag. Most of these have fixed slings with krabs/maillons on them. Please leave these as you find them and do not lower off the trees.

**① Permission** ...... 🏃 E3 6a
The flaky rust-coloured arete is fingery, technical and often dirty.
FA. Gary Gibson 1983

**② Sulphur City** ........ E3 6a
Make fingery moves to a ledge - thread. More hard climbing above gains a shallow groove which leads steeply to the top.
FA. Gary Gibson 1983

**③ Big Pig** ........... HVS 5a
The big piggish groove is quite a struggle to a tree.
FA. Steve Read, N.McLoughlin 1962

**④ The Impending Gleam** .... HVS 5a
Climb a shallow groove and blunt arete right of *Big Pig* until forced left below the vegetation to the tree on *Big Pig*.
FA. Adam Hudson, Gary Gibson 1983

**⑤ Burning Spear** .......... HVS 5a
The groove and crack right of the blunt rib leads pleasantly to a grotty exit. It is better to escape left as for the last route.
FA. Gary Gibson, Derek Beetlestone 1980

**⑥ Nosferatu** ............. E2 5c
Climb cracks that lead up to a tree then move left onto the arete and climb this. A direct start up the lower arete is harder.
FA. Gary Gibson, Derek Beetlestone, Alison Hargreaves 1980

**⑦ Cistron** ........... E1 5b
Climb the blocky crack to a prominent solid tree, then the thinner continuation crack that leads into a final easy groove. *Photo opposite*.
FA. Gary Gibson, Derek Beetlestone, Alison Hargreaves 1980

**⑧ Silenus** ......... E2 5b
Fine climbing, mildly bold but the holds and runners keep coming. Climb the bulge and steep slab to a small ledge then trend left via more interesting climbing into the final groove of *Cistron*.
FA. Gary Gibson 1983

**⑨ Erasmus** .......... E2 5c
Climb the shallow groove into the centre of the face (thread) then head into the hanging white corner above. Follow this delicately as it bends leftwards to joint the finish of *Cistron*.
FA. Gary Gibson, Phil Gibson 1980

**⑩ Stenosis** ............. E4 5c
The blunt rib on pockets then trend right into *Diagnosis*. The upper section is becoming overgrown.
FA. Gary Gibson 1985

**⑪ Diagnosis** ....... E4 6a
Climb straight up the wall passing a thin undercut to reach ledges. Trend right to a bolt lower-off.
FA. Gary Gibson 1983

**⑫ Neurosis** .......... E3 6a
From a ledge, enter the shallow groove and climb this to a difficult exit. Finish as for *Diagnosis*.
FA. Gary Gibson 1983

**⑬ Prognosis** ......... E2 5c
The other best route here. Climb the spidery cracks rightwards, passing the bulge (peg) on thin flaky holds. Continue up the face on lumps to the lower-off.
FA. Gary Gibson, Adam Hudson 1983

North
Southwest
Southeast
Turkey Dip
Masson Lees
Pic Tor
Lorry Park Q.
High Tor
Long Tor Q.
Wildcat
Willersley
Colehill Q.
Harborough
Brassington
Hipley Hill

| | No star | | | |
|---|---|---|---|---|
| up to 4+ | - | - | - | - |
| 5+ to 6a+ | - | - | - | - |
| 6b to 7a | 2 | 3 | 1 | - |
| 7a+ and up | 2 | 9 | 3 | - |

This ugly quarry to the south of Matlock is not a very picturesque place with a car park, some collapsed buildings, lots of illegally tipped rubbish and several tottering soil heaps. Luckily there is also an excellent wall of compact rock  which has been developed for hard sport climbing. It was first discovered years ago but the main development took place in the early 1980s when the Lee brothers climbed all the major crack lines to give 6 routes. This failed to grab the imagination and repeats were few and far between. In the late 90s Pete Cresswell came here and plugged the remaining gaps with a good set of hard sport routes. These have now been cleaned up again and a few even harder routes added by Jon Clark.

## Conditions
The quarry faces northeast, gets a bit of morning sun and is very sheltered from the wind. It stays dry in light rain but the finishes become wet very quickly. The trees can make it slow to dry.

## Access
There is no formal access agreement to this quarry and its inclusion in this guide does not imply that you have right of access to climb there. Access could well change since there is currently development happening on the land near the entrance.

## Approach    **Also see maps on pages 325 and 329**
The quarry is situated just south of Matlock off the A6, 200m south of the Boat House pub. Park as for Pic Tor (page 338) and walk back up the road towards Matlock. The entrance to the quarry is on the left, just before some new houses (being built at the time of writing). Various fences discourage you from entering. The wall is on the far side of the quarry.

Simon Wren moving into the upper crack of *Ground Zero* (7c+) - *opposite* - at Lorry Park Quarry. Photo: David Bond

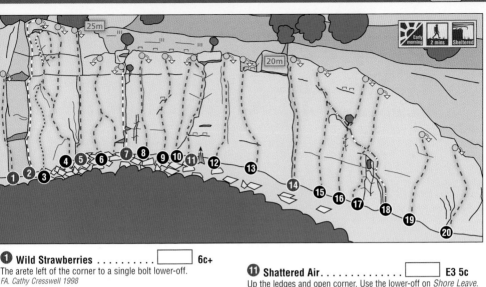

North

Southwest

Southeast

Turkey Dip

Masson Lees

Pic Tor

Lorry Park Q.

High Tor

Long Tor Q.

Wildcat

Willersley

Colehill Q.

Harborough

Brassington

Hipley Hill

**❶ Wild Strawberries** . . . . . . . . . . ☐ **6c+**
The arete left of the corner to a single bolt lower-off.
*FA. Cathy Cresswell 1998*

**❷ On the Road** . . . . . . . . . . . ☐ **E3 5c**
An impressive line up the huge corner. Often damp.
*FA. Dominic and Daniel Lee 1981*

**❸ Ground Zero** . . . . . ☐ **7c+**
The thin wall gives and intense pitch. Continue past the mid-height lower-off to the top for the full tick. *Photo opposite.*
*FA. Jon Clark 2008*

**❹ The Squealer** . . . . . ☐ **7c**
An excellent wall climb. There are two variations.
**Super Direct, 7c+** - break right from the original.
**Direct Finish, 7c+** - straight up from the upper traverse.
*FA. Pete Cresswell 1998. FA. (Finishes) Jon Clark 2009*

**❺ Supercrack** . . . . . . . . . ☐ **7a**
Sustained crack climbing up the thin line with a high crux.
*FA. Dominic and Daniel Lee 1981*

**❻ Dark Matter** . . . . . . ☐ **8b**
Another blank wall climb. Starting from the right is 7c+.
*FA. Jon Clark 2008*

**❼ Edge of Darkness** . . . . . ☐ **6b+**
The clean jamming crack has now been bolted and cleaned.
*FA. Dominic and Daniel Lee 1981*

**❽ Big Spider, Small Bath** ☐ **7b+**
Climb direct to gain a thin crack right of *Edge of Darkness*.
*FA. Pete Cresswell 1996*

**❾ Good Time Emporium** ☐ **7b**
The blank wall past two ledges. The hardest bit is at the bottom but there is another near the top. Staple bolts.
*FA. Pete Cresswell 1996*

**❿ Shore Leave** . . . . . . . . ☐ **7a+**
Technical climbing up the wall left of *Shattered Air*. No bridging allowed into the corner. Staple bolts.
*FA. Pete Cresswell 1996*

**⓫ Shattered Air** . . . . . . . . . . . . . ☐ **E3 5c**
Up the ledges and open corner. Use the lower-off on *Shore Leave*.
*FA. Dominic and Daniel Lee 1981*

**⓬ Deceptive** . . . . . ☐ **7b**
Excellent twin cracks with a tricky section by the second bolt. Much harder than it looks.
*FA. Pete Cresswell 1997*

**⓭ Confidence Trick** ☐ **8a+**
Intense moves up the steep wall.
*FA. Jon Clark 2009*

**⓮ Thunder Road** . . . . . . . ☐ **6c+**
The lone left-facing flake/crack gives sustained pitch.
*FA. Dominic and Daniel Lee 1981*

**⓯ Hell's Angels** . . . . . ☐ **7b**
An intricate lower wall. Staple bolts.
*FA. Pete Cresswell 1998*

**⓰ Sample the Mantel** . . . . ☐ **7b**
A thin wall climb. The mantel is optional.
*FA. Pete Cresswell 1998*

**⓱ Baron Samedi** . . . . . . . ☐ **7b+**
Start up the arete left of the corner of *Desolation Angels*.
*FA. Pete Cresswell 1998*

**⓲ Desolation Angels** . ☐ **E5 6b**
A long diagonal line connecting ledges and flakes with hard moves leads to a tricky finish. A good line and reasonably protected now by bolts on other routes.
*FA. Dominic and Daniel Lee 1981*

**⓳ Game On** . . . . . . . . . ☐ **7a+**
The left-hand of two shorter routes on the far end of the wall.
*FA. Nadim Siddiqui, Dave Simmonite 1997*

**⓴ Go Your Own Way** . . . . . ☐ **7b**
*The last route is much harder than it looks. No grabbing the belay; you have to move past it to get the tick.*
*FA. Nadim Siddiqui 1997*

North

Southwest

Southeast

Turkey Dip

Masson Lees

Pic Tor

Lorry Park Q.

High Tor

Long Tor Q.

Wildcat

Willersley

Colehill Q.

Harborough

Brassington

Hipley Hill

Steve Ramsden on *Original Route* (HVS 5a) - *page 356* -
on the Main face at High Tor. Photo: Adrian Berry
The easiest route on this magnificent sheet of rock is one
of the Peak's premier HVS climbs.

| | No star | ☆ | ☆☆ | ☆☆☆ |
|---|---|---|---|---|
| Mod to S / 4+ | 1 | - | - | - |
| HS-HVS / 5-6a+ | 2 | 1 | 3 | 3 |
| E1-E3 / 6b-7a | 9 | 13 | 2 | 7 |
| E4 / 7a+ and up | 9 | 12 | 10 | 11 |

High Tor is certainly the finest limestone crag in the Peak and is up there with any in the UK for the quality of its climbs. The Main Face is criss-crossed by a magnificent set of multi-pitch outings of stunning quality. The entry tariff for this feast is HVS, but once you get a foot in the door, have no doubt, you will be back for more. As well as the vertical lines, there are also some superb diagonals that sweep majestically across the face, linking unlikely weakness and prolonging the usual pleasure. Many of the pitches here are very big, ensure you bring a large enough rack and plenty of extenders. The far left-hand side of the Main Face has a few slightly easier offerings, as well as a set of butch routes that tackle the impressive overhangs. As an added bonus, there are also the wings - the Left offers routes as good as many of the other buttresses in this book, and the far right has a spanking new set of sport routes.

## Approach     Also see map on page 325

If you drive down the A6, just north of Matlock Bath, then you can't miss High Tor towering above the road. The station car park (pay) is the best place to leave your car at busy times. At less busy times there is a small layby that often has space, about 50m north of where the cable cars cross the road on the A6. Also, roadside parking is allowed on the A6 itself, starting opposite the layby and running towards Matlock. Head towards the cable car station and go around the back of it and follow a path up leftwards to the base of the crag (the main path heads up right to the summit).

It is also possible to approach from Starkholmes. Drive from Matlock to Starkholmes, and park at the brow of the hill on the main road. Walk down High Tor Road (no parking here) and go through the gate. This track leads to the summit, or follow the descent path to reach the crag base.

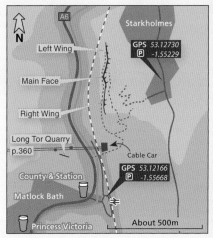

## Conditions

The westerly aspect gives shade until midday, after that the sun swings round and the heat can become a problem later in the day in the summer months. In cooler weather, the crag can be windy but there is little seepage and the face dries fast. There is also no shelter in the rain despite the big caves on the left-hand side of the Main Face especially as westerly winds tend to blow rain onto the face.

## The Left Wing

This is the little brother to the Main Face but it still has some top-notch routes and would rate as a fine crag in its own right were it anywhere else. As it is, it often gets forgotten by climbers who are distracted by the rock to the right. If you do manage to make the effort then you will be rewarded with some fine pitches, but be careful on the loose bands of rock at the top and bottom of the face.
**Approach** - Continue under the Main Face for another minute to arrive at the Left Wing. Some of the routes need a loose scramble to reach the start.
**Descent** - This is awkward and the most reliable is to abseil down the Main Face (see page 352). Also the tree above *V2* is solid enough for abseiling from but ropes will be hard to pull.

*The first seven routes start from a ledge. This can be reached by a steep scramble from below, or an abseil from above.*

**① World's End** . . . . . . . . 🔒 🪣 ☐ **E4 6a**
The first in a series of quality E4s is probably the easiest of the bunch. Start at the far left-hand end of the grassy ledge and climb a crack to a peg. Follow a flake above then trend rightwards (peg) to a grassy finish.
**New World Order, E1 5b** - break left from the peg to an undercut crack and corner on the left.
*FA. Jim Moran, John Reagan 1976*
*FA. (NWO) Geoff Hornby, Suzi Sammut, Mark Turnbull, Simon Lee 1992*

**② No Entry** . . . . . . . . . . . . . 🔒 ☐ **E4 6a**
The second E4 is also at the lower end of the grade. From the middle of the grassy ledge, pull over a small bulge and climb a crack to a peg. Move up, using holds on the right, to an undercut flake. Place some wires and motor up the wall above past a thread to a junction with *World's End*.
*FA. Gary Gibson, Tony Penning, Chris Court 1985*

**③ China Spring** . . . . . . . . 🔒 🪣 ☐ **E4 6a**
High in the grade but consensus suggests that it is probably not really E5. Start at the right-hand end of the grass ledge. Climb a groove (peg) then move left and back right to the break (cam 3 useful on the crux). Continue up the two wobbly grooves above to a grassy finish.
*FA. Pete Livesey, Steve Foster 1976*

**④ Yellow Brick Road** . . . . 🔒 🪣 ☐ **E4 6b**
Another E4 with a hard but well-protected crux move. From the right-hand end of the ledge, clip the peg on *China Spring* then move up rightwards to a big flake. Climb the left-hand edge of this to a hole at the break (peg). Pull up the wall above, just right of the arete, to a peg. Hard moves lead up to easier ground.
*FA. John Codling, T.Saunders 1981*

**⑤ Amber Gambler** . . . . . . 🔒 🪣 ☐ **E4 6a**
The best climb on the Left Wing, with magnificent moves and few rests. From the right-hand end of the ledge, move up rightwards to a big flake (as for *Yellow BR*). Climb the right-hand side of the flake (peg) using a thin crack to gain a hole in the break. Climb up and right from the hole and follow a line leftwards past a flake to finish slightly more easily, eventually reaching grassy ground.
**Beep, E5 6a** - continue traversing right along the break until a hard move can be made direct into the upper groove of *M1*.
*FA. (AG and Beep) John Codling, Steve Allen, Nigel Riddington 1982*

**⑥ A6** . . . . . . . . . . . . . . . 🔒 🪣 ☐ **E4 6a**
A long and devious pitch which is rarely done nowadays despite lots of good climbing. Follow *Amber Gambler* to the hole, then traverse the break rightwards to reach the flakes that now form the upper section of *Roadrunner*. Finish up this.
*FA. Phil Burke 1979. Freed the upper part of the aid route Extender.*

**⑦ High Torquing** . . . . 🔒 🪣 🪣 ☐ **7c+**
A free version of the aid route *Extender*, which goes where *Roadrunner* wanted to go. Fully bolted to the junction with *Roadrunner*. Lower-off here or continue the upper section of *A6*.
*FA. Malcom Taylor 1988*

**⑧ Roadrunner** . . . . . . 🔒 🪣 🪣 ☐ **E6 6b**
A sustained traverse with reasonable protection. Start up the groove of *M1* and, at the bulge, hand-traverse left (large cam useful) past a bolt to reach a short vertical flake. Pull onto this and continue up and left to a thread. Pull into the crack above (good wire below a poor peg) and continue left to a good rest at the base of the prominent groove. Move up and then left (thin) to the lower-off on *High Torquing*. Finish up *A6* or move left to the finish of *Amber Gambler*.
*FA. Ron Fawcett 1981*

**⑨ Wil E. Coyote** . . 🔒 🪣 🪣 🪣 ☐ **7c+**
A good hard pitch crossing *M1*. Follow *Roadrunner* until you are a couple of metres across its traverse. Then make some desperate moves (8a for the short?) on undercut monos direct up the wall to reach the traverse of *M1*, passing 4 bolts. Continue more easily, directly through the roofs to below unstable ground. Lower off from here - a 60m rope is needed to reach the ground.
*FA. Simon Lee, Geoff Hornby 1992*

**⑩ M1** . . . . . . . . . . . . 🔒 🪣 🪣 ☐ **E2 5b**
A fantastic route for the grade taking a strong line up the shield with varied climbing in a superb position. Best done as described, in one pitch, but careful rope work will be needed to avoid drag around the roof. Any in-situ gear should not be trusted, but natural protection is plentiful. Climb the groove, strenuous, but with rests, taking care gaining the sloping ledge (possible belay). Move diagonally left to clear the roof and finish more easily up the groove, which is a touch loose. There is a park-bench belay 15m back from the edge, but it is a stretch to reach it with 50m ropes.
*FFA. Ed Ward-Drummond, Bruce Campbell-Kelly 1969*
*FA. Tom Proctor, Keith Myhill (1pt) 1968*
*FA. Doug Scott, Claud Davies (A1) 1961*

**Approach from Main Face**

North
Southwest
Southeast
Turkey Dip
Masson Lees
Pic Tor
Lorry Park Q.
High Tor
Long Tor Q.
Wildcat
Willersley
Colehill Q.
Harborough
Brassington
Hipley Hill

### 11 Mad Max . . . . . . E6 6b

Once one of the most serious routes on British limestone, originally sieged over two days and done in two pitches. Following a clean up and gear replacement, it is now a hard (E6/7b+) but a fairly well-protected climb of the highest quality, done in one huge pitch. Starting just right of M1, climb a wall to reach and climb a desperate bouldery groove then move left to a runner and rest in M1. Move out right and up the shallow groove and trend right up the wall on pockets (bolt) heading for a peg with a tape and junction with V2. Climb back left with difficulty passing a pair of pegs and an awkward to clip and easy to miss bolt. Pull blindly through the bulges above (further bolts) trending left and then direct to finish, avoiding the loose bits.

*FA. Dominic Lee, Daniel Lee 1983. The regrading of this route made it the first E7 in the Peak, predating Moffatt's Verbal Abuse on Raven Tor. The grade reflected the poor gear (ancient aid bolts) in the upper section. Cleaned again and climbed as described by Graham Hoey in 2004.*

### 15 Lay-by . . . . . . . . . . . . . . HVS 5b

Start left of an ivy-covered tree at the right-hand end of the wall. Climb the corner to a possible belay under the overhang. Follow the groove above then trend left across the wall.

*FA. P.Thompson 1960s*

### 16 Once in a Millennium . . . . . E3 6a

A rockfall may have altered this route - care required. From under the overhang on Lay-by, move left until you are below a groove. Climb this, and the roofs above (2 pegs), to easier ground. Wander across rightwards to finish.

*FA. Gary Gibson, Geraldine Taylor 1985. Gary's 1000th new route.*

### 12 V2 . . . . . . . . . . . . . . . . E5 6b

A worthwhile companion to Delta-G with some extending moves between spaced gear. Slightly marred by the crucial chipped holds. From the peg in the groove of Delta-G stretch left for a handy slot. Pull around and make hard moves up the wall to a poor rest in the scoop of Mad Max. Make a fluttery move up to the break (peg with thread). Then tackle the roofs above with a hard move past a bolt to gain easier ground above. From a thread trend right for the cleanest finish.

*FA. Gary Gibson, Jim Lockett, John Codling 1986*

### 13 Delta-G . . . . . . . . . . . E4 6a

The excellent narrow groove is harder than it looks; tricky to enter (peg in the groove) and desperate to leave. Eventually it spits you out with some haste up the wall to the break. There is an independent and tottery direct finish but it is a much better plan to move right into Entropy to finish.

*FA. Chris Jackson, D.Edwards, Bob Conway 1981*

### 14 Entropy . . . . . . . . VS 4c

A fine route up the long flake/corner towards the right-hand side of the wall. Big cams help along the way or just attack the bold layback with gusto.

*FA. Harry Smith, Hugh Banner 1961*

### 17 The Girdle Traverse . . E5 6b

A great challenge but unfortunately, in its totality, not a great climb. The best pitches are 2, 3, 9 and 10 (the latter two being Debauchery in reverse and Delicatessen). Start on the ledge, as for World's End.

**1) 5c, 20m.** Follow World's End to the break then traverse right to reach the hole on Amber Gambler.

**2) 6b, 16m.** Continue along the break in a magnificent position (well pumpy) then reverse M1 to the small ledge.

**3) 6a, 20m.** Climb back up to the break and continue the traverse all the way to the Entropy flake. Drop down to a belay.

**4) 6a, 18m.** Easier moves lead across Lay-by. Climb up this then move right to a small ledge.

**5) 5b, 12m.** A bad pitch on grassy rock. Take the easiest line rightwards moving slightly up to gain a ledge.

**6) 5a, 18m.** Keep going across more grassy rock to the big gully (High Tor Gully). Drop down to belay.

**7) 4c, 40m.** Drop down and right and pick up a break which leads across into Skylight.

**8) 4b, 35m.** Climb up Skylight into the chimney then go diagonally across the wall, moving up to a hanging belay in a break.

**9) 5b, 24m.** Traverse rightwards to reach Debauchery. Reverse this to its stance.

**10) 5b, 24m.** Move right to Original Route and up to its belay. This is pitch 3 of Delicatessan.

**11) 5a, 12m.** Finish as for Original Route.

*FFA. Pete Livesey, Pete Gomersall 1976. FA. J.Allison, R.Mansfield 1961. The first aided ascent took 25 hours to complete.*

North
Southwest
Southeast
Turkey Dip
Masson Lees
Pic Tor
Lorry Park Q.
High Tor
Long Tor Q.
Wildcat
Willersley
Colehill Q.
Harborough
Brassington
Hipley Hill

North
Southwest
Southeast
Turkey Dip
Masson Lees
Pic Tor
Lorry Park Q.
High Tor
Long Tor Q.
Wildcat
Willersley
Colehill Q.
Harborough
Brassington
Hipley Hill

50m

30m to the cave

45m

45m

35m

The Girdle - p.346

Castellan Cave

## Main Face - Left

Although High Tor is most famous for its clean white sheets of pocketed rock, the left-hand side of the main face is characterised by some huge overhangs and long, towering corners. The great cave of *Castellan* is a hard barrier to cross which means that many of the routes are in the higher grades, however further left are a few orange-spot climbs which are as good as any of their grade in the Peak. Also worthwhile are the cunning routes, like *Laurin* and its near-neighbours, which weave their way through the roofs.

**Descent**- Abseil from the tree above the finish of *Debauchery* or, walk right (facing in) and follow the balcony path until a steep descent gully appears on the right. Descend this to join the approach path.

**❶ High Tor Gully** . . . . . . . . . 🔲 **VDiff**
Of historical significance only, as the cause of a major rift in the ancient Kyndwr Club. The massive legendary cleft on the far left is best described as an experience. It contains mud-slopes, much grass, and piles of rubbish. Best avoided in the wet, and deffo one for the adventurer.
*FA. J.W.Puttrell, William Smithard, A.M.Bennett 1903*

**❷ Lamplight** . . . . . . . . . . . . 🔲 **HVS 5a**
The prominent corner at the left-hand end of the wall. The start is tricky then detour left around the roof at half-height.
*FA. Doug Scott 1960s*

**❸ Sportlight** . . . . . . . 🔲 **7a**
A great line, but with disappointing climbing up the arete left of *Highlight*. Follow the line of bolts past a hard move to easier ground. Above this the arete steepens and the holds becomes rather disposable with some tough moves to the lower-off.
*FA. Gary Gibson, Pete Clark 2008*

**❹ Highlight** . . . . . . . . . . . . [Top50] **HVS 5a**
The long corner with a large capping roof gives a fine route, high in the grade and with a smattering of loose rock for added spice.
**1)** 4b, 18m. Climb the corner to a belay under the bulge.
**2)** 5a, 27m. Pull over the bulge then follow the corner to the roof. Traverse wildly left to gain the finishing corner.
*FFA. Unknown. FAA. Doug Scott, Steve Read 1965*

**❺ Skylight** . . . . . . . . . . . . . [Top50] **VS 4c**
One of the original free routes on the cliff, polished and with some spaced gear, but still well worthwhile.
**1)** 4b, 18m. Climb the corner below the left-hand end of the big Castellan roof, taking care with suspect rock. This is also the approach pitch to the cave.
**2)** 4c, 24m. Climb the crack above then move right and up to gain the chimney. Finish up this. Be aware of loose blocks on this pitch, a result of some severe winters.
A hard alternative to pitch 2 is **Armalite, E4 5c.** Halfway up pitch 2 of *Skylight*, move left under some roofs. Climb a crack then move right around the overhang to a finishing groove.
*FA. Joe Brown 1957. Climbed during a time when free climbing on limestone was rare. FA. (Armalite) John Codling, Steve Higham 1983*

**❻ Approach Pitch** . . . . . . . . . . . 🔲 **6b**
A bolted pitch to allow access to the cave for the sport routes. This is not worth doing in its own right.

**❼ Plight of the Rich** . . . 🔲 **7a+**
Despite recent retrobolting, the wall right of *Skylight* still feels a bit spicy in parts, though less so than when it was E5 6a. Pull over the bulge right of *Skylight* to a rest, then continue directly up the wall on well-spaced pockets for about 10m. Trend right to a rib and continue more easily to a lower-off.
*FA. Gary Gibson 1987*

**❽ Light and Shade** . . 🔲 **7a+**
An impressive line but with the occasional chipped hold. Start 4m right of *Skylight*, usually on a pile of blocks. Pull through the roof and move up to a hidden pocket to the left. Step right and gain the flake and follow this, and the wall above, to a break. Traverse right and finish up a crack - loose.
**A Right-hand Start, 7b+** - join the normal route at half-height.
*FA. Gary Gibson 1987. FA. (RH Start) Jon Clark 2008*

**❾ Pump out the Squealies** 🔲 **7b+**
A route of delightful contrasts. A powerful, fingery lower wall leads to an excruciatingly delicate and scary move to finish. Start below the roof 4m left of *Squeezin' Out Sparks*. Climb the roof to enter the base of a smooth groove from the right. Climb the groove and continue more easily into the smooth corner above. Somehow use the two holds to ascend this to a lower-off.
*FA. Simon Lee, Geoff Hornby 1992*

**❿ Squeezin' Out Sparks** . . 🔲 **7c**
One of the few remaining aid points in the Peak finally succumbed in 2007. Originally split, it is now done in a single pitch. Often damp. From a bolt belay between *Skylight* and *Castellan* in the cave, climb the roof past 2 resin bolts to a fine trad crack (E1) above. Climb a flake on the left to moves right to gain the flake then finish direct. Peg and bolt runners.
*FA. Jon Clark 2007. Nearly freed by Malc Taylor in 1986*

*The blank roof left of Castellan is the old aid route Limelight. This was a long-standing project.*

**⓫ Limelight** . . . . . . . 🔲 **8a**
Climb the roof past three glue-in bolts, by powerful moves and a huge span, to reach the sustained upper wall. It is possible to move left and continue as for *Squeezin'*... if you want to extend the challenge.
*FA. Jon Clark 2007. Nearly freed by Malc Taylor in 1992*

**⓬ Castellan** . . . . . 🔲 **E5 6b**
The impressive roof at the right end of the cave is more reasonable than it appears from a distance. Well-protected but strenuous with generally good holds linked by great moves.
**1)** 6b, 21m. Somehow gain jugs on the lip and follow these into a thrutchy crack leading to a hanging stance. No big cigar?
**2)** 6b, 21m. The crack above the stance has one very hard move and excellent protection throughout.
*FA. Barry Webb, B.McKinnon 1963 (over two days)*
*FFA. Steve Bancroft, John Allen 1976 (also over two days!)*

North
Southwest
Southeast
Turkey Dip
Masson Lees
Pic Tor
Lorry Park Q.
High Tor
Long Tor Q.
Wildcat
Willersley
Colehill Q.
Harborough
Brassington
Hipley Hill

North
Southwest
Southeast
Turkey Dip
Masson Lees
Pic Tor
Lorry Park Q.
High Tor
Long Tor Q.
Wildcat
Willersley
Colehill Q.
Harborough
Brassington
Hipley Hill

**⑬ Laurin** . . . . . . . . . **E3 6a**

Two contrasting pitches, each with a short hard section between rests and lots of exposure. The upper crack can get choked with dirt. It can be done in one long pitch with a few long extenders, thus missing out the tricky stance.

**1)** 5c, 20m. Leave the Castellan cave by the higher of two breaks until you can climb up the right-most of three grooves. Move left on pockets to gain a fine stance below the roof (the best gear for the belay requires a trip to the roof and back).

**2)** 6a, 20m. Climb up to the roof and make a desperate move (easier for the tall) up the steep roof crack above (good thread) in a sensational position. Finish more easily above.

*FFA. Martin Berzins, Chris Hamper 1977. FA. Paul Nunn, Oliver Woolcock 1964*

**⑭ Nightmare of Brown Donkeys**

. . . . . . . . . . . . . . . . . . **E3 5c**

Intricate route finding in wild positions - an underrated classic which needs a steady second. Be aware of the state of the old fixed gear and back it up.

**1)** 5b, 15m. Leave the Castellan cave along the lower break, as for *Delicatessen*, to the stance on *Lyme Cryme*.

**2)** 5c, 15m. Traverse back left for 2m and pull up into a shallow groove from the right. Climb the groove (slightly bold) to gain a crack leading to a bong (a big old peg). Clip this then drop back down and make a hard finger traverse left to a stance on *Laurin*. There are good thread belays under the roof above.

**3)** 5c, 18m. Climb to the roof and undercut leftwards (peg) under the roof. Finish up the loose groove (old gear).

An alternative is **The Phrantic Finish, E3 5c** which tackles the roof direct to a good hold on the lip.

*FFA. Pete Livesey, Pete Gomersall 1975. FA. Charles David Yates, Steve Read 1974. FA. (Phrantic Finish) Ian Parsons, Ian Robb 1987*

**⑮ Party in the Park** . . **E5 6b**

An eliminate that visits some wild spots. *Photo opposite.*

**1)** 6a, 22m. Start as for *Hot Gossip*. After entering the groove traverse left at an easy line above the roof for a couple of metres until below a thin crack. Climb this (one move of 5b to start) then easily up to belay below the cave of *Castellan*.

**2)** 6b, 20m. Follow *Hot Gossip* to the roof (*Laurin* goes right here and *Hot Gossip* straight up). Traverse wildly left into the hanging scoop (knee-lock rest) to good holds and gear (peg). Make the crux moves to and up the rib/crack to jugs and stance.

**3)** 5c, 22m. Move slightly left and up the wall right of the groove of *Hot Gossip* (thread and cam in pocket) to the roof and use the *Phrantic Finish* to cross this. Trend right across the wall to the break and finish up a small flake on the left.

*FA. Neil Foster, Clare Reading, Howard Lancashire, Keefe Murphy 2004*

**⑯ Hot Gossip** . . . . . . **E5 6a**

A complex line, finding its way through some unlikely territory, but with good climbing. Start under the left-hand of a pair of black loose-looking grooves at the cliff base.

**1)** 6a, 21m. Climb into (6b if you don't find the hidden jug) and up the loose black groove below the right-hand end of the Castellan cave to a ledge below the main cave base.

**2)** 6a, 21m. Step right and pull up past a hanging block. Continue through the bulge to gain the middle of three grooves and climb this to the *Laurin* stance.

**3)** 5c, 21m. Climb delicately leftwards then up to a fine groove (peg), as for *Brown Donkeys*.

50m

⑮

⑭

⑬

⑯

35m

*Delicatessen p.352*

25m

**Castellan Cave**

⑬

⑭

⑮

⑯

North
Southwest
Southeast
Turkey Dip
Masson Lees
Pic Tor
Larry Park Q.
High Tor
Long Tor Q.
Wildcat
Willersley
Colehill Q.
Harborough
Brassington
Hipley Hill

Neil Foster on pitch 2 his own route *Party in the Park*
(E5 6b) - *opposite* - at High Tor. Photo: Keith Sharples
This route is an example of that rare thing, a
significant new trad route on Peak Limestone. With his
encyclopaedic knowledge of the crag, Neil was able to
plot a new route up this busy face that included some
significant and independent sections.

**Belays -** The belays at the top of the crag in the middle section are set well back. It is useful to take a short 20m section of rope and leave this at the top if you intend to finish between the top of *Debauchery* and *Original Route*.

*Skylight - p.349*

*The Girdle - p.346*

*Lyme Cryme - p.355*

**❶ Fantasia** . . . . . . . . . . 🌀 ✍ [    ] **E5 6b**
A fine exposed outing with a lot of great climbing. Effectively a high girdle with some wild situations.
**1)** 5c, 35m. Climb *Skylight* to the roof, traverse right (peg) to the arete (bolt above) and down-climb for a few metres until it is possible to traverse right to gain a crack-line which leads to the *Castellan* belay. Apart from nuts in *Skylight* and one in the arete just before the down-climb this pitch is now fully geared.
**2)** 6b, 10m. Traverse right to gain the groove on *Hot Gossip*. Reverse this to the *Laurin* stance.
**3)** 6a, 20m. Reverse *Nightmare..* to the in-situ gear then continue right and up to the twin bolts on *Brompton's Cocktail*. Continue right to belay on *Debauchery*, just left of *Robert Brown*.
**4)** 6a, 20m. Climb up to an overhang and pull out left to a flake. Climb this and the bulges above to finish.
**4a)** 5c, 24m. More in keeping with the diagonal theme. Continue traversing diagonally right across *Ariadne's Thread* into *Darius*. Ascend this to the bolt then continue diagonally right to the thread of *Perseus*. Finish up this.
*FA. John Codling, M.Manson 1981*

**❷ Delicatessen** . . . . . . . . [Top 50] 🧗 [    ] **E2 5c**
A classic journey crossing the main face. With the exception of one short sequence, the climbing is no harder than 5b with delightful balance moves between good pockets. Approach via the 1st pitch of *Skylight* and a long ramble rightwards along the grubby ledge system.
**1)** 5c, 27m. From the *Castellan* cave, follow the lower break to gain a rest at the *Lyme Cryme* stance (possible belay). The juggy crack above is climbed until it is possible to cross the pocketed wall rightwards to the *Debauchery* stance.
**2)** 5b, 24m. Pick-pocket daintily rightwards to *Darius* and follow the juggy flakes up and right until another delicate sequence leads to *Original Route*. Finish up this or abseil off.
**Darius Finish, 5c.** A superb alternative, which improves one of the finest E2s around, is to belay after the delicate traverse on pitch 2 and then finish up *Darius*.
*FFA. Unknown. FA. (Pitch 1) Chris Jackson, John Atkinson 1965*
*FA. (Full route) Jack Street, Ed Ward-Drummond (some aid) 1965.*

North
Southwest
Southeast
Turkey Dip
Masson Lees
Pic Tor
Lamy Park Q.
High Tor
Long Tor Q.
Wildcat
Willersley
Colehill Q.
Harborough
Brassington
Hipley Hill

Walk descent

**A**

**②**

Original Route - p.356

Darius - p.355

**③**

**④**

### Main Face - The Diagonals

Such a magnificent and well-featured piece of rock was always bound to attract those seekers of the less obvious way up the rock. The four diagonals described here are superb and popular too - well, at least the easier ones.

**Descent -** The tree at the top of *Robert Brown* was chopped down by the Council for no apparent reason. Now it is normal to abseil from the tree above the finish of *Debauchery*. To walk down head right (looking in) along the cliff-top path and scramble easily down the steep gully which joins the approach path.

❸ **Debauchery** . . . . . . . Top 50 ⬛ E1 5b

One of top ten E1s in the country, it can be forgiven for the odd bit of polish here and there. The route crosses some remarkable ground with hidden jugs, ample protection and bags of exposure. Back up any old gear that you come across.

*Photo on page 1.*

**1)** 5b, 21m. Traverse left from the base of *Original Route*, moving up to a peg. Keep going up left to 2 cracks (on *Darius*); this can be done high or low with no change in grade. Move left again below the bulge then pull over to the famous stance.

**2)** 5b, 24m. Leave the stance via the left-hand crack to a peg. Make an awkward rising traverse leftwards (pegs) to easier ground below the break. Keep traversing horizontally left (more pegs) until you can pull up to a tree.

*FFA. Pete Livesey, John Sheard 1967. FA. Chris Jackson, John Atkinson (some aid) 1965*

❹ **Decadence** . . . . . . . . ⌘ ⬛ E4 6a

Well-named, the line encompasses some of the best moves and rock on the Tor. While pitch 1 has a sense of urgency about it, pitch 2 probably has the hardest move.

**1)** 6a, 24m. From the left-hand side of *The Pillar* (page 356) move up (peg and bolt above) and traverse left to a semi-rest below flakes. A confident approach will see you up these and onward to a flake. Move across left to the *Bastille* stance.

**2)** 6a, 18m. Step down and left to join the slippy crux of *Flaky Wall*. Continue up the cracks of *Supersonic* then move left, past a rest, up a ramp to the arete (hidden peg). A hard move gains *Original Route*. Climb up this to the belay. Abseil or...

**3)** 5c, 30m. Traverse the upper break leftwards across *Darius* to join *Robert Brown* to finish.

*FA. Arnis Strapcans, Gorden Jenkin 1980*

North

Southwest

Southeast

Turkey Dip

Masson Lees

Pic Tor

Lorry Park Q.

High Tor

Long Tor Q.

Wildcat

Willersley

Colehill Q.

Harborough

Brassington

Hipley Hill

Belay 7m back

Belay 17m back

50m

Walk descent

50m

30m

Delicatessen - p.352

Debauchery - p.353

**Belays -** The belays at the top of the crag in the middle section are set well back. It is useful to take a short 20m section of rope and leave this at the top if you intend to finish between the top of *Debauchery* and *Original Route*.

**1 The Grapevine** . . . . 🏔🧗🗺 ☐ **E5 6b**

A bit of an eliminate, but with some good moves and low in the grade too.

**1)** 6a, 25m. Climb *Lyme Cryme* for a few metres then move diagonally left across the wall to a bulge. Continue above to join the traverse of *Delicatessen* from below and belay on the right. The peg is good and can be backed up with a cam. The direct start is loose and dangerous.

**2)** 6b, 30m. Follow *Brown Donkeys* (page 350) to the bong and then step right and up to 2 old bolts. Make superb moves up then out left into, and out of, a scoop (a small cam above and left of the left-hand bolt provides a good back-up). Join *Debauchery* above and follow it left to finish.
*FA. Howard Lancashire, Ian Parsons 1985*

**2 Lyme Cryme** . . . . . [Top]50🗺📷 ☐ **E3 5c**

A superb route which for many years had a reputation for poor gear, however, protection on the whole is good and the old, bold section can be protected by slight diversion to the right. The first pitch is good value.

**1)** 5c, 23m. Climb the groove past an assortment of pegs, and good wires, until the crack runs out (old bolts up and left). Step right to ledges and move up to hidden slots where good protection is available (large-ish cams). Either drop back down, step left and back up, or simply move left from the gear to gain the hanging groove (peg). Clip the extended peg above and make a hard pull into a hanging groove. Pull out left to a stance and belay on wires (on *Delicatessen*).

**2)** 5b, 23m. Another fine pitch. Follow the cracks above and continue through the crux of pitch 2 of *Debauchery*. Finish direct up a short groove.
*FA. Steve Bancroft, Adey Hubbard 1975*

**3 Brompton's Cocktail** 🏔🧗🗺 ☐ **E5 6b**

An interesting addition which, despite its eliminate nature, deserves more attention than it receives. Pitch 2 makes a good but hard variant on *Lyme Cryme*.

**1)** 6b, 25m. Start up the groove left of *Robert Brown*. From the peg, trend left (bold) to the break. Make a sustained sequence over the bulge and left to gain *Lyme Cryme*; delicate and perfectly protected. Belay as for *Lyme Cryme*.

**2)** 6b, 33m. Follow *Brown Donkeys* (page 350) to the bong then continue to the twin bolts above and right (good small cam up and left of the left-hand bolt as back up). Desperate moves upwards (avoiding the easier detour up the flake on the right) enable you to reach the roof (peg). Finish more easily above.
*FA. Andy Grondowski, Mark Elwell 1981. The name refers to a medicine given to the terminally ill.*

**4 Robert Brown** . . . . . . 🏔🗺 ☐ **E3 5c**

An excellent, direct line up the cliff with just one difficult section on the first pitch. Start left of *Darius*, below a slightly less prominent groove.

**1)** 5c, 32m. Climb the groove to a ledge below the bulge (pegs, new and old - possibly loose). Step left then make a committing pull over the bulge, rightwards onto the face. It starts getting scary if you go up too far left here. Climb the crack above to arrive at the *Debauchery* stance.

**2)** 5b, 20m. Climb the crack at the left-hand end of the ledge leading to a peg at an overlap. Step right below the peg, pull past the overlap and climb a pocketed wall to the upper break. Move left and pull through the bulge on good holds to reach a tree.
*FA. Arnis Strapcans, Jerry Frost 1974. Named in memory of a friend of the first ascensionists who died in a fall at Gogarth.*

**Main Face - Centre**

*Lyme Cryme, Robert Brown, Darius, Perseus* - few walls in the country can compare with this list, and that doesn't include the Diagonals. The other routes may be slightly eliminate in nature but they are still of exceptionally high quality and mostly have fine positions on perfect rock.

**Descent -** The big tree at the top of *Robert Brown* was lopped by the Council some years ago, but you can still abseil from the tree above the finish of *Debauchery*. To walk down, head right along the cliff-top path (looking in) and scramble easily down a steep gully to the approach path.

**5 Ariadne's Thread** . . . . . 🏔🗺 ☐ **E5 6b**

An eliminate with some good climbing; hard sections are broken by easier climbing and good rests. Sufficiently independent. Follow *Robert Brown* to the bulge (thread) and power through to an ancient peg. Climb the flake above (peg on *Robert Brown*) then trend rightwards up the slabby wall to the right of the long bulge. Go over this on the right then move back left to a good flake handhold. Move directly over the bulge and continue up the pocketed wall (thread and good cams) until level with the alarming wafer thin flake on the left. For the full tick move across to the flake when level with its ear. From the top of the flake, either go right as for *Darius*, or left and finish as for *Robert Brown*. Can just be led on 50m ropes although there is a possible stance on *Debauchery*.
*FA. Simon Lee 1987*

**6 Darius** . . . . . . . . . . . [Top]50📷 ☐ **E2 5c**

A gem of a route, but like all gems rather polished - a sign of its allure as one of the best E2s in the country. The route is best done in one pitch, but can be split either at the large break at 20m or right of the flake almost in line with the *Debauchery* stance (in *Perseus*). Start below the prominent groove. Climb the groove to a ledge below the bulge (optional stance to reduce rope drag higher up). Pull through the bulge on the left and follow the crack above until a step right gains another crack. Continue past *Debauchery* into another groove on the left. Continue up the flake above to a position below the big old bolt. Pass this leftwards via a wonderful manoeuvre onto a steep groove to the top. Alternatively climb past the bolt at a polished **E3 6a**.
*FFA. Pete Livesey in 1974. FAA. Oliver Woolcock, Clive Rowland, Paul Nunn 1963. The current bolt was placed by Chris Craggs, 25+ years ago.*

*The next two routes start from the base of Original Route which is reached by scrambling around to the right - see next page.*

**7 Andromeda** . . . . . . . . . . 🗺 ☐ **E3 6a**

An eliminate of limited appeal squeezed into the small gap between *Perseus* and *Darius*. Start as for *Perseus* but pull left onto the wall above the small overlap. Continue in a direct line, past the poor stance on *Darius*, to arrive at the *Darius* bolt from the right. Finish direct.
*FA. Chris French, Ian Milne 1988*

**8 Perseus** . . . . . . . . . . . 🏔📷 ☐ **E3 5c**

A worthy route which deserves more attention and would get three stars on most other cliffs. The upper section feels a little bold but solid gear keeps appearing. Traverse left from the belay beneath *Original Route*. Move up then step left again to a small overlap - reachy. Alternatively, follow *Debauchery* a little further then move back right to the overlap. Climb direct from here (crux) to gain a crack. Climb this (peg and threads) to a final awkward section where the crack ends at a hole. Finish direct. A rather serious direct start is possible up the grassy lower slabs at **E1 5b** - peg runner out right.
*FFA. Pete Livesey, Jill Lawrence 1976. FA. Doug Scott, M.Terry 1968*

North · Southwest · Southeast · Turkey Dip · Masson Lees · Pic Tor · Lorry Park Q. · **High Tor** · Long Tor Q. · Wildcat · Willersley · Colehill Q. · Harborough · Brassington · Hipley Hill

North
Southwest
Southeast
Turkey Dip
Masson Lees
Pic Tor
Lorry Park Q.
High Tor
Long Tor Q.
Wildcat
Willersley
Colehill Q.
Harborough
Brassington
Hipley Hill

*All the routes on this side start by a grassy scramble up to various ledges below the face. Rope-up for this if you are unsure.*

### ❶ Original Route . . . . . . . ⌊50⌉ HVS 5a
A right of passage for HVS leaders - the exposure of the huge face is well felt, a great experience at the grade. Start on ledges below the groove. Move 3m left then climb up and pull back right into the groove. Climb this, past various bits of old gear, and plenty of good wires, to the ledge at the top. Abseil off or continue for a short pitch (4c) to tick the summit direct from a ledge, or up a groove on the right. The obvious direct start is about a grade harder. *Photo on page 342*.
*FFA. Steve Read, Steve Hunt 1958. FA. (as Bastion Wall) Pete Hassell, Peter Biven and another 1953.*

### ❷ Tales of Yankee Power . . E5 6a
The perfect introduction to the E5 grade and on the perfect cliff. Spicy, but safe with a bit of Buoux thrown in. Climb direct from the *Original Route* start to rejoin the route in its main groove. Climb up and place some wires then follow the thin crack in the arete until it runs out. Climb coolly to the jug (one final hard hold?) and regain your composure. Move up the thin wall above (hidden peg on the left) with one final hard move to pass the break and gain the belay on *Original Route*.
*FA. Phil Burke, Nadim Siddiqui, Al Evans 1979*

### ❸ Flaky Wall . . . . . . . . . ⌊50⌉ E4 6a
Another fine route, tracing the easiest line up the shield. Immaculate rock, good protection, a hands-off rest and some brilliant technical sequences. Start lower than *Original Route* as for *Supersonic* (this helps keep the wires on the crux in). Move up left and follow the crack as for *Tales* until the curving overlap on the right can be gained. Pull out right from this to a rest then climb direct up a peg-scarred crack (polished) to a good hold. Wander more easily rightwards up the dinner-plate flake and finish direct from its end.
*FA. Doug Scott, Clive Davies 1961. The upper flake was much more friable making their ascent terrifying. The route was renamed every time someone removed one of the aid points. Ed Drummond called it Hook-Crook Wall (5 skyhooks) and Livesey renamed it Bulldog Wall (1 rest) in 1972. Ironically the FFA isn't known although it was renamed Flaky Wall anyway!*

### ❹ Reproduction . . . . . . E6 6b
High quality climbing up a tenuous line on the blank wall left of *Flaky Wall*, with spaced protection and a lonely feel. Move cunningly rightwards from the old tree (peg) to join the overlap of *Flaky Wall*. Cross this to the rest then climb boldly up discontinuous flakes, bearing left to the thread on *Yankee Power*. Keep going up pockets keeping just left of *Supersonic*.
*FA. Simon Nadin, Richard Davies 1985. Straightened out a route called Musical Women which was a hybrid on Decadence.*

### ❺ Supersonic . . . . . . . . ⌊50⌉ E5 6a
Outstanding face-climbing, continuously interesting with the two hard sections linked by superb moves. All this, plus opportunities to recover in between, make this justifiably one of the most sought after routes of the grade in the country. Start just below the ledge of *Original Route*, below a short, capped groove up and right. Enter the groove (good low wire, peg) and climb it past two pegs to the top. Pull out right (wire) then back left to the rest on *Flaky Wall*. Follow this past its tricky bit and continue in a direct line up the pocketed wall to an exciting finish onto the ledge.
*FA. Ron Fawcett, Geoff Birtles, Al Evans 1976*

### ❻ My New Hat . . . . . . . E6 6c
The hardest route up the shield which, despite the bolts, could barely be described as a sport route. It may not have been repeated. The hard 6c crux occurs with the bolt at your feet, and there's a solid 6b move a long way out. To make matters worse, the first bolt is a grip-clip. Start as for *Bastille*. Make the first move of that route then traverse left and climb boldly and directly, past 2 bolts, to the stance of *Decadence*. Finish up *Bastille* or abseil off.
*FA. Malcolm Taylor, Alison Taylor 1994*

### ❼ Bastille . . . . . . ⌊50⌉ E6 6b
One of the best hard routes in the country with a technical crux, a bold groove and a sting in the tail. Although the crux is well protected, there is a big run-out on only marginally easier territory with ground-fall potential. Scramble up easy rock to a belay under the groove. Climb the wall past two bolts into the capped groove. Climb the groove (heart in mouth, runners in mind) to small wire placements on the right and a peg. Move left with hands above the overhang to a rest on the *Decadence* belay. Make more great moves up the pocketed wall above past bolts until a final swing leftwards gains *Flaky Wall*. Finish as for this.
*FFA. Andy Brown, Jerry Peel 1979. The hard start had been freed by American Mike Graham in 1977, and, although he failed to flash the route, he renamed it 'Basteal'. FA. Brian Moore, D.Land 1963. Aid reduced to 1pt Pete Livesey, Jill Lawrence 1976.*

### ❽ Tumbril . . . . . . . . . . . . . E5 6a
Largely forgotten since the best climbing is also taken by *Decadence* and the start is serious. Start left of *Decadence*, below an undercut slab. Climb up this to flakes, or step in from the first bolt on *Bastille*, both methods being bold. Continue close to the gully then trend left to the top of *Flaky Wall*.
*FA. Ed Cleasby, Rob Matheson 1980. Formerly an aid route.*

### ❾ The Passion Wagon . . . . E5 6b
A worthwhile route but never likely to become popular. It has been given 7b but it isn't really a sport route. Start as for *Decadence*, but from part-way across the initial traverse, climb the steep wall and thin crack right, past 2 bolts. Excruciatingly fingery. Fight up the vegetated gully to find an abseil tree.
*FA. Mark Pretty 1987*

### ❿ The Pillar . . . . . . . . E5 6a
A good introduction to the grade, lacking the big feel of the classic routes of the Main Face, but requiring a deal of care over the placing of protection and handling of the rock, especially towards the finish. Follow the wall past old (and very short) pegs to the roof. Move left then pull over to a good, booming flake. Climb up until you can traverse right to a peg then move up to a bulge (peg). Take a breather then make a hard move right and back left to reach a ledge. Move left into the gully. Tree belay.
*FFA. Jim Moran, Al Evans 1977. FA. Brian Moore, Bruce Andrew 1970.*

### ⓫ Pillar Direct . . . . . . . . E4 6a
An interesting climb which provides a few entertaining moments. Despite the lower E grade, it is only slightly easier than the ordinary route. Start right of the original route and climb up to the right-hand end of the overhang (peg). Pull over to the right then make hard moves back left to join the original at a peg. Finish as for this.
*FA. John Codling, T.Saunders 1983*

### ⓬ Cathy Come Home . . . . . . . . . . E1 5b
Start right of the overhang of *Pillar*. Climb the wall to a groove (peg), continue to a slab which leads to a belay.
*FA. Simon Lee, Phil Dickens 1986*

Descent

30m to ledge

30m to ledge

25m to ledge

④
②
③
④
①
③
⑤
⑥
⑦
⑧
⑨
⑩
⑪
⑫

*Decadence - p.353*

North
Southwest
Southeast
Turkey Dip
Masson Lees
Pic Tor
Lorry Park Q.
High Tor
Long Tor Q.
Wildcat
Willersley
Colehill Q.
Harborough
Brassington
Hipley Hill

## Main Face - Right

If anything, the right-hand side of the Main Face is even better than the *Darius* area. The routes start with the friendly *Original Route* but after that there is nothing to offer but Black Spots. It is all top-notch pocket-pulling - often bold, often technical, mostly on perfect rock and always in a splendid position. After graduating from the classics of the central face, *Yankee Power*, *Supersonic* and *Bastille* provide a worthy trio of ticks for any climbing career.

**Descent -** The tree at the top of *Debauchery* offers the best abseil descent. To walk down head right (looking in) along the cliff-top path and scramble down the steep gully to join the approach path.

## Right Wing

A crag which has been walked past and pretty much ignored by most people for many years has given a new lease of life. Not only are there now a number of good sport routes to go at, the trad climbing here is also well worth the effort. Most routes end at lower-offs - convenient, since the crag top is a bit of a jungle.

**Approach -** The crag is passed on the normal approach walk and is difficult to miss. It consists of four walls, but most interest is in the central two.

**Access -** No more new routes or gardening at this crag.

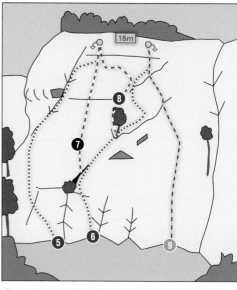

*The first buttress is well-hidden above and left of the main crag.*
**Approach Routes 1 to 4 -** *Continue walking along the main crag to a wall with a cave on the lower right corner. Scramble up and back right under the face to a short wall with three bolted routes and one older trad route.*

**❶ No Way** . . . . . . . . . . . . . . . . . 6b+
The left-hand line.
*FA. Gary Gibson 2010*

**❷ My Way** . . . . . . . . . . . . . . . . 7a+
The central bolted line.
*FA. Gary Gibson 2010*

**❸ Lee Way** . . . . . . . . . . . . . . . . E5 6b
An old trad line past some fixed gear.
*FA. Simon Lee 1986*

**❹ Sideways** . . . . . . . . . . . . . . . 6c
The final route on the right edge of the climbable rock up here.
*FA. Gary Gibson 2010*

*The better climbing is down on the main section starting at a narrow wall with two ramps on it.*

**❺ All the Wubble u's** . . . . . . . . . E3 5c
Skirt the left-hand edge of the wall to gain the diagonal groove. Climb this then swing right to the lower-off.
*FA. Gary Gibson 2010*

**❻ Zed Legs** . . . . . . . . . . . . . . E2 5b
Climb straight up past a thread to gain the base of the lower ramp. Continue up the ramp before moving back left to gain some flakes. Pull over into the next ramp and follow this to its top. Finish up *Memories* (originally it went right to the top).

**❼ That X Factor** . . . . . . . . E4 6a
Good climbing. From the thread in *Zed Legs* move left and climb the wall directly. The upper wall is excellent and has some pegs.
*FA. Gary Gibson 2010*

**❽ Y-Front** . . . . . . . . . . . . . . E2 5b
Slightly eliminate but still worthwhile. Start up *Zed Legs* but continue direct from the base of the lower ramp to the next ramp. Follow this before you can traverse across delicately left to the lower-off.
*FA. C.Cook, S.Berry 1977*

**❾ Memories** . . . . . . . . . . . . 6a
The bolted line on the right gives good climbing and keeps going to the last move.
*FA. Gary Gibson 2010*

*The main section of the Right Wing is a long wall with a dominant central groove (Scimitar Groove). The next routes are on the clean white wall up and left of this.*

**❿ Dutch Moon** . . . . . . . . 6b
Fine technical climbing which is sadly short-lived and escapable. Start up easy rock to gain the wall which is followed on some thin holds.
*FA. Gary Gibson 2010*

**⓫ Venus Eruptus** . . 6c+
More quality thin climbing sharing a big hold with *Dutch Moon* on its upper section.
*FA. Gary Gibson 2010*

**⓬ Black Wedding** . . . . . E5 6a
A pseudo sport route with 2 bolts and three pegs - still more E5 than 7a though.
*FA. Seb Grieve 1985*

**⓭ Sargasso Sea** . . . . . . E4 5c
Bold climbing up the open black groove. Not very appealing.
*FA. Chris Plant 1984*

**⓮ Saga Lout** . . . . . . . . . . . . 6b+
A lovely little climb up the left-hand side of the big pillar.
*FA. Gary Gibson 2010*

**⓯ Endgame** . . . . . . . . . 6c+
The right-hand side of the big pillar gives more quality climbing.
*FA. Simon Lee 1985. Bolted by Gary Gibson in 2010.*

**⓰ Scimitar Groove** . . . . . . . . VS 4c
The central groove has been cleaned up to give a great pitch.

**⓱ My Pedigree Chum** . . . . . . . 6a
The first line of bolts right of the central groove. Friable rock on the last few moves.
*FA. Gary Gibson 2010*

North
Southwest
Southeast
Turkey Dip
Masson Lees
Pic Tor
Lorry Park Q.
High Tor
Long Tor Q.
Wildcat
Willersley
Colehill Q.
Harborough
Brassington
Hipley Hill

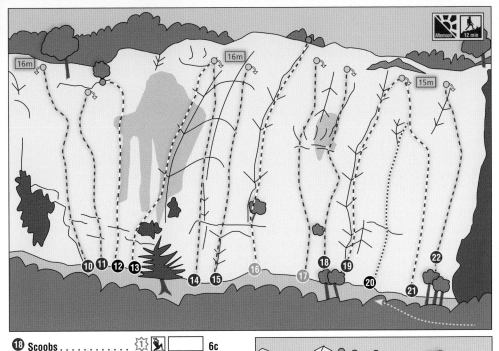

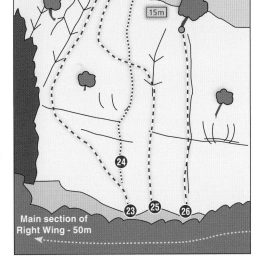

**Main section of
Right Wing - 50m**

**18 Scoobs** . . . . . . . . . . . **6c**
Very thin and technical climbing on the lower wall leads to a
romp up the steeper rock above.
*FA. Gary Gibson 2010*

**19 Prejudice** . . . . . . . . . . **E2 5b**
The shallow groove gives great climbing leading to a steeper
finish past a peg. Lower-off on the right.
*FA. Unknown but claimed later as Pride by Chris Plant in 1985.*

**20 Lulu Belle** . . . . . . . . . . . . **E4 6a**
The direct version of *Memo to Sally* is quite bold.
*FA. Gary Gibson 2010*

**21 Memo to Sally** . . . . . . . **E3 5c**
A worthwhile route which is better protected than it looks. Climb
up a shallow groove then traverse up and left to finish past a
thread to a lower-off.

**22 If Dill Was Here** . . . . . . . . . . . . **6b**
The final bolted line on this section of wall.
*FA. Gary Gibson 2010*

*The final routes are on the clean buttress which is the first
encountered on the approach.*

**23 Still Searching** . . . . . . . . . . . . **E2 5b**
Trend up leftwards to gain a long diagonal groove. Follow this
to the top.
*FA. Chris Plant 1984*

**24 Beautiful White** . . . . . . **E3 5c**
Climb direct past some left-facing undercuts to a break. The
upper wall has a solitary peg to show the way.
*FA. Gary Gibson 2010*

**25 Lower Buttress Route** . . **E3 5c**
Climb a crack (peg) to a slim groove. Cross the white wall
leftwards to gain a finishing crack.
*FA. Chris Plant 1984. Previously an aid route.*

**26 At the Edge of Everything** . . . . . **E2 5c**
Climb a crack (peg on left) to a bulge and thread. Continue up
the crack to a tree.
*FA. Gary Gibson 2010*

North · Southwest · Southeast · Turkey Dip · Masson Lees · Pic Tor · Larry Park Q. · High Tor · Long Tor Q. · Wildcat · Willersley · Colehill Q. · Harborough · Brassington · Hipley Hill

| | No star | ☆ | ☆☆ | ☆☆☆ |
|---|---|---|---|---|
| up to 4+ | - | - | - | - |
| 5+ to 6a+ | - | - | - | - |
| 6b to 7a | 2 | 2 | 1 | - |
| 7a+ and up | 2 | 4 | 5 | 2 |

A steep and shady wall hidden just metres from the busy A6, a short distance north of Matlock Bath. The wall is crisscrossed by a series of hard climbs that provide excellent climbing on microscopic holds. The crag was popular briefly in the 1980s before falling out of vogue. More recently, the locals have given the place a complete face-lift, cleaning up the area, rebolting the original lines and adding many more. The best of the routes here are very good, and many of them are very hard too.

## Approach    Also see map on page 325

Long Tor Quarry is right by the A6, just north of Matlock Bath and opposite the southern end of High Tor. Normal parking is in the station car park but there is also limited roadside parking where the parking restrictions end (care needed, the road is busy). A small gap in the wall with stone steps leads up into the quarry - two minutes away.

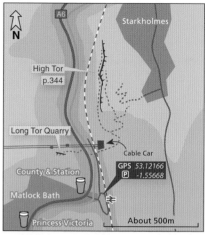

## Conditions

Long Tor Quarry faces north, and effectively receives no sun. The aspect and trees ensure that it is very sheltered from the wind, and will stay dry in light rain, especially when it arrives on south-westerlies.

## Access

There is no formal access agreement to the quarry. The inclusion of the information in this book does not mean that you have right of access to climb there. Its secluded setting has ensured there have been no access problems to date.

Tim Banton starting up the flake of *Jade* (6c+) - *page 362* - at Long Tor Quarry. Photo: David Bond

North
Southwest
Southeast
Turkey Dip
Masson Lees
Pic Tor
Lorry Park Q.
High Tor
Long Tor Q.
Wildcat
Willersley
Colehill Q.
Harborough
Brassington
Ripley Hill

Simon Wren on the upper section of the fiercely technical; *Ruby Fruit Jungle* (8a) - *next page* - at Long Tor Quarry. Photo: David Bond

**❶ Mrs Jackson's Warning.** 6c+
The left-hand route has a high crux. Crimpy and reachy.
*FA. Malc Taylor 1988*

**❷ The Orcadian Donkey's Spotted Tail**
.................. 6c+
Start up *Mrs Jackson's..,* swing along the break to a jug, then
pull up left to gain a niche. Nice climbing gains a bigger hold
and an awkward finale.
*FA. J.Heelam 1988*

**❸ Tatanka Yotanka** ..... 7a+
Follow *Orcadian Donkey* to the jug, then pump all the way along
the break to finish by descending *Exit Wounds*. There and back
is a 7b pump-fest.
*FA. J.Heelam 1988*

**❹ Depravity** ....... 7c
From the large hold on *Orcadian Donkey's* headwall, head right
to eventually reach the lower-off above *Rinsemeal*.
*FA. Jon Fullwood 2006*

**❺ Mosey on Down the Crow Road**
.................. 8a
Climb the wall on tiny holds (stick-clip the second bolt) then
somehow reach the big flat hold up to the left. At the break,
move to a large hold, gain the niche, then make tricky moves
round the bulge. Finish up the wall, trending right.
*FA. Jon Fullwood 2006*

**❻ King of the Jungle** . 8b+
Hard, crimpy climbing above the small ledge to some respite at
the break. From here, continue up *Ruby Fruit Jungle* but finish
direct, making full use of the height of the wall.
*FA. Jon Clark 2009. Includes the Left-hand Finish to Ruby Fruit Jungle.*

**❼ Ruby Fruit Jungle.** . 8a
A good technical pitch with a reachy lower crux and plenty of
hard moves above. Balance and stretch to the break, and pass
it to reach a jug. Fierce fingery moves lead up and right to a
good jug. Trend right to gain the lower-off with difficulty. The
Left-hand finish (now on the previous route) is a bit easier - 7c+.
*Photo on previous page.*
*FA. Andy Pollitt 1988*

**❽ Jungle Fury.** ........ 8a+
The blank wall between *Ruby* and *The Boltest*. Climb *The Boltest*
to the break, then continue straight up via a series of intense
fingery moves to the small slot on *Ruby Fruit*. Move up and right
to finish up the last couple of moves of the *Boltest*.
*FA. Jon Clark 2009*

**❾ The Boltest** ....... 7c
Start at the left-edge of the red-stained rock and stretch and leap
to the break. From here, sustained climbing leads to better holds
and a final stretch to the lower-off. Excellent.
*FA. Steve Lewis 1988*

**❿ Rinsemeal** ........... 7a+
Climb the flake/crack to the break. Continue, using holds on the
wall and the arete, to a tricky finish.
*FA. Jon Fullwood 2006*

Morning | 5 min | Sheltered

North
Southwest
Southeast
Turkey Dip
Masson Lees
Pic Tor
Lorry Park Q.
High Tor
Long Tor Q.
Wildcat
Willersley
Colehill Q.
Harborough
Brassington
Hipley Hill

20m

16m

**14 Future Primitive. . . . . .** 〔1〕 🖾 ☐ **7b**
Gain the crack-line by powering through the overhang.
Precarious moves above this gain the *Exit Wounds* lower-off.
FA. Malc Taylor 1988

**15 Duality . . . . . . . . . . . . .** 🖾 ☐ **7b+**
Climb the flake, then stretch for the ledge above. Gain this
awkwardly, then follow small finger-holds up the wall above.
FA. Jon Clark 2008

**11 Jade. . . . . . . . . . . . .** 〔1〕 🖾 ☐ **6c+**
As for *Rinsemeal* to the break then gain and enter the prominent
groove. Bridge to the lower-off. *Photo on page 360.*
FA. Paul Mitchell 1986

**16 Crystalline . . . . . . . . . . .** 🖾 ☐ **7a**
Layback the awkward crack to a hold, then more precarious
climbing gains the lower-off.
FA. Jon Clark 2008

**12 Pistol Fingers . . . . . . .** 〔3〕 🖾 ☐ **8a+**
Gain the break, then head up and left with increasing difficulty to
reach a final tricky set of moves.
FA. Jon Fullwood 2006

**17 Sac du Sable. . . . . . . .** 〔1〕 🖾 ☐ **6c**
Begin under a shallow groove, then trend up and right to reach the
crack. Steep climbing on mostly good holds gains the lower-off.
FA. Jon Clark 2008

**13 Exit Wounds . . . . . . .** 〔2〕 〔▯〕 ☐ **7c+**
Climb to the break, then undercut and stretch for holds on the
wall above. Hard moves lead to a better hold, then gain the
side-pull to the right. A long reach accesses some small holds
then a shake-out; from here, finish with difficulty.
FA. Jon Clark 2008

**18 Mr Jackson's Yawning . . . . . . .** ☐ **7a+**
Gain the initial ledge and climb the wall to a high crux.

*To the right, beyond much vegetated rock is a rippled wall
with two routes that are reported to be worth the effort of the
approach:* **Human Capital, 6c+** *and* **Scum Manifesto, 7a+**.

| | No star | 1 star | 2 star | 3 star |
|---|---|---|---|---|
| Mod to S | 1 | - | - | - |
| HS to HVS | 3 | 12 | 8 | 1 |
| E1-E3 / 6b-7a | 1 | 1 | 4 | - |
| E4 / 7a+ and up | - | 7 | - | - |

Wildcat has long been a popular crag due to its accessibility, sunny situation and its collection of multi-pitch Orange Spot routes. Many of these follow strong lines on decent quality rock that, generally speaking, isn't too steep - for limestone that is - there are no slabs here! The cliff is very extensive and there is a lot of poor rock and vegetation scattered along its length. Although much of this has all been climbed on in the past, it is best left to return to nature. Only the better buttresses are described in detail here and these are well worth visiting. Many of the routes start with a slightly grotty first pitch leading to a well-placed stance just above the treetops, about halfway up the face. Above this, the quality cranks up, and many routes have excellent upper pitches, with spectacular positions high above the woods and river.

## Approach Also see map on page 325

The crag overlooks the A6 and the River Derwent at the southern end of Matlock Bath. To reach the buttresses described, park in the carpark (pay) for Gulliver's Kingdom (roughly opposite the Pavilion - the large white building between the river and the road). Cross the main road then follow an alley on the right of the Pavilion, past some toilets, and cross the bridge. New Bridge Buttress is directly above in the trees. For the main areas, turn right and follow the riverside path until a smaller path on the left leads up zigzags to a broken wall with a partly-blocked-up-doorway feature on the bend. The main crag is beyond this wall.

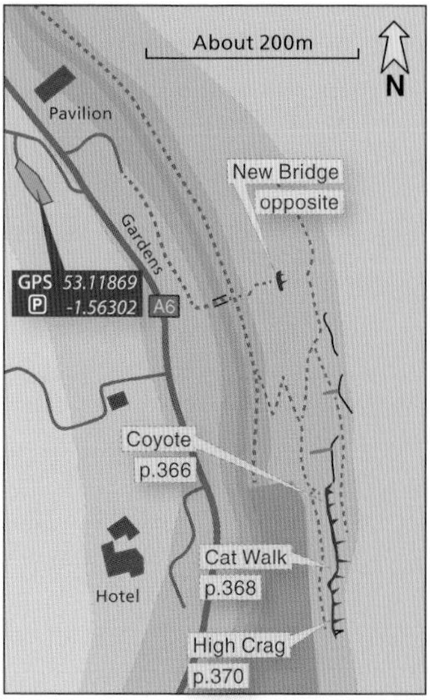
About 200m
N
Pavilion
New Bridge
opposite
Gardens
GPS 53.11869
-1.56302
A6
Coyote
p.366
Cat Walk
p.368
Hotel
High Crag
p.370

## Conditions

The crag faces west, catching the afternoon sun. The lower pitches are shaded and sheltered by the trees, but the upper parts of the crag catch the weather. In summer, the foliage can give the base of the crag an oppressive atmosphere. There isn't much of a seepage problem here and the crag dries fairly quickly after rain, though the earth-slopes below the crag can be a challenge.

## Access

Land near Wildcat is owned by Wesley (Methodist) Guild Holidays. They do not want people wandering into their private grounds, so please use only the approach and descent described. This applies to all the paths beneath the main crag except for the approach path described here.

Coyote Buttress
p.366
Cat Walk
p.368
High Crag
p.370

## New Bridge Buttress

This fine compact little wall is situated directly above the bridge crossed on the approach. It has been floodlit at night in the past but nowadays the tree cover is too dense. The routes are short and intense and the crag is well sheltered and may even stay dry in light rain. The routes were bolted in 2010.

**❶ Criminally Insane. . . . .**    **7a+**
The left-hand line has a reachy and fingery start to gain the good flake on *Trick Psychlist*. Then tackle the powerful upper arete, and finish up the groove-line above.
*FA. Jon Clark  2011*

**❷ Trick Psychlist . . . . . . .**    **7c+**
Very technical climbing up the blank wall to a large flake, then through the bulge onto the upper slab.
*FA. Malcolm Taylor 1987. Originally E6 6c*

**❸ Straight Psychlist. .**    **7b**
A good link-up route. Start up *Strait Jacket* to just below the mid-height break, then move left to tackle the tricky bulge on *Trick Psychlist*. Take a few long quickdraws.
*FA. Matt Fry 2010*

**❹ Strait Jacket . . . . .**    **7a**
The left-hand side of the bulges with good laybacking moves and a tricky 2nd clip.
*FA. Gary Gibson 1985. Originally E5 6b*

**❺ Recoil . . . . . . . . . . .**    **6b+**
A good route up the centre of the buttress gives sustained pocket pulling. Hard moves over the bulge lead to a hanging groove. Finish by moving right around this.
*FA. Gary Gibson 1985. Originally E3 5c*

**❻ Shock Treatment . . . . . . . .**    **7a**
A shorter route to the left of the corner line. Tricky and reachy climbing, especially on the final wall.
*FA. Gary Gibson 1985. Originally E5 6b*

**❼ Lunatic Asylum . . .**    **HVS 5c**
Boulder out the wall and head up the prominent groove to a slightly unstable exit.
*FA. Graham Hoey 1975*

**❽ The Mentalist . . . . . . . . .**    **7a+**
From the jug on *Lunatic Asylum*, reach out right and use an undercut to gain the high break. Climb the short groove above, then move leftwards to finish up the left arete.
*FA. Jon Clark 2009*

North | Southwest | Southeast | Turkey Dip | Masson Lees | Pic Tor | Lorry Park Q. | High Tor | Long Tor Q. | Wildcat | Willersley | Colehill Q. | Harborough | Brassington | Hipley Hill

North
Southwest
Southeast
Turkey Dip
Masson Lees
Pic Tor
Lorry Park Q.
High Tor
Long Tor Q.
Wildcat
Willersley
Colehill Q.
Harborough
Brassington
Hipley Hill

Descent

42m
40m
20m
20m
20m

① **Catastrophe Grooves** . . . . . ★2 ⬜ **HVS 5a**
A Wildcat classic taking the disjointed groove system. Harder than it used to be because of the polish.
**1)** 4c, 18m. Climb the crack and groove above to a stance.
**2)** 5a, 20m. Make balancy moves right into the upper groove. Climb this with moves right at mid-height to finish direct.
*FA. Doug Scott, Steve Read (3pts) 1960s*

② **White Room** . . . . . . . . ★1 ⬜ **HVS 5a**
A right-hand version of *Catastrophe Grooves* sees a lot less traffic.
**1)** 4b, 20m. Climb a wide crack then the wall past bushes.
**2)** 5a, 18m. Continue up the wide flake-crack to its end then head up the short wall to finish as for *Catastrophe Grooves*.
*FA. Gary Gibson, Chris Johnson 1979*

③ **Lyon Route** . . . . . . . . ★1 🦉⬜ **E1 5b**
Good but with a poorly-protected and polished crux.
**1)** 4c, 20m. Climb cracks to a stance under the long groove.
**2)** 5b, 20m. Head up the groove to the bulge and pull past this into the upper section. Continue direct to a tree belay.
*FA. Steve Read, Will McLoughlin 1963*

④ **Coyote Buttress** . . . . . . . . ★2 ⬜ **HVS 5a**
Excellent and varied. Start at a groove left of a short pinnacle, or slightly higher on a ledge to do the route in 1 pitch.
**1)** 5a, 12m. Climb the left wall of the groove to a small stance.
**2)** 5a, 26m. Up the short groove on the right then turn the small roof on its right. Move up and climb the left edge of the buttress and the steep crack above to its top. Escape off right.
*FA. Doug Scott, Ray Gillies, Terry Bolger 1968*

## Coyote Buttress

This tall wall features some impressive black groove-lines and a narrow buttress on its right-hand side. Most of the routes start indifferently but have very good second pitches, in great positions, high above the trees.
**Approach -** Coyote Buttress is the first buttress you reach just past the archway on the approach path.
**Descent -** Walk left (looking in) down the path and through a higher archway before doubling back to the crag.

### ❼ Jackdaw Grooves . . . . . . . . VS 4b
A popular and worthwhile introduction to the crag.
1) 4b, 16m. Start at a long clean groove and climb this until a short traverse left leads to the detached ledge.
2) 4b, 22m. Traverse right below the roof then climb a short wall and long slim groove, right of the deeper one of *BTG*.
FA. (P1) D.Meadows, Tony Watts, (P2) Doug Scott, Ray Gillies 1963

### ❽ Nine Lives Wall . . . . . . . . HVS 5a
5m right of *Jackdaw Groove* climb a shallow groove and the wall over a bulge to ledges and a possible stance on the left. Meander up the steep wall above passing a peg (good holds soon appear) into the prominent groove which leads to the top.
FA. Terry Bolger, R.Shaw 1968

### ❾ Catharsis Wall . . . . . . . . . . . . HVS 5a
1) 5a, 22m. Start at a white groove blocked by a large bulge. Climb the groove and traverse left to avoid the roof. From a ledge, climb back right over broken rock and some vegetation to belay in a fine cave.
2) 5a, 18m. Step left and climb the impending wall and shallow scoop to finish over a small roof.
FA. Sean Golden, Len Pearson 1980s

### ❿ Cat's Eye . . . . . . . . . . . . . . . S 4a
1) 4a, 22m. Climb cracks, 3m right of the white groove, to an overhang. Step left and follow a groove to a stance in the 'eye'.
2) 3a, 18m. Follow cracks out rightwards past a blocky area to a final short wall. Up this to the trees.
FA. B.O'Connel, Bruce Andrews, Steve Bowes, Tony Watts early 1960s

### ⓫ Budweisser Effect . . . . . . . . . . HVS 4c
In the upper part of the cliff is a large deep groove left of a prominent pillar; start directly below this.
1) 4c, 22m. Climb a small rib and groove passing the overhang at its left end. Continue up the wall above to a stance at the base of the crystal-filled groove.
2) 4c, 18m. Climb the crack and groove, moving right at the top up easier but looser ground to finish.
FA. Gary Gibson (solo) 1979

### ⓬ McPlumb Wall . . . . . . . . . HVS 4c
An interesting and satisfying route starting just left of the gully leading up into the recess of *Cougar Cleft*.
1) 4b, 22m. Climb the shallow groove then move left to belay.
2) 4c, 18m. Head up the wall above, passing a small flake, to reach the overhang then follow the traverse line rightwards under this. Finish up broken territory just round the corner.
FA. W.McLoughlin, Steve Read 1963

### ⓭ Cougar Cleft . . . . . . . . . . . . . HS 4a
The rather disgusting lower gully leads up to this pleasant chimney/crack feature suspended high above. The exit is fun.
FA. Nat Allen, Don Chapman 1948. The cliff's first route by 10 years.

### ❺ Derek's Dilemma . . . . . . . . VS 5a
1) 4b, 16m. Climb a groove right of the short blunt pinnacle, moving right to a stance on a detached ledge.
2) 5a, 22m. Climb the black and slippery groove, which has a real lack of good footholds when you need them most.
FA. Steve Read, Steve Hunt 1963

*The next routes start from a slightly raised ledge running along the base of the crag.*

### ❻ Broken Toe Groove . . . . . . . VS 4c
1) 4c, 16m. Climb a flaky groove left of the arete and the wide crack then a bulge to reach the ledge and stance on the right.
2) 4b, 22m. Go left and follow the shallow groove round the right edge of the black bulges, then finish up the crack above.
FA. (P1) Dez Hadlum, Dennis Gray 1960, (P2) Doug Scott, I.Thorlaby 1963

North
Southwest
Southeast
Turkey Dip
Masson Lees
Pic Tor
Lorry Park Q.
High Tor
Long Tor Q.
Wildcat
Willersley
Colehill Q.
Harborough
Brassington
Hipley Hill

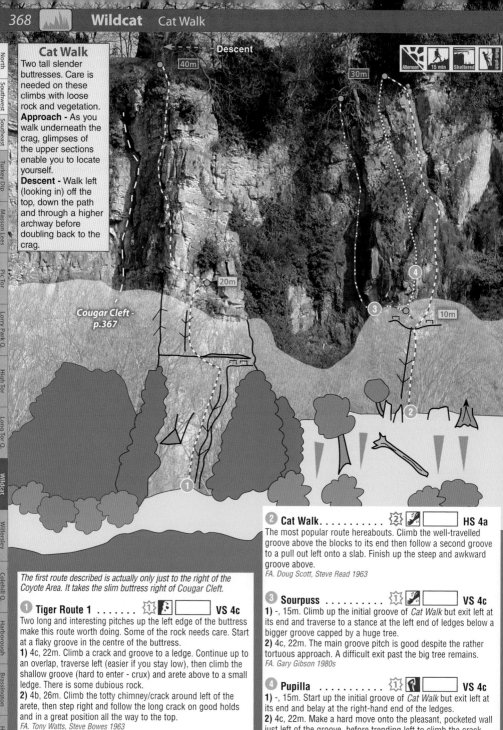

**Cat Walk**

Two tall slender buttresses. Care is needed on these climbs with loose rock and vegetation.

**Approach -** As you walk underneath the crag, glimpses of the upper sections enable you to locate yourself.

**Descent -** Walk left (looking in) off the top, down the path and through a higher archway before doubling back to the crag.

Descent

40m

30m

20m

Cougar Cleft - p.367

10m

---

*The first route described is actually only just to the right of the Coyote Area. It takes the slim buttress right of Cougar Cleft.*

**① Tiger Route 1** ...... ☆1 🔥 VS 4c

Two long and interesting pitches up the left edge of the buttress make this route worth doing. Some of the rock needs care. Start at a flaky groove in the centre of the buttress.

**1)** 4c, 22m. Climb a crack and groove to a ledge. Continue up to an overlap, traverse left (easier if you stay low), then climb the shallow groove (hard to enter - crux) and arete above to a small ledge. There is some dubious rock.

**2)** 4b, 26m. Climb the totty chimney/crack around left of the arete, then step right and follow the long crack on good holds and in a great position all the way to the top.

*FA. Tony Watts, Steve Bowes 1963*

*The next routes require a scramble up under a fallen tree to reach a ledge with two pointed blocks on it.*

**② Cat Walk** .......... ☆2 🔥 HS 4a

The most popular route hereabouts. Climb the well-travelled groove above the blocks to its end then follow a second groove to a pull out left onto a slab. Finish up the steep and awkward groove above.

*FA. Doug Scott, Steve Read 1963*

**③ Sourpuss** .......... ☆1 🔥 VS 4c

**1)** -, 15m. Climb up the initial groove of *Cat Walk* but exit left at its end and traverse to a stance at the left end of ledges below a bigger groove capped by a huge tree.

**2)** 4c, 22m. The main groove pitch is good despite the rather tortuous approach. A difficult exit past the big tree remains.

*FA. Gary Gibson 1980s*

**④ Pupilla** .......... ☆1 🔥 VS 4c

**1)** -, 15m. Start up the initial groove of *Cat Walk* but exit left at its end and belay at the right-hand end of the ledges.

**2)** 4c, 22m. Make a hard move onto the pleasant, pocketed wall just left of the groove, before trending left to climb the crack in the upper left edge of the buttress. There are lots of threads available on this pitch.

*FA. Gary Gibson 1980s*

North Southwest Southeast Turkey Dip Masson Lees Pic Tor Lorry Park Q. High Tor Long Tor Q. Wildcat Willersley Colehill Q. Harborough Brassington Hipley Hill

North
Southwest
Southeast
Turkey Dip
Masson Lees
Pic Tor
Lorry Park Q.
High Tor
Long Tor Q.
Wildcat
Willersley
Colehill Q.
Harborough
Brassington
Ripley Hill

Dom Sellars climbing *Cataclysm* (HVS 5a) - *page 371* - on High Crag at Wildcat. Photo: Dan Lane

## High Crag

The tallest section of Wildcat is bounded on the left by the deep groove of *Manx* and has the prominent straight crack of *The Great Cleft* splitting its right-hand side. Further right, the slim groove of *Cataclysm* pokes out from the trees - its glossy holds glinting in the sun.

**Approach -** As you walk underneath the crag, glimpses of the upper sections enable you to locate yourself. Scrambling leads to the starts.

**Descent -** Walk left (looking in) off the top, down the path and through a higher archway before doubling back to the base.

---

*High Crag is bounded on the left by the big groove of Manx.*

### ❶ Manx . . . . . . . . . . . . . . . . ⌂1 ☐ VS 4b
**1)** 4b, 28m. The deep groove bounding the buttress is popular and low in the grade. Start up a wall on the left then follow the main groove to reach a well-positioned stance out right.
**2)** 4a, 8m. Move left above the groove to finish up a wide crack.
FA. Steve Read, Doug Scott, Ray Gillies 1960s

### ❷ Golden Yardstick . . . . . Top50 ☐ VS 5a
A superb second pitch follows the hanging rib right of *Manx*.
**1)** 4b, 14m. Climb onto a pedestal then continue up the groove to a bizarre stance in a unique cave.
**2)** 5a, 30m. Climb up right then traverse left above the cave to access the right wall of the hanging prow. Follow this with interest to a possible stance and finish up the wide crack of *Manx* over on the left.
FA. Tom Proctor, Al Evans, Keith Myhill 1976

### ❸ Lobo . . . . . . . . . . . . . . . . ⌂1 ☐ VS 4b
**1)** 4b, 14m. Take the first pitch of *Golden Yardstick* to the cave.
**2)** 4a, 26m. Step right and climb the groove passing to the right of the ivy to a zigzag crack. Up this and its continuation to an exit over on the left. A pleasant juggy pitch.
FA. Steve Read, Doug Scott, Ray Gillies 1963

38m

10m

12

11

13

**❻ Lynx** . . . . . . . . . . . . . . . . ⸤50⸥ ⎿⎿⎿⎿⎿ **HS 4b**
A right-to-left diagonal line with plenty of interesting climbing.
Polished in places, though that doesn't detract too much.
**1)** 4b, 30m. From a stumpy pedestal (scratched name) move up
past a tree and take a diagonal line left across slabs to a steep
groove. Climb this to a ledge and tree belay.
**2)** 4a, 16m. Continue across and left following the series of
cracks and corners to a steep final crack (*Lobo*) to finish.
*FA. Steve Read, Steve Hunt 1958*

*Right of the upper groove of Lynx is an impressive steep prow,
in the upper part of the cliff, split by two steep cracks.*

**❼ The Catcuss Furballs Connection**
. . . . . . . . . . . . . . . . . . . . ⎿⎿⎿⎿⎿ **E5 6b**
A fine hard pitch tackling the hanging headwall above the
top section of *Lynx*. Follow *Lynx* pitch 2 for 8m then pull up
diagonally right and climb the wall (several bits of old fixed
gear) to the big tree.
*FA. Darren Hawkins, Malcolm Taylor 1986*

**❽ Clash of Arms** . . . . ⎿⎿⎿⎿⎿ **E4 6b**
From the stance on *Lynx* step right and climb the groove and
crack above then power up the wall on the right to an undercut
overhang. Pull over and follow the crack to the top.
**Mr Dog, E5 6b** - Break left and finish up the steep groove left of
*Tut's Anomalous*.
*FA. Gary Gibson 1980s. FA. (Mr Dog) Malc Taylor 1990*

**❾ Stolen Jewel** . . ⎿⎿⎿⎿⎿ **E5 6b**
A direct line which feels about 7a+. Start up *Lynx* but climb
direct and cross the bulge past an old bolt.
*FA. Pete Cresswell 1987*

**❿ Sphynx** . . . . . . . . ⎿⎿⎿⎿⎿ **VS 5a**
**1)** 4b, 22m. Start up *Lynx* but where it starts to trend left move
out right and climb a groove and rib to a stance and tree belay.
*Photo on page 324.*
**2)** 5a, 18m. Climb the groove on the left then step left (ancient
ring-peg and not much else) and make a short traverse and tricky
mantelshelf to enter a wide crack. Finish more easily up this.
*FA. Steve Read, Will Mcloughlin 1963*

**⓫ Climacteric** . . . . . . ⎿⎿⎿⎿⎿ **VS 5a**
Enjoyable and full-on for the grade. Climb the centre of the wall
to the overlap, and make a difficult pull on to the wall above.
Continue up the steep pockety wall above to a bulge at the top.
*FA. Paul Nunn, D.Goodwin 1968*

**⓬ Cataclysm** . . . . . . . . . ⸤50⸥ ⎿⎿⎿⎿⎿ **HVS 5a**
A shiny classic up a neat hanging groove above a hidden cave.
*Photo on page 369.*
**1)** 4b, 10m. Climb a groove to reach a tree, step right then
continue to another of those strange stances in a cave.
**2)** 5a, 28m. Enter the groove and balance up it to a roof, then
swing right to follow very polished cracks in a fine position.
*FA. Doug Scott, Steve Read (1pt) 1963*

**⓭ Metamorphosis** . . . ⎿⎿⎿⎿⎿ **HVS 5b**
Start just right of a rock nose right of *Cataclysm*.
**1)** 5a, 12m. Climb the wall into a small groove, keeping just
right of the ivy. Continue easily to belay on the left inside the
*Cataclysm* cave.
**2)** 5b, 28m. Make a very hard pull out of the right-hand side of
the cave, then head up the tricky groove and the rib on its right.
Finish up the wall to the right of *Cataclysm's* polished cracks.
Move over left to finish.
*FA. Paul Nunn, D.Goodwin 1968*

**❹ Tut's Anomalous** . . ⎿⎿⎿⎿⎿ **E1 5b**
**1)** 4c, 20m. Start up a short open groove above a fallen flake
then trend left to a flake. Climb this and the bulge above to a
small stance and tree belay.
**2)** 5b, 18m. Follow the ramp of *Lynx* until the undercut flake
on the right can be reached. Power up this by sustained and
dramatic moves - hard to start - and then hard to stop.
*FA. Doug Scott and others (2pts) 1960s*

**❺ Great Cleft** . . . . . . ⎿⎿⎿⎿⎿ **E2 5c**
The long crack system is a strenuous, slippery and awkward
tussle, yet it is a kind of classic despite all of this.
**1)** 4c, 16m. Start left of a block and climb a thin crack to a
groove then a small stance on the left.
**2)** 5c, 28m. Step right and do battle with the crack through a
bevy of bulges. Sustained and strenuous though with good gear
and the occasional solid jam to allow you to catch your breath.
*FFA. Graham Hoey 1975. FA. Doug Scott, Steve Read (3pts) 1963*

North Southwest Southeast Turkey Dip Masson Lees Pic Tor Lorry Park Q. High Tor Long Tor Q. Wildcat Willersley Colehill Q. Harborough Brassington Hipley Hill

North

Southwest

Southeast

Turkey Dip

Masson Lees

Pic Tor

Lorry Park Q.

High Tor

Long Tor Q.

Wildcat

Willersley

Colehill Q.

Harborough

Brassington

Hipley Hill

| | No star | ☆ | ☆☆ | ☆☆☆ |
|---|---|---|---|---|
| **Mod to S** | - | - | - | - |
| **HS to HVS** | 5 | 12 | 5 | 2 |
| **E1 to E3** | 5 | 4 | 6 | 1 |
| **E4 and up** | 4 | 5 | 4 | - |

A fine tall cliff with lots of strong natural lines, many of which are multi-pitch and a good proportion of them are in the ever-popular HS - HVS bracket. What's not to like? Well, the biggest issue is the fact that the cliff faces north and is out of condition in the colder, damper months of the year. Also, there is a smattering of vegetation and loose rock. Despite this, the best of the routes here are very good and well worth sampling.

The left-hand end of the crag has perhaps the finest concentration of quality routes but there are worthwhile climbs scattered all along the cliff. The crag forms a great shady retreat on hot days and the tree cover plus the northerly aspect means that the place is often drier than you might expect when the rains begin.

## Approach    Also see map on page 325

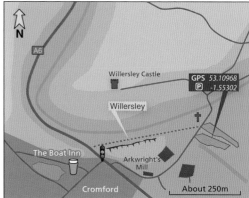

The crag is south of Matlock Bath, near the village of Cromford. From traffic lights on the A6 turn onto the minor road signposted Cromford Station. Continue down this road, passing the large Arkwright's Mill on the left. Just past the mill, there is a right turn into a parking area (pay). Further parking is often available at the next right turn, in the field belonging to Matlock Rugby Club. From the parking, cross the road and follow the footpath past the church to the crag which soon appears on the left.

## Conditions

Willersley is a popular venue on hot summer days. Whilst not seeing much sun, the crag's sheltered position means it is rarely affected by wind and it can give some shelter from rain especially when the tree canopy is full. It is slow to dry but seepage is minimal. In less-than-perfect conditions climbing here is a slippery nightmare. Black Rocks up the hill is a better venue when things are damp.

Dan (climbing) and Graham Parkes catching some late afternoon sun on *Great Corner* (VS 4c) - *next page* - at Willersley, the first route on the crag put up back in 1955.

North
Southwest
Southeast
Turkey Dip
Masson Lees
Pic Tor
Lorry Park Q.
High Tor
Long Tor Q.
Wildcat
Willersley
Colehill Q.
Harborough
Brassington
Hipley Hill

## Access
The crag's owners, the Arkwright's Mill Trust, have stated that they do not wish people to climb at this crag and the information is only included in this book for completeness. If the situation improves then it is worth keeping in mind that the Methodist Guild Holiday Trust owns the hotel across the river and the crag is in full view of guests. Needless to say, swearing and flashing (of body parts - not routes) is to be avoided.

North
Southwest
Southeast
Turkey Dip
Masson Lees
Pic Tor
Lorry Park Q.
High Tor
Long Tor Q.
Wildcat
Willersley
Colehill Q.
Harborough
Brassington
Hipley Hill

## Lime Street Area

The left side of Willersley has some of the best lines around and the trees here are less obtrusive. Most of the routes are single pitches but some venture onto the upper section of the cliff and top-out via easy loose groove-lines. Many of the routes have become very polished.

**Descent -** For the routes which summit, the easiest descent is via the wooded slope to the left of the crag. Please avoid abseiling as this has exacerbated the access situation in the past.

**1 Gripper** . . . . . . . . . . . **E1 6a**
Do battle with the polished roof-crack. Fortunately it relents somewhat above the roof.
*FA. Pat Fearnehough, Ted Howell (1pt) 1962*

**2 Grasper** . . . . . . . . . . **HVS 5b**
The wide crack splitting the roofs is a character-building struggle from start to finish. A bit of grit thuggery helps.
*FA. Dennis Gray 1959*

*The thin hanging crack is* **Close Comfort, VS 5a**.

**3 Great Corner** . . . . . . . . **VS 4c**
The glossed corner crack leads right then back left to a good stance and belay below the roofs. Ever-dry. Abseil descent.
*Photo on page 18 and previous page.*
*FA. Peter Perkins, Peter Strange 1955*

**4 Hangover** . . . . . . . . . . . **E3 6b**
A fighting extension to the previous three routes. Climb the crack in the roof and pull into an easier groove to an overgrown finish. Jungle lurks above so lower off the tree.
*FFA. Tom Proctor 1979. FA. Steve Read, Steve Hunt 1962*

**5 Zombie** . . . . . . . . . . . **E2 5b**
Follow the pocketed seam then tackle the crack-line which is steep, sustained and a bit slippery all the way to a belay above. Abseil off (sensible) or grovel up the gully above (not sensible).
*FFA. Keith Myhill 1970. FA. Steve Read, Steve Hunt 1957*

Not much sun | 5 mins | Sheltered | Restrictions

16m

12m

**Descent**

35m

25m

**❻ Mighty Like a Rose** . . . . . . E5 6a
A bold eliminate up the blank wall right of *Zombie*. The slab at the start is the crux, though the best climbing is higher up.
*FA. Pete Cresswell 1993. First done on bolts, then re-led after some had been removed by person's unknown.*

**❼ Growl Tiger's Last Stand** E2 5c
Low in the grade and excellent. Start up the shallow awkward left-trending groove in the blunt arete to the overhang. Move right and power through the flake that splits the roof then continue up and left on flat holds to the lower-off on *Zombie*. *Photo on page 377.*
*FA. Malc Taylor, Pete Brayshaw 1976*

**❽ Haste, Not Tomato Paste** . . E5 6a
Climb *Growl Tiger's* left-slanting groove in the blunt rib to the overhang. Pass the left edge of the roof with difficulty (and a mono) to gain the wall above then continue by a short flake and easier climbing to the lower-off on *Zombie*. Short but serious.

**❾ God** . . . . . . . . . . . . . E1 5b
A good strenuous pitch, well protected too. Start up the leaning flake system then pull out left on to the wall and up to a rest. Climb the flakes round the edge of the roof then continue until forced to traverse left below the shrubbery to *Zombie*.
*FFA. Ted Wells 1960s. FA. Steve Read, Steve Hunt 1957*

**❿ Sun Chariot** . . . . . . E7 6b
Start between *Lime Street* and *God* with the crux moving rightwards through the overlap (a poor microwire). Fine climbing above, with spaced, but good, gear.
**Crown of Thorns, E4 6a -** Make a detour into *Lime Street Direct* for a few moves then come back left.
*FA. (Crown of Thorns) Martin Roome, D.Bolger 1986. Bolted/de-bolted in 1993. Reclimbed as described and renamed by Matt Fry in 2009.*

**⓫ Lime Street Direct** . . . . E1 5c
One of the best routes here - steep, sustained (and polished).
**1)** 5c, 25m. Climb a slanting groove in the arete to a ledge. Make tricky moves into the main groove - a side-runner on the right may be found useful at the grade, more like stiff E2 otherwise. Head up the groove by superb finger-jamming and bridging to bulges; just above is a stance below an open gully. Abseil off or:
There are 2 alternative starts to pitch 1:
**1a)** 5b. Come in from the crack right of the arete.
**1b)** 6a. The fierce thin crack on the left.
**2)** 4c, 10m. Trend left to enter the gully and climb this.
*FFA. Ted Wells, B.Palmer late 1960s. FA. Steve Read, Steve Hunt 1957*

**⓬ Lone Tree Edge** . . . E1 5b
A fine sustained pitch following the long crack-line to the right of the arete, to the *Lime Street* stance. The crux section is wide and slippery, bring plenty of big gear. From the stance, finish up pitch 2 of either *Lime Street Direct*, or *Lone Tree Groove*.
*FA. M.Harris, Steve Read 1970*

**⓭ Lone Tree Groove** . . HVS 5a
**1)** 5a, 28m. A fine and popular climb up the big groove with its solitary tree. Take care with some loose blocks on this pitch. At the top of the groove traverse left over grass to belay on *L.S.D.*
**2)** 4b, 10m. Trend right up the tottery wall to enter a more solid groove and finish up this.
*FA. Doug Scott, Steve Read 1964*

North
Southwest
Southeast
Turkey Dip
Masson Lees
Pic Tor
Lorry Park Q.
High Tor
Long Tor Q.
Wildcat
Willersley
Colehill Q.
Harborough
Brassington
Hipley Hill

North
Southwest
Southeast
Turkey Dip
Masson Lees
Pic Tor
Lorry Park Q.
High Tor
Long Tor Q.
Wildcat
Willersley
Colehill Q.
Harborough
Brassington
Hipley Hill

*To the right, a huge tree sprouts from behind a big flake of rock - The Sycamore Flake. The next routes start up the front face of the flake.*

**14 Sycamore Flake Direct .** ☆ ⬚ HVS 5b
A good line though with a finish that is a bit of a spoiler.
**1)** 5b, 18m. Climb a thin crack past the edge of an overlap then the groove to a stance below the left edge of the roof.
**2)** 4c, 30m. Continue up the chimney and the floral groove above direct to the top.

*The next two neglected climbs take the bulging wall above Sycamore Flake, to a shared lower-off on the slab above the roof*

**15 Tommy Gun .** . . . . . . . . . . . . ⬚ E3 5c
Climb the crack in the front of the flake then the white wall keeping to the left of the bulges until a finish through a weakness in the roof is possible. Move right to the lower-off.
*FA. Geoff Hornby 1992*

**16 London's Burning .** . ☆ ⬚ E5 6a
Follow the start of *Tommy Gun* but trend right up the wall above the big overhang, passing a peg. Traverse right below the upper roof to finish up a groove splitting its right-hand edge.
*FA. Gary Gibson 1979*

**17 Sycamore Flake** . . . . . ☆ ⬚ VS 4c
A good 1st pitch is spoilt by the grotty finish to the 2nd one.
**1)** 4c, 20m. Swarm up onto the flake containing the large tree. Continue up and left, mantelshelf into the cracks then up these to reach a small but good stance below the notch in the roof.
**2)** 4c, 35m. Climb the chimney and groove above then traverse off right over grass and grot to a finish up *Babylon's* top groove.
*FA. Steve Read, Hank Harrison 1959*

**18 White Riot/Whatta .** ☆ ⬚ E5 6b
A good sustained pitch up the right side of the wall - it has some fixed gear - almost a 7b sport route. Follow *Surplomb* then pull through the left-hand side of the roof and climb the steep fingery wall. Weave through the next roofs then continue joining *London's Burning* at its final roof. Up this to a lower-off.
*FFA. (White Riot) Alan Doig 1984. FA. (Whatta) Simon Lee 1992*
*FA. Doug Scott, W.Bowes (A3) 1962*

**19 Surplomb** . . . . . . . . . . ☆ ⬚ VS 4c
**1)** 4c, 24m. Climb up to the left side of the 'surplomb' and undercut right (occasional seepage) into cracks overlooking the groove of *Babylon*. Climb these to a stance.
**2)** 3c, 16m. Finish up *Babylon's* top groove to the right.

**20 Babylon** . . . . . . . . ☆ ⬚ HVS 5b
A fine line and stout at the grade, with good climbing when dry and a nightmare when damp, as it usually is. Climb the groove throughout (care with loose blocks) passing a tree then the crucial bulge (bristling with old rotten pegs) towards the top.
*FA. Derek Carnell, W.Jackson (aid) 1960*

**21 Sparkle in the Rain** . . . . . . ⬚ E5 6a
From 10m up *Babylon*, move out left on to the wall. Climb this, past a bolt, to a slab. The original route climbed the overhang direct (peg) but is overgrown. Finish up *Babylon*.
*FA. Martin Roome 1986*

**22 Jericho Wall** . . . . . . . . . . . . . ⬚ VS 4c
Pretty overgrown now, this used to be an alternative to the crux section of *Babylon*. Follow *Babylon* and traverse left on a slab just above the tree in the groove. Climb up until a traverse back right leads into the top section of *Babylon* to finish.

**Not much sun** | 5 mins | Sheltered | Restrictions

**Finish of routes 20, 21 and 22**

35m

20m

16

18

22

21

20

*Lone Tree Groove - p.375*

*Lime Street Direct - p.375*

14  15  17  19

North
Southwest
Southeast
Turkey Dip
Masson Lees
Pic Tor
Lorry Park Q.
High Tor
Long Tor Q.
Wildcat
Willersley
Colehill Q.
Harborough
Brassington
Hipley Hill

Ian Fiddeman climbing the upper crack of *Growl Tiger's Last Stand* (E2 5c) - *page 375* - at Willersley. Photo: David Bond

North
Southwest
Southeast
Turkey Dip
Masson Lees
Pic Tor
Lorry Park Q.
High Tor
Long Tor Q.
Wildcat
Willersley
Colehill Q.
Harborough
Brassington
Hipley Hill

## Garroter and Pothole Wall Areas

The central section of the cliff has a fine set of powerful groove-lines, and some open faces. Once these were regarded as equal to the best routes in Wales - well they may not be quite that good - but most are still worth doing. Several routes manage to find their way through unlikely terrain at reasonable grades, without getting involved with anything too dramatic.

**Descent -** Walk off to the right (looking in) from the top and scramble back down and around to the base.

**❶ Last Testament . . .**    E3 5c

The leaning groove left of a large Y-trunked tree is steep and sustained. Pass the bulge (crux - old peg) for more of the same then escape left up the groove. Easier for the long-legged.
*FFA. Ron Fawcett, Pete Gomersall 1976. FA. Terry Bolger, Bill New (2pts) 1968*

**❷ Wind of Change . . . . . .**    E2 5c

The long leaning crack in the sidewall gives a beefy pitch. As the crack runs into *Guts Ache* keep left up the arete until the short easy final corner can be reached.
*FA. Gary Gibson, S.Keeling 1980*

**❸ Guts Ache Groove . . . .**    VS 4c

The slanting groove behind the tree is climbed in its entirety. It gives a fine sustained pitch which is a little easier than it looks from below. Although quite polished, there is still the odd creaky hold to keep you interested.
*FA. Steve Read, K.Beech (some aid) 1959*

Not much sun | 5 mins | Sheltered | Restrictions

32m

20m

**4 Guillotine** . . . . . . . HVS 5a
Climb the steep slanting crack in the left wall of the slabby groove - knobbly. Where it ends, step left into the continuation groove. Up this until *Guts Ache* can be joined. High in the grade.
*FA. Jack Street, Bruce Andrews late 1960s*

**5 Garroter** . . . . . . . . . . . . . VS 4c
One of the original classics of the crag is now very polished but, if you can handle that, the climbing is superbly sustained.
**1)** 4b, 15m. Follow the slabby groove, turn the overhang on the right, then traverse left to a small stance and tree belay.
**2)** 4c, 20m. Head up the fine groove passing an awkward bulge.
*FA. Steve Read, K.Beech 1959*

**6 Halo Left-hand** . . . . . . . . . HVS 5b
A sadly neglected line through the left edge of the bulges that cross the wall. Follow the groove trending right to the bulges then step left and climb steeply into a groove which leads rightwards again up to the top. The vegetation is winning.
*FA. Steve Read, B.Jackson (aid) 1960*

**7 Bagatelle** . . . . . . . . . . . . . HVS 5a
An interesting diagonal expedition.
**1)** 5a, 40m. Follow *Halo Left-hand* to the bulges then traverse right under the roofs passing old pegs and assorted tat before climbing up and right to the stance on *Pothole Wall*.
**2)** 5a, 16m. Traverse right as for *Pothole Wall's* crux then continue up and right to the cliff top.
*FA. Brian Moore, G.Bagg 1967*

**8 Halo Right-hand** . . . . . . . . . . HVS 5b
Follow *Halo Left-hand* to the bulges then traverse 6m right as for *Bagatelle* before pulling steeply leftwards to enter the upper groove. The route is about the same grade as its twin though the rope work is more complicated.
*FA. Steve Read, B.Jackson (aid) 1960*

**9 Tramp** . . . . . . . . . . . . E4 6b
Climb up into the hanging groove and exit steeply from this to reach the traverse on *Bagatelle*. Reach the short diagonal crack up and right with difficulty and power up this to gain the steep final groove just to the left.
*FA. Gary Gibson 1982*

**10 Pleasure Dome** . . . E2 5c
**1)** 5c, 24m. Climb the crack steeply through the bulges then follow the right-trending groove to the small but comfortable stance on *Pothole Wall*. Quite hard work at the grade.
**2)** 5b, 14m. Traverse left to pass the bulges then finish back rightwards up the hanging rib and into the shrubs - exposed.
*FA. Phil Wilson, Mark Walton, John Walker 1978*

**11 Excavator** . . . . . . . . . HVS 4c
Not as loose as the name suggests, though it once was. Start up the steep pocketed slab and trend right to enter the black groove in the steeper rock above. Up this using the occasional disposable hold until the polish of *Pothole Wall* is reached. Finish up this. Low in the grade.

**12 Pothole Wall** . . . . . . . VS 5a
A fine and popular route with just a couple of hard moves which are well protected by fixed gear. The 1st pitch feels quite pushy.
**1)** 4c, 20m. Climb the shallow right-facing groove (polished) then trend left under the ivy on spaced jugs to reach a small exposed stance with good belays.
**2)** 5a, 15m. Passing the pothole involves an awkward and constricted traverse (threads) to reach a ledge. Step back to the left and finish up the hanging groove. An alternative finish out right ends up in an ugly shrubby gully and is best avoided.
*FA. Steve Read, K.Beech (some aid) 1959*

Descent

32m

North | Southwest | Southeast | Turkey Dip | Masson Lees | Pic Tor | Lorry Park Q. | High Tor | Long Tor Q. | Wildcat | Willersley | Colehill Q. | Harborough | Brassington | Hipley Hill

## Gangue Grooves

Just to the right of *Pothole Wall* is *Gangue Grooves* another cracker, devious and continually interesting despite the unfriendly looking rock.

**Descent -** Walk off to the right (looking in) from the top and scramble back down and around to the base.

Not much sun | 5 min | Sheltered | Restrictions

**Descent**

*Pothole Wall- p.379*

32m

**1 Gangue Grooves** .. Top 50 · HVS 5b

Excellent; sustained and varied despite its ugly appearance. Start right of the corner of *Pothole Wall* and trend right then left to reach a vague crack (the same point can be reached from further right as well). Climb the crack up black rock studded with minerals then traverse right across the slab above, stepping down at its end and finishing up a steep groove.
*FA. Doug Scott, Steve Read (some aid) 1964*

**2 Euromess** . . . . . . . . . . . . · E1 5b

1) 5a, 18m. Climb straight up the pocketed wall to the hanging lump and pull right past this before sprinting up a short groove and the wall to a good stance.
2) 5b, 14m. The reddish groove behind the stance leads to a good flat hold. Use this to climb the wall rightwards to the arete and finish up this in a good position.
*FA. Gary Gibson, Adey Hubbard 1979*

**3 Overhanging Wall** . . . . · HVS 5a

1) 5a, 20m. Climb to a small hanging lump from the right and turn this and the next bulge continuing left. Head back rightwards to a stance as for *Euromess* - a pumpy pitch.
2) 4c, 20m. Trend right up the slabby wall of the groove, past a tree and finish up the continuation groove above, exiting right.
*FA. Pete Hassall, Ken Smith 1962*

North
Southwest
Southeast
Turkey Dip
Masson Lees
Pic Tor
Lorry Park Q.
High Tor
Long Tor Q.
Wildcat
Willersley
Colehill Q.
Harborough
Brassington
Hipley Hill

**Boomerang Area**
The right-hand side of the cliff has some good hard routes, as well as the elegant but tired line of *Boomerang*. Many of these routes stay dry in light rain.
**Descent -** Walk off to the right (looking in) and scramble back down and around to the base.

**4 P.T.O.** . . . . . . . . . . . . **E2 5c**
A fine climb with a butch crux that feels a long way off the ground. Climb the long groove to the bulges then power left through these on a series of pockets (old tat) to a tough pull into the groove. Finish direct - sensible, or illogical and guaranteed to increase rope-drag exit rightwards.
*FFA. Keith Myhill 1969. FA. Steve Read, Steve Hunt 1958*

**5 In the Beginning** . . . . . **E5 6a**
Attack the big roof to the right of the crux of *P.T.O.* via a niche (bolts). Exit left from this and sprint up to join the crack that is *P.T.O.*'s right-hand finish. The top section is fully bolted.
*FFA. Gary Gibson 1985. FA. Ken Jones, Zep Dyslewicz 1969*

**6 Diseased Meat** . . . **E4 6a**
Follow *P.T.O.* to the roof then make a tricky blind traverse out right and enter the final hanging groove by some harrowing laybacking. Finish easily.
*FA. Gary Gibson 1985*

**7 Blessed are the Weak** . **7a+**
... for they shall be pumped. A good sport route following the line of fixed gear up the shallow groove and the leaning wall above by sustained intricate climbing. The high 1st bolt means a wire might not go amiss. Popular. *Photo on page 383.*
*FFA. Gary Gibson 1987. Previously aided.*

**8 Boomerang** . . . . **E1 5c**
A once popular route (at HVS 5b) up a good natural line, but it is polished and the old pegs are terrible. Climb the pocketed wall to the overhangs then traverse right to enter the groove. Up this by sustained bridging and jamming until things ease and the vegetation starts to take over.
*FA. Steve Read, Steve Hunt (3pts) 1960*

**9 Hallowed be My Name** **7c**
Climb direct through the bulge. Desperately technical.
*FA. Gary Gibson 1986. It lost crucial holds and was reclimbed by Malc Taylor in 1992 with some extra bolts.*

**10 Mine is the Kingdom** . . **E5 6a**
Climb the bulges above the centre of the traverse of *Boomerang* with difficulty to reach easier-angled rock. Up this then finish up the arete (gear needed) or traverse left to the tree.
*FA. Gary Gibson 1987*

**11 Running Blind** . . . . . . . . . **E4 6a**
Grope up the bulging wall to eventual relief at a juggy flake. Ape right to the arete and climb its left-hand side until forced back left into the corner by the vegetation.
*FA. Gary Gibson 1979*

North
Southwest
Southeast
Turkey Dip
Masson Lees
Pic Tor
Lorry Park Q.
High Tor
Long Tor Q.
Wildcat
Willersley
Colehill Q.
Harborough
Brassington
Hipley Hill

## Cucumber Groove

The far right-hand side of the cliff has another set of good lines in the form of a series of cracks and grooves. These are all in the orange zone so a good day's climbing is on offer here, though sadly all of the best climbs have become polished over the years.

**Descent -** Walk off to the right (looking in) from the top and scramble back down and around to the base.

**1 Cucumber Crack** . . . . . HVS 5a
A butch crack pitch. Follow the fissure in the left wall of *Cucumber Groove* to a ledge and possible belay. Climb into the niche and swing out right on to the wall. Finish more easily, taking care with the rock.
*FA. Steve Read, Steve Hunt 1958*

**2 Cucumber Groove** . . . . VS 4c
A fine line though it is pretty slippery. Climb the well-defined groove throughout; good gear available, though the upper section is quite sustained.
*FA. Steve Read, Steve Hunt 1958*

**3 Cucumber Variant** . . . . . . . VS 4c
A less glossy finish to *Cucumber Groove*. Start up the main groove but swing right into the subsidiary groove at the overhang and then finish pleasantly.
*FA. Steve Read, Steve Hunt 1958*

**4 Sisyphus** . . . . . . . E2 5c
Climb the steep arete and swing right to a steep crack (decent gear at last), layback strenuously up this to a rest. Step back left and follow a second crack to easier ground.
*FA. Len Pearson, Sean Golden 1977*

**5 Adamant** . . . . . . . . . . HVS 5a
Step off the rocking block and power up the right-slanting crack into an easier groove. It gives strenuous jamming and proves to be steeper than it appears from below.
*FA. Steve Read, Steve Hunt 1962. FFA. Geoff Milburn 1966*

**6 Constable Crack** . . . . . . . . E1 5b
A battle which is easier for the ham-fisted. Plod up the wide leaning crack on rattly jams and greasy jugs.
*FA. Doug Scott, Steve Read 1964*

**7 White Wall Corner** . . . . . . . HVS 5a
From the tip of the right-hand block, traverse right to a small tree, then climb the slippery groove with difficulty. Pull left round the blocking overhang to easier ground.
*FA. Des Hadlum, Beryl Turner (aid) 1957*

**8 Beyond Recall** . . . . . . . . . HVS 5a
Climb the steep wall to the tree on *White Wall Corner*, then move out right to follow the arete to the top.
*FFA. Gary Gibson, K.Nowak 1986. FA. Terry Bolger, Bill New (1pt) 1966*

Not much sun | 5 min | Sheltered | Restrictions

North

Southwest

Southeast

Turkey Dip

Masson Lees

Pic Tor

Lorry Park Q.

High Tor

Long Tor Q.

Wildcat

Willersley

Colehill Q.

Harborough

Brassington

Hipley Hill

Graham Parkes pulling through the crux bulge of *Blessed are the Weak* (7a+) - *page 381* - at Willersley. The route is misnamed, it really should have been *Blessed are the Strong*, or *Only the Weak are Spurned.*

North

Southwest

Southeast

Turkey Dip

Masson Lees

Pic Tor

Lorry Park Q.

High Tor

Long Tor Q.

Wildcat

Willesley

Colehill Q.

Harborough

Brassington

Hipley Hill

Rick Gibbon making balancy moves on *Garth was 'ere*
(6a) - *page 386* - typical of the precarious and technical
climbing found at Colehill Quarry. Photo: Chris Craggs

# Wirksworth Area
## Colehill Quarry
## Harborough Rocks
## Brassington, Hipley Hill

North

Southwest

Southeast

Turkey Dip

Masson Lees

Pic Tor

Lorry Park Q.

High Tor

Long Tor Q.

Wildcat

Willersley

Colehill Q.

Harborough

Brassington

Hipley Hill

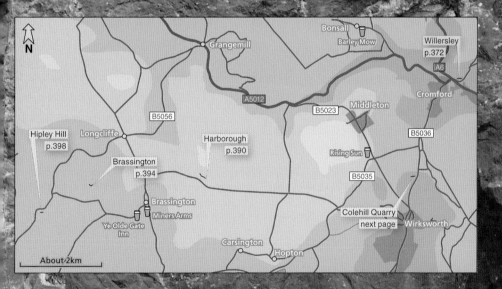

N

Bonsall
Barley Mow

Willersley
p.372

A6

Grangemill

Cromford

A5012

Middleton

B5056

B5023

Hipley Hill
p.398

Longcliffe

Harborough
p.390

B5036

Rising Sun

Brassington
p.394

B5035

Brassington
Miners Arms

Colehill Quarry
next page

Wirksworth

Ye Olde Gate
Inn

Carsington

Hopton

About 2km

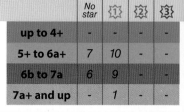

| | No star | ☆ | ☆☆ | ☆☆☆ |
|---|---|---|---|---|
| up to 4+ | - | - | - | - |
| 5+ to 6a+ | 7 | 10 | - | - |
| 6b to 7a | 6 | 9 | - | - |
| 7a+ and up | - | 1 | - | - |

Colehill Quarry is one of many holes in the ground that pepper the Wirksworth/Matlock Area that climbers have been poking around in for over 50 years. It is a secluded venue with an excellent set of routes, many of which rely on sloping holds. The climbing here is more varied and technical than other, more popular, sport-climbing quarries in the Peak - feeling more like well-bolted trad than sport.

## Approach    Also see map on page 385

The quarry is well-hidden just to the west of Bolehill which is 0.65 mile north of Wirksworth. Turn west onto Ravenstor Road and park **sensibly** on the big roundabout in the Business Park. A track leaves the north-east corner of this and a right branch leads into the quarry a couple of minutes away.

## Conditions

The crag faces south and west, getting plenty of sun. It is exceptionally well sheltered and in hot weather, it is a good morning venue; on cold days, it provides a toasty spot if the sun is out. Generally, the quarry is quick drying though it does suffer from some seepage and this makes many of the routes dusty at the start of the season or after rain.

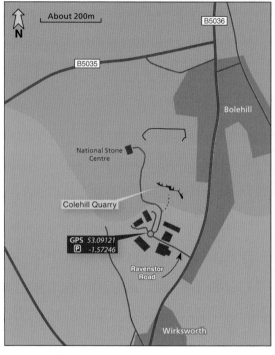

## Access

The quarry is owned by the nearby National Stone Centre and one of the view-points overlooks the quarry. The owners have indicated that climbing is not allowed here, and currently the BMC are looking into the situation. If asked to leave, please be courteous and do so. If there are more than a few people climbing here then please go elsewhere.

*The first routes listed are on the wall on the far left.*

**1 Posing Pouch** . . . . . . . . . 🔾 [ ] 6a+
Soon deteriorates after a puzzling start.
*FA. Gary Gibson, Gordon Jenkin, Dan Jenkin 2009*

**2 Voyeur** . . . . . . . . . . . . . . 🔾 [ ] 6a
The second line from the left is quite taxing.
*FA. Gary Gibson 2008*

**3 Posing till the End** . . . . ☆ 🔾 [ ] 5+
Nice climbing on spaced holds up the arete of the wall.
*FA. Gary Gibson 2008*

**4 I am a Poser and I Don't Care** ☆ [ ] 5+
The face right of the arete has a distinct crux by the flake.
*FA. Gary Gibson 2007*

**5 Garth was 'ere** . . . . . . . ☆ 🔾 [ ] 6a
Decent climbing which eases with height. *Photo on page 384.*
*FA. Gary Gibson 2007*

**6 In Vision** . . . . . . . . . . . ☆ 🔾 [ ] 6a+
The long shallow scoop is high in the grade with a particularly tricky move at mid-height.
*FA. Gary Gibson 2007*

**7 Out-a-Sight, Out-a-Mind** ☆ 🔾 [ ] 6a+
Mantel the initial bulge then bridge the groove above.
*FA. Gary Gibson 2007*

North · Southwest · Southeast · Turkey Dip · Masson Lees · Pic Tor · Lorry Park Q. · High Tor · Long Tor Q. · Wildcat · Willersley · Colehill Q. · Harborough · Brassington · Hipley Hill

Lots of sun | 2 min | Sheltered | Restrictions

18m

North
Southwest
Southeast
Turkey Dip
Masson Lees
Pic Tor
Lovry Park Q.
High Tor
Long Tor Q.
Wildcat
Willersley
Colehill Q.
Harborough
Brassington
Hipley Hill

**8 Above 30** . . . . . . 7b
The start is tough and so is the finish. Low in the grade and easier for the tall.
*FA. Gary Gibson, Mark Richardson 2007*

**9 Just this Side of 30** . . . 7a
Start with difficulty as for *Above 30* but move right and scale the centre of the wall where another hard move lurks.
*FA. Gary Gibson, Mark Richardson 2009*

**10 Taste the Grit** . . . . . . 6b+
Layback and slap-a-way up the left-hand side of the arete.
*FA. Gary Gibson, Mark Richardson, S.Bondi 2007*

**11 What a Pity** . . . . . . . . 6b
The open groove close to the arete and easier ground rightwards.
*FA. Gary Gibson, Gordon Jenkin, Kim Greenald 2008*

**12 Slate Gray Lining** . . . . . . . . . . 5+
The rounded pillar has an awkward start and dirty finish.
*FA. Gary Gibson, Hazel Gibson 2007*

**13 Swooping on Nigel's Ruby** . . . . 5+
Start just right of the bush and climb the wall left of the orange streak. Finish up the right-trending groove.
*FA. Gary Gibson 2007*

**14 The Desperation of Freedonia** . . 6a
Climb slabby rock then steeper ground - all a bit snappy.
*FA. Gary Gibson 2007*

**15 The Reincarnation of Catatonia** . 6a
The odd groove feature leads to a steeper finale.
*FA. Gary Gibson 2007*

**16 The Execution of Dysphasia** . . . . 6a
Climb onto the nose and continue up a steep groove.
*FA. Gary Gibson 2007*

**17 A Revolution for Dyspepsia** . 6b
A tricky mantelshelf gains a shallow groove and steep finish which is especially tricky if tackled direct.
*FA. Gary Gibson, Gordon Jenkin, Dan Jankin 2007*

**18 The Destitution of Threedonia** . . 6b+
The line just left of the broken grassy groove.
*FA. Gary Gibson and the Nottingham Five 2011*

**19 The Evolution of Micradia** . . 5+
This is the tall pillar just to the right of the grassy groove. The 1st bolt is high and there is some grotty rock.
*FA. Geoff Hornby 1990s*

**20 The One in Ten** . . . . . . 6a+
A decent outing up the steep wall left of the big open groove though the crux pull on a dodgy flake is a worry.
*FA. Gary Gibson, Nick Taylor 2010. Gary and Nick did 10 new routes, on 10 different crags, on the same day!*

Routes 1 to 7
50m

**㉑ The Booze Cruise** . . . . . . . 🌙 ⬜ 6b+
The longest line here tackles the wall just left of the open groove
to a finish on the white pillar far above.
*FA. Gary Gibson, Hazel Gibson 2007*

**㉒ Cruisin' for a Boozin** . . . . . . 🌙 ⬜ 6b+
The wall right of the groove has a tricky move low down and a
long reach to gain the hanging flake. The upper wall is easier.
*FA. Gary Gibson, Hazel Gibson 2007*

**㉓ The Crinoid Cruise** . . . . 🌙 ⬜ E3 5c
The long crusty crack may be the best route here, though it
doesn't get much attention. It eases with height.
*FA. Nick Taylor (from the right) 2001*

**㉔ See Me Coming** . . . . . . 🌙 ⬜ 6c
Neat, technical face-climbing up the wall right of the crack.
After the ledge, things ease.
*FA. Gary Gibson, Mark Richardson, S.Bondi 2007*

**㉕ The Scarlet Woman** . . . . . . 🌙 ⬜ 6b
Hard moves (high 1st bolt) past the crescent moon feature lead
to easier face climbing above.
*FA. Geoff Hornby, Suzi Sammut, Alex Sammut 1990*

**㉖ Crocodile Tears** . . . . . . . . 🌙 ⬜ 6c
An eliminate just right until forced into *The Scarlet Woman*.
*FA. Geoff Hornby 1991. FA. (Direct) Gary Gibson 2007*

**㉗ Alligator Crawl** . . . . . . . . . 🌙 ⬜ 6a+
An open groove leads steeply to the easier wall above.
*FA. Geoff Hornby 1991*

**㉘ Tolley put the Kettle On** . . . 🌙 ⬜ 6c
Tricky moves link the flake with the sloping ledge.
*FA. Gary Gibson, Ian Milward 2007*

**㉙ The Convert** . . . . . . . . 🌙 ⬜ 7a
Hard climbing (originally a hairy E3 5b!) with a desperate central
section leading to a steep finish.
*FA. Geoff Hornby, Phil Baker 1988*

**㉚ Forbidden Fruit** . . . 🌙 ⬜ 6b+
Popular, though with a tough, fingery crux.
*FA. Geoff Hornby, Suzi Sammut 1988*

**㉛ Another Roadside Attraction** 🌙 ⬜ 6a
Another route that sees plenty of traffic, up the long groove-line.
*FA. Geoff Hornby, Suzi Sammut, Duncan Hornby 1988*

**㉜ Old King Colehill** . . . . . . . . 🌙 ⬜ 6c
Nice, but sequency, climbing starting up the pale streak. The
crux is low but the interest is maintained.
*FA. Gary Gibson, Mark Richardson, S.Bondi 2007*

**㉝ It's a Hamster Mr. Fawlty** . . 🌙 ⬜ 6a+
The shallow groove left of the edge of the wall is high in the
grade since losing a crucial flake at 2/3 height. Move left and
back right at this grade. The first clip is a bit of a gripper.
*FA. Geoff Hornby, Suzi Sammut 1988*

North | Southwest | Southeast | Turkey Dip | Masson Lees | Pic Tor | Lorry Park Q. | High Tor | Long Tor Q. | Wildcat | Willersley | Colehill Q. | Harborough | Brassington | Hipley Hill

Lots of sun | 2 min | Sheltered | Restrictions

20m

㉑ ㉒ ㉓ ㉔ ㉕ ㉖ ㉗ ㉘ ㉙ ㉚ ㉛ ㉜ ㉝

| | No star | ✪ | ✪✪ | ✪✪✪ |
|---|---|---|---|---|
| **Mod to S** | 20 | 11 | 3 | - |
| **HS to HVS** | 7 | 7 | 1 | - |
| **E1 to E3** | - | - | - | - |
| **E4 and up** | - | 1 | - | - |

Harborough is a popular cliff tucked away in the southern Peak and made from heavily pocketed and solid dolomitic limestone. It is a good place for beginners to experience a first hit on real rock, and a popular spot for more experienced climbers to exercise their muscles and do a bit of soloing. Ticking the whole crag in a session was a good work-out until the roof-crack in the cave was added in 2009!

The routes tend to be steep and fingery so the grades can feel quite stiff. Many of the routes are rather polished, though this is hardly surprising after 100 years of regular usage, and it is popular with groups. The outlook over the High Peak Trail and the grassy base make it a good spot for a picnic although the proximity of the factory detracts a little.

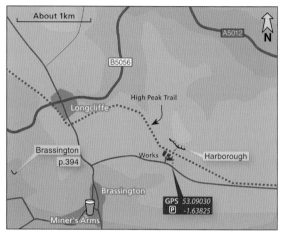

## Approach    Also see map on page 385

The crag is in the southern Peak, to the west of Wirksworth. There is parking on the side of the minor road that runs from Brassington to Wirksworth, just east of the prominent refractory factory. A track leads past the edge of the works and up and over the High Peak Trail to the left-hand end of the cliff by the conspicuous cave and the tower of rock known as The Steeple.

## Conditions

Harborough has a fine, sunny aspect and it is the limestone equivalent of the gritstone cliffs further north. There is no seepage and it dries quickly.

## The Steeple

The left-hand side of the cliff is dominated by the squat tower of The Steeple and a beckoning cave entrance. Some routes here are polished, but are still worth doing.

**1 Introductory Wall** . . . . . . . . . . [ ] **Diff**
The easy arete to the west of the cave then ledgy rock.

**2 Cave Crack** . . . . . . . . . . . . . . [ ] **VDiff**
The crack above the cave and the grass beyond.

**3 Cave Chimney** . . . . . . . . . [ ] **S 4a**
Inside the cave a juggy groove leads, via a bulge, to the first skylight. Often greasy and always gloomy.

**4 Skylight Chimney** . . . . . [ ] **VDiff**
Further into the cave, a second groove to a similar feature glinting high above. Dark and dirty fun.

**5 Gobbler's Roof** . . . [ ] **E7 6c**
And now for something completely different - the dirty horizontal off-width roof crack in the cave. The hardest route at here by a margin of 8 grades!
*FA. Pete Whittaker 2009*

**6 Overhanging Wall Variant** . . [ ] **VDiff**
The groove right of the cave to a ledge then step out right above the overhang for a nicely exposed finish on huge holds.

**7 Overhanging Wall** . . . . [ ] **S 4b**
Climb through the overhang with difficulty, and a polished foothold, to join the previous route on its jugs.

**8 Overhanging Chimney Direct** [ ] **S 4a**
The steep and wide corner-crack by bridging with awkward moves round the bulge.

**9 Overhanging Chimney Indirect** . . [ ] **VDiff**
Avoid the crux on the regular route by a neat bit of side-stepping out right to the ledge, then back left to regain the crack. Finishing direct up the arete of The Steeple is also possible.

**10 Pockets** . . . . . . . . . . . [ ] **S 4c**
The arete on pockets - a sharp start.

**11 Cracks** . . . . . . . . . . . [ ] **HVS 5b**
The finger cracks just right of the arete, by laybacking. A bit of an eliminate and tough too.

**12 Jug** . . . . . . . . . [ ] **VS 5a**
Climb the slippery centre of the steep wall making strenuous use of at least one jug and maybe a finger-jam.

**13 Pedestal Crack** . . . . . . . . [ ] **S 4a**
The polished crack (avoidable to either side) to a ledge and a juggy finish up the slanting groove in the centre of The Steeple.

**14 Concave Wall** . . . . . . . [ ] **HVD 4a**
The scooped wall has a fingery start that is almost 4b.

**15 Steeple Arete** . . . . . . . . . . [ ] **VDiff**
The stepped arete that bounds the wall on the right. The lower arete is slippery and the upper one exposed.

**16 Spider Chimney** . . . . . . [ ] **HVD 3c**
The wide slippery rift to the right wall of The Steeple.

**17 Harborough Crack** . . . . . . . [ ] **HS 4b**
This awkward, slippery groove was first climbed by J.W.P. back in 1898 - a great effort. The star is for historical interest.

**18 Little Arete** . . . . . . . . . . . . . . [ ] **Diff**
A tiny arete right of the brickwork.

**19 Bow Ridge** . . . . . . . . . . . . . . [ ] **VDiff**
The short arete beyond a useful descent gully.

**20 Bow Corner** . . . . . . . . . . . . . . [ ] **HVD**
The short and tricky groove.

**21 Bow-Shaped Wall** . . . . . . . [ ] **VS 5a**
The centre of the fingery wall, passing the bulge on the right.

**22 Bow Arete** . . . . . . . . . . . . . [ ] **Diff**
The short arete on the right.

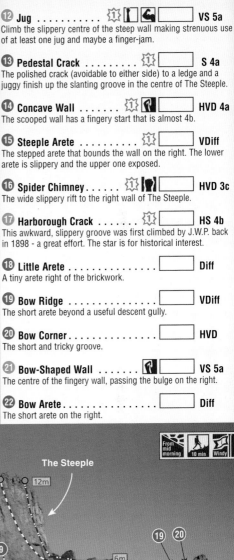

From mid morning | 10 min | Windy

The Steeple

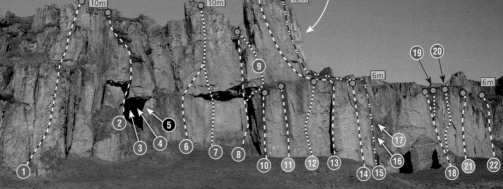

North | Southwest | Southeast | Turkey Dip | Masson Lees | Pic Tor | Lorry Park Q. | High Tor | Long Tor Q. | Wildcat | Willersley | Harborough | Brassington | Hinkley Hill | Colehill Q.

## Creased Wall

The Creased Wall can be easily recognised by its series of thin cracks. Between here and the Steeple Area are some short walls useful for easy bouldering.

**1 Thin Air** . . . . . . . . . . . . . 🎲1 ☐ **VS 4b**
Climb the twin cracks on the far left. The start is tricky.

**2 Creased Wall** . . . . 🎲2 🗿🗿 ☐ **HVS 5a**
The centre of the wall is climbed by a fingery crack-line, sustained and awkward to protect, especially if you layback it.
*FA. Eric Byne 1933*

**3 Crinkle Crack.** . . . . 🎲1 🗿☐ ☐ **HS 4b**
A crack in the right side of the wall leads steeply to a groove. The crucial moves are reachy, a fiddly thread helps protect.

**4 Steep Ridge** . . . . . . . . . . 🎲1 ☐ **VDiff**
The right-hand arete of the wall, passing a ledge at 3m.

**5 Little Gully** . . . . . . . . . . . . . . ☐ **Diff**
The open gully/groove past a ledge is mild.

**6 Adderley's Route** . . . . . . . . . . ☐ **Diff**
Climb the wall on the right and the slanting groove above.

*15m right is a small tower.*

**7 The Furrow** . . . . . . . . . . 🗿☐ ☐ **S 4b**
Plough up the furrowed groove (thread), then finish up the juggy and steep arete of the tower - a very long reach is needed to get started. The groove on the right gives a much easier option, reducing the overall grade to VDiff.

## Little Buttress

A short wall to the left of the taller Trident Buttress has the odd worthwhile route, despite its diminutive size.

**8 The Blaster** . . . . . . . . . . . . ☐ **HVS 5b**
Climb the lower wall with difficulty to a ledge on the left and a tricky finale up a hanging fissure above.

**9 Little Diagonal.** . . . . . . . . . . . ☐ **VDiff**
Climb the right-hand edge of the smooth wall, trending right.

**10 Little Corner** . . . . . . . . . . . . . ☐ **VDiff**
The steep wall just left of a prominent crack.

**11 Little Crack** . . . . . . . . 🎲1 🗿 ☐ **S 4b**
The steep and awkward crack.

**12 Little Wall** . . . . . . . . . . . . 🗿 ☐ **VS 4b**
The wall has one stiff pull and little in the way of gear.

**13 Little Crack** . . . . . . . . . . . . . . ☐ **VDiff**
A little crack immediately left of the chimney.

**14 Little Chimney.** . . . . . . . . . . . . ☐ **Mod**
...is obvious really.

**15 Chimney Arete.** . . . . . . . . . . . ☐ **VDiff**
The right-hand arete of *Little Chimney*.

**16 Scooped Wall** . . . . . . . . . . . . ☐ **VDiff**
A concave feature, trending left to the arete.

**17 Scooped Direct** . . . . . . . . . . . ☐ **HVS 5a**
The steep finish is best done quickly.

**18 Desperation** . . . . . . . . 🗿🗿 ☐ **S 4a**
The steepening right-hand arete of the buttress.

Creased Wall

10m

## Trident Buttress

This is the prominent three-pronged tower on the right-hand side of the cliff. It has some of the best and most popular routes here. The descent off the back is slightly awkward. To the left is a short wall which has the odd worthwhile route.

**19 Trident Face** . . . . . . . . . . . VDiff
A shallow groove leads to a small ledge-system above half-height. Shuffle left and climb the steep upper section by a second groove.

**20 Trident Eliminate** . . . . . HS 4b
Climb the rib in the centre of the face to the break, then step left and pull over the edge of the overhangs on some bounteous jugs. Step right for an exposed finish.

**21 Trident Groove** . . . . . . . . . VDiff
The groove just left of the arete, heading for the gap between the prongs. The upper part is steep and tricky, though good protection is available.

**22 Trident Arete** . . . . . . . . . . VDiff
The right-hand arete is a little tricky in its lower section, the upper section is straightforward and pleasantly exposed. Another offering from J.W.Puttrell back in the late nineteenth century.

**23 Trident Obverse** . . . . . . . . . . . Diff
The reclusive groove in the back of the arete.

## The Arete

Across the grass slopes to the right is the final, small buttress. Although only short, the routes are on good rock. Whip up them all for a quick work-out.

**24 Cracked Wall** . . . . . . . . . . HVS 5b
The fingery twin cracks right of the easy groove.

**25 Overhanging Crack** . . . . . . VS 5a
Climb into the leaning fissure which is a bit beefy.

**26 The Arete** . . . . . . . . . . . . S 4a
The central arete of the buttress, starting on the left then spiralling up the edge. A direct start is **S 4b**.

**27 Blinkers** . . . . . . . . . . . . . VS 5a
The thin crack right of the arete eases with height.

**28 Legs Over** . . . . . . . . . . . . VS 4b
The final offering up the centre of the wall is tricky to start.

Little Buttress

Trident Buttress

North
Southwest
Southeast
Turkey Dip
Masson Lees
Pic Tor
Lorry Park Q.
High Tor
Long Tor Q.
Wildcat
Willersley
Colehill Q.
Harborough
Brassington
Hipley Hill

| | No star | ⚝ | ⚝⚝ | ⚝⚝⚝ |
|---|---|---|---|---|
| **Mod to S** | 16 | 2 | - | - |
| **HS to HVS** | 8 | 3 | - | - |
| **E1 to E3** | - | - | - | - |
| **E4 and up** | - | - | - | - |

The climbing area of Brassington is a diminutive but interesting set of towers in a picturesque landscape. The rock is high quality limestone, riddled with pockets and polished in many places. Sadly the place has been out of vogue for many years and it has become increasingly overgrown, with at least one buttress now completely cloaked in vegetation. Despite this, there is some good climbing to be had here, especially on the East Hill where the multi-pitch outings of the various variations on *The Long Climb,* and the closely-packed routes on the Upper Tier are worth visiting.

In the past there have been access problems here with the landowner charging people to climb on occasions. A right-of-way runs around behind the cliffs so at least you can go and have a look at the place without being bothered. If you are asked to leave then please do so.

**The West Hill -** This is split into two tiers, both of which have been climbed on. The small and clean Upper Tier forms the summit of the hill and is in a fine position with good rock. It has a decent set of short routes similar to the Upper Tier of East Hill in character and worth exploring if you are in the area. The lower tier is more overgrown and has less of interest.

## Approach　　Also see map on page 385

There is parking for half a dozen vehicles in the layby, on the minor road (Pasture Lane), 1km west of Brassington village, from where the cliffs are clearly visible. Walk down the road to a stile and signpost in the wall by the bend, then go through the left-hand gate and follow the track across the fields to the second post. From here, a narrower track runs up the gully (nettles) to the East Hill. The West Hill is most easily reached by another track that starts a couple of hundred metres down the road and goes direct.

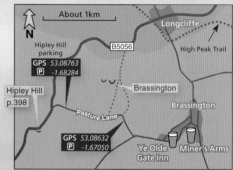

## Conditions

The cliffs cap the crest of Rainster Hill and face south and west. They are rapid drying and catch the breeze. The ten minute walk-in appears to deter just about everybody.

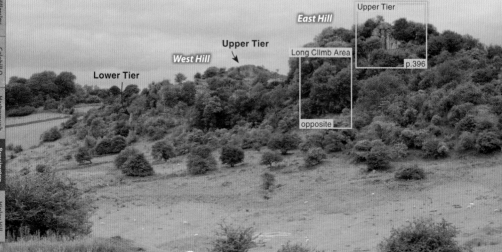

**Long Climb Area**

Originally five multi-pitch routes were described weaving their way up the four tiers, though ivy and other herbage have reduced the choice by one. The climbs listed here are the best. Potential belays and stances are left for you to discover. They all give around 30m of climbing.

Upper Tier next page

Brassington Crack - p.396

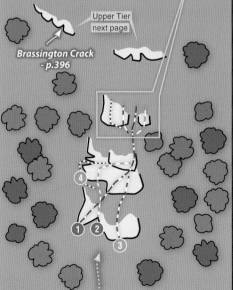

**❶ Long Climb Variants. . . . . . . . ⬜ VDiff**
Partly overgrown nowadays - bring the secateurs. Climb the left arete of the central angular corner on the lower tier. Then the right arete of the groove in the second tier. Continue up the short face and finish by trending right up the open blocky gully (prickly) that separates the two impressive towers.

**❷ Long Climb Indirect . . . . . . . . ⬜ S 4a**
Climb the main corner in the lowest tier then the awkward crack (crux) in the left wall of the corner in the second tier. Climb the short face to a third terrace then the centre of the tall narrow tower on the right.

**❸ Long Climb Direct . . . . . . . ⚃ ⬜ HS 4b**
Climb the front face of the lowest wall and the next wall just above. The widening chockstoned crack is awkward then the final steep buttress (The Ivy Tower) is climbed up its steep right-hand arete.

**❹ International Climb . . . . . . ⚃ ⬜ VS 4c**
Wandering but with a fine climax. Climb the lowest tier by one of the previous routes then follow the ivy-covered ledge around to the left. Climb the right-hand branch of the chimney and the pleasant arete out right. Start up the right arete of The Ivy Tower then trend left and finish up its centre by good fingery climbing.
*FA. Eric Byne, Sten Lindhard 1941*

North | Southwest | Southeast | Turkey Dip | Masson Lees | Pic Tor | Lorry Park Q. | High Tor | Long Tor Q. | Wildcat | Willersley | Colehill Q. | Harborough | Brassington | Hipley Hill

North
Southwest
Southeast
Turkey Dip
Masson Lees
Pic Tor
Lorry Park Q.
High Tor
Long Tor Q.
Wildcat
Willersley
Colehill Q.
Harborough
Brassington
Hipley Hill

## East Hill - Upper Tier

A short series of smart, pocketed walls and steep crack-lines in a fine sunny setting and with a broad grassy base - just the spot for a picnic and a bit of mellow climbing.

**Approach -** Either climb up by one of the Long Climb routes (previous page), or scramble up the path to the right edge of the terrace (see previous page). Some bush-wacking is probably inevitable.

**Descent -** An easy descent is possible over the back of the buttress down a chimney and back round rightwards to the foot of the face.

**①** **Face Climb Number 1** . . . . . . . . [ ] **Diff**
The pleasant thin crack and face above.

**②** **Arete Number 1** . . . . . . . . . . . [ ] **VDiff**
Balance up the right-hand arete of the slab.

**③** **Steep Chimney** . . . . . . . . . . . [ ] **VDiff**
The chimney to a leftward exit, or head through the hole.

**④** **Arete Number 2** . . . . . . . . . . . [ ] **VDiff 4a**
The right-hand arete of the chimney has tricky initial moves then eases above.

**⑤** **Face Climb Number 2** . . . . . . . . [ ] **VDiff**
The centre of the narrow face between the two chimneys is very much an eliminate.

**⑥** **Pedestal Chimney** . . . . . . . . . . [ ] **Mod**
The chimney to the left of the pedestal to a choice of exits.

**⑦** **Pedestal Wall** . . . . . . . . . . . . [ ] **HVS 5a**
A narrow wall and roof above the pedestal taken direct.

**⑧** **Brassington Crack Arete** . . . . . . [ ] **S 4a**
Tackle the arete direct and try to avoid using the pedestal.

**⑨** **Brassington Crack Face** . . . . . . [ ] **HS 4b**
As the name suggests, the face left of the crack without deviation.

**⑩** **Brassington Crack** . . . . . . . ⟨1⟩ [ ] **HVD**
The wide crack can be bridged or laybacked, the latter form of progress is more like HS.

**⑪** **Brassington Face** . . . . . . . . . . [ ] **VDiff**
From just to the right of the crack climb steeply rightwards to a niche then finish up the ivy-covered arete on the right.

8m

Lots of sun   10 min

Upper Tier Right - 20m

*The next routes are situated 20m to the right.*

**12 Easy Arete** . . . . . . . . . . . . . . ☐ **Mod**
Climb the pocketed arete on the left of the buttress.

**13 Snuffer Chimney** . . . . . . . ⟨⟩ ☐ **S 4b**
The narrowing-chimney is awkward. A famous route from yesteryear, if you fell out of it you could consider yourself snuffed.

**14 The Overhang Indirect** . . . . . . ☐ **VS 4c**
Traverse the pocketed wall rightwards below the roof to the arete. Pull over a bugle and climb the juggy wall on the left.

**15 The Overhang** . . . . . . ⟨⟩ 🧗 ☐ **HVS 5b**
Climb the pocketed wall to the roof and pass this using the prominent finger-jug. Continue up the steep wall keeping left for maximum exposure.

**16 Smooth Chimney Outside Route.** ☐ **HS 4b**
An oddly-named climb up the pocketed left wall of the chimney and the wall above.

**17 Smooth Chimney** . . . . . . . . . . ☐ **VDiff**
The obviously-named feature eases with height. Once past the chock, the rest is a doddle.

**18 Elder Rib** . . . . . . . . . . . 🧗 ☐ **VS 4c**
A narrow fin of rock between the two chimneys is fingery but soon eases.

**19 Chockstone Chimney** . . . . . . . ☐ **Diff**
The chimney with the expected threadable feature just before it eases to scrambling.

**20 Crack and Face** . . . . . . . . . . . ☐ **VDiff**
Climb the shallow groove in the right-hand wall of the chimney using holds out right.

**21 Face Direct** . . . . . . . . . . . 🧗 ☐ **VS 4c**
The pocketed wall just right of the groove has a fingery start and taxing finish.

**22 Angel's Crawl** . . . . . . . . . . 🧗 ☐ **VS 4c**
Climb the fingery pocketed arete then step out right and climb the centre of the face direct.

**23 Elderberry Crack** . . . . . . . . . . ☐ **S 4a**
The pair of cracks to the right of the arete are quite steep and pushy, though they can be well protected.

**24 Savoy Crack** . . . . . . . . . . . . . ☐ **HS 4b**
The wider crack just right is a slippery struggle as far as the overhang. Swing right and sprint for the top.

**25 Two Minute Crack** . . . . . . . . . ☐ **S 4a**
The finish has become a little overgrown at the top, secateurs useful but this may slow you down.

| | No star | ⚀ | ⚁ | ⚂ |
|---|---|---|---|---|
| **Mod to S** | - | - | - | - |
| **HS to HVS** | 1 | - | - | - |
| **E1 to E3** | 1 | - | 1 | - |
| **E4 and up** | - | - | - | 1 |

A minor south Peak cliff that sees very little attention. The addition of a quality hard route might put it back on the circuit although this will be too hard for most.

## Conditions
The crag faces northwest and sees precious little sun. It is surprisingly sheltered and seepage doesn't seem to be a big problem

## Approach    Also see map pages 385 and 394
The crag is seconds from the B5056 that links the A515 to A5012. There is no parking on the road near the crag but there is some space on Pasture Lane, the minor road that leads to Brassington. Turn into here and park just past a gate on the right which is about 150m from the junction. This is marked on the map on page 394. It is a 5 minute walk back to the crag.

**❶ The Great Tribulation . .** ⚂ 🪢 ☐ **E6 6c**
An excellent outing, climbing a long-abandoned project up the centre of some impressively steep ground. Climb the pillar between the caves to a jug (peg and thread). A series of hard moves through blocky bulges lead to good holds on the left shoulder (peg) then continue up a steep groove (thread) to a small roof below the leaning headwall. Finish up the hard finger-crack which is climbed on the right with the help of holds in the vague groove. Shady all day and stays dry in the rain, kneepad useful. *Photo opposite and page 13.*
*FA. Jon Fullwood 2009*

**❷ Rabbit Run . . . . . .** ⚂ 🪢 🧗 ☐ **E1 5b**
A striking line up the long groove. Reaching the crack via the technical wall below is the crux, the rest of the route gives good well-protected jamming and bridging.
*FA. Geoff Milburn, Dave Gregory 1966*

*The slabby wall to the right is currently grassy, the following routes are included for posterity - they have not been checked.*

**❸ The Tempest . . . . . . . . . .** 🛡 ☐ **E2 5c**
5m right of *Rabbit Run*, climb straight up the face for 8m, then move left and follow a shallow feature to a grassy exit.
*FA. Sean Golden, Len Pearson, Des Truscott, Ted Wells early 1970s*

**❹ Mistral . . . . . . . . . . . . . .** ☐ **HVS 5b**
Climb slabby rock to the bulge which is climbed direct (thread) on better than expected holds to a grassy finish.
*FA. Sean Golden, Len Pearson, Des Truscott, Ted Wells early 1970s*

*In addition to these routes, the far left-hand side of the crag has four slabby routes - Severe to HVS - and there are a couple of poor grassy Severes up the right arete of the crag.*

North | Southwest | Southeast | Turkey Dip | Masson Lees | Pic Tor | Lorry Park Q. | High Tor | Long Tor Q. | Wildcat | Willersley | Colehill Q. | Harborough | Brassington | Hipley Hill

Pete Whittaker tackling the superb crack of *The Great Tribulation* (E6 6c) - *opposite* - the star (only?) attraction at Hipley Hill. Photo: Mike Hutton Tom Randall is belaying - check *page 13* to see how he got on.

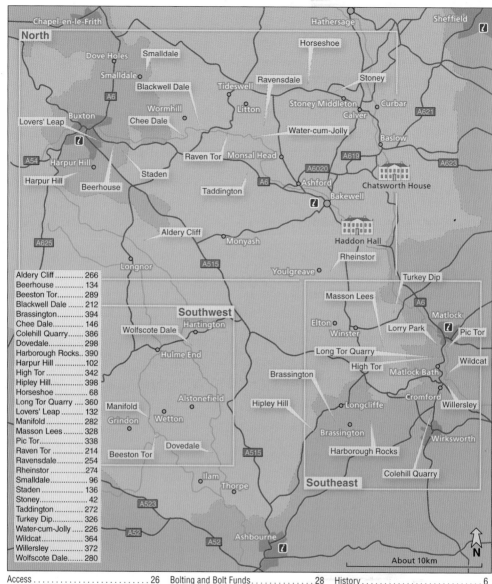

About 10km

N

**Emergencies**
**Dial 112 and ask for**
**POLICE - MOUNTAIN**
**RESCUE.** Have details of
your location and what the
incident involves.